STEVE COHEN, who lives in Colorado in the heart of the Four Corners, is a travel writer, photographer, and editor whose work has appeared in hundreds of publications around the world, including the *New York Times,* the *Los Angeles Times,* the *Washington Post, Travel Holiday,* and the *Whole Earth Review.* He has written, edited, or contributed to a dozen current travel guides and is a member of the Society of American Travel Writers. He is the editorial consultant for this guidebook.

LAURIE ARCHER, a longtime resident of Sante Fe, is the consultant for our coverage of that city and its environs. A former dancer and actress in musicals on Broadway, she is an artist whose works are widely exhibited primarily in the Southwest, and has contributed articles to regional and national magazines such as *Sunset* and *House and Garden.*

NANCY GILLESPIE, a freelance writer and a marketing communications executive, lived in Taos, New Mexico, for a decade and is now a resident of El Paso, Texas. She has contributed to numerous magazines and newspapers, including the *New Mexican, New Mexico* magazine, *Southwest Profile, Southwest Art,* and *Country Inns.*

LARK ELLEN GOULD has worked as a staff reporter and editor for United Press International, the *Las Vegas Sun,* and the McClatchy chain of Senior Spectrum newspapers. She lives in Las Vegas, Nevada, where she works as a freelance writer and teaches journalism to college students.

JUDYTH HILL, a journalist, performance artist, teacher, and published poet, lives near Santa Fe. She is a food columnist for the *Albuquerque Journal,* writes on food for *Crosswinds* magazine, and is a contributor to the *Santa Fe Reporter.* Among many other activities, she coordinates the annual Santa Fe Wine and Chile Festival.

JOHN PENDARIES LA FARGE is the scion of a family that goes back to Alvar Nuñez Cabeza de Vaca, the first Western European to travel through New Mexico. A lifetime Santa Fean, he is a historian, the author of numerous articles, essays, and short stories, and the editor of an oral history of Santa Fe.

BUDDY MAYS, a freelance writer and photographer, is the author and illustrator of ten books on travel, including *Ancient Cities of the Southwest, Indian Villages of the Southwest,* and *A Guide to Western Wildlife,* and has contributed to many others. His articles and pictures have appeared in such magazines as *Travel & Leisure, Travel Holiday, Philip Morris, TWA Ambassador, Delta Sky, Forbes, Sunset,* and *Touring America.* A member of the Society of American Travel Writers, he lives in Santa Fe, New Mexico.

STEPHANIE BOYLE MAYS is a freelance magazine and book editor and travel writer based in Santa Fe, New Mexico. Her work has appeared in the *Chicago Herald,* the *Houston Chronicle, Outdoor Life* magazine, and the *Columbia Journalism Review.*

RICHARD MENZIES is a longtime columnist for *Utah Holiday* magazine. He lives in Salt Lake City, Utah.

SAM NEGRI, a freelance writer based in Tucson, Arizona, covered the Southwest and Mexico for more than 20 years as a staff reporter for newspapers in Phoenix and Tucson. Co-author of *Travel Arizona—The Backroads,* he is a regular contributor to *Arizona Highways* magazine and has published articles on the Southwest in numerous publications.

LYNN NUSOM writes a syndicated newspaper column and articles for several magazines, including *New Mexico* magazine. A resident of Las Cruces in southern New Mexico, he is the author of several books, including *Christmas in New Mexico, The Billy the Kid Cookbook,* and *The New Mexico Cook Book.*

STACY Q. RYCHENER, the co-author of *Out and About in New Mexico,* has lived for 16 years in that state, where family roots go back to 1914. A Taos-based marketing executive, she has served as president of The Association of Historic Hotels of the Rocky Mountain West. SAM RYCHENER, a travel and fiction writer and art critic, has lived in Taos for 15 years.

JOHN STICKLER, who began his career in communications as a stringer for CBS News in Seoul, Korea, has been a marketing executive at southern Arizona's first destination resort and, for 30 years, a freelance journalist. He is a past president of the Society of Southwestern Authors. Now a full-time writer, he lives in the desert northwest of Tucson, Arizona.

LYNN BUCKINGHAM VILLELLA, an Albuquerque-based marketing executive, is a New Mexico native who grew up in the state's Four Corners area. An award-winning journalist, she was writer, columnist, and editor for the *Albuquerque Tribune,* editor of *Albuquerque* magazine, and editor of four regional cookbooks, including the best-selling *Simply Simpatico.* She has lived in Albuquerque since 1966.

MAGGIE WILSON, a native of Arizona whose family roots in the state go back to the mid-1800s, was a columnist and feature writer for the *Arizona Republic* for 30 years, and also travel-promotion manager of the Arizona Office of Tourism. A longtime contributor and contributing editor for *Arizona Highways* magazine, she is a widely recognized expert on Indian cultures and crafts, and is a former member of the board of trustees of the Heard Museum of Art and Anthropology in Phoenix, where she lives.

THE BERLITZ
TRAVELLERS GUIDES

THE BERLITZ TRAVELLERS GUIDE TO THE AMERICAN SOUTHWEST 1993

ALAN TUCKER

General Editor

BERLITZ PUBLISHING COMPANY, INC.
New York, New York

BERLITZ PUBLISHING COMPANY LTD.
Oxford, England

THE BERLITZ TRAVELLERS GUIDE
TO THE AMERICAN SOUTHWEST 1993

Berlitz Trademark Reg U.S. Patent and Trademark Office
and other countries—Marca Registrada

Published by Berlitz Publishing Company, Inc.
257 Park Avenue South, New York, New York 10010, U.S.A.

Distributed in the United States by
the Macmillan Publishing Group

Distributed elsewhere by Berlitz Publishing Company Ltd.
Berlitz House, Peterley Road, Horspath, Oxford OX4 2TX, England

ISBN 2-8315-1786-9
ISSN 1062-3663

Designed by Beth Tondreau Design
Cover design by Dan Miller Design
Cover photograph by Kunio Owaki/The Stock Market
Maps by Nina Wallace
Illustrations by Bill Russell
Editorial assistants: Kathy Clark, Cathy Peck, Jackie Damian
Copyedited by Cynthia Sophiea
Fact-checked in New Mexico by Stephanie Boyle Mays
Edited by Alan Tucker

Printed in the United States of America
1 3 5 7 9 10 8 6 4 2

THIS GUIDEBOOK

The Berlitz Travellers Guides are designed for experienced travellers in search of exceptional information that will enhance the enjoyment of the trips they take.

Where, for example, are the interesting, out-of-the-way, fun, charming, or romantic places to stay? The hotels and resorts described by our expert writers are some of the special places, in all price ranges except for the very lowest—not just the run-of-the-mill, heavily marketed places in advertised airline and travel-wholesaler packages.

We indicate the approximate price level of each accommodation in our description of it (no indication means it is moderate in local, relative terms), and at the end of every chapter we supply more detailed rates as well as contact information so that you can get precise, up-to-the-minute rates and make reservations.

The Berlitz Travellers Guide to the American Southwest 1993 highlights the more rewarding parts of the region so that you can quickly and efficiently home in on a good itinerary.

Of course, this guidebook does far more than just help you choose accommodations and plan your trip. *The Berlitz Travellers Guide to the American Southwest 1993* is designed for use *in* the Southwest. Our writers, each of whom is an experienced travel journalist who lives in the city or region of the Southwest he or she covers, tell you what you really need to know, what you can't find out so easily on your own. They identify and describe the truly out-of-the-ordinary restaurants, shops, activities, and sights, and tell you the best way to "do" your destination.

Our writers are highly selective. They bring out the significance of the places they *do* cover, capturing the personality and the underlying cultural and historical resonances of a city or region—making clear its special appeal.

The Berlitz Travellers Guide to the American Southwest is full of reliable and timely information, revised and updated each year. We would like to know if you think we've left out some very special place. Although we make every effort to provide the most current information available about every destination described in this book, it is possible too that changes have occurred before you arrive. If you do have an experience that is contrary to what you were led to expect by our description, we would like to hear from you about it.

A guidebook is no substitute for common sense when you are travelling. Always pack the clothing, footwear, and other items appropriate for the destination, and make the necessary accommodation for such variables as altitude, weather, and local rules and customs. Of course, once on the scene you should avoid situations that are in your own judgment potentially hazardous, even if they have to do with something mentioned in a guidebook. Half the fun of travelling is exploring, but explore with care.

ALAN TUCKER
General Editor
Berlitz Travellers Guides

Root Publishing Company
330 West 58th Street
Suite 504
New York, New York 10019

CONTENTS

MAPS

THE
BERLITZ
TRAVELLERS
GUIDE TO
THE
AMERICAN
SOUTHWEST
1993

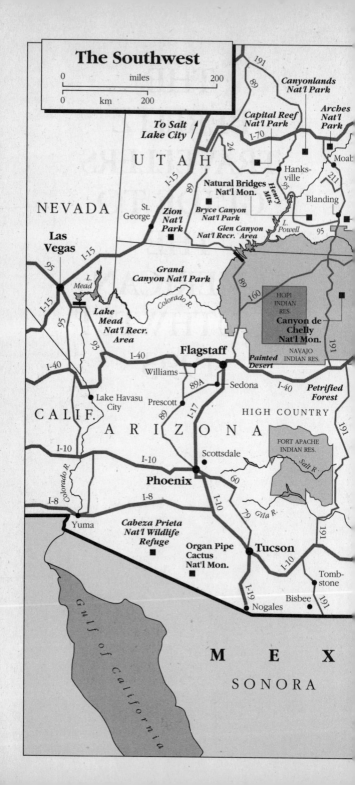

OVERVIEW

By Steve Cohen

Steve Cohen, who lives in Colorado in the heart of the Four Corners, is a travel writer, photographer, and editor whose work has appeared in hundreds of publications around the world, including the New York Times, *the* Los Angeles Times, *the* Washington Post, Travel Holiday, *and the* Whole Earth Review. *He has written, edited, or contributed to a dozen current travel guides and is a member of the Society of American Travel Writers. He is the editorial consultant for this guidebook.*

"You are welcome, but know this land offers scant food or water. Living here will not be easy."

—*Massaw, Hopi deity*

It is a little strange that a region offering abundant beauty and resources (except water) and a promise of hard living should be the epicenter of a modern fashion explosion in arts, design, and cuisine. Yet that is perhaps the strongest current flowing through the Southwest— and one that has become a unifying factor in the minds of outsiders. Southwestern style, whether in architecture and other design arts, clothing, and foods, or in a free and easy sports-filled, sun-drenched lifestyle, is the image portrayed in ads and articles extolling the virtues of this vast swath of land that still echoes with strains of an American frontier. But images can be deceiving. Life has never been easy here where nature reigns, and the people who have survived are a special breed of individuals, far from the dictates of style and fashion.

The expansive American Southwest has long captured the imagination of travellers and explorers of exterior and interior landscapes. With its clear air and bright skies, its spaciousness and corresponding possibilities, it has attracted both nomadic and community-centered Indians (the latter such as the ancient Anasazi and Hopis); Spanish adventurers seeking gold since as far back as the 16th century; and finally Anglos: at first miners of gold, silver, or copper some 150 years ago, soon followed by cowboys and ranchers attracted by epic rangelands, artists drawn to the splendid light, and then scientists employed by military strategists, creating and testing atomic weaponry in the most wide-open, inhospitable places they could find.

While military and scientific efforts put the Southwest on the map, so to speak, it was another modern invention that laid the foundation for a startling population boom after World War II: the air conditioner. With jobs available in burgeoning high-tech industries, and also with a way to cool the hot deserts, modern growth began in earnest. Voila! Dusty desert outposts, including Phoenix, Albuquerque, Tucson, and El Paso were born or reborn. (Las Vegas, which today has a strong economy due to high-tech science and an air force base, became a city as a result of gambling—and Bugsy Siegel.)

But the Southwest is huge, giving people space to spread out. Ranches, horses, and cowboys sporting boots and ten-gallon hats, or greasy baseball caps, are still perhaps the strongest presence here; even many of the Indians dress a lot like cowboys these days. And this hard land, which has not proved well suited to domination by man, has now become a mecca for modern sun-and-fun seekers who crave natural splendor. Not so coincidentally, tourism is virtually the number one industry in the Southwest.

The curious melding of three distinct cultures—Indian, Hispanic, and Anglo—in a remote, long-isolated environment has itself been further shaped by the diverse natural endowments of the Southwest to distinguish the region clearly from, say, the predictable topography of eastern Texas or the Great Plains. The result, for the traveller, is one of America's most distinctive regions. The mix provides interesting eating along with burgers and chili dogs; cowboy bars with live country music; shopping for art, Indian jewelry, blankets, rugs, baskets, or pottery; and accommodations ranging from classic, neon-lit motels to guest ranches, for those who like horseback riding, and pampering retreats. Mainstream activities are well represented by hospitable golf and tennis resorts, while endeavors particularly suited to the scenic, rugged terrain are available for skiers in winter, river rafters in spring, hikers in summer, or mountain bikers in fall, to name just a few examples. A youthful, energetic, sports-minded population means you are nearly as likely to see healthy-looking, Volvo-driving, Patagonia-clad kayakers as you are to see cowboys, whose four-wheel-drive pickup trucks bestow status in these parts.

As a result of the exceptional challenges in taming this dry, sometimes foreboding land for disparate and often conflicting interests, common values have emerged among disparate groups. Self-reliance, a survival skill, has honed clarity of purpose in this epic country with its rugged charms. Despite growing Sunbelt cities, dammed rivers, and missile test sites, a conscious regard for nature is equated with wisdom in these human-dwarfing landscapes, still relatively lightly touched by the human hand. As corny as it may sound, the plaintive existential call to find yourself might not be such a bad bet in the Southwest, where you may find no one else around for miles and yet find nowhere to hide. People confronting themselves, along with the colors and forms of the land, rightly contribute to Southwestern style. The twist is that this is considered fashionable at a time when sameness and conformity prevail elsewhere.

The geographical contrasts within this broad swath of land (extending from below the Mexican border into West Texas, across New Mexico and Arizona's Chihuahuan and Sonoran-type deserts, through the Grand Canyon and Utah's Colorado River country on the Colorado Plateau and into the 14,000-foot peaks of Colorado's San Juan range) have always been impressive: Desert flats speckled with cactus, scrub, and improbable, ancient seabed stone monoliths spread toward distant forested or snow-capped mountains. Canyons drop precipitously to riverbeds, and mesas rise around them. Everywhere the evidence of vanished peoples lingers, and even today large areas are populated not by man but by rattlesnakes, coyotes, and deer, among other wildlife. This is a landscape not always hospitable to human beings; paradoxically, that is no small part of its appeal to seekers of space, time, and distance from more mundane quarters.

Today's Southwest is the result of hundreds of centuries of geological activity. Forces of erosion and wind, volcanoes, and shifting geological plates within the earth's crust have created this visual wonderland of carved sandstone, labyrinthine canyons, and looming mountains. Water, a precious commodity and a primary design force, flows from mountain streams to feed forests and the Southwest's two giant river systems: the Colorado River, draining the 130,000-square-mile Colorado Plateau south through southern Utah and down along the Arizona-Nevada border; and the Rio Grande, flowing south through New Mexico and southeast along the border of West Texas, snaking through deserts for the most part. Neither river system alters the essential nature of the deserts they traverse, yet they retain an unpredictable power that can suddenly overflow the dry creek beds in a fearful, torrential moment. Flash floods uproot trees and swallow cars, only to recede quickly, leaving behind mute evidence of nature's willfulness amid stone arches and towers, twisted canyons, and tall peaks. The land endures, changed but undaunted over eons. Man makes marks even now but has not yet supplanted these elemental forces.

Settlement

This is not to say that man has not tried. Long remote and inaccessible, the Southwest has resisted most efforts at reclamation. Ancient Indians built cities and societies attuned to nature yet not immune to its forces. Abandoned settlements left to become ruins punctuate the entire area and testify to early struggles with drought and subsequent famine. In places, worn tracks are all that remain of once-fertile rangelands, overgrazed and gone to desert. Deserted mines harken back to depleted mineral wealth.

People are newcomers here in terms of geologic time, although spear-point artifacts uncovered near Clovis, New Mexico, indicate prehistoric man's presence as early as 10,000 years ago; the date would place these first primitive New Mexicans among the earliest North American residents. Presumably, these were the ancestors of the Anasazi, the nomadic hunter-gatherers who slowly learned to grow beans and corn. As agriculture developed and became more important, fixed abodes evolved into communities around 2,000 years ago.

Many of the structures built by the Anasazi people over the following 1,500 years remain to this day, most as ruins, but nevertheless evidence of cooperative living, high standards of organization, sophisticated building techniques, and irrigation. Especially fine examples can be seen at such sites as Colorado's Mesa Verde, New Mexico's Chaco Canyon, Arizona's Canyon de Chelly, and

Utah's Hovenweep, among numerous other Southwestern locales.

More than 1,000 years after the development of the communal life of the Anasazi (around 2,000 years ago), nomadic Athabaskan Indians who had crossed the Bering land bridge from Asia headed south from Alaska and the Canadian Arctic, reaching the American Southwest around 600 years ago. The Navajo and Apache are among their descendants. Curiously, "Anasazi" is a Navajo word meaning "the Old Enemies" or "the Ancient Enemies," indicating contact between the tail end of the Anasazi cultures and the arriving Navajo. The gist of the meaning of "Anasazi," "stay away from spirits that were here before," may reflect not only acknowledgment of the Anasazi presence but also the Navajo tradition of literally moving their base from the grounds that hold the bodies of the dead, including the remains of other peoples.

Archaeological evidence suggests that as life became untenable for the Anasazi, various modern Southwestern pueblo-based cultures evolved from these roots. It is believed that the modern Acoma and other Rio Grande–based tribes are likeliest to have descended from Chacoan culture. The Hopi are thought to be related to the Anasazi of Mesa Verde. Pima Indians may have evolved from the Anasazi of northern Arizona. Decisive evidence supporting these claims is one of the many gaps existing in knowledge about the complex linkages among Anasazi (ancestors of the Pueblos), Athabaskan (Navajo and Apache), Pueblo (Hopi, Acoma, and Pima), and other Southwestern Indians. The lingering mysteries are no small part of the attraction of the Southwest to those who find the differences outweigh the similarities among these Indian peoples. Despite their differences, though, most are more comfortable flying in the face of 1990s political correctness and for a number of reasons prefer being called Indians rather than Native Americans. One point often made by Indians is that *anyone* born in the United States is a "native American." Another is that the term "Native American" fails to capture their sense of kinship with the Indians of Canada, Mexico, and elsewhere. But as one Indian comedian says on the subject, "We're just glad that Columbus wasn't looking for Turkey."

After looting and decimating the Aztecs in Mexico, Spanish conquistadors arrived in the mid-1500s seeking gold and silver. They travelled through Texas, Arizona, and New Mexico, but found no riches—only Indians ripe for religious conversion; this force, more than any other, led to the ultimate settlement and taming of the Southwest. Jesuits established communities throughout the region, creating governments along with religious economies. Some of their fortresslike churches still stand in New Mexico.

Anglo hunters and traders were well established by 1825, after the Mexican War of Independence resulted in the establishment of Nuevo Mexico, comprising today's New Mexico and Arizona. In 1848 the treaty that ended the Mexican War ceded 830 square miles of Southwestern territory to the United States, including today's New Mexico, Arizona, Utah, Nevada, and part of Colorado. Indian claims to these ancestral lands were disregarded, only to be grudgingly resolved much later by the establishment of reservation lands. After the Civil War gold, silver, and copper strikes brought prospectors, railroads, shopkeepers, farmers, ranchers, and other forefathers of the modern Southwest.

The land today has been fully explored but not completely settled—and far from tamed. Wild white-water rivers cascade out of the tall peaks in springtime, only to dry into parched summer mudflats. Mountainous areas continue to resist massive development, offering both refuge to wildlife and playground tracts to horseback riders, rock climbers, and fishermen, among other lovers of the outdoors. Deserts and canyons attract seekers of space and natural beauty. Yet in another of the region's contrasts, modern high-tech cities, such as Albuquerque, Phoenix, Tucson, El Paso, and Las Vegas, serve as the gateways to the mysterious and unvanquished lands of the Southwest.

The Southwestern Terrain

The vast spread of the American Southwest truly has no center, but rather several centers, each offering access to surrounding regions. Albuquerque (for New Mexico), Phoenix (for Arizona), and to some degree Tucson (for southern Arizona) are the most important gateway centers. El Paso, Texas, on the southeastern edge of the Southwest, and Las Vegas, Nevada, on the western edge, are also gateways to the region, but they are peripheral ones. (Las Vegas is a gateway for the Grand Canyon's South Rim, as is Phoenix.)

The very definition of the Southwest is somewhat subjective. For this guidebook, we take it to be defined *very* roughly on its eastern boundary by Interstate 25, which

runs north from El Paso through Albuquerque, past Santa
Fe, and up out of the Southwest to Denver. The Sangre de
Cristo Mountains (the tail end of the Continental Divide)
and then the Rockies (the main part of the Continental
Divide) loom to the interstate's left, and the flat-as-a-
board Great Plains stretch off to the right toward the
Mississippi as you drive up to Denver.

The Rockies and other high ranges north of the Colorado Plateau, in central Colorado and in Utah north of the
Colorado River, more or less mark the northern extent of
the region; the Colorado River running due south from
Lake Mead and the Las Vegas area down to the Gulf of
California define the west. Mexico, of course, is the southern boundary.

The geography within this area is dramatically varied—
as is the climate. Albuquerque, with hot summers and
cool, not cold, winters, is in high-desert country that rises
toward the Colorado Plateau in the west, the Sangre de
Cristo Mountains in the north, and the Sandia Mountains
and the Great Plains to the east, with the low-lying deserts
of southern New Mexico and West Texas to the south.
Albuquerque is the main gateway to New Mexico, West
Texas, and parts of the Four Corners. West of Albuquerque there begin to appear volcanic cones and other
indications of the intense volcanic activity that once characterized the Southwest.

The terrain becomes more mountainous and fertile
moving north toward Santa Fe (elevation 7,000 feet), and
by the time you reach Taos you are in the high Rockies,
which continue to dominate with their pine and aspen
forests through Durango and southwestern Colorado.
Here, warm summers with comfortable, cool nights for
sleeping draw the majority of visitors, although skiers
love the deep-powder snow-filled winters with surprisingly warm days and crystalline blue skies, especially
vivid after a storm.

Around Mesa Verde in southwestern Colorado the terrain changes again, extending into Utah and Arizona's
wind-swept mesas and the parched canyons of the Colorado Plateau, on the edge between mountain and desert.
Here, summers are hot, winters are moderately cool, not
often cold. Infrequent snow typically melts in a day.

Into Utah, foliage thins out as the canyons and desert
lands become more pronounced. Summer temperatures
are hotter here and into Arizona, with daytime highs
commonly topping 100°F. The high country around Flagstaff (north of Phoenix) offers respite.

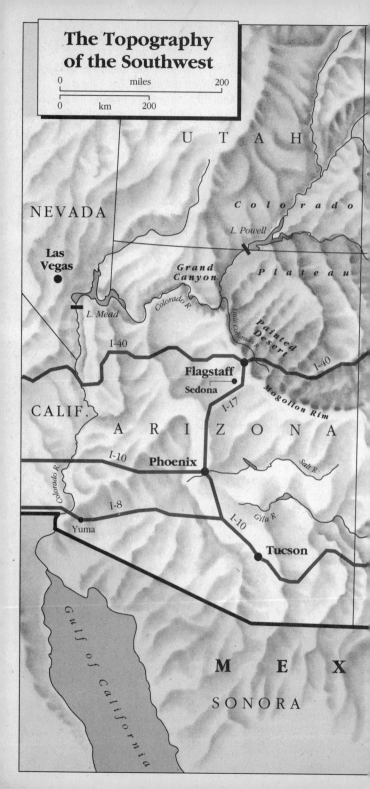

The Topography of the Southwest

UTAH

NEVADA

Colorado

L. Powell

Las Vegas

Grand Canyon

Plateau

Colorado R.

Little Colorado R.

Painted Desert

I-40

I-40

Flagstaff

Sedona

Mogollon Rim

CALIF.

ARIZONA

I-17

I-10

Phoenix

Salt R.

Colorado R.

I-8

Gila R.

I-10

Yuma

Tucson

Gulf of California

MEX

SONORA

Phoenix, the primary gateway to Arizona and the South Rim of the Grand Canyon, lies in a hot valley, but nearby are cooler climes, such as Sedona's Oak Creek Canyon and, farther north on the Colorado Plateau, Prescott. Other hot spots such as Las Vegas and Tucson are themselves other possible gateways. Utah's Canyonlands and River Country may be reached from Salt Lake City or the North Rim of the Grand Canyon, or can be added to a Four Corners loop.

With the diversity of topography comes great variety in climate. One of the most important keys to understanding the variety in the Southwest is altitude. Summers are cooler in mountainous areas but broiling in the deserts— which does little to discourage the vast majority of visitors to the Southwest. The Grand Canyon, for example, one of the hottest spots, draws the majority of its visitors in the summertime, when daytime temperatures can reach 120°F. Elsewhere, and warmer still, Phoenix, Tucson, and Las Vegas consider winter to be high season, with correspondingly higher rates. What few people seem to realize is that although winters can be cold and snowy in mountainous parts of the Southwest, many of the desert areas maintain moderate temperatures, perfect for a hike to visit Indian ruins without breaking a sweat and without facing crowds. Throughout the Southwest spring is mud season, prime time for river runners and crusted hiking shoes. In contrast, fall is perhaps the ideal time to see the region, with a nip in the air sending many visitors home, and the changing foliage providing a colorful backdrop.

A word on the deserts of the Southwest. These are not, in the main, Lawrence of Arabia landscapes with shifting sand dunes, or mile after flat mile of nothing but small rocks typical of western Egypt and parts of southern Israel. The deserts of Arizona and New Mexico are the Sonoran and Chihuahuan desert types, respectively, named after the arid regions extending from the south, in Mexico. (The forms they take are somewhat different; the saguaro, for example, is the trademark of the Sonoran Desert.) They are very much alive, as anyone who has seen those Disney nature films will recall. Mesquite and scrub; wildflowers and flowering cactus; horned toads, gophers, birds— including roadrunners—and, of course, coyotes abound, together with all manner of other plants and wild creatures. These days, with exceptionally high precipitation in the region (for example, in January of this year Phoenix got ten times the month's norm), the deserts may be greener than usual; but after any rainfall the desert immediately and dramatically perks up, like a politician being handed a microphone.

The Southwest for Travellers

NORTHERN NEW MEXICO

Northern New Mexico will be a likely starting place for many travellers, arriving by air to the south in **Albuquerque**, New Mexico's largest city and a repository of historical and cultural influences. Here, in Old Town, are more than 150 shops housed in original adobe structures dating to the territorial period and representing 300 years of Southwestern development. Nearby museums examine the region's natural history and Albuquerque and New Mexico's role in the development of atomic weaponry. The city's Indian Pueblo Cultural Center displays arts, crafts, and historical artifacts relating to New Mexico's various Indian communities. Even with modern conveniences amid the urban sprawl of shopping centers and interstate highways, and with plenty of dining and accommodation possibilities here, the traveller never loses sight of surrounding nature: The Sandia Mountains form Albuquerque's eastern boundary, and to the west dormant volcanic cones protrude from the desert flats—in all offering a gradual introduction from today's urban commonplace to the wonders beyond.

Around Albuquerque the traveller may visit some of New Mexico's Indian pueblo communities as well as portions of several larger Indian reservations. These are the sites of traditional dances and ceremonies, many of which are open to the public. You'll also have ample opportunity to purchase original crafts and artwork directly from the source. In addition to these communities and associated historic and prehistoric Indian sites, the high desert surrounding Albuquerque contains ancient lava flows, historic sites from the period of Spanish exploration, wildlife, wilderness hiking routes, and natural hot springs.

Sixty miles north of Albuquerque—and 2,000 feet higher—is **Santa Fe**, New Mexico's capital and perhaps the single place in the Southwest that lures the most travellers. With its foreign-sounding name offering a hint of the exotic, and with its reputation for fine arts and other cultural pursuits, it somehow combines an elegant historic presence with only a cursory nod to modernity. For some, this is the essence of Southwestern style, sometimes even called Santa Fe style, making the city supremely fashionable—and for good reason. Here is where you find the most eclectic and creative examples of painting, sculpture, weaving, jewelry, and related arts and crafts in all the Southwest. You'll see how the heady mix of nouvelle-Southwestern cuisine, the Santa Fe Opera, hundreds of galleries and artsy shops, and both historic and modern adobe architecture makes Santa Fe "the City Different."

The tall peaks and rugged, arid high desert **Around Santa Fe** contain mysterious canyons, high plateaus, and, for many, an overwhelming sense of peace. Wilderness areas here contain hiking trails and Japanese baths, a Civil War battlefield, Anasazi ruins, and the historic Santa Fe Trail. Small towns, especially along the so-called **High Road to Taos**, offer historic churches and shrines, Spanish-influenced weavers and wood-carvers, Indian pueblos, wildlife sanctuaries, and the still-unchanged vistas and scenery that have inspired artists such as Georgia O'Keeffe.

Fabled **Taos** is perhaps the best-known community north of Santa Fe. Despite its small size and its remoteness in high-desert country, it has been home to artists and writers (such as D.H. Lawrence) for most of this century. The Taos Pueblo is a United Nations World Heritage Site. The Taos Ski Area, not far northeast of town, is consistently rated as one of the best in North America, and many other forms of outdoor recreation draw travellers year-round, including hikers and river rafters who wish to explore the reaches of the surrounding **Enchanted Circle** (an area defined by a series of highways that encircles the Taos mountains north of Taos). The famed mountain man and Indian fighter Kit Carson lived in Taos, and his home is now a museum. And the San Francisco de Asis Church in nearby Ranchos de Taos is possibly the most photographed and painted structure in the Southwest. Add Hispanic and Indian festivals, arts-and-crafts shows, numerous art galleries, surrounding national forests, and designated wild and scenic rivers and you have an inkling of the pleasures to be found here.

THE FOUR CORNERS

The only place in the United States where the borders of four states converge is known as the Four Corners. Straddling the boundaries of New Mexico, Colorado, Utah, and Arizona, the region combines the natural splendors found in various places throughout the rest of the Southwest, from high desert and dominant mountain peaks reaching nearly 14,000 feet to wild rivers, preserved wilderness areas, and rugged canyon country. It contains the most-visited Anasazi ruin in the Southwest, at Mesa Verde, and lesser-known but still very important ruins at Chaco Canyon, Hovenweep, Canyon de Chelly, and Navajo National Monument, among modern reservation lands owned by the Navajo, Hopi, and Ute tribes.

Close to the center of the Four Corners, the evocative Western town of Durango, Colorado, offers plush resorts, guest ranches (formerly known as dude ranches, but rechristened at about the same time wars became conflicts), and a 100-year-old steam-powered narrow-gauge railroad that carries visitors through a time warp to the preserved Victorian mining town of Silverton. Both towns are surrounded by national forests that attract hikers, mountain bikers, fishermen, and hunters stalking bountiful wildlife.

Another part of the Four Corners that is not much different today from the West of 100 or even 1,000 years ago is **Monument Valley**, possibly the most visually distinct landscape in the Southwest. Straddling the Utah-Arizona border within the Navajo Nation, the largest Indian reservation in the United States, its immense rock spires and pinnacles adorn the desert floor like a chess set of the gods. These landforms, photographed to best advantage bathed in sunset's burnished crimson tones, have been popular cinematic backdrops since the 1930s films of John Ford, starring John Wayne. Even today it is doubtful that you could watch a night of television and not see at least one commercial for a sports car, a credit card, or a diet soda filmed in Monument Valley.

THE SOUTHERN TIER

Then we turn to the strip of the Southwest bordering Mexico. **El Paso**, more than the name of a classic Marty Robbins country song, is set hard on the Mexican border, between the confluence of the Franklin Mountains (the southern tip of the Rockies) and the Chihuahuan desert. The border is a mere formality in these parts, by the way; few places convey more of a sense of Spanish America. Whether surveying a historic downtown that reflects the influences of conquistadors and gunslingers, or crossing the border into Mexico at Juárez, you will find an essential blending of Old Mexico and the Wild West in this nevertheless modern city of 600,000 residents.

Outside of urban West Texas the preserved wild lands

of **Guadalupe Mountains National Park** and **Big Bend National Park** offer a different sense of the natural Southwest. In the Guadalupe Mountains, 100 miles northeast of El Paso on the New Mexico border, the parched high desert offers pristine hiking and backpacking trails among prickly pear, cholla, pincushion, and mammillaria cacti that provide habitat for more than 300 species of wildlife, including elk, mule deer, black bears, eagles, and mountain lions. Big Bend, 300 miles southeast of El Paso on the Mexico border, lies between 7,000-foot-tall vertical peaks and canyons that plunge 1,000 feet. It offers 1,100 square miles of Chihuahuan desert filled with eroded gullies and wind-sculpted rock forms. The park contains hundreds of miles of hiking trails and one of the Southwest's premier white-water rafting trips: down the raging Rio Grande, through some of America's most isolated and least tarnished backcountry.

El Paso is the eastern gateway to what we call the Southern Tier of the Southwest: southern New Mexico and southern Arizona around Tucson—the area along the Mexican border. The vast desert lands and isolated mountain ranges of **Southern New Mexico**, north and west of El Paso, have not enjoyed the acclaim heaped upon Santa Fe and Taos—meaning visitors are unlikely to be fighting off crowds in these parts. From the friendly, agriculturally dependent city of Las Cruces, New Mexico's second largest, to the ultimate high-tech White Sands Missile Range test facility, and from Lincoln County, where Billy the Kid became a legend, to the depths of Carlsbad Caverns and the little-known resort oasis of Ruidoso, travellers can find unpretentious hospitality here, far from the trendy and the chichi. There seems to be something old and something new hidden behind every cactus shrub. Southern New Mexico is the antithesis of fashion, but the traveller who does a little digging may uncover a seeming contradiction: The *roots* of Southwestern style are more easily found here than anywhere else in the region.

West across the border into **Southern Arizona**, and at its primary city of Tucson, travellers may deepen their understanding of the blending of the old and new West. Historic desert towns such as Tombstone and Bisbee reflect the rough-and-tumble heydays of gunfighters and copper miners, respectively, while visitors to the Mission San Xavier del Bac, just south of Tucson, may experience a sense of the spirit of the early Spanish explorers and Jesuit missionaries in the only Spanish colonial church in the United States still serving an Indian parish. The epic desert here is grand enough to house monuments to war and peace: the Titan Missile Museum in Green Valley, recently a Cold War defensive site; the more serene Organ Pipe Cactus National Monument, America's largest national monument; and the Cabeza Prieta National Wildlife Refuge, home to desert bighorn sheep and the endangered Sonoran pronghorn antelope.

Tucson itself may be the paradigm of big-city living with a Southwestern flair, combining all the attractions of the regional lifestyle, from terrific Mexican restaurants to modern resorts and evocative guest ranches, along with more of the old and new. The Arizona–Sonora Desert Museum preserves the old and indigenous life forms of this startlingly lively desertscape, while Old Tucson Studios provides a Disneyesque glimpse into moviemaking at a site used by Western filmmakers since the early days of the moving image. Nearby, Biosphere 2, the controversial pseudoscientific experiment in survival within a closed artificial environment, looks the other way, toward the 21st century and beyond.

Heading south past the **Mexican border** provides further insight into the cultural blend that goes into the Southwest experience. From Nogales on the border south to Magdalena and Arizpe, and north again to Naco, travellers will find rural ranching and mining towns, architectural precursors of the mission styles of the American Southwest, people of devout faith, and cultures and attitudes virtually unchanged from the earliest days of the Spanish conquest.

CENTRAL ARIZONA AND THE CANYONS REGION

Central and Northern Arizona offer more desert scenery, although of a quite different variety. North and east of Flagstaff the Great Basin Desert contains plunging canyons, sandstone cliffs, and pinnacles and spires rising more than 1,000 feet. The Painted Desert and Petrified Forest National Park characterize this region, little changed since prehistory. In contrast, the bone-dry Mojave Desert to the northwest, extending beyond the Grand Canyon, reveals undulating dunes and rare, tenacious plant life that is able to exist on less than five inches of yearly rainfall.

This broad area, from Phoenix and the Valley of the Sun up into southern Utah, encompasses six life zones, ranging from lower desert to arctic/alpine, from saguaro cactus–spiked flatlands to the world's largest ponderosa pine forest, and including Colorado's Lake Mead (near Las Vegas), and Lake Powell (in southern Utah), ranked one and two as the world's largest man-made lakes. The towns of Jerome and Prescott, harkening back to wilder Western days, are repositories of mining and Western lore in period architecture, while Sedona attracts New Age types to its scenic red-rock country.

Farther north is the most-visited destination in the entire Southwest: the **Grand Canyon**. Even superlatives fail to describe the mile-deep chasm carved here by the Colorado River. Humanity is humbled by the extravagance of nature contained within the millions of years of geological history revealed by the striated sandstone walls of this very big chasm. The ever popular, highly developed **South Rim** of the Grand Canyon is accessed through the Arizona towns of Flagstaff or Williams. It's a 215-mile drive to the less-visited **North Rim**. Because most visitors reach only one rim, we have acceded to nature and split the canyon down the center, connecting our coverage of the North Rim with Utah's Canyon Country.

Southeast of the Grand Canyon is **Arizona High Country**, tracing the 8,000-foot Mogollon Rim—the dramatic edge of the Colorado Plateau—through forests, mountains, lakes, trails, and scenic drives and offering relief from the sweltering deserts. The southwest portion of the state is again altogether different, revealing lonely deserts, Mexican border towns, and even the original London Bridge, the pride of Lake Havasu City on the Colorado (a developer had it moved here block by block).

In the center of all this lies the **Phoenix/Scottsdale/ Valley of the Sun** megalopolis, reclaimed from the deserts and today an irrigated oasis. Among numerous shops, galleries, and golf and tennis resorts travellers find the Heard Museum, housing one of the world's largest collections of prehistoric and modern Indian artifacts, the Desert Botanical Museum, and Taliesin West, created by architect Frank Lloyd Wright to establish models of design and construction to meet the demands of the 21st-century Southwest.

The works of nature are also stunningly displayed in southern Utah's **Canyon Country**. Spreading north and east from the North Rim of the Grand Canyon and the so-called Arizona Strip "trapped" between the Colorado River ditch and the Utah border, the colorful spires and rock steeples of Bryce and Zion national parks are otherworldly, jagged moonscapes. Lake Powell on the Colorado River offers leisurely houseboat trips through the scenic Glen Canyon area, including the natural stone arch at Rainbow Bridge. Canyonlands and Arches national parks offer more moonscapes, hot, dry, and thoroughly engaging sculpted canyons, and gravity-defying stone arches best seen by the adventurous traveller on a hike, a river-raft journey, a jeep tour, or a mountain-bike excursion.

LAS VEGAS

And last but by no means least, for gamblers and lovers of neon and glitz Las Vegas glimmers on the edge of the desert west of the Grand Canyon, a mecca for travellers seeking lively entertainment and mammoth resorts. There is more to Vegas than craps tables and elaborate shows, however, including designer shopping, extravagant dining bargains, golf, and even family-oriented theme parks and day trips to the Nevada-Arizona border and Lake Mead, created by the Hoover Dam on the Colorado.

If there really is such a thing as Southwestern style, it exists in the people you will meet along the way through this challenging and rewarding wonderland of natural and man-made pleasures. The cowboys and wranglers in Durango's San Juan National Forest have little in common with the bejeweled denizens of Las Vegas's casinos. Rural southern New Mexicans are perhaps even farther in spirit than in geographical distance from the gallery hoppers in Santa Fe or Scottsdale. The Navajo, Hopi, Ute, Pima, and other Southwestern Indians decidedly follow their own historically influenced agendas, while desert rats and mountain men throughout the Southwest survive the inhospitable though often bizarrely beautiful elements of nature, the very elements that attract and challenge skiers, mountain bikers, kayakers, hikers, and river rafters, among many others.

What all these different people share is both ephemeral and enduring. The original Indian peoples are a memory and gunfighters are gone. Grizzled prospectors towing overworked burros are few and far between. No conquistadors will cross your path. But the echo of their presence resounds in cities and towns, large and small. A pioneering spirit still wafts through the canyons and across the deserts, along the rivers, and over the mountaintops in a land ever more accessible, yet remarkably little changed from its earlier incarnations.

Perseverance is no small part of any legitimate Southwestern style, reflecting a state of heart as well as mind.

Its beat can carry you through here on a journey that can bring out the best aspects of yourself—what travel in its highest form is really all about. Food and water may still be scarce, although probably only deep in the boonies, and it may not be easy to comprehend the enormity and complexity of the Southwest, but there has always been room for travellers, and you are welcome here.

USEFUL FACTS

When to Go
If you're not planning a ski vacation to one of Southwestern America's many exciting mountain resorts, the most pleasant time to visit the region by far is during the warmer months.

In the drier, more southerly desert areas of Arizona, New Mexico, and West Texas spring begins early. By mid-April daytime temperatures often range in the high 60s and low 70s, and spectacular quilts of wildflowers—especially in Arizona's Sonoran Desert and the Llano Estacado (High Plains) of West Texas—generally start to bloom about the same time. Strong spring winds occasionally fill the air with dust and make life miserable for campers, hikers, and motorists, but these breezy inconveniences are usually temporary. Temperatures rise dramatically in the lower elevations by the end of May, often reaching 100°F by mid-June.

At higher altitudes, of course, the weather is more moderate. In cities such as Albuquerque, Santa Fe, and Durango—all above 5,000 feet in elevation—jackets and sweaters may be necessary during the day until early June. Late June and early to mid-July are the Southwest's hottest months, with daytime temperatures in low-desert areas surpassing 120°F. Even in the mountains, 90-degree days aren't uncommon. During late July, however, afternoon thundershowers begin to cool and dampen the parched earth, and in south and central Arizona especially, short but fierce rainstorms (so-called monsoons) often slam into the region, sending outdoor lovers scampering for shelter. These storms seldom last for more than an hour or two, and almost always occur during the late afternoon or early evening. The outdoor Santa Fe Opera, for example, starts all performances at 9:00 P.M., so its audiences won't get wet. By mid-September things have usually gotten back to normal with clear warm days and cooler nights. In October the region takes on a magnificent glow as autumn wildflowers bloom and high-country aspen, oak, and maple trees begin their annual color change.

The coolest Southwestern months are January and February, when many of the desert areas may experience below-freezing weather. The busiest periods are over Memorial Day weekend, the Fourth of July, and Labor Day weekend.

Entry Requirements

Believe it or not, thousands of Americans still think New Mexico and Arizona are not part of the United States. Tourism offices in both states receive numerous queries each year requesting information on passports, vaccinations, and currency exchange.

Of course, only foreign visitors must have a valid passport to visit the Southwest. Citizens of Canada, Great Britain, Australia, New Zealand, Japan, and most Western European countries do not need a visa if they are staying less than 90 days and the trip is strictly for pleasure. There are no vaccination requirements.

If you're not a U.S. citizen, always carry plenty of identification when travelling by automobile or bus in the Southwest. Because of the overwhelming number of illegal aliens crossing the Rio Grande from Mexico in search of work, U.S. Border Patrol checkpoints now exist on most major highways, and many smaller ones as well. To be stopped, questioned, and searched by these polite but no-nonsense agents is not something most foreign visitors would enjoy.

Arrival by Air

The major U.S. airlines serve Albuquerque, New Mexico; Durango, Colorado; El Paso, Texas; Las Vegas, Nevada; Phoenix, Arizona; and Tucson, Arizona, while regional carriers provide connections to many smaller communities. Southwest Airlines offers the largest number of daily flights into and out of the region, but America West, American, Continental, Delta, TWA, USAir, and United also provide daily service.

Air France, British Airways, and Lufthansa offer daily or semiweekly flights from many European capitals to Dallas, Houston, and Los Angeles. The nearest international gateway to the Southwest for most other carriers is Los Angeles.

Arrival by Train
Amtrak offers daily train service to many Southwestern cities from Los Angeles and Chicago.

Arrival by Bus
Not recommended.

Renting a Car
If you're not a U.S. citizen you must be at least 25 years of age, hold a valid passport and driver's license from your resident country, show a return ticket for sea or air travel, and have a major credit card to rent a car in the United States. If you don't return the vehicle to the city in which you rented it, be prepared to pay a substantial drop-off fee (as much as $1,000). All Southwestern states now require that front-seat occupants of automobiles wear seat belts.

What to Wear
Travellers who wear anything but lightweight casual clothing during the spring, summer, and fall will be uncomfortable and noticeably out of place. Shorts, tee-shirts, and sneakers are the favored attire for most visitors, though a lightweight sweater may come in handy for cooler evenings in higher altitudes. Winter vacationers should pack for moderate daytime temperatures and cold nights (even Tucson receives an occasional snow). Leave your suits, ties, high heels, and cocktail dresses at home; only the most exclusive Southwestern restaurants require anything but casual dress.

Local Time
From late October through late April the states of Arizona, Colorado, New Mexico, Utah, and the westernmost portion of Texas near El Paso are on mountain standard time—1 hour ahead of Los Angeles and 2 hours behind New York. Nevada falls into the Pacific time zone (the same as California), which is 3 hours behind New York.

In April, however, when the rest of the United States moves to daylight saving time, Arizona automatically reverts to Pacific time. In other words, from the last Sunday in April through the last Sunday in October, Arizona, Nevada, and California will be in the same time zone; Arizona will then be 3 hours behind New York, not 2.

Telephoning

The Southwest uses six area codes: all of New Mexico is 505, all of Arizona is 602, southwestern Colorado (in the Four Corners) is 303, Utah is 801, Nevada is 702, and western Texas is 915. To direct-dial a telephone number from outside the United States, dial 011, the country code for the United States (1), the area code, and the local telephone number. Most pay telephones in the United States take quarters.

Electrical Current

Standard electrical current in the United States is 110/115 volts. Most drugstores and many hotel gift shops now sell adapter plugs for foreign-made appliances.

Cautions

Late-summer thunderstorms in the Southwest are not merely downpours; they are driving tidal waves of vertical force that may deposit a million gallons of water on a single square mile of land in less than five minutes. If you happen into one of these so-called toad stranglers, don't ever attempt to drive across a flooded section of road or highway no matter how insignificant the trickle may seem. In some parts of Arizona, highways—where they cross dangerous gullies and washes—are marked by signs. It's illegal to cross these "posted dips" in stormy weather, even if water is not yet coming over the road.

What happens is this: When the earth beneath the storm has absorbed all the moisture it can handle, torrents of excess rainwater fill nearby gullies and flow downhill at express-train speed. The resulting phenomenon, known as a flash flood, can be and often is deadly. Anything in the flood's path—logs, trees, even automobiles—is simply carried away. If your car's electrical system shorts out in the bottom of a flood-prone gully and you can't reach high ground quickly, the consequences could be unthinkable.

Another basic necessity, in desert areas at least, is to don a wide-brimmed hat if you plan to be outside for more than a few minutes. Sunstroke is a common malady in the hot, dry Southwestern climate, and can absolutely ruin an otherwise pleasant vacation. It's also a good idea to carry a full canteen of water and a roll of toilet tissue in your car. Visitor facilities in the more remote regions of the Southwest, especially on Indian reservations, are sometimes few and far between.

Business Hours and Holidays

Normal business hours throughout the Southwest are
8:00 A.M. to 5:00 P.M., but many shops and stores in resort
areas open from 10:00 A.M. to 6:00 P.M. Banks generally
open at 9:00 A.M. and close at 3:00 P.M. Major holidays are
Easter, Memorial Day, Fourth of July, Labor Day, Thanksgiving, and Christmas; these are good times to stay off the
highways.

Currency Exchange

If you're visiting from another country, change money into
U.S. dollars at your gateway airport. Most banks, shops,
hotels, and restaurants—even in major cities—are simply
not equipped for international currency exchange. U.S.
currency traveller's checks and major credit cards are
accepted virtually everywhere.

For Further Information

Arizona
Arizona Office of Tourism
1100 West Washington Street
Phoenix, AZ 85007
Tel: (602) 542-8687

Phoenix
Phoenix Convention & Visitor Bureau
One Arizona Center
400 East Van Buren, #600
Phoenix, AZ 85004
Tel: (602) 254-6500

Tucson
Metropolitan Tucson Convention & Visitor Bureau
130 South Scott Avenue
Tucson, AZ 85701
Tel: (602) 624-1817

Colorado
Colorado Tourism Board
1625 Broadway, Suite 1700
Denver, CO 80202
Tel: (303) 592-5510

Durango
Durango Chamber of Commerce
P.O. Box 2587
Durango, CO 81302
Tel: (800) 253-1616 or (303) 247-0312

New Mexico
Tourism and Travel Division
491 Old Santa Fe Trail
Santa Fe, NM 87501
Tel: (505) 827-7400

Albuquerque
Albuquerque Convention & Visitors Bureau
121 Tijeras NE
Albuquerque, NM 87102
Tel: (800) 284-2282 or (505) 243-3696

Las Cruces
Las Cruces Convention & Visitor Bureau
311 North Downtown Mall
Las Cruces, NM 88001
Tel: (505) 524-8521

Santa Fe
Santa Fe Convention & Visitors Bureau
Sweeny Center
201 West Marcy Street
Santa Fe, NM 87501
Tel: (800) 777-CITY or (505) 984-6760

Taos
Taos Chamber Of Commerce
P.O. Drawer I
Taos, NM 87571
Tel: (505) 758-3873

Nevada
Nevada Commission on Tourism
5151 South Carson Street
Carson City, NV 89710
Tel: (800) NEVADA-8 or (702) 687-4322

Las Vegas
Las Vegas Convention & Visitor Authority
3150 Paradise Road
Las Vegas, NV 89109
Tel: (702) 892-0711

El Paso & West Texas
El Paso Convention & Visitor Bureau
1 Civic Center Plaza
El Paso, TX 79901
Tel: (915) 534-0600

Utah
Utah Travel Council

Capitol Hall, 300 North State
Salt Lake City, UT 84114
Tel: (801) 538-1030

—Buddy Mays

BIBLIOGRAPHY

CHARLES AMSDEN, *Navajo Weaving, Its Technique and History* (1933). The classic work on one of the great arts of the Navajos.

RUDOLFO ANAYA, *Albuquerque* (1992). The story of a young man's search for his father in present-day Albuquerque. This novel, dealing with the complexities of explosive urban development and the ironies of racial purity in an area where three cultures have collided since 1846, sheds new light on the city.

————, *Bless Me, Ultima* (1972). Small-town life on the eastern plains of New Mexico by this noted contemporary Spanish-American author.

SAM P. ARNOLD, *Eating Up the Santa Fe Trail* (1990). A history of food and recipes from the Santa Fe Trail by a Denver restaurateur and food historian.

BRUCE BABBITT, ED., *Grand Canyon: An Anthology* (1978). Twenty-three authors, from Spanish explorers to present-day adventurers, relate their Grand Canyon experiences in this book edited by a former Arizona governor and U.S. Secretary of the Interior.

TOM BAHTI, *An Introduction to Southwestern Indian Arts and Crafts* (1964), *Southwestern Indian Ceremonials* (1970), and *Southwestern Indian Tribes* (1968). This classic trilogy, periodically updated and revised by the late author's son, Mark Bahti, answers the most frequently asked questions about the wheres and whys of tribal ceremonials; the distinctive "personalities" and lifeways of each tribe; the selection and care of Navajo rugs, Apache basketry, Pueblo pottery, Hopi kachina dolls; the differences between traditional Navajo, Hopi, and Zuni jewelry; and the cross-tribal melding of traditional styles by contemporary artisans.

RUTH LAUGHLIN BARKER, *The Wind Leaves No Shadow* (1948). A novel about one of New Mexico's more colorful 19th-century characters, Doña Tules Barcelo, operator of a gambling casino and one of the wealthiest and most influential women of her day.

RICHARD BRADFORD, *Red Sky at Morning* (1968). An amusing and well-written account of the life of a youth who comes to live in Santa Fe during World War II. Made into a movie in 1970.

ELLEN BROWN, *Southwest Tastes* (1987). Interviews and recipes from the 60 experts of the 1987 Public Broadcasting Service series "Great Chefs of the West." Chronicles the debut of nouvelle-Southwestern cuisine.

J. ROSS BROWNE, *Adventures in the Apache Country; A Tour Through Arizona and Sonora, 1864* (1974). Originally published as a series of articles in *Harper's* magazine in 1864 and 1865. This edition includes an introduction and index by Donald Powell.

HOWARD BRYAN, *Wildest of the Wild West* (1988). Wild but true tales from the frontier town of Las Vegas, New Mexico, 1835–1915. After the railroad came to Las Vegas in 1879 the town was the effective political capital of New Mexico until its downfall in the agricultural depression of the 1920s.

BAINBRIDGE BUNTING, *John Gaw Meem, Southwestern Architect* (1983). This well-illustrated book traces the career of Santa Fe's premier architect, concentrating on the larger elements of the Southwestern style.

WALTER NOBLE BURNS, *Tombstone* (1929; reprinted 1952). Colorful, accurate re-creation of lawless Tombstone in the 1880s.

FABIOLA CABEZA DE BACA, *We Fed Them Cactus,* (1954). A Spanish-American account of ranch life.

ALVAR NUÑEZ CABEZA DE VACA, *Adventures in the Unknown Interior of America* (1983). The author, the first Western European to travel through the Southwest after being shipwrecked on the Gulf Coast in 1528, tells the true and harrowing adventure—without a lick of fiction in it—of how he and three others spent the next eight years trying to get back to their countrymen in Mexico.

SHEILA MACGIVEN CAMERON, *More of The Best of New Mexico Kitchens* (1983). A collection of recipes that have appeared in *New Mexico* magazine. Classic, tried-and-true basic instructions for *rellenos,* beans, and enchiladas in the traditional manner.

ROBERT L. CASEY, *Journey to the High Southwest* (1988). The third edition of a highly detailed, anecdotal traveller's guide to the Four Corners.

WILLA CATHER, *Death Comes for the Archbishop* (1955). One of the most famous novels about New Mexico, the book is a fictionalized account of the life of Archbishop Jean Baptiste Lamy, the first resident bishop of New Mexico, after 1851.

CHILTON, CHILTON, ARANGO, DUDLEY, NEARY, AND STELZNER, *New Mexico, a New Guide to the Colorful State* (1984). A major revision of the 1940 WPA guide to the state, including history, geography, arts and crafts, literature, economy, religion, and 18 tours.

HALKA CHRONIC, *Roadside Geology of Arizona* (1983). Organized along major highway routes, including the national parks and some national monuments, this book is well illustrated with photos, diagrams, and maps.

AGNES MORELY CLEAVELAND, *No Life for a Lady* (1941). A colorful account of Anglo ranch life when New Mexico was still wild and woolly.

BERNICE COSULICH, *Tucson; the Fabulous Story of Arizona's Ancient Walled Presidio 1692–1900's* (1953). A carefully researched history of Tucson from Padre Eusebio Kino's first visit in 1692.

JOHN J. AND FRANK C. CRAIGHEAD, JR., AND RAY J. DAVIS, *A Field Guide to Rocky Mountain Wildflowers* (1974). A richly illustrated guide to common Southwestern wildflowers.

Day Hikes in the Santa Fe Area (1990). Instructions for about 20 hikes, from easy to strenuous, with maps. Published by the Santa Fe Sierra Club.

WILLIAM DE BUYS, *Enchantment and Exploitation: The Life and Hard Times of a New Mexican Mountain Range* (1985). A superlatively researched and well-written account of the cultures of northern New Mexico, their interactions, their effect on the Sangre de Cristo Mountains, and the effect the mountains have had on them.

DON DEDERA, *Navajo Rugs, How to Find, Evaluate, Buy and Care for Them* (1990). The author, a former editor of *Arizona Highways* magazine, gives the history of Navajo weaving, illustrates how it is done, shows traditional regional styles, and offers practical advice.

DAVE DEWITT AND MARY JANE WILAN, *The Food Lover's Handbook to The Southwest* (1992). Chatty, versatile guide to the history of Southwestern foods and an excellent reference for gourmet shops, food festivals, and outdoor markets. Includes classic Southwestern recipes from top regional chefs.

EDWIN P. DOZIER, *The Pueblo Indians of North America* (1970). A fine look into these Indian cultures.

ELDREDGE, SCHIMMEL, AND TRUETTNER, *Art in New Mexico, 1900–1945; Paths to Taos and Santa Fe* (1986). This catalogue, published as an accompaniment to the Smithsonian exhibit of the same name, is a first-rate introduction to New Mexican art and artists.

ERNA FERGUSSON, *Dancing Gods* (1931). A classic about Indian ceremonies and religion.

———, *Mexican Cooking* (1934). A book of classic New Mexican recipes, which differ from those of Old Mexico in that they represent peasant food, less fancy and less varied than its southern cousin.

———, *New Mexico, a Pageant of Three People* (1951). A thorough examination of the three peoples and cultures of New Mexico. A classic.

SEYMOUR L. FISHBEIN, *Grand Canyon Country: Its Majesty and Its Lore* (1991). Spectacular color photography with text that almost matches the sweeping grandeur of Arizona's big canyon.

ROGER AND ETHEL FREEMAN, *Day Hikes and Trail Rides In and Around Phoenix* (1991). Detailed descriptions introduce the parks and wilderness areas of the Sonoran Desert that surrounds Arizona's largest city.

ARRELL MORGAN GIBSON, *The Santa Fe and Taos Colonies; Age of the Muses, 1900–1942* (1983). A popular account of the art colonies of New Mexico.

JOSIAH GREGG, *Commerce of the Prairies* (1967). First published in 1844 and a classic for over one hundred years, this tale of the early trade along the Santa Fe Trail was written by a man who was there.

JOHN R. HAMILTON (photographer), *Thunder in the Dust* (1987). A 30-year chronology in color photography taken behind the scenes and on the locations of numerous Hollywood Westerns, with text by John Calvin Batchelor.

ALICE CORBIN HENDERSON, *Brothers of Light* (1937). A lovely personal account of the author's introduction to the secretive rites of the lay order the Penitentes through her Spanish-American acquaintances. Beautifully illustrated by the author's husband, noted artist William Penhallow Henderson.

MIKE HILL, *Hikers and Climbers Guide to the Sandia Mountains* (1983). Lively, practical, dependable take-along about the Albuquerque area for those who love the outdoors.

PAUL HORGAN, *Great River* (1984). A wonderfully readable history of the Rio Grande, New Mexico's most estimable natural resource, by a highly respected historian of the Southwest.

————, *Lamy of Santa Fe* (1975). This nonfiction accompaniment to Cather's book tells the story of Lamy's life, including the difficulties the straitlaced French bishop had with a people he served well but never quite understood.

MYRA ELLEN JENKINS AND ALBERT SCHROEDER, *A Brief History of New Mexico* (1974). An excellent short history of New Mexico by two of its top historians.

RICHARD E. KLINCK, *Land of Room Enough and Time Enough* (1984). An investigation into the geography, legends, and people of Monument Valley.

JOSEPH WOOD KRUTCH, *The Desert Year* (1985). A naturalist's loving look at and exploration of the Sonoran Desert, including its flora, fauna, and critters, and its glorious sunsets and seasons.

OLIVER LA FARGE, *Behind the Mountains* (1955). A series of vignettes about the descendants of the first European to travel through the Southwest, Cabeza de Vaca, into whose family La Farge married. Amusing and compelling, these stories tell of the family's life on their ranch in Northern New Mexico in the early 1900s, a way of life that is now all but gone.

————, *Laughing Boy* (1929). A writer and anthropologist who devoted his life to the pursuit of Indian rights, La Farge offers an authentic and fascinating look into the hearts, minds, and life of the Navajo Indians through the window of a star-crossed love story, in this, his first novel. Pulitzer Prize winner of 1929.

————, *The Man with the Calabash Pipe* (1966). A compilation of the author's weekly articles for the *Santa Fe New Mexican* and an excellent introduction to the people and times of Santa Fe through the early 1960s.

————, *The Mother Ditch* (1983). A children's introduction to New Mexico, and to traditional Spanish-American village life and agriculture, by way of a story told through the eyes of a boy. This second edition is in both English and Spanish (on alternating pages).

————, *Santa Fe, The Autobiography of a Southwestern Town* (1959). The story of Santa Fe and its people from 1849 to 1953 as told through selected clippings from the local newspaper the *Santa Fe New Mexican.*

RAYMOND FRIDAY LOCKE, *The Book of the Navajo* (1992, revised). A landmark work, eloquently written by the founding editor of *Mankind,* a magazine of popular history. The book covers Navajo history, culture, legends, and lifeways. This volume is so comprehensive it is being used as a textbook at the community college run by the tribe to teach Navajo students their own history.

CARLES F. LUMMIS, *The Land of Poco Tiempo* (1928). A description of New Mexico in the 1880s, the Indians, the Penitentes, the songs, and the religion, by the man who coined the phrase "See America First."

ALICE MARRIOTT, *Maria: The Potter of San Ildefonso* (1948). A classic account of the life of one of New Mexico's most famous artisans, Maria Martínez.

CHRISTINE MATHER AND SHARON WOODS, *Santa Fe Style* (1986). This book on what is popularly perceived as Santa Fe style presents an interesting mixture of the true style—which was really just thrown together and its contemporary, self-conscious form.

BUDDY MAYS, *Ancient Cities of the Southwest* (1982). An illustrated guide to many of the Southwest's archaic Indian encampments, abandoned cliff dwellings, and ruined pueblos.

————, *A Guide to Western Wildlife* (1988). A layman's guide, illustrated by photographs, to the most common species of birds, reptiles, and mammals in the Western states.

————, *Indian Villages of the Southwest* (1985). The writer details the colorful past and present-day activities of the Indian pueblos of New Mexico and Arizona.

EDWIN D. MCKEE, *Ancient Landscapes of the Grand Canyon Region* (1982). An eminent geologist gives a brief account of the evolution of the Grand Canyon area.

TERI C. MCLUHAN, *Dream Tracks* (1985). A study of how the Santa Fe railroad opened up the Southwest and how the Indians were idealized to stimulate travel to the area. With hand-colored lantern slides from the William E. Kopplin collection.

LEON C. METZ, *Border: The U.S.–Mexico Line* (1989). The story of the life and conflicts along the 2,000-mile border from the early days of America's westward expansion through present times.

MARK MILLER, *Coyote Cafe* (1989). The cookbook by the man who put SantaFare on the map and started the tsunami of nouvelle-Southwestern cuisine across America. A "must own" for anyone seriously interested in cooking with chiles, and a good read as well.

JOHN NICHOLS, *If Mountains Die; A New Mexico Memoir* (1979). A lyrical description of Nichols's introduction to New Mexico as a teenager and his move to Taos in the 1970s. His appreciation of New Mexico's beauty and its mores, and the splendid photographs by William Davis, outweigh the author's unfortunate politics.

————, *The Milagro Beanfield War* (1974). This book, well known even before it was made into a movie by Robert Redford, concerns the attempt by a northern New Mexico village to maintain its traditional way of life despite rapacious developers. Amusing, well written, and rather political.

DAVID GRANT NOBLE, ED., *Santa Fe, History of an Ancient City* (1989). A handsomely illustrated history of Santa Fe, selective but done with depth and scholarship.

GEORGIA O'KEEFFE, *Georgia O'Keeffe* (1976). The artist's thoughts about her own work, beautifully illustrated with paintings from throughout her career.

Old Santa Fe Today (1991). Published by the Historic Santa Fe Foundation, the city's premier preservation organization, the fourth edition is an indispensable guide to the historic buildings and features of Santa Fe.

LESLEY POLING-KEMPES, *The Harvey Girls: Women Who Opened the West* (1989). Stories of the women who worked as waitresses at Fred Harvey's restaurants and hotels (of which Santa Fe's La Fonda was one) along the Atchison, Topeka & Santa Fe Railway from the 1880s through the 1950s.

DOUGLAS PRESTON, *Cities of Gold: A Journey Across the American Southwest in Pursuit of Coronado* (1992). A spirited account of the author's re-creation of Coronado's trek, and his exploration of the West and its characters.

EUGENE MANLOVE RHODES, *Pasó por Aquí* (1973). A well-loved novel about cowboy life.

CARLOS A. SCHWANTES, ED., *Bisbee; Urban Outpost of the Frontier* (1992). Six essays and 100 photographs, with a focus on the boom years, 1880–1920.

SANDRA AND LAUREL SETH, *Adobe! Homes and Interiors of Taos, Santa Fe, and the Southwest* (1990). A lavishly illustrated book on the elements of classic Southwestern architecture.

CARL D. SHEPPARD, *Creator of the Santa Fe Style, Isaac Hamilton Rapp, Architect* (1988). The book follows Rapp's life, career, and his invaluable contribution to Santa Fe architecture, including the Museum of Fine Arts and La Fonda Hotel.

JOHN SHERMAN, *Santa Fe: A Pictorial History* (1983). A well-researched and well-produced photographic history of Santa Fe.

MARC SIMMONS, *Albuquerque: A Narrative History* (1982). One of New Mexico's leading historians discusses the city's distinctive mix of landscape, climate, architecture, cultural tradition, and history.

———, *New Mexico, A Bicentennial History* (1977). A first-rate history of the state and part of a series that covered each of the states for the bicentennial.

———, *Yesterday in Santa Fe* (1990). A small, selective book of colorful events that bring Santa Fe history to life.

RICHARD L. SPIVEY, *María* (1979). A handsome photographic essay on Maria Martínez, the famed potter of San Ildefonso Pueblo, and her art.

JOAN AND CARL STROMQUIST, *Santa Fe Recipe* (1989). Wonderful recipes from great restaurants, many of which are now only memories. This amazing cookbook, full of eclectic recipes for every course, reflects the wealth and range of gourmet talent always on the move in the City Different.

CLARA LEE TANNER, *Southwest Indian Painting: A Changing Art* (1957; reprinted 1980). The first complete chronicle on Southwestern Indian art, from prehistoric and historic influences to the development of contemporary artists of the Rio Grande, the western Pueblos, Navajos, Apaches, and others.

ANNE TAYLOR, *Southwestern Ornamentation and Design, the Architecture of John Gaw Meem* (1989). Lavishly illustrated book of the details that made Meem's architecture so influential and important to Southwestern style.

W. H. TIMMONS, *El Paso: A Borderlands History* (1990). The best overview of El Paso available. David J. Weber's foreword reads, "El Paso's history is, in microcosm, the history of the United States–Mexican border region."

NORA B. TRULSSON AND PAULA PANICH, *The Desert Southwest Gardens* (1990). Over 250 color photos and detailed descriptions of 15 Southwestern homes from Texas to Southern California. An architectural odyssey through some memorable historic and contemporary residences.

STEWART L. UDALL, *To the Inland Empire* (1987). A splendid account of the bravery of the Spanish conquistadors, especially Francisco Vásquez de Coronado, written by the former Secretary of the Interior under President John Kennedy. Photographs by Jerry Jacka.

FRANK WATERS, *The Book of the Hopi* (1963). The first, and still one of the best, explorations into the rich ceremonial life of this northeastern Arizona tribe. The discussion of this Fourth World of Hopi evolution, tribal clans, migrations, ceremonial cycles, and history is somewhat esoteric, but then so is the traditional Hopi lifeway. With source material from Oswald White Bear Fredericks.

———, *Masked Gods: Navaho and Pueblo Ceremonialism* (1950). A classic about Indian ceremonies and religion.

HENRY P. WALKER AND DON BUFKIN, *Historical Atlas of Arizona* (1986). This history, complete with many maps (of major trails, explorers' routes, Mexican missions, Indian tribes, military posts, copper mines, etc.), is more than the history of man in Arizona; it defines the terrain, climate, vegetation, geography, and geology of the natural settings that impact upon human life here, and as such it makes Arizona history much easier to understand.

DAVID J. WEBER, *The Spanish Frontier in North America* (1992). A highly skilled and knowledgeable scholar brings the Spanish frontier to life. Accurate, detailed, dramatic, sweeping scholarship and writing.

MARTA WEIGLE, *Brothers of Light, Brothers of Blood: The Penitentes of the Southwest* (1989). An authoritative account of the Penitente religious brotherhood, which has been central to the Spanish-American faith in New Mexico since the early 1800s.

ROBERT R. WHITE, *The Taos Society of Artists* (1983). The best book on the Taos artists.

BARTON WRIGHT, *Hopi Kachinas: The Complete Guide to Collecting Kachina Dolls* (1977). From clowns to ogres, kachina dolls are illustrated and their purposes explained.

Movies

The romantically photogenic New Mexico landscape has attracted moviemakers ever since Thomas Edison shot *Indian Day School* here in 1898. *Pueblo Legend* was filmed in 1912 (the same year New Mexico became a state) by D.W. Griffith and starred Mary Pickford. A series of Tom Mix movies was filmed in Las Vegas between 1914 and 1917.

New Mexico's most famous star, Greer Garson, lived from the 1940s until recently on a ranch in Pecos. Her own Santa Fe movie, *Strange Lady in Town,* was actually shot in Tucson.

Since the 1970s New Mexico has made a concerted effort to attract the movie industry. However, its countryside usually appears without billing, only as a generic "Southwest" backdrop to the action, as in *Young Guns* and *Young Guns II, Greaser's Palace, Twins, Two-Lane Blacktop, Lust in the Dust,* and *The Legend of the Lone Ranger.*

A few movies, however, have captured something of the spirit of New Mexico:

Ride the Pink Horse (1947), with Robert Montgomery, is a *film noir* mystery set in Santa Fe at fiesta, adapted from a book by local author Dorothy Bell Hughes.

Richard Thomas starred in *Red Sky at Morning* (1970), an enjoyable adaptation of Richard Bradford's novel of adolescence during World War II.

The Milagro Beanfield War (1988), based on John Nichols's serio-comic novel, captured much of the book's spirit and whimsy. It was filmed in Truchas on the High Road to Taos, although partially on a set built there for the purpose.

City Slickers (1991), with Billy Crystal and Jack Palance (who won a supporting-actor Oscar for his role), was filmed in Abiquiu and in the new film center made possible by Greer Garson at the College of Santa Fe.

There is also a well-made movie from 1953 about union organizers in Silver City: *Salt of the Earth*. Actor Will Geer, the producer, and the writer were all blacklisted at the time.

—*John Pen La Farge with Maggie Wilson*

NORTHERN
NEW MEXICO
AND
THE FOUR CORNERS

ALBUQUERQUE

AROUND ALBUQUERQUE

SANTA FE

AROUND SANTA FE

TAOS AND
THE ENCHANTED CIRCLE

THE FOUR CORNERS

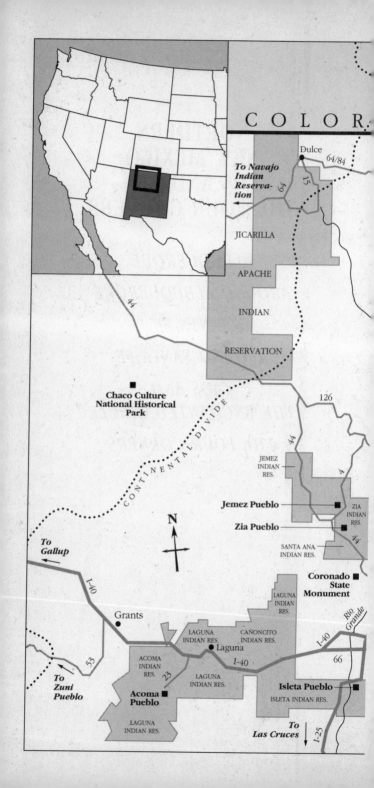

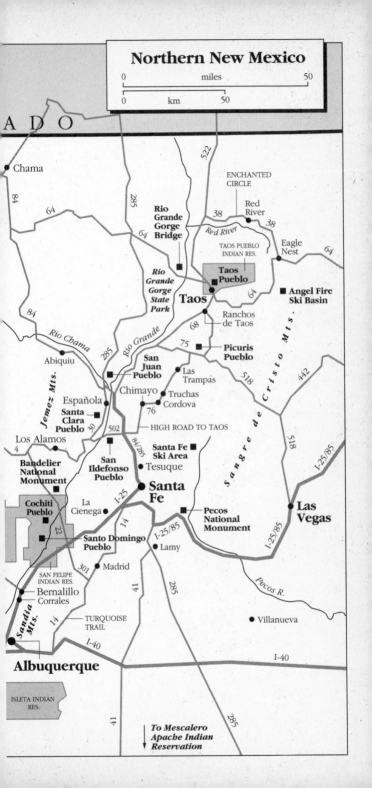

NORTHERN NEW MEXICO

By John Pen La Farge
and Judyth Hill

John Pendaries La Farge is the scion of a family that goes back to Alvar Nuñez Cabeza de Vaca, the first European to travel through New Mexico. A lifetime Santa Fean, he is a historian, the author of numerous articles, essays, and short stories, and the editor of an oral history of Santa Fe. Judyth Hill, who writes on the food of New Mexico at the end of this chapter, is a journalist, performance artist, teacher, and published poet who lives near Santa Fe. She is a food columnist for the Albuquerque Journal, *writes on food for* Crosswinds *magazine, and is a contributor to the* Santa Fe Reporter. *Among many other activities, she coordinates the annual Santa Fe Wine and Chile Festival.*

If you have decided to travel through Northern New Mexico, you have chosen the Land of Enchantment. More than a license-plate phrase, the Land of Enchantment is quite real. The climate, the harsh beauty, the astonishing range of landscapes, the sky and its heaping, wild clouds, the three cultures that make up the population—all of these elements contribute to the magic.

Marvelously diverse opportunities for the traveller are also part of the wonder of this land. The Southwestern food that has become so popular throughout the United States in recent years began in New Mexico, and is at its purest and hottest here—there are no tomatoes in *our* chili. You can travel through landscapes that vary from

43

hot, dry, deeply eroded badlands of black, white, yellow, and red to mountains made lush and cool by the clouds they capture. You can raft the Rio Grande's white water, hike through near desert, fish mountain lakes, ski mountain slopes, visit vibrant Indian pueblos or Indian ruins abandoned unknown centuries ago, buy arts and crafts that range from the most traditional Spanish-American religious icons and Indian pottery to the most avant garde paintings and sculptures—and at day's end plan to hear an opera in summertime Santa Fe. In other words, the enchantment embraces Indian villages that have hardly changed with uncounted centuries, villages that hold to a culture brought from Spain 400 years ago, and the very latest and boldest of American art colonies.

Life in Northern New Mexico is rich, colorful, and relaxed, and as diverse as the personalities of its cities: Albuquerque, Taos, Las Vegas (no, not *the* Las Vegas), and Santa Fe. **Albuquerque**, founded in 1706, is the big city and the usual gateway to New Mexico because of its airport and its central location. From Albuquerque, you can travel east and west along Interstate 40 or north and south along Interstate 25. **Taos**, close to the Colorado border, is still a northern mountain village surrounded by the spectacular scenery that attracted its founders in 1617, but it is growing rapidly in fame because of its art colony and its skiing. **Las Vegas** is the most important town in eastern New Mexico, and has been since it was founded in 1835 to take advantage of the trade along the Santa Fe Trail. Sixty miles east of Santa Fe on the western edge of the Great Plains (Las Vegas means "The Meadows"), it emerged as a major New Mexico rail center in 1879 and, by so doing, became the de facto political capital until the agricultural depression of the 1920s. Because of its poverty Las Vegas has been architecturally well preserved. It looks much as it did 90 years ago, and thus provides a view into the past distinct from that of the pueblos or the Rio Grande villages in the state's central corridor.

Santa Fe in the center of the northern half of the state is, of course, the capital of New Mexico, and has been since 1610, when New Mexico also included what is now California, Arizona, Nevada, Colorado, Utah, Oklahoma, and Texas. Santa Fe is also the unofficial capital of Spanish-American culture and of the newer art-colony culture. It has the mature confidence that only 380 years as a capital city can bring.

Northern New Mexico is decidedly different from the southern part of the state, although the two regions certainly share much history. Southern New Mexico has a larger Anglo population than the north, and its land has been settled for the most part only since the Mexican War of 1846. Prior to that time, "New Mexico" meant the north–south **Rio Grande corridor**, the central portion of the state lying close to New Mexico's major river and its tributaries. Life outside the corridor—especially the lower-elevation, hotter southern part—was too harsh and dangerous to be seriously considered for settlement. There were Anglo-American ranchers in southern New Mexico's Mesilla Valley by the time of the Civil War, but it was only afterward, with the growth in cattle ranching, statehood in 1912, and the extraction of oil and gas also in this century, that the southern part of the state became significantly populated.

Northern New Mexico's climate differs from that of the south. In the north, where cities such as Santa Fe and Taos are at elevations of 6,000 to 7,000 feet, the weather is greatly affected by the Rocky Mountains. Contrary to the expectations of many who believe New Mexico is nothing but desert, the north has four distinct seasons, including a snowy winter in the mountains. Temperatures, as in most semi-arid lands, vary widely within a season and within a day; in fact, you can expect a 20- to 30-degree difference here from any day's high to its low. However, the dryness of the climate mitigates the effect of the temperatures, and both the summer heat and the winter cold are milder than their usual North American counterparts.

Northern New Mexico is different from the rest of the United States in other ways, too, and it views its people differently. It is tricultural, with three groups of people who have maintained their separate identities despite intermingling: Indians, Spanish-Americans, and Anglos. The Indians themselves can be broken into two groups: the once-nomadic Athabaskan-speaking Apaches and Navajos, and the Pueblos, who have lived in their villages since time immemorial. The Spanish-Americans descend from the West's original 17th- and 18th-century colonists, the Spaniards; contrary to popular belief, they are not, with few exceptions, Mexican-Americans. "Anglo" denotes everyone else: Anglo-Saxons, Italians, French, Jews, Lebanese, Chinese, and black Americans.

As you travel through Northern New Mexico the most subtle challenge you will face is to determine what is authentic and what is not. Because of the region's age, because it has been cultivated by three substantially different cultures, because the Spaniards and then the Anglos came as conquerors, and because few people—especially the recent immigrants—are well informed about the state, New Mexico has spawned an astonishing number of myths about its people and its history. The myths sometimes obscure the truth, sometimes embellish it, and at other times replace it altogether. There are myths born of politics, myths born of race or ethnicity, myths born of economics and economic development, and then there are myths born of myths.

Some of these myths assert the inherent cruelty of the Spaniard, or suggest an innate weakness, a corrupt nature. Other myths paint the Indians as nature's noblemen, without blemish, ranging from "perfected beings" to naïfs. Anglos are portrayed as money- and status-seekers, users of both land and people, their culture dominant in importance, playing itself out against the backdrop of the "colorful" native cultures. These myths encourage ignorance and contempt and foster divisiveness. The so-called Black Legend about the depravity of the Spanish character, in particular, has waxed (mostly) and waned (selectively) over the last 500 years—with corresponding pushes and pulls from Spanish-American and Indian perspectives as well. It is quite a complex matter. Suffice it to say that in any history the political context of the times and the power of the prevailing class or culture have dictated the perspective of the recorded stories and myths. The history of the United States has been told basically from the point of view of the English, the Spaniards' great rivals and no lovers of the Indians. Also in the mix are the opinions fostered by two direct wars with Hispanics—the Mexican War (1846–1848) and the Spanish-American War (1898).

There is a brilliant discussion of those shifts, and of the roots of the Black Legend itself, in David J. Weber's *The Spanish Frontier in North America,* especially in chapter 12, to which we refer you rather than dot every i and cross every t of the historical complexities of the Legend in these few pages.

Nearly everyone has a stake in at least one myth. These myths are part of the enchantment of this Land of Enchantment, but they have often caused it harm as well.

Indian Culture

Most everything in the United States changes rapidly and continuously; "tradition" is a word left to the odd cultural festival and to texts. This is not the case in New Mexico. When you stand in an Indian pueblo or, to a lesser extent,

on a Navajo or an Apache reservation, you are surrounded by authenticity and tradition. The Pueblo Indians have been here for thousands of years, descendants
of the ancient, extinct Anasazi, whose culture reached its
peak with the magnificent structures of Chaco Canyon
and Mesa Verde circa A.D. 900–1100. When the Anasazi
deserted their cities and their intricate network of roads
and trade, their people evolved into today's Pueblos, a
culture that has remained largely unchanged.

The traditional religion the Pueblos practice has probably not been altered since primordial times. Because of
Spanish repression in the 17th century (a primary factor
in the famous Pueblo revolt of 1680), certain ceremonies
are celebrated only underground. As a result of the Spanish missionary movement, and because of the open-
mindedness of the Pueblo Indians, the Pueblos have
adopted Catholicism to stand beside—but not in place
of—their own religion. Thus, a Taos or Zuni Pueblo
dance, an age-old prayer to the kachinas (spirits who
bring what is needed), is supplemented by prayer in
church at Mass. If you go to a dance on a pueblo's feast
day, you will see a bower upon the plaza that holds
statues of the patron saint and usually of the Blessed
Virgin. Aside from the practices of the Indians of Guatemala, this is the only example of syncretistic religion
outside of Asia.

If you have the chance to go to a Pueblo Indian dance,
take it. An Indian dance is a long, slow, rhythmic ritual—
ancient and spiritual—in which everything is done in
multiples of four to the beat of drums and to the singing
of the clan. Because the nature of the dance is sacred,
photographs and recordings are sometimes not permitted. (This depends upon the dance and the pueblo.)

Among the problems faced by the Pueblo Indians today
are those that challenge their ability to maintain a traditional life. All aspects of Indian life are informed by their
religion, and the priests of each pueblo are the real
powers that guide daily life, ceremonies, and relationships. Pueblo life is inextricably joined with religion to a
degree that the West has not known since the Middle
Ages. But, as we have learned from European history, it is
difficult to keep tradition alive in a changing world, a
world that demands that our energies be channeled into
areas of life other than the traditional. With American
popular culture ever encroaching through work, television, and sheer proximity, sustaining the old ways becomes more and more difficult.

And then there is the economic poverty of the pueblos. Though rich in tradition, religion, and relationships, the economy of the Pueblo Indians has historically been based on a barter system—a model that cannot compete with a modern economy. The impact of the cash economy and its benefits, through television and direct contact, has fostered dissatisfaction with the more basic trappings of traditional tribal life.

Some Pueblo Indians have chosen to cast their hopes and dreams with the American economy. Some solutions manage to combine traditionalism with capitalism. Under the *portal* (porch, or portico) of the Palace of the Governors in Santa Fe you will see Indians selling arts and crafts of all kinds; you will see the same at many pueblos, and it is here, working for themselves, that those with artistic talent hope both to make a living and to keep to their traditional ways. Unfortunately, life can be bleak and the opportunities few for others.

Despite such attempts to maintain authenticity, myths continue to obscure the reality of the American Indians. They are not unsophisticates who live wholly in harmony with nature. For one thing, not all Indians are communal, as are the Pueblos; the Navajos, for example, are strongly individualistic. The Southwestern Indians do see life and the structure of society through eyes different from those of the white man, but that is a subject for further study on your own if you choose.

Spanish-American Culture

As you travel the Rio Grande corridor and through the rest of north-central New Mexico—the heart of New Mexico's attractions—you will come across many small Spanish-American villages, some in the valleys (towns such as Chimayo, Cordova, Española, Villanueva), some in the mountains (Taos, Trampas, Truchas, Abiquiu).

To begin with, the people here are not, as many outsiders believe, Mexican-Americans, and are therefore not Chicanos. These descendants of Spain were drawn here by their own myth—of gold in the cities of Cíbola and Quivira. Mexico in the 16th and 17th centuries meant riches, and all wealth was measured by the wealth of Mexico.

In 1540 this myth led Don Francisco Vásquez de Coronado to the first exploration north of Mexico. If you see the Pueblo of Zuni, you will see what Coronado had been told might be the first city of Cíbola. Coronado also explored parts of what are now Texas, Oklahoma, and Kansas—an extraordinary journey considering he hadn't the slightest idea where he was, where he was going, or what he would find when he got there. Too often, the achievements of the Spaniards' explorations into unknown lands have been discounted and have gone untaught. Some historians hold instead that the Spaniards were rapacious, base, ignorant, superstitious, and priest-ridden, and that they delighted in violence. The fearlessness, confidence, and faith in God that led them forward and enabled them to explore and conquer South and Central America and the southwestern United States go unsung.

Largely unnoticed was the Spanish conviction that their destiny lay in bringing the Christian faith to the "heathen" and that God would protect them in their duty. It was for this, more than anything, that the king of Spain financed and encouraged expeditions everywhere, and poured money into the dry hole of New Mexico.

During the initial period of conquest, when the Spanish monarchy was still undecided as to its policy toward the natives of the Americas, Indian tribes were enslaved, worked without mercy, and treated brutally. Their forced contribution to the Spanish economy—through labor, crops, and woven goods—became an essential addition. However, it was not long before such treatment became impractical and, additionally, morality intervened. Pragmatic rule dictated that maltreatment of one's subjects offered little and cost much, and the morality of their Most Catholic Highnesses dictated that the natives' place within the divine order be decided clearly and that they be treated accordingly. Thus, upon the urging of the famous priest Bishop Bartolomé de las Casas in the 1550s, Emperor Charles V drew up laws along these lines governing their treatment according to Christian principles. This was a major shift in policy, and one that set the Spaniards apart from the other colonial powers of the day. The Indians, at least in theory, were viewed as human beings with souls to be saved and deserving appropriate treatment according to law. Although it was illegal, the Pueblo Indians continued to be used as serfs until 1680, but their moral standing had risen.

The greedy and arrogant exploitation of the Pueblos, especially from 1610 to 1680, resulted in the famous Pueblo revolt of 1680, when the Indians revolted and tossed the Spaniards out. When Don Diego de Vargas reconquered New Mexico in 1692, he and his successors treated the Pueblo Indians with much more respect.

When you visit the Rio Grande villages and pueblos you will see settlements that barely survived the 18th-century depredations of nomadic Indians who came from the eastern plains and western deserts. The Spaniards accordingly allied themselves with the Pueblos for mutual survival and, after a long campaign, in 1786 allied themselves also with the most feared of the Plains tribes, the Comanches. These alliances went unbroken to the extent that in the 19th century, when Anglo-Americans were unable to travel the Santa Fe Trail without considerable danger, the Spaniards, and later the Mexican-Americans, travelled, traded, and hunted buffalo with impunity.

The lot dealt the Pueblo Indians of Northern New Mexico under Spanish colonialism differed from that served upon those subjugated by the British in North America in two respects: They were accepted in intermarriage as a matter of course, and they were not removed from their ancestral lands. This was not due to graciousness, but because it served the Spaniards economically. Nevertheless, the result is that the Pueblo Indians of Northern New Mexico were not uprooted, torn from their lands, and deposited upon reservations.

The Villages and the Land

The small villages you will see in your travels, whether Indian pueblos or Spanish-American towns, are in many ways the heart of Northern New Mexico. The living museum of Las Golondrinas, south of Santa Fe in La Cienega (The Swamp), is a fine example of how such a village looked 150 to 200 years ago—in effect, a fortress upon a river. The old plaza of Chimayo on the High Road to Taos also shows its origins as a fortress. Acoma Pueblo has been a fortress since time before memory. Nowadays, the outlying areas of Bernalillo, Taos, Villanueva, Chimayo, Velarde, and Truchas, and the pueblos of Santa Clara, Taos, San Ildefonso, and Santo Domingo retain the look of New Mexican villages from a hundred years ago.

New Mexico's climate ranges through six of the seven life zones: from the Arctic and Hudsonian zones to the Lower Sonoran Zone. The climate is affected by the great mountains of New Mexico, the **Sangre de Cristos**. The tail end of the great Rocky Mountains, they begin in the north-central part of the state and grow as they advance northward into Colorado and beyond. These stunning mountains create part of the Continental Divide: Everything to the west of the Sangre de Cristos flows to California and the Pacific; everything to the east flows to the Atlantic through the Great Plains, which come to their end in western Texas, eastern Colorado, and eastern New Mexico. To the west, the south, and the east of the mountains, New Mexico is extremely dry and grows drier and hotter the farther south you go; however, only in the south is any part of New Mexico truly desert. The geography of the state is actually most diverse, ranging from smaller groups of mountains clustered in central and southern New Mexico to scattered lava badlands, dry gullies and hills in western New Mexico, and dry plains of cattle country in eastern New Mexico.

The arid geography of New Mexico and the unpredictability of its weather and rainfall have necessitated the growth of villages along rivers and streams, rather like Egypt but not nearly so grand. The **Rio Grande** and its tributaries dominate the central portion of the state; it is this great river that historically has given life to New Mexico and it is along its banks that most of the traditional Spanish farming villages grew. In addition, whether plains or mountains, much of New Mexico sits at high elevations: Albuquerque at 5,500 feet, and Santa Fe and Taos at 7,000 feet. Thus, the air is clear and quite thin, and the sun is bright and penetrating. All this creates a land of extremes in weather, temperature, and climate, which in turn makes it difficult for the land to be fruitful. What arable land there is must be tended carefully.

Because there is no primogeniture in Spanish law, the land held by Spanish-Americans is often still handed down from generation to generation, divided into smaller and smaller parcels, each one bordering the river that gives it life. It is difficult to tend these plots without damaging them from overuse. For families to make a living, the lands have been used hard, and although each family traditionally helps the others, the yield is rarely enough. In the past the Spanish communities sent families out to create new villages when it was safe to do so. Still, the villages remained dependent upon their common lands and upon the vagaries of nature, and so life here has always been lived close to the bone.

The history of the common lands granted to families

and to communities by the king of Spain or the Republic of Mexico is a complicated one. Much of the Forest Service land you will glory in when you are in the New Mexican mountains used to be part of the land grants. Many who received the grants lost the better part of their lands in the last century largely due to the sharp practices of the immigrant Anglos. The legacy has been resentment and further difficulties for the villagers, who strain to eke out a living, although it can be argued that the Forest Service has kept its lands free from ruination by overuse.

Tales of the poverty of the villages and pueblos, tales of a dignified and warm communal life established upon mutual dependence, honor, and refusal to get ahead at the cost of others are not myths but truths. So are the tales of deep piety and self-effacement, of rugged Spanish self-reliance, and of age-old resentments that still burn. The shoddy practices of some 19th-century Anglos and the swamping of the old ways by American culture are also parts of the truth. The slow disappearance of the traditional life has borne witness to the change from a barter economy to a cash economy, which was ongoing even as late as the 1950s and 1960s. So, it is ironic that the very elements that kept the traditional villages safe from 1846 until recently—their poverty, isolation, and lack of interest in an outside world that reciprocated their disdain—now draw new immigrants who search for authenticity, peace, and beauty amid stability. This, while the villagers leave to find ways to earn cash to buy those things they never before needed but now cannot do without.

Thus, if you go to the tiny and ruggedly beautiful mountain town of Truchas on the High Road to Taos, you will find two art galleries and three bed and breakfasts in a town notorious even as late as the 1970s for its intense dislike of outsiders. Robert Redford was even able to film his version of John Nichols's book *The Milagro Beanfield War* in Truchas when residents of Chimayo, traditionally more receptive to outsiders, refused to let him use their old plaza. And thus it is that Taos, 70 miles (112 km) north along the Rio Grande from Santa Fe, has been transformed from a tough trading center for fur trappers and Plains Indians into an art colony. Rather than rely upon farming, the town now depends upon tourists who are drawn not only by art but by the spectacular Taos mountains that rise suddenly from the western plains, by the Rio Grande gorge that lies like a miniature Grand Canyon to the west, by its famed expert-quality ski slopes, and by the beautiful Taos Pueblo.

The Three Cultures Today

The truth is, when three cultures exist so closely, inter-marrying and interweaving, often stepping on one an-other's toes yet managing to remain true to themselves, the outcome is bound to be complex. The Indians view the Land as integral to life; it provides definition to their lives, it is the source of occupation, and it acts as bound-aries for their gods and their traditional world. The land and the people cannot be separated. The descendants of the Spaniards, who conquered with a belief in destiny (the same belief that the Americans came to hold 400 years later), in time also became part of the landscape, and the land became part of them, though never to the extent it was and is to the Pueblo Indians. The American conquerors mostly ignored the land because it was so poor and what was of value was already taken. Over time the Americans found uses for the land and bought it, stole it, or made it into forest preserves—always acting from their vision of land as commodity.

Today the paradoxes are many. It has been the Anglos who have led the efforts, ever since the 1920s, to preserve the traditional lives and values of the Spanish-Americans and the Indians. It is the Anglos who have brought eco-nomic development and 20th-century art, literature, mu-sic, and scientific colonies to the state, making New Mexico a national center for creativity and fostering creativity among the other two cultures as well. Today it is the Anglos who lead the conservation efforts as preservationists and identify themselves with the Indians, who are, according to one myth, in perfect harmony with the land. The Indians have become symbols, and sometimes the Spanish-Americans are portrayed, once again, as backward fools in need of instruction. Yet when it is politically convenient the Anglos champion the Spanish-Americans and the tradi-tional life, the very life that leads the Spanish-Americans into confrontation with the Anglos on conservation issues. The Spanish-Americans succumb to the temptation to por-tray themselves as victims of the Anglo victimizers. And each group condescends to the other.

There are also myths in the making in New Mexico these days, though they sometimes begin life as issues: They concern growth, development, progress, and the possibility of recovering tradition. Is development good for all, and is it indeed necessary if progress is the goal? Does development inevitably mean the death of older cultures and mores? How growth and development are defined is crucial: Are we talking about growth of the industries that exist, which center around tourism and land development, or do we mean new industries controlled locally by those who work them (for instance, raising sheep for wool)? Can the addition of jobs in the tourism industry and in state and county government be considered progress even when our educated young must leave the state to find work?

The land here is tough and stark and yields only modest riches with trouble and effort. In New Mexico Mother Nature's bones are laid bare to the eye with only the slightest veil of green. The tapestry of human affairs overlaid on that land is woven through struggle and travail, made raw by the unforgiving land and the differences in culture. It is all enchanting, endlessly involved and endlessly interesting. But in the tapestry the thread of myth lies next to the thread of truth, and both are interwoven with the warp of history. They require effort to tease apart. Perhaps this is too much to expect a visitor to do, but maybe you will be inspired to look behind the overwhelming scenery, the colorful people, and the famed artistic creations. For all its faults and myths, New Mexico has been exceptional for the harmony in which its three cultures live and strive. But such harmony is not static; it is constantly being tested, and has to be continually renewed. There is a lesson here for the world at large, which grows smaller every day.

—*John Pen La Farge*

INDIAN PUEBLOS
AND RESERVATIONS
IN NEW MEXICO

The Indians of New Mexico and Arizona are closely related; both states share the Navajo tribe with Utah and, although almost all Pueblo Indians live in New Mexico, Arizona's Hopi villages are culturally related to several New Mexican pueblos. However, New Mexico has the distinction of having more Indians than any other state of the Union, and the percentage of the population they represent is greater than in any other state.

The Indians of New Mexico fall into two broad categories: the Athabaskan-speaking Apaches and Navajos, who are cousins; and the Pueblo Indians, who comprise several linguistic groups. The Pueblos are indigenous to New Mexico, their ancestors having been here for more than 1,000 years. The Apaches and Navajos arrived in New Mexico as raiders in the 16th century, about the same time as the Spaniards; they were settled onto reservations in the second half of the 19th century.

The Pueblo Indians are likely to be of special interest to the traveller because of their proximity to major cities, their marvelously colorful dances, and their arts and crafts, which have been popular for decades, especially since the 1970s.

Pueblo Indian dances are held on important Roman Catholic feast days and also on days sacred to each pueblo. Tourists are usually, but not always, welcome. If the dance is closed, you will not be allowed to enter the pueblo. If the dance is open, be sure to check whether photography is permitted before taking out your camera. Whatever you do, do not try to sneak photographs; the results can be humiliating. Etiquette demands that the visitor neither applaud nor disturb the dancers, for this is not a performance but a religious ritual.

Following is a list of the largest pueblos or those that have arts and crafts of special interest (all telephone numbers are within the 505 area code):

Acoma Pueblo is 55 miles (88 km) west of Albuquerque on I-40 (old Route 66), then 12 miles (19 km) south on NM 23. Called Sky City for its dramatic site, Acoma sits on a mesa far above the valley floor, is still lived in, and is also used for ceremonies. There is a visitors' center at the foot of the mesa. The San Esteban Rey Mission in the Sky City is the oldest church in the United States. Acoma is well known for its excellent pottery, white with black and ocher designs. Tel: 252-1139.

Cochiti Pueblo lies west of I-25 on NM 22 between Santa Fe and Albuquerque. Cochiti makes fine drums and pottery with bold geometric designs similar to that for which Santo Domingo is known (see below). Also, Cochiti has become famous for the "Storyteller" dolls of Helen Cordero. These dolls are now widely imitated. Tel: 465-2244.

Isleta Pueblo, south of Albuquerque about 12 miles (19 km) on I-25, is a large pueblo with a very old church, one that might have achieved the status of the oldest in the United States were it not for reconstruction work done in the early 1700s. The pueblo is known for pottery that is similar to Acoma's. Tel: 869-3111.

Jemez Pueblo can be reached either by heading south from Santa Fe or north from Albuquerque on I-25 to NM 44, from which you head northwest for about 30 miles (48 km). At San Ysidro turn right onto NM 4 and proceed for 5 miles (8 km). Pottery and basket making are the pueblo's strengths, especially pottery of black designs on tan or rust backgrounds. Tel: 834-7359.

Laguna Pueblo is situated about 45 miles (72 km) west of Albuquerque on I-40 (old Route 66). Although not made in great quantity, Laguna's pottery, which resembles Acoma's, is quite good. Tel: 552-6654.

Picuris Pueblo is hard to find. This small but beautiful pueblo is on NM 75, which is off NM 68 en route to Taos. The Picuris Indians are known for micaceous pottery. Tel: 587-2957.

Sandia Pueblo lies 14 miles (22 km) north of Albuquerque on I-25. Although this small pueblo is not known for its own arts and crafts, it operates a large arts-and-crafts center, Bien Mur (Tel: 821-5400), which sells the products of other tribes. Tel: 867-3317.

San Ildefonso Pueblo, on NM 502 off U.S. 84/285, about 22 miles (35 km) north of Santa Fe, is one of the most famous pueblos in the state, not least because of its tradition of black and black-on-black pottery. The Maria and Julian Martínez family carries on the tradition, as do many others in the pueblo. Tel: 455-2273.

Santa Clara Pueblo is near San Ildefonso, just south of Española on NM 30, about 22 miles (35 km) north of Santa Fe. Santa Clara has much the same pottery tradition as San Ildefonso, but also produces red incised pottery, the best-known maker of which is Louann Tafoya. Tel: 753-7326.

Santo Domingo Pueblo, about halfway between Santa Fe and Albuquerque on I-25, has always been one of the most fiercely independent of all New Mexico's tribes. Pottery with bold geometric patterns and necklaces of shell, turquoise, and "liquid silver" are the pueblo's best-known crafts. Its annual **crafts fair**, held in early August, is especially attractive, and draws many craftspeople. Tel: 465-2214.

San Juan Pueblo, 30 miles (48 km) north of Santa Fe and 4 miles (6½ km) north of Española, just off NM 68 (the road to Taos), is close to the site of the first capital of New Mexico, chosen by Don Juan de Oñate in 1598. The crafts of San Juan are wicker basketry and incised red-and-black pottery like that of their cousins at San Ildefonso and Santa Clara. The pueblo is the headquarters of the Eight Northern Indian Pueblos Council, which was established to promote and preserve pueblo life, and it also sells items from all member pueblos. Tel: 852-4400.

Taos Pueblo, just north of the town of Taos, is without a doubt the most famous Indian village in North America. The central pueblo is built as a rising pyramid of apartments, echoing Taos Mountain behind it. This splendid sight has captivated travellers for many years. Consequently, the pueblo is also one of the most crowded at all times of the year. Taos, a producer of drums and some micaceous pottery, plays host to a **crafts fair** on its feast day (at the end of September) that draws Indians from far and wide. Tel: 758-9593.

Zia Pueblo lies between Albuquerque and Santa Fe on NM 44, 18 miles (29 km) west of Bernalillo and I-25. The pueblo is famous for its pottery—especially for its *ollas* (water jars). Tel: 867-3304.

Zuni Pueblo was the first pueblo to be sighted by the Spaniards; from afar they were convinced it was one of the fabled cities of Cíbola. Don Francisco Vásquez de Coronado was consequently rather disappointed when he later saw it close up, in 1540. One of the largest of the pueblos, it lies 40 miles (64 km) southwest of Gallup on NM 53, which meets I-40 at Grants, west of Albuquerque. The pueblo makes pottery and kachina dolls, but is best known for its jewelry, which is characterized by finely cut turquoise-stone patterns inlaid in silver. Tel: 782-4481.

The **Jicarilla Apache Reservation** lies to the north and west of Santa Fe, and is crossed by U.S. 64 and NM 44. The biggest town on the reservation is Dulce, on U.S. 64. The Jicarilla Apaches, famous for their basket making, also promote tourism in the form of outdoor recreation. Tel: 759-3242.

The **Mescalero Apache Reservation** is in the southern part of the state just south of Ruidoso on U.S. 70. This tribe has gone after tourists in a concerted way, offering the **Inn of the Mountain Gods** and encouraging outdoor recreation. Tel: 671-4494.

The **Navajo Reservation** is the largest Indian reservation in the United States, and contains the tribe with the largest population. The reservation covers parts of New Mexico and Utah, and a large portion of northern Arizona. The Navajos are justly famed for their jewelry making and rug weaving. You can find Navajo crafts for sale all over New Mexico, but perhaps the headquarters, aside from Santa Fe, is Gallup, which lies close to the western border of New Mexico on I-40. In addition, the **Gallup**

Inter-Tribal Indian Ceremonial, which takes place in mid-August, has a gathering of Indian artists, craftspeople, and dancers that is second in importance only to **Indian Market**, which takes place in Santa Fe about a week later.

(See also the Central Arizona chapter, or Santa Fe Shops and Shopping, below, for a more detailed discussion of the varying styles of jewelry making among tribes and pueblos.)

—John Pen La Farge

THE FOOD AND DRINK OF NEW MEXICO

Picture driving through the Sonoran Desert, among ocotillos with their showy red flowers atop thorny long tendrils; the sotal agave, with a six-foot spear in golden bloom; and yuccas, their white bell-like blossoms ringing in the scorching sun. Now think of "Southwestern" food: enchiladas, burritos, tamales, and the abundance of wheat, corn, beef, beans, and cheese they bring to mind. These are the result of the cultural melting pot, the offspring of the mating and mingling of Indian, Spanish, Mexican, and Anglo cuisines. How did these dishes evolve from the original diet of the people who inhabited this wild, high desert terrain?

Consider fry bread, that puffy round of soft bread, fried crisp, that is served at every Indian market food booth and forms the basis for the scrumptious Tiwa or Navajo taco, heaped with pinto beans, cheese, ground meat, lettuce, tomato, onions, and chile. We know deep-fat frying can't have been an efficient method of cooking when oils were manually extracted from seeds or rendered from wild game. The present-day Indian diet tends to be high in fats and carbohydrates because most of the foods currently served and eaten in Indian homes reflect the dominion of the Spanish and Anglo cultures, and by the time the Spanish came to the Americas, in the 1500s, European culture had long since adopted white flour and white sugar as a sign of upward class mobility. And in another setback for the Indians' traditional diet, two hundred years later their hunting grounds began to be taken by settlers and pioneers from the Eastern Seaboard, the buffalo and other game killed off, and many of the seasonal migratory gathering patterns broken. Sic transit health.

But this is not the end of the story. Many foods and dishes eaten at the pueblos today *do* hearken back to the original diverse diets of a thousand years ago. The thread of tradition—though just that, a thread—is still strong, and holding. Corn, for example, is still a symbol of ultimate fertility and God's or nature's beneficence, and other pre-Columbian foods such as chiles, beans, and squash are ever present. The buttery piñon nuts and sweet fruits of the cactus are still eaten. And there is a fresh wind stirring the dietary habits of the American people as a whole, as we will see: a creative re-emergence of the flavors and sensibility of the ancient diet in the modern fare of the Southwest.

The Indian Way

Imagine the gray greens, blue greens, and silver greens of that Sonoran-type landscape. Envision the mesas and the pre-conquistador villages, and a diet dictated by the land—when that land is a semi-arid desert. New research suggests that early pueblo societies were almost totally hunting and gathering cultures, that the role of agriculture was limited. Reading about the Hopis' or Pimas' or Yumas' uses of wild plants for food, medicine, and tools—and mind-altering beverages—creates a vivid picture of societies whose members not only were deeply engaged in the cycle of the seasons and weather, but also were observant botanists. Of course. To live here as a gatherer you'd have to know where the various varieties of plants grew and exactly when the fruit would ripen. Missing that week, or day, might mean a year without a certain tool or food.

And the diversity of their diets! Squawberry and choke-cherry (an important source of vitamin C), acorns, juniper, wild lettuces, lambs' quarters (still used as a kind of spinach in Navajo and Tiwa dishes), jojoba, mesquite beans, and agaves were eaten, and all portions of the plants utilized: bark and seeds, pulp, flower, and berry.

The harvesting of the wild plants had to be done quickly, to beat the birds and bears from doing in the winter supply of food, so the gathering often became a group activity, usually with rituals and festivities. A Navajo gathering the *tunas* (fruits) of the prickly pear cactus would pluck a hair from his or her own head, in a gesture of offering something in return to the plant. Harvesting was a fine science of respect, of leaving alive enough to assure a crop the next year, of not stripping the food sources for the wild game. All resources were understood to be part of a cycle of reliance, of sacred relation among the human, animal, and plant worlds. The spines of the prickly pear were plucked, and the pads (*nopales*) boiled; the fruits were picked ripe and eaten as a sweet snack or dessert. (Today the pads may be purchased canned, and many brands of cactus jelly and jam are still made with the sweet fruits.)

Intrepid experimentation must have surrounded the culinary preparation of some plants. A raw agave, for example, is poisonous, mercilessly caustic. Yet the baked heart of the agave is a sweet and nourishing edible, as high in calcium as milk. Bake it, mash it, let the agave ferment, and presto: mescal, that near-hallucinogenic alcoholic beverage. Sweet and nutritious too are the spine-covered buds of the cholla cactus.

Wild game was plentiful, and through hunting and trapping and the making of jerky (dried strips of meat), the ancient native people had a steady protein source from deer, quail, rabbit, and pronghorn antelope.

Every part of the hardy piñon, New Mexico's state tree, was used. The nuts, tasty, nutritious, and calorie-rich, were a food staple: collected, eaten, and traded. Navajos used the wood for fuel, and to build hogans (huts) and fences. The resin was chewed and used as a binder in pottery and baskets. The fragrant incense of the burning branches and needles was an element in many rituals, the dried buds (which are the nuts) a medicine for coughs, fever, and earache.

But the harvest of the tiny nut is difficult. The crop depends on the amount of rainfall from the previous year; the cones containing the nuts become ripe the second year after flowering. In a given region an abundant crop occurs about once every four or five years. When they have ripened, the buttery-tasting nuts are also a favorite of deer, wild turkeys, bears, birds, and squirrels. Native peoples had this figured out, though: At the first snowfall they would follow the ground squirrels' tiny prints to their stashes of nuts, a cache of perhaps 20 pounds of piñons apiece. Today, in the later fall, all over the hills you will see people spreading blankets under the trees and shaking the branches until the nuts drop out of the cones.

As with the piñon, the early people had an intimate relationship with the yucca plant, and used every portion of it. The roots provided soap; the fibers, baskets and sandals; the fruits and flowers, many foods, savory and sweet; and the seeds were ground into meal.

The Indians in Mexico used chile with practically everything they ate, but in southern New Mexico and Arizona the wild chile, *chiltepin,* was scarce and held in special esteem as a valuable delicacy. The *chiltepin* is the closest strain to the ancient species of wild chiles that originated in Brazil and Bolivia long before the advent of Homo sapiens. The seeds of the tiny fruit were probably spread by birds all across South and Central America and then to the American Southwest many thousands of years ago. The *chiltepin* bush, which grows in the transition zone between desert and mountain, requires "nurse" trees to grow beneath. Mesquite, oak, and palmetto provide shelter and humidity, and mesquite fixes the soil nutrient, nitrogen, into the land. The chile bushes can grow large in this environment, with stems two or three inches thick; they would perish in direct sunlight.

Tradition holds that the Papago Indians of Arizona made a yearly pilgrimage into the Sierra Madres of Mexico to gather the tiny chiles, which were used as a seasoning (each person taking a pinch and crushing it onto the food) and as a digestive. The women used the chile on their breasts to wean infants and, of course, chiles induce sweating, which cools and cleanses the body.

The earliest domesticated crops of the ancient Anasazi were beans, corn, squash, and, later, varieties of chile. It is interesting that so many of the foods we take for granted, such as the simple and plentiful bean, have a mysterious origin, a long history, and a debated migration pattern. Beans were grown more than 10,000 years ago in Peru, and apparently made their way northward as a bartered commodity.

Maize—or, as it is known in the Americas, corn— originated in Mexico and came under cultivation 5,000 years ago. To have made a meal of corn must have taken a huge supply, for the cobs of the earliest species were as small as pencil erasers. Prehistoric farmers bred the corn selectively, and ears of corn dating back 3,500 years that were discovered in the 1948 Bat Cave archaeological dig in southern New Mexico were found to be as much as three inches long. Long before Columbus touched the shores of the New World, farmers here had developed more than 200 varieties.

But corn was not simply food. It was also seen as the exchange medium of fertility and beneficence between the natural and sacred worlds. Corn was eaten at various stages of growth, from tiny shoots, after the first thinning, to dried husks, used as wrappings for roasting and baking. Corn was sung to, danced for, and prayed over from seed to harvest. We now know that corn and beans combine amino acids to make a complete protein, as do various beans and rices; a thousand years ago people ate this way as a matter of course.

The squash plant was first domesticated 9,000 years ago in Central America. The blue-fruited Acoma pumpkin and the Santo Domingo squash are among many squash still being cultivated from their ancient beginnings in the Anasazi and Hohokam cultures. This fruit is so beloved by various Pueblo and Navajo peoples that the large, lily-shaped flowers are incorporated into their artwork and jewelry—those treasured silver "squash blossom" necklaces.

Then there's the vital drying and saving of the foodstuffs: sun-drying and parching the grains and corn, making jerky and pemmican from the meat. Long before the invention of pottery, foods were boiled and stewed in tightly woven baskets. Yes, baskets. Stones would be heated on the fire, then put into the baskets with the pumpkin or beans and water, and replaced with newly heated ones until the desired cooking was complete.

So imagine you have pounded the mesquite beans for oil and ground corn on the stone metate, that most excellent kitchen utensil. You've brewed a refreshing ruby-red drink from the squawberry. The thick meat of squash is roasting in the mesquite coals. Is there music, too, and the hum of gossip and children's chatter and games? A picture forms. From a land where it is said that "even a crow has to pack a canteen when he flies over" comes the image of a healthy, varied, balanced, and delicious diet. A diet based on intimacy with the natural, observed universe—ingenuity, harmony, prayer, and gratitude making the crucial difference between scarcity and plenty. Something to think about.

Traditional New Mexican Cuisine

Visiting here you may better understand Georgia O'Keeffe's palette of blues and sandstone reds, and the stunning drama of Ansel Adams's photograph "Moon over Hernandez." Or the poise and sturdy delicacy of pueblo pottery, the fine designs from Acoma, the subtle dimensional work in the black pottery of Santa Clara. Or the turquoise jewelry that mirrors the cerulean sky, and the images of saints and angels in the Hispanic *retablos* and *santos.* These speak of a people in what is perhaps a quixotic balance of culture with the land. This land in turn reminds us, in all its diversity, of the eclectic cultural, geographic, and culinary threads that have been woven together in the evolution of New Mexican cuisine.

Wild game wrapped in corn tortillas, dipped in ground and powdered chile or in chile sauces, accompanied by beans and squash, were already a part of the Indian diet when the Spanish arrived in the late 1500s. The Spanish introduced new food sources, such as cattle and wheat, that added a dimension to the ancient cuisine. It's hard to picture Southwestern food without beef, pork, lamb, cilantro, cumin, onions, lime, wheat flour, rice, beer, and wine, which were all brought by the Spanish settlers and eventually merged with the old foods. The introduction of cattle and lamb had a profound impact on the Southwest. The reliance on wild game was radically lessened with the availability of domesticated beef. The Navajos became sheepherders, and today mutton remains the mainstay of their diet.

In 1580 the Spanish friars brought grapes to New Mexico and El Paso, Texas, making them the two oldest wine-producing regions in the United States. By 1662 priests in the Mesilla Valley were regularly producing sacramental wine for Mass, a hundred years before grapes were planted in California. In Mexico the Spanish planted wheat in such abundance that by the 17th century there was more wheat in the Americas than in Spain. The Pueblo Indians began making bread a staple in their diet, baking the simple, slightly sweet, round loaves that we know as Indian bread in *hornos,* outdoor, beehive-shaped ovens made of bricks of adobe (clay mixed with sand, straw, and water). With the introduction of pork came lard, and the fat to fry the wheat dough into fry bread. Tortillas were now being made from white flour as well as corn.

Under Juan de Oñate in the early 1600s the city of Santa Fe became the end point of the 1,500-mile Camino Real from Mexico City, and thus a center for the influx of many foodstuffs and the development of dishes we have come to recognize as New Mexican cuisine: *carne adovada,* tamales, *huevos rancheros, posole,* enchiladas. While in

Mexico, the Spanish had discovered not only the metallic gold they were seeking but the culinary gold of the Southwest: chiles. A new cuisine was being formed, spicy and unique, combining the dishes of the Indians of the pueblos and the Indians of Mexico with the foods and flavoring of the Spanish.

CHILE AND CHILES

The first step to enjoying the flavors of present-day New Mexican cuisine is to understand that most of the dishes are some combination of chile, beans, beef, pork, chicken, and cheese. The ways they are wrapped in corn or flour tortillas, and what happens next in the preparation of the tasty envelopes, are the keys.

Step number two is to get clear on what is meant by "chile" in New Mexico. Forget bowls of spicy tomato sauce loaded with ground beef and kidney beans; that is chili with an *i*, and though it has its place in American cookery, that place is basically Texas (though probably without the beans). The tin of dried and powdered seasoning on the grocery shelf—chili powder, or ground peppers, cumin, oregano, and other spices for making chili—is also chili with an *i*.

We are talking about chile with an *e*, and by this we mean the fruit (horticulturists consider anything that bears its seed inside, such as tomato or squash, to be technically a fruit) of the genus Capsicum: the pepper plant. There are 150 to 200 varieties of this plant, grown all around the world and spread by trade and cultivation, some measuring up to hundreds of thousands on the Scoville scale of heat (the generally agreed-upon method of judging the gustatory heat of peppers). The hottest of chiles, habeñeros, which come from the Caribbean and the Yucatán area of Mexico, have been rated up to 300,000 units, while the common green bell pepper, still in the same family, has nary a bark, let alone a bite.

Chile peppers were well established in Mexico long before the advent of the Spanish, and many Southwestern Indian recipes using chiles exist in the oral tradition, which suggests the Pueblo people might have been trading with their Mexican neighbors. The Pimas of Arizona eat a simple dish, *chile pasado,* green chile pulp made into pancake shapes and dried in the sun; another very basic recipe made by the Rio Grande Pueblo people is called Indian bacon—red chile pods crumbled and cooked in oil. It is possible these dishes originally were made with the wild chile, the *chiltepin.* Scholars don't know for sure if the story crediting Juan de Oñate with bringing various forms of chile from Mexico to New Mexico is true, or if the extensive trading routes between the Indians of the Southwest and the Indians of Mexico brought chiles northward. One thing is certain: The Spanish took to the fiery fruit with a passion, and began the serious cultivation and use of many chile varieties throughout the Southwest. From Mexico they brought the early forms of *jalapeños, serranos, anchos,* and *pasillas.*

One variety fared exceptionally well in the colder climate of New Mexico, a green chile that ripened on the plant and turned red in the fall. Grown for hundreds of years in various regions of New Mexico, the New Mexico Green, also called the long green chile, is the most widely cultivated chile in the Land of Enchantment. When ripe, it is called New Mexico Red. These are medium-fleshy peppers with a heat that can range from medium to very, very potent; they possess a clear, sweet yet hot flavor that rings with the same intensity as the colors of New Mexico's landscape.

From the time of the Spanish colonization to the late 1800s farmers struggled with the chile. There was no control over what seeds were planted, how hot the chiles would be from year to year, or how large the pods would grow. In 1917 horticulturists at New Mexico State University in Las Cruces developed New Mexico #9, with a flavor range of moderate to very hot, and a dependable pod size of six to nine inches. In the early 1950s the New Mexico chile was further modified with the release of New Mexico #6, which matured earlier, yielded more fruit, and was less pungent than the 9. Further development brought forth New Mexico #6-4, slightly less pungent still, and it remains the most popular commercially grown chile in the state.

This #6-4 chile is mainly grown in the southern part of New Mexico, around Hatch, and they have quite the wingding there over Labor Day weekend to celebrate the harvest. They pick the chiles green from late July through September, then let the rest of the crop ripen to red on the plants to be harvested from October to December. Today New Mexico is the largest grower of various forms of chile in the United States, followed, in order, by California, Texas, and Arizona.

Chile harvest never goes unnoted by avid chile eaters in New Mexico. A significant portion of the harvest is immediately distributed all over the state to be roasted in huge, propane-fired rolling drums of heavy wire mesh, in grocery store parking lots and along the roadsides at small fruit stands. (After the roasting the blistered skin is peeled away.) The pungent, seductive smell of roasting chiles has become as sure a sign of fall in New Mexico as the glowing gold of the aspen meadows in the mountains or the fields abloom with wild iris and purple aster daisies. Then, as the weeks and wildflowers roll on, comes red chile time, when the roadside stands and front porches of homes all over the state are hung with *ristras,* those long, beautiful vermilion clusters of red chiles, set out as decoration or to dry for use during the year in powdered form.

From harvest to harvest the heat of the chile varies; in fact, it can vary on a single plant. When green, chiles are hotter than when ripened and red. New Mexico chile farmers grow all three strains (#9, #6, and #6-4), and the large companies that market frozen and dried chile also buy crops of various Northern New Mexico chile strains, which tend to be hotter, and blend them to produce the mild, medium, hot, and very hot designations that appear on packages in grocery stores. Many restaurants also purchase several varieties of chile to blend, for a specific house flavor.

Green chiles freeze well; large companies that buy them to market year-round to stores and restaurants freeze the roasted, peeled pulp, as do families who buy chiles for long-term consumption. It is possible to buy red chiles dried, puréed with water, and frozen, but by and large red chiles are dried and sold whole in *ristras* and packages, or dried and powdered. The brief appearance of fresh roasted and peeled green chiles on the dining tables of New Mexicans is always welcome, but freshness is not really an issue, because frozen green chiles cook up excellently.

The roasted, peeled green fruit is the basis for the full spectrum of uses as food, sauce, condiment, and overall pleasurable eating experience that New Mexicans call green chile. That term encompasses a variety of consistencies of the pungent, aromatic, piping hot liquid, ranging from sauce to soup to stew, with meat or without.

The chopped pulp of the roasted, peeled green chile is cooked with water and thickened to varying degrees with flour or sometimes—anathema to purists—cornstarch. Green chile is usually flavored with varying amounts of coarse ground beef, although often it is prepared entirely without meat. With a consistency that varies from just thicker than broth to very thick and meaty, chile is both a sauce and a dish. It is poured over and served with numerous New Mexican dishes, and consumed with gusto by chilephiles by itself, in a bowl, with maybe a sprinkling of cheese. Some cooks may add (horrors!) pieces of whole, canned tomatoes or, worse, oregano to their green chile. For shame. Even garlic is inappropriate. Chile, the sauce/condiment/dish, is best enjoyed for the pure Zen flavor of itself.

There is such a thing as green chile stew, however, for which it is permissible to get wild and add potatoes, tomatoes, onions, and meat, seasoning it with garlic. But that is stew, not "green chile" proper.

Red chile, the sauce/spice/dish, has a slightly different lifestyle, because it is dried and used whole, or ground into flakes or powder. Some cooks purée the whole dry red pods with water, simmering until thick, to create the sauce/dish red chile. Some cooks thicken their red chile with flour, some add small amounts of shredded or cubed pork for flavor—all well within the range of an acceptably pure chile experience. When red is used as a marinade, as in *carne adovada,* the whole pods are pulverized and blended with water and other spices. When red chile is used in *posole,* the whole pod is pulverized to the consistency of flakes. And dried, powdered red chile, the spice, is used in a number of dishes, such as guacamole.

As to which is hotter, red or green chile, the answer is that it varies from chile batch to chile batch. Some green roars, some red purrs, but you may experience them the other way around. Most restaurants are willing to let you sample the chile sauces before you order your food. The chemical that produces the fiery flavor of chiles, capsaicin, withstands cooking and freezing, and it's this characteristic that has earned both culinary terror and respect. That on-fire feeling causes the brain to produce endorphins, natural painkillers and stimulants—the reason, many say, New Mexicans become so addicted to chiles.

If you are just at the courting stage of your incipient romance with Southwestern foods, it's useful to remember that in general the smaller the chile, the hotter (or more *picante*). Mere slivers of the little green jalapeño, for instance, often found innocently lolling on a scrumptious platter of nachos (a marvelous snack consisting of a bed of corn chips topped with refried beans, melted cheese, and perhaps ground beef or sliced chicken, and sometimes avocado and sour cream) may send you grabbing for your water glass. The major fire-producing portions of any chile are the seeds and the inner veins; also, chiles tend to be hotter at the top, or stem end, than at the bottom.

If you have overdosed on a too-*picante* dish, the best coolant is not water or beer, but dairy products. A heaping spoonful of sour cream is customarily served on many dishes in New Mexico, and you will come to appreciate it. An icy glass of milk will work well, and ice cream cools the tongue and the revved-up system divinely.

HUEVOS RANCHEROS

To navigate a breakfast menu with savvy, you'll want to know that *huevos rancheros* (literally "ranch-style eggs") are eggs, usually fried, on a flour tortilla covered with red or green chile sauce and topped with melted cheese. *Huevos rancheros,* like most local dishes, can be ordered "Christmas," meaning green chile on one half, red on the other, not mixed, but side by side. This allows you to sample both, but probably you will discover that you are a fan of either red or green, and that splitting your order will mean you don't have enough of your favorite.

(More on coping with culinary heat: You will notice that many dishes, even the *huevos,* come with a desultory-looking toss of chopped fresh tomatoes and lettuce. These are your allies, which, along with a side of sour cream, can safely guide you through many *picante* experiences. Eat them.)

BEANS, POSOLE, AND PAPAS

The *huevos* are almost always accompanied by beans, which in New Mexico means pinto beans prepared in the traditional "soupy" style: whole beans simmered long hours, often with a chunk of salt pork, and served in their own broth. Just as common are *refritos*—refried beans— whole beans mashed to a thick paste with a dollop of heated *manteca* (lard). (If you are a strict vegetarian you'll want to remember that most restaurants prepare beans with some form of meat or animal fat; your safest bet is to ask.)

Another possible side dish is *posole.* This is hominy corn that is rinsed in lime (the chemical, not the fruit) to remove the husk, simmered for umpteen hours in several changes of water, then finally cooked with dried pulverized red chile, pork, and garlic or onion. The result is a thick, hearty stew that can be a meal in itself when eaten with thick, homemade white-flour tortillas. *Posole* is one of the simple glories of Southwestern cuisine. Again, it would be rare to find this dish made without meat; many traditional chefs thicken and flavor *posole* with pig's feet, and swear this is the secret to rich, satisfying flavor.

Papas on a menu means potatoes, usually home fries. A traditional, inexpensive, and delicious dish is *papas con chile,* a large mound of soft home fries covered with red or green chile and melted longhorn or Colby cheese: comfort carbs New Mexico style. Also nice to sample for homey comfort food, by the way, is a cup of Mexican chocolate: hot chocolate with a deep, aromatic cinnamon flavor.

MIGAS AND MENUDO

Some strange breakfast offerings you may encounter are *migas* and *menudo. Migas,* more commonly served in Texas, are eggs scrambled with tomatoes, *chorizo* (a spicy pork sausage made with red chile powder and garlic), onions, cheese, and tortilla chips—a kitchen sink approach to breakfast. *Menudo* is an eating opportunity for the gastronomically adventurous: tripe soup, made from a cow's stomach lining that's been simmered in red chile purée. (Some cooks prefer to make *menudo* with green chile; instead of the red they add peeled, chopped, roasted green chiles to the broth.) On menus all over the state *menudo*'s nickname is "breakfast of champions," and many native New Mexicans swear by its efficacy with morning-after conditions. It is certainly an acquired taste, but lots of macho points can be garnered by saying you've tried some.

SOPAPILLAS

It's possible that you will be offered a choice between tortillas or *sopapillas* with your meal. *Sopapillas* are light, deep-fried, air-filled pillows of bread that you split open to spread their hot, billowy insides with honey butter. Chances are you will become deeply enamored of these and be glad to see that they are a common accompaniment to most every dish on a native-food menu.

SALSA

Even at breakfast you may find that any kind of eggs, scrambled or omelet, comes with a small dish of *salsa* or, better yet, *salsa fresca.* The infinite varieties of this critical item in Southwestern dining are astounding. Some *salsa* (Spanish for "sauce") will blister your mouth, with Scoville points off the scale. When the *salsa* is raging hot, *muy picante,* it is called *pico de gallo,* literally "beak of the rooster," in honor of the macho fierceness of that bird. Other *salsas* are a bland mixture of puréed canned tomatoes, with some chopped green chile, maybe a pinch or two of red chile powder, and some chopped onion. One thing all *salsas* have in common is that, unlike red and green chile, *salsa* is always served cold.

Generally speaking, the best *salsa* is a *salsa fresca,* meaning a freshly chopped—*not* blenderized—mixture of tomatoes, fresh jalapeño or *serrano* chiles, onions, and that royalty of seasonings, cilantro. The flavor of cilantro, the green portion of the plant whose seed we know as the spice coriander, is enticing, indefinable, and seductive. A New Mexican *Rubáiyát* would call for a margarita, a bag of corn chips, and *salsa* with plenty of fresh cilantro.

The Southwest has evidently revealed this important culinary treasure to the rest of the country; the 1993 *Old Farmer's Almanac* says that as of 1991 sales of bottled *salsa* (there's a multitude of makes and models, using every kind of chile imaginable) have overtaken sales of catsup nationally. We are not alone in our passion.

THE MENU BASICS

Clear sailing in reading a New Mexico menu will require you to know that a **burrito** is a white-flour tortilla filled to plump proportions (let us hope) with meat (sometimes chicken) or cheese or beans, or a combination. At breakfast a burrito may be stuffed with bacon, scrambled eggs, *papas,* cheese, and green or red chile, either in the sauce or in the form of green chile strips. The option of "smothered" means covered with red or green chile and melted cheese, always delicious but possibly messy if this is a car-food experience.

A **carne adovada burrito** will be filled with large, lean cubes of pork that have been marinated in pulverized, puréed red chile, garlic, and oregano, then cooked until fork-tender. But be advised that these same dishes will be called *burros* in Arizona, and that frequently this stuffed white-flour tortilla is deep-fried, which transforms it into a **chimichanga**. And in Texas that *adovada* may be called *adobado,* and will be a sour marinade paste of herbs, red chile powder, and vinegar.

An **enchilada** by any other name still remains an enchilada, fortunately. Your choice will be rolled or stacked, which means corn tortillas filled with meat, cheese, beans, etc., either rolled (like a burrito) or stacked flat like pancakes, then covered with green or red chile and melted cheese. Stacked enchiladas are most delicious (and very traditional) when ordered with a fried egg on top; the egg binds all the ingredients and disparate flavors into a symphonic whole and elevates the experience several gustatory notches.

The trendy addition of an ancient foodstuff, blue corn, to Southwestern cuisine has made possible blue corn enchiladas, which are simply enchiladas made with blue corn tortillas. Some folks love them and insist they are tastier than the yellow or white kind. Certainly their lovely blueberry-purple hue adds a certain je ne sais quoi, which might just be nothing more than that feeling of being more native than thou.

Combination platters are a good way to try several items at once. Most combo plates include a taco, a tamale, and a *relleno*. The **taco** can be either soft shell or hard, "soft" meaning the corn tortilla is lightly dipped in hot oil to soften it, "hard" meaning fried to become a crisp, open envelope ready for a selection of fillings. A **tamale** is traditionally shredded, cooked pork moistened and seasoned with red chile and surrounded with *masa* (a dough made with ground corn), wrapped in a corn husk, tied with a bit of the husk, and steamed. Unless they are extremely well made, tamales tend to be more dough than go, but they are tidy travel snacks of the highest order, and almost every gas station has a steamer stocked with tamales for the road. Actually, a well-kept secret of New Mexican cuisine is the wonderful homemade food you may serendipitously encounter at family-run gas stations all over the state. Watch for a counter operated by mom, pop, and their kids, and trust your nose for the mouthwatering odors of freshly made chile. A **relleno** is a long green chile, roasted, peeled, and stuffed (usually with cheese), then either breaded or dipped in an egg batter and fried. A good *relleno,* with real cheese (not made with frightening Cheese Whiz) and not too much breading, is a thing of beauty and a dish you will crave, but unfortunately they are the exception, not the rule. Frozen *rellenos* from hell abound in local restaurants; you might try asking if they are made on the premises, but their quality may still be the unknown factor in the combo-plate equation.

Flautas are deep-fried tightly rolled enchiladas, about as thick as a cigar. Low on taste, high on crunch, they seem best suited to snacking. A **tostada** is essentially a crisp-fried corn tortilla covered with beans/meat/cheese, the usual handful of chopped lettuce and tomato, and maybe guacamole. **Guacamole**, to paraphrase Clifton

Fadiman's memorable line on cheese, is the avocado's leap to immortality, being a sultry, velvety mélange of mashed avocado seasoned with red chile powder, salt, and a quick squeeze of lime, and often studded with chopped onions and tomatoes.

Guacamole will most always grace a **chalupa**, which is a corn tortilla fried into a pretty, rippled cup and filled with burrito, enchilada, and *tostada* makings. Chicken *chalupas*—the flowerlike tortilla filled with refried beans, white meat of chicken, cheese, and chopped lettuce and tomato, then nattily topped with guacamole and sour cream, with a side of green chile or *salsa,* if that is your wont—are very nearly addictive and may engender a serious weekly need for this perfectly New Mexican dish.

THE MARGARITA

Now consider what to drink with this Platonic ideal. Mexican beers are good; the dark ones, Negra Modelo, Dos Equis, and Bohemia, stand up well to the straight-ahead flavor of New Mexican cuisine.

Margaritas are *designed* to add just the right bright, clean taste to accompany these dishes, though. A margarita is a heady mix of tequila, triple sec, and (if you are lucky) fresh lime juice. Tart and full-bodied, they are delicious, refreshing, and definitely mind-altering—so proceed with caution.

The perfect margarita ratio and blend are all in the shaker of the mixologist and on the tongue of the imbiber. The question of the best recipe is a topic that's endlessly argued with great relish in New Mexico. The folks at Maria's New Mexican Kitchen, in Santa Fe advertise, "We serve real margaritas!" and they have written a forthcoming book of margarita recipes, history, and folklore. (The working title is *Maria's Magnificent Margarita Manual,* or *How to Make a Real Margarita,* authored by Al Lucero and John Harrisson.) Owner Al Lucero describes a "real margarita" as one that is made with "real tequila, real triple sec, and real lemon or lime juice, all of which are individually measured into a shaker glass filled with small ice cubes." The stress in that formulation is on the word "real," as we will explain. Al concurs with many margarita cognoscenti that the proper ratio is *exactly* one part triple sec to two parts lime or lemon juice to three parts tequila. The margarita is hand-shaken to break off just enough of the edges of the one-inch-square ice cubes for the addition of a modest amount of water into the drink and to mix all the components properly. "A blender," Al insists, "would add too much water to the drink, while stirring doesn't add enough."

Al describes "real tequila" as "a liquor made and bottled in Mexico that has been double-distilled from the sugary juices of the cooked *pina* (also called the heart) of the blue agave plant." This is the same sweet, baked agave that the ancient Pueblo Indians ate for a sweet and fermented for a mind-expanding drink. For tequila to be considered true it must contain at least 51 percent blue agave juices before sugar and other alcohol may be added, and then the Mexican government stamps the label with the letters *N-O-M* followed by four numbers, a hyphen, and another letter. Cheap tequilas bottled in the United States may contain much more cane sugar, or the agave juices present may be diluted to below 51 percent with grain alcohol. Mescal, which is also made in Mexico from blue agave, is distilled only once, and the government doesn't strictly monitor the percentage of blue agave.

Some margarita connoisseurs are loyal to the rich, elegant flavor of top-of-the-line El Tesoro Tequila, produced with 100 percent blue agave juices, while many locals swear by Jose Cuervo Gold, but with Grand Marnier and lemon juice instead of triple sec and lime. Some prefer Silver Herradura and Cointreau.

Triple sec is a clear, orange-flavored liqueur made from the skins of Curaçao and other exotic oranges and then triple-distilled. For a slightly different flavor, an acceptably upscale margarita may be made, as mentioned, with Cointreau or Grand Marnier. Cointreau is a super-premium triple sec imported from France. Grand Marnier is another French import, a blend of super-premium triple sec with premium Cognac that is aged for a minimum of 18 months.

On the lemon versus lime juice controversy, Al Lucero points out that the real bugaboo—an *absolute no-no* in a real margarita—is the use of any sweet and sour bar mix or, worse, sweetened lemon or lime juice mix. At Maria's, Al uses lemon juice in the margaritas because "limes vary so much in juiciness and quality. We can get more consistent, juicier lemons, and since we add no sweetening, their tartness works well in the drink." Al notes, however, that good, juicy limes make a great margarita.

And as for the salted-rim glasses: Once you have the heady, robust tequila as the predominant flavor, highlighted by the sweet, citrus notes of the orange liqueur of

choice, juxtaposed in turn with the clean "edge" of sour-
ness provided by the lime or lemon juice, sipping the
drink over a salted rim adds the last key element of flavor
that balances and "marries" the other tastes. The salt is
also part of the tradition of drinking tequila in straight
shots: a bite of lime wedge, a lick of salt, and a shot of
fiery tequila down the hatch.

DESSERTS

Traditional desserts are basically simple and soothing,
since this cuisine makes its most luscious taste notes with
chile. **Flan** is ubiquitous, a baked caramel custard dessert,
much like a crème brûlée minus the crunchy broiled
sugar topping. **Natillas** is lighter yet, a custard with fluffy
egg whites stirred in. A dish that originated from the
meatless meals of Lent is **capirotada**, a bread pudding
made rich with eggs, raisins, nuts, cinnamon, and, occasionally, rum. But if you're breathing fire, remember that
a good way to end the meal is simply with a scoop of ice
cream.

A BOWL OF GREEN

At this point, either your next meal will find you longing
for surf and turf and baked potato or about to graduate to
the point where you can think of no finer meal than a
bowl of green. A whole bowl of green chile, just for
yourself, with a spoonful or two of cooked pinto beans
(drained of their broth) stirred in to add some heft, then
topped with cheese that will melt into a gooey pool, and a
fried egg over the top to blend all those quintessentially
New Mexican flavors. You'll order a couple of tortillas on
the side, which are quite fitting to use to wipe the bowl
clean, and eat every drop of the ambrosia. "Bowl of
green, with an egg," you will tell the waiter, and know you
have gone native.

The American Influence

But that, as Dr. Seuss's Cat in the Hat was wont to exclaim,
is not all. After the Spanish established Santa Fe as the
terminus of the Camino Real from Mexico City, the city
became a center for the vigorous trading of foodstuffs
among the caravans of wagons that travelled north and
south along the Royal Road.

The Santa Fe Trail from Missouri was established in the
1820s, making Santa Fe the center of two major trade
routes. (Taos also became a central trading point.) The

Missouri Trail brought the pioneers across the American plains, and with them came the seeds for the produce of gardens back East: tomatoes, asparagus, cabbage, carrots, lettuce, peas, melons, and apples.

The Homestead Act of 1862 and the establishment of the railroad between 1879 and 1882 led to a flood of newcomers and fancy foods; Champagne and oysters became available. The railroad made a walloping difference on the food scene in New Mexico, because with it came railroad hotels and restaurants, including the famous Harvey House chain. New Mexico had 16 Fred Harvey hotels, including five showcases: Montezuma and Castaneda in Las Vegas, La Fonda in Santa Fe, Alvarado in Albuquerque, and El Navajo in Gallup. The Harvey Houses considered the native diet, especially the *picante* chiles, a bit too wild, so they introduced "civilized food" to what they held to be the rough Southwestern palate. Early menus featured baron of beef, turkey stuffed with oysters, chicken croquettes, vermicelli with cheese, and such delicacies as calf's brains scrambled with ranch eggs.

In 1846 the U.S. Army raised the American flag over New Mexico, and the territory was opened to further settlement. Ranchers came to herd the millions of heads of cattle brought by the Spanish that had escaped into the wild. Slabs of beef became standard fare. Ranch life introduced chuckwagon cuisine, and because many of the cowboys were native Hispanic New Mexicans and Mexicans, these *vaqueros* ate their beans with chile.

During the years after World War I Sante Fe and the surrounding environs were discovered by artists Georgia O'Keeffe, Peter Hurd, and Alfred Stieglitz, among others. Attracted by the freer lifestyle, writers (D.H. Lawrence, Willa Cather) moved to New Mexico, as did numerous other poets, musicians, and sculptors. Culture mavens such as Mabel Dodge Luhan and Mary Wheelwright followed. "Sophistication" hit the plates and palates of New Mexico, with the appearance of bistros serving the urbane Italian and French foods the worldy-wise art crowd enjoyed. In the 1940s Rosalea Murphy opened the Pink Adobe Restaurant in Sante Fe and, despite food rationing, began to further the culinary education of Santa Feans with dishes from her Louisiana Cajun upbringing, as well as Continental dishes finessed with touches of chile and other elements of local cuisine.

The mix and mesh have continued. An American standby, the cheeseburger, is served in New Mexico with a generous pour of green chile over the cheese, creating not only a delicious new dish, but one that blends all the culinary influences: wheat and beef from the Spanish, chile sauce from the Indian and Mexican influences, and the sine qua non of down-home American food, the hamburger. Pizzas are served in New Mexico with jalapeños as a standard add-on. Frito pies—bags of corn chips, split open and covered with red chile and cheese—are the state's McLunch.

But New Mexico's population and culture are ever dynamic. The sixties, seventies, and eighties brought yet another influx of newcomers to the state, hipper, more urbane, with even more sophisticated yens. Santa Fe has become the epicenter of a culinary revolution that has exploded the boundaries of Southwestern cuisine and swept American gastronomy along with it. Creative young chefs, trained in many styles and bursting with the spin-the-globe possibilities of menus, have taken on New Mexican food and added their own signatures.

SantaFare

What do you get if you stir Continental gourmet cooking, the cuisines of the Orient, the chow of the chuckwagon, the tango of South American food, the tropical zing of the Caribbean, the lightness of California fare, and the more-is-still-more style of back East with the New Mexican drama *As the Chile Turns*? A light bulb going on in the heads of talented chefs all over Santa Fe and the Southwest.

- What we see in this bright light is a new cuisine, a hybrid, the brainstorm of a culinary elite: techniques, flavors, and ingredients borrowed from the international lexicon of cookery. Thinking globally, cooking locally.
- This cuisine is about a relationship with neighboring farmers, too, especially organic gardeners growing all the latest rage in baby greens and the oldest, heritage strains of native beans, squash, and chiles.
- It also means a commitment to *fresh:* fresh seafood, fresh herbs, fresh vegetables of all makes and models, fresh meats and game. But the contemporary twist to freshness depends not on physical proximity to the land but to a telephone: Most of the world's gourmet offerings are only phone calls and airports away.

- This is food as art, a whirlwind romp through taste, texture, and color, every plate a feast for the tongue *and* the eye.
- This is food about pleasure and what is pleasing: plates served with a knowing flourish to an appreciative audience.

Examples? Take the idea of a *relleno,* a peeled and roasted green chile. Now fill that chile with a subtle mélange of fresh baby shrimp, tender morsels of lobster, a hint of tarragon in a *beurre blanc.* Lightly coat it with an evanescent froth of egg and quickly fry it. What sauce or *salsa* will you pool delicately to one side of the gracefully arching chile? Will it be finished by a signature scribble of crème fraîche? Or take rib-eye steak, dry-rub it with sage—that most desert-suggestive of spices—and coarsely ground black pepper. Grill it over mesquite, and mash up a passel of potatoes to which you add red chile, scallions, garlic, and *queso blanco.*

Add and subtract; use traditional ingredients, then throw in wild fruit notes of mango *salsas,* or add bass notes of smoky chiles, or a treble of edible flowers. It's the new food math.

Spearheaded by chef Mark Miller at the Coyote Cafe in Santa Fe, this style is in fine fettle around the Southwest, as imagined and re-created daily by other superstar chefs such as Dean Fearing and Stephen Pyles in Dallas, Robert Del Grande in Houston, and John Sedlar in California. In Sante Fe this is what you will experience at Santacafe, Geronimo, the Old House, On Water, Edge, Cafe Escalera, and in individual dishes and specials all over this food-crazed town.

But the underpinnings are solid. Remember the desert with its wealth of wild foods, the abundant menu created from the survival-inspired imaginations of those earliest people? Remember also that the essence of any of a number of traditional cuisines is the combination of a basic vocabulary of ingredients. Add to this our young chefs trained in many schools and cultures.

Now rethink your approach to dining in Northern New Mexico. So many restaurants, so little time! Why not try appetizers and margaritas at one place, then have your entrées at another. Savor, sip, and digest. Take a stroll before dessert, look into the windows of galleries, let the art, pottery, and jewelry function as palate cleansers. Sample the local greens, the wild mushrooms, the indigenous sparkling wines. All of this is the flavor of the Southwest of today: the taste of the land but also the taste of its beauty, seasoned—truly, not just poetically—with the light that brought the artists and us here.

—*Judyth Hill*

ALBUQUERQUE

By Lynn Buckingham Villella

Lynn Buckingham Villella is a New Mexico native who grew up in the state's Four Corners area. An award-winning journalist, she was writer, columnist, and editor for the Albuquerque Tribune, *editor of* Albuquerque *magazine, and editor of four regional cookbooks, including the best-selling* Simply Simpatico. *Now a marketing-communications executive, she has lived in Albuquerque since 1966.*

Albuquerque, with close to one-half of all New Mexico's residents, has roots dating to 1706 when Spanish settlers established an outpost along the Camino Real (Royal Road) between Chihuahua and Santa Fe. Provincial Governor Cuervo y Valdez named the settlement in honor of the viceroy of New Spain, the duke of Alburquerque. In the early 1880s the first "r" was dropped from the official spelling by Anglo-American settlers uneasy with the long, unfamiliar name.

To imagine an eagle's-eye view of Albuquerque and its impressive setting, picture yourself in a hot-air balloon drifting silently through the pristine atmosphere high over the city. This sprawling Southwestern metropolis is laid out below you like a vast panoramic postcard that sweeps from 10,000-foot mountain ranges paved with blue-green pine in the east to the legendary Rio Grande (here running north to south) and remnants of extinct volcanoes in the west. Factor in the abundant sunlight, and the arid, buff-colored soil and you have the essential elements of Albuquerque.

Initially, Albuquerque may not seem vastly different from its sister cities in the Southwest—Phoenix, El Paso, Tucson—but only by superficial comparison. With its rich

79

multicultural heritage, enviable physical setting, conge-
nial climate, and colorful history, all of which blends and
emerges again in art, architecture, cuisine, and lifestyle,
Albuquerque just doesn't allow itself to be swept into the
impersonal fog that characterizes so many big cities: A
friendly, laid-back demeanor and persistent small-town
flavor lurk beneath Albuquerque's big-city veneer. Albuquerque has a sense of what novelist Tony Hillerman calls
"room enough and time." And people never fail to com-
ment on the sky here—vast, crystalline, blue. Albuquerque intrigues just because it is close to the heart and
reflects the soul of New Mexico.

Most out-of-staters come into Albuquerque because
it is the major—some would say practically the only—
commercial air gateway to New Mexico. Travellers bound
for Santa Fe and Taos, in particular, usually get there via
Albuquerque International Airport, located at the southern edge of town, where there are various ground connections to Santa Fe and Taos, as well as extensive car-rental
facilities. But Albuquerque itself is worth some time, as
we will show, and also works as a base for the interesting
day-trip attractions nearby. (See Around Albuquerque,
which follows this chapter.)

MAJOR INTEREST

Historic Old Town
The KiMo Theatre
New Mexico Museum of Natural History
Albuquerque Museum
Rio Grande Nature Center State Park
Indian Pueblo Cultural Center
Petroglyph National Monument
University of New Mexico area
Maxwell Museum of Anthropology
National Atomic Museum
Albuquerque International Balloon Fiesta
Sandia Peak Aerial Tramway and Ski Area
Scenic North Valley and Corrales

The Turquoise Trail

Today's Albuquerque—500,000 people and growing—
sits close to the geographical center of the state, where
Interstates 25 and 40 meet. The intersection, a conglomer-
ate of freeway ramps, is referred to as the "Big I," and the

major segments of Albuquerque seem to fan out from this reference point. (To get to the Big I from Albuquerque International Airport, take Yale Boulevard—the airport exit road—north, turn left [west] on Gibson Boulevard to I-25 north. The Big I is about 2 miles/3 km north on I-25.)

Despite the sprawl, you'll find that getting into, around, and out of Albuquerque is really very easy if you get your bearings the way the locals do. Always keep in mind: The Sandia Mountains are due east and the Rio Grande is due west.

The downtown area, just west of the Big I, is roughly defined by Lomas Boulevard to the north, First Street to the east, and Sixth Street to the west. From I-40 take either the Lomas or Central exit west. **Central Avenue**, the fabled Route 66 of song and story, bisects the city from east to west. Old Town Albuquerque is west of downtown by a mile or so and can be reached by taking Central due west to Rio Grande Boulevard, or, from the Big I, by driving west on I-40 to the Rio Grande exit south.

West of the Rio Grande there's a remnant of an old floodplain now spoken of as the West Mesa, the area's newest and fastest-growing suburb. Interstate 40 is the principal link to the West Mesa, although you can also take the new bridge over the Rio Grande at Paseo del Norte to the far north (if you're on I-25 take the Paseo del Norte exit west).

Also on the west bank, due north of West Mesa, is the scenic bedroom community of Corrales, only minutes from downtown Albuquerque but with a character distinctly its own that attracts families seeking a quieter, more rural lifestyle. The most pleasant route to Corrales is to take Rio Grande Boulevard north to Paseo del Norte (take a left); for a quicker trip drive north on I-25 and take the Paseo del Norte exit west across the river.

Northeast Heights (everything north of Central and roughly east of I-25 to the Sandia foothills), the most populous quadrant of the city, is home to the two large shopping malls, Coronado and Winrock centers, and several major chain hotels. The University of New Mexico is in this quadrant, and at just about the northeasternmost extreme is the Sandia Peak Aerial Tramway and access to the Sandia Peak Ski Area.

Kirtland Air Force Base and Sandia National Laboratories, two of the city's largest employers, dominate southeast Albuquerque on its perimeter, east of Albuquerque International Airport.

The telephone area code for Albuquerque is 505.

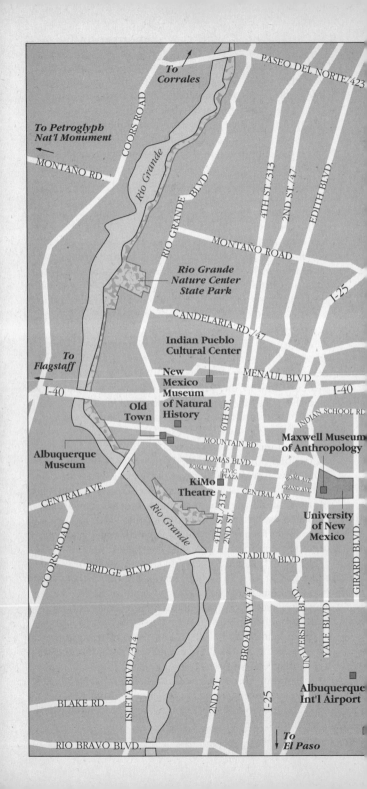

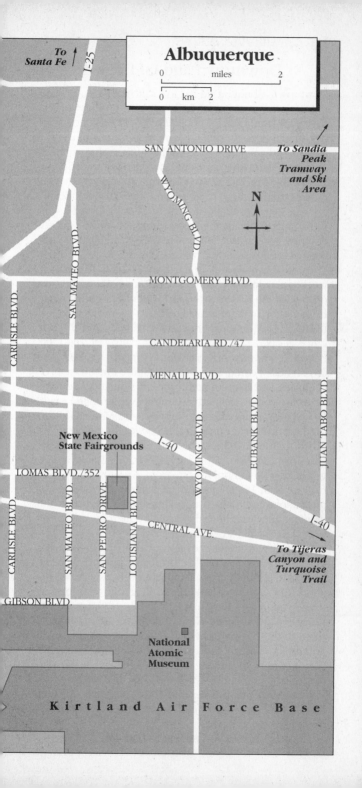

Downtown and Old Town

Downtown Albuquerque has lost much of its charm over the years as government buildings and business towers have supplanted small cafés and retail establishments. Today, however, there remains one treasure from the city's past that, thanks to strong public support, has survived "progress" and the wrecking ball. At Fifth and Central stands the historic **KiMo Theatre**, originally built as a movie palace, then revamped to showcase vaudeville acts—a lovely example of how Art Deco can mesh with Indian motifs. Inside the lobby are murals by well-known Southwestern artists and ornate plaster ceilings reminiscent of the great movie palaces of yesteryear. The KiMo Theatre's art gallery is open from 9:00 A.M. to 5:00 P.M. weekdays; admission is free. Performing-arts groups are onstage at the KiMo year-round with offerings that range from modern and traditional dance to opera and bilingual theater. Local newspapers carry schedules and the box office is open 11:00 A.M. to 5:00 P.M. daily; Tel: 764-1700.

Old Town, the "original Albuquerque," has been the crossroads of community life and culture for almost three centuries, and is undoubtedly the city's number-one tourist attraction. It is defined by Central Avenue on the south, Rio Grande Boulevard on the west, and Mountain Road on the north. From the Big I, head west on I-40 and exit on Rio Grande Boulevard south. Signs clearly indicate Old Town. Or you can get to Rio Grande Boulevard by going west on Central Avenue from downtown.

More than 150 shops and art galleries, housed in historic adobe buildings, are hidden among the patios and winding alleyways here that are Albuquerque's only visible claims to Old World charm.

While it may sometimes appear that only free-spending tourists frequent Old Town and its environs, the truth is that Albuquerque families love rediscovering the area's many attractions and recalling the city's past as expressed in the lovely **plaza**; by the thick adobe walls of historic **San Felipe de Neri Church**, in use continually since 1792; by mariachi bands that play in the small grandstand; and by lively fiestas and religious pageants. Wrought-iron and adobe *bancos* (benches) invite visitors to rest a bit in the shade and enjoy people watching. The five flags that fly over Old Town—of Spain, Mexico, the Confederacy, the United States, and New Mexico— lend historical perspective.

The **Christmas Eve Luminaria Tour** lures legions of

visitors to Old Town time and time again. Once a year all electric lights are extinguished in Old Town and in the Albuquerque Country Club neighborhood, due south across Central Avenue. Softly glowing *luminarias* (meaning "little bonfires" and actually votive candles placed in sand-laden brown paper bags) outline streets, sidewalks, windows, and rooftops. According to traditional Hispanic beliefs, Santo Niño (the Christ child) approaches through the frosty darkness in need of light to find His way to the homes and hearts of the people. Like fireworks on the Fourth of July, the sight is breathtaking no matter how many times you've seen it before. Many visitors choose to inch bumper-to-bumper through the area in their own vehicles; most find it easier on the nerves to take the bus tours offered by the city's Sun Tran bus company; Tel: 843-9200.

Though it ranges from the sublime to the trendy to the downright tasteless, the variety of merchandise available in Old Town is nonetheless impressive. Indians still sell their wares on the plaza, and several shops and galleries feature Indian jewelry, pottery, baskets, and rugs. Prices are generally lower here than in Santa Fe or Taos. Old Town shops also carry art of all types, from abstract to representational, much of it of high quality.

Among the best shops and galleries here are **Mariposa**, 113 Romero NW, for contemporary jewelry, ceramics, and glass (they've also got a gallery in Santa Fe); and **Schelu**, 306 San Felipe NW, for handcrafted pottery, stoneware, Southwestern furniture, weavings, and sculpture. The **Navajo Gallery**, 323 Romero NE in Plazuela Sombra, represents the flamboyant and eccentric Navajo artist R. C. Gorman. The **Covered Wagon**, 2034 South Plaza NW, is a famous trading post and souvenir shop that also houses the American Indian Gallery, a favorite of serious collectors.

There are at least two "must" dining spots in Old Town, both rich with historic charm and significance. **La Placita**, Tel: 247-2204, on the plaza's southeast corner, is an affordable one-stop shop for the classics: enchiladas, tacos, *rellenos, carne adovada* (chunks of marinated pork simmered in red-chile sauce), and so forth. Locals who insist that a New Mexican restaurant's mettle can be tested by a bowl of its chili give La Placita two thumbs up—it's fresh, it's fiery, and it's plentiful. Yes, the restaurant is touristy, but so what?

Without peer when it comes to location, ambience, and the quality of its food is historic **Maria Teresa Restaurant**,

618 Rio Grande NW, a pleasant stroll just a block north of Old Town. The 12-room restaurant occupies one of Albuquerque's oldest adobes, the Salvador Armijo House, built in 1840 and now listed on the National Register of Historic Places. Although the house has been remodeled several times over the decades, it still boasts many cherished family heirlooms that are displayed throughout. The various rooms are named after generations of the Armijo family. (Maria Theresa, by the way, the famous 18th-century empress of Austria, was not an Armijo. The name was picked by an interior designer with a flair for the majestic.) Tel: 242-3900.

Request a table in the Salvador Room just so you can see the Chickering piano. Owner Bill Kouri will be happy to brief you on the building's history and to make suggestions about the menu, which features beef, seafood, and New Mexican specialties. Lamb *fajitas* with mint-and-green-chile jelly are a house favorite. Maria Teresa is so reasonably priced that you'll want to go back for more—maybe for the green-chile waffles at the Sunday buffet.

The Museums of Albuquerque

Don't leave the Old Town area without visiting the **New Mexico Museum of Natural History**, 1801 Mountain Road NW, two blocks east of Rio Grande Boulevard. This fine, high-tech masterpiece, with permanent and changing exhibits on zoology, botany, geology, and paleontology, needs at least three hours if you want to do it justice. But if you're on the run and can see only one exhibit, be certain it's "New Mexico's Seacoast," where there's an "evolator" taking trips back through 38 million years of geologic time to a seacoast setting in which dinosaurs thrived. The museum is open 365 days a year; Tel: 841-8837.

The museum's family-friendly **Museum Café** is located on the balcony. Chef Beauregard Detterman creates easy-on-the-wallet specials and fabulous muffins and desserts, 9:00 A.M. to 5:00 P.M. daily.

Just across the way from the Museum of Natural History is the **Albuquerque Museum**, 2000 Mountain Road NW, which features a large collection of Spanish colonial artifacts—lots of arms and armor, historic maps, and such—as well as changing exhibits of contemporary art. The museum's permanent collection contains works by such artists as Wilson Hurley and Georgia O'Keeffe and by a few notable Taos painters. "History Hopscotch" is an ongoing exhibit (great for kids) that focuses on family ties and on the importance of handing down family traditions and lore. To understand post–Civil War Albuquerque, stay to view "Albuquerque: The Crossroads," an award-winning 38-minute audiovisual presentation given every hour between 10:00 A.M. and 4:00 P.M. The museum is closed on Mondays; Tel: 242-4600.

Your next stop might be the **Rio Grande Nature Center State Park**, just minutes north of Old Town. Located along the east bank of the Rio Grande at 2901 Candelaria NW, the 270-acre nature center preserves the wildlife of the cottonwood groves—what New Mexicans call the *bosque*—along the river. The visitors' center, partially underground, houses exhibits on the ecology, geology, and history of the Rio Grande Valley. Outside, there are nature trails. Tel: 344-7240.

For an excellent overview of the history and culture of New Mexico's Pueblo Indians, and for current information on activities at nearby pueblos, visit the striking **Indian Pueblo Cultural Center**. From I-40 take the Sixth or 12th Street exit north; the center is one block north of I-40 at the corner of Indian School Road and 12th Street. The building echoes the design of the famous Pueblo Bonito, the quintessential example of Chaco culture architecture (A.D. 1100), and provides a setting for exhibiting arts and crafts from all of New Mexico's pueblos, along with interpretive displays. Indian dances are held from May to October along with crafts demonstrations. Don't let indifferent service (or concern for your coronary arteries) keep you from sampling Indian-style cooking— Navajo tacos, fry bread, and *posole* (traditional hominy and pork stew, so bland when eaten alone that locals always top it off with rich red-chile purée)—in the center's restaurant. The gift shop features pueblo arts and crafts, of course, mostly of high quality and at reasonable prices.

(See the University Area section, below, for the Maxwell Museum of Anthropology.)

Petroglyph National Monument

New Mexico was home to some of the earliest residents of North America: Sandia Man, 20,000 B.C., and Folsom Man, 8,000 B.C. By A.D. 1000 Pueblo Indian cultures were well established. To understand something of these ancient peoples and the development of Indian culture along the Rio Grande, you will want to take an excursion to the West Mesa to view what might be the most primitive art gallery in the region. Petroglyph National Monument, on Unser Boulevard a half mile off Montaño Road, sits at the base of a black-rock platform holding five extinct volcanoes. On the smooth faces of hundreds of boulders that lie scattered about the escarpment are an estimated 17,000 engraved and incised figures—people, animals, birds, religious masks, symbols, and a profusion of abstract designs—the work of ancient Pueblo artists who for centuries used the area as a campground.

While camping by modern-day visitors is not allowed, the park has walking trails that range from easy to moderately challenging, and a nice picnic area with running water. The monument is best reached by taking I-40 west to the Coors Road exit north; after about 4 miles (6½ km) turn left on Montaño Road and then right on Unser Boulevard.

The University Area

The architectural vitality of Albuquerque is nowhere more evident than at the **University of New Mexico** (UNM), established in 1889 in what was then considered to be a desert setting on the outskirts of town. (The stretch of Central Avenue connecting Old Town to the university, no longer isolated, is not a section to dally in on your way to the campus. Except for a couple of popular restaurants, this part of old Route 66 is a relatively high-crime area with little of interest to warrant your investigation.) Today UNM has some 25,000 students, major medical and law schools, and a national reputation for excellence in several academic fields. The main campus is south and east of the Big I and is easy to find from the I-25 freeway going east from either the Lomas or Central exit. The campus, which stretches from University Boulevard east to Girard Avenue along Central, is easiest to access from Central Avenue, on its southern perimeter. Parking is always at a premium, for visitors and students alike, so it's best to experience the university by foot.

Pueblo Revival–style architecture had its Anglo beginnings here in the early part of the 20th century. The style of some of the first buildings established a motif that gives today's UNM a distinctive appearance.

In addition to numerous pieces of public art, the university houses several museums, the most noteworthy being the **Maxwell Museum of Anthropology**, located at the west end of the campus at University and Grand NE. Collections emphasize materials from native cultures of the American Southwest. The museum store attracts discriminating shoppers interested in international and Southwestern crafts, and in hard-to-get books about New Mexico. The museum is open Monday through Friday 9:00 A.M. to 4:00 P.M.; Saturdays 10:00 A.M. to 4:00 P.M.; and Sundays noon to 4:00 P.M. Tel: 277-4404 for the museum.

Across Central from the university and one block south at 108 Cornell Drive SE is **Tamarind Institute**, an acclaimed professional center for training, study, and research in fine-art lithography. Tours include a talk about the institute's history, a film on lithography (the art of drawing with a greasy substance on stone or metal and making printed reproductions of the drawings), and a printing demonstration. The gallery is open 9:00 A.M. to 5:00 P.M. weekdays. Tours are offered the first Friday of each month at 1:00 P.M., free of charge, with reservations recommended; Tel: 277-3901.

Head east along Central Avenue from the university and within three blocks you'll find one of the city's best restaurants, **Monte Vista Fire Station**, 3201 Central NE. The menu changes daily, but you can count on fresh ingredients and the most imaginative flavor combinations (mango-chile salsa is one). The pasta dishes, in particular, are *très* California and uncommonly wonderful. On summer evenings the grand old firehouse doors in the Pueblo Revival–style building swing open to allow patio dining, which would be a plus were it not for the traffic on Central. Tel: 255-2424.

Scalo, 3500 Central SE, three blocks farther east on Central in the Nob Hill Shopping Center, is renowned for strictly fresh, artfully simple northern Italian food filtered through a thoroughly Californian sensibility. The exceptional food and reasonable prices guarantee a crowd—and a high decibel level—particularly at lunch. Tel: 255-8781.

The Southwestern Moderne–style Nob Hill Center, which dates from the 1930s, was one of the first centralized shopping centers to be built west of the Mississippi. The **Nob Hill** neighborhood has some fun specialty shops carrying natural-fiber clothing, used books, imported and local crafts, novelty items, natural foods, and such. It also has **Double Rainbow**, 3416 Central SE, a sedate café where locals flock for the best and heartiest breakfasts in town. Early-morning meals just don't get any better than this: muffins of every description (two people can share these minicakes), wonderful egg sandwiches and omelets, gooey sticky buns, fresh seasonal fruit, and honey-spiked yogurt. The café opens every day at 6:30 A.M.

On the other side of the university, about 1 mile (1½ km) to the west down Central Avenue, is **The Artichoke Cafe**, 424 Central SE, small but extremely popular with the business-lunch crowd. Don't just drop in at noon on a weekday; come early or late or prepare for a long wait. The Artichoke offers an interesting mix of classical and innovative dishes in an upbeat atmosphere, and the service is excellent.

Sandia National Laboratories

Sandia National Laboratories, known here as "the Lab," has a work force of more than 7,300. Established in 1949, its lofty mission has been "to enhance the security, prosperity, and well-being of the nation," and this renowned engineering lab has set out to fulfill that mission in a variety of ways.

Its original emphasis—nuclear weapons research and development coupled with monitoring and maintaining the nuclear-weapon stockpile—remains in place today. The nature of that work, however, is shifting more toward activities such as dismantling of nuclear weapons. The lab also owns the country's largest arms-control verification technology program.

Contributions to U.S. industry by way of technology transfer came early at Sandia and have remained strong. In the early 1960s a Sandia physicist invented the Laminar Air-Flow Clean Room, which plays a key role in today's microelectronics industry. Also from Sandia Labs came a modern-day variation of another 1960s invention: the Rolamite, a nearly frictionless switch and deceleration sensor that activates most air bags used in late-model automobiles.

While access to much of Kirtland Air Force Base and Sandia Labs is restricted, the public is invited to visit the **National Atomic Museum** located on the base. Take Central Avenue east to Wyoming Boulevard and then drive south to the base's Wyoming gate (you'll need to stop and obtain a temporary pass at the gate). From the Big I take I-40 east to the Wyoming exit and head south. In addition to mounting displays on the development of atomic energy from 1945 to the present, the museum illustrates energy sources for the future: fission, fusion, light-water reactors, coal gasification and liquefaction processes, solar power, and conservation. Most visitors head straight for Little Boy and Fat Man, two bombs identical and contemporary to those dropped on Hiroshima and Naga-saki near the end of World War II. An especially intriguing exhibit explains in detail the so-called Palomares Incident of January 1966, when, during a peacetime refueling ma-neuver, a tanker and a B-52 bomber collided over Palo-mares, Spain. Four nuclear weapons were dropped inad-vertently and, although they did not "go nuclear," their high explosives dispersed plutonium over a wide area. The United States subsequently embarked on a massive cleanup effort to remove contaminated topsoil. One of the bombs recovered in the cleanup is on display at the museum. Very interesting, if rather unnerving. Admission is free; Tel: 845-6670.

The Albuquerque International Balloon Fiesta

There is always something going on in Albuquerque, but the one event that attracts the most visitors from around the world is the Albuquerque International Balloon Fi-esta, held annually from the first Saturday through the second Saturday in October, and largely responsible for Albuquerque's claim to being "the Balloon Capital of the World." Along with the city's very amiable climate, un-usual (some say weird) weather patterns create near-perfect ballooning conditions. Balloon pilots refer to these patterns as the Albuquerque Box, a phenomenon where prevailing winds at higher altitudes go in direc-tions opposite those nearer the ground. The Box gives pilots great maneuverability; they can go up, forward, down, and back instead of just ascending and heading off in one direction. Another thing that endears Albuquerque to balloonists is the ample availability of open space. It's easy and fun to chase and find balloons after they float away from the launch site.

During the eight-day extravaganza the blue New Mex-ico sky is a veritable riot of color, and marathon sky gazing becomes a local obsession. The mass ascensions—600-plus balloons lifting off at once—are thrilling and the nearest thing to heaven for photographers and film ven-dors. It's also fun to watch the competitions, which test the skills of balloonists and their crews. A favorite is the Key Grab Contest, in which pilots steer their balloons, without ground crew assistance, toward a set of car keys attached to the top of a 30-foot pole. The pilot who grabs the keys first wins the car that goes with them.

A recent enhancement to the Balloon Fiesta is the Special Shapes Rodeo, scheduled toward the end of the week. It's been called an animated cartoon in the sky, because the balloons take such shapes as Mickey Mouse, a giant burger, a witch on her broomstick, a dinosaur, and many more.

For a complete list of Balloon Fiesta events and directions to the launch sites, call the fiesta office; Tel: 821-1000. Because the launch site, located in far north Albuquerque just off I-25 near the Alameda Boulevard exit, is a traffic nightmare during the fiesta, you'll want to investigate the park-and-ride services of Sun Tran bus company that carry Fiesta fans from major Albuquerque shopping centers to the park and back with a minimum of stress. Bus schedules are available from the Fiesta office.

Visitors to the Balloon Fiesta number upwards of 1.5 million, so early planning is advised for those wishing to fly to Albuquerque in early October and for those wanting hotel accommodations during the Fiesta. Last-minute planners often end up staying in Santa Fe or smaller communities to the south, and rental cars are almost impossible to obtain at the airport or around town.

If you fancy yourself floating up, up, and away in one of the balloons at the launch site, you'll need to contact World Balloon Corporation (WBC), the official balloon-ride concessionaire for the Fiesta; Tel: 293-6800. They'll send you a packet of information about what to do and how to dress. WBC's veteran pilots offer rides at $150 per 45 minutes on weekends (a bit less on weekdays), carry appropriate insurance, and are the only pilots who can charge for rides at the launch site. Now, if you know a pilot or know someone who knows a pilot, you are free to schedule rides on your own, either at the launch site or elsewhere. All pilots in the Fiesta are licensed by the Federal Aviation Administration and have passed written and in-flight tests.

While your attention is heavenward and you find yourself rooted to the northern perimeter of the city, make certain you take advantage of the view and the victuals at **The County Line**, 9600 Tramway Boulevard NE; Tel: 296-8822. Travel north on I-25 and exit east on Tramway Road (the east–west road that connects with north–south Tramway Boulevard and the same route that takes you to the tram) to the foot of the Sandias, where this 1940s-style

roadhouse earns rave reviews for Southwestern-style barbecue, smoked prime rib and duck, grilled steaks, and
seafood. The quantities are staggering, so plan to take
your time as you dine, and enjoy the spectacular view of
Albuquerque, day or night.

The Fairs

For two and a half weeks each September, Albuquerque
reverberates with the nonstop activities of the **New Mexico State Fair**, the fifth-largest show of its kind in the
country. In addition to 40 acres of midway, exhibitions,
contests, and horse racing, the fair offers 15 nights of
rodeo contests and concerts featuring nationally ranked
cowboys and major country-music stars. It matters not
that you can't recognize a prize-winning cucumber when
you see one, because the fair offers something for
everyone—mules wearing hats, rockets made by fifth
graders, perfectly coiffed bulls, sweet-potato pie, flamenco dancers, performing pound pups, and lop-eared
rabbits for as far as the eye can see. The fair is no place for
the antisocial, especially on weekends when the crowds
are monstrous. The Indian and the Hispanic villages, both
with traditional foods, crafts, and entertainment, are popular attractions. On Western Heritage Day, usually held on
a Sunday, wear your boots; everyone is declared an honor-
ary cowboy or cowgirl. Gates open each day at 8:00 A.M.
and close at midnight. Admission prices vary depending
on the day, and on Mondays and Tuesdays everyone is
admitted free. The 236-acre fairgrounds are located behind thick stucco walls practically in the middle of town:
north of Central Avenue between San Pedro and Louisiana boulevards. From I-40 take the Louisiana exit south.
Sun Tran, the city bus company, offers an appealing alternative to the fair's parking headaches, with park-and-ride
bus service from two outlying locations; Tel: 843-9200.

Each June, usually on the last weekend, the New Mexico State Fairgrounds are the scene of another major
event, the **New Mexico Arts and Crafts Fair**. The quality,
originality, and variety of the works exhibited by artists
and craftspeople from throughout New Mexico are impressive. The three-day fair includes demonstrations and
free entertainment, and affords excellent opportunities
for browsing and shopping. If you intend to buy, don't
wait until the last afternoon, when pickings are slim.
Parking within the fairgrounds usually is not a problem.

Sandia Peak Aerial Tram and Ski Area

Any visitor to Albuquerque, no matter what time of year, must visit the Sandia Peak Aerial Tramway, one of the city's most important attractions. Open daily except during the second and fourth weeks of April, this is the world's longest single-span tramway. It takes you, very gently, nearly three miles along Sandia Peak above deep canyons and breathtaking terrain from a high-desert setting at the western base of the mountain to the lofty serenity of its 10,378-foot peak. To reach the tram take I-25 north to the outskirts of the city and exit east (right) on Tramway Road (Route 556), then left onto Sandia Heights Road. Or take Tramway Boulevard north from Central Avenue approximately 8½ miles (13½ km); turn right onto Sandia Heights Road.

Tram trips take about 30 minutes each way and are most rewarding late in the day during the incomparable New Mexico sunsets. The view to the west over the Rio Grande and beyond is likely to astonish you. In summer, a refreshing add-on is a modestly priced ride down and back up the east slope of the Sandias on a double chairlift. Because hours vary by time of year and are linked to the beginning and end of ski season, you should telephone to get the current schedule; Tel: 298-8518.

In winter, excellent downhill skiing is available at the **Sandia Peak Ski Area**, at the top of Sandia Peak. The ski season can begin as early as Thanksgiving and usually extends through mid-March. You can ride the tram to the ski area or, if you prefer to drive, take I-40 east to the "other side of the mountain," then NM 14 (the Turquoise Trail) north, and finally NM 165 and NM 536, which lead back west (left) to the base of the ski area (less than a 40-minute drive from downtown Albuquerque). The ski area has 25 miles of trails to accommodate all skill levels, although expert skiers often fault it for being somewhat short on challenge. All right, Sandia is no Taos; on the other hand, at Sandia there are less often lift lines to waste your time (like those at Taos), particularly if you ski on weekdays or toward the end of the ski season. Sandia offers ski rentals and a certified ski school. Instructors are especially good with youngsters and beginning skiers. Tel: 242-9052 for snow conditions and hours.

At the peak, **High Finance** is an excellent year-round choice for casual, affordable dining with an incomparable view. The high altitude adds to the cooking time, so keep this in mind if you're in a hurry. Tel: 243-9742. Another dining choice, back down on the west side of the mountains, is The County Line; see the Balloon Fiesta section above.

Corrales

The most picturesque community in Albuquerque's North Valley (the northwestern area along the Rio Grande) is Corrales, on the west bank, pleasant to visit any time of the year but particularly nice in autumn when the cottonwoods along the river become a blaze of gold. Said to evoke something of the spirit of the Santa Fe of 20 or so years ago, it's an especially fine place for dining, thanks to a fairly dense concentration of first-class restaurants. During the 20-minute drive north from Old Town on Rio Grande Boulevard you'll pass through some truly lovely neighborhoods; be sure to watch for pheasants, doves, and New Mexico's state bird, the roadrunner. Turn west on Alameda Boulevard, cross the Rio Grande, and then head north on Corrales Road (NM 46).

Natives seldom agree on which of Albuquerque's dozens of New Mexican restaurants serves the ultimate enchilada, the definitive burrito. Most folks concede, however, that you can't get much closer to The Real New Mexico Thing than at Corrales's Desert Rose and Rancho de Corrales. **Desert Rose**, 4515 Corrales Road, Tel: 898-2269, features all the New Mexico regulars, realistically priced, plus things that go by such names as Paparito (an enormous chorizo-and-egg burrito), Vegerito (a vegetarian burrito), and El Sonoran (a chicken breast smothered with homemade salsa). Most dishes come with a side of sublime pork-based red-chile sauce. When the weather's right, Desert Rose offers a cool, shady patio for alfresco dining. **Rancho de Corrales**, due north at 4895 Corrales Road, is a fine place to enjoy first-rate *fajitas* and enchiladas. Tel: 897-3131.

While locals readily admit to the addictive qualities of their beloved New Mexican food, they realize one can consume just so many green chiles and blue-corn tortillas. For French and northern Italian cuisine, both innovative and classical and served in a romantic, Old World setting, linger in Corrales and splurge at **Casa Vieja**, 4541 Corrales Road. Chef Jean Peree's menu is long and changes daily. In summer, ask to be seated on the shady, intimate patio of this wonderful old adobe hacienda; Tel: 898-7489.

The Turquoise Trail

Allow yourself a half day or more to experience the scenic and historic route between Albuquerque and Santa Fe, NM 14, known as the Turquoise Trail, once the haunt of robbers waiting for shipments of gold and silver from some of the richest mines in North America.

Start your journey by driving east on I-40 into **Tijeras Canyon**, following a route travelled through the centuries by Indian traders, miners, and settlers. By some accounts early Albuquerque inhabitants experienced anxious moments during the full moon in September when Comanche raiding parties would sweep down from Tijeras Canyon to attack the valley settlements and carry off the harvest.

As you approach the canyon from the Big I you'll have the Sandia (Watermelon) Mountains to your left and the Manzano (Apple) Mountains on your right. The early Spaniards gave the mountains their names, respectively, because of the melon-pink glow they often exude at sunset, and because of the apple orchards planted in the foothills by Spanish settlers. The main mass of the mountain ranges is granite, with layers of limestone on top. The limestone is rich with fossils, having once formed the bottom of a shallow sea that covered the entire region.

Leave I-40 at exit 175, marked Cedar Crest and Tijeras (the exit forks). For hiking maps and other information about the national forest lands in the Sandias, follow the arrow leading to Tijeras and NM 337 South (right). The Tijeras Ranger Station, open daily, will be on your left about 1 mile (1½ km) south of the exit. If you don't wish to stop at the station, follow the exit's left fork, which will take you on a curve under I-40. You'll now be heading north on NM 14, along the eastern side of the Sandia Mountains, toward Santa Fe.

As you drive north you'll pass through **Cedar Crest**, a small but energetic community spread out among the piñons and junipers. Continuing north on NM 14, you'll pass through the revived "ghost towns" of Golden, Madrid, and Cerrillos. The earliest gold rush west of the Mississippi (in 1825) led to **Golden**, and in **Cerrillos** the Cash Entry Mine was rumored to have a vein of silver so pure that you could carve the ore out of the wall with a butter knife. By one account, "at night, the prospectors' campfires were so numerous that they covered the hills like a blanket of stars." The future looked golden for the mining communities, but the quality of ore declined and then the Great Depression caused their demise. It is said that gold dust still can be found in Galisteo Wash near the village of Cerrillos, and on weekends you'll usually see a few "prospectors" scrutinizing the area.

All these towns remain partially inhabited by modern-day settlers, mostly artists and craftspeople, who have brought a renewed frontier spirit to the old ghost towns. Today these towns are alive with galleries, crafts shops, antiques shops, little museums, and restaurants, most of them open year-round.

Madrid, in particular, is worth exploring. Originally a coal-mining town, Madrid depended on mines that contained both anthracite and bituminous coal—a rare geologic occurrence. The mining-company row houses are being restored to life with great integrity, and old company stores now house art galleries and specialty shops. On Sunday afternoons during summer, jazz and bluegrass festivals are held here in the old ballpark.

For an interesting dining experience on the Turquoise Trail, stop for lunch or dinner at the **Mine Shaft Tavern** in Madrid; Tel: 473-0743. Specializing in burgers, steaks, and margaritas, the tavern goes to great lengths to celebrate its Old West theme. If you're saving up for haute cuisine in Santa Fe, the Mine Shaft is still a great place to stop for coffee en route.

"A country café in the European tradition" is what owner Susan Macdonell calls her popular **San Marcos Cafe**, located a bit off NM 14 beside the San Marcos Feed Store 8 miles (13 km) south of the NM 14 and I-25 junction. If you're lucky, you'll visit the San Marcos on a day when Susan is serving her green-chile chicken lasagna, a celestial New Mexican variation on the basic Italian theme. The most requested menu item, however, is the San Marcos burrito. Susan wraps fresh tortillas around stewed roast beef and potatoes—with outstanding results. In the summer try fresh berry pie for dessert; at any other time of year the best bet is bourbon apple pie served hot with ice cream. The San Marcos opens seven days a week, but on Sundays serves only brunch and closes at 2:00 P.M. Tel: 471-9298.

NM 14 joins I-25 5 miles (8 km) south of Santa Fe. Just before you leave the state road you'll see a row of small conical hills to your left. These hills embrace the site of the turquoise mines from which the Turquoise Trail gets its name. The last mine to operate in this area was owned by the famous Tiffany company. Though plenty of turquoise remains in the ground, the quality of the ore is less than optimal. The turquoise mines are on private land; amateur prospectors are not allowed.

Staying in Albuquerque

Albuquerque has no dearth of places to stay. Most of the major chains are represented and dozens of moderately priced motels and all-suite inns can be found along I-25 and I-40. You don't need us to find those.

Five minutes to the east from Old Town is a small hotel of historic proportions, **La Posada de Albuquerque**, on Second Street NW. This true New Mexico masterpiece one block north of Central Avenue (old Route 66) is strong on charm as well as on modern amenities. While you probably won't want to wander about downtown Albuquerque amongst the parking garages and office towers, you are well positioned at La Posada to launch excursions in any direction. There's plenty of space for your car in a parking structure next door. You can afford to indulge yourself at quiet, candlelit **Eulalia's**, La Posada's popular dining room, which, particularly at noon, will probably have a crowd.

Take a fast-forward careen into the ultramodern at the **Hyatt Regency Albuquerque**, two blocks north of Central Avenue on Tijeras Avenue NW. The tower of this 390-room showpiece and its adjacent professional building dominate the Albuquerque skyline in a most agreeable fashion, and the multimedia art exhibited in the public areas is stunning. The hotel has a large underground parking area. A bonus of basing yourself at the Hyatt Regency is proximity to **McGrath's**, perhaps the best hotel restaurant in town. More than half the dishes reflect a nouvelle-Southwestern approach. Try the Hatch chicken: a chicken breast stuffed with Hatch chile (New Mexico–grown green chile), cheese, and smoked pork. The Sunrise Burrito for breakfast is spicy and hearty, and the Caesar salad at lunch or dinner is the city's best.

Casas de Sueños (Houses of Dreams) one block south of Old Town on Rio Grande Boulevard SW, faces a golf course and stands out rather brashly from the modest older residences that characterize the quiet, vintage Albuquerque country club neighborhood. To gain access you have to walk under the blue-tiled belly of a snail. That's what neighbors call the curved wooden-and-Plexiglas creation that hovers in symmetry above the bed and breakfast's entrance. Beyond the snail and within the adobe walls are 13 guest studios positioned amid flower beds and garden paths. Sunlight floods through the studios' spacious windows, and each suite has a different theme and character designed to reflect the area's mix of cultures. Some have kitchens, some have fireplaces. A different breakfast menu appears each morning.

Three-quarters of a mile (1 km) east of Old Town is an eight-room bed-and-breakfast inn, the **W. E. Mauger Estate** (pronounced "MA-jor"), on Roma Avenue NW. A recent renovation has transformed what was a trashed-out flophouse into one of the best examples of Victoriana in the city. Built in 1897, the home is on the National Register of Historic Places, its rooms done in frilly pink furnishings, each with its own stuffed animal as well as private bath and refrigerator. The stately home has a big front porch with wicker furniture and several secluded patios as well. Breakfasts in the indoor/outdoor dining room include crab-corn soufflé, a layered green chile–bacon concoction, and vegetarian burritos. Ample parking is provided on the grounds.

Just north of the Rio Grande Nature Center, 100 yards east of Rio Grande Boulevard on Candelaria Road in a quiet neighborhood of adobe residences old and new, is the lovely **Las Palomas Valley Bed and Breakfast**. Lori and Andrew Caldwell are gracious hosts who have restored an old family home and filled it with antiques and objets d'art, including items that belonged to Oliver Cromwell and to Napoléon. Flower gardens and orchards surround the inn, providing a setting both calming and restorative. There are eight suites, most with private patios. Guests are invited to use the tennis courts (rackets are provided) and the hot tub. Also provided, free of charge, are trail bikes and the use of a mobile telephone, a fax machine, and laundry services. The Caldwells serve a lavish sit-down breakfast: three fresh breads, flavored coffees, specialty omelets. All this for a price that's standard bed and breakfast.

You can soak up some laid-back Corrales atmosphere at the secluded **Corrales Inn Bed and Breakfast**, on Perea Road, just off Corrales Road. Co-owners Laura Warren and Mary Briault designed and built the inn in 1986 to offer their guests comfort, privacy, and quiet—not to mention fabulous breakfasts. In Corrales you will actually hear roosters at dawn, and there are miles of pathways here to wander along the Rio Grande and through the *bosque*. All six moderately priced rooms, which are situated around an attractive courtyard, have full private baths and individual controls for heat and air-conditioning.

Windchaser Farm Bed and Breakfast, on Angus Road in Corrales, just north of the Corrales Road–NM 528 intersection, offers a little bit of country along with two spacious suites, each with private bath. The nicely affordable lodgings are in an authentic adobe on a busy horse farm, and guests leave feeling they have truly experienced New Mexico. Host Helen Kruger serves a Continental breakfast of fresh breads and fruits.

The **Albuquerque Hilton Hotel,** at University and Menaul boulevards NE, just east of the Big I (take the Menaul-Candelaria exit east off I-25), is big and has indoor and outdoor pools and two top restaurants, one a most reliable source of affordable New Mexican cuisine, both traditional and new. With almost any lunch or dinner choice at the Hilton's **Casa Chaco,** you'll get fresh salsas made with such exotic chile varieties as *chipotle* and *poblana,* and with fresh fruit. Subdued and pricey, the hotel's **Rancher's Club** is where local business executives take clients they want to impress. To call it a steak house is to do it a great injustice. The dinner menu is primarily grilled meats, seafoods, and vegetables, and the grilling is done in French ovens over exotic woods such as sassafras, cherry, hickory, apple, and mesquite. The atmosphere is very formal and the service excellent.

One of the best views of the Albuquerque International Balloon Fiesta is available from the **Holiday Inn Pyramid,** on the corner of San Francisco and Jefferson NE, just east of the launch site. From I-25 take the Paseo del Norte exit and turn back (south) on the one-way frontage road. While not all of its 311 rooms have a view to the west—hence to the balloon show—you need only step outside for a ringside seat. The nouveau-Aztec design is easy to spot—impossible to overlook, actually—as you head north from Albuquerque toward Santa Fe on I-25. Pastel elegance, impeccable service, and a familiar Continental/international menu are the hallmarks of the hotel's popular restaurant, **The Gallery.** Set in a windowed area at the ground level of the hotel's six-story atrium, it's a worthy splurge.

There is also a handful of chain hotels and all-suite inns in the moderate price range near the balloon grounds.

If a rustic setting in the mountains sounds appealing, plan a stay at **Elaine's, A Bed and Breakfast,** on Snowline Road, left off NM 14 (the Turquoise Trail) just at the four-mile marker north of the I-40 turnoff. This three-story log bed and breakfast set on four glorious acres offers traditional comfort and gracious hospitality, compliments of host Elaine O'Neil. Two rooms share a bath, but the large suite has its own bath—and a big brass bed to boot. Breakfasts are lavish, and O'Neil has opted to forgo televisions and, instead, to fill the house with books for her guests. Prices are slightly higher here than at most area bed and breakfasts, but you get your money's worth.

GETTING AROUND

Albuquerque, a major transportation hub for the Southwest, embraces the intersection of two important interstate highways, I-40 (east–west) and I-25 (north–south).

Situated on a mesa on the southern perimeter of the city, 5 miles (8 km) from downtown just east of I-25, Albuquerque International Airport is one of the busiest airports in the region, and is the usual gateway for a trip to New Mexico. The airport itself has lately undergone a major transformation, with welcome improvements in facilities and atmosphere. Compared to some large airports, this one is easy to negotiate.

Albuquerque is served by many carriers, including American, America West, Delta, Continental, Northwest, Southwest, TWA, United, USAir, and Mesa, which provides daily service to Farmington, Alamogorda, Las Cruces, Roswell, and several other communities in the state. Taos Air Charter serves the Taos Ski Valley from Albuquerque airport.

Most major car-rental companies have outlets at Albuquerque International, either in the airport or two or three minutes away by shuttle bus.

As you depart the airport (on Yale Boulevard), I-25 is easily reached by turning west (left) on Gibson Boulevard.

All major chain hotels and nearby motels provide complimentary shuttle service; use the courtesy phone at the hotel/motel board near the luggage-claim areas.

Taxi service from the airport to downtown Albuquerque costs about $9 and takes 10 minutes. Ride sharing for two or more people to a maximum of two destinations is permitted.

Buses headed for Santa Fe leave the airport almost every hour. T.N.M. and O. Coaches (Tel: 243-4435) has departures three times a day (late morning, afternoon, and evening), seven days a week, charges $10.50 one-way, and deposits passengers at the T.N.M. and O. terminal at 858 St. Michael's Drive in Santa Fe (far south of the plaza). Shuttlejack (Tel: 243-3244) has ten departures a day between 6:50 A.M. and 10:15 P.M.; the fare is $20. Their buses stop in downtown Santa Fe at El Eldorado hotel and The

Inn at Loretto. Both shuttle services leave from a location near the Albuquerque airport's baggage-claim area.

Amtrak's *Southwest Chief* links the city to the West Coast and to Chicago. Trains arrive daily from Los Angeles via Flagstaff, Arizona, and from Chicago via Kansas City, Missouri, and Topeka and Dodge City, Kansas. It's a 16-hour trip from Los Angeles and a 25-hour trip from Chicago. The Amtrak depot is at 314 First Street SW, three blocks south of Central Avenue at the eastern edge of downtown. For information and rates, Tel: (800) 872-7452.

Albuquerque is served by the Greyhound/Trailways Bus System, which has a terminal at 300 Second Street SW in the downtown area (Tel: 247-3495), and by various charter companies.

ACCOMMODATIONS REFERENCE

The rates given below are projections *for 1993. Unless otherwise indicated, rates are for a double room, double occupancy, and do not include meals. Price ranges span the lowest rate in the low season to the highest rate in the high season. As rates are always subject to change, it is wise to double-check before booking.*

The area code for Albuquerque—and all of New Mexico—is 505.

▶ **Albuquerque Hilton Hotel.** 1901 University Boulevard NE, **Albuquerque**, NM 87102. Tel: 884-2500; Fax: 889-9118. $89–$109.

▶ **Casas de Sueños.** 310 Rio Grande Boulevard SW, **Albuquerque**, NM 87104. Tel: 247-4560; Fax: 842-8493. $85; $175 (three-room suite for two).

▶ **Corrales Inn Bed and Breakfast.** 4763 Corrales Road, **Corrales**, NM 87048. Tel: 897-4422. $55–$65.

▶ **Elaine's, A Bed and Breakfast.** P.O. Box 444, 72 Snowline Road, **Cedar Crest**, NM 87008. Tel: 281-2467 or (800) 821-3092. $66 (shared bath); $83 (private bath).

▶ **Holiday Inn Pyramid.** 5151 San Francisco Road NE, **Albuquerque**, NM 87109. Tel: 821-3333 or (800) 465-4329; Fax: 828-0230. $92–$102.

▶ **Hyatt Regency Albuquerque.** 330 Tijeras Avenue NW, **Albuquerque**, NM 87102. Tel: 842-1234; Fax: 766-6710. $95; $345 (suite).

▶ **La Posada de Albuquerque.** 125 Second Street NW, **Albuquerque**, NM 87102. Tel: 242-9090; Fax: 242-8664. $82–$102.

▶ **Las Palomas Valley Bed and Breakfast.** 2303 Candelaria Road NW, **Albuquerque**, NM 87107. Tel: 345-7228; Fax: 345-7328. $65–$95.

▶ **W. E. Mauger Estate**. 701 Roma Avenue NW, **Albuquerque**, NM 87102. Tel: 242-8755. $99 (largest double).

▶ **Windchaser Farm Bed and Breakfast**. 246 Angus Road, **Corrales**, NM 87048. Tel: 898-4607. $60.

AROUND ALBUQUERQUE

By Buddy Mays

Buddy Mays, a freelance writer and photographer, is the author and illustrator of ten books on travel, including Ancient Cities of the Southwest, Indian Villages of the Southwest, *and* A Guide to Western Wildlife, *and has contributed to many others. His articles and pictures have appeared in such magazines as* Travel & Leisure, Travel Holiday, Philip Morris, TWA Ambassador, Delta Sky, Forbes, Sunset, *and* Touring America. *A member of the Society of American Travel Writers, he lives in Santa Fe, New Mexico.*

In the high-desert landscape surrounding Albuquerque lies a cornucopia of interesting and attractive visitor attractions. Indian villages, historic Spanish churches, ancient pueblo ruins, and distinctive geological formations are just a few of the numerous offerings in this part of the state. An arid but enchanting fragment of the American Southwest, this spectacular land of rocky peaks and sandstone buttes, grassy plains, juniper-covered mesas, and tortured lava flows has changed little since the time of the Spanish conquistadors.

Unless you plan to join an organized motorcoach or van tour, the most reliable way to get around in this portion of the state is by automobile. Roads here are in excellent shape, and while driving distances between destinations may occasionally seem outrageous (especially to city dwellers), most legitimate touristic sights lie just a few miles off east–west I-40 or north–south I-25, which intersect at Albuquerque. Locals usually recommend sticking to the "four lanes" whenever possible, unless you happen to be a back-road junkie or command unlimited time. Try for an early start each day, especially in the summer; the coolest, most pleasant time for long drives in hot weather is during the early morning.

MAJOR INTEREST

West of Albuquerque
Laguna Indian Pueblo
Acoma Indian Pueblo
Lava flows and wilderness hiking at El Malpais
Historic Spanish inscriptions at El Morro
Zuni Indian Pueblo

South of Albuquerque
Isleta Indian Pueblo
Spanish missions and Indian ruins at Salinas
Wildlife watching at Bosque del Apache
The Very Large Array radio telescope

North of Albuquerque
Coronado State Monument
Jemez Pueblo
San Diego Mission
Geothermal activity
Battleship Rock and natural hot springs
Trout fishing
Jemez Falls
Valle Grande volcanic caldera
Bandelier National Monument
Wilderness hiking

(For **east of Albuquerque**—Sandia Peak and the Turquoise Trail—see the Albuquerque chapter.)

Though it's certainly possible to do each of the tours described below as separate one-day excursions (and return to Albuquerque for lodging), your trip will be more enjoyable if you spend two or three leisurely days exploring each area, taking time to absorb the region's complex history, to meet and talk with locals, and to savor the traditional hospitality for which New Mexico is known worldwide. Opportunities simply don't get any better.

North on the Jemez Mountain Trail you can visit the pueblos of Zia and Jemez, then soak your cares away in a natural hot spring or fish for rainbow trout in a tumbling mountain stream. There are no accommodations along

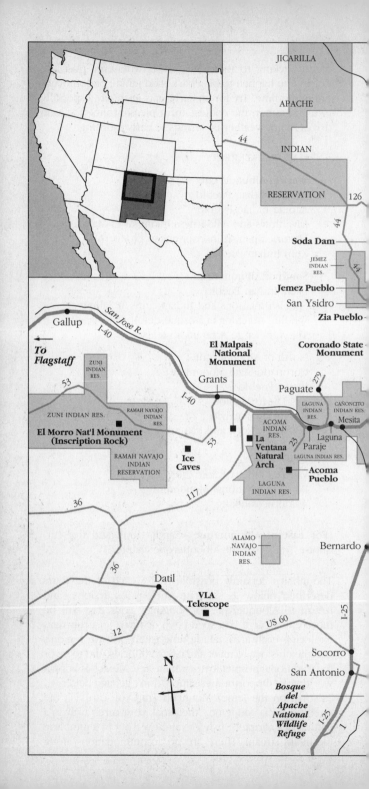

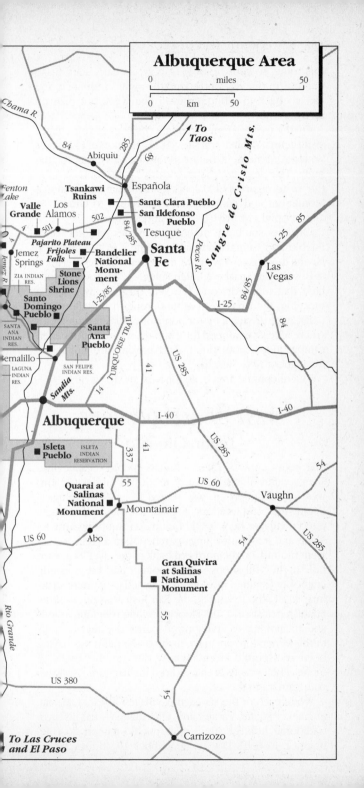

this route, so your best bet is to get an early start, make the tour in one day, and spend the night in Santa Fe. You can go back to Albuquerque if you wish, but plan on arriving late.

On the western tour you might consider taking a day to visit Laguna, Acoma, and the NM 117 portion of El Malpais National Monument before returning to Grants for the night. The next day you might drive south on NM 53 to the western part of El Malpais, go on to El Morro National Monument and Zuni Pueblo, then return to Grants for another night or drive back to Albuquerque.

On the southern itinerary, consider visiting Isleta Pueblo and Salinas National Monument in the morning, having lunch at the Owl Café, then spending the afternoon at Bosque del Apache Wildlife Refuge. Make Socorro your base that night, drive to the Very Large Array the next morning, then return to Albuquerque in the afternoon.

If you're driving a motor home or pulling a trailer, or if you're at least equipped for camping, so much the better; campgrounds, both public and private, are numerous throughout New Mexico.

The telephone area code for New Mexico is 505.

WEST OF ALBUQUERQUE
Laguna Pueblo

The community of Laguna Indian Pueblo, nestled in a sleepy valley along the San Jose River 45 miles (72 km) west of Albuquerque, was settled in 1699 by refugees fleeing the conquistadors of Spain. The oldest of six small pueblo villages here is Old Laguna, a crumbling array of stone and adobe dwellings perched atop a "tell," or ancient mound, on the northern bank of the river. Scattered hole-in-the-wall shops display pottery and other handicrafts, but Laguna's most interesting and prominent structure is a Catholic church, the **San José Mission**, built by Spanish priests in 1701. Floor-to-ceiling religious murals and ancient Spanish paintings decorate the interior walls of this venerable sanctuary, many of the paintings having been transported from Mexico City on the backs of mules. Photographs aren't allowed in the church, so leave your camera in the car.

While each of the six Laguna villages—Seama, Mesita, Encinal, Paguate, Paraje, and Old Laguna—has its own traditional holidays, the entire pueblo gathers to celebrate St. Joseph's Day on September 19. Indian dances and a colorful crafts fair are usually part of this festival (the public is welcome). Christmas dances are held in December, but for exact dates and times you should call the pueblo administration; Tel: 552-6654.

To reach Laguna from I-40, take exit 114 and follow the frontage road west to the community's entrance.

Acoma Pueblo

A few miles west of Laguna along I-40 is the turnoff to Acoma Indian Pueblo, at exit 108. Roosting like a vulture atop a burly sandstone mesa 12 miles (19 km) south on NM 23, this venerable village, aptly nicknamed Sky City because of its lofty position high above the arid valley floor, was built around A.D. 900. Today it is among the oldest occupied communities in America (though with a very small population), and certainly one of the most dramatically situated.

From the pueblo entrance on top of Acoma Mesa, views of the desolate, brown, desertlike landscape below are spectacular. Especially prominent to the north is the towering bulk of Enchanted Mesa, a neighboring sandstone uplift atop which Acoma residents once took refuge from attacking Spaniards.

Vandalism has necessitated an unfortunate restriction in the pueblo; all non-Indians must now be accompanied by local guides. Tours last slightly more than an hour and take place seven to ten times a day depending upon the number of visitors. When you arrive at the mesa leave your car in the designated area and pay a $6 fee per person at the visitors' center (children between the ages of six and 17 pay $4; free for children five and under). A small bus will carry you from the parking lot to the village itself.

A slow meander through the dusty town streets is like a stroll back in time. The ancient stone and adobe walls and *vigas* (roof beams) here are all original. Some of the structures are dilapidated, but remember that most of the Acoma buildings were constructed more than a thousand years ago. The highlight of the tour is an architectural treasure known as the **San Esteban Rey Mission**, constructed by the pueblo when it was ruled by Spanish priests in 1699. The mud and stone walls of the church are nine feet thick, and roof beams that were carried from a mountain 40 miles away (they were never allowed to touch the ground in transit, according to Indian legends) are 40 feet long.

Artisans of one kind or another make up most of the 50 or so permanent Sky City residents. Souvenir hunters can buy their pottery, beadwork, and other pueblo handicrafts from vendors' stalls and tables along the tour route. Note that Acoma pottery, normally characterized by complex Mimbres designs (geometric, angular, and curvilinear patterns), is highly prized by collectors. The works for sale on the streets are for tourists, but if you're interested in higher-quality items, ask your guide. One tip to remember when buying pottery or other handicrafts in any Southwestern pueblo: Don't accept the first price offered. Vendors expect to bargain and generally price their work accordingly.

Normal visiting hours are 8:00 A.M. to 7:00 P.M. April through September, and 8:00 A.M. to 6:00 P.M. from October to March. Unscheduled, Indians-only religious ceremonies may close the pueblo at any time (it's always a good idea to call before you go; Tel: 252-1139). An Acoma experience is doubly enjoyable on St. Lawrence Day (August 10), or on San Esteban Feast Day (September 2). Both celebrations feature Indian dances and tables piled high with traditional food. You can take pictures during the tour—but not on feast days—for a fee ($5 for each still camera shot; camcorders have recently been prohibited), but don't attempt to photograph an Acoma resident without first obtaining his or her permission.

Grants

A jumping-off point for many of western New Mexico's attractions—such as Acoma and, below, El Malpais and El Morro—Grants is located just off I-40, 72 miles (115 km) west of Albuquerque. The onetime hub of the country's uranium industry, the city offers little in the way of visitor entertainment, but if you plan to poke about here, visit the **New Mexico Museum of Mining** to see how the local uranium boom began.

Modest motels are abundant in Grants, with many located at the eastern end of town just off the first I-40 exit. One of the best digs at this end of town is **The Inn** (part of the Best Western chain); the **Sands Motel** downtown is another comfortable, quiet choice.

El Malpais National Monument

Hikers and wilderness lovers will especially appreciate the ravaged landscape of hardened volcanic lava, blackened cinder cones, and eroded sandstone buttes of El Malpais National Monument, 10 miles (16 km) south of Grants between NM 53 and NM 117. Translated as "Badlands" from the Spanish, this 126,000-acre preserve was created by erupting volcanoes during the age of dinosaurs. The last lava flow here spewed forth from the earth's bowels just a thousand years ago.

The monument has no visitor facilities on site, but you may obtain trail maps and brochures of the region in Grants at the El Malpais Information Center, 620 East Santa Fe Avenue; Tel: 285-4641. The longest, most scenic walkway in the monument, the **Acoma-Zuni trail**, begins at a well-marked trailhead 18 miles (29 km) south of Grants on NM 53. There's little change in elevation on this seven-and-one-half-mile-long path of the ancient Anasazi Indians, but footing in the lava is uneven and hiking is sometimes strenuous, so wear sturdy boots.

A shorter hike off NM 53 is to the dramatic cinder cones and lava tubes near **El Calderon** (the trailhead is south of where the Acoma-Zuni trail crosses the highway). The trail is well marked. Bat lovers might enjoy the night tour offered by the U.S. National Park Service (summer weekends only) to watch the creatures as they leave El Calderon's Bat Cave (it's not usually open to the public); contact the El Malpais Information Center in Grants (see above) for times and dates. Another fairly short walk off NM 117, also south of the Acoma-Zuni trail crossing, leads to the forested sandstone bluff country of the **Cebolla Wilderness**.

Sections of El Malpais are accessible by car for visitors not interested in endurance walking. At the commercially operated **Ice Cave**, 20 miles (32 km) south of Grants on NM 53, you can explore a huge, ice-filled underground lava tube. **Sandstone Bluff Overlook** and **La Ventana Natural Arch**, 10 miles (16 km) and 17 miles (27 km) south of I-40 on NM 117, respectively, are the best places from which to get dramatic overviews of El Malpais Monument without overworking your feet. (The NM 117 turnoff is between Acoma and Grants).

El Morro National Monument

From El Malpais, NM 53 continues southwest a few more miles through sparse forests of scrub juniper and ponderosa pine to El Morro National Monument. Named by 17th-century Spanish explorers, this 1,300-acre preserve is one of the state's most visually appealing places. You'll see El

Morro's centerpiece—a slab-sided, 200-foot-high sandstone bluff known as **Inscription Rock**—long before you reach the preserve itself.

For centuries travellers chiseled their names and messages into the soft sandstone base of Inscription Rock for all who passed by to read. The oldest carvings (there are hundreds) were left by Don Juan de Oñate, founder of the first Spanish settlement in New Mexico. Oñate and his band of soldiers were returning from an expedition to the Hopi villages of present-day Arizona and Mexico's Sea of Cortez when he camped at El Morro and wrote, "Passed by here the Adelantado Don Juan de Oñate from the discovery of the Sea of the South, the 16th of April of 1605."

Stop at El Morro's visitors' center for a short lesson in area history before visiting the famous inscriptions. The two-mile-long, self-guided trail to the base of Inscription Rock leads also to ancient Pueblo Indian ruins near the bluff's summit. Panoramas of the surrounding terrain from this high point are staggering, so be sure to take your camera.

Zuni Pueblo

Thirty-eight miles (61 km) west of El Morro on NM 53 you'll come to Zuni Indian Pueblo, thought by early Spaniards to be one of the fabled Seven Cities of Cíbola. Known originally as Hawikuh and first visited by Europeans in 1539, the village has numerous crafts shops selling fine "needlepoint" jewelry (silver-encased designs formed with bits of turquoise, jet, and coral), and black-and-red-on-white animal-design pottery. The old Spanish church here (visitors are welcome) was constructed in the late 1600s and totally renovated in 1968. Little of the old pueblo, in fact, remains; clusters of modern houses with tin roofs, telephone lines, grocery stores, and gasoline stations hide the few ancient buildings that are left.

Zuni has no feast day but observes Shalako, a celebration of life, all year long. The public portion of the ceremony takes place in late November or early December and is well worth watching; call the pueblo from October on for exact dates and times; Tel: 782-4481.

SOUTH OF ALBUQUERQUE
Isleta Pueblo

To begin your southern itinerary drive south on I-25 to exit 209 and follow the access road to historic Isleta Indian Pueblo. Occupied since the 13th century, this old mud-and-stone village of 3,000 inhabitants sits in a wide, cottonwood-filled valley on the Rio Grande just 15 miles (24 km) south of Albuquerque.

Pueblo residents won't mind if you walk or drive slowly through town, but you should steer clear of areas marked "restricted" (these are often religious sites), and try to make as little ruckus as possible. You'll find a number of small shops here selling locally made pottery, silver and turquoise jewelry, and other local handicrafts, so don't hesitate to stop and browse. Most Isleta handicrafts aren't traditional. The pottery designs (usually red and black on white) are borrowed from Laguna Pueblo, which borrowed from the pottery of Acoma; the jewelry styles are copied from the Navajo.

As in most Southwestern Indian pueblos, life revolves around the old, centrally located plaza. Many of the adobe houses here date from the time of the Spanish, but modern refurbishing and the addition of rooftop television antennas have taken their toll on the community's charm. Dominating the north end of the plaza is **St. Augustine Mission** (constructed in 1720), one of the oldest and most legend-surrounded churches in the Southwest. Probably the strangest tale from the church concerns Fray Juan José Padilla, buried beneath the St. Augustine altar in 1756. According to local storytellers, the padre's coffin suddenly bulged up through the packed earthen floor one day, scaring churchgoers half to death and severely startling the resident friar. Padilla was quickly, apologetically reinterred, but not for long. Every so often, up popped the priest while parishioners paled. When the coffin appeared again in 1962, church officials had finally had enough. The Movable Priest was once again buried, this time under six inches of concrete. Padilla was likely forced to surface because of a variable water table that actually floated the coffin upward during extremely wet years. Many Isleta residents, however, say the good friar had just been keeping an eye on his flock.

The pueblo is perhaps best known among visitors and locals alike for its scrumptious fresh-baked Indian bread.

Twice daily—early morning and midafternoon, usually—pueblo women slide freshly kneaded loaves into *hornos* (mud ovens), and 45 minutes to an hour later retrieve them golden brown and delicious. You'll see Bread for Sale signs tacked both to shops and private homes in the village; the going price per loaf is about $2.

Isleta holds two public feast days, August 28 and September 4, during which non-Indians are welcome to partake in pueblo events. Visitors may photograph the mission and other structures without paying a fee but shouldn't point a camera at residents without their permission.

Salinas National Monument

From Salinas it's a 40-mile (64-km) drive south on I-25 to Bernardo, where U.S. 60 turns east to Salinas National Monument. There are three large, widely separated archaeological sites at this remote monument, each displaying a crumbling 17th-century Spanish mission and an abandoned prehistoric Pueblo Indian town.

Mogollon Indians (pronounced "Muh-gee-OWN") from northern Mexico first occupied the Salinas Valley around A.D. 700, but were later joined and assimilated by the Anasazi from what is now the Four Corners region. By A.D. 1100 a total of 11 large pueblos had been established in the area, and though agriculture was undoubtedly often difficult in the arid valley, the towns flourished and grew.

In 1598, however, the pueblo at Gran Quivira, one of the three sites, was visited by New Mexico's first governor, Don Juan de Oñate. Immediately afterward Franciscan missionaries arrived to quash Indian religious practices and convert pueblo inhabitants to Christianity. By 1630 three huge missions had been built: San Gregorio de Abo at Abo, San Buenaventura at Gran Quivira, and Nuestra Señora de la Purisima Concepción at Quarai. Demanding massive quantities of salt, corn, and other tribute from the Indians, the priests did little more than aggravate an already difficult situation. Crop production in the Salinas Valley had barely been adequate to feed the puebloans before the Spaniards arrived; now there was simply not enough food to go around. A severe drought in 1666 brought on famine, and habitual raids by nomadic Apaches made things worse. By 1677 both the missions and the pueblos had been abandoned, left to erode in the wind.

Today, although the mission walls are crumbling away and the prehistoric Pueblo Indian towns are blanketed with rubble, Salinas remains one of the state's most engrossing archaeological sites. Hiking trails around the ruins are short, self-guided, and not strenuous—and you probably won't see more than one or two rattlesnakes.

The Abo Unit lies 26 miles (42 km) east of I-25 and north of NM 60; Gran Quivira Unit, the largest and most developed of the three, is 25 miles (40 km) directly south of Mountainair on NM 55; Quarai, with the best-preserved mission, is 8 miles (13 km) north of Mountainair, also on NM 55. To fully explore all three units requires about three hours (if you start early from Albuquerque and don't spend too long at Isleta Pueblo, you can complete the tour before lunch). If your time is limited, bypass Abo and Quarai and go directly to Gran Quivira, the only site with a decent museum. The monument is open every day year-round; hours are 9:00 A.M. to 5:00 P.M. in winter and 8:00 A.M. to 6:00 P.M. in summer.

South to the Owl Café

South of Bernardo on I-25 you'll notice that the sage-covered plains and soft, rolling hills of central New Mexico have been replaced by a harsher, rockier, rough-edged landscape, known as the Chihuahuan desert. Welcome to the land of coyotes, rattlesnakes, and cactus, where everything alive either stings, stabs, stinks, or sticks.

Socorro, 25 miles (40 km) south of Bernardo, is a welcome retreat if you need gas or just a stretch. (Most stations are at the north end of town just a few blocks off I-25; we discuss its accommodations and food possibilities below.) If not, stay on the interstate for another 8 miles (13 km) to exit 139 (U.S. 380) and the tiny hamlet of San Antonio. Start licking your chops at the edge of town, then go directly to the **Owl Cafe**, reputedly the best hamburger joint in the state. A required layover for beef lovers (order your cheeseburger doused with green chile and be sure to try the French fries), the restaurant sits at the junction of U.S. 380 and NM 380 in the center of town.

Bosque del Apache
National Wildlife Refuge

NM 380 continues south through corn and grain fields along the western bank of the Rio Grande 8 miles (13 km) to Bosque del Apache National Wildlife Refuge, a large sanctuary that attracts bird and animal lovers from all over the world. Among the many larger species here are mule deer, coyotes, bobcats, wild turkeys, and upland game birds, but from October through March most visitors come to observe the waterfowl, especially the Bosque's small flock of whooping cranes. These large, ungainly white birds arrive around mid-October (accompanied by hundreds of thousands of ducks and sandhill cranes) and usually remain through February. They're sometimes difficult to spot, but birders seem to have a lot of fun trying. Another crowd pleaser here is a flock of snow geese—between 20,000 and 30,000 strong, depending upon the previous year's hatch—that can turn the sky black when they lift off the fields in unison.

The $2-per-car entrance fee is worth every penny. A graveled tour loop takes one to three hours depending on how fast you drive and the number of stops you make; most animal viewing can be done right from your car. If you want to explore the refuge on foot you may do so at any of several self-guided trails that skirt the edge of the wetlands. Binoculars are helpful, especially for observing the whoopers.

The cold months are the best times to see truly large numbers of animals at Bosque, but no matter when you visit, critters of some kind—mammals, birds, or reptiles—will always be in abundance. One of America's premier wildlife sanctuaries, Bosque is well worth an hour or two of your time.

If you run out of daylight, feel hungry, and need a place to stay, return to **Socorro**, which has several pleasant, inexpensive motels in which to overnight and one great spot for dinner. Among the most comfortable accommodations are the **Golden Manor** (Best Western) and the **San Miguel Motel**, both on California Avenue, the main north–south drag. For dinner, try the historic **Val Verde Steakhouse**, 203 East Manzanares Street, specializing in steaks and New Mexican fare.

The Very Large Array

From Socorro drive 49 miles (78 km) west on U.S. 60 to be greeted by one of the strangest sights in the American Southwest. Scattered across the midsection of a large natural bowl called the Plains of San Agustin, the **National Radio Astronomy Observatory**—better known as the Very Large Array, or VLA—reminds most travellers of a scene from the *Star Wars* sci-fi thriller *Return of the Jedi*.

Reputed to be the world's most powerful radio telescope, the VLA is not one structure but many—an array of

28 huge dish antennas, each 82 feet in diameter, electronically connected to create a single radio telescope 20 miles in diameter. Completed in 1979, the unit gathers solar and stellar information for astronomers and scientific organizations the world over.

The VLA is located in the isolated Plains of San Agustin for several reasons. Because of the 7,000-foot elevation and smogless desert climate, atmospheric water vapor (and, consequently, photograph-blurring clouds) is minimal here. Surrounding mountains block interference from television and radio station signals as well as transmissions from military bases. Finally, the wide, grass-covered bowl makes it relatively simple to move the monster telescopes, each weighing 235 tons and standing 94 feet above its foundation.

A small, unmanned visitors' center offers a self-starting slide show and a serve-yourself gift shop, but little else. The real attraction here is a self-guided, 30-minute round-trip trail to the foundations of several of the huge antennas.

NORTH OF ALBUQUERQUE
Albuquerque to Santa Fe on the
Jemez Mountain Trail

Beginning 18 miles (29 km) north of Albuquerque at Bernalillo, branching west off I-25, the **Jemez Mountain Trail** bisects the Indian areas of Santa Ana, Zia, and Jemez before looping east through the heart of the mountains, finally to descend into Santa Fe from the north. Comprising NM 44, NM 4, NM 502, and U.S. 84/285, and about 120 miles in length, the trail can easily be driven in one day and is by far the most picturesque route north out of Albuquerque. (For a discussion of other routes to Santa Fe from Albuquerque, see the end of this chapter.)

The Jemez Mountains themselves, jutting upward from the desert some 20 miles northwest of Albuquerque and extending northward along the western edges of the Rio Grande and Chama River valleys, are among the state's most scenic chain of peaks. Once the principal hunting grounds for large bands of prehistoric Pueblo Indians, today this verdant quilt of forested peaks, aspen-filled valleys, and roaring mountain streams is a mecca for fishermen, hikers, backpackers, animal watchers, and touring motorists.

Most highways in the Jemez region are well maintained

and open year-round, but if you plan to drive on snowy days, check local road conditions with the New Mexico State Police, Tel: 827-9000, before you go. Storms are fairly common in north-central New Mexico from December through March, and trying to negotiate a narrow mountain highway in a blizzard is not much fun.

Coronado State Monument and Points West

To begin your sightseeing leave I-25 at exit 242 in Bernalillo, and drive northwest on NM 44. (Bernalillo has little to offer travellers. It does, however, host the New Mexico Vine and Wine Festival on the first weekend in September.) As you cross the Rio Grande bridge watch for the signs to Coronado State Monument and the 14th-century Indian town of **Kuaua**, one of 12 large Rio Grande pueblos still occupied when Spanish explorer Francisco Coronado arrived in 1540. These ruins aren't as classic or as well preserved as those in Salinas Valley, but the murals of masked dancers unearthed in one of the pueblo's large underground kivas (now located in a special exhibit room) are wonderful examples of the region's prehistoric artistry. The monument is open from 8:00 A.M. until 5:00 P.M. daily.

The pueblo of **Zia**, 17 miles (27 km) northwest on NM 44, was occupied before the Spanish arrived. (Our coverage does not include the nearby Santa Ana Pueblo as it is open to outsiders only ten days each year.) In 1688, however, eight years after a region-wide Indian revolt against European occupation, Spanish conquistador Domingo Cruzate burned Zia to the ground and killed more than 600 Indians in the process. The town, a scattered collection of low-slung stone-and-adobe houses, was rebuilt atop a 300-foot-high lava-covered mesa in 1692 and has changed little in appearance since. The permanent population today is about 650.

Zia potters are talented artisans, and the pueblo's polychrome ceramics (typically black, dark brown, and red on a pure white background) are considered good investments by most collectors—especially the large water jars, or *ollas*. The Zia bird, a long-legged, long-necked avian with widespread wings and tail, is the best-known design. You can buy pottery and other locally made handicrafts (jewelry, beadwork) here in several small pueblo shops.

Visiting hours at Zia are 8:00 A.M. until 5:00 P.M. except on religious holidays, when the village is closed to non-Indians. Zia's feast day, August 15, is usually celebrated with a corn dance and crafts fair and is always the most exciting time for a visit. Whenever your visit, be sure to stop by **Our Lady of Assumption Mission**, dating from 1692.

Jemez Pueblo

At the village of San Ysidro, NM 4 bears right off NM 44 toward the mountains and Jemez Pueblo, 5 miles (8 km) from the intersection, on the left side of the highway.

Tribal legends claim Jemez ancestors originated in a great northern lagoon called Uabunatota, then slowly migrated southward until they found a home in the rugged escarpments of the Jemez Mountains. The Spaniards first visited the region in 1541, but European domination did not sit well with the Jemez people, and they staged a bloody revolt in 1680. The present-day village, mostly dilapidated and ancient-looking one- and two-story adobe buildings occupying a shallow river valley on the west side of the highway, was settled around 1696 after the Indians had been soundly defeated by soldiers under the command of Diego de Vargas.

Walking tours through the village are typically frowned upon except on the pueblo's feast day, November 12, and other public holidays. But by turning left at the sign that reads General Rules to Abide By, you may drive to the **San Diego Mission**, constructed in the early 1700s. As you negotiate the pueblo's narrow streets, notice that nearly every house has an *horno,* or bread oven, located in the front yard. Fresh-baked bread is a daily custom at Jemez, and a popular item to sell to tourists.

Little exists in the way of shops in the village itself, but on most summer days a colorful outdoor crafts market thrives at **Red Rock Scenic Area**, 3 miles (5 km) north of Jemez. Here you can buy willow baskets, moccasins, drums, and, of course, warm, oven-fresh bread from pueblo vendors. Also available for purchase is handmade polychrome pottery, typically heavy, all red or black, or sometimes red on white; it is not of traditional design and is made solely for sale to tourists. An especially picturesque time at Jemez is feast day, when a harvest dance and an arts-and-crafts fair generally accompany the celebration.

The Cañon de San Diego

Following the Jemez River (on NM 4) up Cañon de San Diego from the pueblo, you'll enter the tiny village of Jemez Springs. If you didn't pack a picnic, **Los Ojos Restaurant and Saloon** here is a great place to stop for lunch. A funky old structure whose interior is adorned with deer antlers, bear rugs, and rusty rifles, this local hangout boasts that it is the "Home of the famous Jemez Burger; one Jelluva Jamburger." Across the street you can buy thick deli sandwiches and picnic supplies at another Jemez Springs favorite, the **Jemez Mercantile**.

At the northern end of the village on the east (right) side of the highway, **Jemez State Monument** encompasses the abandoned Indian town of Gyusiwa, one of the original Jemez pueblos occupied before the Pueblo revolt. The old Spanish mission at the monument was destroyed in 1680 by angry puebloans, but even in its crumbly state it still has eight-foot-thick adobe walls and a bell tower 42 feet high. You'll find a small museum at the visitors' center displaying relics and artifacts from both the prehistoric and Spanish eras.

A five-minute drive beyond Jemez State Monument along the river on NM 4, **Soda Dam**—a 40-foot-high natural barrier of mostly pure, hardened sulphur—partially blocks the stream and displays the first signs of the vast geothermal activity bubbling and boiling beneath the Jemez Mountains. Swimming and bathing aren't allowed here; but the dam is a great place for photographs.

Ten miles (16 km) farther on, NM 4 passes a towering slab of black basalt known as **Battleship Rock**, jutting from the canyon bottom. By taking Forest Trail 137, which starts at the northeast end of Battleship Rock Campground (right at the base of the rock itself), hedonists can hike two miles to **McCauley Hot Springs**, another Jemez Mountains geothermal site. A pleasant half-hour's soak in the naturally heated water is guaranteed to make driving stiffness disappear. Yet another set of thermal pools, **Spence Hot Springs**, lies just past the Battleship Rock Campground on the opposite side of the Jemez River. Look for a large, unmarked parking area on the right (the trail starts at the end of the lot). You can don a swimsuit or not at either location, but most local folks bathe in the nude. A really pleasant time to take advantage of the hot springs is midwinter, when air temperatures fall well below freezing and the forest is blanketed with snow.

Spring, summer, or fall, you can enjoy excellent **trout fishing** for rainbows and German browns in the heavily stocked Jemez River. Stop at the High Country Store at the junction of NM 4 and NM 126 for fishing information, a temporary license, and whatever bait and tackle you didn't bring.

The Jemez Mountains

At the junction of NM 126 and NM 4 you can take the left fork to Fenton Lake or the right to Santa Fe. The lake, 8 miles (13 km) to the northwest on NM 126, is often crowded with fishermen—not a place for travellers who appreciate forested solitude. The right turn (NM 4), however, leads along the east fork of the Jemez River to Bandelier National Monument, which we cover below; traffic is generally light en route and the scenic attractions memorable. The road is twisted, steep, and narrow in places, so take your time.

On the right side of NM 4 a few minutes' drive east from the NM 126 junction you'll see the entrance to Jemez Falls Campground. **Jemez Falls** itself is a lovely 50-foot-high cascade located a quarter of a mile by a moderately easy (and pretty) trail from the far end of the campground. You can't reach the water itself, but the view of the falls is stunning from a rocky outcrop at the end of the path.

Another scenic hike begins where NM 4 crosses the east fork of the Jemez, five miles east of the campground entrance road (there's a small parking area for cars alongside the highway). The trail meanders along the grassy banks of the river through a narrow, steep-walled, shady canyon; bird life in the summer here is abundant, and there's always the chance of spotting deer and elk.

A "must stop" is at **Valle Grande** (Great Valley), a massive extinct volcanic caldera several miles farther to the east, visible from NM 4. When the volcano last erupted one million years ago, the explosion must have been stupendous; fragments of volcanic rock from Valle Grande have been discovered as far away as Kansas. The valley is private land, but sightseers may park and take pictures in the official viewing area adjacent to the highway.

If you appreciate unheralded picnic spots, watch for Forest Road 289 where it turns south off NM 4 about 2 miles (3 km) beyond the Valle Grande scenic viewpoint. A five-minute drive down this gravelly track, past the Bandelier National Monument boundary, lies one of the prettiest meadows in the Jemez. Stop and park when you see a rail fence on the right. Unless you have a four-wheel-drive vehicle, however, don't try to go any farther—and don't attempt to reach the meadow in snowy or muddy conditions. The road is closed in winter.

A few miles beyond the Forest Road 289 turnoff, NM 4 drops out of the mountains to invade the sprawling, canyon-slashed mesa country of the Pajarito Plateau. Here, NM 501 branches north (left) to the small mountain city of **Los Alamos**, birthplace of the atomic bomb. Except for the Bradbury Science Museum and its atomic weapons display, Los Alamos offers few attractions for travellers. In winter, nearby **Pajarito Ski Area** (8 miles/13 km west of Los Alamos on Camp May Road) attracts many visitors. The area, though small and without accommodations, usually has excellent snow conditions. Pajarito offers 40 separate runs and three double lifts in season (mid-December to mid-April); open Wednesdays, weekends, and federal holidays only.

Bandelier National Monument

If you elect to stay on NM 4, the turnoff to Bandelier National Monument is well marked on the right about 6 miles (10 km) past the intersection of NM 501. The visitors' center, museum, major ruins, and principal trailheads at the Frijoles Canyon section of the monument lie about 3 miles (5 km) from the entrance station.

Public access to much of the Pajarito Plateau is restricted by the U.S. Department of Energy, the agency that runs Los Alamos National Laboratory, but about 50 square miles (mostly on the southwestern side) fall within Bandelier's jurisdiction. The Indian tribes who once inhabited the region arrived in the late 12th century, and by the mid-1400s they had settled into several large pueblos in a harsh but survivable lifestyle. Not long afterward, however, and shortly before the arrival of the Spanish, the settlements were suddenly abandoned in favor of new homes along the Rio Grande to the east. Abundant in wildlife and dotted with hundreds of prehistoric Indian dwellings, the monument is one of those rare sanctuaries that is as much of a wilderness today as it was a century ago.

Major archaeological sites here are located fairly close together, making sightseeing easy for day visitors. A pathway (with wheelchair access) meanders up Frijoles Canyon from the visitors' center to the Anasazi ruins of

Tyuonyi, **Talus House**, **Long House**, and **Ceremonial Cave**. If you want to take your time you'll need about two hours for the round trip. Another trail to magnificent Upper and Lower **Frijoles Falls** requires about three hours round trip.

If you're a truly dedicated hiker, make the eight-hour round-trip hike through Bandelier's rugged piñon- and pine-dotted canyon country to **Stone Lions Shrine**—an age-old Pueblo Indian religious site comprising a huge stone circle decorated with deer antlers. Another prehistoric backcountry site you shouldn't miss is **Yapashi Ruins**, located on the trail to Stone Lions. Unexcavated Yapashi is little more than a hillside of large dirt- and cactus-covered mounds; nonetheless, it is astonishing: a sprawling, 800-year-old ruined city in the middle of absolutely nowhere.

No matter where you hike in Bandelier, wear a hat and good shoes or boots, carry your own water, and stay on or near the trails. The Pajarito Canyon country is uneven, unforgiving terrain in which even expert hikers can easily get lost.

On to Santa Fe

From Bandelier, the drive to Santa Fe via NM 4, NM 502, and then south (right) on U.S. 84/285 takes about an hour. Motorists returning to Albuquerque on I-25 should add another 70 minutes to that. If time permits, stop at **Tsankawi Ruins**, a roadside segment of Bandelier 11 miles (18 km) east of the monument on NM 4 that contains a cluster of Anasazi cliff houses similar to those in the Frijoles Canyon area. Another short side trip might be to **San Ildefonso Pueblo**, located just east of the Rio Grande bridge on the left (north) side of NM 502. Direct descendants of the Pajarito Plateau Anasazi, San Ildefonso folk are friendly and outgoing, and make some of the most exquisite (and expensive) black ceramics in the state. The late Maria Martínez is the great maker's name here. Signs direct sightseers to the better-known shops, in which they are welcome to browse or buy. There's little else to see in the pueblo itself except the exterior of the traditional kiva and a recent replica of a Spanish mission that was burned during the Pueblo revolt.

The fastest (and least scenic) way from Albuquerque up to Santa Fe is, of course, I-25 north from the city center. It takes about one hour. An alternate and longer route (though not as long as the Jemez Mountain route), which we discuss in the Albuquerque chapter, is the so-called Turquoise Trail (NM 14): east from the city center on I-40, then left (north) on NM 14 at Cedar Crest, and on up through the old mining towns of Golden, Madrid, and Cerrillos into Santa Fe. The Turquoise Trail runs along the far, or eastern, side of the Sandia Mountains that loom over Albuquerque.

GETTING AROUND

The most practical way to explore the area around Albuquerque is by automobile. Avis, Budget, Dollar, Hertz, National, and several other car-rental companies have offices at the Albuquerque International Airport. (If you're planning a trip during the annual Albuquerque International Balloon Fiesta in October, be sure to reserve a car well in advance.) Highway maps may be obtained from most car-rental agencies and gasoline stations, or from the N.M. Tourism and Travel Division, 491 Old Santa Fe Trail, Santa Fe, NM 87501; Tel: 827-7400.

Most highways in this portion of the state are in good condition and are open year-round. If you plan to drive the Jemez Mountain Trail (NM 44 and NM 4) during the winter, however, check a local weather report before you leave; Highway Hotline, Tel: (800) 432-4269. The road is sometimes closed between Jemez Springs and the Parjarito Plateau–Los Alamos area for short periods after heavy snows.

As in most other regions of the Southwest, automobile traffic is usually heaviest from Memorial Day to Labor Day. April, May, September, and October are perhaps the prettiest months to visit, and also the least congested. Don't be surprised, however, if a stiff breeze threatens to remove your hat during April, especially in the southern regions. Spring winds are a fact of life in most areas of the state during March and April, but they are usually played out by the first of May.

Each of the trips described in the Around Albuquerque section can be driven in a single day, but the destinations will be far more enjoyable and you'll have much more time for sightseeing if you allow at least two days for each segment.

If you prefer travelling by sightseeing coach, **Piper Tours**, Tel: 242-3880, offers escorted bus tours to many of the region's better-known attractions.

ACCOMMODATIONS REFERENCE

The rates given below are projections *for 1993. Unless otherwise indicated, rates are for a double room, double occupancy, and do not include meals. Price ranges span the lowest rate in the low season to the highest rate in the high season. As rates are always subject to change, it is wise to double-check before booking.*

The area code for New Mexico is 505.

▶ **Golden Manor.** 507 North California, **Socorro**, NM 87801. Tel: 835-0230 or (800) 528-1234. $43–$47.

▶ **The Inn.** Exit 85, 1501 East Santa Fe Avenue, **Grants**, NM 87020. Tel: 287-7901 or (800) 528-1234. $62.

▶ **Sands Motel.** 112 McArthur, **Grants**, NM 87020. Tel: 287-2996 or (800) 424-7679. $38–$42.

▶ **San Miguel Motel.** 916 California Avenue NE, **Socorro**, NM 87801. Tel: 835-0211 or (800) 548-7938. $39.

SANTA FE

By John Pen La Farge

"This villa ... in the final analysis ... lacks everything. Its appearance is mournful ... the Villa of Santa Fe consists of many small ranches at various distances from one another, with no plan as to their location. In spite of what has been said, there is the semblance of a street. . . ."

—Fray Francisco Atanasio Domínguez

Santa Fe has progressed considerably since the town was described by Fray Domínguez in 1776. Santa Fe has progressed even since it was called, in the early 19th century, a "prairie-dog town." Happily, its people have progressed in popular description, too. Early-19th-century general and explorer Zebulon Pike called them "a lazy gossiping people always lounging on their blankets and smoking cigarillos"; they were noted by the Americans mostly for fandangos, raucous music, corrupt politics, cowardly soldiers, shameless women (who also smoked), and vice-ridden priests; their favorite sport was said to be gambling.

Today Santa Fe is seen, even if only in the imagination, as an entrancing, slightly foreign, artistic place, filled with creative and vaguely rustic people who nevertheless are astonishingly cosmopolitan. Here is Shangri-la on a trickle that is called a river, a place to lose oneself if one needs to be lost, or to find oneself if already lost. An artistic, social, familial, or spiritual transformation can very likely happen here. Maybe all four.

Here in the hardscrabble land that only a few generations ago meant a tough and often poverty-stricken life for even the best of families is a lively city of multiple cultures and the arts: music, painting, sculpture, literature, poetry, and performance art. Here is Indian culture and Spanish-American culture in all their forms—pottery, jewelry, weaving, tinwork, embroidery, carving, religious and folk dances—all rooted in the lives of the people.

The climate is dry but temperate; there is little rain and plenty of pure sunlight in a clear blue sky that dazzles. Although the temperature will usually change 20 to 30 degrees in a day, the thermometer almost never rises above 90 in the hottest summer or sinks below zero in the coldest winter.

The city itself is brown and even those buildings not made of adobe appear to be. The soft feel of the walls and surfaces, the illogical but organic layout of the roads and streets, the haphazard arrangement of the houses—here tightly bunched, there widely spaced—and the idiosyncratic decorations all conspire to make the city feel as though it had sprung naturally from the earth.

La Villa de Santa Fe was named after Their Catholic Majesties' 1492 encampment outside the Spanish city of Granada just before the final reconquest of Spain from the Moors. Santa Fe means "Holy Faith," and this plain designation tells much about the town. It was founded upon faith: faith in God, in the Roman Catholic religion, in the Spanish monarchy, and in the willingness of the Spanish people to advance into unknown, harsh regions to begin new lives and to convert the native populace to Catholicism. This simple name represents much that Spain gave to the New World and holds within it all of the bitter times suffered by its people because of their unending faith in themselves, in their duty, and in God.

If you ask at the Chamber of Commerce or at City Hall what the city's name is, however, you will be told it is La Villa Real de Santa Fé de San Francisco de Asis (The Royal City of the Holy Faith of St. Francis of Assisi). This rather more magnificent name was mistakenly ascribed to the city in the 1920s, and tells much about how Santa Fe has changed over time and what you may expect. This second name stresses royalty and the faith of one great exemplar rather than the bone-tough life and the faith of an entire country. More in line with a 20th-century tourist destination, this name demands rather less of the imagination and the spirit than did the previous title. It is a flowing name that deserves a better river.

Santa Fe's nickname is probably its best: the City Different. This appellation came about earlier in this century, when Santa Fe was developing into the city that has become so famous today. Despite the whimsical character of this nickname, a whimsy entirely characteristic of the people who created the town's cosmopolitan and unpretentious mixture, the name would have been deserved at any point in its history. This name is also the most endangered.

Santa Fe was the first capital city in what is now the United States. It was founded in 1609 as the capital of an area that looked almost exactly like the land the Spanish colonists had left behind in hopes of better things. Santa Fe is the capital of one of the harshest lands in America with one of the most difficult climates. It is ironic that the Spaniards travelled halfway around the world only to find a place just like home and just as unforgiving.

Today Santa Fe itself is green, but just outside the city proper the land is as it always has been. With the exception of the mountains to the north, the country is all dry hills covered with scrubby piñon and juniper trees and traversed with arroyos—dry gullies that run only after a heavy rain. The land is not desiccated desert, but it is stark and bony.

Santa Fe was central to a land where the Indians, initially subjugated by the Spaniards, eventually came to live side by side in comparative harmony with their rulers some years after the revolt of 1680. Together, both peoples fought to survive the depredations of the "wild" Indians such as Apaches, the nomads whose pleasure it was to despoil the region at every opportunity. In 1821 the City Different, with a population of only 5,000, comprised two cultures that remained relatively separate and distinct yet cooperative and friendly. With the American conquest of New Mexico in 1846, the City Different became, and still is, the capital of a *tri*cultural realm, the only such model in the Americas: three distinct cultures despite their interweaving.

The City Different remained a backwater of empire and then a backwater of two successive republics from 1610 until this century. Nonetheless, its romance captured the imaginations of many generations, and its name was known considerably beyond what its actual importance suggested. Furthermore, the stark physical beauty of its setting and the qualities of its people ultimately captured the hearts of thousands who at first found it a disreputable collection of mud hovels.

In this century Santa Fe came of age, and with the advent of artists, poets, writers, eccentrics, and remittance men (those who came from abroad but were supported by monies from home) it became celebrated for its unique qualities. The tricultural backwater—literally miles from anywhere, difficult to get to (thankfully, it still is) and even more difficult to leave, the capital of a harsh and often forgotten land—became an artists' colony, a center of creativity. After World War II the addition of a substantial number of top scientists (Los Alamos is nearby, and the Manhattan Project was headquartered here) increased the intellectual ferment of the unlikely mixture.

All of these factors have attracted a wide range of visitors from around the world: One is just as likely to see Japanese or Germans as New Yorkers. Earlier in the century visitors were primarily educated adventurers, often from the East, looking for the unusual. Another core group was neighboring Texans, who, despite their history of friction with New Mexico and the Spanish-Americans over land and trade, have remained Santa Fe's most faithful visitors. Today Santa Fe increasingly attracts Californians, and especially the Hollywood crowd, who find in the city a quiet second home (this has sparked controversy as real-estate prices, and therefore taxes, have correspondingly skyrocketed).

Away from the fast-paced world, away from industry, hucksters, and deal makers, away from American culture that in most of the United States recognizes itself only, La Villa de Santa Fe offers color and vibrancy, the living culture of its three communities, and the beauty of its physical setting.

Is this not perfection?

Well, perhaps. But for each person who finds purpose in the freedom and intellectual climate of the city, another is lost in the slow pace that demands little. For each paradise found, another discovers a trap instead.

Santa Fe's coming of age has occasioned yet another controversy, this within the last decade or so: the debate over just what exactly is "Santa Fe style." The commercialization of the Santa Fe "look" in decoration and clothing came in the early 1980s with splashy stories in numerous newspapers, in magazines such as *Esquire* and *National Geographic,* and with Ralph Lauren and a thousand others who decided that money could be made from marketing that look. Found in bars and stores from Los Angeles to Washington, D.C., and now in EuroDisney, the look comprises bold geometric patterns, pastel colors, cacti, howling coyotes, skulls of various herbivores, updated cowboys and Indians, brightly painted snakes, arts and crafts from Mexico, flowing skirts, and leatherwear. Several books have attempted to catalogue the style. Almost all of it is fake.

Santa Fe style as it actually evolved prior to, say, 1960,

was informal, thrown together without great self-consciousness. As anywhere, people naturally tended to decorate their houses with local arts and crafts, i.e., with what was available. That meant Indian pots and blankets, perhaps Indian baskets and kachina dolls; Spanish-American handcrafted furniture, *bultos* (religious statues), and *retablos* (icons); tableware, ironwork, tinwork, and leather furniture from Mexico. Whether because of Georgia O'Keeffe or not, skulls were occasionally hung outside because of the natural beauty of the bones. The rest of the house was then filled with whatever the owner made or brought from back home, be it Chippendale, Louis XIV, Japanese prints, Victoriana, Danish Modern, or Bauhaus. In other words, true Santa Fe style was eclectically assembled from whatever was at hand; its guiding spirit was relaxed and funky rather than stylized, and, aside from a love of native crafts and local sensibilities, was not self-conscious.

It was the same with clothes. Santa Feans have always worn leather, long intricate skirts, neckerchiefs, cowboy or Stetson hats, and Indian jewelry, but this too has now become more forced as a result of being marketed to the nation. Now there are "elements" to the style, and the elements have been catalogued and categorized, available for purchase from a store rather than thrown together upon inspiration. What once flowed from the place and time is now contrived.

Santa Fe is not paradise, though it has much to recommend it. Many have been drawn here to grab all they can from a land that seems to hold infinite possibility. The town you find will be in some ways utterly charming but in other ways lost and confused. You may be enchanted by the City Different or you may become a detractor, but it is unlikely that you will be unaffected.

MAJOR INTEREST

The Plaza Area
Palace of the Governors
Museum of Fine Arts
La Fonda Hotel
St. Francis Cathedral
Sena Plaza
Padre Gallegos House
Pinckney R. Tully House
Felipe B. Delgado House
The Santa Fe River

Palace Avenue
Staab House/La Posada Hotel

Canyon Road
The First Ward School/Linda Durham Gallery
El Zaguán
Olive Rush House and Studio
Borrego House
Cristo Rey Church

Guadalupe Street Area
El Santuario de Nuestra Señora de Guadalupe
Agua Fria Street

Old Santa Fe Trail/Old Pecos Trail
Loretto Chapel
Barrio de Analco
San Miguel Mission
The Oldest House
Pink Adobe Restaurant
Carlos Vierra House

A Santa Fe Drive
Randall Davey House/Audubon Center

Other Museums
Museum of International Folk Art
Museum of Indian Arts and Culture
Wheelwright Museum of the American Indian

Santa Fe, founded in 1610, is an ancient city by American standards, but because it was for centuries the capital of an impoverished province, the city grew slowly, most of its growth occurring in this century. Thus the majority of what is old and interesting in the city is concentrated around the plaza and on three of the streets leading from it: San Francisco Street, Palace Avenue, and Old Santa Fe Trail (so-called).

The **plaza** is the heart of the city, and it is where our coverage begins. Most of the important sights are located within a few minutes' walk in any direction from the plaza: The Palace of the Governors has been the center of the town since 1610; the Museum of Fine Arts, built in 1917, set the visual style for Santa Fe from that time on: Sena Plaza is one of the oldest intact houses in Santa Fe and one of the most beautiful; La Fonda Hotel, like the Museum of Fine Arts, has influenced the look of the town, and for decades was the center of Santa Fe's social life; the **Santa Fe River**, although physically unimpressive, is

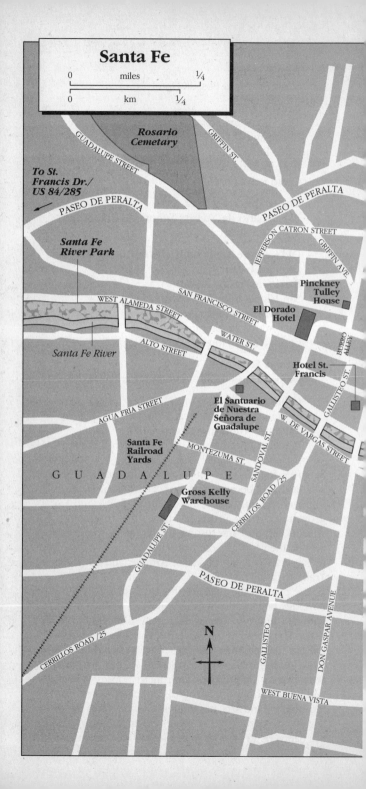

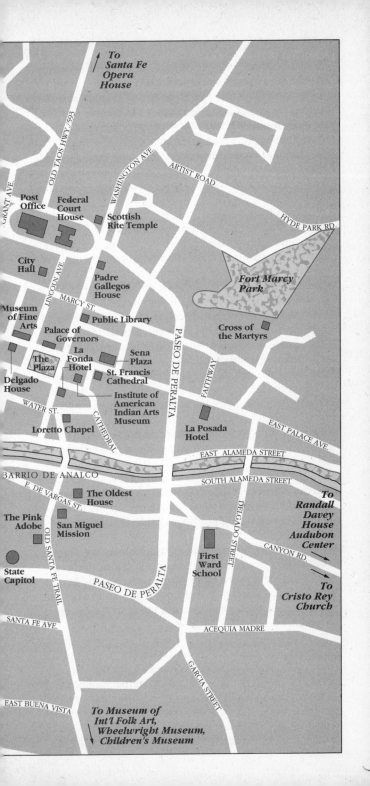

the reason for the city's existence, and was for centuries the blood to the city's heart, the plaza.

The streets off the plaza provide a glimpse into the various periods of Santa Fe's history. **San Francisco Street**, the southern boundary of the plaza, is a record of the town's architecture from the end of the 19th century into the early 20th. **Palace Avenue**, the northern boundary and a fashionable residential street throughout this century, is where the best of the best have often lived—thus the Staab House.

Canyon Road is our next venue, an ancient street that runs up Santa Fe Canyon from the southeastern part of the town center. It is charming both because of its authentic and unpretentious New Mexican houses and because of the quiet and simple ambience that remains in stretches. Canyon Road is also the center for the arts colony of Santa Fe, and has been for the last 70 years.

Guadalupe Street, which defines the western edge of the town center, is a fairly old street named for venerable El Santuario de Nuestra Señora de Guadalupe; the stretch of Guadalupe south of the river is a new center of activity that holds the key to the future of downtown Santa Fe.

Old Santa Fe Trail, which we discuss next, is not quite what its name declares, but it *is* the old entrance into the plaza, at the eastern end. On Old Santa Fe Trail, the Loretto Chapel contains a beautiful staircase proclaimed to have been built by miraculous intervention; the so-called Oldest Church, the San Miguel Mission, is a ruggedly handsome recollection of New Mexico's oldest architecture; and the Barrio del Analco along De Vargas Street where it crosses Old Santa Fe Trail at San Miguel Mission is one of Santa Fe's oldest neighborhoods, with some of its oldest houses.

At the end of our coverage of specific areas we suggest a Santa Fe drive because much of the charm of the city lies not in the obvious sights but in the streets and houses that look as though they had simply sprung up from the earth. Among them you'll discover the town that has often been least touched by "progress."

A note about the weather and planning your trip. Although the sights of Santa Fe change little with the seasons, the peak time to see them (from the standpoint of weather, not of avoiding crowds) is during the summer months, when the days are warm but not unbearable. Santa Fe sits 7,000 feet up in the foothills of the Rocky Mountains, an elevation that cools the summer, moderates the winter, brightens the sun, and makes exhaustion more likely and intoxication easier until you've adjusted to the altitude.

Hotel reservations during the summer months should be made well in advance. Spring, really May and June, can be most pleasant, although June can also be the hottest and driest month of the year. September and October are distinctly cooler than the summer months, but on the other hand the city is freer then of the masses who converge on the plaza in the high season. Unless you are a skier and New Mexico is having a good snow year— something that does not always happen but has for the past several years—November through April offer little inducement for a visit. November, March, and April in particular are frequently the dreariest months, and in March especially the wind can be horrid for anyone with allergies.

The one bright spot in the winter months is Christmas, celebrated in a uniquely Santa Fe fashion with *luminarias* (small bonfires) and *farolitos* ("little lanterns," small brown grocery bags with an inch or so of sand and a votive candle). The lanterns are placed along the streets and walls of the old east side of town and around the plaza on Christmas Eve. Those who walk among the lights will also smell the rich piñon and juniper smoke that characterizes cold nights in Santa Fe. The effect is magical, and visitors are beginning to catch on to this, too. (South of Santa Fe *luminaria* is taken to mean the little lantern and *farolito* to mean a bonfire.) In early December there is Las Posadas, a reenactment in the plaza of Joseph and Mary's search for a room in Bethlehem.

The telephone area code for Santa Fe is 505.

The Plaza

The Santa Fe plaza has been the heart of the city since its founding in 1610 by Don Pedro de Peralta at the behest of the king of Spain. When people speak of Santa Fe, it's the plaza area they speak of, just as when we say "New York" we usually mean Manhattan. The archetypal Spanish city is laid around a central square, on which are located the most important buildings of government and religion and the houses of the leading citizens. From such a plaza radiate the less important buildings and the less prominent citizens. Thus the plaza is both the literal and metaphorical heart of a Spanish town whether in Spain, South America, Mexico, or here in Santa Fe.

Because of the concentration of interesting buildings and history around the plaza, to say nothing of arts and crafts, Indian art galleries, shopping, and museums, you could easily spend a full day exploring the area. If you are a real shopper or museum aficionado, plan for more.

Almost all the significant events of the city's history have occurred in the plaza, where the people have gathered and lived out their lives for nearly 400 years. The heart of the heart is the **Palace of the Governors**, built on the north side of the plaza soon after the founding of the city. This is where the king of Spain's representative lived, and so it was known originally as "*las casas reales.*" Because the building stood for royal power it was by far the grandest in the territory, and under Mexican rule even acquired glass windows years before any other building in Santa Fe, in 1832.

From the plaza the proud Spanish dons did their best to dominate the immense territory of New Mexico by force, only to be humbled and thrown out by the Pueblo Indian revolt of 1680. The Pueblos made the plaza theirs until the reconquest of 1692, when the Spaniards under Diego de Vargas decided to try cooperation and *compadrazgo* (binding friendship) rather than rule by force. The governors in the palace then had the unenviable duty of trying to keep whole a territory bounded by wilderness, desert, scarcity, hostile nomadic Indians, and independent-minded colonists who cared little for cooperation. From this small stronghold in a city of only a few thousand the representative of Spain ruled an area that included all of the western United States, extending eastward, at times, to the Mississippi River.

From 1821, after the Mexican revolution, the task faced by the governors was not much easier, but it was in the plaza that the residents of Santa Fe first saw the Mexican flag raised. Typically for New Mexico, the ceremony was arranged by an American, because the presiding government felt he alone had the requisite knowledge of how to celebrate independence. Also typically, the ceremony took place weeks after Mexico had achieved its independence from Spain, when the news, which must have been exceedingly surprising, arrived. The best news was that the Mexican government had opened its poorest province to trade with the United States—and so was born the Santa Fe Trail. You will find a historic marker to this vital trade route in the form of an upright stone in the southeast corner of the plaza.

Facing the palace on the northern side of the plaza is a

monument to General Stephen Watts Kearny, the man
who initiated the next episode in the plaza's history: the
American conquest of New Mexico from Mexico. When
he rode in, in 1846, General Kearny promptly appeared
in the plaza to reassure the frightened population that the
women would not be dishonored, property rights would
be respected, people would be protected from the hostile Indians, and they would enjoy all the rights of American citizens.

In the center of the plaza is an **obelisk** commemorating
several events. Dedicated in 1867, the monument honors
Union soldiers who died in the battle of Glorieta (east
of Santa Fe; see the following chapter) against the
Confederates—who were actually intent upon the conquest of California. New Mexico was seen only as a gateway
to this conquest, but it was here that the Confederate plans
failed. This same monument also honors soldiers and
settlers who died in battle against the "savage" Indians.
(The word "savage" was chiseled out in the 1970s by an
offended party.)

For the Americans the Palace of the Governors served as
an all-purpose government building; here the legislature
met, various departments had their offices, the Territorial
Library was estabished, and there was also a bank. During
the territorial period Governor Lew Wallace completed
his novel *Ben Hur* in the palace. The governmental uses
continued until the early 20th century, when the building
was nearly torn down as being too dilapidated to be of any
value except for the land it occupied. Fortunately, in 1909
the legislature established the Museum of New Mexico, to
be housed in the palace, and put it under the supervision
of the School of American Research. The palace was then
renovated and restored from its Victorian Territorial style
to the Spanish Pueblo style it reflects today. (Territorial
architecture differs from Spanish Pueblo architecture in
its use of bricks or adobe with brick coping, and in
its Neoclassical details of milled woodwork. Bricks and
milled lumber, as well as cast-iron pillars, tin roofs,
pressed-metal ceilings, and Anglo architectural tastes all
arrived in New Mexico with the railroad in 1879.)

The Palace of the Governors is now the **Museum of
New Mexico**'s headquarters and history museum, and
within it you will find excellent displays and a good
museum shop. One of the most interesting exhibits is that
of the Segesser hides—buffalo hides painted by Spaniards in the 18th century to record important battles. They
are the only surviving records of their kind. The hours of

the palace (and all Museum of New Mexico facilities) are 10:00 A.M. to 5:00 P.M., except in January and February, when the museums close on Mondays; Tel: 827-6483.

It is now an old Santa Fe tradition that the palace's **portal** (arcade) is one of the best spots to buy Indian crafts, especially jewelry. The Indians—primarily from the local pueblos—and the palace's administration are strict as to the quality and authenticity of all that is sold here; and the sight of all the Indians gathered under the long stretch of the *portal,* their wares displayed on blankets, is splendidly and authentically Santa Fe.

The palace today is only a fraction of its original size; its protective towers are long gone. In 1680, when taken over by the Pueblo Indians, the palace was large enough to hold 1,000 people, 5,000 sheep and goats, 430 horses and mules, and 300 head of cattle without crowding. In 1993 it is unknown how many tourists it will hold comfortably, but at the rate Santa Fe is gaining fame, we will probably soon find out, goats or no goats.

At the turn of the century, when the government considered ridding itself of the palace because its *vigas* (rough beams made of peeled logs) were sagging and its dirt roof was sifting slowly down into the rooms, Midwestern American architecture was the prevailing style of the town as a whole. The old Spanish or Pueblo architecture was considered vulgar and poor, fit only to be torn down or remodeled. Thus Santa Fe might have come out looking rather like Denver had it not been for the remodeling of the palace; for Carlos Vierra, who built a splendid house on Old Pecos Trail (see below); for the Chamber of Commerce, which decided that encouraging the Santa Fe look was a good commercial idea; and, most importantly, for the New Mexico exhibit of the Panama-California Exposition in San Diego in 1915, which was housed in the first example of what is now known as Spanish Revival style (designed by architect I.H. Rapp and inspired by Acoma Pueblo's church and convent built in the 1600s).

Across Lincoln Avenue to the west of the palace is the **Museum of Fine Arts** (Tel: 827-4455). Along with the palace, this building has set the style for the City Different since its construction in 1917 in the manner inspired by the exposition. Rapp designed the museum to incorporate elements from the Acoma church and convent, elements that have become classic Santa Fe style: uneven wall surfaces, rounded, soft corners, no hard edges, small windows in massive walls, an avoidance of the linear and the regular, and a second story set back from the first.

You'll see the Spanish influence in the layout of the building as it wraps around the patio, which has several good murals by Will Shuster, one of the Cinco Pintores— five painters who made their homes in Santa Fe in the 1920s. In summer, when the flowers are in bloom, the patio is particularly worth seeing. Be sure to raise your eyes to catch the massing of walls and *vigas,* their juxtapositions, and their shadows. The museum itself shows contemporary art or retrospectives on the first floor; Southwestern paintings from its permanent collection and prints from the first, "classic," half of the 20th century on the second. The museum's St. Francis Auditorium, directly modeled upon Mission church architecture, is the handsomest in Santa Fe. It contains romantic murals of Columbus and the Spanish conquistadors. This is where the Santa Fe Chamber Music Festival holds forth every summer.

The Museum of Fine Arts is important to the history of Santa Fe in another way. When artists first gathered in Santa Fe—and, indeed, until the 1960s, there were no art galleries—they showed their work either in their studios or at the museum. Because of the museum's open-door policy, it acted as a great encouragement to the art colony, which today benefits from 150 galleries.

Diagonally across the plaza from the museum, on San Francisco Street, is **La Fonda Hotel**, for decades the town's largest building and the only one with an elevator. This structure, too, contributed to the resurgence of the Spanish Pueblo style when it was reconstructed in the 1920s. Because it was the largest building, because it was the hotel where everyone who was anyone stayed, and because it was at the center of the city's social life, La Fonda's architectural style had great impact. Today, by law, its height defines the limit to which any downtown building can be constructed. Inside, La Fonda is no longer quite the grand hotel of former days—its spaces have been poorly cut up and its walls are too busy visually—but the vibrant Indians and Spanish-Americans painted by Gerald Cassidy, the windows and furniture decorated in the Mexican style, the Mexican tinwork, the elegant Santa Fe meeting room, and the welcoming atmosphere bespeak its classic period. And the elevator is still worth a ride.

Opposite La Fonda Hotel on San Francisco Street is **Packard's**, named for Al Packard, a much-respected Indian trader, now retired. The store carries rugs, pottery, and jewelry of consistently high quality.

Aside from the buildings of architectural and historical interest, other points of historic interest surround the plaza. On the west side is the First National Bank, the oldest in Santa Fe. In the middle of the block the Plaza Restaurant is virtually the only unpretentious downtown restaurant left, and, aside from La Fonda and the Shed (a beloved Santa Fe institution that always has long lines for its New Mexican food), is the only downtown eatery that predates 1970. Its attendant dive, the Plaza Bar, filled with marijuana smoke and questionable characters, exists no longer.

The **Catron Building** on the northeast corner is the only building on the plaza, aside from the palace, that has not been altered out of recognition. It was built in 1891 by Senator T. B. Catron, a leader of the notorious Santa Fe Ring, a group of politicos who controlled much of the wealth of the territory in the latter part of the 19th century. Through his machinations Catron was once the largest landholder in North America—and has a New Mexico county and a Santa Fe street named after his family to show for it.

The east side of the plaza is the newest side. Originally, the plaza stretched farther east to what is now the cathedral and was a gathering place for all the wagon trains, traders, fur traders, and merchants that made the Santa Fe Trail famous. At one time it also held a bullring.

In the middle of the south side of the plaza you will find a plaque commemorating La Castrense, the military chapel for the presidial company of Santa Fe. From the 1600s until 1894 the presidio occupied a large tract of land behind the palace. A building just behind the Museum of Fine Arts is one of the last remaining officers' quarters from the 19th century. La Castrense is gone, but in its day it was said to be the finest building in the territory. Its strongly carved stone reredos (altar screen) is now in Cristo Rey Church on Canyon Road, and its *vigas,* corbels, and choir loft are in the Santuario de Guadalupe on Guadalupe Street.

Also on the south side of the plaza, in a building that is not one of the finest in the territory, is Woolworth's. Woolworth's, the observant visitor will note, is the only store left on the plaza—and virtually the only store downtown—that serves the populace of the city rather than the tourist trade. Thus we are brought up to the modern day, in which the historic heart of the city is no longer the heart physically. For a city to have a real heart, its populace must live its life there, walk and talk and shop there, find it important not merely for what it is but because that is where they are centered. London, San Francisco, Paris, New York, Rome, or, for that matter, Bath and Segovia, are vital because when you visit you are surrounded by and caught up in the life of the people. Such a city is not a Disneyland, nor a Williamsburg, nor an overgrown outdoor shopping mall; it is alive. Although the city and county governments of Santa Fe remain downtown, the connection between the plaza and its citizenry has been increasingly sundered since the late 1970s.

Woolworth's is notable for another reason; it serves an excellent Frito pie, which comes heartily recommended if you like serious junk food. If the day is nice, get your Frito pie to go and eat it on the plaza.

One block to the east of the plaza is **St. Francis Cathedral**, built in the 19th century by the territory's first resident bishop, Jean Baptiste Lamy, a Frenchman. The Romanesque-style cathedral was built over what had been the old *parroquia* (parish church), but it has never been finished. Its main doors tell the story of the Church in New Mexico. Inside, the cathedral is of only minor interest, except for the new reredos that depicts saints of the New World, and for the Chapel of Our Lady of the Rosary to the altar's left. The chapel is the only remaining part of the original 1718 *parroquia,* and holds a 16th-century statue of the Virgin. The statue, called La Conquistadora and credited with the peaceful reconquest of 1692, is the most revered icon in New Mexico—which is saying a great deal, as Spanish-Americans are a more than ordinarily pious people.

To the north of the cathedral are the **Sena and Prince plazas**, commonly known as Sena Plaza. This long, low building was built in many stages during the 19th century along the classic hacienda pattern. Its primary builder, Don José D. Sena, a scion of one of Santa Fe's most notable families, was a major in the Union army during the Civil War. What was the upstairs ballroom, reached by outside stairs, became the territory's legislative chamber when the capitol burned in 1892. The western portion of Sena Plaza was bought by territorial supreme court justice L. Bradford Prince in 1879; hence Prince Plaza. In their day these houses entertained the cream of the capital city's society. Since the 1930s the plazas have held shops, bookstores, offices, and restaurants.

In 1927 the eastern end of Sena Plaza was deeded to famed New Mexico Senator Bronson Cutting together with the Misses Elizabeth and Amelia White; the three hired artist William Penhallow Henderson to restore the building. Number 109 East Palace was the office out of which the Manhattan Project (the wartime effort that resulted in the creation of the atomic bomb) was headquartered after 1943.

There is a brand-new museum in downtown Santa Fe, across the street from the cathedral, toward the plaza. The **Institute of American Indian Arts Museum** is the new gallery of the institute, an organization established to keep alive the traditional culture and arts of American Indians. The gallery shows the work of current and past students of the institute. The most interesting rooms are those dedicated to the founding artists, innovators whose imagination has had profound impact on Indian art, and the room dedicated to traditional crafts. As you would expect with what is primarily student art, much of the rest of the exhibited art is derivative and of indifferent execution. Hours are 9:00 A.M. to 6:00 P.M. Monday through Saturday, until 8:00 P.M. Wednesdays, and noon to 5:00 P.M. Sundays; Tel: 988-6278.

Up Washington Avenue, one block from the plaza's northeast corner, you will find the **Santa Fe City Library** on the right. The library, although altered, was originally designed by New Mexico's patron saint of architecture, John Gaw Meem, as city hall, and is still a fine building in the Territorial style.

In contrast, across Washington Avenue to the west, the oppressively massive and graceless building dominating the street is what Santa Feans call the Ugly Building, formally the First Interstate Bank Building. The remarkable thing about the Ugly Building is that it complies with every code the city has enacted with the purpose of encouraging harmony in the historic downtown. "It takes times to ruin a world, but time is all it takes," as Fontenelle said.

One block north on Washington Avenue, the **Padre Gallegos House** sits opposite the Federal Oval at numbers 227–237. This splendid example of the hacienda style was built in 1857 by one of New Mexico's most colorful 19th-century characters. During his life Padre Gallegos was first a priest, educated by the controversial Padre Martínez of Taos, then, when he was defrocked by Archbishop Lamy for vice and dabbling in politics, he married within the Episcopal Church and was variously elected to the territorial assembly and the U.S. Congress.

To the east, on Paseo de Peralta, is a pathway leading

uphill to the **Cross of the Martyrs**, honoring the 23 Franciscans martyred during the Pueblo revolt of 1680. Above the cross once stood Fort Marcy, which was built after 1846 in the hope of keeping the Mexican-American population in awe of its new government. It was never really used, however, and has crumbled into dust. The view from up there is one of the best in the city.

North of the padre's house is the Scottish Rite Temple, often known as the Pink Monstrosity for obvious reasons. The temple, built by the Masonic Order in 1911 as a foursquare statement of the Order's importance and universality, is rumored to be modeled upon La Alhambra in Granada, but any resemblance is purely coincidental. Inside, you will find well-preserved and imaginative rooms and a theater, all representative of the Masons' philosophy.

Just south of the temple, the Federal Oval contains the **Federal Courthouse**, completed in 1889 after 36 years of on-again, off-again construction. It is a fine, honest statement of Anglo-American governance. Inside are six WPA murals by William Penhallow Henderson; at the southern entrance is a monument to Kit Carson.

South of the Federal Oval is City Hall, which used to be the high school. Next door, Sweeney Convention Center once served as the high school's gymnasium; its tarting-up barely conceals its origins.

At the west end of the Federal Oval is Grant Avenue. If you go to the end of Grant and look north toward the ridge, you will see the Hayt-Wientge Mansion, a fine Victorian house, on top of the ridge. South, down Grant Avenue, is the handsome First Presbyterian Church, designed by John Gaw Meem in 1939. Just to the west is a large white building that was the headquarters for the "I Am" cult in the 1940s.

Where Griffin Avenue meets Grant is the **Pinckney R. Tully House**, an excellent example of Territorial architecture. The bricks it appears to be made of are actually painted plaster. Another good example, opposite, is the **A. M. Bergere House**, one of Fort Marcy's officer quarters from the 1870s.

At the southern end of Grant Avenue is **Burro Alley**, named for the burros that brought firewood into Santa Fe until the 1930s. There is a mural in the alley by Howard Coluzzi.

West of Burro Alley, where Palace Avenue makes a wide turn, sits a hugely imposing structure that, despite a resemblance, is not a Mexican prison but **El Dorado** hotel, the largest hotel in town. From the vantage point of the alley you will see enormous, intricate wrought-iron gates set into a massive entryway that looks for all the world like the gateway to the Temple of Isis. The hotel occupies land that once contained one of the most historic structures in town, part of the gambling establishment of the famed Doña Tules. Doña Tules's political connections and charm made her the territory's most powerful woman in the 1830s and 1840s. The building, the last bit of her history, was allowed to collapse and the hotel built in its place in 1986. The city fathers also delayed the passage of the Streetscape Ordinance for two weeks so that the building of the hotel, which violates all standards, might begin before the law could confine it. Despite this miserable beginning, the management of the hotel has gone out of its way ever since to contribute to the city. El Dorado also serves a fine Sunday brunch.

East of Burro Alley on Palace Avenue is the two-story, balconied **Felipe B. Delgado House**, now part of the First National Bank. The Delgados were another of Santa Fe's most prominent families, and Don Felipe's 1890 house is another outstanding example of Territorial architecture. John Gaw Meem restored the house in 1970.

South of the plaza, along the Alameda (La Alameda is the name given the street that follows a river in any Spanish town), is the **Santa Fe River**. The river is not notable for its size or volume, but without it Santa Fe wouldn't be here at all. The immense satisfaction a Santa Fean receives from seeing a really strong flow in a good year is ineffable. There is a pleasant park along the river, complete with tables that can be used for picnics. Upstream, where Delgado Street crosses the river, is the bridge where the stolen secrets of the atomic bomb were passed to the Rosenbergs to transmit to the USSR in the late 1940s.

Palace Avenue

Palace Avenue, from Sena Plaza east, was the most desirable address in Santa Fe until the most recent decades. (Now the fanciest addresses are in the foothills and out in the green Tesuque Valley, north of Santa Fe along Bishop's Lodge Road.) On Palace Avenue many of the "best" families lived and called on one another. As the avenue is well preserved, it is worth a walk to enjoy the architecture and atmosphere.

At the northwest corner of Palace Avenue and Paseo de

Peralta is the Willi Spiegelberg House, built in 1880 by the same artisans who built the cathedral. The Spiegelbergs were one of the many Jewish merchant families who came to New Mexico in the 19th century, bringing American goods, construction materials, credit, and honest dealings to even the remotest corners of the state. Jewish money helped build the cathedral, for which favor it is said that Archbishop Lamy had an inscription of the Tetragram made in Hebrew lettering over the main doors.

Next to the Episcopal Church of the Holy Faith is the dead-end Faithway Street, on which the delightful Queen Anne–style **George Cuyler Preston House** sits at number 106. The house was built in 1886; its roof is metal, and its second story is sheathed not in wood shingles but in metal pressed to resemble shingles. The Preston House is now a bed and breakfast.

Opposite on Palace Avenue is **La Posada Hotel**, once the home of the Staabs, another of the Jewish mercantile families. The original front of the house can be seen inside the lobby; it leads into one of the nicest bars in Santa Fe.

Most of the rest of this tree-shaded street passes through a quiet residential neighborhood with houses dating from the last part of the 19th century and the early decades of the 20th. The architecture is, for the most part, neither Pueblo nor Territorial, but rather the substantial brick-and-stone bungalows and other Midwestern styles of the times. If you continue east for several blocks you will end up near Cristo Rey Church, the point of demarcation between Canyon and Upper Canyon roads.

Canyon Road

You may either start Canyon Road where it begins, just south of the Paseo de Peralta crossing of the river, as we do here, or, if you have come up Palace Avenue, take a left on Canyon Road and continue in an easterly (Upper Canyon) direction, or a right turn to head back to Paseo de Peralta. Walking the road slowly and going into the many shops and galleries on Canyon Road from its beginning east up to Cristo Rey Church will occupy the better part of an afternoon.

(Because there are no real blocks in the old part of Santa Fe—it was laid out by soldiers trailing pikes they were too tired to carry—all distances given are approximate.)

Canyon Road is one of the oldest streets in Santa Fe. Originally it followed an Indian trail along the Santa Fe

River canyon to the Pueblo of Pecos. The burros that ended up at Burro Alley often came down the canyon from the hills, where their masters cut piñon wood to sell. Well into this century the road passed by unpretentious houses and small agricultural plots. The street and the houses are well maintained and charming, but the atmosphere has changed almost entirely from the agricultural past. Few houses on Canyon Road below the crossing of the *acequia madre* ("mother ditch," from which the fields drew water) remain residential. Instead, Canyon Road now calls itself "the Art and Soul of Santa Fe," which, although a bit cute, is not far wrong.

In the earlier part of the century artists moved onto Canyon Road and opened their studios. There were no galleries in those unpretentious days, aside from the Museum of Fine Arts, as we have mentioned, so the studios were the artists' only outlet. Gradually Canyon Road became famous for its artists, and as it has metamorphosed, the lower part of the road has been almost wholly given over to arts and crafts.

At the southeast corner of Canyon Road and Garcia Street is the **First Ward School**, built in 1906 by I. H. Rapp, who also designed the Museum of Fine Arts. Now the Linda Durham Gallery, the red-brick schoolhouse is a classic of its kind. If you like avant garde art, Linda Durham has some of the most challenging in town.

Half a block up from Delgado Street, at 545 Canyon Road, is **El Zaguán**, one of the truest gems of Santa Fe. The house, which is rented out as apartments by the Historic Santa Fe Foundation, was built in two phases; the product of the earlier phase, pre-1849, has four-foot-thick walls, the later, walls three feet thick. The *zaguán* (vestibule) for which the building is named is the covered corridor between the patio and the garden. The garden was installed by anthropologist Adolph Bandelier, for whom Bandelier National Monument is named.

Another half block father on the right, at number 630, is the **Olive Rush House and Studio**, now a Friends' meetinghouse. This ancient building of unknown date is one of the few houses left in Santa Fe that is stuccoed, as all the town's buildings originally were, with adobe.

About a block farther and to the right, where tiny Gormley Lane goes off to the south, is an unpretentious building with "Gormley's" in fading paint up above. Until recently this was an actual, live, no-foolin' neighborhood grocery store. In the earlier part of the century, when the economy was still often cashless, the Gormley family had enormous sheds (now unfortunately torn down) behind the store, where Spanish-American families came to trade hides and piñon nuts for goods or cash.

In the same block with Gormley's store once stood Claude's Bar. For decades, until the mid-1970s, Claude's was *the* artists', homosexuals', poets' wild-life bar, and was quite notorious. If you were a bohemian, this is where you went. As with the Plaza Bar, it has vanished into orderly civilization's maw.

Also on the right, where Camino del Monte Sol meets Canyon Road, is the **Borrego House**, now, for the moment, Geronimo Lodge, a restaurant. The house was built in several stages, the first presumed to have been prior to 1769. The *portal* and large front room, a 19th-century addition, together are another fine example of Territorial architecture.

To the east, beyond the intersection of Canyon Road and Palace Avenue, the road becomes mostly residential, and the personality of the neighborhood has not changed noticeably in decades. The block above the crossing of the *acequia madre* under the road is one of the most charming in town; here the old houses directly front the road, which is not as commercialized as the lower portion with its shops, restaurants, and galleries. It dazzles the eye less, offering instead a feeling of comfort and age.

Canyon Road makes a sharp right by Manderfield School, and just beyond is **Cristo Rey Church**. Cristo Rey (Christ the King) was designed in classic Spanish Mission style by John Gaw Meem in 1940 to honor the 400th anniversary of Coronado's exploration of New Mexico. More specifically, the church was built to hold the beautiful stone reredos of 1760 that had originally been carved in La Castrense, the military chapel on the plaza.

The Guadalupe Street Area

If you follow the Alameda, which is south of the plaza, along the river three blocks west you will come to Guadalupe Street. Cross the bridge to the south bank for **El Santuario de Nuestra Señora de Guadalupe**. Probably begun in 1776, the *santuario* was built in classic, unpretentious 18th-century New Mexico style, although it has been somewhat altered over the years. When La Castrense, the plaza's military chapel, was torn down, Guadalupe inherited its choir loft, corbels, and *vigas*. The painted reredos, dated 1783, is by José de Alzibar. When the Denver and Rio

Grande Railroad ran, it came right by the church. Two buildings south of the *santuario,* a stone warehouse faced with red brick dates from 1885.

As the plaza has been given over to tourists, Guadalupe Street has become a prime area for shops and restaurants, and it is here that the future of downtown Santa Fe lies. If you go south past Montezuma Street you will come to the old railroad yards. This area, which in toto lies between Montezuma Street and Cerrillos Road, was condemned in 1988 by the city council as a "blighted area." The decision was controversial, and set off a hot debate as to who owns it and what should be done with the last large, undeveloped parcel of land in downtown Santa Fe. Low-income housing? A convention center? Hotels? A shopping area? Should it serve tourists or residents? Industry, perhaps? A park? Should city hall move here or remain on Marcy Street? Should some portion of the railroad remain as a commuter line to the areas south of town? Does the city own the land? The railroad? Or does it revert to the original owners whose land was condemned for the railroad? This area may not look like much, but it is one of the most tempestuous sites in town.

Within the yards are the old railroad office and train station. Inside the latter is one of Santa Fe's most popular Mexican restaurants, **Tomasita's**; be prepared for a long wait. To the south and in the middle of the yards is the old Gross-Kelly Warehouse, once one of New Mexico's premier mercantile houses.

The Santuario de Guadalupe lies on the corner of Guadalupe Street and **Agua Fria Street**, (the latter stretches all the way out through a tiny village, also named Agua Fria, almost to the Santa Fe Airport on the southwestern edge of town). You will not necessarily want to drive the entire length, but on any drive along Agua Fria you will see an old, poor, still authentic area of town. The architecture is vernacular, rather whimsical, and has touches of Old Mexico in it.

Old Santa Fe Trail
and the Barrio de Analco

Old Santa Fe Trail is the old entrance to the plaza from the south—and thus from Chihuahua in Mexico—although this is not in fact the old Santa Fe Trail. To walk the street and the Barrio de Analco, stopping at all the sights, will probably take two hours. If you walk all the way to the Carlos Vierra House from the capitol, add another half hour. As the Vierra House is a private residence, the walk may not be worth the effort unless you are intrigued by Santa Fe architecture.

Half a block south of La Fonda is the charming, Gothic **Loretto Chapel**, built between 1873 and 1878 for the nuns and students of Loretto Academy for girls. The Order of Loretto was brought to New Mexico by Archbishop Lamy in the 1850s. The chapel is remarkable for its miraculous staircase, which has become famous around the world. After the chapel was finished, the sisters realized there was no room for a stairway to get to the choir loft. The nuns then did the natural thing and prayed to Saint Joseph, the carpenter. A while later a carpenter appeared, one whom no one seemed to know. He set to work with a will and constructed a beautiful, wooden, circular staircase that employed no nails and had no obvious means of support. When he finished he disappeared without seeking payment. Tradition has it that the unknown carpenter was Saint Joseph himself.

Across the river, veering off to the west, is East De Vargas Street, the remains of the **Barrio de Analco** and the oldest part of Santa Fe in terms of Spanish history (aside from the plaza); this area south of the river was the site of a prehistoric pueblo. The barrio was the home of the Christianized Mexican Indians who came from Mexico with the conquistadors. On the north side of the street, at number 129–135, is the **Roque Tudesqui House**, which was extant when the record of Italian-born Tudesqui's purchase of it was made in 1841. The wisteria vine here, when in bloom in spring, is a marvelous sight. Across the street, at number 132, is the **Gregorio Crespin House**, the date of which is unknown, although tree-ring specimens from its *vigas* date between 1720 and 1750.

On the southeast corner of East De Vargas Street and Old Santa Fe Trail is the **San Miguel Mission**, built to serve the Barrio de Analco in 1626. Although San Miguel claims to be the oldest church in the United States, it is not; the mission churches at Isleta and Acoma pueblos have prior claim. The original church was burnt in the 1680 revolt and rebuilt in 1710. The peace and strength of the chapel inside cannot be conveyed in words. The thickness of the walls, their uneven quality, and the plainness of the decorations, except for the elaborate reredos, are powerful. If the chapel is full of tourists and you cannot detect these qualities, you might consider returning for 5:00 P.M. Mass on Sunday. The statue of Saint Michael in the reredos was brought from Mexico to Santa Fe before 1709, and the paintings on the reredos are from 1756 to 1760. The screen itself is from 1798. On display underneath transparent panels set into the floor of San Miguel are remains of the prehistoric Pueblo occupation of Santa Fe, including parts of ancient pueblo buildings and artifacts of their inhabitants.

In 1859 Archbishop Lamy brought the Christian Brothers to Santa Fe to found a boys' school. San Miguel served as their chapel until they sold St. Michael's College to the state in the 1960s. The college has since become the College of Santa Fe and now has a burgeoning film and theater department made possible by Greer Garson and her husband, E. E. "Buddy" Fogelson. The Fogelsons spent many summers at the Forked Lightning Ranch, about 30 miles (48 km) east of Santa Fe in the lush Pecos Valley. The handsome, plain St. Michael's College Dormitory, built in 1878, is just south of San Miguel Mission.

It should be noted that until the city had a commercially oriented fit of historicity, Old Santa Fe Trail was called College Street, named for St. Michael's College. Old-timers are still annoyed at the change.

Across East De Vargas Street from San Miguel chapel is the "**Oldest House**." The origins of the house are shrouded in time, but the tree-ring dates of the *vigas* are from 1740 to 1760. To quote the Historic Santa Fe Foundation's *Old Santa Fe Today,* "The western part remains a unique remnant of the type of building once prevalent in the city— part Indian, part Spanish, low-ceilinged and crude, with dirt floors and thick adobe walls."

Eastward, at the corner of East De Vargas and Paseo de Peralta, is another old Territorial adobe, the **José Alaríd House**, which dates from around 1835.

Just south of and across the street from San Miguel Mission is the **Pink Adobe Restaurant**, begun in the 1940s by Louisiana artist and local character Rosalea Murphy. She and the Pink Adobe have prospered ever since thanks to the ambience, good food, and now-famous bar (the Dragon Room).

Next to the Pink Adobe Restaurant is **Arrowsmith's Relics of the Old West**, a shop that carries just what it says, and some of the finest old traditional jewelry in Santa Fe, too. The store has been run by Mark Arrowsmith since his father, Rex, an Indian trader from way back, retired.

At the corner of Old Santa Fe Trail and Paseo de Peralta is

the new state capitol building, also known as the Round House for its shape. The old state capitol, the Bataan Memorial Building, lies behind it to the west. (The 200th Coast Artillery was made up of New Mexico men when it was sent to the Philippines in 1941. The 200th was captured by the Japanese and, consequently, New Mexico contributed disproportionately to the Bataan Death March. Of the original 1,400 men, 577 died, including 488 New Mexicans.)

If you travel farther up Old Santa Fe Trail about three city blocks, the trail splits into a Y; to the right the road becomes Old Pecos Trail. About one more block south, on the southwest corner of Old Pecos Trail and Coronado Road, at number 1002, is the **Carlos Vierra House** (a private residence). Vierra was an artist who came to Santa Fe for his health and stayed to work on the restoration of the Palace of the Governors. Between 1918 and 1919 he built the house as a paean to the Spanish Pueblo style, of which the house was meant to be "the last word." An editorial upon his death said, "It was Vierra's insistence upon purity of style that saved Santa Fe from many an architectural monstrosity. . . . That Santa Fe is not only a 'City Different' but a 'City Beautiful' is . . . largely owing to him. . . ."

A Santa Fe Drive

Because much of the charm of Santa Fe is hidden in the winding streets of the old east side, among houses that might or might not have great architectural or historical value, it may be worth your while to drive around at will to sightsee. Be careful; the streets are narrow and, if it is summer, there is likely to be considerable traffic. If you desire an itinerary, or are likely to become lost in Santa Fe's wandering streets, this one will do for getting the general feel of the town outside the plaza area.

From the plaza drive east one block on San Francisco Street to its end at St. Francis Cathedral on Cathedral Place. A right turn will take you to the Alameda. Turn left on Alameda and go one block to the Paseo de Peralta. Cross the river and follow the Paseo for a couple blocks to where it veers off to the right. At this intersection take a left onto Acequia Madre Street (Fenn Galleries will be on your left). After one block take another left onto tree-lined and elegant Garcia Street. At the end of Garcia turn right onto Canyon Road and follow it until you come to

the Borrego House, where a right turn will take you onto
Camino del Monte Sol.

Although only somewhere between 50 and 70 years of
age, the Camino, as it is known, is a tightly packed street
of idiosyncratic adobe houses and walls that has the
appearance of agelessness and natural growth that gives
Santa Fe much of its charm. It was named by its first
residents, artist William Penhallow Henderson and his
wife, poet Alice Corbin Henderson. Before then it had
been prosaically named Telephone Road. With the Hen-
dersons the Camino became the place to live for artists
and their crowd; most famously, the Cinco Pintores—Will
Shuster, Josef Bakos, Freemont Ellis, Walter Mruk, and
Willard Nash—built houses here in the 1920s: five little
nuts in five mud huts, it was said.

Follow the Camino up to its junction with Garcia Street,
where a right turn onto Garcia will take you (stay right)
back down to Acequia Madre Street, where you should
take another right.

La acequia madre, the "mother ditch," is the most
important irrigation ditch in any town. It feeds all the
smaller ditches, and in a town that grows crops—which
Santa Fe did until the 1930s, at least—it is of central
importance. The *mayordomo* of any *acequia madre* is a
man of great sway.

Acequia Madre Street, which follows the *acequia,* is
narrow and tree lined, and has many little bridges that
cross the ditch to quiet dead-end streets. All of this makes
for a neighborhood that is quintessential Santa Fe.

Follow Acequia Madre Street along the *acequia* until
you reach Abeyta Street, where Acequia Madre becomes
one-way; turn right onto Abeyta and then almost immediately left onto Camino del Poniente (for its one block),
cross Camino del Monte Sol, and you are once more on
Acequia Madre. Continue until the *acequia* debouches
onto Canyon Road and go right up Canyon Road, then left
where Canyon Road turns in front of Cristo Rey Church.
This part of Canyon Road still has a semi-rural feel and
seems separate from the rest of the city. Continue all the
way up Canyon Road, even when the road becomes dirt.
At the end you will find the house of one of Santa Fe's
most important artists, Randall Davey. The house is now
owned by the Audubon Society, which operates a nature
center here. The **Randall Davey House** was built in 1847
as a sawmill for lumber to build Fort Marcy. Davey lived
in the house from 1920 until his death in a sports-car
accident in 1964. The house and grounds are well worth

the visit for their beauty and serenity, and for the views of Santa Fe Canyon they offer.

Return the way you came until you reach the intersection of Canyon Road and Cerro Gordo (Fat Hill) Road. Take a right and follow Cerro Gordo's twists and turns. Be careful on the narrow road as you admire Santa Fe Canyon falling steeply to your left, then rising on the right into the hills. At the end of Cerro Gordo Road turn right onto Palace Avenue and continue until you reach the plaza.

Other Museums

Several fine museums in Santa Fe that are not on the plaza deserve mention. All but one are on Camino Lejo, which is about 2 miles (3 km) southeast of the plaza off Old Santa Fe Trail.

The **Santa Fe Children's Museum**, on Old Pecos Trail 1 mile (1½ km) south of the plaza just beyond the Carlos Vierra House, is an interactive museum open Thursday to Saturday from 10:00 A.M. to 5:00 P.M., and Sundays noon to 5:00 P.M.; Tel: 989-8359.

CAMINO LEJO

On Camino Lejo, off Old Santa Fe Trail, is the **Museum of International Folk Art**. This museum is exactly what its name says: It draws on worldwide folk culture for its exhibits. The museum is charming, but becomes positively magical in its new wing, dedicated to the massive collection of toys, dolls, miniatures, and children's entertainments of architect Alexander Girard. Despite the size and complexity of the exhibit, only one-third of Girard's collection is actually shown. The museum's hours are 10:00 A.M. to 5:00 P.M. daily except in January and February, when it is closed on Mondays; Tel: 827-6350.

Next to the Museum of International Folk Art is the Laboratory of Anthropology, designed by John Gaw Meem, and its new wing for exhibits, the **Museum of Indian Arts and Culture**. The Indian arts museum concentrates on Southwest Indian cultures and has an excellent collection of pottery. The hours are the same as the folk-art museum; Tel: 827-6344.

Behind the Museum of International Folk Art is the **Wheelwright Museum of the American Indian**. Founded in 1937 by Mary Cabot Wheelwright and famed Navajo medicine man Hosteen Klah with the intention of preserving Navajo culture, the museum is now given over to all

American Indian arts. The museum shop—the Case Trading Post—on the lower floor is a reproduction of a Navajo reservation trading post. Tel: 982-4636.

Spectator Sports

Every mid-July Santa Fe's rodeo is celebrated with a parade and much hoopla. The rodeo itself is held in grounds off Rodeo Road, which meets Cerrillos Road—a horribly over-commercialized main artery—at the far southwest end of town. If you have never seen a rodeo, this one is marvelous true-west fun. **Rodeo de Santa Fe**; Tel: 471-4300.

Southwest of Santa Fe about 10 miles (16 km) on I-25 are the **Downs at Santa Fe**, a track for horse racing. The season runs from mid-June until early September.

Fiestas and Other Local Events

Fiestas de Santa Fe is a celebration for the entire city. Traditionally, it took place on Labor Day weekend. Now, because of the crowds and violence it attracted in the mid-1970s, it is scheduled for the second weekend in September. Fiestas commemorates the reconquest of New Mexico in 1692 by Don Diego de Vargas from the rebellious Pueblo Indians. As discussed above, when the Spaniards returned they brought with them a small statue of Our Lady of the Rosary, which, it was believed, enabled the Spaniards to complete a relatively peaceful reconquest. The statue has been known ever since as La Conquistadora. De Vargas's wish was that she be honored every year, and so in 1712 the fiesta was begun.

Although the origin of Fiestas is religious, the celebration itself is more of a citywide party, frequently inundated by tourists. These days the religious element consists of a mass said in the cathedral on Sunday evening followed by a dignified but celebratory candlelight procession to the Cross of the Martyrs. Fiestas begins, however, on Friday at Fort Marcy Park, north of the plaza, with a 40-foot puppet, Zozobra—Old Man Gloom—into whom participants pour their angers, frustrations, pettinesses, sorrows, and resentments. When dark descends upon the baseball field crowded with as many people as can fit, the lights are turned out and Zozobra lectures the crowd upon its faults and failures; then, in the most pagan ceremony still legal in the United States, Zozobra is burned and all hell breaks loose. From then on fiesta is a series of balls, parades, food and crafts booths, parties, and even a melodrama.

If you are looking for a traditional, unself-conscious local celebration intended simply for the people of the town, you will not find it here any more than in New Orleans's Mardi Gras or Munich's Oktoberfest. As with both the others, Fiestas can be good fun, but here, as there, you will be in the midst of a great crowd—locals and tourists combined—that has somewhat lost its bearings.

In August, the peak of the high season, comes one of the most popular events in Santa Fe, and—be warned— the most crowded weekend in town: **Indian Market**. Collectors come from around the country to the premier market for Indian arts and crafts. Although Southwestern tribes traditionally dominate the market, Indians from as far away as Alaska and Florida also participate. If you have an interest in pottery, weaving, jewelry, kachina dolls, baskets, and, to a lesser extent, sculpture and painting, this is an event you should consider, despite the crowds. Much-coveted awards are given by experts on Indian arts and crafts. Inevitably, the pieces given awards are sold immediately. Indian Market takes place on the first weekend after the third Thursday in August. The market begins with a benefit auction on Thursday and a membership preview of award-winning pieces on Friday. In order to reserve accommodations *anywhere* in Santa Fe for Indian Market weekend, the wise begin months, if not at least a year, ahead.

Less well known is **Spanish Market**, which takes place on the last full weekend in July. Spanish Market is an exposition of such traditional Spanish-American crafts and arts as carved pine furniture, *bultos* (religious statues), *retablos* (painted icons), straw appliqué, tinwork, and embroidery. The Spanish Colonial Arts Society, sponsor of the market, gives awards. There are also artists' demonstrations, and traditional music and dance.

The New Age in Santa Fe

Santa Fe has always been a haven for people with bohemian attitudes and unusual beliefs. In the 1960s, when the Age of Aquarius was declared, Santa Fe and Taos became centers of hippie communes and culture. Gradually, during the 1970s, the Age of Aquarius became the New Age, and one of its centers is Santa Fe. (Another is Sedona; see the Central Arizona chapter.) If you have an interest in astrology, tarot, channeling, crystals, shamanism, aura balancing, lectures by gurus and psychics, or any one of a number of metaphysical, esoteric, and occult pursuits, this is your vortex. Santa Fe is also a center for such alternative health therapies as rolfing, acupuncture and acupressure, aromatherapy, Ayurvedic medicine, and dozens of other treatments. Advertisements for treatments, gurus, and workshops appear on billboards all over town.

Without a doubt, one of the best occult bookstores in the United States is in Santa Fe, **The Ark Bookstore** at 133 Romero Street off Agua Fria Street. The Ark also has books on science, as well as magazines, crystals, tarot cards, greeting cards, incense, and numerous other items.

THE PERFORMING ARTS IN SANTA FE

For a town out in the middle of nowhere, surrounded by high mountains and semideserts, great distances in all directions from what one might call major civilization, and populated mostly by poor, struggling people, Santa Fe is an astonishingly cultured city with a cosmopolitan attitude, developed over the better part of this century.

Classical Music

Far and away the most famous of Santa Fe's cultural offerings is the **Santa Fe Opera**. The opera was begun by a dreamer, John Crosby, who believed he could create an opera company in a mountain town of 25,000, perform during July and August in the open air at an altitude of 7,000 feet, and make it a success. The first season was in 1957, and the opera has since become justifiably world renowned.

The Santa Fe Opera does not put its efforts into attracting the biggest names in the field, but rather into developing young talent and coupling it with first-rate mature talent both in front of and behind the curtain. The apprentice program is especially admired for giving singers at the beginning of their careers honest work and training. Each season's five operas represent a spectrum of works: Familiar older pieces, such as those by Mozart, Puccini, and Rossini, will appear with the occasional comic opera (Strauss, Offenbach), or pre-Mozart opera (Cavalli, Monteverdi), and always an American or world premiere of a more difficult, avant garde work—Henze,

Sallinen, Penderecki. Maestro Crosby's particular obsession is Richard Strauss, and one of his operas habitually is produced. In other words, there is something for everyone, and encouragement to appreciate operatic works unknown to the listener. If you go to one performance of each opera during the season, which is possible to do in August in a mere week, you will come away impressed and edified by the breadth of the Santa Fe Opera.

Both the site and the architecture of the Santa Fe Opera house are spectacular. The opera is on the top of a hill overlooking the Tesuque Valley, which lies beneath the Sangre de Cristo Mountains. The graceful and uplifting new building was constructed after a devastating fire in the original in 1967, and, as was its predecessor, is partially open to the elements. Thus you should dress warmly, and if your seats are in the open section, bring protection in case of rain (if there is rain you may move to the standing room section in the rear).

The opera is 7 miles (11 km) north of town on U.S. 84/285; if you prefer not to drive, take Shuttlejack, a bus service from the Cerrillos Road motels and the major downtown hotels; Tel: 982-4311 for schedules and reservations. If you drive, arrive at least 15 to 30 minutes early. Performances start punctually at 9:00 P.M., and latecomers are not seated until intermission. Standing-room tickets go on sale at 8:00 P.M. Tel: 982-3855.

The other major cultural events of the summer season are the Santa Fe Chamber Music Festival, which is becoming almost as well-known as the opera, and the **Santa Fe Desert Chorale**. The chorale, the only professional vocal ensemble in New Mexico, performs in a variety of places, but primarily at the historic Santuario de Guadalupe, southwest of the plaza at the corner of Guadalupe and Agua Fria streets. The chorale has performed music from ancient to modern for the past ten years, and has been critically praised for the quality and imagination of its performances, held from June to August. Tel: 988-7505.

The **Santa Fe Chamber Music Festival** began in 1972 and quickly became an event of great note. The festival brings composers, ensembles, and soloists of national and international stature to Santa Fe for its July and August season. Since 1976 the festival has also had a composer-in-residence during the season. The range of music performed, from Baroque to avant garde, is impressive, and includes a "Music of the Americas" series that presents folk music from North and South America. The

Chamber Music Festival also offers open rehearsals daily, and features talks on Sunday afternoons and before concerts. Performances are held on the northwest corner of the plaza in St. Francis Auditorium in the Museum of Fine Arts, just about as perfect a place for a chamber music concert as you could wish. Tel: 983-2075.

If you come to Santa Fe during the off-season—that is, during the fall, winter, and spring—you will still find the city alive with both music and theater. To those who live in the town, it is a matter of wonder that the community manages to support not one but two orchestras. They started off as one, the Orchestra of Santa Fe, in 1974. Following an ugly dispute ten years later several musicians left and began their own orchestra, the Santa Fe Symphony. The result is that the people of Santa Fe have been double winners, for both orchestras are worth hearing and are of consistently high quality.

The **Orchestra of Santa Fe**, a chamber orchestra, plays music from the Baroque period to the 20th century, and has premiered several works over the years. The orchestra performs at the Lensic Theater, a classic movie palace from the 1930s on San Francisco Street, about one and a half blocks west of the plaza; the season runs from February to May and performances are also given in December. Tel: 988-4640.

The **Santa Fe Symphony** is a full-size symphony orchestra with, consequently, a different repertoire that emphasizes 19th- and 20th-century works, most of them not the standard fare. In fact, one of the most satisfying elements of the two orchestras is their great range and lack of predictability. The Santa Fe Symphony gives six subscription performances a year one block north of the plaza at the Sweeney Convention Center, a converted school gymnasium that no amount of mutation has been able to disguise; Tel: 983-3530.

Theater

South of the plaza, just past the Carlos Vierra House on Old Pecos Trail, the former National Guard Armory has been transformed into a theater and is now the home of the **New Mexico Repertory Theater**. The company produces six plays a year, between October and May. Unlike the orchestras, however, the quality of the performances is decidedly variable. Nevertheless, the effort is usually worth the price. Tel: 983-2382.

The College of Santa Fe, far south of the plaza on St.

Michael's Drive near Cerrillos Road, has a first-rate theater school. The quality of the student productions, which take place in the Greer Garson Theatre (Garson and her husband were longtime patrons of the college) is uneven, but when one of their productions is good, it is terrific. Tel: 473-6511 (box office).

GETTING AROUND

By Car

Because Santa Fe has been physically isolated from the rest of the world for so long, it has managed to maintain much of the character that makes it the City Different. The city still takes some effort to get to, but travelling has become easier with the advent of the interstate-highway system.

Most of Santa Fe's visitors arrive by car. Interstate 25 will bring you from the east and north—Denver—or from the south and west—El Paso and Albuquerque. Interstate 40, which goes east to Texas and west to Arizona, runs through Albuquerque and intersects there with I-25. NM 14, the Turquoise Trail from Albuquerque (see the Albuquerque chapter), meets I-25 just south of Santa Fe (follow the directions given below for I-25 entrances into town). U.S. 64/84 will also bring you down from Colorado.

When coming into Santa Fe **from the north**—from, say, Taos—follow U.S. 84/285 until it becomes St. Francis Drive. If you want to go downtown, follow St. Francis Drive to Alameda, the street along the river, then turn left and follow Alameda until it intersects with Sandoval Street (you are, at this point, effectively downtown); turn left at Sandoval and follow it until it turns right and becomes Palace Avenue. Palace Avenue reaches the plaza after another block. If you want to get to one of the Cerrillos Road motels, from Alameda turn right at Sandoval Street and follow it to Cerrillos, another ¼ mile (½ km).

When you are coming **from the south**, Cerrillos Road will be the main, most southern, and ugliest entrance to town off I-25 (it is a motel and fast-food strip). If you are coming from the south but do not want to come in by Cerrillos Road, there are two more exits off I-25. The first alternate will bring you in by St. Francis Drive, a main artery, from which you can turn either left when it meets Cerrillos Road, and head for the motels, or right on Cerrillos Road, and go into the heart of town. This route is probably the quickest.

The other alternate is rather out-of-the-way and will bring you in from the east along Old Pecos Trail, a semirural route; go left at the stoplight that is directly to your left as you come off the exit ramp. If you take the trail all the way into town, you will wind up at the plaza (the last stretch being Old Santa Fe Trail).

Parking is scarce in Santa Fe, and can make travel a problem at all times of the year, but especially during the summer. The streets are narrow, old, and laid along mainly historical or accidental lines instead of in a grid pattern. The one attempt at planning a downtown roadway—Paseo de Peralta—created a loop around the downtown area that facilitates getting from one side of town to the other.

A public transportation system began at the onset of this year; however, if you are staying downtown you should walk as many places as possible. If you are not staying within walking distance of downtown, park in a public lot and then walk. The main city parking lots are all close to the plaza: on the corner of Sandoval and San Francisco streets; on the corner of Don Gaspar and Water streets; on the corner of the Alameda and Cathedral Place; next to the city hall on Marcy Street; and between Marcy and Palace on Sheridan Avenue. Several of the large hotels also have public parking, but you will probably pay more for it (the city lots charge less). If you must drive, bring your patience.

By Air

Most Santa Feans are grateful that the town has no real airport, just a small landing strip for commuter planes, because visitors to the city have to make an effort to get here—crowd control at its most basic. So if you fly to New Mexico you will probably fly into Albuquerque International Airport (a grand name for an airport that once upon a time had an occasional flight to Mexico) on Southwest, Continental, United, American, Delta, America West, USAir, Northwest, TWA, or Mesa airlines.

From Albuquerque there is a fairly expensive air commuter service to Santa Fe Airport four times a day during the week, twice on Saturdays, thrice on Sundays. Call Mesa Airlines, Tel: 473-4118. Or you can rent a car at the Albuquerque airport, or take the ground shuttle up to Santa Fe. The shuttle runs between the Albuquerque airport and Santa Fe's two main downtown hotels—El Dorado and The Inn at Loretto (and others upon request)—ten times a day from May to October, seven times a day in the winter; allow 1½ hours travel time. The fare is $20. Call Shuttlejack; Tel: 982-4311.

Buses for Santa Fe leave the Albuquerque airport almost every hour. T.M.N. and O. Coaches (Tel: 243-4435) has departures three times a day (late morning, afternoon, and evening), seven days a week to its terminal on St. Michael's Drive. The fare is $10.50 one-way.

Car-rental pickup locations in Santa Fe are at the airport, along Cerrillos Road, and at various downtown hotels. However, prices at the Albuquerque airport are usually less expensive.

By Train

Despite the name of the famed Atchison, Topeka & Santa Fe Railway, the City Different is not actually on the main line. However, Amtrak trains do stop at about 2:30 P.M. at the hamlet of Lamy, 20 miles (32 km) south of Santa Fe, once a day in each direction, west to east and east to west, with terminuses in Chicago and Los Angeles; Tel: (800) 872-7245. There is a shuttle service from the station to and from Santa Fe's hotels and motels. Reservations are preferred and may be made either through Amtrak or by calling the Lamy Shuttle; Tel: 982-8829.

By Bus

Santa Fe is served by five arrivals daily each from the south (Albuquerque) and from the north (Denver). The bus company is Texas, New Mexico, and Oklahoma, known as T.N.M. and O. (From the Albuquerque hub you can make connections to any place in the country.) The bus depot in Santa Fe (also known as the Greyhound Station) is inconveniently located far south of the plaza on St. Michael's Drive, and transport to and from town is by taxi. Tel: 471-0008.

Tours

Tours of Santa Fe and of the surrounding area fall into two categories: commercial and scholarly.

Commercial tours: **Santa Fe Detours** is one of the oldest tour companies here, with a history that goes back to the famed Santa Fe Indian Detours begun by Erna Fergusson for the Harvey Hotels. Santa Fe Detours offers walking tours (2½ to 3 hours) and motor tours (1½ to 2½ hours) of Santa Fe, as well as motor tours of northern New Mexico—to cliff dwellings, to Taos—and air/land tours to such outlying areas as Canyon de Chelly in

Arizona, balloon trips, rafting trips, and horseback rides. The Santa Fe tours begin at La Fonda Hotel on the plaza; for motor tours, you may be picked up at your hotel. Tel: 983-6565.

Rojo Tours conducts tours of Santa Fe, New Mexico, southern Colorado, southern Utah, and Arizona. All tours are customized for individuals and groups, including conventions and retreats. The service is multilingual. Tel: 983-8333.

Grayline Tours of Santa Fe offers two city tours: a 2½-hour bus tour that picks up its passengers from their hotels between 8:45 and 9:30 in the morning, and the less expensive Roadrunner open-vehicle tour, which leaves every hour on the hour from the corner of Shelby and Water streets. The latter lasts an hour and a half. Grayline also offers an all-day tour of Chimayo and Taos (passengers are picked up between 8:15 and 9:00 A.M.). Tel: 983-9491.

Rocky Mountain Tours offers customized group and individual tours of Santa Fe and the area, rafting trips from May to August, balloon trips, and tickets on the Cumbres & Toltec Scenic Railroad, a narrow-gauge railroad that begins in the northern New Mexico town of Chama. Santa Fe tours last 90 minutes and leave several times a day from the plaza. Rocky Mountain Tours will also arrange car-and-driver tours. Tel: 984-1684.

There are also two walking-tour companies. **Santa Fe Walks**, the first of its kind, leaves at 9:30 A.M. and 1:30 P.M. from La Fonda Hotel on the plaza, and covers three and a half miles in 2½ to 3 hours, including a coffee break. Tel: 989-8811. **Afoot in Santa Fe** leaves the same times (Sundays at 9:30 A.M. only) from the Inn at Loretto on the Alameda south of the plaza, and takes about 2½ hours. Tel: 983-3701.

Scholarly tours. Two outfits make a great effort to hire and consult experts so as to give in-depth educational experiences:

Recursos de Santa Fe Tours, a nonprofit organization, offers tours to groups only, although the group may be as small as five or six people. The tours are intended for those with a serious interest in the arts, nature, pueblos, the Southwestern states, New Mexico, or Mexico. The groups that most frequently take advantage of Recursos de Santa Fe are museum and academic travel groups, though there is no restriction to any kind of group. Recursos also offers seminars on arts and literature in addition to its study tours. Tel: 982-9301.

The **Museum of New Mexico**'s Palace of the Governors

has recently begun a series of walks, May through September, called Palace Walks, History Talks. These walks are given by staff members of the Palace of the Governors or by other experts in history, architecture, and archaeology. The tours begin at 10:00 A.M. daily from the History Library on Washington Avenue, to the east of the plaza; they last 1½ hours. Proceeds go to the Palace of the Governors' Endowment Fund.

ACCOMMODATIONS

During the past decade Santa Fe's hotel scene has truly come of age. Where once bed-seeking visitors had few choices—two or three rundown hotels in the historic district or a bevy of circa-1940 roach traps on the outskirts of town—today the city offers an extraordinary range of rooms, suites, and apartments capable of meeting any traveller's needs.

But while accommodations in Santa Fe may finally be plentiful, so too are sightseers; several million visitors tour this popular resort community each year, and the vast majority stay overnight. The simple fact is, if you show up during the May to September "high season" expecting to find a quality room without reservations, you may be disappointed. The way to avoid this all-too-common situation, of course, is to make your sleeping arrangements as far in advance as possible (six months ahead is not unheard of).

When doing so, remember that most of Santa Fe's truly memorable accommodations, those that offer top-notch service, quality restaurants, traditional styling, and true Southwestern ambience, lie in or near the downtown historic district. Basing yourself within walking distance of the major attractions can be advantageous (the non-hotel parking situation in the downtown area during the height of the season is absolutely abysmal; you can spend all morning simply looking for a place to leave your car). If being close to everything matters, ask how far your chosen hotel is from the plaza before making reservations; anything more than a dozen blocks away is well out of the city's heart.

Except where we have noted, architecture and views are *not* a part of selecting accommodations in Santa Fe. Ninety-eight percent of all of Santa Fe's hotels are large, brown-stucco, pueblo-style affairs. As for views, with few exceptions what visitors see from their rooms are brown rooftops, trees, and power cables or telephone lines. Or parking lots.

You might also prepare yourself for what some travellers call "price shock." True, Santa Fe lies in the hinterlands of northern New Mexico and is fairly small, but hotel rates, meals, and other essential travel necessities aren't cheap here. There are off-season exceptions, but during the height of the summer expect to pay $90 to $300 for double-occupancy rooms, even more for suites. If your visit happens to coincide with a local "event," such as Indian Market or Fiestas de Santa Fe, expect room costs to increase by at least 30 percent. There are, of course, less expensive accommodations in town (all the major motel and motor-hotel chains have establishments on commercialized Cerrillos Road, the main access route from I-25), but $45 to $75 per night is the *low-end* range even there during high season. Naturally, most of these lower-priced establishments are nowhere near the historic district, plaza, or Santa Fe's other principal attractions.

The following accommodations have been selected for their ambience, location, service, and amenities. The rates given are *projections* for 1993, and unless otherwise indicated are based on double room/double occupancy. Price ranges span the lowest rate in the low season to the highest rate in the high season. As rates are always subject to change, it is wise to double-check before booking. The telephone area code for Santa Fe (and all of New Mexico) is 505. The postal zip code for Santa Fe is 87501.

Large Hotels near the Plaza
El Dorado. When it was completed in 1986, the towering El Dorado, three blocks west of the plaza, became highly controversial. Local residents didn't fancy this squat, block-wide, fortresslike structure suddenly appearing in what had traditionally been a low-slung downtown. Today, however, all is forgiven and most residents have stopped complaining. Operating very much like a fine Swiss timepiece, this huge structure (218 rooms and 20 suites) is presently among Santa Fe's most popular and publicized hotels.

El Dorado caters to conventions, but celebrities such as Mick Jagger, Carol Burnett, and Sam Shepard also stay here when they're in town. Standard rooms, decorated in a muted Navajo/Pueblo style, are large and comfortable; suites, some with private terraces and kiva fireplaces, are absolutely huge. A top-floor outdoor pool and sunning area have the town's best views of the nearby Sangre de

Cristo Mountains. On the ground floor the **Old House Restaurant & Tavern**—with offerings such as pan-seared venison and lobster grilled with shiitake mushrooms—is expensive but worth every penny. For outdoor dining in warm weather try the large, atrium-like Eldorado Court. Underground parking is available for guests.

309 West San Francisco Street. Tel: 988-4455 or (800) 955-4455; Fax: 988-5376. $190–$600.

Inn at Loretto. This luxurious four-story landmark two blocks south of the plaza is hard to miss. Built in 1975 and modeled after the ancient Indian pueblo at Taos, it looms over the surrounding historic district like a great brown toad hung with strings of red chile peppers.

A cool, dark lobby cubbyholed with shops, galleries, and salons may remind Tolkien readers of an elegant hobbit hole. Rooms and suites, some with private or shared balconies, are standard (room furnishings might be called "late Holiday Inn") but spacious and attractive. Pueblo Indian–style murals splash the walls with intricate designs and pastel colors. A fourth-floor outdoor patio provides guests with an exquisite view of the city.

Bimi's restaurant, known for its traditional New Mexican specialties, offers indoor and outdoor dining, the latter beneath a great white awning near the pool; live entertainment is provided in the bar. Complimentary parking is available in a walled compound adjacent to the hotel.

211 Old Santa Fe Trail, at East Alameda. Tel: 988-5531 or (800) 727-5531; Fax: 984-7988. $90–$189.

La Fonda Hotel. The grande dame of Santa Fe sleepovers, La Fonda is still the only hotel actually right on the plaza, at the southeast corner. Once part of the famed Harvey House chain and probably the town's most traditional hostelry, it has long been the favorite resting place of upscale and upbeat visitors (Kit Carson, Ulysses S. Grant, and President Rutherford B. Hayes were but a few of the hotel's famous guests) who like to mingle in the mainstream.

La Fonda's crowded reception area forever bustles with staff, guests, Indians selling jewelry, and ogling sightseers. Chronic shoppers can buy or browse for everything from fine photography to Paris fashions in the colorful lobby bazaar. A recent renovation has upgraded room quality immensely; pricier chambers and suites have fireplaces, balconies, and mountain or city views. New Mexican decor is standard throughout.

For breakfast try the French Pastry Shop, loitering place

for celebs and famous for its croissants and fine coffees (credit cards not accepted). The outdoor La Terraza (open seasonally) is great for lunch, while just off the lobby the skylit **La Plazuela Courtyard Restaurant** features a gardenlike atmosphere and sumptuous Northern New Mexico food; the top-floor, outdoor **Bell Tower Bar** (open seasonally) is the place to go for afternoon margaritas, views of the city, and summer sunsets. Covered and protected parking is available underneath the hotel.

100 East San Francisco Street. Tel: 982-5511 or (800) 523-5002; Fax: 988-2952. $130–$415.

Smaller Hotels near the Plaza

Inn of the Anasazi. Potted designer cactus simply doesn't complement this fine hotel's dark, low-ceilinged lobby, polished flagstone floor, huge fireplace, and piped-in classical music, but otherwise the Inn of the Anasazi is as fashionable as they come. Managing director Merry Stephen states simply, "We like people [Oprah Winfrey and other celebrities among them] to think they aren't coming to a hotel but to a private home."

Fifty-one guest rooms and eight suites sport a nouvelle-Southwestern motif with their gaslit kiva fireplaces, four-poster beds, and massive *trasteros* (Spanish-style armoires); aspen *vigas* (roof beams) blend with antique Indian rugs and handwoven fabrics to create a pleasant if somewhat gallery-like atmosphere. Extra guest niceties include all-cotton robes and linens, VCRs, minifridges, safes, and honor bars.

Just off the lobby the **Anasazi Restaurant** offers a pricey prix-fixe menu for epicureans; the standard menu ranges from mesquite-grilled chicken to mushroom-dusted rainbow trout (regional organic farmers grow much of the inn's food). A wine cellar (cum private dining room) is perhaps one of the best in Santa Fe. Evening cocktails are served in the Living Room (buzzers summon waiters), while the adjacent Library is for reading, chatting, and high tea. Parking is underground and protected.

113 Washington Avenue. Tel: 988-3030 or (800) 688-8100; Fax: 988-3277. $195–$365.

Hotel Plaza Real. Convenient, charming, and expensive might succinctly describe the spiffy new Plaza Real (completed in 1991), half a block north of the plaza on Washington Avenue. Newly arrived guests appreciate the bright, warm Territorial-style lobby; world-wise travellers may find the narrow fountain-and-sculpture-dotted central patio reminiscent of a favorite "bistro" street in Rome or Madrid.

Rooms and suites, many with private balconies and wood-burning fireplaces, are spacious and cheerful, though some northside chambers face a side street where noise may be a factor. Massive wood beams, Mexican-style furniture, and four-poster beds complement the hotel's obvious Southwestern motif.

Plaza Real has no restaurant, but room service is available from the fine adjacent Inn of the Anasazi (see above). Deluxe Continental breakfast (homemade pastries, bagels, fruit, coffee, tea) is served in an airy second-floor library-like dining room just above the lobby. The Rendezvous Bar, just off the lobby, serves drinks in the late afternoon and evening; a street-side outdoor coffee bar (open seasonally) is the place to see and be seen. Other offerings are in-house covered parking and an excellent concierge service.

125 Washington Avenue. Tel: 988-4900 or (800) 279-7325; Fax: 988-4900. $95–$425.

Hilton of Santa Fe. Not as ponderously chic as some of Santa Fe's accommodations, the Hilton is one of the city's older hotels (built before Santa Fe style was stylish). It is typical of its brand name: trusty, clean, and unremarkable.

Families like this establishment because of its familiar and casual atmosphere, its location (a five-minute walk west of the plaza), and its family rates. The recently upgraded rooms are still a bit motel-ish, but most are spacious and bright. For breakfast or lunch the Chamisa Courtyard Cafe, once the courtyard of the 250-year-old Spanish home around which the hotel was built, is open and airy. A bit fancier is the **Pinon Grill**, with moderately priced cuisine and live music most nights. There is a parking lot on the hotel grounds; pets are accepted.

100 Sandoval Street, at West Alameda. Tel: 988-2811 or (800) 336-3676; Fax: 988-1730. $85–$230.

Hotel St. Francis. On lively Don Gaspar Avenue, two blocks south of the plaza across from a large open parking lot and set off from its surroundings by its cavernous street-side verandah and its blue-framed windows, the St. Francis is one of Santa Fe's great success stories. New owners and a complete renovation in 1986 transformed what was once a second-rate, circa-1920s youth hostel sliding quickly toward oblivion into *the* place to stay for connoisseurs of quiet grace and simple elegance.

A spacious ground-floor lobby—the fireplace is nearly

walk-in size—offers tranquil respite from the noisy plaza crowds; tea and drinks are served here in the afternoon. Though rooms and suites are small (elevated ceilings help, but avoid the rooms under the eaves), they are nicely appointed with brass beds and lots of antiques. The classy **On Water Restaurant**, specializing in seafood, duck, and poultry, is reasonably priced; weather permitting, guests (and the public) can dine outdoors in a lovely walled courtyard.

210 Don Gaspar Avenue. Tel: 983-5700 or (800) 666-5700; Fax: 989-7690. $75–$300.

La Posada de Santa Fe. Enveloping a lovely, century-old French Second Empire–style mansion three blocks east of the plaza, La Posada has one thing other Santa Fe hotels do not: its own ghost. The spirit of Julie Staab (wife of the original owner), who died in 1896 in what is now room 256, is often spotted by staff and guests alike lounging about the common rooms or wandering the mansion's halls.

There's little wonder Mrs. Staab's ghost refuses to leave. Spread over six beautifully landscaped acres on Palace Avenue, La Posada offers guests a peaceful retreat at the edge of Santa Fe's boisterous downtown area. Some guest rooms in the mansion itself are cramped and noisy, but the 100-plus spacious adobe *casitas* (little houses) scattered throughout the compound offer plenty of seclusion. Most of them also include fireplaces, hand-painted tiles, skylights, flagstone floors, and private parking (right outside the *casitas*). Some have small, private, walled terraces in front.

The Staab House restaurant in the main building, specializing in Continental and Southwestern cuisine, seems still to be finding its way; a Victorian-style **bar** comprising several antiques-filled chambers, also in the main building, is a favorite hangout for upscale locals (try the spicy nachos here; one serving is an entire meal).

330 East Palace Avenue. Tel: 986-0000 or (800) 727-5276; Fax: 982-6850. $88–$395.

Inn on the Alameda. This quiet but expensive little hostelry five blocks southeast of the plaza offers 47 fairly standard rooms (though some have fireplaces and private balconies or patios), but general manager David Oberstein says guests appreciate the inn's privacy and location. Only a short stroll from the downtown activity but well beyond the noise range, the hacienda-style walled compound sits just opposite Santa Fe's verdant Alameda, or river park.

There is no in-house restaurant here, but the South-western-style Agoyo Room sports a full-service bar and lots of lounging space. A better place to meet for drinks, however, is the quiet open-air patio just off the lobby. Skiers or tired strollers appreciate the wonderful outdoor Jacuzzi. A fancy Continental breakfast is included in the room rate; there is protected parking on the grounds.

303 East Alameda. Tel: 984-2121 or (800) 289-2122; Fax: 986-8325. $130–$330.

Hotel Santa Fe. General manager James Reed compares this brand-new establishment to a bolo tie. "It's warm, friendly, and casual," says Reed, "like something a Southwesterner would wear with an open shirt."

Located in an old, noisy, but almost totally renovated neighborhood near the state capitol, the Hotel Santa Fe sits on the corner of Paseo de Peralta and Cerrillos Road five blocks southwest of the plaza. It is partially owned by the Picuris Indian Pueblo of Northern New Mexico and boasts a staff that is 40 percent Indian. Outside, the neat, adobe-brown pueblo-style architecture is complemented by one of the city's most colorful wildflower gardens. The lobby and other common areas are expansive and open, decorated in Pueblo Revival style and dotted with Alan Hauser sculpture; the rooms and suites are large and bright, all furnished in Santa Fe style. In-room amenities include microwaves, honor bars, safes, and remote-control cable television.

The inn has no restaurant but lies just a block from several of Santa Fe's best-known eateries, among them Tomasitas and the Guadalupe Café; a lobby deli serves sandwiches, snacks, and finger food (a catering service will prepare a Pueblo Indian–style banquet for groups on request). The lobby lounge offers full bar service; round-trip shuttle service to the plaza—a 15-minute walk to the northeast—is available.

1501 Paseo de Peralta at Cerrillos Road. Tel: 982-1200 or (800) 825-9876; Fax: 984-2211. $60–$205.

Peripheral Hotels

These hotels are not within walking distance of the plaza.

Marriott Residence Inn de Santa Fe. The Residence Inn sits just 3 miles (5 km) southeast of the plaza (drive south on St. Francis, then east on St. Michael's), but what a different world. Lacking any sort of charm whatsoever, the area is next to a major hospital in what many locals call "Strip City."

Location aside, this sprawling, condominium-like affair

is perfect for families. Apartments and suites, all decorated in Southwestern motifs, are bright and spacious.
Rooms come with fireplaces and fully equipped kitchens,
and the more expensive penthouse suites have private
balconies. Three outdoor Jacuzzis, an outdoor pool, and
basketball and racquet-tennis courts in the large central
courtyard are shaded by aspen, pine, and maple trees.
Chile *ristras* (strings of red chile peppers) add a bit of
New Mexican flavor to the perfectly manicured grounds.
Shuttle service to the Santa Fe airport, van service to
the plaza, and an "extended" complimentary Continental
breakfast are included in the price. Residence Inn has no
restaurant.

1698 Galisteo Street, at St. Michael's Drive. Tel: 988-
7300 or (800) 331-3131; Fax: 988-3243. $155–$195.

Picacho Plaza Hotel. Translated from Spanish, *picacho*
means "peak" and *plaza* means "town square." But this
former Sheraton, 1½ miles (2½ km) north of the plaza,
isn't built on a mountain and has no real plaza. Strange
are the ways of those who name hotels.

What Picacho Plaza does have are large and comfortable if somewhat motel-type rooms and suites, nice views
of the Sangre de Cristo Mountains (and the national
cemetery just across the street), and the **Maria Benitez
Flamenco Troupe**. The troupe, which performs at the
hotel from July through September (reservations are a
must), is one of Santa Fe's most popular attractions and
worth every penny of the high-priced ticket.

Guests here have free use of the adjacent Santa Fe Spa,
a popular and well-equipped health club; there is complimentary shuttle service to the plaza area. The hotel's
Petroglyph Restaurant and Lounge serves good if not
notable food.

750 North St. Francis Drive. Tel: 982-5591 or (800) 441-
5591; Fax: 988-2821. $78–$394.

Bishop's Lodge. A live stream, a shimmering waterfall,
and a Duck Crossing sign on the entrance road quickly
inform visitors that Bishop's Lodge is a country resort.
Nestled in the rolling, piñon-covered foothills of the
Sangre de Cristo Mountains a little more than 3 miles (5
km) north of Santa Fe (views of the Jemez Mountains are
unfortunately blocked by a nearby ridge), it was originally
built as a private retreat for Archbishop Lamy (famous in
Willa Cather's *Death Comes for the Archbishop*) and later
became the summer home of the Pulitzer family.

Impersonal and sprawling but perfect for outdoors-
loving families, this 1,000-acre "ranch" has miles of beauti-

ful hiking trails, and offers guided horseback trips, skeet and trap shooting, tennis, and off-site golf (guest courtesies are available for golfers at three local courses). For overburdened parents the lodge offers a supervised children's program seven days a week.

Accommodations are comfortable but not fancy. Both European and modified American plans are available. Standard rooms in Southwestern decor are small but well-appointed; the more expensive suites have fireplaces, balconies, or private terraces. The **Bishop's Lodge Restaurant** (attire is casual for breakfast and lunch, but jackets and dresses are required at dinner) is well-known and well-appreciated by Santa Fe locals.

Bishop's Lodge Road. (Washington Avenue, which runs north from the plaza, becomes Bishop's Lodge Road.) Tel: 983-6377 or (800) 732-2240; Fax: 989-8739. $135–$345, European plan (credit cards not accepted; cash, personal, and company checks only).

Rancho Encantado. Hospitality, great sunsets, and spectacular views of the Jemez Mountains make up for whatever this famous ranch resort lacks in landscaping maintenance (grounds are left au naturel for the most part). Privacy is an important amenity here; if you want to be left alone, this is the place.

Rambling over 168 acres, Rancho Encantado, built in 1932 and now, as it always has been, the personal estate of wealthy socialite Betty Egan, hosts lots of celebrities, but the not-so-rich are welcome too. Accommodations are widely varied—everything from bedrooms in the main lodge and adobe *casitas* (little houses) to spacious private villas. Horseback riding, tennis, swimming, and hiking are available to guests. The **Rancho Encantado Restaurant** is well-known to Santa Fe residents for its excellent seafood and Continental cuisine; reservations are usually necessary, even for guests. The resort has no room service.

To get to Rancho Encantado drive 7½ miles (12 km) north on Washington Avenue from the plaza (it turns into Bishop's Lodge Road) through the village of Tesuque; about a mile (1½ km) past Tesuque turn east on NM 592 (toward the mountains) and continue another 2 miles (3 km) to Rancho Encantado (signposted).

Route 4, P.O. Box 57C. Tel: 982-3537 or (800) 722-9339; Fax: 983-8269. $100–$300.

Small Inns and Bed and Breakfasts

Alexander's Inn. This comfortable bed and breakfast lies six blocks east of the plaza on quiet Palace Avenue, well away from the downtown fuss but within easy walking distance of shops and museums. The inn is ensconced in a large shake-roofed Victorian house (built around the turn of the century), a well-kept structure that has the woodsy ambience more typical of Seattle than of Santa Fe.

Five bright, newly renovated rooms (plus a private *casita*)—some with fireplaces, stained glass windows, and skylights—are fastidiously furnished with Victorian antiques (check out the four-poster bed in number 5); two rooms share bathrooms. Amenities include down comforters.

The common areas at Alexander's are tidy and spacious; a shady enclosed patio in back contains a breakfast area, as does the wide verandah in front. Light breakfast and afternoon tea are included in the rates. Parking is off-street and protected.

529 East Palace Avenue. Tel: 986-1431. $65–$140.

Grant Corner Inn. Walk two blocks west of the plaza on Palace Avenue and one block north on Grant, pass from the street through the shaded gazebo at the Grant Corner Inn, and you enter a lovely Victorian world. Pleasantly renovated, this spectacular turn-of-the-century structure—from its shady verandah to the flocked wallpaper on the bedroom walls—is as gorgeous and traditional as they come.

Every chamber here is exquisite. Common areas, of which there are several, are open, bright, and uncluttered, while the 11 guest bedrooms—some spacious, some tiny, some with shared baths—are appointed with tenderness, care, and abundant antiques. Oriental rugs cover the hardwood floors throughout; huge brass beds sport colorful handmade quilts. Monogrammed towels, clawfoot tubs, and ceiling fans are among the inn's numerous niceties.

Lemon waffles and orange granola pancakes are two of the many delicious entrées on the breakfast menu; afternoon wine and cheese are also included in the price. During warmer months most guests take both on the shaded, brick-floored verandah.

122 Grant Avenue. Tel: 983-6678. $55–$135.

Inn on the Paseo. You can spot the Inn on the Paseo, three and a half blocks northeast of the plaza, by looking for the white picket fence. Quaint, comfortable, and just a five-minute walk from the plaza, this painstakingly renovated hostelry, which was once three side-by-side homes, is a charming new addition to the City of Holy Faith.

Bubbly innkeeper A. J. Gordon (everyone calls her

A. J.) delights in showing off the place. Nineteen pleasant rooms boast four-poster beds, down comforters, and lots of Southwestern art; most have private outside entrances and one-step access to a rustic wooden deck. The honeymoon suite, complete with Jacuzzi, has the third floor to itself. Colorful hanging quilts in the rooms and common areas are handmade by owner Nancy Arseneault and give the interior a Northern New Mexico farmhouse atmosphere. A full breakfast created in the inn's kitchen (*sans* eggs or meat) is included in the room price; no other meals are served in the inn, but **Josie's**, one of Santa Fe's premier New Mexican restaurants, is right around the corner. Parking is off-street and protected.

630 Paseo de Peralta, between Marcy and Otero streets. Tel: 984-8200; Fax: 989-3979. $89–$149.

Dancing Ground of the Sun. The bare brown exterior of this small, streetside inn resembles a motel, but its great location (three and a half blocks east of the plaza), pleasant innkeepers, and large apartments make up for whatever is lost in atmosphere.

Owners David and Donna McClure go all out to make guests feel comfortable. While there's no lobby or other common area here, the four accommodations are spacious and spotless, decorated in Santa Fe style; some are equipped with sofas and fireplaces, and all have queen- or king-size beds. Other amenities include cable television, fully equipped kitchens, and a substantial Continental breakfast. Parking is off-street (the day's first three guests park in the compound; others across the street).

711 Paseo de Peralta. Tel: 986-9797 or (800) 645-5673. $115–$135.

Dos Casas Viejas. Location—a ten-minute walk west of the plaza and smack in the middle of one of Santa Fe's roughest neighborhoods—is about the only thing wrong with this gorgeous little bed and breakfast. (The area is slowly being gentrified, however, and over the past several years has lost much of its snarl.) Owners Jois and Irving Belfield have lovingly transformed what were once run-down 19th-century homes into an elegant and beautifully decorated retreat. One large room and two suites (three more suites to be added this year) are furnished in luxurious Santa Fe style, with traditional furniture, wood-burning fireplaces, terra-cotta tile floors, and beamed ceilings. Amenities include private walled patios, fine linens and towels, and fresh flowers in the rooms daily. Common areas include an exquisitely furnished library, a dining area, and a lap pool. The half-acre compound is surrounded by a seven-foot-high adobe wall (parking is within the protected compound); guests gain access through a coded electronic gate. A deluxe Continental breakfast is complimentary; two great eateries, **Encore Provence** and **La Tertulia**, are just up the street.

610 Agua Fria Street. Tel: 983-1636. $125–$185.

Water Street Inn. Twenty years ago the West Water Street area, five blocks due west of the plaza, was a barrio; the Salvation Army shelter, in fact, still occupies a busy nook just around the corner. Today, however, a segment of the area has been transformed into a stylish mixture of upscale nightclubs and offices. The Water Street Inn, once a run-down adobe apartment complex, exemplifies what time, work, and money can accomplish—even in a not-so-nice neighborhood.

Innkeepers Dolores and Al Dietz treat guests like family and keep the bed and breakfast's seven large rooms, some with terraces and fireplaces or antique wood-burning stoves and each with private bath, as neat as a pin. Indian rugs, Taos-style furniture (hand-carved wood), ceiling fans, and beamed ceilings add style to simplicity.

Water Street Inn has no restaurant, but **Vanessie's**, a dine, drink, and dance club just next door, serves steak and seafood (late-night noise from the club is a problem for some rooms on the north side). Or you can head over to **Maria Ysabel's**, at 409 West Water (just off Guadalupe), for their famous *huevos rancheros* green and other Mexican delights, any time after 11:00 A.M. Complimentary Continental breakfast is served in your room; wine and hors d'oeuvres are available in the common room at 9:00 P.M. There is off-street parking.

From downtown Santa Fe drive west on Alameda Street, turn right on Guadalupe (go half a block), then left on Water Street.

427 West Water Street. Tel: 984-1193. $85–$130.

Territorial Inn. From manicured grounds and towering shade trees to neat brick walkways, a pitched roof, and smooth adobe walls, the exterior of this gentrified 19th-century structure is a sight for sore eyes. Its location is perfect for shoppers and museum-goers–just one and a half blocks north of the plaza on Washington Avenue.

The inn has ten guest rooms (eight with private baths); complimentary breakfast, afternoon tea, and brandy at night are included in the price. Other amenities include a gazebo-enclosed hot tub and near-instant access to Santa Fe's museums, shops, and galleries. The innkeepers here can be sharp at times and a bit stuffy, however, and the common areas—heavily "harumphed" in Victorian appointments—are dark and fusty. Overlarge paintings droop from the walls, and dark drapes on the windows partially block light. The Territorial is not to everyone's liking.

215 Washington Avenue. Tel: 989-7737; Fax: 986-1411. $70–$150.

—*Buddy Mays*

DINING

Some say it's the light. The extraordinary, clear, honeyed air that frames every juniper-dotted mesa, every softly nipped adobe wall, that makes paintings in the sky each evening at dusk. Some call it "God's country." Well, there are certainly divine things here, and that includes the food.

That also includes the pace, if you give yourself over to it. Remember: They don't call this mañana land for nothing. If your enchilada happens to wait under the heat lamp a little, relax (which is all you can do in most places). Getting riled up will just ruin your mood to no avail. You'll find that no line divides the quality of service between the trendy and the home-style places, either; willing, warm service will be just where you encounter it. Also, many of the people bringing those luscious platters of *carne adovada* know a lot about what's happening around town: art, hiking and camping spots, the secret hot springs, where to get a good haircut (Lennon/Erickson, off Agua Fria) or where to buy cowboy boots (Santa Fe Boot Company, on Cordova). You know, the real town jewels. All you have to do is ask.

It's pretty recent in Santa Fe's restaurant world to happen upon "professional" wait-persons; it used to be that every waiter had a master's in Postmodern Expressionism or pre-Columbian creation myths. This is a town where many of the service people are artists or Ph.D.s, or have some kind of real life percolating. Meanwhile they are bringing you another side of green or extra sopapillas, your latest food addictions. The burgeoning of the au courant Southwestern gourmet style may have brought a certain level of professionalism into the dining rooms about town, but in most cases exceptional table service is still a cause for celebration and large tips. New Mexican wait-persons are usually not even paid minimum wage; good service needs to be acknowledged, and a little appreciation will go a long way.

DOWNTOWN

Breakfast or Lunch

The thing about Santa Fe is that the eating options are deep and wide. If you want to take a look at the local politicians and downtown gallery/business folk, then buy the morning paper and visit **Tia Sophia's**, two blocks west of the plaza at 210 West San Francisco Street, which boasts down-to-earth prices and is open just for breakfast and lunch; Tel: 983-9880. The green chile cheese-and-ham omelet is state of the art, not nouvelle anything. It's mama food—if your mother happened to be born in New Mexico. Coffee is brought around in metal pots until you beg for mercy; tortillas are homemade; and the beans are half refried, half soupy—a science. The waitresses have all been here since the Jurassic age, a rarity in this economically volatile burg.

Another popular restaurant downtown is **Cafe Pasqual's**, 121 Don Gaspar Avenue at the corner of Water Street. There may be lines outside for all three meals here, especially Sunday brunch. Bring something to read, or at least be willing to enjoy the sunshine and a chat; you may wait a while. Still, service is good and portions are huge. Black-bean *huevos,* the "Monterey omelet," and all pancake permutations are the dishes of choice at breakfast here. At lunch and dinner "traditional" foods are done with considerable twists toward the gourmet; beer and wine are available. Reservations are accepted at dinner only; Tel: 983-9340.

On the weekends, the most civilized brunch imaginable, not "native," but with gentle touches thereof (like a peep of red pepper in a crab frittata), may be enjoyed on the willow-shaded patio of **Grant Corner Inn**, 122 Grant Avenue, one block north of Palace Avenue. You'll face a choice of only two entrées, which will seem like a relief after the assorted voluminous, occasionally bilingual, menus everywhere else. A harpist is playing; there's a basket of fresh, warm sweet breads and muffins; and there's a chilled fresh-fruit frappé to quaff while you plan the next leg of your New Mexico journey. Here is sanctuary for the road- and flight-weary. Reservations are mandatory; Tel: 983-6678.

A 180-degree spin in mood is **Real Burger**, at 227 Don Gaspar Avenue between Alameda and Water Street, for a hefty breakfast burrito. For incredibly little money you can get a big fresh flour tortilla filled with eggs, *papas* (potatoes), cheese, chile sauce, and bacon if desired— incredibly fast. This is not about classy atmosphere in subtle pastels. At Real Burger you place an order at the window, then, *muy pronto,* they call your number and produce a tray of food for your consumption at the funky wooden tables or on the little street-side patio. You may need to return for lunch, along with myriad Santa Feans in the know, as the green chile cheeseburgers send a sensory memorandum straight to the brain.

If you are the "don't talk to me about food, it's morning" type, the **Galisteo News**, at the corner of Galisteo and Water streets, may be for you. The News has umpteen magazines, postcards, and cards, a strong, specially blended brew of coffee, pastries culled from all the town's good bakeries and a few home bakers, all those de rigueur espresso drinks, and a good view of local street life. And many writers writing. In fact this is the site where local author Natalie Goldberg wrote the famous literary how-to, *Writing Down the Bones.* The News stocks film, city maps, and tickets to most of the town's major cultural events.

Many locals also frequent the **Plaza Bakery**, 56 San Francisco Street at the plaza. The too-bright light and formica setting are not exactly conducive to a read and a schmooz, but note the location because this is also the Häagen-Dazs place, and is open very late at night for serious chocolate experiences. The daytime pluses are high-test coffee and excellent croissants, easily portable for outside enjoyment on the old cast-iron benches around the plaza. There you can watch the younger crowd (a.k.a. plaza rats) at play, and maybe see some "cherryed-out" low-rider vehicles (that's car talk for customized, reconditioned older models—a Northern New Mexico obsession now recognized as national folk art). The bakery, across from the Palace of the Governors Museum, is convenient for an investigatory stroll along the blanket-, jewelry-, and pottery-lined sidewalk display of the creations of native Pueblo artisans. You might find fresh *horno*-baked Indian bread (an *horno* is an outdoor oven that looks like a beehive), and maybe even *pikki,* the delicate rolled bread of the Hopi people.

A quiet and peaceful coffeehouse, **Café Romana**, is tucked neatly along Burro Alley, to the west of the plaza between San Francisco Street and Palace Avenue, up a ways from the wonderful Lensic Theatre, Santa Fe's grand old movie house and home of the Santa Fe Symphony. Café Romana provides all the necessary versions of espresso drinks and a carefully chosen selection of local baked goods. The walls feature changing shows of photography or paintings, and there are no stampeding crowds here. Closed Sundays.

Lunch

If you find yourself downtown along with the hordes at the noon hour, try to take in lunch before noon or after 1:00 P.M. to avoid a wait at the walk-in places. For any of the trendy or upscale restaurants, make a reservation. Downtown Santa Fe is hopping at lunchtime, when businesspeople and tourists alike try to wolf down an enchilada and a sopapilla and get on with their day.

An example of one such superpopular spot is **Josie's Casa de Comida**, a traditional *comida nativa* restaurant at 225 East Marcy Street near Paseo de Peralta. The lines at this lunch-only place are long, and though some local folk swear by Josie's chile, forsaking all others, it's all in the stomach of the beholder. Don't worry if it's not to your liking; there are many other home-style New Mexican eateries to discover.

Other hot spots frequented by locals are **Carlos Gosp'l Cafe**, at 125 Lincoln Avenue at the corner of Marcy Street, and **The Shed**, at 113½ East Palace Avenue east of the plaza in a wonderful 300-year-old hacienda enclosed by a pretty, private courtyard. At Carlos's, very fairly priced homemade soups and sandwiches are featured in a make-yourself-to-home atmosphere. Their green chile corn chowder, "hangover stew," is serious medicine for the morning after a margaritas-about-town night (the best are at Maria's New Mexican Kitchen and at Tomasitas; see below). And, glory be, they serve perfect lemon meringue pie, no small feat for baking at an altitude of 7,000 feet. The Shed, very tastefully, calmly, old-style New Mexican, is known for its red chile cheese enchiladas and its mocha cake, both great, and for holding its own for 40 years. Tel: 982-9030. Open for lunch only.

Looking for fabulous green chile cheeseburgers, margaritas, and homemade soup—consistent good food and service in a place that can handle kids and big groups? Hands down, that would be **San Francisco Street Bar & Grill**, in the **Plaza Mercado** at 114 West San Francisco Street. In the summer they sport a little bratwurst stand around back for fast, cheap street eats. SFSB&G has continuous service, 11:00 A.M. to 11:00 P.M. This is important;

most restaurants here close between lunch and dinner, and 3:00 to 5:00 P.M. can be difficult hours to find a good meal. Likewise, there's a dearth of places for après-movie or post-concert meals.

While in the Plaza Mercado, visit **The Santa Fe School of Cooking** (Tel: 983-4511) and take a cooking demo of Southwestern food from a local chef. The results of the couple hours you spend here are yours for the feasting.

Many diners swear by **Fabio's**, an endearing, village-pretty Florentine bistro over in Santa Fe Village, a quaint, rambling collection of clothing and curio shops at 227 Don Gaspar Avenue (before you reach Alameda and the river), next to Real Burger. The *gnocchi* are angelic tid-bits, all the pastas are made on-site, there's a well-selected wine list and a patio with a wood-burning pizza oven, and they try hard to please; Tel: 984-3080.

A down and dirty, fast and guiltily good lunch can be had right on the plaza, from **Woolworth's** on San Francisco Street. Their frito pie and their chile dog, heaped with Abuela-style red chile sauce from scratch and hot, melted cheese, are well respected by many townies.

At 104 West San Francisco Street, the **Santa Fe Emporium** stocks all the beans, salsas, and sopapilla mixes you by now will have come to need, and also dispenses fresh fudge and Ben and Jerry's ice cream. They will gladly wrap and ship all purchases out of town. A special note: The Emporium is in the miraculous position of being able to sell wine by the bottle on Sundays. This is by dint of designation as the official tasting room for Anderson Valley Vineyard, one of New Mexico's oldest wineries. For a refundable dollar you can sample the Anderson line and pick up everything for a picnic seven days a week—and even get a locally made basket to transport it.

Even picante diehards take an ethnic break occasionally, and the City Different cheerfully houses many seductive "cuisines different," in the moderate price range. For Japanese, there's **Shohko-Cafe** at 321 Johnson Street at the corner of Guadalupe, with convenient parking in the rear. Green chile tempura, anyone? It's actually very good, and the sushi bar here is one of the city's best sites for art-gossip eavesdropping and celeb-spotting (big stars all seem to love raw fish, or at least Shohko's spicy tuna hand-rolls). You must make a reservation; Tel: 983-7288.

A spin of the globe may stop at **India Palace**, 227 Don Gaspar, for an all-you-can-eat lunch buffet that never lapses into steamed foods from hell. The curries are authentic and subtle, and the baskets of just-made onion *paratha* and *chapati* bread are tasty. India Palace, however, can be tricky to find. From the front of the St. Francis Hotel on Don Gaspar, head across the street and through the city parking lot. The restaurant's entrance is at the back of the building facing the parking lot.

The long and leisurely lunch is traditional in Hispanic and Mexican cultures. A lot of Santa Feans like to do it Italian style, namely at the **Palace Restaurant**, 142 West Palace Avenue, a half block west of the plaza. Though the red-flocked wallpaper is scary, the food is self-assured, predominantly serious Italian, and many a big deal in the gallery world has been closed here, over Caesar salads tossed at the table, and salmon filets wrapped in fresh spinach and phyllo. Make a reservation, and eat on the lovely patio; Tel: 982-9893. Barkeep Alphonso runs a fun bar in the separate lounge area, and wins local popularity contests year after year for his cast-of-thousands drink list and genial personality.

Lunch can be the perfect opportunity to sample high-end fine-dining places, like **Cafe Escalera** (Tel: 989-8188), which is a bit less pricey during the day; the menu features that clear, clean, semiveggy California cuisine that goes great with sunny days. Chef David Tanis, the Zen master of bread in town, serves pan-fried oysters with not a lick of grease and salads of locally grown baby greens. The dining space is pop stark, and the acoustics a bit loud, but the food is innovative and studious. They make a doozie of a martini here, too, which merely meditates on vermouth. You will find Escalera up the escalator and to the right at 130 Lincoln Avenue, one-half block north of the plaza, a location many Santa Feans will describe to you as "the old Sears Building." This is simply Santa Fe time-warp direction giving. Many locals carry, in their mind's eye, a sort of ten-years-back overlay map of used-to-be's. Ask where some place is, and you may first need to hear what was there two, three, or even four restaurants ago. (The local passion for reciting a litany of incarnations for various restaurants is a hint that restaurateuring in Santa Fe is a high-stakes version of "Wheel of Fortune.")

Lunch may also be the way to check out the very pricey **Inn of the Anasazi**, which for all its chic dry-stack masonry and expensive pottery has a pretty checkered food record. Sometimes a meal there will soar into the creative realms of Pueblo-Continental-cowboy cuisine, a fascinating high-wire act. When pulled off successfully, such a meal goes on record with the great ones. But they can be off, way off, and the service so diffident as to rattle a saint.

It's worth the gamble. One thing to trust is the desserts; chef Kathy Redford goes to the wall with showstoppers like homemade red chile peach ice cream, billowing out of a hand-made white-chocolate casing lavishly strewn with fresh blackberries and raspberries. For reservations (and to see if she is still there), Tel: 988-3236.

Dinner

All jazz and jitter is **Edge**, on the corner of Palace and Grant avenues west of the plaza, at 135 West Palace Avenue. The food is creatively simple Southwest: green chile, bacon-breaded baby clams served steaming in pearly shells, or a thick smoked-turkey sandwich with two cheeses, grilled poblano chiles, and pickled onions. Open from 11:00 A.M. to 2:00 A.M., Edge can fill a number of sustenance needs, because this is the bistro side of Santa Fe's high-tech disco meet-and-greet, and a late-night haven for Real Food. The decor is uptown suave, toney stainless steel, three shades of glamour gray. And the razzmatazz and multi-amp sound stay nicely put in the next-door dance space. You can visit the disco side, but you don't have to eat there.

You have heard this before: Go up the escalator at 130 Lincoln Avenue (remember Cafe Escalera in the old Sears Building?). But this time, at the top go to the left, to **Babbo Ganzo**. Succulent pillows of ricotta-filled ravioli swirl sensuously amidst wild-boar meat sauce and Roma tomatoes; a wood-burning pizza oven produces crusts to end all arguments over thin versus thick forever; and almondy, crisp biscotti await a dip in a sweet wine for dessert. Babbo Ganzo sells the biscotti to go, and they are just the thing for dunking in your morning coffee. If you don't buy some, you will wish you had. Be sure to make reservations; Tel: 986-3835. (If it sometimes seems as if the actual native food of Santa Fe is Italian, it probably reflects the population pool of transplanted urbanites from New York and California. Promise them anything, but give them fresh pasta, al dente.)

Being a town's best-kept culinary secret is a double-edged sword. The customer has the best end of the deal, as the object of dedicated gastronomic attention, but being a secret is no restaurant's goal. There are a few special restaurants here that are just on the cusp of gaining their deserved recognition for outstanding quality of food, service, ambience, and a generous helping of the personal touch. Not accidentally, two of the finest are inside hotels.

The thought of hotel food usually conjures up vegeta-

bles boiled into submission and whimpering on the plate
next to a pool of something gelatinous over chicken. Not
so at the Eldorado Hotel's **Old House Restaurant**, in a
beautifully appointed, romantically lit room, highlighted
by playful folk art. Dine in large comfortable armchairs,
served by practiced and attentive waiters. The food is
prepared with élan; a steak will be finished with fresh
shiitake mushrooms and the potatoes mashed with red
chile. The wine list has a flair for adventure. At press time
word has hit the streets that the talented John Sedlar,
chef/owner of the noted restaurant Bikini in Santa Mon-
ica, California, and a native Santa Fean, may be taking
over operation of Old House. This would probably mean
a remodeling of the space and a redesign of the menu—
and could be the start of Something Big, bigger even than
the already excellent restaurant here. The hotel is located
at 309 San Francisco on the corner of Sandoval Street; Tel:
988-4455. Across the lobby, the **Eldorado Court** features
live entertainment and, truth to tell, exceptional dining as
well.

And then there's **On Water**, inside the Hotel St. Francis
at the corner of Don Gaspar Avenue and Water Street.
Here you'll find a welcoming, airy, serene room, with a
continually changing menu that keeps the kitchen and
staff lively and alert. Chef-owners Don Fortel and Rocky
Packard cook in the international vernacular: curries not
for the fainthearted; *feuilletages* of thin-sliced mushrooms
redolent with chive and tarragon; peasant-sturdy pâtés
with down-home pickles Americana. The service here is
dedicated, with a feeling of warmth and esprit de corps.
The bricked-in patio, with the swoop of swallows in summer and old, old peach trees, is a heartthrob of a space.
Don't be surprised if you find yourself drawn back again
and again, because this is the kind of place you will be glad
to say you discovered. Tel: 982-8787.

The Hotel St. Francis itself serves an exquisite proper tea
every afternoon, with scones, clotted cream, chocolate-
covered strawberries, perfectly brewed tea, Champagne,
or, still more calming, a glass of fine Sherry. Take your tea
in the overstuffed armchairs in the lobby or outside on the
front verandah. Marvelously proper, yet decadent.

Also on the cusp of recognition is the virtuoso food
performance over at **Paul's** on West Marcy Street between
Lincoln and Washington Avenues, a small, engagingly
decorated dining space; the folk art is familiar, but the
food stylings are completely original. With great respect

for fresh, clear flavors, Paul's offers thoughtful, imaginative treatments of Continental standards. Tel: 982-8738.

THE MECCAS

And then there are the heavyweight foodie meccas. Like **Coyote Cafe**, 132 West Water Street, between Galisteo and Don Gaspar, winner of scads of food and wine awards, and written up almost to obsession. The Coyote is, simply, a great restaurant. Effervescent atmosphere, coyote art in metal and glass, brilliantly painted folk-art denizens of the desert, and a tad noisy—but it all contributes to a "happening" mood. But who cares about the atmosphere if the food isn't cutting-edge? Well, it is. No basking in past glory here. Coyote's menu, which changes daily, reinvents a cross between rough-and-ready Western food, ancient Pueblo, Mexican, and classical New Mexican, with a zip from South America and some resonance from founder Mark Miller's New England. A tight team of line cooks led by chef Mark Kiffin produce consistent excellence. And the food is fun: ancho chiles and crème fraîche scribbled across cumin-dusted swordfish fillets grilled over pecan wood; sweet-hot mango salsa; blue-corn crab cakes; a squash-blossom *relleno;* tuna tartar with avocado *crema.* There's lots of range-fed game; wild herb-marinated venison with prickly-pear sauce; hibiscus quail. Yes, Coyote is at the top of the market, but it's worth the money. If you love to eat, do it here. And don't be a reverse food snob; let yourself be seduced. Chef Susie Dayton's desserts are right up there, and the wine list, culled from around the world, merits its heaps of accolades as well.

The dress code at Coyote Cafe prohibits shorts in the dining room for dinner, and the menu formula is a prix fixe four-course affair. Don't even consider walking in; reservations are a must. Tel: 983-1615.

Coyote has an outdoor **Cantina**, open in the summer, serving lunch, hors d'oeuvres, and drinks. And what drinks! *Muy picante* Bloody Marys made with tequila, and a triple-rum daiquiri that is instant rhumba. Don't forget to visit the **Coyote Cafe General Store**, downstairs on Water Street, for a mind-boggling collection of salsas, all forms of dried chiles, specialty ingredients, and a definitive supply of Southwestern cookbooks and knickknacks.

You must also make reservations to visit the **Santacafe**, in an 18th-century adobe at 231 Washington Avenue between Paseo de Peralta and Marcy Street, because this highly touted, grandstanding restaurant tends to cram

'em in. The food here is exquisite. Not eccentric, but
clever; not wild, but imaginative. Santacafe is known for
an Oriental spin on the Occidental, and for superlative
fresh ingredients. This is another great restaurant, with
salads of the tenderest local greens, chile-roasted pecans,
sliced pears, and Maytag blue cheese; melt-in-your-mouth
dim sum; and entrées that look like small, perfect Kan-
dinskys. Service tends to be a bit on the chilly side, but
the place hums. If Coyote is Beethoven, this is Bach:
elegant, precise combinations of flavors set neatly. The
dining room is intimate, done in uncomplicated, spare
lines, with a tiny bar, best just for pre-dinner cocktails.
This is not a hang-out; neither is it a good place to bring
children. Dress up and bring the gold card; Tel: 984-1788.

La Casa Sena, Tel: 988-9232, is set like a jewel, just east
of the plaza on Palace Avenue, in the shop- and gallery-
lined courtyard of Sena Plaza; in summer the courtyard
becomes a bewitchingly lovely garden, from the first
daffodils and hyacinths through cascades of fragrant lilacs
and a gala of Shasta daisies. This is a grande dame of a
location, in the historic home (circa 1860) of Major Jose
Sena, at number 125, and she wears her years like fine
pearls. La Casa Sena centers firmly on stylish, scrumptious
renditions of New Mexican entrées with luxury accents
and the finest ingredients, such as free-range piñon-
breaded chicken with chile-lingonberry sauce. But nothing is gratuitous; the flavors make a rich and satisfying
marriage. The wine list of more than 700 vintages is
worth reading for its sheer grandeur and educated
breadth. The warm, quiet dining room is hung with a
connoisseur's collection of paintings and exudes an amiable elegance. The calm assurance of the place suggests
that everything will be right with your dining experience.
This is a class act in every respect.

And there's more to La Casa Sena. The **Cantina**, next
door, offers some of the best fun to be had in Santa Fe on
any given evening: whopper margaritas made with the
king of tequilas, El Tesoro, and cabaret-scale performances
of Broadway's big-ticket shows and perennial classics, performed by a handpicked staff of up-and-coming singers.

CANYON ROAD

If we were to nominate an out-on-a-limb new star (it's not
even downtown but out on Canyon Road), it would have
to be **Geronimo**. Chef Gina Ziluca (she's also executive
chef at Edge, for which see above) puts a kick and twirl
on every dish, and the plates come out as eye-popping

visuals. The food here is cowboy hearty cum nouvelle light, with the full lexicon of chiles in play.

The rooms are lovely in the old Borrego House (circa 1756), re-envisioned with rubbed stainless-steel tables, subtle Mexican fabrics, and an intimate bar for before and after anything that matters. The patio in the inner court-yard has a fountain, and the front porch invites a long, relaxed stay. Either are excellent for sipping margaritas and sampling the shrimp, scallops, and green-onion cakes with *chipotle* sauce and *salsa fresca;* or the tortellini with roasted duck, goat cheese, toasted pine nuts, and green chile with cilantro pesto *crema;* or the fresh *papparadelle* pasta with green onion, Anaheim chile in Champagne butter with fried oysters and Dungeness crabs. This style of cuisine draws from a wide range of references and then homes in gracefully on the center of eating pleasure. Geronimo, 724 Canyon Road, serves lunch and dinner (until 10:30 P.M.) seven days a week, and the bar stays open until 2:00 A.M. Tel: 982-1500.

East of Geronimo at 808 Canyon Road is a cool late-night hors d'oeuvre scene at **El Farol**. There's live music, often of the loud, rockin' Western type, and a huge assort-ment of *tapas,* both hot and cold. Definitely a Santa Fe moment. Tel: 983-9912.

The one really noteworthy Chinese restaurant in town is across from Geronimo on Canyon Road. At the **Impe-rial Wok** the dishes are made with fresh vegetables and are never precooked to that stage of bland limpness commonly served. The spareribs and assorted appetizers make a good light meal, and the cocktails are fun. The dining room is a lush atrium, quiet and civil. The Wok is open seven days a week for lunch and dinner but the hours change daily. Call ahead; Tel: 988-7100.

Canyon Road offers a stroll through the art world, through galleries set amongst towering horse-chestnut trees that bloom in the summer and fragile salt cedars that wave feathery pink branches. The current gallery scene is an exciting mingle of modern with Western and Indian art. The trick to enjoying this sensory flood is not to cram. Take time to try a meal at **Celebrations**, at number 613. This charming patio and small, comfy din-ing room is a good choice for a hearty fruit-topped pancake breakfast, or a lunch of southern Louisiana–style cooking—gumbos, cheese grits, and such—an in-teresting rest from Santa Fe fare.

Or take your coffee-and-cake break at **Downtown Sub-scription**, 376 Garcia Street at the corner of Acequia

Madre, a mere two blocks south of Canyon. This is a
superb shop for small-press quarterlies, periodicals, newspapers, and all manner and make of magazines—and the
poppyseed cake is a great dunker. There is no table
service here; order at the counter, where service is quick
but tends to be impersonal. The coffee is *muy fuerte,* and
will put the "go forth and travel" spirit back in your day.
Many locals enjoy the Subscription for morning coffee,
but the upright wooden chairs and the uptight vibes don't
invite lingering—a problem if you want to browse Canyon Road's shops; many don't open until later in the day.

   On Canyon Road at number 616, the small, nookish
Bookroom Coffeebar is set behind the fun, funky collection of "functional" art, hand-crafted teapots, glasses, and
such at Off the Wall. The Bookroom Coffeebar has a
peaceful hum, a tree-filled patio out back, and a tea/
espresso/coffee-and-cake menu. A hot spot of the literati,
the Coffeebar hosts readings every Wednesday night.

THE OLD SANTA FE TRAIL AREA

To Pink or not to Pink is the question. And it's best to mull
over this major culinary dilemma about the famed Pink
Adobe at their adjacent lounge, the **Dragon Room**, the lair
of the famous Pink Adobe grande dame herself, Rosalea
Murphy. Hung with Rosalea's paintings and her witty art
collection, this is the see-and-be-seen spot for artists on
the make, and others merely making it. Elbows rub over
the picante Bloody Marias, the ever-replenished bowls of
popcorn, and the **Pink Adobe**'s famous green chile stew.

   This decision isn't about food, it's about trend and
tradition and the little-known fact that over the years
many of the artists in town waited tables, tended bar, or
prepped enchiladas at the Pink, 406 Old Santa Fe Trail
across from San Miguel Mission. Rosalea would take art in
trade for tabs, and so has kept a lot of people going until
their careers kicked in. The question is, do you eat here
or merely kiss the threshold? Answer: Eat. The steak
Dunnigan, the pork Napoléon—consistency has kept this
place in the pink for over 40 years. Don't even think of
taking a chance; make a reservation. Tel: 983-7712.

   Across the street from the Pink is yet another "Oldest
House in the United States." True or not, you can trust
that the **Upper Crust Pizza** here has a great Greek pie,
with feta cheese and olives, and calzones that make perfect munch-and-stroll food. They deliver; Tel: 983-4140.

   If you're on the roam out of town, take time to stop at
the little shopping center at the southeast corner of Paseo

de Peralta and Old Santa Fe Trail. Over in the corner is **Ohori's Coffee, Tea and Chocolates**. Most of the excellent, full-bodied coffees at all the town's finer establishments come fresh from Susan Ohori's roasters. Try a pound or two of the house blend, or design your own mix. While there, have a cup of coffee or an espresso and sample the delectable truffles and baked goods. Susan makes sure that everything in the shop—art postcards, a tempting selection of hand-crafted art and housewares, and those chocolate-covered espresso beans—is of the utmost quality.

Farther out of town Old Pecos Trail splits off on Old Santa Fe Trail and goes on to become the Old Las Vegas Highway (U.S. 84/85/285), parallel to I-25, where you'll find the little roadside café **The Bobcat Bite**. Among the few things townies agree on is that Bobcat Bite has superlative green chile cheeseburgers, real home fries, and the best hummingbird show in town (look out the big window behind the counter). It's a tiny place, casual, reasonable, and very much part of the Real Life of these parts; no reservations.

On the way to Bobcat you will have passed the private club El Gancho, on your left, and it restaurant, **The Steaksmith at El Gancho**, which is open to the public. If you must have a steak-and-potato dinner, surf and turf, or other varieties of that kind of all-American "don't show me anything with chiles or arugula" food, have a dinner here. Don't miss the spinach cheese-ball appetizers. It's very crowded in summer; call for reservations. Tel: 988-3333.

THE GUADALUPE STREET AREA

Guadalupe Street may be where the true culinary heart of Santa Fe beats. For years this was the low-rent district closest to the plaza, so you'll find many longtime establishments serving New Mexican food the way the locals love it: red, with a sweet, steady burn, and green, with an endorphin-producing yowl of heat for tongue and mind. And there are many great shops, including the gourmet-equipment kingdom of **Cookworks**, three charming brick buildings filled with the right stuff for pantry, cupboard, and breakfront. They're a fun visit if you're the Williams-Sonoma type and realize that a *comal* is the very thing for cooking tortillas, or if you just need to know the latest fashion colors for kitchen aids.

But don't leap into the day too quickly. No one else in Santa Fe does. Except, perhaps, at the **Aztec Street Cafe**, off Guadalupe at 317 Aztec, which opens and begins to fill

promptly at 7:30 A.M., mostly with artists. It's a real slice of
Santa Fe life, lots of dogs and spiral notebooks, purple
mohawks, and nose rings. The bulletin board offers rides
to anywhere, strange musical instruments for sale, and
healing for parts of yourself you may not have even heard
of yet. Aztec offers utterly delicious coffee, enough to get
any engine going; good assorted baked goods; and great
bagels from Fred's in Albuquerque (so far, still the chewi-
est bagels in New Mexico).

Or check out the **Sanbusco Market Center**, at 500
Montezuma, one block west of Guadalupe Street, a mini-
mall of sorts, but one that houses a great toy store
(Pookinoogan) and The Winery, a terrific resource for
fine wines, including the good wines of New Mexico, and
locally produced gourmet treats such as Salman Ranch
raspberry jams and the Sweetwood Dairy line of herbed
goat cheese. Superb Italian foods and a west-facing rooftop patio are to be found at **Pranzo Italian Grill** in the
market center. Pizza and pasta are prepared here by chef
Steve Lemon, one of Santa Fe's stars, known for his creative rock 'n' roll with pan-regional Italian cuisine complemented by fresh local products. The well-bred wine list
and skilled mixology in the separate lounge area make
this a great hors d'oeuvre or late-night stop for antipasto
or pizza. Tel: 984-2645.

You want to remember the Sanbusco Center, 500 Montezuma, for several reasons, not the least of which is
Portare Via, the trattoria aspect of Pranzo's. Also in the
market center, Portare Via opens at 7:30 A.M. for coffee
and buttery cinnamon buns. This is also a great place to
purchase a full-tilt picnic lunch to take on a sightseeing
day around Santa Fe. The homemade buffalo mozzarella
with fresh basil and sliced Romas is a good choice, and
the "Tuscan rolls" with a slab of soft Fontina and a handful
of olives, chased down with a bottle New Mexico's award-
winning Gruet sparkling wine (from The Winery), should
be just the thing to take on that drive to Abiquiu to see the
mesas that taught Georgia what she wanted to know
about color.

However, if you can't get to the hinterlands they'll
come to you, at least in vegetable form, on Tuesday,
Thursday, and Saturday mornings in spring, summer, and
fall from 7:00 A.M. until noon in the Sanbusco parking lot.
Farmer's Market is sheer bliss for wild honey, flowers,
chiles, Abe's corn, Jake's melons in season, and whatever
the green world is gracing us with at the time. Much is

organic. You will see very special local items: choke-cherry jam, Rose Trujillo's tamales and fruit pies from Nambe Pueblo, dried-flower wreaths, and handmade red-willow baskets.

From the western end of the Sanbusco parking lot, an exit now leads to 548 Agua Fria Street, the exquisite location of Santa Fe's romantic new French restaurant, **Encore Provence**. Set in an adobe home with a resplendent garden, Encore Provence serves light, modern French cuisine, including seafood dishes topped with delicate sauces, prepared from fresh seafood flown in daily from Maine. Attentive waiters scurry between three intimate dining rooms appointed with Provençal decor. Definitely expensive, but well worth it. Open daily for dinner only. Call for reservations; Tel: 983-7470.

Now, are you wondering what happens to all those chiles from the market? If it's 11:00 A.M., you're in luck. **Maria Ysabel's** at 409 Water Street (just north across the river, right behind the Hilton) is open, and you should—no, you *must*—have the *huevos rancheros* green (two fried eggs on corn tortillas laden with green chile and melted cheese), with a side of beans and *posole* (a hominy corn, red chile, and pork stew). Be sure to convince a fellow diner to order the *carne adovada* burrito (a flour tortilla stuffed with tender chunks of pork marinated in red chile, garlic, and oregano), so you can swap and swoon. This is so down-home native that only the local cognoscenti are aware of the heights of Belle Mondragon's completely-from-scratch cooking. And the *huevos* aren't even on the menu.

The Chile Places

Lines are the name of the game at **Tomasita's Cafe**. You can't make reservations, but don't let that dissuade you from a visit. Most locals will tell you this is *the* place for green-chile chicken enchiladas with sour cream, or otherworldly frozen margaritas. The *chalupas* (a crisp, fried corn tart filled with chicken), *refritos,* guacamole, and cheese would have had Brillat-Savarin himself asking for seconds. Expect loud and busy. Fast, competent service and moderate prices more than make up for the pre-meal wait. If you go for dinner get there early, or enjoy the sunset out over the train yard while you sip your margarita (that little building across the parking lot was the original Santa Fe line stop). There's a great, cheap kid's menu (with a no-chile option) and a nice patio.

Tomasita's is open Monday through Saturday, from 11:00 A.M. until 10:00 P.M. at 500 South Guadalupe Street in the old railroad yards, across from the Guadalupe/Garfield intersection. Tel: 983-5721.

Down the road a piece back toward the plaza at number 313 is the other local favorite, **Guadalupe Cafe**, for bulging *chimichangas,* enchiladas Christmas (in other words, topped with red and green chile), and at lunch a turkey sandwich on grilled whole wheat with green chile and Swiss cheese, which comes with a sybaritic cup of jalapeño cheese soup. The fresh fruit pies are terrific, as is anything with raspberries; Tel: 982-9762.

A slightly off-the-wall treat is **Diego's Cafe and Bar** in the De Vargas Mall at the intersection of Paseo de Peralta and Guadalupe, on the other side of downtown. Diego's features good margaritas, okay atmosphere, and great chicken-wing appetizers with chile dip. Fabulous for-real New Mexican food for low prices. Locals tend to jam the place, so call for reservations; Tel: 983-5101. The owners of Diego's, Tomasita's, and Tia Sophia's (see Downtown, Breakfast or Lunch, above) are sisters and brothers, and the quality is high across the board at all three places.

Many guidebooks will suggest you try La Tertulia over on Agua Fria Street between Dudrow and Guadalupe. Housed in a former convent, it's a pretty place with authentic Hispanic decor, but the food is merely adequate. If you must go, have the sangria and nachos and dine elsewhere.

If at this point you are in need of a cleansing lunch of fresh celery or carrot juice, and a nut burger, falafel, or outrageously good vegetarian Reuben, made with tempeh (a chewy meat substitute made from soy), and topped with soy cheese (for the no-dairy lover in you), **Healthy David's Cafe** over in the Design Center Mall between Cerrillos Road and Sandoval Street is the place. And the bulletin board here is a rhapsody of the metaphysical. Actually, bulletin boards are required reading and a time-honored spectator sport for those on any restaurant line in Santa Fe.

A gem of a Thai place has recently opened on Garfield Street, between Sandoval and Guadalupe streets, in an elegant, graciously lit little house decorated with antiques from Bali and Thailand. **Thao's** food is high-style French-Thai, very unusual, ringing with lime leaves and fresh ginger. This artfully prepared food will reawaken even the most jaded or scorched palate. Dinners are pricey; lunch is a deal. Call for reservations; Tel: 988-9562.

CERRILLOS ROAD

Whatever you're doing here on The Strip (the main feeder road from I-25 into Santa Fe), let's hope it includes breakfast at **Tecolote Cafe**, 1203 Cerrillos Road, especially if it's Sunday. Owner-chef Bill Jennison's house specialty, shirred chicken livers, is glorious. All the muffins and breads are baked in-house; the omelets, *huevos rancheros,* chile and home fries are excellent. This is a much-loved, sunny breakfast spot, offering generous portions and great service. There are lines on the weekends, so bring a friend or a good read.

Of lesser fame, but you'll be glad to know about it, is the **Horseman's Haven Cafe**, way, way out at 6500 Cerrillos next to the Texaco station. This is the best steak-and-eggs deal in town, and not just for the price. The meat is full flavored, the chile is hotter than at Tomasita's, and the home fries bring tears of joy. The plate-size green chile cheeseburgers need to be attacked with a knife and fork. Tel: 471-5420.

While we're into the truly fundamental gastronomic glories of Santa Fe: Do the drive-through at **Baja Tacos**, 2621 Cerrillos, south of downtown. It looks as if it would be fast but awful food, heavy on the vitamin G, but no, this is all from scratch, authentic family-recipe native cooking. You haven't achieved gourmand bliss until you've had the green chile cheese fries here. Just pray you get the happy-hour smiling face on your receipt; it means your meal is free and you'll just have to return to try their tofu tacos and burritos, because yes, this is a secret veggy health-food haven. Great lemonade, too.

If it's cocktail time and you're ready to decide which margaritas are for you, frozen or up? Cuervo Gold or El Tesoro 100% Blue Agave? Herradura Silver? Can you detect the nuances between cointreau and triple sec? Not yet? Then go to **Maria's New Mexican Kitchen**, at 555 West Cordova Road just off St. Francis Drive, designate a driver, and spend the evening running your own tests. Order the tender chile-barbecue ribs, and the bacon-chile quesadillas, oozing with melted cheese. Owner Al Lucero, a native Santa Fean, has incorporated many of his family's recipes into the menu of this long-established eatery. Check out the "soupy" beans and have a side of the *posole.* Al recommends an egg on any enchilada, "to tie the flavors together." No glitzy atmosphere (they added on as they grew), just wonderfully authentic local funk. And oh, those margaritas!

Just remember that for the morning after, anything with chile will set you back right with the sunny, blue-skied day awaiting you. *Huevos rancheros* Christmas style, with a side of *refritos* and *posole,* for example, will do the job—and now you know where to find them.

SANTA FE WINE AND CHILE FIESTA

Santa Fe has become an international mecca for serious foodies, and the star of the culinary show is the chile. Talented chefs from local restaurants have created myriad signature styles, from the very traditional to the wild nouvelle. A few of the local restaurateurs decided to celebrate and show off this fabulous eclectic cuisine. They invited 50 of the best restaurants and 50 hand-picked wineries from California, Spain, France, and New Mexico to demonstrate that this fine cooking style can make a successful, if sometimes adventurous, marriage with fine wines.

The result is a yearly party for a week in September, at harvest time, including cooking classes with famous visiting and local chefs; guided tours of the chile, garlic, and fruit farms in northern valleys; and early-morning trail rides up mesas culminating in campfire breakfasts.

There are wine classes, wine tastings, and wine dinners at the local restaurants, a Champagne brunch in a bucolic setting, and a black-tie "big bottle" auction, with wines served by all the participating wineries and hors d'oeuvres from the invited restaurants. The Grand Tasting takes place on Saturday at the Hotel Eldorado, where each of the 50 restaurants serves samples of a dish of its own design involving chiles, and the 50 wineries pour up to four different vintages each. The sheer abundance of great food, show-stopping cookery, and superb wines is staggering.

The dates of the third annual Wine and Chile Fiesta are September 21 to 26 this year. For reservations, prices, and more information, write The Santa Fe Wine and Chile Fiesta, 112 West San Francisco, Suite 303-68, Santa Fe, NM 87501; Tel: 982-8686.

—*Judyth Hill*

NIGHTLIFE

Santa Fe has very recently begun to develop a nightlife. Of sorts, that is. This is not the town that never sleeps. This is a town that pulls its covers up over its head, snuggles in, and oversleeps the snooze alarm. But as a result of an influx of newcomers from California and New York in the past few years, Santa Fe has stretched, yawned, and managed to extend its hours to after 10:00 P.M.—but not much after.

Actually, there have always been a few fun places to drink and dance, to meet and mingle. What was missing was somewhere decent to eat out late, other than the American road-food scene on the strip along Cerrillos Road. But that need has now been met in high style, and if you take it in stride that Santa Fe is just not much of a late-night party animal, you may find that the après-dinner amusements available will do nicely.

BARS

If real Santa Fe ambience is your desire, the classy, classic environs of the **Dragon Room**, the lounge adjunct of the famous Pink Adobe Restaurant at 406 Old Santa Fe Trail, should do nicely. This is where both the real artists and those who want to be hang out. Especially the wannabes on dates; this is the town's socially correct singles scene, where you might meet someone you could introduce to your family. The Dragon Room makes great margaritas and bloody Marias, and serves bar snacks that verge on minimeals, like the excellent Pink Adobe green chile stew. Plus there's the ever-replenished bowls of free popcorn. The Dragon Room is open seven nights, with live classical and Hispanic guitar every night except Fridays and Saturdays. There is no cover charge—that would be déclassé. Call for hours; Tel: 983-7712.

If you're desiring a romantic tête-à-tête, the **Staab House** bar in La Posada Hotel at 330 East Palace Avenue is an elegant Victorian parlor, with a glowing fireplace in the winter. In the summer you can drink out on the pretty patio, which has a fountain and overlooks a rose bower and the manicured swimming-pool area. The lounge features a series of small antiques-filled rooms with cushioned love seats that hearken back to a more graceful era. This wonderful place is open seven nights and, of course, there is no cover charge.

A good piano bar is always a treat, and Santa Fe has a couple. The **Palace Restaurant**, at 142 West Palace Avenue, has for years been the place for the local business folk and politicians to belly up and sing along. Mixologist Alphonso, who has been at the Palace for nigh-on always, wins the local paper's Best Bartender Award year after year. Open seven nights; no cover charge. Tel: 982-9891.

Vanessie's, formally Vanessie of Santa Fe, at 434 West San Francisco Street, has talented barkeeps as well: They keep a card file of crazy drinks, and an evening of stump-the-bartender is always fun. Piano player Doug Montgomery knows all and plays all. Open seven nights, with no cover charge; Tel: 982-9966.

A bar with a great view? The **Ore House** on the plaza, upstairs at the southwest corner of Lincoln and San Francisco streets, was in years past an excellent restaurant. These days the balcony bar, which is the town's only bar directly on the plaza, is its best attribute. They have live music on the weekends, but avoid the "blue margaritas." The Ore House is open seven nights; Tel: 983-8687.

Words fail to convey exactly the charms of **Evangelos**, 200 West San Francisco at the corner of Galisteo Street. Affectionately known as Nick's to the many locals who frequent this Santa Fe landmark, Evangelos, with its bizarro/Polynesian decor, is a "must visit." All the opera stars do; in fact, the downstairs pool hall is frequented by the most unlikely combination of superchic and basic barfly to be found in town. Proceed with the singles scene here at your own risk; this is the kind of place to meet people you may need to support. Nick's motto is "No Bud," and he carries a fabulous assortment of international beers. The jukebox is the best in town. Open every night; there is a cover charge only one night a year: Fiesta Friday. Tel: 982-9014. (But there's not really any reason to call Nick's other than to look for a wayward mate, and the bartenders are trained not to tell: It's that kind of place.)

The swanky **Eldorado Hotel Courtyard and Lounge**, at 309 West San Francisco, is a terrific place to relax in an elegant space on comfortable couches. There is live music nightly, ranging from classical Spanish guitar to jazz to the excellent local pianist/icon, John Gooch. There is no cover charge unless there is a special show, and the appetizers, especially the nachos, are first-rate. The Eldorado is open seven nights; Tel: 988-4455.

The very chic restaurant **Geronimo**, up at 724 Canyon Road, has an intimate bar with a kiva fireplace and a pretty patio with a fountain. They also have a long front porch that's a superb place to end an evening on the town with a quiet drink under the stars. Geronimo's is open seven nights; Tel: 982-1500.

La Casa Sena Cantina, in Sena Plaza at 125 East Palace next door to La Casa Sena Restaurant, provides one of the best nights out to be found in Santa Fe. Manager—and lyric baritone—Greg Grissom heads up a team of rigorously rehearsed, star-quality singers and performers (all of whom are doubling as your waiters and waitresses) in cabaret-style performances of Broadway show music, as well as popular selections from the 1940s to the present. The sheer vocal quality of the performances is dazzling, as is the prevailing good mood. The margaritas are top-notch, and the bar is serviced by La Casa Sena's kitchen, so the food is excellent. Open seven nights; there is never a cover charge. Tel: 988-9232.

DANCING

Chez What, at 213 West Alameda, features live bands to bop 'til you drop on Tuesday, Friday, and Saturday nights. Mondays, Wednesdays, and Thursdays a disc jockey spins dance music. There is a small cover charge. No food is served, but a full bar is available. Closed Sundays; Tel: 982-0099.

Luna, at 519 Cerrillos Road, is Santa Fe's latest addition to the night scene, with a stylish bar, gallery, pool parlor, and dance-hall combo that has taken the town by storm. Luna books local artists and au courant national acts, and the huge warehouse dance floor (and the *80-foot-long bar*) is usually packed. There are go-go dancers on Friday and Saturday nights, and a cover charge that varies depending on the event. Luna is open evenings. It is best to call for exact days and hours; Luna tends to close on Mondays, unless. . . . Tel: 989-4888.

The very trendy nightclub **Edge**, on the third floor at 135 West Palace, also has a hip, creative booking style and high-energy vibes. There are live blues acts, "trash disco" (pop jumpin' jivey stuff), raucous dance music, classy songsmiths, a state-of-the-art dance floor, a king's ransom in high-tech lighting, and video screens. Edge also happens to be one of the best restaurants in town, and that puts them tops in the late-night eats department. The kitchen usually stays open until 1:00 A.M.; full bar service, of course. Edge is open seven nights and the cover charge varies; Tel: 986-1700.

LATE-NIGHT EATERIES

Eleven at night may not seem terribly late to you, but for Santa Fe, it's pushing the limit. That's what makes **Pranzo Italian Grill** at 540 Montezuma Avenue such a standout— not to mention wonderful pizzas and antipasti, a very impressive wine list, and great bartenders. This is a very popular place to burn the candle at the late-night end. This is also a good place for that slice of something rich and chocolatey with a steaming cup of cappuccino. Pranzo has recently added a second-floor balcony patio, where you can sup and sip with a lovely view of the town. Open seven nights; Tel: 984-2645.

The **San Francisco Street Bar & Grill**, at 114 West San Francisco Street, makes great margaritas and the best green chile cheeseburger in town. Their homemade soups are also excellent. The Grill is open seven days, and they serve continuously from 11:00 A.M. until 11:00 P.M.; Tel: 982-2044.

—Judyth Hill

SHOPS AND SHOPPING

Santa Fe is a shopper's dream come true. Whether it be such special things as Indian-made silver-and-turquoise jewelry, custom-fitted cowboy boots, Moorish folk art, or paintings by Frederic Remington, you can buy it in the City Different.

Many visitors here quickly fall in love with the Indian-made arts and crafts sold in Santa Fe; these include handwoven wool rugs, pottery, kachina dolls, fetishes, sand paintings, and, in particular, jewelry. All but the latter should be purchased from reputable dealers to ensure quality and authenticity. Stores that belong to the Indian Arts & Crafts Association—a self-regulating group of dealers in Indian crafts—for instance, can usually be trusted. Buying Pueblo or Navajo Indian jewelry, on the other hand, requires a different shopping strategy, because top-quality items are available not only from stores but from street vendors as well. A few basic facts about the history and manufacture of silver and turquoise jewelry might help when making a purchase.

Silver. Although Southwestern Indians have worn jewelry created from shell, turquoise, and other materials for centuries, the Indian love of silver originated shortly after the arrival of the Spanish, in the early 17th century. Navajo warriors often stole silver bridles and other horse trappings from the conquistadors, for instance, and in later times traded sheep to Mexican silversmiths for jewelry.

Contemporary ideas of "Indian jewelry" began to evolve in the Southwest only about 100 years ago, however. In the late 19th century Mexican silversmiths were employed by the Hubbell Trading Post in Arizona (see the Four Corners chapter) to teach Athabaskan Navajos the art of metalworking, and sometime between 1884 and

1899 chunks of turquoise set in silver belts, bracelets, and rings began to appear. Until the 1970s, the major characteristic of Navajo jewelry was that silver settings were created to fit stones that had been shaped by nature, not cut to fit settings (as in Zuni jewelry). However, today Navajo jewelry employs slices, nuggets, and cabichons (dome cuts) of turquoise, and occasionally coral. The Navajo are known as the silver beads masters, and their silver is also sometimes stamped with geometric designs, which accent turquoise and other stones.

The pueblo-dwelling Zuni Indians learned silversmithing from the Navajos, but quickly developed their own stone-to-stone inlay style by cutting and shaping turquoise, lapis, mother-of-pearl, coral, and other stones to fit silver settings. Some of their work today also employs thin silver "channels" between the stones, known as channel work. With their needlepoint or petit point methods they create individual bezels for tiny domed pieces of turquoise, which are then set into a brooch, bracelet, ring, or pendant. The Zunis' carved fetish work creates tiny animal or bird forms from various stones that are then strung with tiny "heshe" beads to form colorful necklaces. Hopi Indians, in turn (also pueblo dwellers), learned from the Zuni, but developed an entirely new style by using silver-on-silver overlays—the top layer cut out, usually in the shapes of animals, the bottom layer often blackened for contrast—in place of turquoise.

Turquoise. In the romantic world of lovers and legends, turquoise is known for its powers of protection; wear it and no harm will come your way. In the no-nonsense world of geological science, the stone is called cuprous aluminum phosphate; its blue and green colors are determined by varying chemical combinations of copper.

Turquoise is found naturally in the Southwest and in other parts of the world in a wide variety of shades and compositions, but is usually a soft, porous stone colored blue, blue green, or green. Turquoise nuggets are often injected with plastic resins to produce "stabilized turquoise," used by some craftspeople in carving fetishes. These stabilized stones are of little intrinsic value, however, and jewelry containing this type of turquoise is generally considered costume jewelry. Gemstone quality, nonstabilized turquoise, hard enough to cut and polish to a high luster, is what you should look for. The best way to tell the difference is color: Quality, nonstabilized turquoise is usually many-hued and has a matrix (a network of tiny veins) of copper; stabilized turquoise is a solid color, usually bright blue, and bears a strong resemblance to the plastic resin with which it has been injected.

Nearly all of the Indian tribes in the Southwest now make some type of silver or silver-and-turquoise jewelry. Among the most prolific are the people of Santo Domingo Pueblo, but the art form is widespread and lucrative; many local artisans, from a number of different tribes, have become wealthy from the sales of jewelry. The search for these beautiful items—concho belts (round or oval-shaped pieces of silver, often decorated with chunks of turquoise or coral, that are strung together with leather), rings, necklaces, earrings, and so on—can lead shoppers on a wonderful and exciting treasure hunt through Santa Fe. Keep in mind, however, that you get what you pay for. If you're looking for an investment, don't hesitate to spend the money; prices are astonishingly high for older, often better-made silver, or silver-and-turquoise, jewelry referred to as "pawn." If you just want an attractive addition to your jewelry collection, on the other hand, there are extraordinary, beautiful pieces in Santa Fe that will fit every budget.

The Plaza Area

The historic Santa Fe plaza, old and new heart of the city, is where most visitors head first. Many shoppers could stay within a few blocks of this ancient, tree-shaded square for their entire Santa Fe stopover and still manage easily to fill several suitcases with fine Southwestern goods.

On the plaza's southeast corner at 61 Old Santa Fe Trail, **Packard's Indian Trading Company Inc.** boasts a huge collection of one-of-a-kind and beautifully made jewelry, pots, rugs, kachinas (spirit dolls), and fetishes. Prices can run high here, but Packard's reputation is first-rate. Next door to the north on Old Santa Fe Trail is **Eagle Dancer**, also dealing in silver-and-turquoise jewelry and pottery.

On the northeast corner of the plaza, at the junction of Santa Fe Trail and Palace Avenue, **Santa Fe Dry Goods** sells cowboy boots, denim shirts, and expensive designer jeans—the ensemble to go with all your new jewelry. A right turn onto Palace will take you to **James Reid Ltd.**, which features silver belt buckles, bolo ties, concho belts, bracelets, and earrings as well as museum-quality antiques, Indian weavings, and pottery. Santa Fe craftsman James Weller's furniture is also sold here.

If you want to outfit your dream home (or one-room

apartment) in Santa Fe style, stop in next door at **Tara Tucker Ltd.**, where graceful wrought-iron bed frames and pseudo cowhide-covered throw pillows are part of the offerings. Across the street **Ross LewAllen Jewelry**, at number 105, specializes in original silver pieces inspired by designs from Africa, Egypt, and South America, at reasonable prices. **Frank Patania**, whose shop is a few doors east at number 119, has been designing silver jewelry in Santa Fe for 65 years; in addition to Patania's own work, the shop also features Navajo silverwork and New Guinea tribal art. Farther away from the plaza, a few doors east from Patania's, **Barbara Zusman's Art and Antiques** sells pawn and Mexican jewelry, Russian icons, exotic textiles, folk and pre-Columbian art, and stained glass paintings.

In **Sena Plaza**, a small shopping complex on Palace Avenue half a block east of Santa Fe Trail, **Soap Opera** offers a fine collection of soaps, lotions, and bath oils. Here, too, is **Gusterman's**, appealing to shoppers who appreciate modern silver and gemstone designs, and **Pachamama**, specializing in antique and traditional folk art from Latin America. If you're in need of sweet sustenance, return to Palace Avenue by detouring through **Señor Murphy's Candymaker**; a hunk of Murphy's delicious piñon fudge will revitalize your spirit if not your pocketbook.

Back toward the plaza, then north (right) about 20 feet on Washington Avenue, is the **Museum Shop** of the **Palace of the Governors**, where you can buy books on the Southwest, posters, fetishes, postcards, jewelry, and Pueblo Indian pottery. It's more fun to buy Indian-made wares from the Indians themselves, however. On the plaza's north side beneath the Palace of the Governors *portal,* local pueblo people display all sorts of handcrafted wares at fairly reasonable prices, from sand paintings and rugs to pottery and jewelry. All goods sold here, by the way, must meet the museum's quality standards (don't be afraid to ask questions about how, and by whom, any item was made, when shopping "under the portal"). To the west of the portal at the corner of Lincoln and Palace, the **Museum Shop** of the **Museum of Fine Arts** offers a fine selection of books on international and regional art. Contemporary Northern New Mexican crafts, silk scarves, pottery, and blown-glass pieces are also sold here.

Shops selling Navajo and Pueblo Indian jewelry, Navajo textiles, Pueblo pottery, Southwestern art, and similar items are plentiful on **San Francisco Street**, the plaza's southern boundary, directly across from the Palace of the Governors' portal. The stores with the best reputations here are probably **Ortegas Turquoise Mesa**, **Ray Tracy Galleries**, and **Simply Santa Fe**. **Dewey Galleries**, at 74 East San Francisco, also sells Mexican and New Mexican-style furniture, while **Tom Taylor**, at number 100 (street-side in La Fonda Hotel), offers a fine selection of custom-made cowboy boots.

West San Francisco Street and the Galisteo Street Area

About a block west of the plaza on San Francisco Street **Nambé Mills Showroom**, 112 West San Francisco, sells Nambé Ware, a locally made metal serving- and dinner-ware with an international reputation for quality and beauty. A few doors farther west you'll find beautiful but expensive hand-knit Southwestern-motif sweaters in **Jane Smith Ltd.**; directly across the street at **Base Camp**, sports enthusiasts are welcome to meander through a complete line of high-quality camping, hiking, and cross-country skiing gear. Not to be missed is **Margolis and Moss**, at 120 West San Francisco, specializing in rare books and photographs; browsers are also welcome at **Origins**, at number 135, with its collection of ethnic clothing, jewelry, and artifacts from around the world.

West San Francisco is also home to three other fine bookstores: **Santa Fe Booksellers** (number 203) specializes in art publications and new and out-of-print books on the Southwest; **Collected Works Bookshop** (number 208B) sells books on poetry, travel, and photography, along with the latest fiction and nonfiction; **Caxton Books and Music** (number 216) carries a wide range of maps, hard- and soft-cover books on travel and the Southwest, and a large assortment of CDs, cassettes, and records.

Galisteo Street turns south off San Francisco two blocks west of the plaza. **Montecristi Custom Hat Works**, at 118 Galisteo, produces expensive Panama hats, but also sells less-costly headgear and an excellent selection of hat bands. Across the street at exotic **Vi Vi of Santa Fe** you'll find "blanket coats," leather-fringed jackets, tapestry vests, and crushed-rayon-and-taffeta broomstick skirts.

Quilt lovers should stop by **Quilts to Cover Your Fantasy** at 201 Galisteo and ogle the collection of South-western-design quilts and wall hangings. The **Elizabeth Drey Collection**, number 209, carries an eclectic mix of custom-made leather furniture and clothing, African baskets, jewelry, and rugs. At **Foreign Traders**, 202 Galisteo, and nearby **Artesanos Imports** you can buy handcrafted furniture, pottery, hand-painted tiles, and lots of other imported goodies from Mexico and Latin America. **Seret and Sons Rugs and Tapestries**, 224 Galisteo, offers large selections of rugs and carpets, mostly from foreign climes. They will also reupholster your furniture in the carpet of your choice. **Taos Furniture**, on the corner of Galisteo and Alameda, sells handmade ponderosa pine furnishings designed and built by local craftspeople.

On the corner of West Water and Don Gaspar streets, one block south of the plaza, **Doodlet's** features charming porcelain ware, tin boxes, cards, stocking stuffers, and other trinkets. For chile addicts **The Chile Shop**, 109 West Water Street, boasts a wide array of dried chiles, chili powder and sauces, chile-decorated dinnerware, and even chile-shaped Christmas lights.

The Guadalupe Street Area

Four blocks due west from the plaza is Guadalupe Street, one of the city's principal north–south thoroughfares. The northern end of Guadalupe is lined with hotels, banks, and parking lots. South across the Santa Fe River past the historic Santuario de Guadalupe, however, eight or ten refurbished blocks of the street (officially known as the Guadalupe Railroad Historic District) offer a turn-of-the-century atmosphere as well as some of Santa Fe's finest shops.

If you're fond of pictures, for instance, drop in at **Scheinbaum and Russek Ltd.**, 328 South Guadalupe, dealing in rare and contemporary photography, and representing such internationally known photographers as Henri Cartier-Bresson, Eliot Porter, and Laura Gilpin. Several doors down at **Pierre Mahaim Rugs and Antiques**, 405 South Guadalupe, examine the collection of Moorish decorative accessories, tribal rugs, pottery, and folk-art furniture. **Worldly Possessions**, with an entrance on Guadalupe but actually located at 330 Garfield Street, specializes in tribal and folk art and artifacts, textiles, and wood carvings. If you like to fish, or simply talk about it, head for the **High Desert Angler** at 435 South Guadalupe. The shop sells licenses and quality fishing gear, and the staff is happy to offer advice on the best fishing spots or set you up with a guide.

Sanbusco Market Center—once a huge lumber warehouse and now the anchor of the Guadalupe Railroad

Historic District—is one block west of Guadalupe on Montezuma Avenue (turn west at the only stoplight). **Los Llanos Bookstore** here has one of the largest collections of Southwestern and Indian books in Santa Fe. In **The Winery** you can sample (and purchase) the best wines New Mexico has to offer. Clothing freaks might like **Sew Natural**, which sells patterns and fabrics for "broom" skirts and other Southwestern-style clothing, and **Santa Fe Outfitters**, which specializes in designer jeans and "soft" outdoor wear. The Farmer's Market is also held in the Sanbusco parking lot Tuesday and Thursday mornings, spring through fall.

The Canyon Road Area

Canyon Road, a ten-minute walk southeast of the plaza along Paseo de Peralta, was the nucleus of Santa Fe's art community during the 1920s, and not much has changed since then. A bumper sticker proclaims the neighborhood is the "art and soul of Santa Fe," and, with few exceptions, businesses here are centered on showing and selling art of one form or another.

One of the best known of Santa Fe's art showplaces is **Fenn Galleries**, at 1075 Paseo de Peralta, a long block south of the Canyon Road–Paseo de Peralta junction. Fenn's superb collection includes paintings and sculptures by Frederic Remington, Charles Russell, and Georgia O'Keeffe, as well as works from the Taos and Santa Fe schools.

Mabel's, on the corner of Canyon Road and Paseo de Peralta, is a must for animal lovers. Inside you'll find whimsical, handcrafted items with animal motifs, such as bear chairs for adults and children, for example, and hand-painted sweaters, mirrors, and hooked rugs that also feature animal designs.

The compound at 225 Canyon Road has several shops of interest, among them the **Munson Gallery**, which represents 25 regional artists, and **Spider Woman Designs**, which sells antique Southwestern and Mexican textiles. Two blocks east, in a historic red-brick schoolhouse, is the **Linda Durham Gallery**, where you can see the works of several well-known New Mexican painters and sculptors. **Copeland-Rutherford Fine-Arts Ltd.**, in the rear at 403 Canyon Road, and **Galeria Capistrano**, at number 409, also feature contemporary New Mexican artists, painters, and photographers, among them T.C. Cannon, Helen Hardin, and Tony Ortega.

At the intersection of Canyon Road and Garcia Street,

Blue Door Art and Antiques sells affordable furniture, antiques, and sculpture, while **Robert F. Nichols**, a few doors east, features decorative folk art such as 19th- and 20th-century hand-carved birds, antique quilts, and furniture. **Economos Works of Art**, at 500 Canyon Road, displays an eclectic mix of fine-quality Indian, African, Oceanic, and pre-Columbian art, as well as antique Mexican and New Mexican colonial furniture and decorations. **Morning Star Gallery**, located in a 19th-century Spanish hacienda, is the largest dealer of antique Indian art in the United States (the collection here is museum quality), and sells textiles, jewelry, kachinas, pueblo ceramics, basketry, and carvings.

Colonial and contemporary Latin American art, jewelry, textiles, and pottery are the specialties of **Throckmorton Fine Arts** at 550 Canyon Road. Close by, at number 555, **Nedra Matteucci Fine Arts** displays the work of Southwestern Impressionists, Realists, and landscape painters. The **Claiborne Gallery**, number 558, is well known for its extraordinary collections of primitive Mexican furniture, and half a block east **Al Luckett, Jr., Fine Paintings and Antiques** deals in fine-quality New Mexico furniture and religious wood carvings.

Weaver Alice Parrott has been designing and creating tapestries, rugs, and textiles for more than 35 years; many are featured at **The Market—Alice Kagawa Parrott's Handweaving Fabrics**, at 634 Canyon Road. Across the street the **Zaplin-Lampert Gallery** shows watercolors, drawings, and prints of the American West by 19th- and 20th-century artists. At **Quilts Ltd.** aficionados will find an extensive collection of traditional, current, and vintage creations, and at nearby **Kania-Ferrin Gallery** the collection of antique Indian basketry, kachinas, and pottery is worth a look. **Umbrello Showroom**, 701 Canyon, beautifully displays antiques, metal photograph frames, dinnerware, and cotton fabrics from Mexico; across the street at **Gypsy Alley** working artists give studio tours to visitors.

Other Shopping

Perhaps the best bargains on Indian-made silver-and-turquoise jewelry in Santa Fe can be found at **Sissel's Fine Indian Jewelry & Leather Goods**, at 2900 Cerrillos Road (about 3 miles/5 km south of the plaza). Quality here is excellent, and everything in the store is permanently reduced by 50 to 70 percent. In other words, the same pair of earrings that cost $150 at a downtown store will cost you about $45 at Sissel's.

Four blocks south of the plaza on Old Santa Fe Trail, **Arrowsmith's Relics of the Old West** is a browser's heaven. You never know what you'll find here, but the shop specializes in quality Indian jewelry and beadwork, saddles, old guns, and pottery. And if you follow old Santa Fe Trail south to the junction of Camino Lejo (about 1½ miles/2½ km) and turn right to the Santa Fe Museum complex on Camino Lejo, you'll find the **Museum Shop** of the **Museum of Indian Arts and Culture**. The store boasts a nice assortment of handmade jewelry, inlaid belt buckles, turquoise-studded silver boxes, kachinas, books on the Southwest, pottery, fetishes, and Apache, Navajo, and Hopi baskets. In the same complex the **Museum Shop** of the **Museum of International Folk Art** sells arts and crafts ranging from jewelry to handmade toys. At the **Wheelwright Museum of the American Indian**, also in the museum complex, the **Case Trading Post** has a fine collection of old (pawn) jewelry, Pueblo pottery, Hopi baskets, Navajo blankets, fetishes, and kachina dolls.

—*Stephanie Boyle Mays*

AROUND SANTA FE

By Buddy Mays

The vast and varied patchwork quilt of the Northern New Mexico terrain surrounding Santa Fe boasts a scenic and historic grandeur enjoyed by few other regions of the Southwest. Towering peaks stand guard over an arid but nonetheless bounteous landscape of blue shadows and golden earth that has been occupied by human beings for more than 12 millennia. Neolithic nomads hunted mammoth and long-horned bison here on the high, grass-covered plains; it was here too that, later, wandering clans of Anasazi Indians emigrated when they were driven from their traditional northern homes by ferocious Shoshone newcomers.

Decades before the Pilgrims stumbled ashore at Plymouth Rock, Spanish conquistadors and Catholic priests searched Northern New Mexico for El Dorado (treasure) and for saveable souls. Close on their heels came travel-weary Spanish colonists, carving a nouvelle-European civilization from the isolated and untamed countryside. Last to arrive, much later, were the North Americans—trappers and traders at first, then paradise-bound settlers aboard giant Conestoga wagons on the Santa Fe Trail.

This heterogeneous, tricultural stew rich in history, tradition, and scenic beauty has created in Northern New Mexico one of the Southwest's most rewarding vacation destinations. It has been said that most visitors see more of Northern New Mexico with their hearts than with their eyes, and few who have been here will disagree. "When your spirit cries for peace," wrote one lover of the land earlier this century, "come to a world of canyons deep in

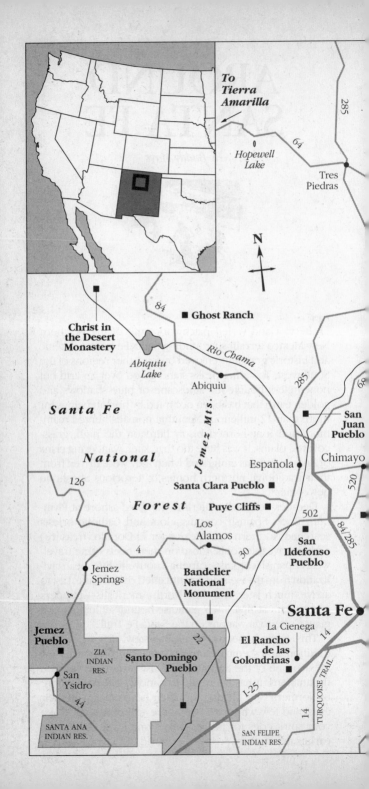

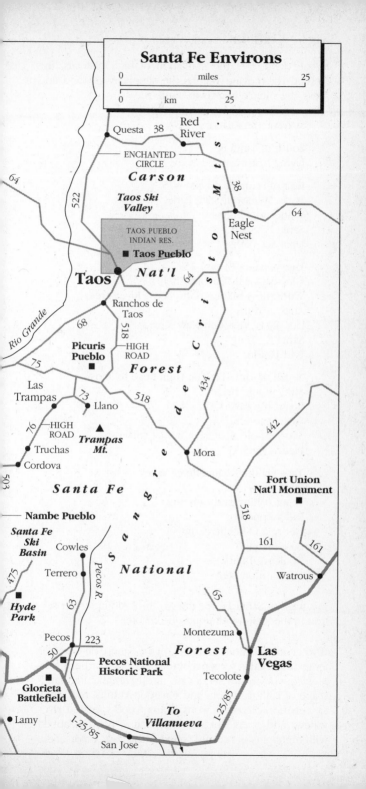

an old land; feel the exultation of high plateaus, the strength of moving waters, the simplicity of sand and grass, the silence of growth." Still true.

MAJOR INTEREST

South of Santa Fe
Living historical museum

East of Santa Fe on NM 475
Hyde Memorial State Park
Wilderness hiking
Santa Fe Ski Basin
Japanese baths

East of Santa Fe on I-25
Glorieta Civil War battlefield
Wilderness hiking in the Pecos River area
Anasazi ruins
Las Vegas: Victorian New Mexico
Santa Fe Trail
Fort Union

North of Santa Fe: The High Road to Taos
Miraculous shrine
Spanish weavers
Wood-carvers
300-year-old Spanish colonial villages
Picuris Pueblo

Taos via the Chama River Valley
Puye Cliffs
Trout fishing and camping
Indian pueblos
Georgia O'Keeffe country
Bass fishing
Zoological park
Desert monastery

For **west of Santa Fe** see the North of Albuquerque section in the Around Albuquerque chapter.

If you could clamber to the top of the Sangre de Cristo or Jemez mountains for a panoramic view of Northern New Mexico, you would see a vast, mostly uninhabited landscape of rolling, piñon- and pine-dotted hills, rocky mesas, erosion-carved canyons, cottonwood-speckled river valleys, and open, grass-covered plains. Brown dabbed with highlights of red and yellow is the basic color of the earth here, splotched by a hundred different shades of green. Because of the rugged terrain, human habitation is minimal. Most people reside on small farms and ranches and in tiny mountain villages and Indian pueblos; with the exception of Santa Fe and Española, cities simply do not exist.

If you could measure distances from your lofty vantage point you would find that all of the attractions discussed in this chapter can be easily reached by car from Santa Fe in less than a day. Accommodations are available in some outlying areas, but with a few notable exceptions—the Plaza Hotel in Las Vegas, Hacienda Rancho de Chimayo in Chimayo village, the Truchas Farm House Bed & Breakfast in Truchas, and Ghost Ranch near Abiquiu (see the Accommodations Reference at the end of the chapter)—they are usually small, inexpensive, and sometimes not too clean motels without style or tradition. Restaurants, too, are basic (again, there are a few notable exceptions), and neither offer nor know the meaning of "fine cuisine." Most visitors find that it's far less of a hassle in most cases to base themselves in Santa Fe, explore the surrounding countryside during the day, then return to the City Different at night.

Several of the suggested drives in this chapter end in the historic art colony of Taos to the north. You can also reach Taos from Santa Fe by a more direct and much faster route: U.S. 84/285 north to Española, then northeast on NM 68. (Take St. Francis Drive north out of Sante Fe; it becomes U.S. 84/285 at the city limits.) This direct drive, which follows the Rio Grande for much of the way, takes slightly more than an hour. (That sinister-looking gap running across the plateau to your left as you near Ranchos de Taos on NM 68 is the dramatic and deep Rio Grande gorge.)

The telephone area code for New Mexico is 505.

SOUTH OF SANTA FE

An elderly, black-clad señora using a hand-carved wooden paddle slides crisp brown loaves of fresh-baked bread from a squat adobe oven. Nearby, on the porch of a weathered log cabin, another Spanish matriarch cards newly sheared wool with hand-hewn tools. In a neighboring barn her sun-wizened husband butchers a hog while a girl of ten—probably a granddaughter—grinds kernels of dried corn to meal on a stone *metate*. Wood smoke pours from the cabin's mud chimney, farm animals wander unattended, and the tangy odor of roasting chiles permeates the summer air.

If you think you're in a small Spanish village somewhere near Barcelona, that's understandable. The sights, sounds, and odors at **El Rancho de las Golondrinas** (The Ranch of the Swallows), 10 miles (16 km) southwest of Santa Fe, can play tricks on your senses. In reality the ranch is a 200-acre living historical museum located in the village of La Cienega. Originally a *paraje* (rest stop) on the old Camino Real from Mexico City to Spanish-occupied New Mexico, today this incredible attraction weaves an absorbing tapestry of colonial life in the 18th- and 19th-century Southwest.

A network of well-marked pathways leads visitors to a working blacksmith shop, an 18th-century grist mill, a restored Penitente *morada* (church), an ancient mountain village, and scores of similar exhibits. On special festival days (the first weekends in June, August, and October) traditionally dressed Hispanic volunteers offer demonstrations in the arts, crafts, farming techniques, and other daily activities of early New Mexico settlers. Museum visitors can also sample traditional Spanish colonial food, dance to 300-year-old music played on handmade instruments, help weave a wool rug, or even learn how to skin a hog.

The creator of the museum was Y. A. Paloheimo, a retired Finnish diplomat who for 30 years collected colonial buildings and artifacts from throughout New Mexico. In 1971 Paloheimo leased the ranch to the Colonial New Mexico Historical Society, which, with the help of volunteers from the state's tiny mountain villages, operates it today.

The easiest way to the ranch from Santa Fe is via I-25 south for about 5 miles (8 km) to exit 271; then follow the signs. The museum is normally open from June through August, but special tours can be arranged at other times by calling ahead; Tel: 471-2261. Hours are 10:00 A.M. to 4:00 P.M. Wednesday through Sunday; there is a small entry fee.

Just south of Santa Fe, NM 14—the Turquoise Trail, which we cover in the Albuquerque chapter—branches off from I-25 and runs down to I-40 a bit east of Albuquerque. A few miles down NM 14 is the **San Marcos Cafe**, which serves good New Mexican–style food. The carpet is dingy, service is slow, the chairs, tables, and flatwear are mismatched, and the small dining room is dimly lit and cluttered with tacky antiques. Nonetheless, the café, adjacent to the San Marcos Feed Store 12 miles (19 km) south of Santa Fe on NM 14 (the Turquoise Trail) offers burritos, chile stews, a variety of ever-changing daily specials (usually European in nature), and home-baked desserts that will melt in your mouth.

San Marcos is open Monday through Saturday, 8:00 A.M. to 2:00 P.M. and 5:30 to 8:00 P.M., and offers live entertainment on Friday and Saturday evenings; Sunday brunch, also with live entertainment, is served from 8:00 A.M. until 2:00 P.M. You can eat on the small outdoor patio in warm weather. Reservations aren't usually necessary.

EAST OF SANTA FE ON NM 475

Known as Ski Basin Road, Hyde Park Road, and Artist's Road, depending upon who is giving directions and where you are on it, manicured NM 475 whisks travellers from Santa Fe's rather cosmopolitan ambience northeast to the towering peaks, lovely forests, and tranquil seclusion of the Sangre de Cristo Mountains in a matter of minutes. The highway (known here as Artist's Road) begins just four blocks north of the Santa Fe plaza, where it turns east off Washington Avenue.

Hyde Memorial State Park, 8 miles (13 km) up the mountain, was established in 1938 as New Mexico's very first mountain-forest park. Bisected by the Little Tesuque River and encompassing 350 acres of steep pine- and piñon-covered terrain, this undeveloped mix of mountain slope and river canyon is a soothing contrast to the busy streets of Santa Fe a few miles to the west.

The land on which the park was established was a gift to the state from noted educator and naturalist Benjamin Talbot Babbit Hyde. Five well-marked, well-maintained nature trails wind through the reserve, two of them joining longer wilderness trails in the nearby Santa Fe National Forest. The hiking routes are steep (if you plan to hike far, take it easy at first; remember that elevations here range from 8,500 to 9,000 feet), but they offer great views of the nearby high plains and of the Sangre de Cristo Mountains. All major pathways begin at the easily spotted manager's office, roadside.

Winter visitors enjoy the park's ice-skating rink, sledding area, and cross-country ski trails; for hiking, the weather is best from April through October. Autumn is especially lovely here as the leaves of the willows and aspen trees along the Little Tesuque change from green to gold. Playgrounds, picnic areas, and several large campgrounds lie scattered along the river, the campgrounds with tables, fireplaces, and Adirondack-style shelters. Overnight camping fees are $7 to $14 per night.

Ten miles (16 km) beyond Hyde Park on NM 475, and surrounded by the Santa Fe National Forest, **Santa Fe Ski Basin** nestles in a chain of Alpine valleys just below Penitente Peak at the end of the road. In winter the basin's bonus is some of the most skiable snow (an average of 250 inches a year) in the Southwest. Eight major ski lifts and 38 groomed runs let powder lovers choose whatever terrain and difficulty level best matches their ability. The season is generally from Thanksgiving through mid-April. Lift lines are short and parking is no problem on weekdays, but if you don't like crowds stay away on weekends and major holidays.

In warmer months, if you're in good physical condition, consider making the all-day, eight-mile round-trip hike from the ski basin to Kathryn Lake via the **Windsor Trail**. The trailhead, on the north side of the ski basin parking lot, is well marked. This is serious trekking, with strenuous slopes and scree crossings (you may want to overnight at the lake), but the terrain and views are magnificent.

Windsor also connects to other trails that give hikers and backpackers access to most of the 167,000-acre **Pecos Wilderness**, part of the Santa Fe National Forest. This huge area of mountainous terrain, encompassing several 12,000-foot-high peaks, a dozen Alpine lakes, and hundreds of square miles of forest, is one of New Mexico's most beautiful and popular wild areas. Trail maps are available for a small fee at the U.S. Forest Service office at 1220 St. Francis Drive in Santa Fe.

On your return drive down the mountain to Santa Fe (the same way you came), try soaking your cares and stiffness away in refreshing seclusion at the **Ten Thousand Waves** Japanese bath house, about 5 miles (8 km) east of the city limits on the north side of NM 475. The private outdoor tubs are steaming hot, the air is clean, and the mountain views are spectacular at this upmarket, fairly expensive spa. Massage and other body and skin treatments are also available, for an additional fee. The use of robes, sandals, and towels, however, is included, as is the East Asian atmosphere.

EAST OF SANTA FE ON I-25

The wee village of **Lamy**, 8 miles (13 km) south of Santa Fe and just south of I-25 (exit the interstate at the U.S. 285 South junction and follow the signs; Lamy is down a road to the left off 285), barely borderline where cartographers are concerned, just large enough to rate a spot on the map. Among the hamlet's more notable structures are an Amtrak train station, a slightly askew community church, and a strangely asymmetrical house made of white plastic foam that resembles a Turkish mosque. A bit more orthodox and located just across the street from the train station is one of the area's best and oldest steak houses, the **Legal Tender Restaurant**. Besides lunch and dinner, this country bistro also renders a luscious Sunday brunch.

Glorieta Battlefield

It's a 13-mile (21-km) drive east on I-25 from the U.S. 285/Lamy turnoff to exit 299 and Glorieta Battlefield, site of the last Civil War battle fought in New Mexico. Once you've left the interstate, cross back over the highway, turn right on NM 50, and drive about 1 mile (1½ km). You'll see signs marking the site.

It was here in a rocky, cottonwood-lined canyon near old Pigeon's Ranch that volunteer Union forces under the command of onetime Methodist preacher Major John Chivington destroyed a Confederate wagon train of supplies and virtually broke the back of the Confederate army in the Southwest. Without food, ammunition, or horses, the Southerners, led by General Henry Hopkins Sibley, were forced to give up their northward march and flee into the unforgiving New Mexico desert south toward El Paso. Fragments of the adobe buildings of Pigeon's Ranch still exist, and a historical marker alongside the highway details the events of that bloody March day in 1862.

The Pecos Canyon

Farther east along NM 50, in the string village of Pecos ("string" indicates a community stretched along a river or creek like a string), the road ends in a T in the center of town. If you turn left onto NM 63 north (discussed in the NM 475 section, above) you'll follow the Pecos River up a steep-sided canyon toward the Santa Fe National Forest and the southern end of the Pecos Wilderness.

Monastery Lake, a few miles from the village, offers good fishing, but the trout are larger and feistier in the adjacent Pecos River. Most of the land between the northern boundary of the lake and the Dalton Fishing Area a few miles beyond is private, but starting at the Dalton Fishing Area you can cast a fly or dunk a worm wherever the stream isn't posted. Another fine but smaller stream for trout is Holy Ghost Creek, entering the main river near the tiny town of Terrero, some 5 miles (8 km) farther north along the Pecos River and the parallel NM 63. There's a spacious and seldom used campground at the end of the Holy Ghost access road; a hiker's trail over the mountains to the Santa Fe Ski Basin (a two-day hike; see NM 475, above) also begins here.

Past the Terrero store, NM 63 negotiates another 6 mountainous miles (10 km) through fir forest and aspen glade to end at the summer-home area of Cowles. From the road's-end parking lot, hikers (or cross-country skiers in winter) can access the Pecos Wilderness on several trails.

Pecos National Historic Park

If you turn right at the stop sign in Pecos, you'll take NM 63 south to Pecos National Historic Park, 2 miles (3 km) from the village. Straddling a low, grass-covered ridge, the crumbling Spanish mission at this ancient archaeological site is a structural wonder. Built like a fortress, the church was not meant to be destroyed easily; the walls in some places are seven feet thick and the roof beams weigh several tons each. Though it is nowhere officially proclaimed, perhaps the bastionlike building was a reminder from the Spanish priests to their Indian converts that God and the Church were invincible.

The Anasazi Indians who once resided in what is now a destroyed pueblo adjacent to the mission first arrived in the upper Pecos Valley about A.D. 1100. The pueblo village itself was probably constructed sometime in the 1400s, though scientists seem unsure about exact dates. When Spanish priests took up residence in the early 17th century they constructed the mission using conscripted Indian labor, then immediately attempted to extinguish traditional Indian beliefs. The mission was partially destroyed in the Pueblo revolt of 1680 but was rebuilt when the Spaniards returned in 1692. In 1781, however, an epidemic of smallpox wiped out many of the pueblo's inhabitants, and 57 years later the last 17 survivors of the town moved to the pueblo of Jemez.

Be sure to visit the monument's small but excellent museum before walking the self-guiding trail—beginning at the visitors' center—that wanders through the mission ruins and the unexcavated remnants of a five-story Anasazi pueblo. You'll need about an hour to visit the entire monument, but most visitors take longer.

Toward Las Vegas

NM 63 continues south from the monument, eventually to rejoin I-25 at the village of Rowe. The piñon-dotted hill country through which the road travels on its way to the interstate is part of the Forked Lightning Ranch, once owned by movie star Greer Garson but recently given to Pecos National Historic Park. Uninvited visitors aren't yet welcome on the ranch, but eagle-eyed motorists can spot the huge main house in the river valley to the left.

Return to the interstate at Rowe and for the next 30 miles heading east enjoy one of the most eye-pleasing arrays of high-speed highway scenery in the state. Skirting the southern foot of the Sangre de Cristo Mountains, I-25 slices through a mellow landscape of ocher hills, wind-swept valleys, and staggering vistas before angling east into the Great Plains and north near Las Vegas toward Denver. Part of this region's scenic charisma stems from the tiny and timeless Hispanic villages dotting the country-side alongside the interstate. Isolated hamlets such as San Jose, Tecolote, San Ysidro, and Villanueva have seemingly escaped the march of civilization, except for the addition of automobiles and television antennas. Older residents here often do not speak English, babies are born at home, and village men still make simple but adequate livings by farming, ranching, or cutting firewood on nearby Rowe Mesa.

Villanueva State Park

For a closer look at some of these villages, leave I-25 at exit 323 about 1 mile (1½ km) past the crossover of the Pecos River, and drive south for about 14 miles (22 km) on NM 3 to Villanueva State Park. This stretch of narrow but maintained pavement follows the Pecos River through one of the prettiest canyons in the state, and cuts through the tiny villages of Ribera, El Pueblo, and Villanueva in the process. On the right about 6 miles (10 km) from the turnoff, the **Madison Vineyards & Winery** welcomes visitors with sips of their excellent wines (the vines here are some of the oldest in the state).

At Villanueva State Park, 3 miles (5 km) south of Villanueva village in a lovely canyon of cottonwoods adjacent to the river, you'll find picnic tables and campsites with electricity and water. If the New Mexico Department of Game & Fish hatchery truck has recently stocked the stream with rainbow trout, fishing can be excellent.

To continue to Las Vegas retrace your route to the interstate and head east about 40 highway miles (64 km) around the southern foot of the Sangre de Cristo Mountains.

Las Vegas

Founded in 1835, Las Vegas, New Mexico, has none of the glitter of its larger Nevada cousin. Nonetheless, this old railroad stop and mercantile hub for wagon trains and traders on the Santa Fe Trail is a fascinating town to visit.

Start your city tour in the historic downtown plaza. In earlier years local farmers and merchants gathered here to welcome newly arrived wagon trains negotiating the Santa Fe Trail with carts of cheese, chiles, bread, firewood, and other goods. Today a showcase of Victorian architecture, the town's peaceful, cottonwood-shaded common is an amicable meeting place for strollers, shoppers, and sightseers.

Perhaps the most interesting plaza structure is the three-story **Historic Plaza Hotel**, built as the town's principal hostelry in 1882 shortly after the arrival of the Atchison, Topeka & Santa Fe Railway. With its elegantly appointed lobby, comfortable rooms, and excellent Victorian-style dining room, the Plaza has always enjoyed a certain renown. During the era of silent films, for instance, stars like Romaine Fielding and Tom Mix enjoyed the hotel's hospitality, while more recently it was seen in the movies *Easy Rider* and *Red Dawn*. Restored to its Victorian splendor in 1982, the Plaza presently provides one of the best accommodation bargains in town.

A few doors down from the Plaza Hotel's main entrance, **Los Artesanos Bookstore** is another of the plaza area's fascinating structures. The original building, with its crenellated parapet and linteled windows, vintage light fixtures, and fine white-oak floors, was constructed in 1921 as the Louis Ilfeld Law Office and was one of the first structures in the Southwest to boast an air-conditioning system. Today browsers will find that Los Artesanos contains a truly impressive collection of first-edition Western Americana books.

From the plaza you can stroll or drive through the historic districts along Fifth, Sixth, Columbia, and Washington streets to inspect the city's unusual stone architecture and Victorian- and Queen Anne–style homes. The Carnegie Library, Immaculate Conception School, D. T. Lowery House, and Our Lady Of Sorrows Church are among the best maintained, but nearly 900 Las Vegas buildings have been placed on the National Register of Historic Places, and the area is considered one of the most prominent architectural jewels in New Mexico. Tour maps and walking guides to the historic areas are available in most shops and hotels.

A more nature-worthy Las Vegas treasure lies 11 miles (18 km) to the northwest, nestled in the lower slopes of the nearby Sangre de Cristo Mountains. (Las Vegas itself sits at the base of these mountains on the edge of the Great Plains.) Follow NM 65 through the small town of Montezuma and past Armand Hammer's United World College of the American West (you can't miss the college; this huge, red-sandstone Victorian–style structure sits on a hill on the north side of town). At the fork in the road several miles past the college, turn right on Forest Road 261 to **Porvenir Campground**. Snug in the shadow of towering granite cliffs, this quiet forest park offers picnic grounds, overnight camping, and a shallow but praiseworthy trout stream. Hiking trails lead to nearby Hermit Peak and the Elk Mountain area of the Pecos Wilderness.

For a steamy end to the afternoon stop at the convenient highway pullout directly across from the United World College on your return trip to Las Vegas. A few yards off the highways lie side-by-side natural hot springs in which car-weary travellers are welcome to soak away their aches. Few locals will tell you about the place, but it's easy to find.

The Santa Fe Trail

If you drive northeast from Las Vegas on I-25 through the grasslands toward Watrous and the turnoff to old Fort Union, watch for lines of eroded wagon ruts alongside the highway. All that remain of the 800-mile-long Santa Fe Trail, they are usually most visible on the slopes of small hills. Starting in Old Franklin, Missouri, and ending in Santa Fe's plaza, this famous caravan route was utilized from 1821 to 1879 by traders, trappers, and land-seeking emigrants. The ruts can often be seen running north to south on both sides of the interstate.

Fort Union

A few miles north of Watrous take NM 161 northwest to Fort Union, located on a grassy plain where two forks of the Santa Fe Trail—the Mountain Branch and Cimarron Cutoff—came together. Built in 1851 to solve what the U.S. Army once called the "Indian problem," it was the largest army fort on the trail, and is credited with saving the lives of virtually hundreds of travellers. Not only did the fort provide hospital care for the weary, wounded, and ill, it offered security as well. Westbound wagon trains were easy targets for roving bands of Utes, Kiowas, Apaches, and Comanches, but when Fort Union troops began patrolling the region and escorting the trains to safety, Indian attacks and harassment declined dramatically.

When the railroad arrived and traders and migrant families no longer travelled west by wagon train, Fort Union was closed and abandoned. It was declared a national monument in 1959, and though little restoration has been done the site is still worth viewing. In addition to a cluster of disintegrating adobe barracks and a small museum, Fort Union boasts the largest visible network of wheel ruts on the entire trail. The prettiest time of day here is late afternoon, when the setting sun transforms the crumbling brown buildings to a deep, theatrical, rusty red.

From Fort Union, return to I-25 the way you came. If you drive north on the interstate for 52 miles (83 km), you can take NM 58 west via Cimarron to Taos, about 70 more miles (112 km). Otherwise, you can return to Santa Fe via I-25.

NORTH OF SANTA FE: THE HIGH ROAD TO TAOS

Many of the tiny villages on the western slope of the Sangre de Cristo Mountains north of Santa Fe were origi-nally settled in the 17th and 18th centuries during New Mexico's Spanish colonial period. Far removed from provincial bureaucracy and linked to Santa Fe and each other only by horse or wagon trails, these isolated outlying communities were virtually left on their own—at least where day-to-day survival was concerned. Vulnerable to Indian attack, drought, disease, and a hundred other whims of man and nature, they became tiny, autonomous mountain kingdoms loyal only to God and to themselves.

Today the horse and wagon trails have been paved and are known collectively as the High Road to Taos. Most villages along the route, however—still remote, still independent, and to a degree still obstinate toward governmental edict—retain an archaic aura present in few other regions of America. Witchcraft, for example, is a common practice here, and superstition plays a major role in everyday life. Some towns, in addition to a Catholic church, still have *moradas*—meeting halls for an ancient religious brotherhood, the Penitentes, notorious for flagellation and human crucifixion rites.

Few visitor attractions exist on the High Road, but the picturesque architecture of these 17th-century villages, combined with panoramic views of the mountains to the east and the high desert to the west, create a drive that shouldn't be missed. Accommodations are limited here, but several small bed-and-breakfast inns are available to travellers who make reservations in advance. Most visitors, however, prefer to make the High Road tour in one day and return to Santa Fe in the afternoon, or spend the night in Taos. If you don't stop for lunch at Rancho de Chimayo (see below) and if you don't spend the night at a bed and breakfast, you can easily drive from Sante Fe to Taos via the High Road in three to four hours. (One alternative route to Taos, discussed below, is via the Chama River Valley, about three hours; another, more direct, route is to follow the Rio Grande on NM 68 north from Española, something less than one and a half hours overall from Santa Fe.)

The logical place to begin a tour of the High Road is in the colonial community of Chimayo, 25 miles (40 km) northeast of Santa Fe. Originally founded as a penal colony in the late 17th century, the village was constructed in fortress style (with only one entrance to the outside world) around a central plaza atop an abandoned Indian pueblo. Today it is the only surviving fortified Spanish town in the Southwest. The most scenic route to this old village is to take U.S. 84/285 north 15 miles (24 km) to the junction of NM 503 (just past the Los Alamos exit) and turn right toward the Sangre de Cristos. After 7 miles (11

km) turn left again on NM 520, which will take you
directly into the village.

Just before you reach the NM 503/NM 520 junction,
you'll see signs to **Nambe Pueblo** (first occupied around
A.D. 1300). The pueblo is small, fairly modern (even the
church is new), and offers little for travellers. Pueblo
artisans produce a few woven belts, beaded hair clips,
and mica-flaked black or red utility pottery, but these
items are usually offered for sale only in private homes.
(Nambé Mills, makers of Nambé Ware, an expensive
serving- and kitchenware sold from outlets in Santa Fe
and nearby Cuyamungue, has no connection with the
pueblo.) For a fee visitors may fish, camp, or picnic at
Nambe Lake a few miles east of the pueblo.

El Santuario de Chimayo

El Santuario de Chimayo, often called the "Lourdes of
America," sits in a snug cul-de-sac just south of the main
village (watch for a small sign on the highway that reads
Santuario). Built as a family chapel between 1813 and 1816
by wealthy landowner Don Bernardo Abeyta, this lovely
structure is another of New Mexico's myth-surrounded
churches. Legends claim that in 1813, when Don Abeyta
lay sick and dying on his bed, a vision summoned him to a
field near his hacienda, where he was immediately cured
of his ailment. In devout appreciation for the miracle he
ordered that a church be constructed on the site.

Today, cluttered with religious folk art and spiritually
oriented icons, El Santuario de Chimayo is regarded as
one of the state's holiest sites by New Mexico's large
Hispanic population. During Holy Week, the week before
Easter, some 30,000 pilgrims from throughout the Southwest walk, drive, and sometimes crawl to the shrine to
pray and partake of holy dirt from a hole in the floor of a
room just off the main chapel. Interior walls of the
santuario are adorned with crutches and canes left by
pilgrims who claim to have been healed. Sightseers, of
course, are welcome to visit the shrine at any time during
regular hours.

Three-tenths of a mile (½ km) past El Santuario, **Restau-
rante Rancho de Chimayo** bears a well-deserved international reputation for gourmet New Mexican cuisine
created from recipes passed down through seven generations. Owned by the Jaramillo family, residents of
Chimayo since the 1700s, this country restaurant with its

whitewashed adobe walls, cozy dining rooms, excellent service, and superb entrées is the former home of two brothers—Hermenegildo and Trinidad Jaramillo. It has an outdoor terrace for dining in good weather.

The chef's favorite is *platon especial,* which includes guacamole salad, a rolled enchilada, a tamale, a taco, a *torta de huevo,* rice, and beans—all smothered in local red or green chile sauce. Most entrées are prepared with locally grown products. Reservations are recommended if you plan to stop for lunch, and are absolutely necessary for dinner. The restaurant is closed Mondays; Tel: 351-4444.

Just across the street, **Hacienda Rancho de Chimayo** offers distinctive bed-and-breakfast accommodations in another restored adobe building that once housed other members of the Jaramillo family. Seven guest rooms, each opening onto a lovely enclosed courtyard, are adorned with local antiques and family treasures, and each has its own piñon-burning fireplace. The inn serves a hearty Continental breakfast of fresh pastry, fruit, juice, and coffee or tea. Reservations are a good idea, especially in the summer.

Chimayo is Northern New Mexico's principal Hispanic weaving town, and is *the* place to purchase a fine wool rug or blanket. Prices are high but quality is excellent. Of the many talented weavers here, the Ortega family is perhaps the best known. Residents of Chimayo since the early 1700s, the Ortegas opened their first store in 1918, selling family-made blankets to neighbors and the occasional passerby. Today the **Ortega Weaving Shop**, at the junction of NM 520 and NM 76, is open every day. (They also sell their own fine New Mexico–style chili powder.) Next door to the main shop an Ortega-owned gallery displays other types of Northern New Mexico crafts.

For a look at the town's old fortified plaza follow the dirt road in front of Ortega's to the south (left), and take the first right-hand fork. The plaza is about half a block farther on the left.

The Mountain Towns

CORDOVA

Just past the Ortegas' shop at the stop sign, turn right onto NM 76 and continue east for about 4 miles (6½ km) to the wood-carving village of Cordova. Situated in a river valley south of the main highway (the access road is a bit rough), this tiny Spanish town was originally known as El

Pueblo Quemado, and was settled in the early 1700s. The most prominent artisans here are the Lopez family, who have been creating *santos* (saints) and other religious figures from aspen, cottonwood, and pine for generations. Visitors are always welcome in the town's several shops. The two largest are the studios of **George Lopez and Sabinita Ortiz** and that of **Gloria Lopez**.

TRUCHAS
The Cordova access road returns to NM 76 about a mile beyond the town. Another 3 miles (5 km) up the mountain, perched like a vulture on the edge of a high mesa, is the village of Truchas, the principal filming location for the popular movies *Red Sky at Morning* and Robert Redford's *The Milagro Beanfield War.* At **Los Siete**, just off the highway near the western lip of the mesa, you'll find lots of local Hispanic arts and crafts at fairly modest prices.

Where NM 76 makes a sharp left turn, go straight to visit the town's mom-and-pop art galleries, crafts shops, and quilt stores. The only accommodation here is the **Truchas Farm House Bed & Breakfast**, ½ mile (1 km) from the junction on the same road. Surrounded by 30 acres of farmland, the three spacious guest houses are more than a hundred years old, and boast two-foot-thick adobe walls and modern furnishings. Prices are a bit high for a place like Truchas, but the hospitality shown overnight visitors by owner Aurello Lopez and his wife is Southwestern traditional and worth every penny. Reservations are a good idea in the summer.

LAS TRAMPAS
Las Trampas, founded circa 1750 to give valley residents below warning of imminent attack by Comanches, lies 8 miles (13 km) farther north on the High Road, within shouting distance of Jicarilla and Trampas peaks. The picture-postcard church here, **San Jose de Garcia**, was constructed just a few years after the village was settled, so that local residents would not have to travel the nine difficult miles to the mission at Picuris Pueblo. Legends say that only 12 men (for the Twelve Apostles) were permitted to work on San Jose, so construction took 20 years. When the church was completed, two gold and silver bells—Maria de Refugio, which announced funerals and other solemn occasions, and Maria de Gracia, which called residents to weddings and feasts—were placed in the bell towers. Gracia has since been stolen, but Refugio is still working and safe in the tower. Histori-

ans claim the church is probably the finest remaining example of Spanish colonial religious architecture in New Mexico.

Picuris Pueblo

Beyond Las Trampas NM 76 drops into a wide, tree-filled valley and intersects with NM 75. Picuris Indian Pueblo, occupied by Anasazi descendants since about A.D. 1200, lies to the left. The entrance road is well signposted.

Spaniards first visited Picuris about 1598. According to historical documents, the pueblo at that time was among the largest in colonial New Mexico, housing a population of more than 3,000 people. The original Spanish church here was burned in 1680 and the replacement, **San Lorenzo Mission** (still standing today), was constructed in the late 1700s.

The present population of Picuris has dwindled to less than 300, and time combined with erosion, has all but destroyed the original pueblo. Mostly farmers, the Picuris people have developed little in the way of pueblo industry except for a small prehistory **museum** located just east of the governor's office, and a **restaurant**, in the same complex, which offers traditional Pueblo Indian food.

The bronze-colored, mica-flecked pottery made by Picuris artisans can be found in several small shops in town. Local gourmets say that frijoles—pinto beans—cooked in a Picuris pot taste far better than those cooked in other types of containers. There's also a lake adjacent to the pueblo in which visitors, for a fee, can fish for rainbow trout. The pueblo's feast day, dedicated to San Lorenzo, is August 10, when there are corn dances, foot races, and pole-climbing contests.

Santa Barbara Recreation Area

Among the best-kept secrets of Northern New Mexico is the lovely and underused mountain campground called Santa Barbara Recreation Area. Located in an aspen-filled valley at the northern end of the Pecos Wilderness, it's a difficult place to find. From Picuris return to NM 75 and continue east (left) through the village of Peñasco to the NM 73 junction. Turn right on NM 73 toward Llano, drive 1½ miles (2½ km), then turn left onto County Road 116. Two hundred yards past the turnoff you'll pass a small brown *morada* (church) and cemetery on the left side. Follow this rough hillside road 6 miles (10 km) along the

Santa Barbara River through a gorgeous valley until you can't go any farther.

Of all the Forest Service recreation areas in the state, this is one of the prettiest. Campsites and picnic areas along the river are surrounded by dense groves of quaking aspen, fir, and blue spruce, and visitors can often spot mule deer, elk, grouse, and even an occasional black bear feeding or meandering along the stream. Forest Trail 24 begins a few yards beyond the valley's last official campsite and winds through meadows of wildflowers to the Santa Barbara divide and to a number of Alpine lakes deep in the Pecos Wilderness backcountry. The river here is filled with cutthroat, German brown, and rainbow trout. An exceptional time of year to hike in the area is autumn, when the aspen and red willow leaves are turning gold. The campground is closed in winter, but cross-country skiers can use the trails whenever they wish. Trail maps are available at the U.S. Forest Service office in Peñasco.

On to Ranchos de Taos

The few remaining miles of the High Road via NM 75 (east) and NM 518 (north), although certainly a beautiful drive, offer few attractions of interest. At U.S. **Hill Vista**, however, you might want to pull over for a moment to read the historical marker at the small parking area on the right. In 1598 Don Juan de Oñate sent colonists along this route, El Camino Real, the oldest road in the United States, to settle Spain's new acquisitions. In 1847 Colonel Sterling Price and his men dragged heavy cannons to Taos along the same route to quell a rebellion against the new American government. On clear days scenic views of the Taos Valley and Wheeler Peak, New Mexico's highest mountain, are stunning.

At Ranchos de Taos (site of the famous San Francisco de Asis Church; see the Taos chapter) you will run into NM 68; a right turn onto NM 68 will take you into Taos.

TAOS VIA THE CHAMA RIVER VALLEY

The first part of this three-hour drive traces the route discovered by Spaniards Silvestre de Escalante and Francisco Domínguez as they unsuccessfully tried to force an

overland route to Monterey, California, from Santa Fe in
1776. Beginning at the base of the Jemez Mountains, then
following the starkly beautiful Chama River Valley for
nearly 30 miles before turning east to bisect the Carson
National Forest, it is an alternative, though somewhat
lengthy, route to Taos. You'll need a full day and a full tank
of gas to investigate properly the numerous attractions
found along this enchanting segment of asphalt.

To begin, drive north on U.S. 84/285 from Santa Fe to
the Los Alamos turnoff (NM 502), about 16 miles (26 km).
At the junction turn left and drive about 7 miles (11 km),
cross the Rio Grande, then about a mile (1½ km) farther
on, turn right on NM 30 north toward Santa Clara Pueblo
(the exit is marked Española). Visitors are also welcome
to examine the lovely and expensive black pottery in
local shops at San Ildefonso Pueblo (see the Around
Albuquerque chapter), on your right just before you
cross the Rio Grande.

Santa Clara Canyon

The well-marked road to Santa Clara Canyon leaves NM
30 about 6 miles (10 km) beyond the NM 502 junction
and heads west (left) into the heart of the Jemez Mountains. As you drive, watch for washouts and large chuck-
holes, which often mar the pavement after heavy rains.

The abandoned Anasazi Pueblo of **Puye Cliffs** is situated picturesquely in the south-facing tufa cliffs on the
right side of Santa Clara Canyon Road, a few miles beyond
the turnoff. Most noticeable are hundreds of small asymmetrical cave entrances—each one laboriously carved by
hand in prehistoric times—but a larger set of apartment-
like dwellings known as **Top House Ruins** sits directly
above, atop the mesa. Combined, the two sections of this
ancient village have about 2,300 rooms, and were probably one of the ancestral homes of the Santa Clara people.

Similar in design to the ruins at nearby Bandelier
National Monument (see the Around Albuquerque chapter), and probably built by the same people according to
archaeologists, the cave-room and mesa-top structures at
Puye were constructed between A.D. 1450 and 1475, about
the time of the great Anasazi migration. Both sections of
the village were more than likely occupied at the same
time, the lower rooms being utilized as winter quarters,
the upper used in summer. Peak occupation was circa
1540, the same year Spanish conquistador Francisco Coro-

nado arrived in the Southwest from Mexico, but by 1550 the town had been abandoned.

Trails here are self-guided and, because of the altitude, fairly strenuous. Caretakers ask that you remove nothing, especially pottery shards, from the ruins. Local legends claim that during the excavation of Puye in the 1930s Indian workers heard spirit voices telling them not to remove bones or artifacts from the old town. Some did not heed the warnings and immediately died. Strangely enough, the "Puye curse," if there is one, still seems to be guarding the ruins. Until just a few years ago intertribal dances and a popular Indian arts-and-crafts fair were held at the mesa each summer, but after several spectators were killed by lightning in 1981, festivities were permanently canceled.

Santa Clara Pueblo

If you continue west on Santa Clara Canyon Road beyond Puye the road soon turns to gravel and follows a tiny winding creek to a chain of shallow, man-made lakes. For a fee visitors can fish for rainbow trout, hike in the surrounding pine and fir forest, and picnic or overnight at maintained but often busy roadside campgrounds. Land and facilities here are owned by Santa Clara Pueblo, so be sure to read the visitors' list of rules and regulations posted along the road.

If you retrace your route from the canyon to NM 30, a left turn will take you to the Indian pueblo of Santa Clara. Once known as K'hapoo and renamed Santa Clara by the Spanish, the village lies about 3 miles (5 km) north of the canyon entrance just off NM 30 on the banks of the Rio Grande.

First settled in the 14th century, Santa Clara today is a fairly modern and progressive community of farmers, businesspeople, and artisans that hardly resembles in layout or design the original pueblo. The Santa Clara Mission, for instance, is fairly new, constructed about 1918 after the original 18th-century church collapsed in a storm, and many of the historic stone and adobe homes have been replaced by new and far less traditional government housing.

Of the many Santa Clara artisans, perhaps the most respected are the pueblo's internationally known potters such as Margaret Tofoya and Teresita Naranjo. Handmade and sometimes carved or sgraffito black-on-black, solid red, and polychrome vases and bowls, created using techniques passed down through scores of generations and usually sold from vendors' homes, fetch top prices from collectors and ordinary travellers alike. The village has also produced a number of excellent Indian painters. The work of the most famous, Pablita Velarde, graces the walls of homes and galleries all over the world.

Indian dances and other public ceremonies are held throughout the year at Santa Clara, but times and dates vary so you might want to call before you visit. The most important celebration is the Santa Clara Feast Day, held on August 12.

San Juan Pueblo

In Española, where NM 30 joins U.S. 84, turn left and drive 6 miles (10 km) north of town. Turn right at the U.S. 285 junction and follow the highway across the Rio Chama to the entrance of San Juan Pueblo.

Spanish conquistador Castano de Sosa was the first European to visit this ancient pueblo. "The very sight of us frightened the inhabitants," wrote Castano in 1591, "especially the women, who wept a great deal." It would not be the last time Indian women at San Juan cried. Seven years after Castano's visit the town was made the official capital of New Mexico province by Juan de Oñate. The Indians were ordered to move out while Oñate, his soldiers, and thousands of cows, goats, and horses moved in. Everything the pueblo people left in their hurried relocation was confiscated, of course.

Modern San Juan, headquarters for the Eight Northern Pueblos Council, plays an important role in formulating statewide Indian policy. It has also been a pacesetter in revitalizing Indian arts and crafts in New Mexico. The **Artisans' Guild** here retails traditional and contemporary crafts from all the state's pueblos, and the **O'ke Oweenge Arts and Crafts Cooperative** offers an excellent selection of San Juan handicrafts. Coral and turquoise jewelry, bead-work, baskets, and pottery are a few of the handicrafts produced by pueblo artisans.

About a hundred original structures still stand in the old part of town, but you need permission from the tribal governor in order to wander, and permission is usually granted only to those with friends living in the pueblo. A **museum** in the headquarters building, however, offers a small selection of artifacts. The feast day here is June 24, and generally includes the Comanche dance.

Abiquiu

When artist Georgia O'Keeffe moved to the Chama River Valley in 1949 she came in search of solitude, painterly terrain, and peace of mind. O'Keeffe found all three—and immense inspiration as well—in the tiny Chama River village of Abiquiu, about 12 miles (19 km) north of San Juan Pueblo on U.S. 84. "All the earth colors of the painter's palette," the painter wrote of the surrounding landscape, "are out there in the many miles of badlands."

Founded in the 1740s, then abandoned and resettled several times over the next few years because of Indian attacks, Abiquiu finally became a staging center for trappers, merchants, and migrants heading west to the California coastal village of Los Angeles. It was really Georgia O'Keeffe, however, who put the town on the map. When O'Keeffe's husband, photographer Alfred Stieglitz, died in 1946, she purchased a large hilltop adobe home in the village, and remained there until her own death in 1984.

O'Keeffe's property rambles across a hill on one side of town, but while motorists are welcome to drive by and look, the compound itself is closed to the public. In the central village area the church of Santo Tomas dominates the plaza, but little else here attracts visitors. You might consider stopping at modest **La Cocinita**, however, for a quick but delightful lunch. The tiny roadside café, specializing in a native concoction known as an Indian taco (a deep-fried sopapilla stuffed with ground beef, tomatoes, lettuce, cheese, and spicy red chile sauce), sits a few hundred yards south of the Abiquiu turnoff. La Cocinita opens whenever the cook arrives.

Abiquiu Lake State Park

Abiquiu Lake, a five-minute drive up the valley on U.S. 84 from the village of Abiquiu, then left on NM 96, is one of those tiny angling meccas that has been overlooked by everyone except a few tight-lipped locals. Part of a U.S. Army Corps of Engineers flood-control project, the reservoir was completed in 1962 and is presently managed by the New Mexico Department of Game & Fish. About four miles in length, with two-thirds of its shoreline enclosed by steep sandstone walls, Abiquiu is filled with bass, crappie, catfish, trout, and kokanee salmon. Local anglers say it is one of the most productive small fishing lakes in the state. Lakeside camping and picnic areas, the former with shelters and grills, are plentiful.

Ghost Ranch

A three-minute drive north on U.S. 84 from the Abiquiu Lake turnoff and 2 miles (3 km) east off the main highway (a sign marks the entrance road), secluded **Ghost Ranch**— nestled amid the severe and barren hills that Georgia O'Keeffe found so appealing—offers superb accommodations for those who have made reservations in advance. O'Keeffe actually owned a small getaway cabin on this one-time working ranch before she moved to Abiquiu.

The ranch took its name from nearby canyons that are supposedly inhabited by witches and ghosts. Now operated by the United Presbyterian Church, the ranch facilities are used principally for adult study seminars on conservation and cultural education, but extra rooms and *casitas* (small houses) are offered to the public when space is available, on a reservations-only basis. Travellers are welcome to drive the main ranch roads, however, and visit the small archaeological **museum** near the headquarters. If you're a moviegoer and the terrain seems somewhat familiar, you're probably remembering the film *City Slickers,* which was shot on the property.

A short drive north on U.S. 84 from the ranch entrance road, **Ghost Ranch Living Museum** provides a pleasant home to nearly a hundred different species of Southwestern flora and fauna. Displays include a wide variety of indigenous plants and geological exhibits, a walk-through fire tower, and a walkabout watershed that compresses an entire Northern New Mexico forest into just two acres. Among the most unusual zoological exhibits are a six-foot-long diamondback rattlesnake that eats just once a year and a native magpie with a ten-word vocabulary. Mountain lions, Mexican wolves, beavers, elk, and bears also reside here; most were donated to the museum after being found injured in the wild. The museum is closed on Mondays during December and January; summer hours are 8:00 A.M. to 6:00 P.M.; winter hours are 8:00 A.M. to 4:30 P.M.

Christ in the Desert Monastery

Benedictine monks constructed a remote monastery in the Chama River Canyon about 1964 and today work its large gardens and keep bees here. The 13-mile-long dirt road along the Rio Chama that leads to the isolated complex—a beautiful drive through Chama River Canyon country—leaves U.S. 84 to the left about 1 mile (1½ km) past the Ghost Ranch museum. (Don't attempt to negotiate the access road in wet or snowy weather unless you have a four-wheel-drive vehicle.) The monastery's main quarters and small chapel (there are also a few guest quarters) nestle beneath the steep sandstone walls of the Chama River Canyon on lovely grounds dotted with piñon, juniper, and cottonwood trees. There's a small gift shop at the monastery but little else.

Cumbres & Toltec
Scenic Railroad

Not far from where the monastery entrance road leads off the main highway, U.S. 84 leaves the Chama River Valley for a time and climbs upward through piñon-dotted foothills to the higher, pastoral landscape and mountain villages of the isolated Brazos Valley (U.S. 84 is joined by U.S. 64 from the east in the process). You'll find few visitor attractions here, but the scenery is gorgeous.

About 13 miles (21 km) north of the village of Tierra Amarilla, U.S. 64/84 passes through the bustling little resort town of Chama (population 1,090). In winter Chama is a popular center for cross-country skiers and snowmobilers. During the summer and fall, however, most visitors come here to ride the **Cumbres & Toltec Scenic Railroad**, which runs between Chama and Antonito, Colorado. Daily, from Memorial Day weekend until mid-October, this little narrow-gauge, coal-burning steam train carries passengers on a 64-mile-long round-trip journey through some of Northern New Mexico's most beautiful mountain country (you can also ride the train one-way and return to Chama by van). The cost is $45.50 per person round trip. Reservations are usually necessary; Tel: 756-2151. Credit cards are accepted.

If you wish to head for Taos instead of Chama, turn right on U.S. 64 east just before you reach the village of Tierra Amarilla. Bisecting the Carson National Forest, this well-maintained but twisty highway meanders east across the rugged Tusas Mountains to Hopewell Lake, the tiny village of Tres Piedras, and finally joins NM 522 just north of historic Taos. This final leg across the mountains, 85 miles (136 km) from Tierra Amarilla to Taos, takes about two hours without stops. U.S. 64 is often closed during the winter due to snow.

GETTING AROUND

As in most other areas of New Mexico, touring the northern part of the state is best accomplished by car; this is an area to which van or motorcoach tours simply do not go. Most national car-rental agencies have offices at the Albuquerque airport or in Santa Fe. You'll also need a good highway map of the state, available at car-rental agencies, gas stations, or from the New Mexico Department of Tourism, 491 Old Santa Fe Trail, Santa Fe, NM 87501; Tel: 827-7400.

Each of the trips laid out in this chapter can be accomplished in a day (some in far less time), so you can lodge in Santa Fe each night if you wish. A visit to El Rancho de las Golondrinas south of the city, for instance, shouldn't take more than a few hours and will leave you plenty of time to spend the afternoon hiking in Hyde Memorial State Park or in the Pecos Wilderness to the east. The longer tours, east to Fort Union via I-25 and north to Taos on the High Road or on U.S. 84 via the Chama River Canyon, normally require a full day to enjoy minimally; you can always spend the night in Las Vegas or Taos if more time is needed.

Highways in this part of Northern New Mexico are, for the most part, well-maintained and open year-round. A notable exception is U.S. 64 from its crossing with U.S. 84 south of Tierra Amarilla east to Tres Piedras; because of drifting snow, this road is generally closed from December to April.

Traffic tends to be heaviest from Memorial Day through Labor Day (especially through the Chama River Valley) but lightens considerably during the fall, winter, and spring. Probably the loveliest times to visit are in April, when spring wildflowers bloom in profusion alongside the highways, and in late September and early October, when the leaves of cottonwoods and aspen trees turn gold in anticipation of winter.

Most larger towns have a Chamber of Commerce or visitors' bureau to help with directions and accommodations, answer questions, and generally assist in whatever manner necessary.

ACCOMMODATIONS REFERENCE

The rates given below are projections for 1993. Unless otherwise indicated, rates are for a double room, double occupancy, and do not include meals. Price ranges span the lowest rates in the low season to the highest rates in the high season. As rates are always subject to change, it is wise to double-check before booking.

The telephone area code for all of New Mexico is 505.

▶ **Ghost Ranch.** Ghost Ranch Conference Center, **Abiquiu**, NM 87510. Tel: 685-4333. $36.75 per person, double occupancy (includes three meals a day).

▶ **Hacienda Rancho de Chimayo.** NM 520 between Santuario and Chimayo. P.O. Box 11, **Chimayo**, NM 87522. Tel: 351-2222 or (800) 477-1441. $54–$86.

▶ **Historic Plaza Hotel.** 230 on the Old Town Plaza, **Las Vegas**, NM 87701. Tel: 425-3591. $55; $80 (suite).

▶ **Truchas Farm House Bed & Breakfast.** County Road 76 in town. P.O. Box 410, **Truchas**, NM 87578. Tel: 689-2245. $75.

TAOS AND THE ENCHANTED CIRCLE

By Stacy Q. Rychener and Sam Rychener

Stacy Q. Rychener, co-author of Out and About in New Mexico, *has lived in the state for 16 years, with family roots going back to 1914. A Taos-based marketing executive, she has served as president of The Association of Historic Hotels of the Rocky Mountain West. Sam Rychener, a travel and fiction writer and art critic, has lived in Taos for 15 years.*

Y ou must first be impressed by Taos's remoteness: one hundred thirty miles from the nearest airport, in Albuquerque, 70 miles from Santa Fe, and 300 miles from Denver, with not much in between. Taos is one of those uncommon spots that thrives in spite of its isolation. And that isolation has helped create in the people of Taos a rugged, self-reliant individualism characterized by suspicion of government and business—and people whose roots don't go back as far as theirs.

Pueblo cultures appeared here in the 13th century, probably after a prolonged worldwide drought between A.D. 1000 and 1275 led to the disappearance of the earlier Anasazi and Chaco cultures. The Spanish came next, colonizing the valley in the 1600s, subjugating and converting the Pueblo tribes—and intermarrying with them. The

233

next wave was of northern European descent: French and Yankee trappers and mountaineers who began working the mountain valleys in the early 19th century. In the beginning of the 20th century another wave of Easterners arrived, led by an unlikely group of artists attracted to the landscape. Successive migrations have put their own stamps on Taos: hippies in the 1960s, yuppies in the 1980s.

Today Taos is a mosaic of many peoples: Indians, Hispanic professionals and subsistence farmers, Anglo New Agers, shopkeepers, outdoor enthusiasts, retirees, and artists—the last both commercially successful ones who zip around in BMWs and starving types who must wait tables on the side. What continues to draw people to Taos today is what has drawn each of these groups through the years: a setting of great natural beauty and bountiful resources where individual customs, art, and architecture flourish.

MAJOR INTEREST

Indian cultural sites and ceremonies
Art scene
Crafts
Outdoor recreation

Ranchos de Taos
San Francisco de Asis Church

Taos
Taos Plaza, Bent Street Galleries, and Kit Carson
    Road
Kit Carson Historic Museums
Millicent Rogers Museum
Taos Pueblo
Taos Ski Valley
Festivals and special events

Side Trips from Taos
The Enchanted Circle
Carson National Forest
Rio Grande Gorge
Orilla Verde State Park
BLM Wild and Scenic Rivers at Cerro

Taos's remoteness has long challenged both those who have sought to make it home and those who have tried to govern it from afar. The northernmost point of New Mexico reached by the Coronado expedition of 1540,

Taos Pueblo welcomed Captain Hernando de Alvarado and invited him to lodge here. Not finding the treasure Coronado had sent him scouting for, Alvarado pushed on. In 1598 Don Juan de Oñate led a group of colonists to settle in San Juan (near present-day Española, 40 miles southwest of Taos). The settlement failed, but by 1628 the population of the new capital of New Mexico, Santa Fe, had swelled to 1,500. The distance of more than 1,500 miles to Mexico City through deserts inhabited by hostile tribes made administration costly and difficult.

By 1615, or possibly earlier, the first Spanish settlers had come to Taos Valley, and not long afterward the *encomienda* was in place here too: Each landholder had "commended" to him Indians who lived on, worked, and defended his land in return for the assurance of their spiritual and physical welfare. (In the English colonies this practice came to be known as slavery.) Because of this forced servitude, and because of the persecution and murder of Indians up and down the Rio Grande for practicing native religions, a great degree of enmity began to build up, and by as early as 1650 revolt was in the air.

At some point a man by the name of Don Fernando Durán y Chavez received a land grant near the mouth of Taos Canyon. The river flowing out of the canyon and meandering through town bears his name today—the Rio de Don Fernando. On August 10, 1680, Don Fernando, his son, and his nephew were the only three Spaniards to get out of Taos alive when the Pueblo Indian revolt erupted. They beat a hasty retreat to Santa Fe and then to El Paso. Don Fernando never returned.

The causes of the Pueblo revolt are generally attributed to discontent with the *encomienda* system and religious persecution. The mastermind behind the 1680 revolt was a San Juan medicine man named Popé who, after being arrested and beaten by the Spaniards for his religious practices, escaped hanging and vowed revenge. He then spent five years in Taos laying out a complex plan for pueblos up and down the Rio Grande to rise up and eradicate all evidence of the white man by destroying churches, buildings, and other trappings of Spanish civilization. Smoke signals and runners spread the news from pueblo to pueblo, and on the appointed day Spanish haciendas were sacked and burned and the occupants killed or driven out.

For 12 years afterwards New Mexico was free of the Spanish. It wasn't until well after reconquest, in 1692, that they returned. Taos Pueblo, the original hotbed of revolution, didn't capitulate until 1696. In 1710 the Don Fernando Durán y Chavez grant was awarded to Cristobal de la Serna, who never used it. His heirs sold the land in 1724 to Diego Romero, a man of mixed Spanish and Indian ancestry. Romero settled on the Rio de Don Fernando while his son appears to have been the first settler along Rio de Las Trampas, known today as the Little Rio Grande. Early settlements were built along streams from which the settlers irrigated fields through a system of *acequias* (ditches), just as the Indians taught them. These *acequias,* still in use today, are protected for their historic and agricultural value. Teams of men cleaning ditches and shoring up their banks are a common sight around Taos in April. If you keep your eyes open you'll notice these ditches everywhere.

Accounts of early-18th-century Taos are rare. Undoubtedly settlement paralleled what we know of other areas in the state: Scattered, agrarian-based communities, or haciendas, gradually developed while nearby missions converted natives and administered the spiritual needs of the colonists. Continuing raids from Utes, Apaches, and Comanches undoubtedly encouraged close cooperation between the Spanish and Taos Pueblo against their common enemies.

Taos As Art Colony

In May 1898 Ernest Blumenschein, 24, and Bert Phillips, 30, two artists who had studied together at the Academie Julian in Paris decided to make a sketching and painting trip to the American Southwest. In Denver they outfitted themselves with wagon and horses and headed south for Mexico. In early September a wagon wheel broke down near Questa, and they flipped a three-dollar gold piece to see who would take the wheel to Taos for repair. Blumenschein lost. On horseback the next day he rode into the Taos Valley and had "the first great unforgettable inspiration of [his] life."

Phillips and Blumenschein soon settled down here to paint and to extoll the area's virtues. They painted the first landscapes of Taos, paying special attention to the exotic architecture and the two distinct cultures, especially the Pueblo Indians, whom they often adorned with headdresses (even though Pueblo Indians didn't and don't wear them). Their enthusiasm for Taos—not to mention the commercial success they began to enjoy—brought other artists. In July 1912 Phillips, Blumenschein, and friends Herbert Dunton, Joseph Sharp, O.E. Couse, and Oscar Berninghaus met at the home of Dr. T.P. Martin (today, Doc Martin's Restaurant in the Taos Inn) and formed the Taos Society of Artists. The society dedicated itself to organizing travelling exhibitions and promoting member artists, thereby acting as Taos's first publicity firm. Soon more than a hundred other artists had arrived. A steady stream of them continues to visit, and many choose to make Taos home.

Today the Taos phone directory lists more than a hundred studios and galleries featuring hundreds of artists at all levels of accomplishment and in all mixes of media. And this doesn't count the inns, restaurants, and banks that show art as a sideline. The Taos Yellow Pages lists art brokers, dealers, consultants, curators, workshops, and artists' agents. One gallery becomes a ski shop in winter. Another advertises "two convenient locations." Most galleries accept major credit cards and offer monthly payment plans. Buildings that only a few short years ago housed hardware and grocery stores are now galleries. Some represent dozens of artists while others are working studios of a single artist. And, just as in any art colony, you will find a heavy helping of schlock, or "art-type stuff," as Larry Bell, a Taos artist with work in the Guggenheim, calls it. You begin to wonder how those early members of the Taos Society of Artists might view this hyping of the arts today, especially as they were the ones who set the self-promoting ball in motion.

It's problematical here to try to judge galleries by how long they've been in existence. Most artists, even successful ones, change galleries from time to time, and galleries shuffle artists even more frequently. The sale of art (in contrast to the making of it) is a fluid business, especially from the boom of the 1980s to the near bust of the early 1990s. That so many galleries here stay open year-round is a testament to the vibrancy and pull of the arts community, or at least to the marketing powers of certain individuals within it. In the mid-1980s the state Department of Tourism published statistics showing that art sales in the Albuquerque–Santa Fe–Taos corridor were third in the nation, behind only New York and Chicago. That the department credits these sales to tourism is not surprising. In Taos galleries you'll see lots of Southwestern sunsets, romanticized images of Indians, and adobe courtyards abloom with hollyhocks. We discuss many of the reputable galleries below.

If you're interested in openings, special exhibitions, and lectures, check the calendar section of *Taos Magazine,* available free in most hotel and motel rooms, or see the more complete and up-to-the-minute listings in the *Tempo* section of the *Taos News*.

VISITING TAOS

Taos today consists of three towns: Taos Pueblo in the north; Taos proper in the middle; and Ranchos de Taos in the south. Spaced at approximately three-mile intervals, they are slowly growing into one another along the connecting main road, Paseo del Pueblo Norte (U.S. 64)/ Paseo del Pueblo Sur (NM 68). Local residents use "Taos" to identify not just these three communities but also rural settlements for many miles around. Really, when someone tells you he lives in Taos, it could mean almost anything, for as D.H. Lawrence who once lived here said, "Taos is a state of mind."

Regardless of the direction from which you approach Taos, your first impression is of its striking physical beauty. From the north on NM 522 and from the west on U.S. 64, Taos and its environs glitter against the sheer backdrop of the Sangre de Cristo Mountains to the town's east. Approaching from the east, on the other hand, U.S. 64 winds through scenic Cimarron and Taos canyons. The famous High Road from Santa Fe, NM 518, drops out of the mountains and parallels the Little Rio Grande.

From the south, the direction from which most travellers come, NM 68 climbs out of Pilar, dips around a horseshoe bend, and rises onto a mesa—where you see Taos sprawling below you to the right and the Rio Grande Gorge zigzagging parallel to the mountains like a thunderbolt laid down on the earth. This view rarely fails to stop motorists, and a rest area provides an excellent photo opportunity. A wide, straight downgrade from there on will tempt you to speed down into Ranchos de Taos and then Taos itself, but the 55 m.p.h. speed limit is rigorously enforced here.

With the opening of Taos Ski Valley in 1955, Taos became a two-season, year-round destination. In winter Taos generally belongs to the skiers; nonskiing visitors flock in from April until November, when the weather is crisp but generally predictable and colors have turned. A large and varied calendar of events makes summer a great time to visit, but it is the many festivals and special events in September and October that make fall probably the best time. Don't avoid this season because it's popular; the Taos Fall Art Festival and San Geronimo Day at Taos Pueblo are solid reasons to brave the crowds.

Whatever the season, the weather can be volatile. At 6,950 feet elevation, temperatures dip into the 50s at night even in the hottest part of summer, and a cloudburst can drop the temperature 15 or 20 degrees in minutes, so take sweaters and a water-resistant jacket.

Taos is unrelentingly casual. In Taos it's your God-given right to dress down. Travellers should bear in mind that Taos is a playground for those who live here, too. Don't be put off if a barkeep or waitress seems distracted. They may be artists or writers by day. Or skiers. Or river rafters. Though other smaller communities match or exceed Taos's physical beauty, none offers so much in activity and accommodation.

It's conceivable that if you are in a hurry you could tour Taos Pueblo, circumnavigate the plaza, and visit a museum or two in a day. But to explore the art colony, take in some seasonal outdoor recreation, or study the history of the region while meeting a colorful character or two you'll need anywhere from three days to a week. Whether you're coming for an extended visit or just passing through, the sight that should go at the top of your agenda is Taos Pueblo—the historical and spiritual center of Taos. Without it, the Taos Valley would be a very different place indeed, and certainly never would have been called Taos.

We begin our coverage approaching from the south, as do most travellers to Taos, with Ranchos de Taos and its beautiful San Francisco de Asis Church. From there it's on to Taos proper, with its historic district, art galleries, and museums, and then north of the historic district to Taos Pueblo and the Millicent Rogers Museum.

Around Taos you'll find the ski areas, which we cover next; the Enchanted Circle, a 100-mile auto loop of spectacular scenery; Carson National Forest; and the Rio Grande Gorge, to name just a few highlights.

The area code for Taos County is 505.

RANCHOS DE TAOS PLAZA

Ranchos de Taos is the first community you enter as you approach from Santa Fe or Albuquerque. A yellow caution light hanging precariously on NM 68 in front of the U.S. Post Office is your signal to slow down and park in the plaza on the east side of the highway. The Ranchos de

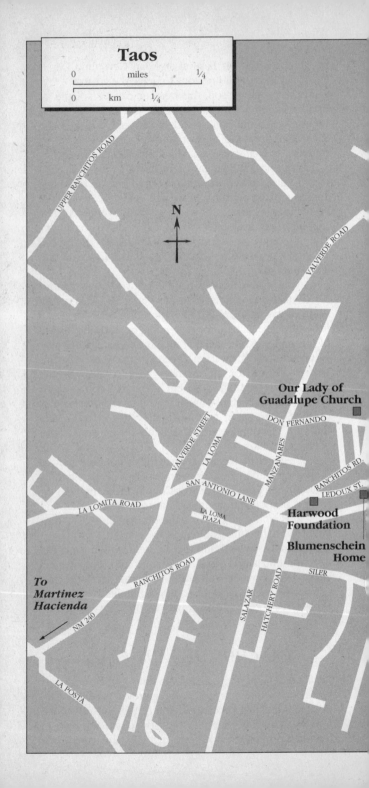

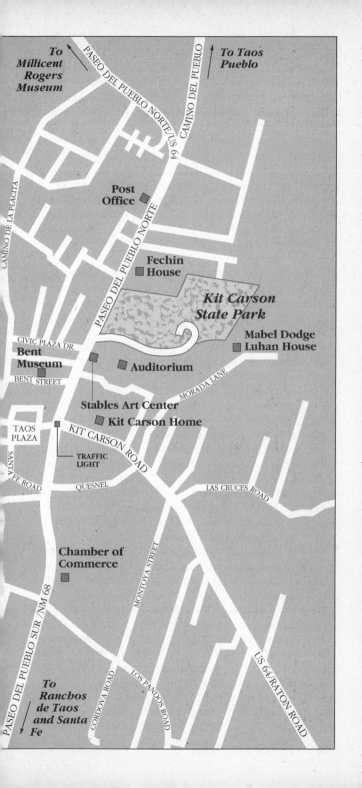

Taos Plaza, about 4 miles (6½ km) south of Taos's historic district, is believed to be the first of many such plazas in the valley. The towering structure in the plaza's center is the often-photographed **San Francisco de Asis Church**, a national landmark—and probably the subject of more paintings than any other church in America. (Georgia O'Keeffe's are probably the best known.) It's de rigueur for Taos artists to paint the church, and there's rarely a day when you won't see at least one easel fighting for parking space with cars. The church's date is variously put between 1725 and 1815, but no baptismal, burial, or marriage records exist to corroborate a date before 1815.

Early colonists wanted churches to match those in Europe and Mexico, cathedrals that would soar to the sky. The nature of adobe before the days of concrete footings, however, ensured that most structures would at some point return to the earth. The huge buttresses at the back of San Francisco de Asis were placed there to keep the five-foot-thick walls from doing just that.

Before you enter the church be sure to visit the parish office for an introductory slide show on the church's history and a viewing of the "Mystery Painting" owned by the parish. The mystery in this 19th-century painting of Jesus is the presence of a cross over his shoulder, visible only when viewing the artwork in darkness. Because the painting was made before the discovery of radium or the use of luminescent paints, its ghostly image has baffled art scholars. But the real historic treasure here is the San Francisco de Asis Church itself. If you wish to attend services, check times and arrive early, as they are always crowded. Inside the church notice the old paintings and *retablos* in the nave. In the north window stands a huge cedar carving of Saint Francis of Assisi by Leonard Salazar.

Santo (saint) carving is another of the traditional native crafts that survives from Spanish colonial days. Taos's remoteness necessitated furnishing churches locally, including pews, altars, and *retablos*. However, *santo* carving came to be looked on with disfavor by religious authorities because in their eyes, *santos* were primitive and thus sacrilegious. Archbishop Lamy of Santa Fe even tried to put an end to this art form by official decree. What survives today are more stylized figures, often rendered in cedar burls, that are sold all over town.

The date of Ranchos Plaza itself is put at 1779; remnants of the plaza's early fortifications sit crumbling on the north side. The plaza is known to have once been much larger, extending across what is now Paseo del Pueblo

Sur to include a similar plaza behind what is today the post office. The smooth mud-plastered building next to the post office is the old El Cortez movie theater, now a vacation home of actor-director Dennis Hopper.

In the last five or six years Ranchos Plaza has come back to life. The church draws tourists, and in Taos tourists mean art galleries, of which there are a number here.

Ranchos Plaza Grill is a great place for sandwiches and luncheon specials like green chile, and burgers and fries (possibly the best in Taos). Breakfasts here are generous and tasty, too.

Three-tenths of a mile south of Ranchos Plaza, on NM 68, sits the **Adobe and Pines Inn**, a bed and breakfast housed in a beautifully restored 150-year-old adobe home. With only three rooms, the inn provides service and tranquillity, and the house has some interesting construction details, such as a secret tunnel from the kitchen pantry to the old well-house. Though off limits to guests, the tunnel is further evidence of the once-serious threat from Indians. Rooms are appointed with Southwestern furniture, and their lack of phones can be considered a plus if you like quiet. Rural bed and breakfasts in and around Taos offer some of the most delightful accommodations here, with the additional benefit of more easily meeting people, especially inn owners who have lived in Taos for years and can direct you to their favorite haunts.

From Ranchos de Taos to Taos

In the past 15 years Taos has been "discovered" by a wide variety of vacationers. Its distance from large population centers hasn't really protected it from being trampled. Even so, the town manages to retain its small-town, artist-colony flavor in spite of an increasingly tourism-oriented economy. On the plus side of this boom, jobs (mostly low-paying) have multiplied for the resident population, which has grown from 2,500 in Taos and 17,500 countywide to 4,000 and 23,000, respectively, since 1960. On the minus side greed and traffic jams have increased as well. In the old days a wagon ride from Ranchos de Taos to the Pueblo took two hours; now, during summer traffic, the ride seems to take almost that long in a Mazerati. No wonder the local population, more dependent on tourism than ever, exhibits such startling ambivalence toward visitors. On Taos Plaza, in the height of summer, you occasionally find notes on shop doors proclaiming, Gone Fishing or Closed All Week.

The **Sagebrush Inn**, ½ mile (1 km) northeast of Ranchos de Taos on the west side of NM 68, opened its doors in 1929. Georgia O'Keeffe stayed here and painted in the third-story room. Try to get accommodations in the older, original hotel, where smaller rooms have had their common walls removed and have been remodeled into suites. The inn's bar offers live two-step music in the evenings, and is Taos's most consistently popular night spot.

About 1½ miles (2½ km) north of the inn, on the east side of the highway, **La Ultima Restaurant**, at 703 Paseo del Pueblo Sur (NM 68), serves reasonably priced, authentic New Mexican dishes: enchiladas, tacos, *rellenos,* and everything in between. If you're really hungry after a day of skiing or shopping try one of the combination plates, which are more than most people can eat. **Taos Gems and Minerals**, at 637 Paseo del Pueblo Sur, in the next block north and across from Holy Cross Hospital, sells possibly the widest and best selection of same in Northern New Mexico. Zeke Lambert, chef and co-owner of **Lambert's of Taos**, at number 309, was chef at both the Apple Tree Restaurant and Doc Martin's Restaurant (see below for both) before opening Lambert's in 1990. He serves daily lunch specials and changes his dinner menu every other night to feature such specials as grilled quail, crab cakes, and pepper-crusted lamb. Lambert brought a huge local following with him, so reservations are a must; Tel: 758-1009.

At the quiet corner of Los Pandos Road (which meets Paseo del Pueblo Sur at Pueblo Motors) and Cordova Lane, just three and a half blocks from Taos's historic district, is the **Casa de Las Chimeneas** bed-and-breakfast inn, two rooms and one suite that open onto a walled courtyard with formal gardens—in continuous summer bloom—and sparkling fountains. The inn's common areas are tastefully decorated with regional art and Southwestern furnishings. Breakfasts here feature a daily special entrée along with fresh fruit and pastries. Appetizers and complimentary juices served each afternoon provide a welcome respite for gallery-weary guests and make this one of the premier lodgings in Taos.

TAOS HISTORIC DISTRICT

Roughly six blocks long and four blocks wide, Taos's historic district radiates in each direction from Taos Plaza

at its center, a landmark most easily located by the traffic light at the intersection of U.S. 64, NM 522, and NM 68. (The streets directly fronting the plaza—it couldn't be easier—are North Plaza, South Plaza, East Plaza, and West Plaza.) Scores of historic buildings housing galleries and museums line the streets surrounding the plaza as well as Ledoux Street, home also to the Blumenschein Home and Museum, full of artworks and a glimpse into Taos life at the turn of the century; Bent Street, also great for shopping; and Paseo del Pueblo Norte, the main drag. After exploring these venues our coverage of Taos then heads east of the plaza along Kit Carson Road, home of more galleries and shops, and to the southwest along Ranchitos Road before continuing north to Taos Pueblo the Millicent Rogers Museum.

Taos Plaza

Taos Plaza is a relative latecomer, taking on its role as a commercial area long after other plazas in the valley had been established. We know it existed during the Civil War, because records show that Kit Carson and a handful of volunteers defended it after Union soldiers defeated a Confederate contingent near Santa Fe at Glorieta Pass.

Today Taos Plaza remains the heart of this community. During Fiestas de Santiago y Santa Ana or, simply, **Fiestas**, on the last weekend in July, the plaza closes to traffic and fills with food vendors and amusements, including Tio Vivo, one of the oldest operating merry-go-rounds in the United States. The whole town becomes one big, uncontrollable party—a homecoming for Taos natives who live elsewhere, complete with parades and special events such as chile cook-offs and live entertainment in the plaza gazebo. Visitors are likely to feel ignored and inconvenienced. Driving is nearly impossible, many shops and galleries are closed, and rooms are hard to find. It's a wild time, a sort of mini–Mardi Gras.

Because of its small commercial district, narrow streets, and traffic bottlenecks, Taos lends itself well to walking. For a nice introduction to the town and its citizens, past and present, you might want to consider **Taos Walking Tours**, which depart from the Kit Carson Home and Museum (east of the Taos Plaza traffic light, on Kit Carson Road) daily, except Sundays and holidays, at 10:00 A.M. from June through October. Visitors are guided through Taos's old streets and past the homes of mountain men,

artists, and assorted shady characters. The charge for the hour-and-a-half tour includes museum fees to the Kit Carson Home and Museum (for which, see below). Tel: 758-4020.

Or you might try the **Pride of Taos** trolley cars, which depart the southeast corner of Taos Plaza five times daily and from hotels and motels along their route. Guides narrate a brief history of the area, drop you off at any of the trolleys' destinations, and pick you up later. It's a great way to stay out of your car while taking in the rural and historic sights of Taos. The trolleys operate from early May to late October.

To experience the countryside around Taos, bicycling is a great choice. Gearing Up, at 129 Paseo del Pueblo Sur, rents both touring and mountain bikes by the day or week; Tel. 751-0365. However you get outside town you'll discover that, despite the hubbub in town, Taos is a rural place.

TAOS PLAZA GALLERIES

Taos Plaza is a good place to begin "doing galleries." From the center of town the galleries fan out like spokes of a wagon wheel. Itself the subject of numerous paintings, the plaza has its own colorful history, having witnessed mobs, hangings, gunfights, murders, and countless fires. Paintings by the Taos Six and other early Taos masters today command prices in five and six figures—when they can be found and if the owners want to sell, which is seldom.

There are, however, paintings on view by the old Taos Artists on the second floor of the old county courthouse, now called **North Plaza Art Center**. In the old courtroom are the valuable frescoes of Emil Bisttram, John Ward Lockwood, Bert Phillips, and Victor Higgins. To keep artists as well as steelworkers and road crews at work during the depression, the U.S. government commissioned these murals to adorn a new courthouse built to replace one destroyed by fire in 1932. The WPA project started in the fall of 1933 and was completed the following summer, earning each artist $56 a month. The general subject of the murals is the use and misuse of law. On the first floor of the art center, in the **Michael McCormick Gallery**, you can view the work of contemporary Taos artist Miguel Martinez. Works by other painters hang in the old jail cells—with upgraded lighting, of course. This jail briefly held actors Dennis Hopper, Peter Fonda, and Jack Nicholson in the 1969 movie *Easy Rider*.

The **Fernandez de Taos Bookstore**, a few doors west of

the old courthouse, sells a wide variety of out-of-state newspapers and magazines, and an excellent selection of books on Taos and the Southwest. Also on North Plaza is **Broken Arrow**, showing possibly the best collection of Indian jewelry, weavings, pottery, fetishes, and kachinas in town—which is saying something because everybody here sells Indian crafts.

The last vestiges of "sleepy little Spanish town" Taos can still be seen at the soda fountain in the Taos Trading Company and in the hardware department at El Mercado. Gone are the barber shop, grocery stores, mercantile companies, and lawyers' offices. Even the gas stations that not long ago occupied all four corners at the plaza–Kit Carson Road intersection have been replaced by a realty office, a restaurant, a parking lot, and Plaza Real, a mini mall.

East Plaza is entirely taken up by Plaza Real, with Ogelvie's Bar and Grille upstairs. The patio overlooks the plaza and is mobbed during Fiestas. The lower floor of Plaza Real is filled with shops, including the retail room of La Chiripada, Taos County's only winery, which is 30 miles (48 km) south in Dixon. They also sell locally grown herbs and chiles. Also on the lower floor, **Open Space, A Cooperative Gallery** features the work of local artists and craftspeople in a variety of mediums, from clothing to sculpture and paintings.

Adjacent to Plaza Real is the newer (1934), elegantly expanded McCarthy Plaza. There, in **Maison Faurie Antiquities**, antiques and one-of-a-kind curiosities cram every corner of the store, and most days owner Robert Faurie is on hand to explain each item's significance in his thick Parisian accent. If you're looking for a great place to observe local color, sample local beer with a sandwich or daily special, or pick up fixings for a picnic try **Murray's Delicatessen** next door. And next to Murray's, shop at the **Millicent Rogers Museum on the Plaza**, which features many of the same crafts and artifacts as those sold in the store at the museum (for which see North of the Historic District, below).

Across McCarthy Plaza, **Village Weavers** is a colorful and inviting shop filled with Zapotec Indian, Native American, and contemporary blankets and rugs. Wool growing and weaving have a long and important history in Taos, as the first settlers of the valley were sheepherders. Often a local weaver is on hand demonstrating the craft.

Halfway down the block, on South Plaza, is the **Hotel La Fonda de Taos**. No stroll around the plaza is complete without a stop here to view the private art collection of hotelier Saki Karavas, which includes a Gaspard portrait of his mother and works by Emil Bisttram, Howard Cook, Miguel Martinez, and many others. Karavas inherited the hotel from his uncle in 1953 and acquired a collection of D. H. Lawrence paintings in 1957 from the third husband of the novelist's widow, Frieda Lawrence. Pay the front-desk clerk one dollar and follow her into Karavas's office to see the Lawrence works. Banned from exhibition in London because of their erotic nature, the paintings were embroiled in controversy until they came home to Taos. However, Lawrence's artwork is not on a par with his writing; most viewers express relief that he only dabbled in painting. If you come by in the afternoon Karavas may be in his office, a small, unheralded museum of sorts that, besides the Lawrence paintings, contains memorabilia of the hotelier's long life in Taos: a letter from Einstein and photographs of Taos personalities and visitors such as author Frank Waters, Dennis Hopper, Lady Dorothy Brett, and Richard M. Nixon. (The picture of the former president was taken at the formal ceremony marking the return of Blue lake to Taos Pueblo. The Lake, a sacred shrine of the Pueblo, had been appropriated by the U.S. government and absorbed into Carson National Forest in 1906.) The office itself has been featured in numerous magazine articles about this engaging and garrulous Taos character. Just don't let him hustle you in checkers.

La Fonda, as it's known locally, is no relation to the hotel of the same name in Santa Fe. The rooms are clean but generally lacking in amenities such as television. Lack of parking also detracts. But the hotel has so much history and its location is so great—convenient to good restaurants and shopping—that it has to be recommended. **Taos Mountain Outfitters** just west of La Fonda is the best place to pick up a forgotten article of camping or climbing gear, or simply to ask advice on a good hiking or cross-country ski trail. They rent Nordic ski equipment, mountain bikes, and camping gear, and sell a wide array of casual wear, sweaters, and jackets.

West Plaza is a collection of adobe buildings with a long, beautiful portal that looks 200 years old. It's not, of course. Fires and the nature of adobe construction have necessitated the rebuilding of the plaza many times. The architecture and appearance of West Plaza is of interest, but unfortunately the stores here specialize in kitschy tourist items such as tee-shirts, coffee mugs, and rubber tomahawks. However, as you stroll north, completing your circumnavigation of the plaza, head up narrow Teresina Lane. A few steps north on the lane is **El Patio de Taos**, a restaurant housed in possibly the oldest building in Town of Taos, and believed to predate colonization. The menu is varied, the atmosphere charming, and native specialties quite good, especially the tamales and *rellenos*. **Old Taos** here is the shop to explore if you're in the market for really old collectibles, such as Southwestern weavings, furniture, or jewelry.

Ledoux Street

From the corner of West Plaza and South Plaza head south for the **Clay & Fiber Gallery**, which shows a wide array of contemporary New Mexican fine crafts, including glass, pottery, weavings, and jewelry. A hundred yards southeast of Clay & Fiber, in the Design Center at 105 Camino de la Placita, is the **Rod Goebel Gallery**. One of the new breed of artists who located here after World War II, Goebel shows works from both his Impressionist and new Abstract styles in addition to art from his personal collection. The gallery is one of the few places where collectors can find old Taos artists' work on sale, including *santos* by Patricinio Barela and paintings by Walter Ufer and Howard Cook.

At the southeast corner of Camino de la Placita and Ledoux Street, enter the delightful courtyard of **Collins-Pettit Gallery**, which features a strong collection of paintings by Taos artists Walt Gonske and Ron Barsano. Gonske's landscapes and Barsano's nudes have attracted collectors from all over the world.

Ledoux Street, a narrow lane maybe only a hundred yards long, is rich with the history of both the old and the new Taos art scenes. If you follow the dirt alley behind Marciano's Cafe Espresso you can see that all the houses on Ledoux's east side are connected; these are probably some of the oldest buildings in town, and they may have formed an exterior wall of some larger plaza. Two doors west of the Collins-Pettit courtyard (which is south on Ledoux Street) stands the **Navajo Gallery**, studio of R. C. Gorman, the Taos artist with perhaps the widest international reputation and certainly the most commercially successful one. His work can be purchased at the gallery, and some days you may even glimpse him in the process.

A "must see" is the **Blumenschein Home and Museum**, halfway down Ledoux Street at number 222. It's operated by the Kit Carson Historic Museums, a nonprofit organization that runs three museums here, one from each epoch of Taos history. (For the other two—Kit Carson Home and Museum and Martinez Hacienda—see below.) The Blumenschein Home, meticulously maintained, contains one of the better collections of early Taos art. It was common (and still is) for artists to trade work among themselves, and the collection here, which grew from bartering among Blumenschein and his circle, is noteworthy (though the lighting could be better). The house has a genuine homey feel; the parlor, where the Blumenscheins entertained, had the best dance floor in town. It was not unusual in the old days for people to sell rooms or parts of these common-wall houses as the need arose. New doors were cut through the adobe and old doors sealed off. In this way the Blumenscheins turned their four-room house into a 12-room, parts of which date from 1797. Art aside, the Blumenschein Home provides a delightful glimpse into Taos life at the turn of the century. It's as if Ernest and Mary (Mary was an artist too) might return from a sketching trip any moment.

The **Harwood Foundation**, at 288 Ledoux Street just before Ledoux meets Ranchitos Road, was the home of Lucy and Case Harwood. South windows in the Harwood Library and the Blumenschein Home look downhill, and you can imagine what the views must have been like before the ubiquitous Chinese elms matured. The Harwood Library is noted for its collection of art books. Upstairs, a gallery holds special exhibitions of contemporary Taos artists and a rotating display of early legendary Taos artists such as Brett, Blumenschein, Phillips, Dasburg, and many others—a collection so large it is hoped by many that a new location can be found so it can be on permanent view. Gallery lectures and receptions are common throughout the year.

The Bent Street Area

Backtrack up Ledoux Street and head north on Camino de la Placita to Civic Plaza Drive. At the corner of these two streets stands the Town of Taos Civic Plaza, where the important **Taos Invites Taos** art exhibition highlights the three-week-long Taos Fall Arts Festival from mid-September to early October. (To visit Taos at this time of the year, plan on making reservations anywhere from one to three months in advance—more if your stay overlaps the San Geronimo Day festivities on September 29 and 30.) Arguably the most impressive exhibition of

Taos-based artists, Taos Invites Taos is a juried show and sale featuring artists who have been invited by the festival committee. This is a chance to see the best contemporary Taos painters under one roof. Last year marked the first time that a cash award of $5,000 was presented for the best piece in the show. (There is also a Spring Arts Celebration; see the Paseo del Pueblo Norte section, below.) During the same period the Taos Open (next door in the Bataan Hall) features younger, less-established artists in a juried show and sale.

Improbably enough, the **Taos Fire Station**, located on Camino de la Placita behind the Town of Taos Civic Plaza, contains one of the best permanent collections of Taos art. Although it's open to public viewing, it's one of the best-kept secrets in Taos. The volunteer fire department was established after the 1932 fire destroyed most of North Plaza. So many local artists have made their annual donations with paintings that today it's an honor to have one's work hanging at the fire department. The atmosphere is just what you'd expect of any fire station day room: lots of linoleum and folding chairs, and a panting coffee urn in the corner. It's a volunteer fire company, so donations are appreciated.

Retrace your path down La Placita and enter Bent Street from the west. The wide variety of shops on Bent and in the John Dunn House Shops makes this one of the most engaging shopping areas in town. On Bent see the country furnishings and linens at the **Partridge Company**, in the old Maxwell House. In the shop's Christmas room you can find unusual handmade and imported Christmas ornaments all year long. In earlier times the white-clapboard-and-adobe building that houses the **Apple Tree Restaurant** earned distinction as a brothel. Today it's noted for its casual elegance and its food, including Southwestern dishes, seafood specials such as salmon and roughy, vegetarian specials, and a respectable wine list. A bit of advice on eating out in Taos: Don't eat anywhere where locals aren't apparent. By that standard Apple Tree fares well. Four intimate dining rooms and the popular patio in summer have brought the Apple Tree a wide following among visitors and Taoseños alike. Reservations are a must for dinner and even for lunch in peak tourist seasons; Tel: 758-1900.

The John Dunn House Shops across from the Apple Tree holds an intriguing variety of stores. **G. Robinson Old Prints & Maps** sells antique maps and prints; if you don't see anything that grabs you on the spot, sign up for the catalogue mailing list. **Native Furniture of Taos** is the retail outlet of Hispanic furniture maker Greg Flores, who has made a name for himself at a relatively young age. His style is simple, close to the WPA styles of the 1930s. Samples are on display, and there is a catalogue from which you may order. **The Taos Company** shows a wide variety of upscale Southwestern decorations and furniture. **Moby Dickens Bookshop** sells a good selection of contemporary fiction and nonfiction and hosts frequent book signings. Taos has long attracted writers in abundance, and Moby Dickens is one of the better bookstores that services them.

Across the street from the Bent Street entrance of the John Dunn House Shops you'll find the **Governor Bent Museum** in the Taos home of Charles Bent, first American governor of the New Mexico territory, who earned the position because he had already been a longtime resident of the area when the United States annexed it. At Christmas in 1847, while Bent was home from the capital in Santa Fe, he was ambushed on the front porch by a mob of Indians and Mexicans. Wounded, he attempted to escape through a hole in the adobe wall of his living room through which his family had already crawled. But the mob found him, and scalped and shot him while his family looked on. The hole in the wall is still there (or perhaps it's a facsimile thereof), along with artifacts from that wilder era.

Morgan Gallery at 4 Bent Street presents the embossed engravings of Ed Morgan, the oil landscapes of William Scott Jennings, and the color-pencil drawings of Reina, among others. This is one of the most inviting galleries in town, with a personable staff.

If you continue east on Bent for another 50 feet you'll come to the end of Bent Street at Paseo del Pueblo Norte, one block north of the Taos Plaza stoplight.

Paseo del Pueblo Norte

As you look south toward the plaza light from the Bent Street–Paseo del Pueblo Norte junction you see what tourism and "progress" have wrought since Oscar Berninghaus painted his well-known portrait of this intersection. Traffic is bumper-to-bumper at peak season, and even at certain times of the day in off-season. Curiously, Taos artists seem to shy away from depicting this sort of social phenomenon today. If you'd like to talk to some artists about this or weightier matters, the Meet-the-Artist

Series at the historic Taos Inn (a few steps south of this junction) provides an excellent opportunity. Every Tuesday and Thursday in both spring and fall artists discuss their subjects and techniques and show slides or take visitors on studio tours that may include demonstrations. Meet-the-Artist is so popular that reservations may be required; Tel: 758-2233.

In the early days in Northern New Mexico, small, individual plazas incorporating Pueblo and Spanish colonial architecture were created by connecting adjoining adobe dwellings around a central courtyard into which livestock could be driven at night. A well was also located within the plaza, and the buildings, focused inward, had few exterior windows. Parapets circumnavigated the roofline and towers were installed at regular intervals for defense. Many of these little plazas, or *placitas,* can still be seen all over town.

One that most visitors come across is now the lobby of the historic **Taos Inn**, a national and state landmark. After the death of her husband, Dr. Thomas P. Martin, Helen Martin bought the adjoining houses, covered the *placita* with a high log ceiling, and turned the whole structure into a hotel, which it has remained since 1936. One wall near the swimming pool reportedly dates to the 1600s. The lobby itself—the *placita* in its time—was surrounded by houses that today hold Doc Martin's Restaurant, the hotel library, and the Adobe Bar. The lobby fountain sits directly over the spot where the original well stood. Today the Taos Inn has 39 rooms centered around three courtyards, but it is still the quaintest and most historic hotel in town. Many rooms have kiva-style fireplaces; all are furnished in Southwestern decor. You'll need reservations well in advance of a stay here. Try to book into the back courtyard, where the rooms are large and quiet.

Doc Martin's Restaurant serves three meals a day, with a varied and excellent menu including native specialties like *carne adovada* (pork cutlet marinated in red chile) and an extensive, award-winning wine list. The **Adobe Bar**, which features occasional live entertainment, often overflows into the lobby; it is used like a living room by many Taoseños, just as it was when the Taos Six formed the Taos Society of Artists in the Martins' living room. A fire generally crackles in a cozy corner of the lobby during fall and winter.

One door south of the Taos Inn, **Martha of Taos** sells Martha Reed's own distinctive Southwestern fashions as well as "fiesta" and "broom" skirts. The brown, two-story building across the street from Martha's was once the old Traveller's Hotel where, in a certain room on the second floor, Leopold Stokowski and Greta Garbo reportedly carried on an affair.

The **Stables Art Center**, one door north of the Taos Inn, is one arm of the Taos Art Association (the other "arm" represents the performing arts). The Stables Gallery puts on many juried and invitational shows throughout the year, including the popular annual members' show in the spring. Also in the spring, for three weeks in May, the **Taos Spring Arts Celebration** involves the arts community in gallery shows, print-signing ceremonies, special exhibits, and gallery demonstrations. Besides the Fall Arts Festival, this is another great time to visit Taos; a large number of activities in the performing, visual, and literary arts are held in venues all over town. Ask the Chamber of Commerce for a schedule of events and locations; Tel: 758-3873.

The building housing the Stables was built by one of the most nefarious Taos characters of all time. Arthur Rochford Mamby came to Taos at the turn of the century as an investor in a Red River silver mine, 25 miles to the north. One quirk in his history of investing: His partners' bodies always seemed to turn up partially decomposed and missing some important part, usually the head. His partner in Red River was no exception. Paying slave wages to local Indians, Mamby then tried to build a hotel north of town over some hot springs near the community of Arroyo Hondo. (The remains of that hotel can most easily be viewed by renting a copy of the movie *Easy Rider*. You can bathe in the hot springs by negotiating a steep but hard-to-find trail—ask locally—or by taking a raft trip down the Taos Box portion of the Rio Grande.) Most of Mamby's money seems to have come from the wealthy widows he courted and later bilked. When investigators showed up at his home one day to serve judgment in favor of one of the widows, they found that Mamby had suffered the same fate as his old partners. Dr. T. P. Martin declared Mamby's death to be of natural causes. However, the mutilation of the head, which some attributed to the viciousness of Mamby's own dogs, made positive identification uncertain and led to speculation that Mamby may have staged his own death to escape prosecution. Mamby's lone positive contribution to Taos, other than building this house, are the trees he planted up and down Paseo del Pueblo Norte.

Behind the Stables Art Center is the Taos Community

Auditorium, the heart of Taos's performing-arts community. Here you can attend the Taos Art Association's dance, theater, and musical performances throughout the year.

Last year marked the 30th anniversary of the **Taos School of Music**, which brings together internationally famous faculty and promising students from the best schools across the country for a two-month-long period from June to August. It's the oldest such arrangement in the United States. Classrooms and lodging are provided at the Hotel St. Bernard in Taos Ski Valley (see below), but performances are held here at the Taos Community Auditorium. The American String Quartet, resident faculty since 1979, and their students give two weekly recitals at the Taos Community Auditorium from mid-June through early August.

Music From Angel Fire performs in late August and early September with its all-star lineup of musicians presenting classical and chamber music from around the world (musical genres change each year). Concerts are given at the Taos Community Auditorium, at Village Haus in Angel Fire (see The Enchanted Circle, below), and at the magnificent old Shuler Theatre in Raton, 90 miles (144 km) northeast of Taos via U.S. 64 and I-25.

Kit Carson Memorial State Park, north of the Stables and the Community Auditorium, is a welcome expanse of greenery in the middle of town. Follow the driveway or any of the gravel footpaths back to the cemetery where Kit Carson, Mabel Dodge Luhan, Long John Dunn, Arthur Mamby, and other historic figures are buried. In late September the **Wool Festival** brightens up Kit Carson Park with demonstrations and exhibits from Northern New Mexico's wool industry. Wool has roots far back in Taos history. The earliest Spanish settlers tended huge flocks, and today weaving still thrives here. At the Wool Festival you'll find everything from ram skulls (now popular decorator items) to colorful, handwoven wearables. Across the street from the park, **Weaving/Southwest** in Yucca Plaza Mall offers weaving and knitting supplies, demonstrations, and decorator items year-round.

The **Fechin House,** at 227 Paseo del Pueblo Norte, just north of the park, is the former residence of famed Russian artist Nicolai Fechin, who came to Taos at the turn of the century. It's a work of art in its own right—one that has been featured in many publications. All of the interior woodwork was done by Fechin as an escape from painting; the staircases, doors, and window frames are loaded with interesting architectural details that combine form with function. The Fechin House operates as a museum, hosting special exhibitions of paintings from such places as China, Russia, and Costa Rica, and including exhibits of Fechin's work as well. During the summer the Fechin Institute, a nonprofit arm of the museum, hosts intensive five-day fine-art workshops at the Branham–Donner Ranch in San Cristobal, 10 miles (16 km) north of town (see The Enchanted Circle, below). Classes in oil painting, photography, pastel, drawing, and sculpture are taught by nationally recognized artists. The Fechin House restoration is yet to be completed and, because of an ancient heating system, the museum is open daily only from late May through late October. It is closed during the winter except for tours by prior arrangement; Tel: 776-2622.

Across the street, **Los Rios Anglers Inc.** at 226C Paseo del Pueblo Norte can help you plan a fishing or rafting adventure (Tel: 758-2798). In the next block, **Michael's Kitchen** is an adventure itself. Michael Ninneman serves up a wide assortment of pancakes, waffles, hamburgers, tacos, and enchiladas in a noisy, crowded atmosphere. Every visitor to Taos eats here at least once, perhaps because it's so popular with local clientele as well. You may have to stand in line to get a table, but service is fast.

Hensley Gallery Southwest, across the street and a half block north of Michael's Kitchen, occupies space that was once the old Taos Hardware. The exposed brick walls serve as a striking backdrop for the outsize landscapes of Jackson Henley and the impressive anatomical drawings of his son, Michael, and internationally acclaimed Gustave Rehberger. This is one of the most impressive galleries in Taos, with a stable of fine painters who passionately explore the human form. Hensley Gallery thus offers a sharp contrast to the Southwestern themes of the many more commercially oriented galleries here.

In the next block north, Shriver Gallery and the Taos Gallery are two of the nicest in town. **Shriver Gallery**, in a beautiful old adobe home with hardwood floors, shows many artists, including Ray Vinella and Ron Rencher, who paint landscapes in oil and watercolor. Adobe courtyards with hollyhocks and cashmere pastures dotted with cattle are rendered skillfully and in abundance. **The Taos Gallery**, which first opened its doors in 1957 on Kit Carson Road, today represents Julian Robles and Robert Daughters, two popular Impressionists who first came to Taos in the 1950s. Daughters's work is done with a palette knife in a style that makes you think of Van Gogh (a comparison that infuriates the artist). Robles's work is filled with imaginative use of the human form coupled with Southwestern themes.

Paseo del Pueblo Norte then swings northwest as NM 522/U.S. 64 and leaves town (continuing straight instead of veering left will take you to Taos Pueblo). **Country Furnishings of Taos** at 534 Paseo del Pueblo Norte carries the latest creations by area furniture makers, painters, and folk artists. Two miles (3 km) north of town is the factory and showroom of **Overland Sheepskin Company**, with full-length sheepskin coats, gloves, hats, and other products that attract shoppers year-round.

Kit Carson Road

Kit Carson is emblematic of the sort of person who was attracted to Taos as the frontier began to spread west. The popularity of beaver-skin hats in the East during the early 1800s and the resulting high price for pelts—six to eight dollars apiece—made illegal entry by Americans into Spanish Territory worth the risks: confiscation of goods, fines, even hanging. In 1821 the success of the Mexican revolt ended Spanish authority, and the new Mexican government was even less equipped to halt the influx of Yankee and French trappers who would, over the next 20 years, take beaver pelts valued at an estimated $100,000 a year from New Mexico. Laws against foreigners were ineffective, as it was easy for them to bribe local officials, form partnerships with Mexicans, or take on false citizenship. The Pueblo had been a bustling, vibrant community for hundreds of years by that time, and these mountain men and trappers (Kit Carson being only the most famous) chose Taos as their center for operations.

Two factors ended the beaver trade: a shift in fashion because of the importation of silk from Asia, and the near extinction of the beaver. Though the livelihood of the mountain man dwindled, many, such as Carson, stayed on to work as guides for wagon trains and military expeditions. (Another was a Frenchman named Ledoux, for whom Ledoux Street was named.) Carson married a Mexican woman, Josefa Jaramillo. His knowledge of the land and of Indian ways and language earned him positions in military campaigns, the most infamous being his command role in the subjugation of the Navajo at Canyon de Chelly and the forced relocation of their entire nation to

Bosque Redondo, near present-day Fort Sumner in the eastern plains of New Mexico. For this reason Carson is an ambivalent figure even in his adopted home town. He bought his home on the street now named after him in 1843 and retired here after the Navajo campaign in 1864.

Kit Carson Road (which becomes U.S. 64) runs east from the Taos Plaza stoplight on NM 68. It's a short block and the signs for all establishments can be seen from anywhere on the street. The **Kit Carson Home and Museum,** operated by Kit Carson Historic Museums, is situated halfway up the first block on your left. Open seven days a week, the home offers glimpses into Carson's life here in Taos, and as mountain man and soldier elsewhere. Built in 1825, the house also embodies pueblo construction methods. The **Carson House Gift Shop** sells everything from affordable gifts and Christmas ornaments to collectible Indian art, folk art, and the hand-carved furniture of Mark Romero.

To the west of the Carson House lies some of the original centuries-old boardwalk. The carved posts in front of Del Fine Art Galleries predate sawmills in the area. Also on the old boardwalk, **Gallery A** is one of Taos's oldest, having first opened its doors in 1960. Today it represents 80 artists, including Gene Kloss, Carlos Hall, and Charles Collins. The gallery seems busy with so many styles, everything from Impressionist to Western paintings as well as etched-glass pieces.

To the east of the Carson home and still on the north side of the street is **El Taller Taos**, the gallery of artist Amado Peña, whose colorful and highly stylized images of Indians have brought an international following. Next door to the east, **Casa Benavides Bed and Breakfast Inn** combines luxurious accommodations with in-town convenience. Once the gallery, studio, and home of Taos artist Thomas Lewis, the compound recently underwent renovation and now lets 22 rooms appointed with Mexican furniture. It also serves scrumptious and bountiful breakfasts.

The south side of Kit Carson Road is loaded with history and art. And food: **Caffe Tazza** serves up a huge selection of espresso and cappuccino beverages, and baked snacks. Long a hangout for the literati of Taos, Caffe Tazza hosts poetry and prose readings throughout the year. Next door, the **Taos Book Shop** specializes in art books and rare or first editions on the Southwest.

Chef Robert Garcia and wife, Patsy, opened the doors of **Roberto's Restaurant** in 1965. Located off the street in a quiet courtyard just a step east of the Taos Book Shop, the building, dating to the early 19th century, radiates Old World charm with its high ceilings and thresholds worn down like bars of soap. Native New Mexican specialties— such as tamales, *rellenos,* and sopapillas—keep visitors and local residents coming back year after year; Tel: 758-2434. If you forget to make reservations, give your name to Patsy and browse the **Total Arts Gallery**—in the alley between Roberto's and Kit Carson Road—which shows a broad spectrum of art from traditional to modern, sculpture to oils, and even posters.

Head up Morada Lane, which intersects Kit Carson Road at the bottom of the hill (as you head east). At 239 Morada Lane **Lumina** features fine art and photography by Ansel Adams, Pamela Parsons, Paul Pascarella, and Jim Wagner in the **Victor Higgins home**. Higgins was one of the founders of the Taos Society of Artists at the turn of the century. Like many buildings here, the house itself is a work of art, growing over the years with rooms or stories added, outdoor staircases plastered over; its age and rounded contours give it the appearance of a large hobbit house.

At the end of Morada is the **Mabel Dodge Luhan House**, which is now a bed-and-breakfast inn, and also an educational and conference center. Mabel Dodge Luhan, Taos's early patroness of the arts, came from big, Eastern banking money. When her third husband, Maurice Stern, travelled west to paint, she followed, but didn't go back with him. She married a man from Taos Pueblo, Tony Luhan, and began building this magnificent adobe mansion. Soon she was bringing her artistic friends and acquaintances from all over the world: Lady Dorothy Brett and D. H. Lawrence from England; artists and photographers Ansel Adams, Edward Weston, Georgia O'Keeffe, and Nicolai Fechin; writers Willa Cather, Aldous Huxley, and Frank Waters; and musician Leopold Stokowski. The list is long of artists and notables whom Mabel Dodge Luhan "turned on" to the beauties of Taos. The education foundation organizes group conferences and special educational retreats, and is available for individual lodging as well. All 20 rooms, ranging in price from expensive to reasonable, have private baths and views of Taos Mountain to the north, while guests have the run of the huge rooms in the main house. Breakfasts are served buffet style, with Southwestern specialties. Box lunches are available if you want to picnic.

RANCHITOS ROAD

Ranchitos Road (NM 240) is a lazy, meandering two-lane road that follows the Pueblo River from the west part of town to Ranchos de Taos. Local residents call it the back road, but if you take it you'll find it's a lot more pleasant and sometimes even faster than Paseo del Pueblo Sur (NM 68), the commercial route.

Head out the southwest corner of Taos Plaza to get onto Ranchitos Road, which runs past the *Taos News* building. If you're walking, cycling, or driving it's only 300 yards to San Antonio Lane, which branches off Ranchitos to the right and climbs La Loma ("The Hill," in Spanish), at the top of which you can tour La Loma Plaza.

There is a great deal of evidence that the people of Taos Pueblo and others, notably the Utes and Apaches, coexisted peacefully with the colonists. The Comanches, however, were a different story. After the massacre of 1760, when the Comanches carried off 50 women and children from Taos, a royal decree went out that, for defense, houses had to be constructed on high ground using common walls to create a kind of fort. **La Loma Plaza**, atop La Loma, is one of the oldest of these constructions, dating to the late 18th century. Most houses on La Loma wear National Register plaques. **Taos Hacienda Inn** abuts the southwest corner of the plaza and seems to combine all that is historic and beautiful in Taos; part of the inn served as fortification for La Loma Plaza. As a private residence the structure has been home to a Carson National Forest supervisor, who planted many of the inn's towering spruce and cottonwood trees, and later to an artist, who used upstairs rooms as studios. Lovingly restored and opened as a bed and breakfast in 1991, the inn has seven rooms, all with fireplaces, private baths, and phones. Suites are equipped with kitchenettes. Breakfasts include a daily special, fresh juices, and baked goods, and afternoon snacks consist of Southwestern hors d'oeuvres and beverages, or homemade cookies with cappuccino and espresso. The grounds and living areas are so peaceful and beautiful you may not want to leave to go sightseeing.

One legacy of Spanish colonialism that still flourishes in Taos is furniture making, and over the years it has developed a style of its own. Begun of necessity because of Taos's isolation, furniture making here today has evolved to fine craftsmanship, even art. Taos furniture is generally made with larger-dimension pine lumber in rectilinear shape with exposed joinery—a heavy Southwestern Shaker. The better furniture makers adorn their work with ornate carving. One mile (1½ km) from La Loma Plaza, west on Ranchitos Road, is the workshop of **Roberto Lavadie**, one of several quality designers and furniture makers in Taos. The altar screen at St. Francis Cathedral in Santa Fe, for example, is a Lavadie creation.

Continue a bit farther west on Ranchitos Road and turn north onto Upper Ranchitos Road, which bears off to the right by the sign for the Martinez Hacienda. About a third of a mile up that road, the moderately priced **Casa Europa** bed-and-breakfast inn and gallery occupies a picturesque walled compound. Though parts of the inn are nearly 200 years old, the six guest rooms are as contemporary as you'll find, some with fireplaces and all with queen- or king-size beds. Generous and delicious breakfasts are served in the main dining room, and during ski season *après*-ski hors d'oeuvres and drinks are served every evening.

Continue north one-tenth of a mile on Upper Ranchitos to Karavas Road, a dirt lane on your left. **Rancho Rio Pueblo Taos Country Inn** is located on this quiet country road only about 2 miles (3 km) from town. With the Rio Pueblo outside the door and the cottonwoods filled with magpies and grackles, you will feel as if you are a thousand miles from nowhere. The core of the house dates from the early 1800s. All rooms are suites with fireplaces, hand-carved furniture by local craftsmen, private baths, telephones, and televisions.

Head back to Ranchitos Road, which here parallels the Rio Pueblo, and turn right (southwest). Notice the many *acequias* in the floodplain. Travel a little over a half mile (less than 1 km) to the **Martinez Hacienda**, the third of the three museums operated by the Kit Carson Historic Museums (the Kit Carson Home and Museum and the Blumenschein Home and Museum, above, are the other two). The Martinez Hacienda, the oldest parts of which date to the 1780s, shows what hacienda life was like during the Spanish colonial and Mexican territorial periods. The fortresslike building, with thick adobe walls and no exterior windows, proves how real the threat of Indian attack was to early valley settlers. During its day the Martinez Hacienda was most likely a trade and cultural center in and of itself. In the 1960s hippies occupied it, allowing goats to graze on the roof, and by the time Kit Carson Historic Museums acquired it in 1972 much of the structure had fallen into ruin. The National Parks Service designated it a National Historic Building, and restoration brought the hacienda's 21 rooms back to their original condition. Archaeological work was required to find the placement of original walls, remnants of which are on display behind glass enclosures in a back room. This "must see" gets better with each passing year. As part of its living-museum program you can view demonstrations of early colonial crafts such as smithing, weaving, and furniture making. The museum recently acquired four rare Spanish colonial horses, directly descended from stock brought by conquistadors to the New World more than 400 years ago.

Long before recorded history Taos Pueblo was an important trading center among Indians. In the 1700s there were fairs at Taos Pueblo where goods from French traders were available. The tradition grew in the early 1800s, when fairs were attended by Yankee trappers and mountain men. The past comes alive at the Martinez Hacienda during **Old Taos Trade Fair**, the last weekend of September: two days of fine native foods, mountain men, Indians, music, dancing, demonstrations of traditional Northern New Mexican skills, and other performances, including a reenactment of the arrival of Padre Martinez, an early Taos educator and son of Don Severino Martinez, *dueño* of the hacienda. Old Taos Trade Fair is another of the events that make Taos such a special place in early fall.

Ranchitos Road now turns south and crosses the Rio Pueblo twice more before you reach the stop sign at Los Cordovas Road. If you turn right and travel a little less than a mile south on Los Cordovas you'll come to **Chavez Millwork**, home of furniture maker and carver Miguel Chavez, known for his ornate carving of colonial-style designs and doors. As a youngster Miguel was the subject of a book and movie, *And Now Miguel . . .*, which documented the life of the sheepherding Chavez family.

A left turn at the stop sign (east on Ranchitos Road, NM 240) will take you to number 90, the private residence of **Mark Romero**, dean of Northern New Mexico's woodcarvers and furniture makers. (His home is not open to the public, but you can see his furniture at the Carson House Gift Shop on Kit Carson Road.) Romero began carving in his teens, and in 1953 formed a partnership with designer and artist R. W. Dicus to make furniture and doors. Many Taos furniture makers worked or apprenticed at Romero's woodshop. Today his work is seen in fine homes, offices, and universities across the United States.

One-half mile (less than 1 km) farther is the junction with NM 68; a left turn will take you back to Taos, a right turn to Ranchos de Taos and Santa Fe.

NORTH OF THE HISTORIC DISTRICT

The **Millicent Rogers Museum** houses one of the finest all-around collections of historical artifacts in New Mexico. Founded in 1953, the museum was seeded with items from Millicent Rogers's personal collection of Indian jewelry, textiles, baskets, pottery, and paintings. To get to the museum take NM 522 about 4 miles (6½ km) north of the Taos Plaza stoplight. Just before the blinking yellow traffic light at the intersection of U.S. 64, NM 150, and NM 522 there's a Texaco station on the left, and behind it a dirt road: Museum Drive. Follow Museum Drive 1 mile (1½ km) and you're there. The museum has undergone several expansions since the fifties, and includes artifacts of both religious and colonial New Mexico. Special exhibits are always noteworthy and keep local residents coming back. The museum is open year-round except for major holidays and San Geronimo Day (September 30). The **Millicent Rogers Museum Store** here is a good place to find local crafts and folk art.

Three restaurants in the neighborhood stand out, all within a mile of each other. On NM 522 a little less than a mile north of the blinking light is **Villa Fontana**, where chef Carlo Gislemberti, who trained in some of the great hotels of Europe, plies his trade. The cuisine of the house is classical northern Italian, but the menu expands to include seasonal dishes such as wild-mushroom soup, a house specialty and a local favorite. Gislemberti's creations stand up to the best anywhere, but the wine, on a fairly extensive list, is overpriced. Tel: 758-5800; closed Sundays. The **Brett House**, in the former home of Taos artist Lady Dorothy Brett, sits at the corner of NM 522 and NM 150. Open for dinner Tuesday through Sunday, it serves a wide range of Continental and American dishes including steaks, seafood, and regional specialties. They even experiment with ethnic cuisine one evening a week. Try to get a table with a view of Taos Mountain. Tel: 776-

8545. A mile (1½ km) north of the Brett House on NM 150 is the softly lit **Carl's French Quarter** at the Quail Ridge Inn. Carl's, with its big, blazing fireplace in winter, is noted for seafood and Creole and Cajun specialties, including blackened redfish, blackened prime rib, and Cajun popcorn. Tel: 776-8319.

Taos Pueblo

At the base of 12,000-foot Pueblo Peak, Taos Pueblo ranks as one of the most important historic sites in the Southwest, not to mention most picturesque. As the largest pueblo structures anywhere, the two main multistoried dwellings have long captured the imaginations of travellers from all over the world. The Pueblo's nomination in 1988 as a United Nations World Heritage Cultural Site has validated that fame, placing Taos Pueblo in a class with the Taj Mahal and the pyramids of Egypt. To get to the Pueblo from the center of Taos go north on Paseo del Pueblo Norte (U.S. 64) for a quarter mile, veer right at the Allsup's store, and drive 3 miles (5 km) north. If you opt to walk from Taos Plaza instead, it will take 45 minutes to an hour.

As you leave Taos behind and pass onto Pueblo land, the scenery quickly turns rural and the speed limit drops to 35 m.p.h. Keep alert for the tribe's stray horses. A mile (1½ km) up the road sit **Tony Reyna's Indian Shop** and **Sonny Spruce's Indian Shop**, two great places for Indian crafts of all types, especially from the New Mexico pueblos. Each of the eight northern pueblos is noted for a particular craft: Santa Clara, for example, for its black pottery; Taos for its drums. Less than a mile north of Sonny Spruce's is **Red Shirt Yu-Neek Drums Shop**, the largest of the drum-makers' shops located at the Pueblo. There's no sign out front, so look for hollowed-out cottonwood logs surrounding the house; owner Mike Red Shirt fashions them into drums. Because of the current popularity of drums as decorator items, inventory may be low, so you may have to shop the retail stores in town or those ahead at the Pueblo itself.

Continuing north, you will pass the homes of some of the Pueblo's roughly 1,800 residents. Follow the cars through an intersection, stop at the entrance gate, and sign the register. You'll pay a fee to park and additional fees for permits to sketch or take videos and photographs. Tours, which run from May 1 through November 1, are officially free (though the tour guides will expect a tip) and are highly recommended; the guides will escort you through restricted areas, explaining construction methods and describing significant ruins, the historical and cultural interest of which may be lost to the casual observer. If you elect to strike off on your own be sure to respect the no-trespassing barricades—or you will be abruptly escorted back to the parking lot. Remember, this is not a museum, and while the residents are happy to let you visit, they will not tolerate you popping into places where you don't belong.

Looking north from the parking area you will see the bald face of Pueblo Peak, whose summit wears a mantle of snow for all but a few months of the year. If you could somehow be transported to the top you would look down on Blue Lake, Taos Pueblo's sacred religious shrine and the source of the Rio Pueblo. The river supplies water for those who live in the multistoried pueblos and for irrigating the surrounding fields.

Neither pueblo structure has plumbing or electricity, in deference to tradition. About 70 families still live here, but most prefer homes with modern conveniences. Even so, the pueblos remain the oldest continually inhabited structures in North America. (Some scholars have argued that these pueblos were not the ones seen in the area by white men in 1540 when Coronado came through Northern New Mexico in search of Cíbola; however, no records of an Acoma-like destruction of those original structures have been found.)

Taos means "place of red willows" in the Tiwa language, which most of the Pueblo's residents struggle to keep alive. Related to the Anasazi peoples of Mesa Verde and Chaco Canyon, Taos Indians settled here almost 1,000 years ago. No one knows precisely when, and the Tribal Council repeatedly turns down requests from archaeologists who would like to resolve the debate. This area was probably attractive to settlement because the Rio Pueblo proved reliable in a time of prolonged drought. No wonder, then, that the Taos Indians regard Blue Lake and its watershed as sacred, at the center of their religion. And no wonder they fought so hard to get Blue Lake back from the U.S. government, which, in 1906, absorbed it into the Carson National Forest. They succeeded: In 1971 Richard Nixon signed House Resolution 471, ending the 64-year-old legal battle and returning the lake and surrounding land to Taos Pueblo.

The U.S. government was not the first to chip away at Pueblo lands. When the conquistadors arrived the Taos homeland stretched over much of present-day Taos, Colfax, and Mora counties, with Blue Lake its spiritual center. It was an important trading area, too, where Pueblo tribes met Plains Indians from the east, Navajos from the west, and Apaches, Comanches, and Utes. Despite treaties giving Taos Pueblo possessory rights, land grants from the Spanish crown, fraudulent titles issued by corrupt Mexican administrators, and squatters reduced their lands at the same time that disease and oppression were reducing the tribe's population from an estimated 15,000 in Coronado's time to fewer than 500 when Blue Lake was appropriated. Along the way the Spanish converted the Pueblo to Catholicism, using force when persuasion failed. (The Inquisition coincided with the colonization of the New World; Pueblo tribes up and down the Rio Grande were persecuted for practicing native religions until the Pueblo revolt of 1680 expelled the Spanish for a dozen years.) Today most Pueblo residents worship in the Roman Catholic San Geronimo Chapel here while simultaneously preserving the sacred ways of their ancestors. As you face the north pueblo you can see ladders emerging from kivas, where elders keep alive a religion based on the sanctity of nature and the interconnectedness of all things.

As you leave San Geronimo Chapel, turn left down the lane from which you entered the pueblo. Turn right at the stop sign and you'll see the ruins of the original San Geronimo Chapel. In 1847 Mexicans and Taos Indians revolted against the growing American presence in New Mexico. They killed the territorial governor, Charles Bent, and retreated to this chapel. Two weeks later the U.S. cavalry laid siege, reducing the chapel to rubble and killing 150 inside. The bell tower, all that remains today, is left standing in commemoration of those who died 146 years ago.

All structures within the historic plazas are constructed of adobe (sun-dried mud brick). The bricks are cemented together with mud and, finally, plastered over with a mud slurry as protection against the elements—a job that must be redone every year or so. It's hard work, but materials are free. The many small gift shops in the Pueblo's lower floors allow you to observe more construction details, such as the logs, called *vigas,* which support the ceilings and the roofs of mud, not to mention the apartments above, which are stacked up to five stories high. Explore a few shops, then sample the fry bread sold by women in the plaza. Both the fry bread and bread baked in the beehive-like *hornos* (ovens) were introduced by the Spanish.

If you're fortunate enough to be in Taos on September 29 and 30, don't miss the festivities of San Geronimo Day, when the Pueblo teems with hundreds of Indian arts, crafts, and food vendors, and is the scene of Indian dances and merriment. San Geronimo is the Spanish-christened patron saint of the Pueblo, but the tribe puts a Taos twist on the festivities: A dozen "ceremonial clowns" move through the crowds, exacting tribute from vendors and playing practical jokes on tribal members—only occasionally on a tourist. A pole climb caps the ceremony, when one of the ceremonial clowns reaches a cache of food atop a 40-foot pole.

Dances are common throughout the year, so check local listings when you get to town. Other dances of note are the deer dance, or Matachines dance, performed on Christmas Day, and the inspiring buffalo or deer dance on January 6. Keep in mind that these dances, including the festivities during San Geronimo, are religious in nature, and photography is therefore not allowed. The Pueblo is closed to visitors in February.

Photographers get their chance at the annual Taos Pueblo PowWow during the second weekend in July. Hundreds of Indians from all over the United States and Canada congregate in pastures near Overland Sheepskin Company, just off NM 64, 4 miles (6½ km) north of Taos Plaza, for three days of dancing and singing. Troupes try to outdo each other in costumes and dance competitions, with prizes awarded to the winners. (Take folding chairs or blankets to sit on.) An Indian arts-and-crafts market does brisk business. You'll pay an entrance fee for all the colorful entertainment, but camping is free if you'd like to pitch your tent alongside a real tepee.

AROUND TAOS

The natural beauty of the Taos area is what strikes most people first. Here the planet's bone structure is on display, the product of the Sangre de Cristo uplift, which created the mountains east of Taos, and of volcanic activity to the west, which created the cinder cones and basalt flows that the Rio Grande proceeded to carve even as they were being formed. What all this boils down to is spectacular scenery for armchair athletes and lots of fun for outdoor enthusiasts.

Think of a circle with Taos on the southwest perimeter. This is the Enchanted Circle (the roads forming the circumference of which we'll discuss later). In the middle of the circle are situated Mount Wheeler, the tallest peak in the state at 13,131 feet, and Taos Ski Valley, both accessible via NM 150, which runs northeasterly from the blinking light at the junction of U.S. 64 and NM 522 in Taos.

Our coverage around Taos begins with Taos Ski Valley—one of the most impressive places to enter the mountains no matter what the season—as well as a brief discussion of other Northern New Mexico ski resorts. Then we'll introduce you to the Enchanted Circle, a 100-mile loop from Taos through gorgeous countryside: Angel Fire, Eagle Nest, Red River, and Questa. Carson National Forest surrounds Taos Valley, and after covering Questa and the western perimeter of the Enchanted Circle we offer a glimpse into the valley's many wonders next, as well as some information on the rivers and deserts of this area.

Taos Ski Valley

There's no question but that more people visit the mountains around Taos during winter than at any other time of the year. With four downhill ski areas close by—Angel Fire, Red River, Sipapu, and Taos Ski Valley—Taos gets much of its national exposure from winter-sports enthusiasts who glimpse Taos's other assets and vow to return. What sets Taos Ski Valley (TSV) apart from other world-famous ski areas is its small size and decidedly European atmosphere. Here Taos's remoteness translates into short lift lines during all but holiday seasons. With only 900 pillows for rent at the base and a moratorium on water hookups, Taos will never have the traffic of a Vail or an Aspen. And the Blake family, who own and operate TSV—children of founder Ernie Blake—want to keep it that way: a resort for the serious skier. With 2,600 feet of vertical drop, nine chairs, and 72 runs, many of which are marked "expert," TSV has a well-deserved reputation for difficulty. But there is a lot of intermediate and beginner terrain, too. To get to TSV from Taos take U.S. 64/NM 522 northwest 4 miles (6½ km) to the blinking yellow light and turn right, then follow NM 150 15 miles (24 km) north.

Salsa del Salto, 1 mile (1½ km) north of the village of

Arroyo Seco on NM 150, is a real gem of a bed-and-breakfast inn: Only eight rooms furnished with local furniture and down comforters, it's close to the ski valley (only 10 miles/16 km) while not too far from Taos (only 9 miles/14½ km). Designed by architect Antoine Predock, the inn's rooms have striking views of the mountains and numerous amenities, including use of the pool, spa, and tennis court. All this, plus terrific breakfasts and afternoon appetizers, make this a superb choice in any season.

True "powder hounds" who must spend every second skiing will prefer, however, to stay at the slopes. Most lodges at the base rent by the week—Saturday to Saturday—and are on the European plan: all meals included. While most accommodations are only ordinary, the overall experience at Taos is not. The food is some of the best you'll find anywhere, and virtually all your needs are attended to, so you can concentrate on what you came for. About $1,300 a week buys your lodging; three meals a day, including wine at dinner (if you wish); and lift tickets and morning lessons at the ski school, which experts continually rank as one of the best in the country. All you have to worry about are the bar tab and ski tune-ups, available at several ski shops nearby.

The **Hotel St. Bernard**, an old stone-and-log structure that makes you think of bear-trap bindings and lederhosen, is owned by Jean Mayer, of French ski-racing fame. One of the first lodges built here, it sits high on the bunny slope and is famous for its food; the beef Wellington is especially popular. The St. Bernard depends almost entirely on return guests, which says volumes about the quality of its food and service. The **Hotel Edelweiss**, owned by Mayer's brother, Dadou, is also noted for its food, as is the **Thunderbird Lodge**, across the Rio Hondo about a hundred yards from the main lodge.

Don't expect much nightlife at the ski valley. The notable exceptions are the St. Bernard, which occasionally hosts two-step music in the bar, and the Thunderbird Lodge, which hosts the January Jazz Festival, when it brings in a dozen big names such as Ralph Sutton, Scott Hamilton, and Butch Miles.

If European plan isn't your scene, there are a number of condominiums with full kitchen facilities. Among the nicer ones are **Rio Hondo Condominiums** and **St. Bernard Condos**. At the latter, lodgers may elect to purchase a meal plan at Hotel St. Bernard. Like the hotels, the condos also rent from Saturday to Saturday during ski season. If you don't want to backtrack to Taos after checking in, be sure to buy groceries and supplies before you head into the mountains.

One unpublicized, word-of-mouth find here is the **Chalet Montesano**, a small inn with a lap pool, an exercise room, and a ski-in/ski-out location; all suites are equipped with kitchenettes. Unlike other accommodations near the resort, the inn is open year-round.

Whether you stay in a condo, a bed-and-breakfast inn, or park your RV in the lot, you can dine at the Thunderbird, the St. Bernard, the Edelweiss, or the Hondo Lodge. **Tim's Stray Dog Cantina** in the base area at TSV specializes in Mexican food, and is open year-round for breakfast, lunch, and dinner, serving not only skiers but summer visitors too—of which TSV has more every year. (For other dining choices between Taos and Taos Ski Valley, see North of the Historic District, above.)

Taos School of Music (see Paseo del Pueblo Norte, above) occupies the Hotel St. Bernard in June and July, filling the ski valley with the sound of music. Lectures on specific musical compositions are open to the public at no charge one night each week. The Rio Hondo Condominiums and others book summer rentals, which lets you put an Alpine face on a warm-weather Taos vacation. If you visit in summer, try to make the hike to Wheeler Peak, the tallest in the state; the ten-mile trail to Mount Wheeler takes off behind the Thunderbird Lodge. A shorter, less demanding hike to Williams Lake takes off to the left of ski lift number one.

Northern New Mexico Ski Areas

Taos Ski Valley (TSV) is 19 miles (30 km) north of Taos on NM 150 and partially situated on 1,300 acres of Carson National Forest, with 1,050 skiable acres. TSV offers 72 slopes, three quad lifts, five double chair lifts, one triple chair lift, and two surface lifts. The average annual snowfall is 306 inches, and TSV pridefully acknowledges a 2,612-foot vertical drop. Snowmaking is used when needed. The village elevation is 9,207 feet, with a summit elevation of 11,819 feet. The longest run at TSV is five and a half miles and the terrain is 24 percent novice, 25 percent intermediate, and 51 percent advanced. Daily, weekly, private, or group lessons are available all season, seven days a week. Multiple children's programs for ages six weeks to 12 years are offered by the day or week. Handicap access is available. Snow boards are not permitted. Retail shops and downhill and cross-country rental equipment are available, but there is no full grocery store in the valley. Round-trip ski shuttles leave from town hotels and the TSV parking lot daily. TSV is open from Thanksgiving to the first week in April. Tel: 776-2291; 776-2233 or (800) 776-1111 (reservations); 24-hour snow phone: 776-2916.

Angel Fire Ski Area, 26 miles (42 km) east of Taos on 365 mountainous acres, has four double and two triple lifts, a base elevation of 8,500 feet, and a summit elevation of 10,680 feet. Angel Fire's vertical drop is 2,180 feet and the area boasts 57 trails. Its average snowfall is 140 inches and its longest run is three and two-tenths miles. The terrain is 40 percent novice, 45 percent intermediate, and 15 percent advanced. Snowmaking capacity covers 50 percent of the mountain. Snow boards are permitted. Handicap access is available as are daily, weekly, private, or group lessons and children's ski programs (ages three to 12). You can rent downhill and cross-country equipment at the ski area. Angel Fire's season runs from December 10 to March 28. Tel: (800) 446-8117 or (800) 633-7463; snow phone: 377-4222. (For more on Angel Fire, see below.)

Red River Ski Area, 37 miles (59 km) northwest of Taos, sits on 204 acres of Carson National Forest. It has three double chairs, two triple chairs, and one surface tow to reach 49 ski runs. Snowmaking covers 75 percent of the terrain. Red River's longest run is two and a half miles and its terrain is 32 percent novice, 38 percent intermediate, and 30 percent advanced. The ski area's base elevation is 8,750, while the top elevation is 10,350, giving a vertical drop of 1,600 feet. The ski area offers child care for ages six months to four years, and daily, weekly, private, or group lessons. Snow boards are welcome. Downhill ski-equipment rental and retail shops abound in the ski area and in the town of Red River. Cross-country equipment is available only in town. Red River ski season runs from Thanksgiving to April 1. Tel: 754-2382. (For more on Red River, see below.)

Sipapu Ski Area is only 25 miles (40 km) southeast of Taos via NM 518, and has three lifts: one triple chair and two poma lifts. The base of the mountain sits at 8,200 feet and the top elevation is at 9,000 feet, giving a vertical drop of 800 feet. Sipapu's longest run is one and one-third miles. The terrain is 10 percent novice, 70 percent intermediate, and 20 percent advanced. Daily, weekly, private, or group lessons are offered for ages four and up. Services are limited, so check to see if they have what you need before going. Sipapu opens when there's snow and closes when there's not; the season is roughly Christmas through mid-March. Tel: 587-2240. (For more on Sipapu, see below.)

If you plan on doing a lot of skiing during your stay, you might want to invest $15 in a SKI 3 Card. The card entitles you to $6 off the regular lift-ticket price during the week and $3 off on weekends at Taos Ski Valley, Angel Fire, and Red River. Write to SKI 3, P.O. Box 15425, Santa Fe, NM 87506.

The Enchanted Circle

This 100-mile auto loop can be driven safely in about three and a half hours—without stops—in good weather. The scenery is so spectacular you may decide to do just that, or you might want to at least take the time to enjoy a picnic en route. But because the Enchanted Circle passes through or by several quaint, fun-loving communities that serve up various events throughout the year, you may want to make points on the circle vacation destinations, as many visitors do, and visit Taos on day-trip excursions. Whatever you decide, there's a lot to do here.

The Enchanted Circle loop to the north of Taos in effect encircles Taos Ski Valley and 13,161-foot Wheeler Peak. The "bottom" third of the route is U.S. 64 as it runs through Taos and east through Carson National Forest, over Palo Flechado Pass into the Moreno Valley, past the turnoff for the Angel Fire Ski Area and past Eagle Nest Lake up to Eagle Nest. (At Eagle Nest you can leave the loop for a side trip east, staying on U.S. 64, through Cimarron Canyon.)

NM 38, the "top" third, travels from Eagle Nest up and around through the town of Red River and over the mountains (more of the national forest) west to the town of Questa. The last, western third is straight-as-an-arrow NM 522 south from Questa and back into Taos—a hilly and scenic leg that will get you back to Taos while exposing you to lots of wide-open Northern New Mexico vistas to the west.

You can make the loop either clockwise—by leaving Taos to the north on NM 522—or counterclockwise, the route we follow, through Taos Canyon to the east from the Taos Plaza traffic light on U.S. 64 (here, Kit Carson Road). Fall is the most popular time of year for this excursion, and the road, especially where two narrow lanes wind through Taos Canyon, can be heavily travelled. If so, relax and enjoy the scenery. There are plenty of places to stop and pass the time in camp and picnic grounds maintained by the Carson National Forest (for which, see below).

About 7 miles (11 km) east of Taos Plaza on U.S. 64 is the turnoff to **Shadow Mountain Ranch**, where you can horseback ride by the day or half day. In winter many of these forest roads make excellent cross-country ski trails, most notably the Garcia Park Road and La Junta Canyon. (A map of all these roads is available at the Carson National Forest Visitors Center at the corner of Paseo del Pueblo Sur and Paseo del Cañon in Taos.) It's about 18 miles (29 km) east on U.S. 64 from Taos Plaza to 9,017-foot-high Palo Flechado Pass, once commonly used by Indians, Spanish, and Anglo settlers travelling west from Cimarron. On the other side of the mountain you begin a rapid, hairpin descent into the Moreno Valley. Turn south onto NM 434 and you're in Angel Fire.

ANGEL FIRE

In 1966 Texas oil and cattleman Roy Lebus bought 12,000 acres of the Moreno Valley and built his dream resort, including a championship 18-hole golf course and a ski area. **Angel Fire Country Club and Golf Course** is a jewel of a course, perhaps one of the prettiest—and definitely one of the most challenging—in the Rockies. In summer the country club's dining room serves Rocky Mountain trout, steaks, and New Mexican specialties, and is a valley favorite. **Angel Fire Ski Area** is a full-service, well-managed resort with snowmaking on all runs and high-capacity chair lifts (lift lines are unheard of except on peak holidays). However, its snow is not as reliable and its runs are not as challenging as Taos Ski Valley, and without the vertical drop of Taos it's probably destined to live in TSV's shadow. On the other hand, lift tickets aren't as expensive here, and with so many condominiums for rent at the base—see Accommodations Reference at the end of the chapter—it's not as pricey as Taos either, and thus is attractive to families. It's also great for intermediate skiers. (For more detailed ski information, see Northern New Mexico Ski Areas, above.)

Angel Fire, the Moreno Valley's major attraction, qualifies as a four-season resort because of the special events it hosts. **Balloons Over Angel Fire**, in mid-July, exploits the crisp mountain air to send acres of colorful ripstop nylon climbing against the Sangre de Cristo Mountains backdrop. The **Angel Fire Repertory Theatre** produces 15 shows under the stars during their summer season. In

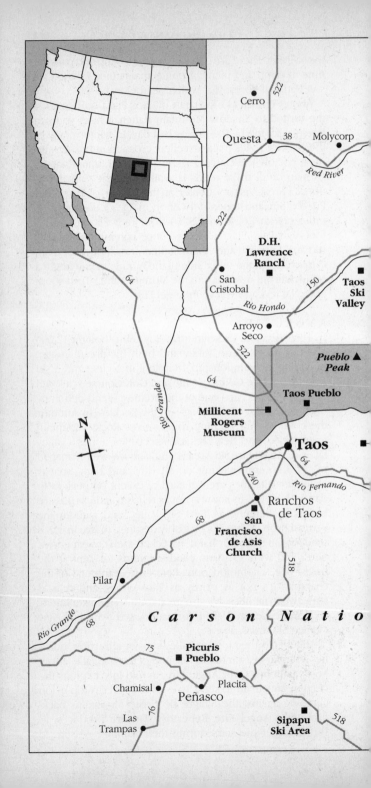

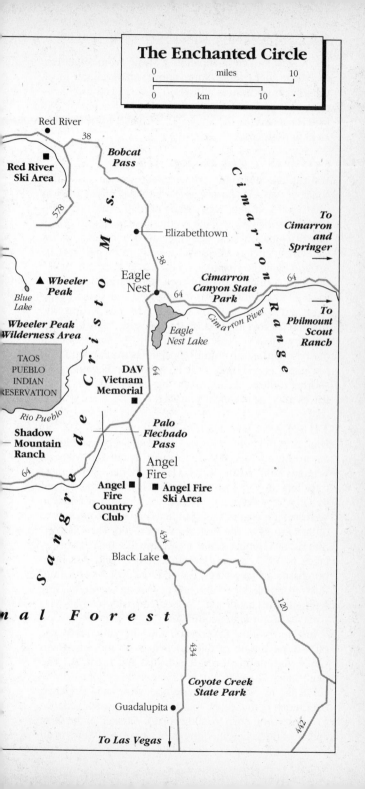

late August and early September **Music From Angel Fire**
(see Paseo del Pueblo Norte, above) unites all-star musicians from orchestras all over the world and gives concerts (classical and chamber music this year) at the Village Haus here, at the Shuler Theatre in Raton (90 miles/
144 km northeast of Taos), and in Taos.

COYOTE CREEK AND SIPAPU
You can detour from the Enchanted Circle and continue
south on NM 434 (known as Black Lake Road) all the way
to Mora if you like. This stretch of road, which parallels
Coyote Creek, is one of the prettiest and most inspiring of
America's back roads. Recently paved in order to allow
valley residents a safer drive down to Las Vegas (see the
Around Santa Fe chapter), it now lets visitors experience
the high country, **Coyote Creek State Park**, and the tiny
town of Guadalupita. From there you can swing northwest and return to Taos via NM 518 past **Sipapu**, the
smallest ski area in Taos County, discussed above in Northern New Mexico Ski Areas. With only one small lodge at
the base and a "small hill," Sipapu has trouble attracting
the experienced skier, but it's great for beginners. (A
shorter route to Sipapu from Taos is via NM 518, which
leaves town near Ranchos de Taos.)

THE EAGLE NEST AREA
High on a hill between Angel Fire and Eagle Nest, off U.S.
64, in the middle of Moreno Valley, is the DAV Vietnam
Veterans National Memorial, a landmark that catches most
travellers' eyes before they know what it is. Constructed
by Dr. Victor Westphall, whose son David was killed in
Vietnam, the chapel was completed in 1971, long before
other shrines to the Vietnam War existed. The Disabled
American Veterans came to Westphall's financial assistance in 1977. Since then additional acreage has been
purchased and a visitors' center added, where a continuously running video is shown. During Memorial Day
weekend the chapel and grounds teem with veterans who
come to honor fallen comrades.

Just north of the DAV turnoff and a hundred yards east
off U.S. 64 is one of the quiet finds on the Enchanted
Circle, the **Monte Verde Ranch Bed and Breakfast**. The
main "Rock House," built in 1935, served as home for the
Lebus family, whose ranching operation once stretched
over much of the valley. Today it provides guests a chance
to enter a time warp from the forties. Situated in the dead
center of the valley, the inn offers astonishing views in all

directions. If you want to fish or hike, you have a thousand acres and teeming trout streams to do it in, plus the run of neighborhing national forest lands. Four moderately priced, antiques-filled rooms make this a great travel value. Too bad it's closed in winter.

Eagle Nest Lake, a 2,200-acre sports-lover's paradise, has two outfits where you can rent or launch your own boat. The lake is a favorite fishing spot and well stocked with trout and kokanee salmon. It's also popular with windsurfers, who find challenge in the volatile mountain winds. The town of **Eagle Nest**, where U.S. 64 turns east and the Enchanted Circle continues north on NM 38, doesn't have much to recommend it, except an arts-and-crafts fair each year in late July and Kaw-Lija's Restaurant, where you can get a great hamburger and ice cream cone. Fishing tackle, bait, groceries, and gasoline are also available in Eagle Nest.

CIMARRON

Leave the Enchanted Circle and head east on U.S. 64. After 2½ miles (3½ km) you'll enter scenic **Cimarron Canyon**, loaded with camping and fishing spots on the Cimarron River, including those in Cimarron Canyon State Park. From Eagle Nest it's 24 miles (38 km) to the town of Cimarron, once synonymous with the Wild West. Today its biggest attraction is the **Philmont Scout Ranch**, 137,000 acres of mountains, valleys, rivers, forests, and archaeological sites where thousands of Boy Scouts from all over the world convene for ten-day visits each summer. Scouts select from 27 different programs for their visits, ranging from archaeology and rock climbing to "living history." The huge ranch was a gift to the Boy Scouts of America from Waite Phillips, prodigal son of the Phillips Petroleum family, who built Philmont and then left to seek his fortune elsewhere. Since the summer of 1939 Philmont has enriched the lives of countless Boy Scouts. The whole story is told at the Philmont Museum, which serves as a visitors' center, 10 miles (16 km) south of Cimarron on NM 21.

Only six miles (10 km) south of Cimarron on NM 21, **Casa del Gavilán** nestles in the east slope of the Sangre de Cristo foothills. Built in the early 1900s by Eastern industrialist J. J. Nairn, Casa del Gavilán is today a sprawling adobe bed-and-breakfast inn with seven rooms and large common areas suited to small retreats and conferences. The inn serves full breakfasts and will accommodate with picnic lunches and light suppers for an additional charge. The **Old Mill Museum** in Cimarron, housing four stories of exhibits on Wild West and Cimarron history, is worth a visit. If you're bound for points farther east keep your eyes open for pronghorn antelope and deer in the plains between Cimarron and Springer.

THE RED RIVER AREA

To continue on the northern leg of the Enchanted Circle, leave U.S. 64 at Eagle Nest and head north on NM 38. It's about 13 miles (21 km) from Eagle Nest to 9,820-foot-high Bobcat Pass. Along the way, at 5 miles (8 km), you pass Elizabethtown—what's left of a once-bustling gold town. Few buildings remain standing from the day when almost 1,500 miners called it home. If you want a closer look, turn down the driveway (on the west side of the highway) with the cattle guard—a bed of pipes that prevents cattle from exiting their pasture. It's the only road leaving the highway along that stretch.

As you descend Bobcat Pass on the northwest side watch out for loose rock on the road. On a certain Sunday in late September you should also watch out for bicyclists doing the Enchanted Circle Century Bicycle Tour, a 100-mile loop that begins and ends in the thriving community of **Red River**, a gold-mining boomtown that had a population of more than 3,000 in the early 1900s. Today the permanent population remains stable at about a tenth of that, most of whom "mine" the visitors who make this a boomtown each winter when they come in search of "white gold." The mostly intermediate runs of **Red River Ski Area** (see Northern New Mexico Ski Areas, above, for ski details) are popular with families from West Texas who help give the town a decidedly Texan flavor.

In winter Red River's well-groomed Nordic ski center, **Enchanted Forest**, offers 18½ miles of groomed trails, lessons, and clinics. In late February the Enchanted Forest hosts Just Desserts Eat and Ski—a workout for a worthy payoff; Tel: 754-2374. In summer Red River's several stables offer horseback riding, while companies situated on Main Street offer four-wheel-drive tours, back-country treks, and trips to old mines. **Michael Martin Murphey's Westfest** turns Red River into a boomtown for one weekend in June. Two days of country music and scores of Western arts, crafts, and food vendors highlight the festivities.

Lifts West Condominium Resort Hotel in Red River offers hotel rooms of all sizes up to spacious three-bedroom suites with fireplaces. The dramatic lobby of the main building boasts huge spruce-log construction and a three-story courtyard. Lifts West is a decade old, but the rooms still seem new and quiet. Suites are equipped with kitchenettes; most have fireplaces. (See also Condominiums in the Accommodations Reference at the end of the chapter.) Dining in Red River is decidedly Texan; don't even think about health food or nouvelle cuisine. Both **Brett's Steakhouse** and **Texas Red's Steakhouse** are open for lunch and dinner, serving traditional steak-and-spirits fare.

Continuing west on NM 38 toward Questa you pass through scenic **Red River Canyon**, with several campgrounds maintained by the Carson National Forest. Molycorp mine, a molybdenum operation that is the last extractive industry left in the county (and one of its biggest employers), dominates the northern scenery for this part of the tour. During World War I the Allies captured one of the big German guns and assayed the metal to determine how those ingenious Germans could hurl their shells so far. They found that the steel had been hardened with molybdenum, and thus the mine was born. Today, with cheaper sources of molybdenum available overseas, the Molycorp mine is an on-again, off-again operation.

SOUTH TO TAOS

In the town of **Questa** at the junction of NM 38 and NM 522 you can see the well-maintained **Iglesia de San Antonio** on old Questa Plaza. This is clearly an old church, judging from the *vigas* (beams) protruding well below a tin roof (which must have been added later). But no information sheet or plaques exist.

It's roughly 20 miles (32 km) from Questa straight south on NM 522 through rolling piñon country to the blinking light just north of Taos. Halfway, you pass the turnoff east to San Cristobal and the **D. H. Lawrence Ranch.** After visiting Taos arts patroness Mabel Dodge Luhan, Lawrence decided to live and work here for a time. Today the ranch is a retreat owned by the University of New Mexico. A couple hundred yards up a steep, boulder-strewn trail is a small shrine containing Lawrence's ashes.

Going down NM 522 toward Taos you pass over a rise similar to the one the painter Ernest Blumenschein must have traversed when he saw Taos for the first time and received the "first great inspiration" of his life. As you near the blinking light you will see a large residential compound on the east side of the highway that overlooks several sculptures in the fields to the south. This is home of famed Navajo artist R. C. Gorman.

The Carson National Forest

The Carson National Forest literally surrounds Taos Valley, and much of it is accessible through campgrounds and hiking trailheads positioned along major highways. Carson maintains 39 campgrounds with varying levels of service. Drinking water and toilets are available at 11 of them. Don't see a campground to your liking? It's your legal right to camp anywhere on U.S. Forest lands. If you're the adventurous type head up any forest road you see and "throw down" wherever you like. Hiking trails vary too in length and level of effort. Carson has a total of 330 miles of trails; some of these, however, are in the forest's seven wilderness areas, which do not permit mountain bikes or any motorized vehicle. One such hike, to Divisidero Peak, takes off from U.S. 64 in Taos Canyon, across the road from El Nogal Picnic Area; climbing two and a half miles uphill rewards you with views of the Taos Valley.

If you want to explore trails outside of the wilderness areas, Red Dawg Rentals on Main Street in Red River rents trail bikes and ATVs. They can also direct you to the best spots for riding. Gearing Up at 129 Paseo del Pueblo Sur between Taos and Ranchos de Taos rents bicycles to match your objectives, or can repair the one you brought with you.

Rock climbers find Taos a mecca. A guidebook to Taos rock climbing, called *Taos Rock III,* is a photocopied edition put out by local climbers and sold at Taos Mountain Outfitters on Taos's South Plaza. They also sell topographical maps if you need them for hiking. Whatever you want, the Carson National Forest Visitors Center, in the same building as the Taos County Chamber of Commerce (on the corner of the Raton bypass and Paseo del Pueblo Sur), will provide you with maps and advice on campsites, backcountry trails, wilderness areas, and cross-country skiing. Open Monday through Friday.

THE RIVERS
AND THE DESERT

The many mountain streams around Taos afford unlimited opportunities for fishing. Taylor Streit Flyfishing Service (Tel: 751-1312) gives expert instruction to all levels of anglers and provides a guide service to the best fishing holes in Northern New Mexico. Casting, selecting a fly, reading water, and "thinking like a trout" are some of the skills Taylor shares. The state's game and fish department stocks most of the area's major streams, such as the Little Rio Grande, Rio Hondo, Rio Fernando, Red River, Rio Costilla, and Rio Grande in addition to most lakes and reservoirs. With so many vacationers in and around Taos, your ability to "limit" is mostly determined by your perseverance in getting to inaccessible spots, especially along the Rio Grande. During the summer at the Red River Fish Hatchery on NM 522 just south of Questa, your kids (11 years and younger) are almost guaranteed their limit— while *you* watch.

THE RIO GRANDE GORGE

The Rio Grande Gorge, which cuts through Taos Valley, offers most challenging fishing because of its inaccessibility and because of the variety of fish swimming in it. Native species of trout and northern pike have been stocked over the years. Information about how to get into the gorge can be obtained from the Carson National Forest Visitors Center (see above) or the U.S. Bureau of Land Management. And you need a fishing license, which you can buy at sporting-goods stores or fishing shops all over town.

Even if you don't plan to fish, you can experience the gorge, expending as little or as much energy as you wish. The easiest way is to drive north from Taos on NM 522 to the blinking yellow light, then take U.S. 64 west 7 miles (11 km) to the **Rio Grande Gorge Bridge**. It's a 650-foot drop to the water, so you will see why many call this a mini–Grand Canyon. It's exactly that to people who live here, each of whom has his or her favorite way to enjoy it.

A more logical way to appreciate the gorge is to get down into it. The truly adventurous who don't mind a windy, gravel road can enter the gorge at **Orilla Verde State Park** by taking NM 68 some 2 miles (3 km) south of Ranchos de Taos, and then NM 570 about 6 miles (10 km) west to the park entrance. Beyond the entrance the road turns into a steep, white-knuckle affair as it descends into the gorge. Less ambitious travellers can find Orilla Verde State Park by driving to the town of Pilar 20 miles (32 km) south of Taos on NM 68 and following the signs. At Pilar you're already in the gorge. You'll find five well-maintained campgrounds on the narrow road that runs the length of the park. Slow-moving water lets you wade or swim safely, and guided hikes leave the Taos Junction Campground parking lot daily at 10:00 A.M. in the summer.

The unqualified best way to enjoy the gorge is to take a rafting trip during the high-water months of April, May, and June. Some years are better than others depending on snowfall, rain, and when the farmers in the San Luis Valley of southern Colorado begin to irrigate. This section of the Rio Grande, called the Taos Box, runs from John Dunn Bridge north of Taos to the Taos Junction Bridge in Orilla Verde State Park. It has several class III and IV rapids, so this is not a do-it-yourself excursion. Far Flung Adventures (Tel: 758-2628 or 800/359-4138), Los Rios River Runners (Tel: 776-8854), and Native Sons Adventures (Tel: 758-9342 or 800/753-7559) are the best of many outfitters in terms of equipment, professionalism of guides, and the all-important lunch. They take care of everything, including rubberized gear, transportation, life preservers, and, of course, food. All you need to bring are old tennis shoes. All three companies provide expert guide services on the Rio Chama as well as through the Taos Box and the "Racecourse" sections of the Rio Grande south of Pilar. (The Rio Chama, about 80 miles/128 km west of Taos, flows southeasterly from its headwaters near the town of Chama to the Abiquiu Reservoir, and then to its confluence with the Rio Grande at San Juan Pueblo, just north of the town of Española.)

A more strenuous way to experience the desert and gorge is at the Bureau of Land Management **Wild and Scenic Rivers Recreation Area**. Take NM 522 north of Taos to Questa; 6 miles (10 km) north of Questa turn left and follow the signs through the village of Cerro. The staff of the visitors' center can direct you to many hiking trails that plunk you into the Rio Grande Gorge in one of its most untamed spots, where all wildlife is protected. The Big Arsenic and Little Arsenic springs trails are two of the prettiest hikes down; it's two miles to the river. You may fish; many two-pound lunkers hide out among boulders as big as cars. There are a few shelters, and hundreds of unimproved sites. Water from the springs is filtered through a mile of granite and several miles of lava, and so is some of the sweetest found on earth. Be sure to fill your water bottle for the trip back up.

GETTING AROUND

Automobiles provide the most flexibility and freedom for a short or extended stay in Taos. However, if you absolutely refuse to drive there are alternatives. **Grayline Tours** offers half-day and all-day side trips to Taos from Santa Fe. Of course, that's not enough time. **Pride of Taos** (Tel: 758-8340) has tours of the valley and gives special sightseeing tours by prior arrangement; it also operates shuttles directly to and from Albuquerque Airport. **Step On Guide Service** (Tel: 758-4020, P.O. Box 8, El Prado, NM 87529) has personal guides who ride in your rented car or taxi. Faust's Transportation (Tel: 758-3410, P.O. Box 1050, El Prado, NM 87529) runs a taxi service and charter-bus service, including in-town transportation or airport service to Albuquerque and to the Amtrak stations in Lamy (south of Santa Fe) and Raton (90 miles/144 km northeast of Taos). In winter both Pride of Taos and Faust's Transportation operate ski shuttles from lodges in Taos to Taos Ski Valley.

Four active Chambers of Commerce are eager to help you plan your vacation to Taos County:

Taos County Chamber of Commerce, P.O. Drawer I, Taos, NM 87571, Tel: 758-3873 or (800) 732-TAOS;

Angel Fire Resort Chamber of Commerce, P.O. Box 547, Angel Fire, NM 87710, Tel: 377-6661 or (800) 446-8117;

Eagle Nest Chamber of Commere, Box 3224, Eagle Nest, NM 87718, Tel: 377-2420;

Red River Chamber of Commerce, P.O. Box 870, Red River, NM 87558, Tel: 754-2366 or (800) 348-6444.

ACCOMMODATIONS REFERENCE

Many of these specially chosen accommodations have a small number of rooms, so advanced reservations are a must. Nonsmoking rooms are available or even the rule, and pet policies vary, so ask about both when making reservations. Many in-town properties offer off-season rates in late spring or early winter. Taos Ski Valley lodging is open from Thanksgiving to the first week in April unless otherwise indicated.

Private homes and condominiums as vacation rentals are especially appealing to large families or those who are staying for extended periods; listings are at the end of the reference section.

The area code for all of New Mexico is 505.

Toll-Free Reservation Services

▶ **Central Reservations.** Route 434, P.O. Drawer 457, Angel Fire, NM 87710. Tel: 377-3072 or (800) 635-9633; Fax: 377-3869.

▶ **Taos Central Reservations.** 314 Paseo del Pueblo Norte, P.O. Box 1713, Taos, NM 87571. Tel: 758-9767 or (800) 821-2437.

▶ **Taos Valley Resort Association.** P.O. Box 85, Taos Ski Valley, NM 87525. Tel: 776-2233 or (800) 776-1111; Fax: 776-8842.

The rates given below are projections *for 1993. Unless otherwise indicated, rates are for a double room, double occupancy, and do not include meals. Price ranges span the lowest rate in the low season and the highest rate in the high season. As rates are always subject to change, it is wise to double-check before booking.*

▶ **Adobe and Pines Inn.** P.O. Box 837, **Ranchos de Taos,** NM 87557. Tel: 751-0947 or (800) 723-8267; Fax: 758-8423. $85–$110.

▶ **Casa Benavides Bed and Breakfast Inn.** 137 Kit Carson Road, **Taos,** NM 87571. Tel: 758-1772. $80–$175.

▶ **Casa de las Chimeneas.** 405 Cordoba Road, Box 5303, Taos, NM 87571. Tel: 758-4777. $110–$158.

▶ **Casa del Gavilán.** Highway 21 South, P.O. Box 518, **Cimarron,** NM 87714. Tel: 376-2246 or (800) 445-5251; Fax: 376-2203. $65–$100.

▶ **Casa Europa.** 157 Upper Ranchitos Road, Taos, NM 87571. Tel: 758-9798 or (800) 525-8267. $70–$110.

▶ **Chalet Montesano.** Pattison Loop, P.O. Box 77, **Taos Ski Valley,** NM 87525. Tel: 776-8226; Fax: 776-8226, ext. 110. $122–$220 per unit/per night; $793–$1,430 per unit/per week.

▶ **Hotel Edelweiss.** P.O. Box 83, **Taos Ski Valley,** NM 87525. Tel: 776-2301. $1,200 per person/per week, includes 2 meals, all-day lift tickets, and morning ski lessons.

▶ **Hotel La Fonda de Taos.** 108 South Plaza, P.O. Box 1447, Taos, NM 87571. Tel: 758-2211 or (800) 833-2211. $65–$85.

▶ **Hotel St. Bernard.** P.O. Box 88, **Taos Ski Valley,** NM

87525. Tel: 776-2251. $1,300 per person/per week, includes all meals, all-day lift tickets, and morning ski lessons.

▶ **Lifts West Condominium Resort Hotel.** Main Street, P.O. Box 318, **Red River**, NM 87558. Tel: 754-2778 or (800) 221-1859; Fax: 754-6617. $55–$219.

▶ **Mabel Dodge Luhan House.** 240 Morada Lane, P.O. Box 3400, **Taos**, NM 87571. Tel: 758-9456 or (800) 846-2235; Fax: 751-0431. $75–$125.

▶ **Monte Verde Ranch Bed and Breakfast.** Highway 64, P.O. Box 173, **Angel Fire**, NM 87710. Tel: 377-6928. Open mid-May to October 31. $55–$75.

▶ **Rancho Rio Pueblo Taos Country Inn.** End of Karavas Road, P.O. Box 2331, **Taos**, NM 87571. Tel: 758-4900 or (800) 866-6548; Fax: 758-0331. $100–$150.

▶ **Rio Hondo Condominiums.** P.O. Box 81, **Taos Ski Valley**, NM 87525. Tel: 776-2646; Fax: 776-2825. 7/1–10/10: $65–$85 per night; 11/20–4/15: $1,150–$3,300 per week.

▶ **Sagebrush Inn.** Highway 68, P.O. Box 557, **Taos**, NM 87571. Tel: 758-2254 or (800) 428-3626; Fax: 758-9009. $85–$140.

▶ **St. Bernard Condos.** P.O. Box 676, **Taos Ski Valley**, NM 87525. Tel: 776-8506. $1,044 per person (in a party of four) per week, includes all-day lift ticket, morning ski lesson, and dinners at Hotel St. Bernard.

▶ **Salsa del Salto Bed & Breakfast Inn.** Highway 150, P.O. Box 1468, **El Prado**, NM 87529. Tel: 776-2422. $85–$160.

▶ **Taos Hacienda Inn.** 102 La Loma Plaza, Box 4159, **Taos**, NM 87571. Tel: 758-1717 or (800) 530-3040; Fax: 751-0155. $95–$295.

▶ **Taos Inn.** 125 Paseo del Pueblo Norte, **Taos**, NM 87571. Tel: 758-2233 or (800) 826-7466; Fax: 758-5776. $80–$155.

▶ **Thunderbird Lodge.** 3 Thunderbird Road, P.O. Box 87, **Taos Ski Valley**, NM 87525. Tel: 776-2280; Fax: 776-2238. $126 per person/per night, includes all meals; $1,170 per person/per week, includes all meals, 6-day lift ticket, and morning ski lessons.

Condominiums and Rentals in Private Homes

▶ **Bandanna Red River Properties.** Main Street, Box 555, **Red River**, NM 87558. Tel: 754-2949 or (800) 521-4389; Fax: 754-6246.

▶ **Del Norte Vista Properties.** 715C Paseo del Pueblo Sur, **Taos**, NM 87571. Tel: 758-2031 or (800) 258-8436; Fax: 751-0867.

▶ **Resort Properties of Angel Fire, Inc.** Angel Fire Village, P.O. Box 829, **Angel Fire**, NM 87710. Tel: 377-6441 or (800) 338-2589; Fax: 377-3814.

▶ **Zirkel Realty.** 207F Paseo del Pueblo Sur, P.O. Box 406, **Ranchos de Taos**, NM, 87557. Tel: 758-2263 or (800) 658-6928; Fax: 758-2263.

THE FOUR CORNERS

By Steve Cohen

The view across four states from Park Point, near the entrance to Mesa Verde National Park in the southwestern corner of present-day Colorado, was known to the Ute Indians who hunted these mesas and canyons in the late 1880s as "the rim of the little world." From this highest spot in the park, on clear days—which are the norm year-round—it is possible to see as far as 200 miles in any direction. The view encompasses the 13,000-foot snow-caps of Colorado's La Plata Mountains, and the San Juan range to the northeast. Utah's Blue Mountains and perhaps the faint La Sals can be glimpsed to the northwest. Sleeping Ute Mountain lies to the west, with Arizona beyond it. And Shiprock, an ancient volcanic plug encircled by flatlands, can be seen looming 1,700 feet over New Mexico to the south. Though the actual geographic convergence of four states—Colorado, Utah, Arizona, and New Mexico—is about 40 miles south of here, this is pretty close to the spiritual center of the vast area known as the Four Corners.

Ranging through these four Western states, which meet at the Four Corners National Monument, the region represents an ephemeral spiritual/historical linkage that defies state lines. Combining elements of longtime Indian traditions with resonances of the Old West, the area we will look at roughly spans 20,000 square miles, extending from Colorado's San Juan Mountains west into the valleys and canyons of Utah and Arizona, and south into New Mexico's high desert. It is a landscape characterized in the northeast quadrant by the high Alpine topography of the Continental Divide: jagged snow-topped rock peaks, mountain streams, waterfalls, wildflower meadows populated by deer and elk herds, fragrant pines, and golden autumn aspens (below 10,000 feet). The Western towns of Durango and Silverton anchor this Colorado portion of the Four Corners.

Most of the Four Corners region lies within the 130,000-square-mile extent of the **Colorado Plateau**, an elevated rocky tableland close to the size of California. This plateau includes Mesa Verde National Park, Ute Mountain Tribal Park, and Hovenweep National Monument, as well as most of the Navajo Nation and the separate entity of Hopiland.

The high-desert land here is much drier, perfect for the growth of small cactus and yucca, the strong fibers of which were used by ancient Indians for sewing. Lizards slither under rocks, seeking shade in the broiling sun. Giant rock monoliths adorn the desert flats, while striated red-rock canyons, resembling upside-down mountain vistas, trail from an average 5,000-foot elevation to the lowering desert beyond.

It is rugged territory and without large cities. Water is generally scarce and dependent upon winter snowmelt. Summers in the desert bring daytime temperatures of more than 100 degrees. Winters can bring fierce wind-driven storms dumping more than 300 inches of snow yearly in the mountains. On the other hand, the mountain and desert topography is dramatically spacious, with expansive vistas revealing tall peaks, exotic rock forms, and mysterious canyons. Wildlife is common. The air is clear and clean, and the sunlight seems more brilliant due to the ever-lower oxygen content at increasing altitudes. Despite climatic extremes, with temperatures often dropping 50 degrees after sundown, the sun shines in a blue sky perhaps 300 days a year, and colorful wildflowers and raspberries reappear reliably in the high country each July and August. Even the desert puts on a flower show most years, though it comes early, in spring, before temperatures start topping 100°F around mid-June.

While virtually any direction you set off in within this little world will lead to the quiet of nature and to solitude—if that is what you are seeking—the Four Corners is clearly not for everyone. Thus it is home to certain persevering strains of humanity, notably the Ute and Navajo peoples, as well as the Hopis (who have probably been here the longest). The Hopis may be directly descended from the ancient so-called Anasazi, whose intriguing, though not completely understood, desert-preserved ruins, dating to before A.D. 1000, are scattered across private lands, historic sites, national monuments, and parks throughout the Four Corners. Hispanics explored the area in the late 1700s, giving names to towns and geographic features that stuck and still spice the cultural mix today. The relative upstarts, the Anglo-Americans, came 100 years later: gold and silver miners, cowboys, shopkeepers, and bankers, each pioneering group bringing its own cultural context to the frontier.

This period signaled the opening of the Ute peoples' little world to the big world. Towns sprang up, some to prosper, others to return to ghosts when the mines played out. The railroads came through during the 1880s to service the mines. Agriculture, including cattle ranching, took hold—and a couple of cowboys from Mancos, the Wetherills, wandered into a small box canyon and discovered the Mesa Verde ruins in southwest Colorado in 1882, ultimately leading, in 1906, to the establishment of the first U.S. national park on land set aside to preserve man-made ruins.

Today the mines are mostly gone, though their history lingers in abandoned "glory holes" and towns such as Silverton, Colorado. A train very much like the one used in the mining era still calls on this Victorian town, only now it carries tourists, not miners. The mountains, canyons, and mesas that challenged settlers and explorers like the Wetherills are still used agriculturally, but now they also serve as a playground for the recreationally minded who come here for hiking, biking, and skiing; to ride horses, fish, and hunt; or to ogle the still largely natural geography, reveling in its immensity and beauty. Others come to consider the widespread archaeological evidence fanning out from Mesa Verde to Canyon de Chelly in Arizona and Chaco Canyon in New Mexico, making the Four Corners a treasure trove of prehistoric Indian life. And for those interested in present-day Indians, approximately three-fourths of the Four Corners is on reservation land. The Navajo Reservation is the largest in the United States. As for the Utes, their little world now includes casino gambling.

There currently seems to be room enough here for everyone, and a wide variety of approaches for dealing with tourists. On the one hand there's the efficient and helpful Colorado Welcome Center in Cortez, which demonstrates efficient know-how and enthusiasm: Questions are answered; you're in and out quickly with no problems. Tourism, after all, is bread and butter out here.

The Navajos, on the other hand, seem almost like a quirky foreign bureaucracy within the U.S. borders. There is no tourist information center in Window Rock, Arizona, the Navajo capital, only a very hard-to-find tourism office in one unmarked trailer among many. If you can find it, however, the Navajos manning it are happy to provide information. Tourism is a bright spot for the Navajos, who are coping with 56 percent unemployment on the reservation. It's just that their view of it is as different as their way of looking at the world in general. Part of the charm of the area is the journey through these diverse cultural attitudes.

Our discussion of the Four Corners assumes a car and a starting point in central or Northern New Mexico, around Albuquerque, Santa Fe, or Taos. It is a three- to four-hour drive from these cities just to begin this minimum week-long loop tour (ten days to two weeks would be better).

We start at Chaco Canyon National Historic Park, a World Heritage Site in northwestern New Mexico, and travel in a counterclockwise loop around the Four Corners point itself: first up into southwestern Colorado (Durango is the central town here), the site of Mesa Verde National Park and Ute Mountain Tribal Park.

From there we move west into southeastern Utah (Valley of the Gods), then south into Monument Valley and down into northeastern Arizona for the Navajo and Hopi lands—ending at the famous Canyon de Chelly ruins near the border with northwestern New Mexico.

MAJOR INTEREST

Northwestern New Mexico
Chaco Canyon National Historical Park (World
    Heritage Site)
Bisti Badlands
Salmon Ruins
Aztec Ruins National Monument

Southwestern Colorado
The Durango Area
Victorian/Western towns of Durango and Silverton
Durango & Silverton Narrow Gauge Railroad
San Juan National Forest and Weminuche
    Wilderness Area
Mesa Verde National Park
Ute Mountain Tribal Park and Four Corners
    National Monument

Anasazi Heritage Center, and Escalante and
    Domínguez Ruins
Hovenweep National Monument and Lowry
    Indian Ruins

Southeastern Utah
Edge of the Cedars State Park
Valley of the Gods
Goosenecks State Park
Monument Valley Navajo Tribal Park.

Northeastern Arizona
Navajo National Monument
Hopiland
Hubbell Trading Post National Historic Site
Canyon de Chelly National Monument

NORTHWESTERN NEW MEXICO

Chaco Canyon National Historic Park

There is evidence here, in a barren, high New Mexican
desert 60 miles from the nearest modern town, of Indian dwellings and artifacts—pottery and ornamental
turquoise—that indicates the ancient residence of a culture more advanced and complex than the cliff dwellers
of neighboring Mesa Verde, a short drive north across
the Colorado state line.

Mesa Verde is better known, though, drawing more
than 700,000 visitors yearly, perhaps because of its national park status as well as for its intriguing, mysterious
cliff dwellings. Chaco Canyon's designation as a national
historical park has meant fewer visitor services, such as
paved access roads, and this, in turn, has kept crowds
away. Chaco Canyon was, however, dedicated as a World
Heritage Site on October 22, 1988, acknowledging its
historic worldwide significance in the rarefied company
of the Egyptian pyramids and Mayan ruins of Central
America.

You do not just stumble onto Chaco Canyon. You must
drive 20 miles (32 km) north on NM 57 from the southerly I-40 corridor (via NM 371). Or you can drive 30
miles (48 km) south on NM 57 from the northerly NM
44. Both dirt-road entrances reach the park headquarters, which consists of a small museum and information
center, bathrooms, and a freshwater spigot that offers
the only potable water for many miles. A mile farther,

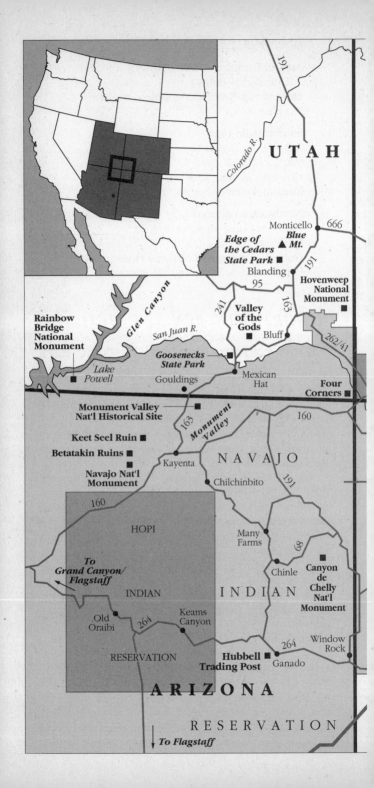

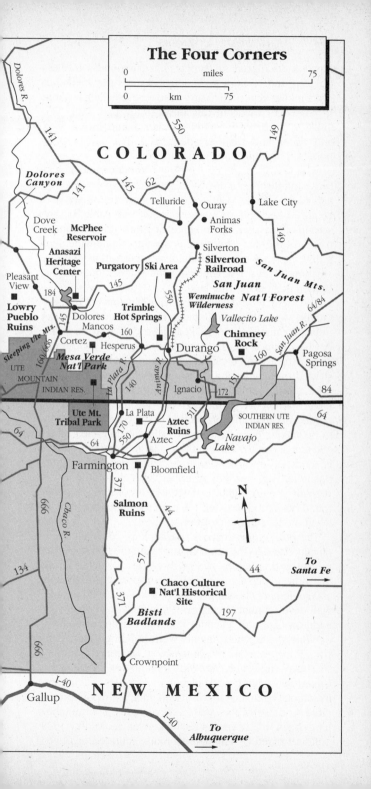

low, wind-sculpted sandstone cliffs surround a treeless campground. Cold-water bathrooms are provided, but no drinking water. The entry roads are usually navigable in passenger cars, but call ahead to the park (Tel: 505/ 988-6727) for road conditions after a rain. Bring food and water and plan to spend as full a day here as possible, or camp out and stay longer.

Most visitors begin by watching a 20-minute movie and browsing through a display of artifacts—pottery, jewelry, and tools—at the visitors' center, where trail maps and required backcountry permits are also available, before setting off on a self-guided hike, driving tour, or a combination of the two. The route is through a mile-wide, ten-mile-long, rock-strewn sandy desert that was as close as anything to an urban center for the Anasazi Indians who farmed this once-fertile land.

The site may well have been magical to ancient Indians. Carved petroglyphs and pictographs painted on rocks indicate ritual sites. In 1972, at the top of a ravine at the Penasco Blanco ruins, scientists discovered a pictograph portraying a star, a crescent moon, and a handprint on the shaded underside of a 20-foot-tall cliff. Astronomers believe this long-hidden artwork may represent a supernova that occurred in A.D. 1054, one that was also recorded in China and that burned bright enough in the sky to be visible in daylight for two years. Atop Fajada Butte, 400 feet above the canyon floor, a large spiral petroglyph is scratched into the sandstone. Three slabs of rock are positioned against the inscribed wall. Until the rocks recently shifted slightly, a narrow beam of sunlight penetrated between them and fell onto the spiral precisely at noon on the summer solstice.

The peak of the Chaco Anasazi culture has been scientifically dated to the tenth century, with the first construction of large pueblos two or three stories high. During that time Chaco Canyon grew to support approximately 400 settlements housing a total of 5,000 to 10,000 people, with developments in masonry construction allowing the addition of fourth and fifth floors to existing structures.

While the isolated Anasazi were building Chaco Canyon, Europeans were constructing far more complex structures (and soon cathedrals), yet no other tribe in the United States left behind elaborate architecture, cunning irrigation systems, or sophisticated trade highways comparable to those of the Anasazi. Seventy-five communities have been discovered stretching over more than 300 miles of carefully engineered roads centered at Chaco

Canyon. The longest ran 42 miles. Outlying settlements fanned out like spokes of a wheel in travel intervals of one day.

Seeds found among the ruins and preserved in the dry desert air have been traced to varieties of corn, beans, and squashes that originated in Mexico. Distinctive black-and-white ceramics, turquoise, chalcedony, obsidian, and shell jewelry, yucca-fiber baskets, and painted wooden ritual objects suggest contact with Indian societies in Mexico and Central America.

Pueblo Bonito, the largest and best-known ruin in Chaco Canyon, was apparently occupied from around A.D. 900 to 1200. Over the years it grew into a cluster of 800 rooms rising four stories high, built around 37 kivas. These large, round pits, apparently used for gatherings or for religious services, could hold hundreds of people at one time. Jewelry and possible ritual objects have been found in caches in the great houses and kivas.

At other Chaco Canyon ruins you can see successive layers of masonry built upon one another, from primitive to increasingly sophisticated. Developing construction techniques made possible more expansive designs. **Casa Rinconada, Chetro Ketl, Pueblo del Arroyo**, and **Pueblo Alto** are several of these sites, which sit within yards of a paved park loop road; others can be reached along marked hiking trails of one-half to five miles.

A major distinction between the Chacoans and Mesa Verde's cliff dwellers, who built apartment-like structures directly into caves on vertical cliff faces, can be seen in a typical ruin here, which consists of freestanding brick or masonry walls several stories high, built on the canyon floor. (At Mesa Verde you mostly look down at ruins that blend into the scenery as if camouflaged. At Chaco Canyon, structures are adjacent to the loop road on the canyon floor. You can walk a few steps and be standing in a ruin.) These people had no metal technology, no draft animals, no wheeled vehicles. They left no written records. Chaco Canyon's elaborately telling remains are the only indication that it was the center of an economic, spiritual, and social system that stretched over an area of 30,000 square miles for six generations.

One school of archaeological thought holds that when these ancestors of today's Pueblo Indians first lived here, the earth was covered with soil and vegetation, grasslands and forests. Over the centuries the Indians evidently cut down thousands of trees to build their giant pueblos and to use as fuel. Without trees the soil lost its vitality and, over time, its ability to hold moisture and support crops. Sustained droughts and compromised topsoil are believed to have led to the apparently rapid disintegration of the local and peripheral Indian cultures. Grasses that may have survived were probably later consumed by grazing cattle and sheep introduced by Anglo settlers, destroying any remaining ground cover. As a result, wind whistles over eroded, cracked, dry desert land here today.

By the 1300s Chaco culture had completely disappeared, its people dispersed, its empty structures left behind intact—offering mute testimony to the skills and creativity of a vanished race.

For information on Chaco Canyon contact the Park Superintendent, Star Route 4, Box 6500, Bloomfield, NM 87413.

Chaco is literally in the middle of nowhere, 115 miles from Santa Fe, 95 miles from Durango, Colorado, 72 miles from Farmington, New Mexico. The closest town is Bloomfield, New Mexico, 60 miles (96 km) to the north via NM 57 and NM 44, where you can buy gas and food, or a meal at a truck-stop café.

Farmington

After the drive from, say, the Santa Fe area and the balance of the day exploring Chaco Canyon, you might choose to spend the night to the north in Farmington, a charmless town on the eastern edge of the Navajo Nation but the largest in the Four Corners. Farmington's population of 34,000 is largely dependent on nearby oil, gas, and coal reserves. Its airport is served by Continental Express, United Express, and Mesa Airlines, for those who might want to fly from Albuquerque and rent a car here, and it does have a number of chain motels and restaurants, as well as several Indian crafts shops where you might find some relatively good buys, compared with Santa Fe or Taos prices. For local information contact the Farmington Convention and Visitors Bureau, 203 West Main, Suite 401, Farmington, NM 87401, Tel: (800) 448-1240 or (505) 326-7602.

As for dining here, **The Trough**, located behind the Country Palace Bar 2 miles (3 km) east of town on U.S. 550, serves enormous Western-size steaks, pork chops, and seafood in an atmosphere that might be called upscale casual around here (meaning, please scrape your boots before dining). After dinner, Farmington's Lions Wilderness Park is the site of an outdoor summer drama, *Anasazi,* *the Ancient Ones,* performed Wednesday through Saturday nights, mid-June to early September. Call the visitors bureau (see above) for schedules and reservations.

Outside Farmington

Thirty-two miles (51 km) south of Farmington on NM 371—which runs south of I-40, passing to the west of Chaco Canyon—are the **Bisti Badlands**, a federally protected wilderness area containing bizarre soft-clay formations that resemble images from a strange dream, or perhaps another planet. There are no services whatsoever out here; bring water and food along on any excursions into this moonlike, barren landscape that appears to have remained unchanged for 65 million years.

On the way out of Farmington, heading toward Durango to the north, two sites in New Mexico provide further insight into the Anasazi.

San Juan Archaeological Research Center and Library at Salmon Ruins, actually east of Farmington 2½ miles (4 km) before Bloomfield on U.S. 64, has a museum containing artifacts from the largest Chacoan settlements of the 11th century. The site also contains ruins of an 11th- to 13th-century apartment complex and a hands-on Heritage Park where visitors (attended by a guide) can learn to throw a dartlike *atlatl*, used for hunting by the Anasazi prior to the bow-and-arrow era. Other displays, which may be entered, include life-size replicas of Navajo, Ute, and Apache dwellings and other Indian structures. Tel: (505) 632-2013.

After an hour or two at Salmon Ruins, continue east on U.S. 64 to Bloomfield, then 8 miles (13 km) north on NM 544 to the town of Aztec and the **Aztec Ruins National Monument**, on U.S. 550. This is the site of the world's largest reconstructed kiva and a rather compact but extensive array of pueblo ruins that may be toured in about an hour. Tel: (505) 334-6174.

From these ruins NM 173 heads east to connect up with NM 511. A short distance to the north on 511 is New Mexico's largest reservoir, **Navajo Lake**, 38 miles (61 km) east of Farmington. Fishing for German or rainbow trout, kokanee salmon, bass, bluegill, and catfish can be very good here, and boating, swimming, waterskiing, windsurfing, camping, and picnicking attract 250,000 recreational users each year to the 15,000-acre reservoir and adjacent **Navajo Lake State Park**; Tel: (505) 632-2278.

North of Navajo Lake, on CO 151 (follow NM 511, which

becomes CO 172, to get to CO 151), is the **Chimney Rock Archaeological Area**, the remains of 16 excavated ruin sites clustered around two natural rock towers. Long held sacred by the Southern Utes and nearby Taos Indians, Chimney Rock is the most remote community directly connected with Chaco Canyon. Tel: (303) 264-2268.

From Chimney Rock it is 41 miles (66 km) west to Durango via U.S. 160.

SOUTHWESTERN COLORADO

For an excursion into modern Indian territory, consider **Ignacio**, Colorado, the tribal headquarters of the Southern Utes, about 30 miles (48 km) southeast of Durango on CO 172. The tribe runs a small, contemporary Southwestern-style motel, the **Sky Ute Lodge and Restaurant**, high-stakes bingo every Friday night, a Cultural Center **Museum and Gallery**, and an excellent public radio station, KSUT (92.1 FM), featuring music and nationally syndicated programs. Seasonal events include a four-day-long Bear Dance in the spring, a Sun Dance in July, a September powwow and fair with members of many other tribes from around the country, and numerous rodeo and riding events throughout the year at **Sky Ute Downs** equestrian center. For information on events contact the Southern Ute Tourist Center; Tel: (800) 876-7017 or (303) 565-4531.

Also in the tiny town of Ignacio is the small shop **Custom Boots by Larry Smith**, at 655 Browning Avenue, for that hand-made pair of cowboy boots you have always wanted. Smith has more than 30 years' experience as a boot maker, and he guarantees boots that fit.

The Durango Area

North on U.S. 550, about an hour from Farmington, is Durango, a recommended base for at least two days, maybe more. The town has a good airport, serviced from Albuquerque, Denver, or Phoenix. Most, if not all, the car-rental companies in town—among which are many of the major firms and a number of local outfits—also rent four-wheel-drive vehicles. Motor-home rentals are available as well. Probably 50 or more restaurants service this town of 13,000. In addition, there are many places to stay, ranging from inexpensive motels to guest ranches, from bed and breakfasts to slope-side condos, from historic hotels to a plush full-service resort and an ultra-exclusive wilderness resort.

These air and ground services, combined with the cozy Western ambience of the town and the presence of numerous galleries and factory-outlet stores, make Durango an increasingly popular destination in itself. Add to that the access it offers to the mountains for hiking, camping, mountain biking, or skiing, to rivers and lakes for fishing, canoeing, kayaking, or river rafting, and you have an ideal base for exploring much of the Four Corners on day trips.

The more distant reaches, beyond a 50- to 75-mile (80- to 128-km) radius, will probably necessitate staying overnight outside of the Durango area, where choices are more limited the farther from town you go.

Durango

Durango is unusual among thriving Colorado mountain towns in that it is not really a ski town. There is skiing at the Purgatory-Durango Resort, but that's 26 miles (42 km) north of town. Durango sits in a high, fertile river valley at 6,700 feet. Summer is the main tourist season, and the outdoors is what most people come for, to hike, backpack and camp, raft rivers, ride horses, and fish. Deer and elk hunting have long dominated the calendar for a few weeks each fall, but only recently have savvy travellers begun to catch on to the benefits of this season, which boasts cooler weather, smaller crowds, and colorful autumn leaves.

Durango is also one of the increasingly rare towns where Main Avenue is still the heart of local commerce. There is a shopping mall south of downtown, but the small, completely walkable central business district (a designated historic area between Fifth and 12th streets) holds sway with classic Victorian architecture of formidable cut-stone and brick buildings; crafts shops and art galleries featuring contemporary and earlier Indian, cowboy, and Southwestern-inspired paintings, pottery, and weavings; restaurants and hotels alongside hardware stores, haircutting shops, Western outfitters, and sporting goods dealers; and of course the factory outlets. An important Main Avenue tenant anchors the start of the avenue just below Fifth Street: the train depot, starting point of the famous Durango & Silverton Narrow Gauge Railroad, which we discuss in its own section, below.

Another historic district spreads out along Third Avenue, two blocks east of Main, and includes numerous

19th-century houses featuring gable roofs, bay windows, and elaborate Victorian trim work. Both districts can be covered easily on foot in several hours. A good place for historical information is a block east of the train depot at 175 East Fifth Street, at **Southwest Book Trader**, a used-book store featuring antiques and collectibles, including Western and railroad memorabilia.

A new municipal parking lot is located in Durango at West Eighth Street and Camino del Rio, two blocks west of Main.

STAYING IN DURANGO

A block north of the depot, at 567 Main, is the **General Palmer Hotel**, built in 1898 and named after the gentleman who brought the railroad to town in 1881. It is popular with the historically minded and comfort-conscious for its elegant Victorian setting, carried out with mostly reproduction furnishings in individually decorated rooms that include all modern amenities.

The **Strater Hotel**, one block farther north on Main, is a redbrick downtown showcase, an impeccably restored historic hotel filled with museum-quality furnishings. It too features deluxe modern amenities, as well as the largest collection of antique walnut furniture west of the Mississippi, spread through 93 rooms, no two of which are decorated alike. The Strater's **Diamond Circle Theatre** hosts Gay Nineties melodramas June to September, nightly except Sundays; Tel: (303) 247-3400. The hotel's **Diamond Belle Saloon**, an opulent Western-style bar, comes complete with swinging doors, an antique back bar, garter-clad barmaids, and a honky-tonk piano player.

Jarvis Suite Hotel, one block west of Main on West Tenth Street, feels like a cozy residence hotel. Modern suites in the remodeled 100-plus-year-old building have kitchens.

DINING IN DURANGO

The best restaurant in Durango is the **Red Snapper**, one block east of Main at 144 East Ninth Street, which offers fresh seafood every day (remarkable for land-locked Durango), an enormous salad bar, debilitating desserts such as Death by Chocolate, and nondebilitating prices.

The **Durango Diner**, 957 Main, is not fancy and serves simple, solid diner fare for breakfast or lunch. Sit at the counter to eavesdrop on local gossip. **Carver's Bakery and Cafe**, at 1022 Main, is another option for fresh food served in a casual atmosphere; they brew their own beer in the back. One block north, **Wolf Creek General Store**, at number 1130, can supply all the goodies for a picnic, or you can dine here on the best sandwiches, pastries, and breads in town. For vegetarian tastes try **Durango Natural Foods**, eight blocks east of Main at 575 East Eighth Avenue. This is a grocery store, not a restaurant, but one of the few places in town for fresh veggies and organic foods.

The restaurant selection in downtown Durango as we see it may look thin, but that would not be literally true. There are downtown steak houses (reputedly "fine dining" establishments), Chinese, Mexican, and Italian restaurants, along with burger joints, an authentic Woolworth's lunch counter, and **TJ's All-American Hot Dog & BBQ**, at 1050 Main, where you should make it a point to sample one of their tiny, conical "sport peppers" for a taste of what may be the hottest bite available in Durango. However, many of these offer safe, unimaginative cuisine with indifferent service. As most of the restaurants are located between Sixth Street and 11th Street on Main, you may want literally to follow your nose to a restaurant that appeals to you. And as restaurants tend to come and go downtown with some frequency, you might discover something new and appealing. Menus are often posted outside the door. By the way, yearly ratings by locals routinely name Pizza Hut the town's favorite pizza place, so claims to top honors should probably be taken with a grain of salt.

As for Western-style nightlife, there are two seasonal dinner shows from Memorial Day to Labor Day. The **Durango Jamboree** at the Iron Horse Inn, 5800 Main, 3 miles (5 km) north of town, serves a barbecue chicken-and-ribs dinner with a 90-minute "Hee-Haw"–style show featuring Western, bluegrass, folk, country, waltz, pop, and old-time gospel music. The **Bar-D Chuckwagon** is located 9 miles (14½ km) north of Durango at 8080 County Road 250, which runs parallel and to the east of U.S. 550. Their sliced beef and baked beans dinner is served before the show—the songs, stories, and Western comedy of the Bar-D Wranglers. The property includes a miniature train that carries travellers around the Bar-D spread; a record shop that sells tapes, videos, and CDs of the Wranglers; and of course the inevitable gift shop.

Non-Western–style nightlife, primarily consisting of rock or reggae bands (yes, reggae), is available nightly at **Farquahrt's**, in the heart of downtown Durango, at 725 Main.

SHOPPING IN DURANGO

One of Durango's best collections of authentic Navajo rugs, jewelry, sculptures, and paintings (for purchase or just great browsing) is at **Toh-Atin Gallery**, 145 West Ninth Street, one block west of Main. Prints, posters, and art wear can be found at their other store, **Art on Main**, at 865 Main Avenue. One block south and west of Main, **Thompson River Trading Company**, at 140 West Eighth Street, specializes in museum-quality Southwestern and Indian art, baskets, blankets, rugs, and jewelry. Altogether there are at least another dozen or so good galleries in the downtown area. Also downtown, across the street from the General Palmer, at 598 Main, **O'Farrell Hat Company** makes made-to-order cowboy hats.

National travelling art shows, local artists, educational exhibits, and children's shows are featured at the **Durango Arts Center**, 835 Main, upstairs in the Main Mall. The Arts Center also sponsors concerts and other local events. One of the prime venues for concerts, films, lectures, and other special programs is Fort Lewis College (Tel: 303/247-7010), located at College Heights on a hill overlooking Durango, a five-minute drive east on Sixth Street from Main Avenue. The school's **Center for Southwest Studies** exhibits Indian and Southwestern artifacts such as pottery and cowboy gear, and has a research library; Tel: (303) 247-7456. The 18-hole public links at Hillcrest Golf Course are across from the college; Tel: (303) 247-1499.

DURANGO AREA OUTFITTERS AND TOUR OPERATORS

The national forest and wilderness areas around Durango can be accessed with a minimum of hassle through a variety of local tour operators and outfitters. For an overview of the area, **New Air Aviation** (Tel: 303/259-6247) offers charter helicopter service throughout the region, as well as sightseeing tours. **Gregg Flying Service** (Tel: 303/247-4632) offers fixed-wing "flightseeing" trips over the Continental Divide to the east of Durango, with charter service throughout the Four Corners.

Glider flights are available at **Val Air Soaring** (Tel: 303/247-9037), located 3 miles (5 km) north of Durango on U.S. 550. Hot-air balloon flights over the Animas Valley, the fertile river valley stretching north of Durango to the high peaks of the San Juans, can be arranged by **New**

West Adventures (Tel: 303/385-4940). New West also operates a variety of other trips, including jeep tours and photo safaris from late April to mid-October.

Adventure Touring

For the more actively inclined, **Southwest Adventures** (Tel: 800/642-5389 or 303/259-0370) offers courses and guided trips at various skill levels of mountaineering, rock climbing, white water rafting and kayaking, and mountain biking. Among them is a guided rafting trip on the class IV and V rapids of the Upper Animas, rated one of the roughest 26-mile stretches of white water in the United States. Participants must pass a physical-fitness test before departures, which are usually limited to June 1 through July 30 (depending on water flow). Less demanding rafting trips, on the far more predictable Lower Animas, are offered by **Mountain Waters Rafting** (Tel: 303/259-4191) and **Durango Rivertrippers** (Tel: 303/259-0289). Camping equipment may be rented at **Backcountry Experience**, 780 Main; Tel: (303) 247-5830.

Fishing

Fly-fishing excursions can be arranged through **Duranglers** (Tel: 303/385-4081), and any number of operators offer horseback rides, pack trips, guided hunting trips, and sleigh rides, including **Rapp Guide Service** (Tel: 303/247-8923) and **Buck's Livery** at Purgatory (see below); Tel: (303) 385-2110. A couple of outfits even offer day hikes with llamas to carry your gear; for information contact **Buckhorn Llama Company** (Tel: 303/259-5965) or **Turnbull Llama Company** (Tel: 303/259-3773).

Mountain Biking

And then there is mountain biking, the one activity above all others that has put Durango on the world sports map as the "Mountain Biking Capital of the World." The area's reputation was cemented when the first unified World Mountain Bike Championships were held at Purgatory (see below) in 1990. Riders from 23 countries participated, and the overall champion was a Durango rider. Many of the world's top riders continue to live and train in southwest Colorado.

The world championships were a one-shot deal, but annually, on Memorial Day weekend, hundreds of bike riders converge on Durango for the Iron Horse Classic, a road race that has pitted fearless bicyclers against the narrow-gauge train since 1972. The best bikers always beat the slow train to Silverton (see the next section), but for many noncompetitive riders it is thrill enough just to complete the 50-mile course, which clears two 10,000-plus-foot mountain passes. There are easier bike rides, of course, including hundreds of miles of roads and trails rated from easy—which may be harder than you expect at an altitude higher than 6,500 feet—to seriously hard. Purgatory, for example usually hosts several major professional and amateur biking events each summer, and a daily option here is to haul your bike up on a chairlift, then ride *down* the slopes from Purgatory's heights.

The best bet is to check with one of Durango's several bike shops for information on the roads and trails, and for maps and equipment rentals. Contact **Mountain Bike Specialists** (Tel: 800/255-8377 or 303/247-4066) for a full array of biking services, including rentals and a variety of completely outfitted, guided bike tours from a half day to five days; custom tours can also be arranged. One of their trips includes riding the narrow-gauge train to Silverton, followed by biking back along an old stagecoach trail to Purgatory, finishing the three-day, two-night trek with a soak at Trimble Hot Springs (see below for Purgatory and the hot springs).

Additional information about all Durango-area activities and amenities is available from Durango Area Chamber Resort Association, P.O. Box 2587, Durango, CO 81302; Tel: (800) 525-8855 or (303) 247-0312.

THE DURANGO & SILVERTON NARROW GAUGE RAILROAD

The train depot at 479 Main Avenue, established in 1881, is the home of the Durango & Silverton Narrow Gauge Railroad, one of Durango's biggest attractions. A ride in restored antique train cars behind a coal-fired engine on the 90-mile round trip to Silverton gives a sense of what things were like in the short heyday of the area's gold and silver booms.

Originally used to haul miners, equipment, and ore out of the gold- and silver-rich San Juans, the railroad carries more than 200,000 people each year between May and October, and in 1992 service was restored for a Winter Holiday Run, November 25 to December 31. This is a dramatically scenic train route at any time, but particularly in the autumn, when the leaves are changing, or in winter, when the steep hillsides are banked in snow. The track follows El Rio de las Animas Perdidas Purgatorio (the Spanish-named "River of Lost Souls in Purgatory," today known as the Animas River) north from Durango through 45 miles of the two-million-acre San Juan National Forest, notable for numerous 13,000- and 14,000-foot peaks along the Continental Divide. The train edges the enormous Weminuche Wilderness Area (see below), where hikers who wish to get away from motors, mountain bikers, and developed campsites can hop off, fend for themselves in the wilderness, then flag the train down for a ride back to civilization (Durango or Silverton) when they want to get out. The only other way to get into these woods is on foot, by horseback, or on cross-country skis.

The train travels on a narrow-gauge track only three feet wide; in places there is no room for anything larger. It chugs slowly, belching steam and cinders, and you can lean out and nearly touch giant boulders on one side, while mere feet away on the other side there may be a sheer 400-foot drop into the churning waters of the Animas. Though no longer a lifeline for miners and ore shippers working remote camps, the train moves through a world remarkably little changed today.

The clean yellow-and-black train cars may as well be clattering time machines. Your choice is between an antique parlor car or an open gondola car, where you are free to walk around, soot and black ash blowing into your face and hair as you literally hang out with everyone else, gawking at the pristine scenery, pointing, smiling, and shooting photos. Mammoth aspen groves, massive rocks, evergreens, rushing waters, and a purple-melting-into-blue sky evoke classic images. Parts of *Butch Cassidy and the Sundance Kid* were filmed here, at Baker's Bridge. The baby cow named Norman and the rest of the herd that starred in *City Slickers* were Durango natives, and the ranch is just over yonder.

One of the sites along the way is exclusive guest ranch **Tall Timber**, situated next to the train tracks about two-thirds of the way to Silverton. Guests lacking the time or inclination for taking the train to Tall Timber can fly in or out by private helicopter. The closest road is five miles away from this highly rated resort. Popular activities at Tall Timber, open May to October and one week at Christmas, include fine dining, helicopter picnics, heli-hiking, fishing, and horseback trips. Or you can just sit in peace and silence, on a rock or a rocker, and watch summer thunderheads crackling across a wildflower-speckled valley.

Nearby ranches, though not on the train route, include

Colorado Trails and **Wilderness Trails**, both offering family vacations, log-cabin accommodations, horseback riding, overnight pack trips, and even gold panning.

The train rumbles along at under 20 miles per hour for most of the three-and-a-half-hour (one-way) trip, with a 3,000-foot gain in elevation by the time you reach Silverton. Information can be obtained at the train depot in Durango; Tel: (303) 247-2733.

Silverton

For many, the two-hour train layover in Silverton, at 9,300 feet elevation, is plenty of time to cover the whole town on foot. This once-thriving mining center now survives on train-passenger lunches and gift-shop purchases. The last mine here closed a few years ago, but the town remains a living legacy of Western lore, not to mention perseverance. The Victorian architecture of historic buildings throughout town is authentic, and the entire town, all 24 square blocks of it, has been designated a National Historic Landmark.

Though there's not all that much to do in Silverton, the surrounding countryside is impressively mountainous and remote, and the local bars are authentically Western (several sport bullet holes embedded in aging walls from the town's wilder days). After a day on the train, a jeep ride in the mountains, an evening in the town, and a night in a historic hotel might be fun before catching the train back to Durango the next morning.

On Greene Street, the main drag, almost every structure between 12th and 14th streets has historic significance. Blair Street, one block south of Greene, was the red-light district, at one time housing 34 saloons and brothels. Today, the train stops at 12th and Blair.

Silverton's historic hotels, decorated in varying degrees of ornate Victoriana, include the **Grand Imperial Hotel** (1219 Greene), the **Alma House Hotel**, on the corner of Blair at 220 East Tenth Street, and the **Wyman Hotel** (1371 Greene). Overnight stays can be booked at the train depot in Durango or Silverton along with return train passage for the following day. The Silverton Chamber of Commerce can provide complete visitor information, including details regarding a number of Silverton firms offering jeep rentals: P.O. Box 565, Silverton, CO 81433, Tel: (800) 752-4494 or (303) 387-5654.

The scenic-drive possibilities from Silverton include the **Alpine Loop Back Country Byway**, operated by the Bureau of Land Management; Tel: (303) 247-4082. Best negotiated in a four-wheel-drive vehicle, the 65-mile Alpine Loop splashes through streams and past the ghost town of Animas Forks before rising over two mountain passes, including 12,800-foot Engineer Pass, which gives a 360-degree view of the San Juan range from above the tree line. On the way back the route passes through **Lake City**, with the largest concentration of late-19th-century buildings in the state, as well as abandoned mining camps, lakes, waterfalls, campgrounds, and hiking trails among some of Colorado's most rugged and remote scenery. Cinnamon Pass, at 12,260 feet, is close to Animas Forks and the road back to Silverton.

It is, of course, possible to drive to Silverton from Durango, skipping the train altogether. The 50-mile (80-km) ride along U.S. 550 North is a portion of another designated and well-signed scenic road, the **San Juan Skyway**, administered by the U.S. Forest Service. This justifiably renowned road, all paved, offers incredible views from hairpin turns high on mountain passes, wildlife, historic sites—the works. But lines must be drawn somewhere, and the line for our Southwest runs somewhere south of Ouray and Telluride, which are at the northern end of the skyway. Other portions of this 236-mile loop do, however, pass through parts of the Four Corners we cover, west of Durango, through Mancos, Cortez, and Dolores, which are described below. Nonetheless, the entire San Juan loop is a worthwhile day trip to consider (see Getting Around, below).

North from Durango to Purgatory

A motel/fast-food strip leads out of the Durango downtown area onto North Main Avenue, alias U.S. 550 North. **Griego's Taco House**, one block east of Main at 1400 East Second Avenue, is a classic tiny drive-in serving great, cheap Mexican food. For sit-down service, Griego's North Main, at 2603 North Main, is said to have the same food, but somehow it tastes better at the drive-in.

The restaurant is across the street from La Plata County Fairgrounds, 2500 North Main Avenue, site of an annual county fair in mid-August, and the **Durango Pro Rodeo**, with shows scheduled Tuesday and Wednesday nights, June through August, as well as on other selected dates Memorial Day through October; Tel: (303) 247-1666. The **Animas School Museum**, about 1 mile (1½ km) north of downtown and one block west of Main at 31st Street and West Second Avenue, includes a turn-of-the-century classroom and other historical exhibits relating to the Durango area. Considering history of a different sort, the **Sundowner Saloon**, at 3777 North Main, usually has a country band playing, and offers free Western swing-dance lessons.

Past the city limits and north in the Animas Valley, striated red-sandstone cliffs rise over the river as Main Avenue becomes U.S. 550 North. Six miles (10 km) out of town, at Trimble Lane, is **Trimble Hot Springs**, once well-known to the Ute Indians for their healing properties. Today's modern facility includes an Olympic-size pool, two therapy pools, and two hot tubs heated by the natural hot springs; Tel: (303) 247-0111. After a soak in the pool go for Durango's best pizza, 2 miles (3 km) north of the hot springs at **Mama's Boy**, 32225 U.S. 550 North.

Ten miles (16 km) farther north is the **Tamarron Resort**, a well-run operation in a truly spectacular mountain setting, with red-rock cliffs on one side of the property and the tall peaks of the San Juans trailing into the distance on the other. The resort has tasteful "Southwestern meets Rockies"–style lodge rooms and condos, one of the state's top-rated 18-hole golf courses, a health club, an indoor-outdoor pool, horseback riding, jeep tours, river rafting, fishing, tennis—and an Italian restaurant complete with singing waiters on Thursday, Friday, and Saturday nights. But there is no hula show. In winter Tamarron features cozy horse-drawn sleigh rides and cross-country skiing on the undulating golf course, and is within shooting distance of the **Purgatory-Durango Ski Resort**, located another 10 miles (16 km) up U.S. 550 North.

PURGATORY

"The Area," as Purgatory is known to locals, is most popular between Thanksgiving and April, when it consistently records some of the state's deepest levels of feathery powder snow, along with some of the sunniest winter weather around. It is not unusual for a couple of feet of fresh snow to fall overnight, followed by a bright sunny day warm enough for skiing in the knee-deep powder without a parka by noon. Particularly in springtime, southwestern Colorado is one of the best places to work on your ski technique and your tan at the same time. The year-round resort area includes restaurants, shops, hotel and condo accommodations, and a program of summer activities to boot: classical music concerts and a variety of mountain-biking events and activities, as well as hiking, fishing, jeep tours, horseback trips, and a quarter-mile-long Alpine slide; Tel: (800) 525-0892 or (303) 247-9000.

The condos at the **Purgatory Village Hotel** range from studios to three bedrooms, and most include kitchens, fireplaces, and balconies as well as Jacuzzi-equipped bathtubs (a great comfort after a day of hiking, mountain biking, or skiing). The best restaurant near the ski area is **Cafe Cascade**, located 1 mile (1½ km) north of Purgatory, at 50827 U.S. 550 North. It is also probably the most expensive restaurant in the Durango area, but the only game in town if you're looking for fresh Louisiana alligator, venison tenderloin, quail with Animas Valley plum-and-juniper *demiglacé,* or rabbit loin. As for dining and shops at the ski area, the choices are mostly utilitarian and can be scoped out within a half hour or so. There's a modestly stocked deli, Sterling's cafeteria, and sporting goods and ski/bike shops—all a little overpriced, in keeping with the resort-style ambience.

San Juan National Forest

San Juan National Forest surrounds Durango, covering two million acres of southwestern Colorado from Telluride to the New Mexico border, from McPhee Reservoir in Dolores to Pagosa Springs, 47 miles (75 km) east of Durango. Deer, elk, bears, coyotes, and eagles are more common than people in parts of these evergreen forests, but human amenities are plentiful: hundreds of miles of trails for hikers and mountain bikers; numerous camping and picnicking sites; the San Juan Skyway (mentioned above under Silverton); and rivers and reservoirs for fishing, swimming, and boating—all set amid crystalline Alpine lakes fed by mountain streams, waterfalls, and cataracts. There are also canyons, abandoned mines, Indian ruins, and impressive elevations averaging more than 10,000 feet, with at least a dozen rising higher than 14,000 feet—amid the highest mountain range in the Lower 48. Contact the National Forest office; Tel: (303) 247-4874.

Fall colors, led by the blazing gold of fluttery aspen leaves, are so spectacular here that communities surrounding the forest have banded together to promote a month-long **Colorfest**, in September and October, when a packed calendar of special events and activities awaits leaf peepers (the committee hopes always to beat the high-country snows, which are not uncommon any time between September and July). For information, Tel: (303) 247-0312.

Vallecito Lake, 20 miles (32 km) northeast of Durango, is one of many popular fishing spots in the forest, good also for swimming, boating, and windsurfing; boat rentals are available. **Wit's End Guest Ranch**, 254 County Road 500, at the north end of the man-made reservoir, features plush accommodations in modern log cabins.

WEMINUCHE WILDERNESS AREA

Within the national forest, roughly bordered by Vallecito Lake on the east and the narrow-gauge train tracks to the west, is the Weminuche Wilderness, one of the country's largest wilderness areas. Its 459,000 acres are protected to preserve a primitive character—meaning no roads, improvements, or permanent dwellings are allowed. Elevation here averages 10,000 feet, laced by more than 400 miles of trails for hiking or horseback riding. Mountain bikes and motorized vehicles are not permitted, but there is access to the wilderness on hiking trails from Vallecito Lake, Silverton, or Purgatory, or from the Durango & Silverton Narrow Gauge Railroad, all of which are discussed above.

West from Durango to Hesperus

West of Durango on U.S. 160 the mountains rise into the La Plata range before giving way to mesas, canyons, and the hint of desert flats to come. About 20 miles (32 km) southwest of Durango, off U.S. 160 on County Road 140 in Hesperus (population 200 or so) is the **Blue Lake Ranch**, an exclusive small bed-and-breakfast inn on a private lake surrounded by flower and vegetable gardens, and with exceptional mountain and mesa views. **Chip's Place**, a nondescript cinder-block edifice in the Canyon Motel at the corner of U.S. 160 and County Road 124, serves a renowned super chili cheeseburger that has been enshrined in the Hamburger Hall of Fame.

Up the road from Chip's is **La Plata Canyon**, on County Road 124, north from U.S. 160. The steep road gains nearly 4,000 feet in elevation as it follows the La Plata River for 14 miles from the Canyon Motel to Kennebec Pass at more than 12,000 feet. Mountain bikers or hikers who top the pass can ogle the snow peaks of the Continental Divide; the *truly* intrepid may begin the **Colorado Trail** at this point, connecting with its western terminus on Junction Creek, and walk or ride a bike for the next

470 backcountry miles to Denver (see Getting Around at the end of the chapter for information).

Mancos

Little Mancos, about 29 miles (46 km) west of Durango, is a blur to many travellers on U.S. 160. They don't know what they're missing. First, alongside the highway at the crossroads of U.S. 160 and Main Street, is **Millwood Junction**, 101 West Railroad Avenue, arguably the best restaurant in the Four Corners and occasionally a scene for live music by nationally known groups such as Wind Machine (they recorded a song named after the restaurant). People come from as far as Telluride—100 miles away—for Millwood's Friday-night seafood buffet. Any night here is good, though, with inexpensive specials and a moderately priced menu of imaginatively prepared steaks, chicken, and seafood, all with a Southwestern flavor. Dress, as usual, is casual for this intimate setting. Tel: (303) 533-7338.

South two blocks and around the corner on Grand Avenue, a Western-crafts renaissance blooms in a block of long-abandoned historic storefronts. One shop now displays whittled wooden sculptures, and another—the **Bounty Hunter**, 119 West Grand Avenue—makes custom cowboy hats, boots, and Western clothing as well as furniture and luggage for discriminating buyers. Across the street, the **Cowboy & Indian Gallery** displays a suitably cluttered selection of Western antiques and collectibles. Next door, the **Mesa Verde Stage Line**, at number 122, offers mule-drawn stagecoach rides through Mancos Valley in coaches they make right in town; Tel: (303) 533-7264.

Northeast of town, the national forest is home to the **Lake Mancos Guest Ranch**, a family ranch located ¼ mile (½ km) north of Mancos on CO 184, then 5 miles (8 km) northeast, following signs to 42688 County Road N. Carpeted family cabins feature bedrooms with king-size beds, two bathrooms, and a porch. Lodge rooms are also available for singles or couples, although this is not the place to go to get away from kids.

Mesa Verde

Mesa Verde National Park is a 37-mile (59-km), 45-minute drive west from Durango via U.S. 160, or an 8-mile (13-km) drive west from Mancos (watch for signs indicating the turnoff). The cliff dwellings, ruins, and museum displays of Indian history here, detailing the puzzling abandonment of this site of a complex culture, are the most extensive in the Southwest: 52,074 acres, or 80 square miles. More than 4,000 ruin sites and 600 cliff dwellings remain; you won't see them all, of course, but plan to spend at least a day looking around, maybe longer.

Mesa Verde is believed to have been settled sometime after the peak of the Chaco culture; like Chaco Canyon, it was mysteriously abandoned near the end of the 13th century, suggesting that Anasazi Indians lived in the area from approximately A.D. 600 to 1300, growing corn and beans, weaving baskets, and creating pottery before disappearing from their nearly inaccessible cliff dwellings and pueblos. These homes, which have been carefully restored and stabilized, are visible today as ruins in the only national park established to protect man-made artifacts, including well-preserved pit houses, kivas, and architecturally distinct stone-and-masonry communities.

Some of the famous cliff dwellings seem to be embedded in sheer rock walls. The only access would have been by primitive ladders that reached as high as 80 feet. Today's visitor should be prepared to do some walking and possibly some ladder climbing to reach various ruins, although a number of sites can be seen at a distance, from overlooks. The trails are well marked and well maintained (off-trail hiking is prohibited). An offbeat way to see Mesa Verde in winter is on cross-country skis. There will be no one else around—just you and the winter wind.

Mesa Verde contains five major cliff dwellings and many more mesa-top dwellings, revealing various generations of inhabitants from the earliest basketmakers to the later pueblo builders. Facilities include a museum, several gift shops, ranger-guided tours, a campground, restaurants, and **Far View Lodge**, a motel where reservations are very hard to come by during the busy summer season.

Summers here can be uncomfortably hot and plagued by traffic jams. Mesa Verde is a better bet in the spring, which is wildflower season, or in the fall, when the colors provide a pretty contrast to the stone-and-mortar ruins. Off-seasons at Mesa Verde offer cooler weather, with fewer people around, resulting in more peace and quiet to savor the ruins—although many of the ruins, the motel, the campground, and all but one restaurant are closed mid-October to mid-April. For information and reservations, contact Mesa Verde, P.O. Box 277, Mancos, CO 81328; Tel: (303) 529-4461.

Cortez

Cortez, on U.S. 160 some 10 miles (16 km) west of the entrance to Mesa Verde, might be a good choice as a base for several days' activities. The Ute Mountain Tribal Park; the Four Corners Monument; Crow Canyon Archaeological Center; the Dolores area with its museums, ruins, and reservoir; and the Hovenweep National Monument (all of which are covered below) are all within day-trip range from this town. Cortez itself is less Old Western than just Western, as compared with Durango or Silverton. That means you will find fewer historic buildings and more mobile homes, modular structures, mostly modest chain motels, and uninspired cuisine. Nothing fancy. The spiffiest place to stay is the **Holiday Inn Express** on U.S. 160 (Main Street), at the east end of town. The best food may be at the M&M Truckstop, 7006 U.S. 160, at the south end of town. **Francisca's**, a restaurant at 125 East Main, makes good margaritas and decent Mexican food.

As you come to Cortez from Mesa Verde, your eyes will be bombarded by a strip of shops along U.S. 160 selling Indian goods ranging from schlock to art. Less than a mile west from the edge of town is the Cortez Colorado Welcome Center, next to City Park, 928 East Main Street on the corner of U.S. 160 and Mildred Street; Tel: (303) 565-4048. This is the best place in the region to stock up on brochures and information about the entire Four Corners. On summer nights, except Mondays, free Indian dances and storytelling convene at 7:00 P.M. in the park.

A few blocks west and one block north of the Welcome Center is the **Cortez-Colorado University Center**, at 25 North Market Street. This museum, closed Sundays, features displays from various periods of Anasazi history. Nightly summer lectures are given here, and a traditional hogan (home), constructed by a Navajo family, is open to visitors. Crafts demonstrations and traditional foods are offered; prices for crafts tend to be more reasonable here than elsewhere in the region.

Think of Cortez as the doorway to Indian Country. This friendly and unpretentious town is a more convenient base for excursions to the north, west, and south than Durango. Keep in mind that attractions in the Cortez area are spread out. Allow yourself one full day to tour, for example, the Ute Mountain Tribal Park, the Four Corners Monument, and the Ute Casino. Crow Canyon Archaeological Center, the Dolores area, and Hovenweep Na-

tional Monument each merit a full day. Returning to
Cortez for accommodations is recommended in all cases,
although the option of continuing on to Blanding, Utah,
via UT 262 and U.S. 191 North from Hovenweep is a
possibility. It's about the same distance from Hovenweep
to Cortez or to Blanding.

Ute Mountain Tribal Park

Twenty-two miles (35 km) south of Cortez on U.S. 160/
666 is the entrance to one of the most evocative ruin sites
in the Southwest, the Ute Mountain Tribal Park. Most of
the thousands of people who visit Mesa Verde every year
have never heard of this park, which is on Indian land
surrounding Mesa Verde on three sides, and is more than
twice its size. Ute's 125,000 acres contain hundreds of
still-unexcavated archaeological sites. Last year a mere
3,000 connoisseurs of Indian ruins explored the Ute
Mountain Park, which was last populated circa A.D. 1250.

This park is totally different from Mesa Verde. There is
no concrete, asphalt, or steel. It is quiet and primitive—
low-key, the way the Indians want it.

Ute Mountain Park is only 30 miles (48 km) northwest
of the Four Corners National Monument, where the Colorado, New Mexico, Arizona, and Utah borders meet. As
you drive south out of Cortez—past the used-car lots and
truck stops outside town, past **Mesa Verde Soaring** (Tel:
303/565-6164), which offers glider rides over Anasazi
ruins—the hills lengthen, and striated sandstone buttes
and grass-topped mesas rise out of the desert, with cattle
or sheep grazing between clusters of scrubby brush. To
the west is Sleeping Ute Mountain, a series of contiguous
peaks that are said to resemble a chief lying on his back
with his arms folded across his chest. You are now in
Indian Country.

Unescorted visitors are not allowed here, and reservations are required for the park's various tours, which
consist of a pair of Indian guides driving a pickup truck,
followed by a small caravan of private cars. Tour participants must provide their own vehicles, and should make
sure they are well stocked with gas, food, and water for the
day-long excursion over nearly 100 miles of dusty dirt
roads. The Utes simply lead you; they offer no provisions.
The guides stop at various spots to conduct short hikes and
offer archaeological and historical interpretations from an
Indian perspective. (Mesa Verde, by contrast, is guarded by
rangers and protected by many rules, as it should be. But it

is almost as if the cowboys are telling the Indians' story there.)

No one lives within the Ute Mountain Park. A few Indians keep livestock on the summer range, and access to outsiders is limited to 50 people per day for these guided tours. This is an archaeological record left almost as it was found, not reconstructed as at Mesa Verde, or commercialized as in Monument Valley (see below), where Indians in costume charge tourists to pose for photos. Here, the cumulative grandeur is less apparent. If you do not know what you are looking at, you may see only rocks. Yet the best-preserved Anasazi sites of the Southwest are here, protected on the reservation.

The first tour stop is an underground kiva, a mound of earth melting almost invisibly into the desert color scheme. You climb down a wooden ladder, then duck through an underground tunnel and into the kiva, which is lighted by a hole cut in the ground above your head. As part of an ongoing description of Indian life, the guides explain the ceremonial significance of the kiva as a place for gatherings.

A few miles down the road you hike over barren-looking hills in a field littered with thousands of pottery shards from the region, as well as from Arizona and New Mexico (indicating trade with distant peoples). Beneath the hills are unexcavated ruins, ancient Indian home sites that were dug out below ground in the fashionable architectural style hereabouts circa A.D. 1150. You are free to touch the fragments of painted pottery, water jugs, and cup handles made from coiled clay, and the petroglyph rock carvings, all hidden among many more rock mounds and flowing sandstone cliffs along a steep, rocky trail.

The arid 25-mile-long Mancos River Valley, in which the park is situated, was carved by the Mancos River over eons, before the fertile years when this area last supported human life. As you overlook the scrub and cactus here, the theory that years of drought caused the Anasazi to abandon their homes in this area and in Mesa Verde will ring true.

The tour continues up steep rock cliffs by way of ladders or ancient hand-holds to reach more petroglyphs and faded, centuries-old rock paintings. Deeper into the park the road climbs out of the bare desert into thickening juniper, piñon, and cedar forests. After you eat the lunch you brought with you, a hike down over the mesa top will bring you to the only housing sites that have undergone any excavation in the vast park. From the lip of the mesa you can barely see **Tree House Ruin**, carved out of the cliff sides, its natural camouflage hiding it for centuries until discovery by the Wetherills, the Mancos ranchers who reported the finding of Mesa Verde as well.

After climbing down a series of short ladders that step down the side of the mesa, you walk single file along a good trail that hugs precipitous ledges, careful to avoid the poison ivy pointed out by the guide. Tree House is composed of 27 living rooms and three kivas. In stone are carved a pair of century-old signatures, "A. Wetherill 1-1-88" and "J. W. Wetherill 1-14-90." The structure had been a three-story dwelling; remnants of wooden ceiling beams still plug holes carved in the rock. Low ceilings and narrow doorways indicate the small stature of the Anasazi. Eight-hundred-year-old corncobs, more pottery, and bone shards all suggest a ghostly presence.

Lion House, nearby, was named for the mountain lions that are still found around here. The ruins are four stories high, with 47 rooms and six kivas, making them the largest excavated ruins in the park, although many others undoubtedly remain hidden by the centuries. A quarter mile farther, Morris Five ruin, named after Earl Morris, who excavated here in 1913, has 17 rooms, two kivas.

Mesa Verde, with its larger, impeccably kept remains, seems sanitized compared to this place, which retains its ancient spirit along with its artifacts. Even Chaco Canyon, another fabulous Indian site protected from tourist hordes by daunting dirt roads, has a museum and park rangers. Here at Ute Mountain Park you can almost feel the spirits of primitive people and you can touch their history. At **Eagle's Nest**, for example, the last stop on the tour, you climb a 30-foot-tall ladder to 17 rooms and one kiva, another small enclave abandoned to the ghosts. By late afternoon you can feel the dust on your skin and taste it in your mouth. Scale the ladder for a bird's-eye view of the box canyon around which these long-gone people built their homes and lives, and you'll see from the top, shielded by the overhanging lip of the mesa, the farthest ruins. The scents of dry earth and evergreens mingle, and you can all but see residents plying these trails, hauling water in jugs from the river below.

The Ute Mountain Park is open daily for guided tours, depending on the weather and the dryness of roads; Tel: (800) 847-5485 or (303) 565-3751, ext. 282. Camping is available in a small, primitive campground. Individual backpacking trips to more remote areas for 24 hours or longer are also available, with an Indian guide. Durango's

Mountain Bike Specialists, Tel: (800) 255-8377 or (303) 247-4066, offers guided mountain-bike tours in the park, and **Rapp Guide Service,** Tel: (303) 247-8923, offers horse-back trips.

Four Corners National Monument

Four Corners National Monument, the only place in the United States where four states—Colorado, New Mexico, Arizona, and Utah—meet, is about 30 miles (48 km) southwest of the Ute Mountain Park on U.S. 160. A brief stop here is most conveniently accomplished from the tribal park.

The monument is not much more than a cement slab in the ground, surrounded by numerous souvenir stalls operated by Navajo merchants. Most people drive up, get out, snap a few photos of junior contorting to be in all four states at one time, and drive away. One recent visitor climbed out of his car on a rainy spring night and exclaimed, "This is what I came here from Germany to see?" Well, it is probably worth a visit, if only to say you did so, although there is not much to see in this boring spot at the epicenter of all this beauty. The overblown buildup and blatant commercialism here make for a dramatic contrast to the spirituality of the Ute park.

If you're heading back to Cortez for the night you might want to stop for some low-stakes gambling, including blackjack, craps, and slots, at the **Ute Mountain Casino,** located behind the Ute Mountain Pottery Plant on U.S. 160, 12 miles (19 km) south of Cortez.

Crow Canyon Archaeological Center

About 5 miles (8 km) west of Cortez, off U.S. 666, the Crow Canyon Archaeological Center, 23390 County Road K, is a modern research and educational institution devoted to studying the Anasazi of the Four Corners. Research expeditions, workshops, field trips, and study programs provide hands-on experience; students of all ages learn to excavate, analyze artifacts, and document new archaeological sites in the region. Offerings range from one-day programs that include tours of labs and a working archaeological dig to week-long residency programs where you go out in the field daily to dig at an ongoing excavation. Botanical studies and seminars are also offered. But do not just drop in here; there is no staff to handle unscheduled visitors. Perhaps this is why directions, involving a maze of dirt roads, are not publicized. Call first—reservations are required at least one day in advance; Tel: (800) 422-8975 or (303) 565-8975.

The Dolores Area

No reservations are required for the **Anasazi Heritage Center**, 27501 CO 184 in Dolores, about 10 miles (16 km) north of Cortez via CO 145. Displays in this museum for the study and interpretation of the prehistory of the Four Corners include a replica Anasazi dwelling, artifacts, and interactive exhibits where visitors can grind corn with a stone or weave fabrics on a primitive loom. Tel: (303) 882-4811. Outside the museum a steep walk up a short trail leads to the **Escalante and Domínguez Ruins,** two small pueblo excavations that may have been the first ruins discovered by Spanish explorers, in 1776. They overlook the south end of the **McPhee Reservoir**, a ten-mile-long man-made lake. Many of the two million artifacts stored at the Anasazi Center were retrieved from this valley before it was flooded in 1984 to create the lake.

There are several boat ramps, campgrounds, and picnic areas around the 50-mile shoreline. Besides boating, sailing, swimming, and waterskiing, activities include fishing for rainbow, cutthroat, or German brown trout; kokanee salmon; large- or smallmouth bass; yellow perch; and bluegill. A state fishing license, required of all anglers in Colorado, is available at any sporting-goods store, bait shop, or boat-rental shop throughout the state. Hiking trails are another option. Elk, antelope, and deer are frequently sighted—and the targets of hunters in the fall. For McPhee information, Tel: (303) 882-7296.

The reason for building the reservoir was to control the waters of the **Dolores River**, which still offers some of the best white water rapids in the West in May and June after heavy winter snows. Check with **The Outfitter**, 410 Railroad Avenue in Dolores, for white water trips; Tel: (303) 882-7740. The 12-mile stretch from the McPhee Dam to County Road 505 is considered by *Trout Magazine* to be one of America's 100 top trout streams for catch-and-release fly-fishing. The Dolores area, the last Alpine forest before we drop down to the Colorado Plateau, rises up from the valley to the river's headwaters among 14,000-foot peaks. The fall colors north of Dolores are almost beyond belief, with mountainsides of aspens glittering golden in the high sun.

The **Old Germany Restaurant**, in the center of the town

of Dolores at 200 South Eighth Street, serves moderately priced Bavarian dishes along with German beers and wines. Information on the Dolores area is available from the Cortez Colorado Welcome Center; Tel: (303) 565-4048.

Hovenweep National Monument and Lowry Indian Ruins

About 50 miles (80 km) due west of Cortez lies Hovenweep National Monument. It is a little hard to reach. From Cortez take U.S. 160/666 south for 4 miles (6½ km) to McElmo Canyon Road (also known as County Road G). Turn right and stay on this road for 29 miles (46 km). Clock the distance. It will be 25 miles (40 km) to the Utah state line; then 4 miles farther look for a small sign pointing to Hovenweep. Turn right and clock another 4 miles before turning right again. Drive 6 miles (10 km) to the Hovenweep Visitors Center (Tel: 303/562-4248), which is well signposted on your right.

On the way there you might call ahead to inquire about stopping in at **Kelly Place**, 14663 County Road G, a living history farm complete with Indian ruins surrounded by orchards and vineyards on a 100-acre property. Workshops are offered in gardening, Anasazi pottery techniques, photography, Southwest archaeology, and weaving. Tel: (303) 565-3125.

Straddling the Colorado-Utah border, Hovenweep is the site of six groups of ruins—some in Utah, others in Colorado—noted for a variety of multistory masonry towers. There is a well-maintained campground at the park, with a ranger on duty, but the closest reliable facilities other than a water fountain and a soft-drink vending machine are in Cortez, or in Bluff or Blanding, Utah. Make sure your gas tank is full, and bring food and water along if you plan to visit this remote spot.

Hovenweep's towers, which postdate the Mesa Verde period, overlook small, narrow canyons from every possible vantage point to view the mesa tops and valley bottoms at the same time. Was protection the motive? Historians don't know. The canyons contain permanent springs, but after 400 years or so of habitation the Hovenweep communities were abandoned, around A.D. 1300.

It takes only a few hours to hike the easy trail looping around the **Square Tower** group of ruins. There is even a parking lot next to the ranger station at one part of the loop. A chat with the ranger (on duty from 8:00 A.M. to 5:00 P.M. daily) is a good idea before further exploration to more distant sites. If you want to do some independent backcountry hiking to top-notch ruins, this might be the place; other sites in the region (below) may require hiring a guide or hooking onto a tour group. Biking is also a good way to get around the fairly level terrain of Hovenweep, though bikes are restricted to park roads and are not allowed on trails.

After visiting Hovenweep, you can head west to Blanding (via UT 262 and U.S. 191 North), where there are several motels—and where even less happens than in Cortez. Or return to Cortez by reversing your route or via a different route past more interesting ruins.

Assuming you opt for the latter, turn right upon exiting Hovenweep (you'll be travelling northeast on an unmarked dirt road) and drive 25 miles (40 km), until the road ends at County Road CC, which may or may not be marked. One mile (1½ km) to the left is **Lowry Indian Ruins**, a National Historic Landmark, just west of Pleasant View. There is no camping here and no ranger, only a few picnic tables. Still, this is a fine place for an unhurried walking tour of Anasazi architecture that will reveal good examples of the progression of masonry styles used in structural additions made over time. You can clamber up short ladders to take in the views of Sleeping Ute Mountain, now to the east, and the vast Colorado Plateau spreading in all other directions. Or climb down into a rare painted kiva, where bits of original 900-year-old painted plaster are visible in the underground chamber.

To continue your return to the home base of Cortez, travel 9 miles (14½ km) east on County Road CC to Pleasant View, and then 20 miles (32 km) to the southeast on U.S. 666 to Cortez.

Thirty-five miles (56 km) north of Cortez, on the way north into Utah on U.S. 666, is agricultural Dove Creek, the "Pinto Bean Capital of the World." The Adobe Milling Company, 535 East U.S. 666, sells tasty Anasazi beans that look like speckled pintos but are easier to digest, as well as a pungent hot sauce: Dos Gringos. The label says it's great for "barbecues and meats, casseroles and bean dishes, Southwestern and Mexican recipes, soups and stews, cocktails and Buffalo wings. Also keeps feet warm in winter. Apply directly to socks."

Just before you reach Dove Creek you'll see the

marked turnoff for the **Dolores Canyon overlook**, 11 miles (18 km) to the northeast. The sign, on your right when travelling north, reads Public Lands Access, Dolores River Canyon and Overlook. The winding river is visible at the bottom of a red-walled, half-mile-deep canyon.

SOUTHEASTERN UTAH

From Dove Creek continue northwest along U.S. 666 for 23 miles (37 km) to Monticello (covered in the Utah Canyonlands chapter of this guidebook). At Monticello turn left onto U.S. 191 South to reach Blanding, 25 miles (40 km) down the road. Though this route from Cortez to Blanding may seem longer than others on your map and to take you out of your way, the marked, paved roads we've suggested make for a much smoother ride than the alternative dirt roads, many of which are unsignposted.

Blanding, on U.S. 191, is worth a stop, if only for a short visit to **Edge of the Cedars State Park**, at 660 West 400 North, in the northeast part of town. The small museum here contains excellent displays of artifacts, tools, and artwork relating to Anasazis, Utes, Navajos, and early Anglo settlers, and there is a multiroom ruin on the site. There is also the clean, unexceptional **Best Western Gateway Motel** in town if you need to stay overnight.

Those not travelling from Colorado first (as we do in this chapter) can get to Hovenweep National Monument from Blanding by heading south on U.S. 191 to UT 262 (take a left), which will take you to the site.

South of Blanding, U.S. 191 passes through Bluff, a small town offering an unusual restaurant and stunning sheer rock cliff scenery, such as the **Navajo Twin Rocks**, which are visible from the highway. The **Cow Canyon Restaurant**, 163 Mission Road, overlooks the San Juan River at the south end of town. Traditional dishes such as squash-blossom stew are served, as are hybrids, like teriyaki chicken cooked the Navajo way: seared over a wood fire then slowly cooked over the embers. This casual spot, with a rough wooden interior and river views from the patio, will give you change back from a twenty for dinner.

At Bluff you will probably want to pick up U.S. 163 West, a designated scenic byway and the road leading to Monument Valley. On the way, about 15 miles (24 km) southwest of Bluff on the right side of the road (only a small sign marks the entrance), a 17-mile scenic-loop drive passes through the **Valley of the Gods** (the route is best for four-wheel-drive vehicles). It is like a deserted mini–Monument Valley. Rugged dirt roads that see little traffic trail among isolated volcanic rock spires and desolate buttes.

The Valley of the Gods loop concludes on UT 261. Eight miles (13 km) south on UT 261, just before you rejoin U.S. 163, there is a turnoff onto UT 316, where a 1-mile (1½-km) leg followed by 4 miles (6½ km) more on a paved access road brings you to **Goosenecks State Park**. From the park **overlook** you can see the sinuous San Juan River, 1,500 feet below, travel six serpentine miles to move only one mile closer, as the crow flies, to Lake Powell. The small town of Mexican Hat—named for a big balancing rock that looks a little like a sombrero—is about 5 miles (8 km) south of the intersection of UT 261 and U.S. 163. Its name is its only claim to fame.

Monument Valley

Monument Valley Navajo Tribal Park, straddling the Arizona-Utah border southwest of Mexican Hat, and accessed by U.S. 163, has seen the shooting of numerous classic Hollywood Westerns, including *Stagecoach* and *How the West Was Won*—not to mention countless commercials, calendar photos, and fashion layouts. The vast valley is filled with towering monolithic rocks, volcanic spires, buttes, and mesas that may therefore look familiar, bearing names like the Mittens, Three Sisters, Thunderbird, and Rain God. The immense freestanding rock forms are among the classic images ingrained in so many of us as "the American West."

It would be easy to spend a few days exploring the Anasazi sites, with their rock art, and the natural sandstone arches within the approximately 30,000-acre boundaries of the tribal park. And seeing at least one sunset in Monument Valley is a must: The huge sandstone forms rising out of the gullies and canyons take on bright shades of orange and red, accented by deep shadows created by the rays of the descending sun.

A self-guiding 17-mile unpaved **loop road**, beginning at the visitors' center, drops down through the broad valley, past sheep ranches and private farms shadowed by the giant vertical rocks, past John Ford's Point, named for the Hollywood director who made the valley famous by posing John Wayne in front of this imposing scenery. Very few signs appear on this self-guided loop, so you'll probably have several opportunities to see the sites from various vantage points—if not to get completely lost.

Because absolutely no off-road travel is permitted without a Navajo guide, and because the dirt road can be very rugged, many visitors prefer to explore the park as part of a guided tour, which can be anything from an hour to several days long, by jeep, horseback, or combining hiking and camping. Arrangements should be made at the visitors' center (Tel: 801/727-3287), 4 miles (6½ km) east of U.S. 163, directly east of the town of Gouldings. All the guides are Navajos. Moonlight, sunrise, wildlife, and photography tours are among the offerings.

Adjacent to the visitors' center, a 100-site campground overlooks the entire valley and the most famous view of the park: the Mittens, two giant buttes that epitomize the imagery of Monument Valley. Along the entry road to the park, vendors sell jewelry, rugs, mutton stew, or fry bread (a deep-fried, delicious Navajo specialty that tastes like an unsweetened doughnut) from rickety wooden stalls. Across U.S. 163 is **Goulding's Lodge**, a modern motel that evolved from a trading post established in 1924. Now there is a private landing strip here, as well as the motel, a restaurant, a gift shop, a gas station, a supermarket, and more. A **museum** inside the original trading post includes Anasazi artifacts and a film set from the Ford-Wayne collaboration *She Wore a Yellow Ribbon.*

Be prepared for crowds and 100-degree temperatures in Monument Valley in the summertime. Arrive early for a campsite, or make sure you have a reservation at Goulding's. The alternative accommodations closest to the tribal park, other than a small, unsavory-looking motel in Mexican Hat, 24 miles (38 km) north, is a clean **Holiday Inn** in Kayenta, Arizona, 25 miles (40 km) south. The fried chicken at the Thrift Way gas station in Kayenta, by the way, is "to die for," according to several independent taste testers. And a Burger King in town contains an interesting museum-like display relating to Navajo code breakers in World War II, right under an ad for a Whopper. Welcome to the 16-million-acre Navajo Reservation.

NORTHEASTERN ARIZONA
Navajo National Monument

The largest of the pueblo-type ruins in Arizona are located at Navajo National Monument (from Kayenta take

U.S. 160 west for 20 miles/32 km, then AZ 564 north for 9 miles/14½ km). The **Keet Seel Ruins** are open Memorial Day (late May) to Labor Day (early September) only, and are a strenuous eight-mile hike from the monument's visitors' center, which is impossible to miss at the end of AZ 564. Access to Keet Seel is limited to 20 people daily. The round trip takes all day for fit hikers, but you can also hike in, camp near the ruins, then hike out the next day. Arrangements can be made at the visitors' center for a guided one-day horseback trip to the site with a local Navajo; Tel: (602) 672-2366 or 672-2367.

The **Betatakin Ruin**, visible from an overlook close to the visitors' center, nestles in the alcove of a south-facing rock across a narrow canyon. The only way to see Betatakin close up is on a ranger-guided hike conducted daily, May to September, but, again, limited to 20 people. This round-trip hike takes about five hours; the return from the ruins is the equivalent of walking up a 70-story building at 7,300 feet elevation. Bring water. Make reservations for the limited-attendance tours to get close to the ruins here.

Hopiland

Due south of the Navajo Monument, along AZ 264, lies Hopiland, a reservation belonging to the Indian group thought most likely to have descended directly from the Anasazis. To get to Hopiland from the Navajo Reservation it is inadvisable to take any of the numerous unmarked dirt roads that run through the reservations. They may or may not eventually get you to your destination, and road conditions are unpredictable, particularly in bad weather. Instead, we recommend turning right onto U.S. 160 from AZ 564 and heading southwest 31 miles (50 km) to Tuba City, a large town by Navajo standards but without much to recommend it to travellers (except gas). From Tuba City turn left onto AZ 264 and head southeast to Hopiland along this, its main paved road.

The relatively small Hopi Reservation—it is one-tenth the size of the Navajo lands—is at the southern end of Black Mesa, where three steep, flat-topped mesas rise sharply out of the desert. Villages are scattered across the simply named First Mesa, Second Mesa, and Third Mesa. One village, Old Oraibi, was settled in 1150 and may be the oldest continually inhabited village in North America.

The Hopi are bound by tradition in many ways. For

example, when you walk through a Hopi village after harvest you see mounds of colorful corncobs laid in the sun to dry, heaped in front of the small stone-and-wood houses. Visitors always want to buy the corn for decorations. The Hopis could make a fortune selling it, but after many centuries of growing the multicolored food for their own use, they have no plans to change their course. The red corn is eaten fresh or cooked in hot sand (popcorn). The white corn is used for hominy and in ceremonies. The blue corn is used in cooking and ground into flour for traditional *piki* bread. Yellow corn is sweet corn; first baked in underground pits, it is then hung outside to dry, to be boiled and eaten in the winter. The Hopis say it tastes fresh. None is sold.

At the very old village of **Old Oraibi** on First Mesa you can see ancient houses (still occupied) that look a lot like the many Anasazi ruins you have been viewing rising out of the scrubby desert terrain. Satellite dishes and modular housing are mixed in, looking out of place among rocks larger than houses, strewn like pebbles or piled into bluffs, larger rocks that form tall outcrops, and finally, mesas. In the distance more spectral mesas and pastel sandstone cliffs shimmer like hallucinations in the desert heat.

The name "Hopi" means "Good, Peaceful, or Wise," and Hopis have traditionally been farmers rather than warriors. But the Hopi Reservation, created by Congress in 1892, is surrounded by the 26,000-square-mile Navajo Reservation, and relations are historically tense between the two groups, exacerbated by cultural differences. Navajos are nomadic, or were. Their families tend to live at a distance from one another, even today, by tradition. Hopis are pueblo people, farmers, and are long settled here in communal-minded villages. Conflicts between the two tribes have often focused on land disputes involving the low-lying deserts and gullies, the buttes, and mesas ranging as high as 7,200 feet.

No doubt these tensions have contributed to the Hopis remaining the most private of Indians. No photos can be taken, no drawings or tape recordings can be made in the villages, and certain ceremonial dances are closed to outsiders. At other times, particularly during summer weekends, colorful dances are open to the public, though the no-camera rule applies—cameras are confiscated from those who fail to comply—and "neat attire and a respectful disposition" are suggested in guidelines handed out by the Hopi. Visitors are more or less welcome in all the Hopi villages, unless otherwise posted, but it is hard to avoid feeling like an outsider here.

No problem, though, if you want to buy the Hopis' famed silver-overlay jewelry (cutouts of silver placed over a bottom layer of blackened silver), a rug, or a carved wooden kachina doll (fashioned from cottonwood roots, then painted and clothed to represent various Hopi spirits; the ones for sale are subtly different from those used ceremonially by the Hopi). Hopis, who also raise livestock and farm the mesas, have long been recognized for weavings, pottery, carvings, and silver jewelry of the highest order. A museum at the **Hopi Cultural Center** in Second Mesa, on AZ 264, displays historical tribal artifacts, including silver and baskets. Several stores in the complex (often marked only by a small hand-lettered sign in a front window) sell tribal artwork and a few crafts. It's all very low-keyed, but you could get lucky and find silver work or a kachina doll you really like. Some of the shops are set among the houses, others cluster around the **Hopi Cultural Center and Motel**. Reservations are a must for the tidy, plain 33-room motel—which is the best place to stay for many miles. There is also a restaurant here, serving burgers and eggs as well as Hopi specialties such as *chil-il-ou-gyava,* a bean chili, and *nok-quivi,* a stew of lamb and corn. For information on Hopi ceremonies phone the Office of Public Relations at tribal headquarters in Kykotsmovi; Tel: (602) 734-2441.

Hubbell Trading Post
National Historic Site

Situated east of Hopiland and just a few miles west of Ganado on AZ 264, Hubbell Trading Post National Historic Site is the only operating trading post within the U.S. National Park Service jurisdiction. The Navajos were removed from these ancestral reservation lands in 1864 by U.S. Army forces, then returned in 1868, after everything they ever had was gone, to start a new way of life from scratch. Exchange with the Anglos became necessary for sustenance, and trading posts opened to supply Indians with the sugar, coffee, canned goods, tools, and cloth on which they were growing dependent. In return, Indians traded what they had: rugs, pots, baskets, and jewelry—never using cash.

Well into the 20th century the Hubbell Trading Post and others like it were the only points of contact between many Indians and the members of the culture that had defeated them. The Hubbell store first opened on this site in 1876, and was operated by descendants of John Lorenzo Hubbell until it was sold to the Park Service and opened to the public in 1965. Hubbell died in 1930 and was buried on a hilltop overlooking the trading post. You can tour his antiques-filled house and barn, or buy candy, canned peas, a galvanized bucket, a string of beads, or some of the better Navajo rugs and blankets available anywhere (prices tend to run high). The good stuff is kept in an antique safe. Local artisans conduct weaving and silversmithing demonstrations here daily in the summer. Much of Navajo silver work, distinctive from that of the Hopis in that it combines silver with turquoise or coral (in bracelets, concho belts, and squash-blossom necklaces), reflects the Spanish influences of the Mexican silversmiths who taught the Navajo their skill in the 1800s.

Although it may be difficult to locate the Navajo tourism office, as we said at the beginning of the chapter, it's not hard to find Navajo crafts. For quality turquoise-and-silver jewelry, baskets, rugs, and pottery the **Navajo Arts & Crafts Enterprise** has one of the most extensive selections in the Four Corners. The shop is near the intersection of AZ 264 and Navajo Route 12 North, 31 miles (50 km) east of Ganado and Hubbell in the Navajo capital Window Rock, at the New Mexico border. Sharing the building with the shop is the **Navajo Tribal Museum**, containing displays depicting traditional aspects of Navajo life, and offering a good selection of books and article reprints related to Navajo culture.

Canyon de Chelly
National Monument

Convincing evidence of ancient and modern Indians living in concert with the environment can be found at Canyon de Chelly National Monument near **Chinle**, about an hour north from Ganado/Hubbell off U.S. 191. Deep sandstone canyons here were home to Pueblo Indians 1,000 years ago. Today the canyon is still occupied and farmed, but by Navajos. In summer the glimmering river-fed canyon bottom offers a visual contrast to the stark sandstone rim. Though unoccupied in winter, the canyon is nonetheless considered a spiritual center by the Navajos.

Because of its proximity to the canyon, the city of Chinle is relatively prosperous compared with other Navajo towns. It has two better-than-average motels, the venerable, Spanish-influenced **Thunderbird Lodge**, next to the campground at the mouth of Canyon de Chelly, and the newer, cleaner, friendlier **Canyon de Chelly Motel**, 1 mile (1½ km) outside the park on AZ 7, the road that continues along the south rim of the canyon.

The 100-mile-long canyon and the adjacent **Canyon del Muerto** house numerous Anasazi sites dating to as early as A.D. 200, alongside corn and bean fields, peach orchards, and horses grazing in the fertile canyon bottoms. From its shallowest, westernmost point, at around 200 feet, the canyon descends to 1,100 feet in the east, spanning 11 million years of geology and nearly 2,000 years of human occupation, with more than 100 ancient ruin sites and numerous examples of rock art.

The best place to begin is at the visitors' center (Tel: 602/674-5436), about 2 miles (3 km) east of AZ 191 on AZ 7. Maps and information about tours and special ranger-led programs are available here. There is also an informative small museum. From the visitors' center AZ 7 heads east for 19 miles (30 km) along the south rim. Various scenic overlooks are well signed along the route, which changes from pavement to dirt after 19 miles (only high-ground-clearance, four-wheel-drive vehicles should attempt to go any farther east). There is one site here, **White House Ruin**, to which visitors are allowed to descend unescorted into the steep canyon. Otherwise, a Navajo guide is required for four-wheel-drive vehicle, horseback, and hiking tours along the canyon bottom, which is, by the way, notorious for shifting quicksand.

From the visitors' center the north-rim drive, AZ 64, also contains many signposted canyon overlooks. Beyond Canyon de Chelly AZ 64 (all of which is paved) continues to AZ 12, which, taken north, connects with U.S. 191 to U.S. 160 (the road to Farmington, New Mexico, and Durango, Colorado). AZ 12 South leads to Window Rock and, just beyond, to I-40, the connecting highway to Albuquerque. (We also cover Canyon de Chelly in the High Country section of the Central Arizona chapter.)

You can easily spend a day or longer exploring the canyon. But even if you only have time for a quick half day of stops at all the canyon overlooks spaced along either the north- or south-rim drive, it's worth it for the glimpse of tiny ruins 1,000 feet below the sometimes sheer, sometimes gracefully billowing canyon walls, the thriving farms, and the tenacious foliage growing out of the rock. The canyon offers a respectful blend of old and new, which is what, at its best, a visit to the Four Corners is all about in the first place.

GETTING AROUND

It is virtually mandatory that you have a car to cover the Four Corners. You can drive from the Albuquerque–Santa Fe–Taos area in a few hours to the start of a Four Corners loop. It is possible to fly from Albuquerque, Denver, or Phoenix to Durango, Colorado, on Continental, United Express, Mesa Airlines, or America West. The airport at Farmington, New Mexico, is served by Continental, United, and Mesa. Several major and numerous local car-rental firms have either airport or in-town locations or both in Durango and Farmington. A Durango airport-to-town shuttle is offered by Durango Transportation, Tel: (303) 247-4161. In Farmington you need to call a cab.

Greyhound/Trailways, Tel: (303) 259-2755, offers regional bus routes. The Lift, Tel: (303) 247-3577, operates bus service in Durango, as well as a Durango–Purgatory shuttle in winter.

It is also possible to begin the Four Corners loop from the west via the Grand Canyon, Lake Powell (Page, Arizona) or Flagstaff, through Tuba City, Arizona; or from the north in Utah, via Moab to Blanding.

Various driving routes are included throughout the text. It may look easy; there are relatively few roads from which to choose. But road signs can be poor or nonexistent off main roads, and a wrong turn could lead you many miles out of your way. Good maps are essential and readily available in local bookstores and sporting-goods shops. Fill up with gas whenever you can. Always carry drinking water. A four-wheel-drive vehicle is not necessary in summer for any of the routes suggested in the text, although in certain spots, such as parts of the Alpine loop near Silverton, Colorado, it would be a good idea. In winter, although roads are carefully and conscientiously plowed, four-wheel drive is *always* the best idea.

None of the towns in the Four Corners is very large. Most are laid out in simple grid patterns. Parking is generally not a problem, although in downtown Durango, in midsummer, it is becoming so.

At the end of the tour suggested in the chapter, you are in Canyon de Chelly, about a three-hour drive from Durango, Farmington, or Albuquerque.

There is no single phone source for complete area-wide information; however, there is a mailing address. Contact the Four Corners Tourism Council, P.O. Box 540,

Mancos, CO 81328. For information on accommodations, dining, and activities including tours, bicycle and camping-gear rentals, and places of interest in Durango contact the Durango Chamber of Commerce, P.O. Box 2587, Durango, CO 81302; Tel: (800) 525-8855 or (303) 247-0312. Information, including maps, on the San Juan National Forest, which surrounds Durango; the 236-mile San Juan Skyway, connecting Durango, Silverton, Ouray, Ridgway, Telluride, Dolores, and Cortez; the 470-mile Colorado Trail, which extends northwest from Durango through Silverton, Salida, Buena Vista, Leadville, Copper Mountain, and Breckenridge to Waterton Canyon, south of Denver; and the Weminuche Wilderness Area, within the San Juan National Forest, is all available from the U.S.D.A. Forest Service, 701 Camino del Rio, Durango, CO, Tel: (303) 247-4874.

For information on the Mesa Verde–Hovenweep area contact the Mesa Verde–Cortez Visitor Information Bureau, 1 West Main, P.O. Box HH, Cortez, CO 81321; Tel: (800) 253-1616, ext. 310, or (303) 565-3414. For information about Hopiland, including scheduled dances and special events, contact the Office of Public Relations at tribal headquarters in Kykotsmovi, Tel: (602) 734-2441; or the Arizona Office of Tourism, 1100 West Washington Street, Phoenix, AZ 85007, Tel: (602) 542-8687. For Navajo Nation information contact Navajo Tourism Department, P.O. Box 663, Window Rock, AZ 86515; Tel: (602) 871-6659 or 6436.

ACCOMMODATIONS REFERENCE

The rates given below are projections *for 1993. Unless otherwise indicated, rates are for a double room, double occupancy, and do not include meals. Price ranges span the lowest rate in the low season and the highest rate in the high season. As rates are always subject to change, it is wise to double-check before booking.*

Colorado
The area code for Colorado is 303.

▶ **Alma House Hotel.** 220 East Tenth Street, P.O. Box 359, **Silverton**, CO 81433. Tel: 387-5336. $45–$48.

▶ **Blue Lake Ranch.** 16919 County Road 140, **Hesperus**, CO 81326. Tel: 385-4537. $85–$225.

▶ **Colorado Trails Ranch.** 12161 County Road 240, **Durango**, CO 81301. Tel: 247-5055 or (800) 323-DUDE. Summer only. $850–$1,110 per person weekly, includes meals and activities.

► **Far View Lodge** (in Mesa Verde National Park). P.O. Box 277, **Mancos**, CO 81328. Tel: 529-4421. Open mid-April to mid-October. $69–$85.

► **General Palmer Hotel.** 567 Main Avenue, **Durango**, CO 81301. Tel: 247-4747 or (800) 523-3358. $75–$145.

► **Grand Imperial Hotel.** 1219 Greene Street, P.O. Box 57, **Silverton**, CO 81433. Tel: 387-5527. Closed some winters. $46.

► **Holiday Inn Express.** 2121 East Main, **Cortez**, CO 81321. Tel: 565-6000 or (800) 626-5652; Fax: 565-3438. $70–$72.

► **Jarvis Suite Hotel.** 125 West Tenth Street, **Durango**, CO 81302. Tel: 259-6190. $73–$113.

► **Lake Mancos Guest Ranch.** 42688 County Road N, **Mancos**, CO 81328. Tel: 533-7900. Summer only. $920–$1,840 weekly, includes meals.

► **Purgatory Village Hotel.** P.O. Box 666, **Durango**, CO 81301. Tel: TRY-PURG or 247-9000. $49–$190.

► **Sky Ute Lodge and Restaurant.** P.O. Box 550, **Ignacio**, CO 81137. Tel: (800) 876-7017. $34–$42.

► **Strater Hotel.** 699 Main Avenue, **Durango**, CO 81302. Tel: 247-4431 or (800) 247-4431. $62–$145.

► **Tall Timber.** SSR Box 90, **Durango**, CO 81301. Tel: 259-4813. May–September: $2,200 for four days, three nights; $3,100 for seven days, six nights. October only: $1,800 and $2,500. Rates includes meals, all facilities, and r/t transportation to resort via narrow-gauge train or helicopter.

► **Tamarron Resort.** 40292 U.S. 550 North, **Durango**, CO 81301. Tel: 259-2000 or (800) 678-1000. $85–$365.

► **Wilderness Trails Ranch.** 23486 County Road 501, **Bayfield**, CO 81122. Tel: 247-0722 or (800) 527-2624; Fax: 247-1006. June–September only. $975 per adult per week, includes meals, horseback riding, and ranch activities.

► **Wit's End Guest Ranch.** 254 County Road 500, **Vallecito Lake**, CO 81122. Tel: 884-9263 or 884-4113. $154–$190. Rates include meals.

► **Wyman Hotel.** 1371 Greene Street, P.O. Box 780, **Silverton**, CO 81433. Tel: 387-5372 or 249-4646 in off-season. Closed mid-October to mid-May. $58.

Utah
The area code for Utah is 801.

► **Best Western Gateway Motel.** 88 East Center, **Blanding**, UT 84511. Tel: 678-2278 or (800) 528-1234 (reservations only); Fax: 678-2240. $36–$69.

► **Goulding's Lodge.** P.O. Box 1, Monument Valley, UT 84536. Tel: 727-3231; Fax: 727-3344. $52–$88.

Arizona
The area code for Arizona is 602.

► **Canyon de Chelly Motel.** P.O. Box 295, Route 7, Chinle, AZ 86503. Tel: 674-5875. $86–$94.

► **Holiday Inn.** Box 307, **Kayenta**, AZ 86033. Tel: 697-3221 or (800) HOLIDAY. $49–$102.

► **Hopi Cultural Center and Motel.** P.O. Box 67, **Second Mesa**, AZ 86043. Tel: 734-2401. $55–$60.

► **Thunderbird Lodge.** Box 548, **Chinle**, AZ 86503. Tel: 674-5841. $79–$84; $140–$152 (suites for up to four people).

THE SOUTHERN TIER

EL PASO

BIG BEND

GUADALUPE MOUNTAINS

SOUTHERN NEW MEXICO

TUCSON AND SOUTHERN ARIZONA

SIDE TRIPS INTO MEXICO

EL PASO
BIG BEND AND THE GUADALUPE MOUNTAINS

By Nancy Gillespie and Buddy Mays

Nancy Gillespie, a freelance writer and a marketing communications executive, lived in Taos, New Mexico, for a decade and is now a resident of El Paso, Texas. She has contributed to numerous magazines and newspapers, including the New Mexican, New Mexico *magazine,* Southwest Profile, Southwest Art, *and* Country Inns. *She contributes the El Paso section. Buddy Mays, who covers Big Bend and the Guadalupe Mountains here, also wrote our chapters on Around Albuquerque, Santa Fe Accommodations, and Around Santa Fe.*

No other area in the United States endures so many slings and arrows as the Borderlands, the vast swath of land that begins in California and ends at the Gulf of Mexico. The United States–Mexico border is undoubtedly thought of by many outsiders as ridden by poverty and ignorance, a haven to illegal aliens, drug lords, and "coyotes" (smugglers of goods and people), and finally, merely a hostile desert inhabited by thorny plants and venomous creatures. While problems and disadvantages peculiar to the border definitely do exist, they all too often overshadow the distinct, exotic subculture that has arisen along this international boundary. This is to the detriment of travellers who bypass the Borderlands—and so miss the benefits of La Frontera, the "nation" created here by the merging of the United States and Mexico. There is no such nation as La Frontera in the atlases, of course, because they concentrate on political boundaries. But there is a La Frontera in reality, reality being less in thrall to the dictates of politicians over the years. For La Frontera the Rio Grande is not so much a boundary as a unifying element, one that has helped develop and define the region.

This land—and the Indians on it—was claimed first by Spain, then by Mexico. Despite nearly 150 years of American rule, this is Spanish America, and it will probably always remain so. Nowhere is this more evident than in the El Paso corner of West Texas, the eastern gateway to the Southwest.

While West Texas is semi-officially defined as the strip of land that runs from the panhandle down to Mexico, and as far east as Abilene and San Angelo, a funny little nib juts out where the Lone Star State meets Old and New Mexico. Here, West Texas becomes an integral part of the Borderlands.

This is a tough and starkly beautiful land, its spirit formed by the contrast of mountain and desert landscapes. The Franklin Mountains, the last of the Southern Rockies in the United States, slice through El Paso with a vengeance and plunge to a sudden stop at the obelisk in Tom Lea Park. The obelisk sits a few feet from the edge of a bluff beneath which El Paso dreams under the Chihuahuan Desert sun.

As the crow flies, the distance between the bluff and the Rio Grande is only two miles. El Paso is on one side of the border, Ciudad Juárez, Mexico, on the other, separated by the river. The legendary Rio Grande is a tangible threshold, but aside from that you won't perceive many differences between these two diametrically opposed cultures down here.

Outside of El Paso and the Mission Trail southeast of the city along the river, there are two other major attractions in Far West Texas, both of which are scenic areas of great grandeur: Big Bend National Park, along the Rio Grande farther to the southeast, and the Guadalupe Mountains east of El Paso along the New Mexico border. We cover them in this chapter following El Paso and environs.

Whereas the rest of Texas is on central standard time, El Paso and the area around it are on mountain standard time, an hour earlier. The telephone area code for El Paso and environs is 915.

MAJOR INTEREST

Historic District
University of Texas at El Paso

EL PASO

El Paso del Norte carries the musical ring of the Spanish language, and an implied mystique that is four centuries old. In April 1598 Don Juan de Oñate declared the territory surrounding the Rio Grande a Spanish acquisition and named it El Paso del Rio del Norte, "the Pass of the River of the North." Oñate was the first to colonize the area, but his arrival was predated by the army of the Rodríguez-Chamuscado expedition, which reached the Pass of the River of the North in 1581.

The El Paso of the 1990s, seen by night from the crest of the Franklin Mountains, is a sea of lights that sprawls across the desert. The wedge-shaped mountains narrow to a slender tip that points to the south like an arrow to downtown El Paso, a densely populated district compressed into the two-mile strip between the end of the Franklins and the Rio Grande. By day, in the blinding light of a desert sun, El Paso takes on another persona. Joined to Juárez like a Siamese twin, El Paso both captivates and repels. It is, in fact, a city that positively inspires ambivalence. Some love El Paso, but just as many loathe it.

For too many years travellers have merely passed through the city on their way to another destination, shunning the border experience. Yet El Paso/Juárez, their combined population two million and climbing, is the largest metroplex on the United States–Mexico border, the linchpin of the *maquila* (twin plant industry) and, quite possibly, a key player in the free-trade arrangement being developed by Canada, the United States, and Mexico.

A city both isolated and insulated from mainstream America, El Paso is closer to Albuquerque and Phoenix than to Austin, the capital of Texas. Diehard Texans consider the city an extension of New Mexico—it was in fact once part of Neuvo Mexico in New Spain—and periodic rumors suggest that that state may "annex" El Paso or that El Paso will secede. Nobody takes these notions seriously, but the topic manages to surface on a regular basis. The Hispanic population of El Paso, growing by leaps and bounds, has reached a clear majority: approximately 71 percent of the city's 600,000 residents. And this majority, flexing its political muscles for the first time, is chipping away at the power base long held by the Anglos.

The Tigua Indians, the oldest identifiable group in Texas, are meanwhile trying to recapture tribal lands claimed by the city. The imminence of the free-trade agreement polarizes El Paso even more. Even the Franklin Mountains divide the city into several distinct geographical and political units: Upper Valley, Lower Valley, Westside, Eastside, Northeast, and Central.

The many voices of El Paso add to the mystique of the city. What is El Paso all about? It is a city that consists of a mix of Anglo, Hispanic, and Indian—with a touch of Western Americana thrown in for good measure. But it's also a city that, in the face of many political and economic problems, can laugh at itself. El Pasoans have mastered ironic humor. Where else could a television anchorman refer to an unidentified body as *Juan* Doe, or a newspaper sponsor the Great Car-Theft Contest? Then there is the quixotic side: On November 25, 1991, with the blessing of the city, a group of latter-day "Spanish conquistadors" rode into Plymouth, Massachusetts, to divest the Pilgrims of the first Thanksgiving. If El Paso has its way, rewritten history texts will read, "The first Thanksgiving was celebrated by Don Juan de Oñate on April 30, 1598, on the banks of the Rio Grande."

To Oñate and his expedition, a celebration by any name was appropriate. From Santa Barbara in what is now southern Chihuahua, Mexico, the conquerors travelled across 350 miles of mountains and deserts. They reached the Rio Grande nearly dead from hunger and thirst. The end of the journey inspired a thanksgiving feast of fish and fowl shared with local Indians.

El Paso also displays a demonstrative nature. Over the past 50 years the five-point Star on the Mountain, which lights up the western flank of the Franklins, has grown to 459 by 278 feet, a moving sight visible to airline passengers from 100 miles away. *Viva! El Paso,* staged every summer in an outdoor amphitheater at the base of a cliff in McKelligon Canyon, re-creates the city's history in song, dance, and dialogue (an event well worth braving the heat to attend). During mild weather the canyon is a favorite place to picnic.

Home to Fort Bliss, the largest Army Air-Defense Base in what until recently was referred to as the free world, El Paso is so fiercely patriotic it renamed the North–South Freeway "Patriot Freeway" at the end of Desert Storm.

El Paso's diverse and often conflicting elements create a city that does not subscribe to the norm. Trying to compare El Paso with anywhere else in Texas, or the rest of the country, is like comparing kumquats with campesinos. The search for the real El Paso requires an adventurous spirit and an open mind. Once you accept its eccentricities, El Paso "grows on you," as loyal El Pasoans will tell you (always with a bemused look).

Wrapped around the Franklin Mountains like a horseshoe pointing north, El Paso does not follow a consistent grid pattern. It's easiest to visualize the city as an irregularly shaped wheel with spokes radiating out from the hub formed by the confluence of Interstate 10 and U.S. 54 (Patriot Freeway), a junction commonly known as the Spaghetti Bowl. Destinations east and west are reached by I-10, including downtown, Westside, Upper Valley to the west, and Lower Valley in the extreme southeastern part of town. Gateway Boulevard East, a one-way street heading east, and Gateway Boulevard West, one-way west, are local access roads that run parallel to I-10.

Points north and south are accessed by Patriot Freeway/ U.S. 54, including Fort Bliss (to the north) and the Cordova, or Free, Bridge to Juárez (to the south). Gateway Boulevards North and South flank Patriot Freeway and, like their east–west counterparts, are one-way access roads. The downtown area, which begins just a few blocks north of I-10 (on the west edge of the city before I-10 turns to the north) and extends south to the Rio Grande and the United States–Mexico border, encompasses the business district and Civic Center Plaza. It contains more historic sites per city block than any other section of El Paso.

We begin our coverage in historic downtown El Paso, followed by short excursions to nearby neighborhoods, historical sites, and the university. Next we head east to El Paso Museum of Art and Concordia Cemetery; the beautiful grounds and history of Fort Bliss, northeast of downtown; and into Franklin Mountains State Park on the Woodrow Bean Transmountain Drive. We then follow the

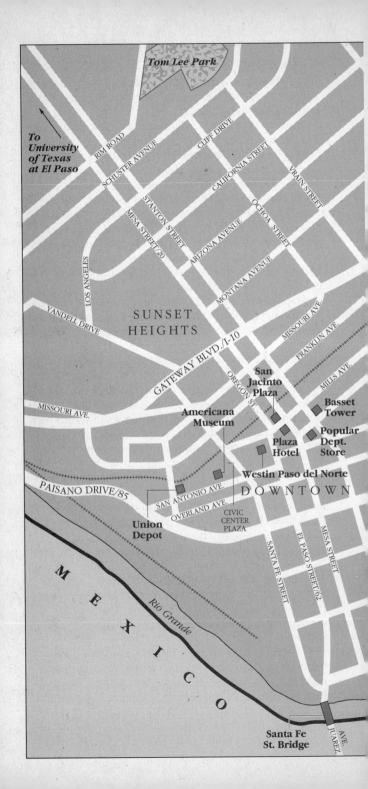

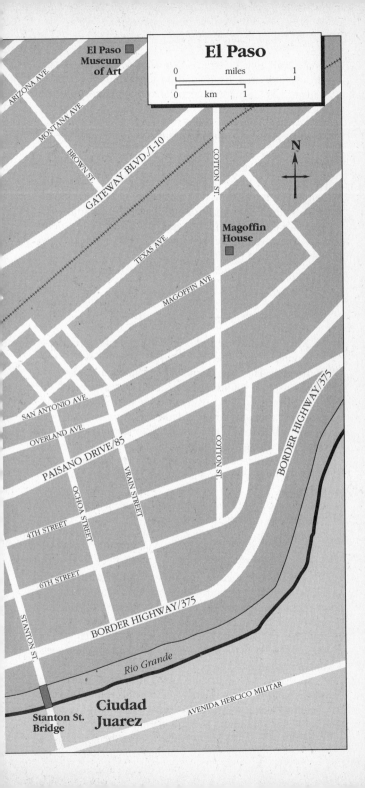

Oñate Trail, which retraces Don Juan de Oñate's passage through the area; head south to Ciudad Juárez, Mexico; return to El Paso and Hueco Tanks State Historical Park; and finish our coverage of the area with a tour of the Mission Trail southeast of El Paso.

Lastly we cover Big Bend and Guadalupe Mountains national parks farther out in Far West Texas. To reach the Guadalupe Mountains on the Texas–New Mexico border to the east of El Paso, take Montana Avenue (which becomes U.S. 62/180) east. To travel from Guadalupe Mountains National Park to Big Bend National Park, follow TX 54 south through Van Horn and pick up I-10 east to Fort Stockton, where you connect with U.S. 385 South. U.S. 385 will take you to Big Bend.

The telephone area code for El Paso and environs is 915.

Downtown El Paso

In every downtown block you will sense the paradox of La Frontera: high energy tempered by ennui, with a predominantly Hispanic population bustling in and out of Anglo-inspired buildings. The high-rise towers of the international banking district segue into the mom-and-pop operations of South El Paso without missing a beat. Nearly a hundred outdoor murals in downtown El Paso treat everything from immigration to AIDS. The resurgence of this traditional Spanish art form recalls the days of Mexican masters; the aesthetics range from gaudy to gorgeous.

If El Paso went Hollywood and cast the footprints of its star players in concrete, the imprints would bear the names of an amazing array, from Bat Masterson and Pancho Villa to Villa's nemesis, General John "Blackjack" Pershing, and President William Howard Taft. And as for impressive architecture, the **Downtown Historic District** alone, which centers roughly on San Jacinto Plaza and encompasses 33 blocks in the city center, includes 25 historical landmarks, 16 of which are in the National Register of Historic Places, and most of which are on Paisano Drive, Stanton, Oregon, and South El Paso streets, and a section of Santa Fe Street.

To orient yourself while taking in a good number of these buildings, you might want to begin your visit with a **walking tour** of the downtown area. Every Saturday during spring, summer, and fall members of the El Paso County Historical Society guide visitors through the historic district after an 8:00 A.M. breakfast at Ramada Inn's View from the Top Lounge. Limited tours are available from December through March, and special group tours can be arranged; Tel: 566-8621. The **El Paso Downtown Walking Tour** and the **Architectural Legacy of Henry C. Trost Tour** overlap in central downtown and can be accomplished simultaneously. Brochures for these and other self-guided walking tours are available at the kiosk in Civic Center Plaza on Santa Fe Street.

The Trost architectural style weds the influences of Louis Sullivan and Frank Lloyd Wright with Spanish Mission and Pueblo styles of architecture. Trost arrived in El Paso in 1903 and over the following 30 years played a key role in the city's development. A pioneer architect and an innovator in the use of reinforced concrete, Trost designed more than 200 El Paso buildings. The tour highlights the glazed terra-cotta façade of the Popular Department Store (at the meeting of Texas Avenue and Mesa and San Antonio streets) and the intricately carved frieze of plant designs on Bassett Tower at 307 Texas Avenue. One of the few Art Deco buildings in the city and a classic example of the Trost style, the tower carries the name of one O. T. Bassett, who arrived in El Paso in 1880. It was Bassett's intention to build four towers, one on each corner of the block, but only one came to fruition. The first floor, where an exhibit displays the building's history, is open to the public. The Plaza Hotel and the Westin Paso del Norte buildings are part of the Trost legacy as well.

The **Westin Paso del Norte**, 101 South El Paso Street, actually at the corner of Santa Fe Street across from the Civic Center, is the "uptown" place to stay downtown. Built in 1912 to withstand earthquakes and fire, and modeled after the great hotels of San Francisco, the Westin still has many of its original features, including the Tiffany Dome, reportedly insured by Lloyd's of London for over $1 million. In keeping with the elegant decor, the **Dome Grill** serves Continental cuisine, steak, and seafood in a formal atmosphere; Tel: 534-3010.

The hotel provides a self-guided-tour brochure (inquire at the front desk) that focuses on the 1850s, an era so bloody that the city was then known as the "Six-Shooter Capital of the U.S." In the courtyard of the Westin a plaque marks the site of the "Four Dead in Five Seconds" gunfight, which took place on April 14, 1881. The melee arose from an inquest into the murder of two Mexican ranchers near Canutillo (a little west of El Paso) in which the prime suspect was cattle rustler and gunman Johnny Hale. Because the witnesses were Mexican, Gus Krempkau, a former Texas Ranger who spoke Spanish, acted as interpreter. Hale was irate over Krempkau's translation of the events, and when the court recessed he simply shot and killed him. City Marshall Dallas Stoudenmire, also on the scene, whipped out his gun: His first shot killed a Mexican bystander, the second killed Hale. Then a Hale supporter and former city marshall jumped into the fray, but he had barely drawn his gun when Stoudenmire shot and killed him, too. Stoudenmire himself died in another gunfight the following year.

The Westin also marks one end of the **Paseo de las Luces**, actually one block of South El Paso Street and part of a downtown revitalization project. Turn-of-the-century lampposts installed by the city give the Paseo a romantic aura at dusk. El Paso Street leads into the **South El Paso** district—in effect, Juárez—only briefly interrupted by the Santa Fe Street Bridge across the Rio Grande, and has more sensory impact per block than anywhere else in the city. El Paso Street in particular is filled with shops—for shoes, dresses, children's clothing—and pawnshops. Locals consider them some of the city's best, with bargain-priced antiques, silverware, leather, and electronics. Exploring the Paseo and South El Paso after dark, however, is not recommended.

A stone's throw from the Westin's main entrance are three highly touted restaurants. Directly across the street from the Westin is the **San Francisco Grill**, at 127 Pioneer Plaza, where the house specialty—freshly made Maui chips with clam dip—precedes lunch or dinner. Be assured of a good meal: Owner Anthony Duncan is the youngest president in the history of the Texas Restaurant Association. Tel: 545-1386. **Cafe Central**, at 1 Texas Court and visible from the Grill, gets the lunch crowd for an upscale Mexican and Continental menu; Tel: 545-2233. **Antonio's** in the Plaza Hotel, at Oregon Street and Mills Avenue, has built its reputation on Mexican cuisine and draws businesspeople and politicians for breakfast and lunch; Tel: 532-5885. The Plaza Hotel itself, Conrad Hilton's first project, is now a historic landmark. Only the first three floors are in use, and no sleeping rooms are available.

On the north side of the Plaza Hotel towering palms and Mexican elders line **San Jacinto Plaza**. In the 19th century passengers on the Butterfield Overland Stage disembarked at San Jacinto beside a pool filled with alligators. The reptiles were given to El Paso as a joke, and the city promptly turned around and built a fountain and pool for its acquisitions.

Downtown El Paso was once known as Ponce's Rancho, named after the four settlements founded in 1827 by Juan Maria Ponce de León (not the same man who sought the Fountain of Youth). Fifty-some years later Chinese laborers followed the railroads to El Paso, and Chinatown sprang up in an area that ran from St. Louis Street (now Mills Avenue) to Fourth Avenue and from Stanton Street west to El Paso Street. At its peak Chinatown held nearly 1,000 residents, most of whom lived on South Oregon Street between Overland Avenue and Second Street. Their business enterprises—mostly restaurants and laundries—thrived, as did the opium traffic. By 1890 many of the Chinese workers had returned to native soil and the population dropped to 300. Chinatown is only a memory now.

The railroads ushered in all of the dubious accoutrements of the Wild West era, including a full-fledged tenderloin district in which both prostitution and gambling flourished. On a visit in 1891 President Benjamin Harrison publicly noted the deplorable state of affairs in "Sin City." Two years later the city had also made way for the El Paso Symphony, which gave its premier performance. Sin notwithstanding, culture was here to stay.

Today many of the city's cultural events take place in the three-building **Civic Center** complex directly across from the Westin on Santa Fe Street. A full schedule of performances from rock and pop to classical music are staged in the sombrero-shaped performing-arts theater. On the lower level of the theater building the **Americana Museum of Southwestern Cultural History** displays dioramas and artifacts dedicated to the pre-Columbian history of the Southwest. Trade shows, expositions, and arts-and-crafts exhibitions are held in the Great Hall.

To finish the downtown walking tour head south on Santa Fe Street from the Civic Center to San Antonio Avenue and turn west (right) onto Durango Street. **Union Depot**, at 700 San Francisco Street, was an integral part of a civic improvement program started by El Paso in the early 1900s. Built in 1906 by the architectural firm of Daniel H. Burnham, designers of Washington, D.C.'s Union Station, Union Depot's initial cost was $260,000, a hefty sum in those days.

The Magoffin Home
State Historical Park

To get to the Magoffin Home at 1120 Magoffin Avenue, drive east on San Antonio Avenue past the new County Courthouse—you can't miss the green-glass façade—until you come to a Y intersection. Magoffin Avenue, a one-way street running east, is the left branch of the Y and can be easily overlooked, so drive slowly. The home, about five blocks east of the intersection, is marked by a large sign on the right. A splendid example of Territorial adobe architecture (1865–1880), the home was built by Joseph Magoffin, a prominent politician and business-man, in 1875. Seven of the 19 rooms are open to the public and many include Magoffin family furniture. Guided tours are available. Open Wednesday to Saturday from 11:00 A.M. to 4:00 P.M. Future funding for the home-stead is in limbo, so call the park superintendent before you go; Tel: 533-5147.

To return to downtown from the Magoffin Home continue east on Magoffin Avenue to Cotton Street; turn right and head south to West Paisano Drive, and turn right again. West Paisano will take you back downtown.

Hart's Mill and Oñate's Crossing

Oñate's Crossing, Hart's Mill, and Old Fort Bliss, three sites considered significant by local historians, are simply not for everyone; you'll need your imagination to appreci-ate them. Take West Paisano Drive west until you see the brown-and-white signs that will guide you to the sites. After you pass beneath a bridge, get into the left lane and prepare to make a U-turn at the brown-and-white sign. This will take you onto the access road running parallel to Paisano Drive.

The first three houses you'll come to were once offi-cers' quarters at **Old Fort Bliss**, 135 acres at Hart's Mill (see below) purchased by the army in 1881 to serve as its fifth post. During the Apache Indian wars in Arizona the post was a way station. Abandoned by 1893–1894, when the wars ended, the once-vital fort sheltered flood victims and refugees from the Mexican Revolution of 1910–1920. Now private residences, the homes are not open to the public.

Hart's Mill, established by Simeon Hart with the help of his father-in-law, the well-to-do flour miller Don Leandro

Siqueiros, supplied flour to the United States–Mexico Boundary Commission, military posts in Texas, Arizona, New Mexico, and northern Chihuahua. Hart's son, Juan, founded the *El Paso Times*.

All that remains of the rambling adobe hacienda built by Hart in 1849 is **La Hacienda Cafe, Inc.**, next door to Old Fort Bliss. The decor shows the Spanish influence but the interior is plain and no two El Pasoans can agree on the quality of the Mexican food it serves. Some say good, others groan. La Hacienda is worth visiting because it still carries the aura of times long gone. Tel: 546-9197.

Directly across from the entrance of La Hacienda is the historical marker for **Oñate's Crossing**, where Don Juan de Oñate first forded the Rio Grande. The name conferred an identity upon the area and the impetus for the first settlement, Paso del Norte (present-day Ciudad Juárez) and eventually El Paso, Texas. Juárez, founded in 1659, is the area's oldest community.

Return to West Paisano Drive and retrace the route east to Santa Fe Street. A left turn onto Santa Fe will take you back downtown.

Sunset Heights Historical District

The Sunset Heights Historical District, northwest of downtown, is bordered by I-10 to the south and west and Mesa Street to the east, and extends north to Schuster Avenue, one block south of the University of Texas at El Paso. Access the district by driving north on Santa Fe Street and west on Yandell Drive, a one-way street at this point. The brainchild of a New York emigré in the 1880s, Sunset Heights was the first planned subdivision in the country.

Over the last several years, many of these fine old homes have been restored to their former grandeur, but the district remains a mishmash of down-at-the-heels and downright splendid. The latter applies to the recently renovated and elegant **Sunset Heights Bed and Breakfast Inn**, at 717 West Yandell (the extension of Yandell Drive). Two pairs of Tiffany doors, antiques-filled rooms, and its own wine cellar create a first-class accommodation.

The University of Texas at El Paso Neighborhood

UTEP, as it is called locally, is at the north end of Sunset Heights. Follow Schuster Avenue east to Oregon Street,

turn left and drive north past Sun Towers Hospital to
University Avenue (about five blocks). Take a left on
University and stop at the gate house for a visitors' pass
and to ask the guard for directions to public parking
areas. The campus is renowned for its Bhutanese architecture, reminiscent of the Palace of the Dalai Lama. The
style is simple and striking, perfectly suited to the desert.
UTEP is small enough to tour on foot; the Campus Walking Tour brochure includes a good map with an easy-to-
follow key.

Rim Road and Old Kern Place

From the university, on University Avenue, go one block
east to Mesa Street; a right turn and four blocks will bring
you to Rim Road, where you should turn left into one of
the oldest and most beautiful residential areas in El Paso.
Any left off Rim Road, which climbs steadily toward the
Franklin Mountains, will lead you through El Paso's most
elite neighborhood of old money (sprinkled liberally
with the nouveau riche), spacious homes, mature trees,
and sweeping views of El Paso and Juárez. Homeowners
on Rim Road are accustomed to a procession of sightseers; scarcely a visitor passes through El Paso without
driving through.

At **Tom Lea Park**, ½ mile (1 km) east of Mesa Street on
the south side of Rim Road, park your car and walk over
to the obelisk at the official end of the Southern Rockies.
The park after dark affords great views of the sister cities
of El Paso and Juárez.

Rim Road runs east to become Scenic Drive. A right
turn on Scenic Drive leads to the first lookout, located at
4,222 feet elevation, for a view of three states (counting
Chihuahua) and two nations. The drive curves high above
the city and eventually becomes Richmond Avenue.

A left turn on Scenic Drive takes you to Robinson
Avenue and Sierra Crest on Crazy Cat, a residential development perched precariously on the top of a mountain.
(Crazy Cat is not a mountain but a semi-stable landslide,
the name allegedly deriving from the tale of a mountain
lion gone loco.) In a town where real-estate values esca-
late with the altitude, Sierra Crest, one of the city's highest
vantage points, is one of the most expensive, a high-
security area guarded by a gate house and not accessible
to the public.

Below Sierra Crest, any road running to the right of Robinson Avenue cruises through **Old Kern Place**, an older, highly desirable neighborhood developed in 1910. A microcosm of El Paso's diverse architecture, tree-shaded Old Kern runs the gamut: Colonial, English Tudor, Southwestern stucco with bright tile roofs, and bungalows that might have sprung from a Frank Lloyd Wright atelier in Mason City, Iowa. The juxtaposition of distinct styles that have risen from regional fashions is an ongoing source of fascination for visitors to El Paso. Nearly every regional residential style in the country can be found in Old Kern.

Old Kern ends quasi-officially at Stanton Street, one block east of Mesa Street. A left on Mesa will take you back downtown.

The Museum of Art
and Concordia Cemetery

Another pleasant day trip covers the area east and northeast of downtown El Paso. From downtown take Mesa Street north to Montana Avenue, where a leisurely drive east will give you a good idea of typical El Paso residential architecture. White-pillared plantation-style homes attest to the Texas affinity for anything Southern, but fanciful Victorians crop up along with early-20th-century bungalows.

At 1211 Montana sits the **El Paso Museum of Art**, once the gracious home of former Senator W. W. Turney. In the west wing the Kress Collection of European masters shines against walls of forest green, deep scarlet, and dark royal blue. The east wing, reserved for changing exhibitions, spotlights contemporary and Hispanic art.

From the museum proceed east on Montana Avenue to Copia Street, south on Copia for two blocks to Yandell Drive, and left on Yandell to **Concordia Cemetery**, the last stop in the old days for law enforcers and lawless alike. Defending their honor or lack thereof, nearly all ended up in Concordia, described by historian Leon Metz as "a resting place for the good, the bad and the very ugly." Although the cemetery is in need of T.L.C. it is nevertheless El Paso's version of Boot Hill, and many a notorious character, including gunslinger John Wesley Hardin, is buried here.

Fort Bliss

From Concordia Cemetery return to Montana Avenue and proceed east (right) to the North–South Freeway (U.S. 54); take the access ramp marked Highway 54/Alamogordo. The exit at Pershing Drive takes you directly to Fort Bliss. If you're coming from downtown, take I-10 to U.S. 54 and follow the directions given above from there. Civilians must supply a driver's license and/or proof of insurance at the gate house.

Today's serene, well-maintained grounds and high-tech weaponry give no hint of the fort's modest origins and wandering location. Fort Bliss began in 1847 as a temporary campsite for the First Dragoons who arrived to protect American and Mexican settlers from Apaches who went on the rampage during the Mexican-American War. More troops arrived in 1849 to set up a post on the site of what is now the Civic Center. The post changed location several times during the rest of the century—though at one point it was altogether defunct for a couple of years—being upgraded from post to fort along the way, and surrendered to the Confederacy during the Civil War. The army finally settled in at La Noria Mesa in northeast El Paso, the current site, in the early 1890s.

Of the four museums at Fort Bliss, **Fort Bliss Replica Museum** is the most appealing to a general audience. Adobe buildings re-create the fort of 1854–1868; a living-history program provides insight into the daily lives of soldiers in 1857.

Woodrow Bean Transmountain Drive

Take U.S. 54 north to Loop 375, the Woodrow Bean Transmountain Drive exit. From there head west to the **Wilderness Park Museum** at 4301 Transmountain Drive, less than 1 mile (1½ km) past the freeway. The indoor-outdoor museum introduces visitors to the lifestyles of indigenous Indians through dioramas. Exotic plants of the desert are identified on the path leading to the museum entrance. Closed Mondays.

Follow Transmountain Drive west up a steep incline. One of the highest roads in Texas, the ten-mile, four-lane highway, which crests at 5,250 feet, was once a steep, narrow pass called Smuggler's Gap. Literally blasted through the Franklin Mountains, Transmountain Drive is the only route that connects northeast El Paso with the Westside. The views of the Rio Grande Valley are spectacular, and there are plenty of places to pull over and take pictures.

Transmountain Drive ends at I-10; take I-10 east to return to downtown.

The Oñate Trail

The newest of El Paso's historic venues, the Oñate Trail retraces Don Juan de Oñate's passage through the area. The trail begins at Placita Santa Fe, at the intersection of Mesa Street and Doniphan Drive (take I-10 west from downtown or from Fort Bliss to the Doniphan exit) and extends along Doniphan to Bazar de Artesanos at Thorn Drive. Along the trail several art galleries, boutiques, and antiques shops provide ample occasion to shop for pottery, paintings, silk scarves, jewelry, and Southwestern antiques in turn-of-the-century rock and adobe buildings.

The Riviera Restaurant at 5218 Doniphan features authentic Mexican food, including, house specialties, red or green enchiladas; Tel: 584-1542. If you prefer an informal atmosphere, the Riviera delivers food next door to **Aceitunas**, one of El Paso's well-kept secrets. Aceitunas looks small from the outside, but out back there is a large outdoor garden with trees, a stream, and a waterfall—a beer garden if you will. Only liquid refreshments and popcorn are served, but Aceitunas doesn't mind a bit if you bring your own food. At 5200 Doniphan, Aceitunas is open from 4:00 P.M. to 2:00 A.M. during the week and from 3:00 P.M. on Fridays and Saturdays; Tel: 581-3260.

From Placita Santa Fe, Mesa Street, which is bordered here by shopping strips, fast-food chains, and restaurants, runs south. Any road off Mesa leads to residential areas where the landscaping points out the conflict between Eastern embellishments and a chronic water shortage. Rosebushes cluster beneath palm trees and pines and mingle with bougainvillaea, wisteria, cactus, and rosemary—an herb that flourishes in the arid climate. "Xeriscaping," the newest local buzzword, emphasizes the use of drought-resistant plants that help conserve water.

Looking south from the intersection of Mesa Street and Sunland Park Drive you'll see Mount Cristo Rey rear up on the far side of I-10. On top of the mountain, Christ of the Rockies, a 42½-foot-tall statue, marks the junction of Texas, Mexico, and New Mexico. Created by Urbici Soler, a master sculptor who also worked on the Christ of the

Andes monument, the statue is the largest of its kind in North America. To the north of Mount Cristo Rey is the fertile swath of land that borders the Rio Grande, a section that includes El Paso's lush residential Upper Valley.

El Paso Outdoors

In El Paso leisure time is spent outdoors year-round, a tribute to the steady desert sunshine. The sun has failed to shine only 50 days in the past 18 years. Golf ranks high in Sun City, thanks to native son Lee Trevino, for whom a boulevard is named. (Lee Trevino Drive is one exit before Zaragosa Road off I-10 in east El Paso, and many of the residential streets in that part of town carry the names of golfers.) **Painted Dunes Desert Golf Course**, touted by *Golf Digest* as one of the top-ten best new courses of 1991, features splendid mountain views and a brand-new Southwestern-style country club. It's a 25-minute drive from downtown; take Patriot Freeway/U.S. 54 north past Transmountain Drive and exit on McCombs Street. Turn west and look for the country-club entrance on the right; Tel: 821-2122.

The not-so-faint of heart can rock climb or rappel in Hueco Tanks State Historical Park (see below). **Commercial Sales** at 520 West San Antonio Avenue carries a full range of climbing equipment. **Franklin Mountains State Park**, limited to daytime use, offers hikers an opportunity to experience the desert. While numerous footpaths meander through the 16,108-acre park, the only formal trail (the Ron Coleman Trail) begins at Smuggler's Pass and ends in McKelligon Canyon. From Patriot Freeway/U.S. 54, drive 5⅓ miles (8½ km) west on Transmountain Drive/Loop 375; from I-10 take the Canutillo exit and drive east about 6 miles (10 km) to Smuggler's Pass. You'll see the turnaround where you can park your car. On the south side of the road look for the ruins of a stone gate that mark the trailhead. The trail is about three-and-a-half-miles long one-way and the elevation ranges from 4,880 to 6,700 feet with intervals of steep climbing balanced with easy walking. Allow four to five hours to make the round trip. Take along a snakebite kit and a canteen of water, and familiarize yourself with emergency procedures before you go.

For spectator sports the city's stellar attraction is the annual John Hancock Bowl. Held in UTEP's Sun Bowl Stadium on December 31, the oldest independent college football classic attracts about 50,000 fans and live cover-age on network television. (Not a good time to try to get a hotel room here if you're not interested in football.) The game is sponsored by the El Paso Sun Carnival Associa-tion, the umbrella for 17 major sporting events that fill the calendar from October through the first week in January.

October is crammed with sports activities: the Sun Carnival El Paso/Juárez International Classic Run, SunWest America's Bicycle Classic, the John Hancock Col-lege All-American Golf Classic, the Sun Carnival Handball and Racquetball Tournament, and the Intercollegiate Ten-nis Tournament. November brings the Sun Carnival Thanksgiving Day Parade and the Tournament of Champi-ons Band Pageant. December features the Sun Carnival Basketball Classic. The schedule culminates with the New Year's Eve bowl game. The Sun Carnival office is located at 2609 North Stanton Street, a half block north of Robin-son Avenue; Tel: 533-4416.

The **Amigo Airshow**, held in October every year at Fort Bliss's Biggs Army Airfield, attracts 80,000 to 100,000 spec-tators. The weekend event features acrobatic and other aerial maneuvers by civilians, military pilots, and war birds. Performers have included the U.S. Air Force Thun-derbirds Jet Team, the U.S. Army's Golden Knights Para-chute Team, the U.S. Navy's Blue Angels, Manfred Radius, Jimmy Franklin, and the F-16 Taco Squadron; Tel: 532-5387.

Staying in El Paso

With the exception of the historic Westin Paso del Norte, Sunset Heights Bed and Breakfast Inn, and Cliff Inn (deco-rated with an exceptional collection of European an-tiques), El Paso accommodations are contemporary in style and appointment. The city has more than 6,000 rentable rooms, but during large conventions or meet-ings the hotels quickly fill up and rates increase. The slow season is September/October and December/January, when some, but not all, hotels reduce their rates.

The rates given below are *projections* for 1993. Unless otherwise indicated, rates are for a double room, double occupancy, and do not include meals. Price ranges span the lowest rate in the low season and the highest rate in the high season. As rates are always subject to change, it is wise to double-check before booking.

The telephone area code for El Paso is 915.

Airport Vicinity

The airport is east of downtown via I-10. **El Paso Airport Hilton.** Light and airy, within walking distance from the airport. 2027 Airway Boulevard, 79925. Tel: 778-4241; Fax: 778-6871. $81; $89–$99 (suite); and $65 Friday through Sunday with a two-day advance.

El Paso Marriott Hotel. High-energy **McGinty's**, the in-house disco, draws locals and visitors alike. 1600 Airway Boulevard, 79925. Tel: 779-3300; Fax: 772-0915. $64–$129.

Embassy Suites Hotel. Inside the plant-filled atrium, guests and visitors enjoy cocktails at umbrella-shaded tables. A glass-enclosed elevator services the upper floors. All accommodations here are two-room suites (separate living and sleeping quarters), and include galley kitchens and many amenities. 6100 Gateway East, 79905. Tel: 779-6222 or (800) EMBASSY; Fax: 779-8846. $104–$124.

Holiday Inn-Airport. Recently remodeled to include a large central atrium. 6655 Gateway Boulevard West (at the intersection of Airway Boulevard), 79925. Tel: 778-6411; Fax: 778-6517. $64.

Radisson Suite Inn. Completed in 1991, this is a Southwestern-style pink stucco all-suite inn with an inviting façade. 1170 Airway Boulevard, 79925. Tel: 772-3333; Fax: 779-3323. $83–$99; $69 (weekends). Ask about special rates.

Downtown

Cliff Inn. El Paso's best-kept secret, contemporary on the outside, has been filled with priceless paintings, ceramics, and furnishings by its owners, the Schiavo family of Rome, Italy. Two miles (3 km) northeast of downtown in north-central El Paso, Cliff Inn provides a quiet, lovely retreat. 1600 Cliff Drive, 79902. Tel: 533-6700; Fax: 544-2127. $55–$65.

Holiday Inn Park Place. Superbly located one and a half blocks northeast of San Jacinto Plaza; definitely upscale, like other El Paso Holiday Inns. 325 North Kansas Street, 79901. Tel: 533-8241; Fax: 544-9979. $69; $59 (weekends).

Ramada El Paso. Standard Ramada, with one exception: outstanding views in every direction from its **View at the Top Lounge.** The popular cocktail lounge serves the best banana daiquiris in Texas and is perfect for a twilight visit, when the city lights go on in El Paso and Juárez and the view is stunning. 113 West Missouri Street (on the corner of El Paso Street about three blocks north of the Civic Center), 79901. Tel: 544-3300. $78.

Sunset Heights Bed and Breakfast Inn. An elegantly restored Victorian home within walking distance of downtown and the university. The inn offers fine eight- to twelve-course dinners to guests and non-guests by reservation. 717 West Yandell Avenue, 79902. Tel: 544-1743 or (800) 767-8513; Fax: 544-5119. $70–$165.

Westin Paso del Norte. Historic, beautiful, and conveniently situated—the ultimate in El Paso accommodations. 101 South El Paso Street (across from the Civic Center), 79901. Tel: 534-3000; Fax: 534-3024. $110–$140.

Westside

El Paso's Westside begins at Schuster Avenue (the northern fringe of the Sunset Heights Historic District) and runs north to the intersection of Doniphan Drive and Mesa Street, and east from I-10 to the Franklin Mountains. The neighborhood, close to downtown, with stunning residential architecture and landscaping, numerous restaurants and small shopping centers, and the Sunland Park Mall, invites a junket.

Holiday Inn Sunland Park. Five minutes north of downtown across I-10 from Sunland Park Mall. Fresh, contemporary Southwestern decor, cool and inviting. 900 Sunland Park Drive, (at I-10), 79922. Tel: 833-2900; Fax: 833-6338, ext. 646. $72.

Dining in El Paso

El Paso lives up to its name as the "Mexican Food Capital of the United States." If you're not fond of dishes smothered in chile sauce, remember that most Mexican restaurants also carry standard American fare. Try tortilla soup as an appetizer (the recipe varies with the restaurant but basically it's a broth of onions to which tortilla chips are added, and sometimes vegetables), and expect chips and salsa with every meal.

Part of the fun of dining out in El Paso is discovering small, obscure Mexican restaurants. **Rosa's Cafe**, directly across from the power plant on Doniphan Drive (between Executive Center Boulevard and Sunland Park Drive) is one such place. No listing in the phone book, no street number, no fancy decor, but a complete lunch for around $3 including soup and entrée.

Second in dining popularity in El Paso is Texas steak and barbecue, the latter usually served with beans. But East Asian, Italian, and German are also on hand. In this landlocked city good seafood is available, but it is not the star of El Paso menus. Sheer numbers make it impossible to cover even one-tenth of the dining possibilities in town, and omissions should not be construed to mean the places are lackluster. Local opinions vary widely and one person's perfect bowl of chili is another's heartburn.

Mexican

Forti's Mexican Elder, at 312 Chelsea, is El Paso's top-of-the-line Mexican restaurant. A fountain in the main dining room, gaily painted tiles, and hanging plants provide the perfect setting for *fajitas* or tacos *al carbón*. Take I-10 east to the Paisano Street exit and continue to drive east on Gateway Boulevard East to Chelsea. Take a right on Chelsea and look for Forti's, just before the Coors plant (the total driving time is 15 to 20 minutes); Tel: 772-0066. Forti's has opened a second restaurant with the same good food and ethnic decor at 7410 Remcon Circle on the left (west) side of North Mesa Street between Resler Drive and I-10, just before Wal-Mart. Tel: 585-0086. At 15644 Gateway West, **Alexandro's** (ah-le-HAN-dros) is another Mexican favorite, with good food and fast service even during a busy lunch hour, and the usual hanging plants and painted tiles. As at Forti's, the combination plate is massive. Tel: 779-6773.

Taco Cabana, a Mexican fast-food establishment, is surprisingly good. You order at the counter, but a waitress brings your food to the table. On the Westside at 5866 North Mesa Street (at the intersection with Shadow Mountain Drive); at 150 South Americas Avenue, in the far Eastside off I-10; at 1777 North Lee Trevino Drive, off I-10; and in Cielo Vista Mall (exit I-10 east at Hawkins Boulevard and head north).

Jaxon's puts El Paso's history on the wall and Mexican food on the table. Good margaritas and enchiladas. Try the one on the Westside at 4799 North Mesa Street; Tel: 544-1188. The second Jaxon's is a few blocks from the airport at 1135 Airway Boulevard; Tel: 778-9696. Reservations are suggested for dinner. At **Avila's**, fresh tortillas or sopapillas accompany Tex-Mex meals. On the Eastside at 10600 Montana Avenue (Tel: 598-3333); on the Westside at 6232 North Mesa (Tel: 584-3621). **Antonio's**, in the Plaza Hotel at Oregon Street and Mills Avenue, deserves its reputation for good Mexican food (breakfast and lunch only); Tel: 532-5885. **Cafe Central**, 1 Texas Court, serves what locals call "gourmet Mexican" (and Continental dishes) in a comfortable but distinctly upper crust setting adorned with paintings; Tel: 545-2233.

Steak and Barbecue

The king of El Paso steak houses is **Cattleman's** at Indian Cliffs Ranch, a 35-minute drive from downtown on I-10 east to Fabens, exit 49. At Fabens, go 5 miles (8 km) north into the desert and watch for the signs. Indian Cliffs comprises a dude ranch with party facilities, a "Western town," a covered-wagon camp, and movie sets, and the steak house is one of the primary attractions. Steaks come in an array of cuts from the two-and-a-half pound "Cowboy" on down, but seafood, chicken, and barbecue are also on the menu. Pork and beans and cole slaw with pineapple are served in heavy black metal pots with all meals. The setting is Old West, complete with wall decorations of saddles, cowboy hats, and other Western memorabilia. On Sundays from Easter through November, weather permitting, guests are treated to a free hayride. Tel: 544-3200. Reservations are recommended on weekends for groups of 15 or more; all others are accommodated on a first-come, first-served basis.

The Great American Land and Cattle Company, "home of the two-pound Texas T-bone," has three locations: in the northeast at 7600 Alabama Street (Tel: 751-5300); on the Westside at I-10 and Vinton—take the Westway/Vinton exit from the freeway (Tel: 886-4690); and on the Eastside at 22 Yarbrough (Tel: 595-1772). The ambience is rustic Western, and the menu includes fine steaks and barbecue.

For barbecue check out the exclusive **Stateline**, at 1222 Sunland Park Drive, where diners select their cut of meat and the type of charcoal used to cook it. The interior is 1940s roadhouse—memorabilia, jukeboxes, old photographs—and the restaurant attracts people from West Texas and southern New Mexico. Take I-10 west and exit at Sunland Park Drive; go south for about ⅛ mile. Tel: 581-3371. **Doc's Barbecue**, at 8220 Gateway Boulevard East, features barbecued beef, pork, and chicken. "Springfire," a musical comedy satire of El Paso enacted by the owners, is performed Wednesday through Saturday at 8:30 and 9:45 P.M. You don't have to be a local to enjoy this act. Reservations are recommended; Tel: 593-3627. To get to Doc's, go east on I-10 to the Lomaland exit (between Yarbrough and Lee Trevino drives); Doc's is on the corner of Lomaland Drive and Gateway Boulevard East.

Other

Gunther's Edelweiss Restaurant, located on Lomaland Drive at I-10, serves German food in a Bavarian atmosphere; Tel: 592-1084. Restaurants connected with major hotels, such as the Westin, Marriott, Radisson, Hilton, Embassy Suites, and Holiday Inns, are consistently good and are the main source of Continental-type cuisine in El Paso. The **San Francisco Grill**, 127 Pioneer Plaza, also serves Continental dishes in the intimate atmosphere of a hometown bar and grill; Tel: 545-1386. Outstanding among dining choices is the **Three Continents Restaurant and Lounge** in Cliff Inn, 1600 East Cliff Drive (take Mesa Street north of downtown for about ½ mile/1 km, then go east on Cliff Drive for 1½ miles/2½ km). Its name derives from a menu that features American, Mexican, and Italian cuisine; the atmosphere could best be described as serene; Tel: 533-6700. **Applebee's Neighborhood Grill and Bar**, at 5800 North Mesa Street, has an ambience similar to what you'll find at San Francisco Grill and is patronized primarily by Westside residents. A superb sandwich menu and exotic desserts; Tel: 833-8899.

Both Furr's and Luby's cafeterias—chains that are Texas institutions, very inexpensive and family oriented—have several locations. Fast-food chains are scattered throughout town but clustered on Mesa Street and Lee Trevino Drive. Casual attire goes anywhere in El Paso; jeans and boots are widely accepted.

Shopping in El Paso

No one should leave El Paso without a pair of fine Western boots. Unsurpassed for quality and quantity, El Paso's skilled boot makers gave impetus to the city's nickname as the "Boot Capital of the United States." The Tony Lama and Lucchese families in particular have contributed greatly to El Paso's reputation as the premier town for purchasing this traditional footwear.

Tony Lama factory outlets are found at 7156 Gateway Boulevard East in central El Paso, on the Westside at the intersection of Mesa Street and I-10, and on the Eastside at 12151 Gateway Boulevard East. The **Lucchese Factory Outlet** is located at 6601 Montana Avenue. **Bootrader**, at 10787 Gateway Boulevard West, boasts 10,000 pairs of boots and also carries Western apparel. **Cowtown**, a few blocks west at number 11401, also carries a full line of Western boots and apparel. Leathers and denims are especially good buys at Cowtown.

Two specialty shops on the Westside carry an unusual inventory. It's easy to spot **Elodia's**, at 5410 North Mesa Street, with its large sparkling lizard logo painted across the storefront. Elodia buys exotic clothing from around the world. The surprise here is her collection of marble for sale—tables, credenzas, and other furniture pieces. **Tres Mariposas**, at number 5857, just a few blocks north of Elodia's, carries an ever-changing line of offbeat, stylish women's fashions.

Mexican, Central and South American, and Indian goods are best purchased in Juárez, but bargains follow the rise and decline of the peso. Check out the prices on the American side first by browsing at **El Paso Saddleblanket Company**, at the corner of Missouri and Oregon streets. Owner Dusty Hensen, who describes himself as "an ole Texas trader," has stocked two floors with an enormous inventory. Rugs appear in all shapes, sizes, and types, from Mexican and fine Orientals to reindeer, sheepskin, and cowhide. Pottery, Southwestern-style jewelry, baskets, and kachinas fill the shelves, and if you have a yen for unusual furniture, look for chairs and loveseats made of cattle horns and upholstered in cowhide. Plan at least an hour to shop here.

For the ultimate in Southwestern gourmet items, stop by **El Paso Chile Company** at 909 Texas Avenue, a few blocks east of downtown. Choices include six kinds of salsa, chile-spiced peanuts, jalapeño mayonnaise, a Louisiana hot sauce called "Hellfire and Damnation," and honey jalapeño mustard.

CIUDAD JUAREZ

The two primary tourist crossings from El Paso into Juárez are the downtown Paso del Norte Bridge, also called the **Santa Fe Street Bridge**, and the Cordova Bridge, or Free Bridge. To reach Juárez by the Cordova Bridge, drive east from downtown on I-10 to the Spaghetti Bowl and take the first exit ramp, marked Highway 54/Alamogordo *and* Juárez. At the Y bear to the right (south) and follow the signs to Juárez. To walk across the Santa Fe Street Bridge, park your car in a lot on the American side (do *not* leave it unattended on the street). The Mexican side of the bridge leads directly to shop-lined Avenida Juárez and the Mercado Juárez open-air market, open from 9:00 A.M. to 7:00 P.M. Monday to Saturday and until 6:00 P.M. on Sundays.

Throughout Juárez major American credit cards are accepted, although not all retailers take American Express. Most shops handle shipping.

A word of warning: While the *mercado* is well worth exploring, this area reflects the poverty of the city. Expect aggressive pursuit by big-eyed children selling chewing gum or cheap trinkets, and street vendors hawking their wares. And while the cholera epidemic in the Mexican interior has not yet reached Juárez, there's still a chance of catching the *tourista,* or Montezuma's Revenge. It is inadvisable to buy food from vendors, particularly fresh fruit. Bottled water or soft drinks are recommended even in the better restaurants.

The international telephone country code for Mexico is 52.

SHOPPING IN JUAREZ

Don't buy the first item that catches your eye in the *mercado,* but compare prices from one stall to the next. Be prepared to bargain—merchants routinely price their goods at about 30 to 40 percent above what they expect to put in their pockets. The best buys here are leather, pottery, rugs (look for handwoven rather than machine made), and perfume. To visit other shopping areas, simply flag a cab.

The fastest route to the new Pueblito Mexicana Mall is via the Free Bridge, which runs into Juárez's Avenida Abraham Lincoln, the city's main drag. The mall, at Avenida Lincoln and Calle Zempoala, is visible immediately after you pass the Chamizal Monument park on the Mexican side of the border, a mirror reflection of the one on the American side. (The two public parks honor the final settlement of a dispute between the two countries that went on for over a century. In 1864 the Rio Grande flooded and shifted 400 acres of land to the north [U.S.] side of the river. The subsequent bickering over ownership continued until September 1964, when Presidents Lyndon Johnson and Gustavo Díaz Ordaz signed the final agreement that returned dominion over the land to Mexico.)

If you drive to the Pueblito, take advantage of the underground parking provided at the mall. Don't hesitate to pay one of the young men who hang out for the sole purpose of "watching" cars for tourists.

The multimillion-dollar **Pueblito Mexicana Mall** is Juárez's newest tourist attraction, designed to resemble a Mexican shopping village. Storefronts are painted in bright colors and lined with plants and flowers. The mall's high arched roof is flanked on either end by magnificent stained glass murals. Inside, you can buy everything from ponchos to piñatas. Just off the central atrium, a cosmetics shop carries a complete line of American-made products including Clinique cosmetics and Shalimar perfume. Prices are generally lower than in the United States. Open 10:00 A.M. to 10:00 P.M. daily.

From the mall follow Avenida Lincoln south to several outdoor pottery shops that feature garden statues of Saint Francis, glassware, and wall hangings. Tarahumara pots, priced at several hundred dollars in Santa Fe or Taos, go for $50 or less here. A block or so south, in front of the PRONAF Center, watch for **Curiosidades Decor**, the place to buy Mexican blue glass, Mexican colonial-style furniture, jewelry, and an alabaster or hand-carved wooden chess set at half the U.S. price. The shop also carries some kitsch as well, like the conversation-piece coffee table, a nearly life-size lion lying on his back with paws in the air to support the glass top. Open 10:00 A.M. to 7:00 P.M. Sunday to Friday and until 8:00 P.M. Saturdays; Tel: 12-27-21.

At one time the PRONAF (Programa Nacional Fronterizo, established to enhance the appearance of the city of Juárez and to promote the sale of Mexican products) was *the* place to shop for Mexican arts and crafts, but the shopping center, eclipsed by Pueblito Mexicana, is in the process of being razed.

Travelling more than four or five blocks beyond Pueblito Mexicana Mall is not wise unless you are accustomed to heavy traffic and Mexican-style driving—and have a good sense of direction. Juárez is the fourth-largest city in Mexico, with a population of nearly 1.5 million, and at peak hours traffic is mayhem. Driving here requires skill, finesse, and nerves of steel. It is easier to take the El Paso–Juárez Trolley Company tour of Juárez, which currently makes ten stops. You can jump off at the destination of your choice, browse or have lunch, and pick up the trolley on its return trip. The trolley company supplies a complete list of stops and the approximate time the trolley will return for pickups. The round-trip ride in itself takes about an hour; the tour, known as the **Border Jumper**, begins and ends at the Convention Center Plaza Terminal, but tickets must be purchased at the Civic Center in El Paso. Juárez tours leave hourly Wednesday to Sunday, 10:00 A.M. to 5:00 P.M. April through October and 9:00 A.M. to 4:00 P.M. November through March. Schedules and times are subject to change; in El Paso, Tel: 544-0061 for information and 544-0062 for reservations.

DINING IN JUAREZ

Several good restaurants in Juárez serve steak, seafood, and, of course, Mexican fare. **Chihuahua Charlie's**—"we don't speak English, but we promise not to laugh at your Spanish"—claims the freshest seafood. (Generally speaking, Juárez seafood surpasses what you'll find in El Paso.) The restaurant, part of the popular Carlos Anderson chain, is a stop on the El Paso–Juárez Trolley Company tour, which allows ample time for lunch before the trolley returns. If you drive take the Cordova Bridge to Avenida Lincoln and drive south past the Plaza de las Americas to Paseo Triunfo de la Republica 2525; Tel: 13-99-40.

Casa del Sol in the PRONAF Center (at the east end of Plaza de las Americas) features the same menu with more of a Continental flair. Though the quality of the food has gone down somewhat, the restaurant continues to be popular. Tel: 13-65-09. The **Montana Steakhouse**, Avenida Lincoln 1142, specializes in corn-fed beef as well as steak and barbecued ribs; Tel: 13-32-68.

One rule of thumb applies to dining out in Juárez: Go to places that have been personally recommended or don't go. Better yet, stop by the El Paso Convention Bureau (1 Civic Center Plaza, Tel: 534-0600) for directions and recommendations other than those given here. The best information source in Juárez is the Federal Tourism Office, located in the Municipal Building (Unidad Administrativa Benito Juárez) at Avenida Malecon and Francisco Villa, about a block east of the end of the Santa Fe Street Bridge. Tel: 15-24-23, 15-23-01, or 14-66-92. Open 9:00 A.M. to 8:00 P.M. Monday through Friday and 9:00 A.M. to 1:00 P.M. Saturdays and Sundays.

CROSSING THE BORDER

U.S. residents may visit Ciudad Juárez for 72 hours and travel 18 miles (29 km) into the interior without a special permit or tourist card. Be prepared with proof of citizenship or residency: birth certificate, driver's license, voter registration card, or green card. You may be required to show the same documents on the return trip.

Purchases of up to $400 (U.S.) are duty free but must be declared. Duty-free items also include one liter of liquor and one carton of cigarettes for personal use.

Visitors planning to travel farther into the interior of Mexico need a Mexican Tourist Card, available at the port of entry with proof of citizenship. Citizens of other countries should check with the U.S. Immigration Office or the Mexican Consulate before crossing the border. Those who drive into the interior can obtain a permit at the port of entry by showing proof of vehicle ownership. *Mexican automobile insurance is required,* and can be obtained at one of several agencies in El Paso; check the Yellow Page listings.

For Further Information
U.S. Consulate in Juárez: (16) 13-40-48; Mexican Consulate in El Paso: 433-4082.

HUECO TANKS
STATE HISTORICAL PARK

Take a picnic basket and plan at least a half day at Hueco (pronounced "WAY-co"), where "mountains" of massive granitelike rocks are scattered over 860 acres northeast of El Paso. The name derives from the natural hollows in the rocks that catch and trap water. The availability of water drew nomadic tribes to Hueco Tanks as early as 10,000 years ago. Over the centuries other cultures left their imprints in thousands of pictographs and petroglyphs. Park rangers give guided tours of the rock art here from June through August. A popular destination for rock climbers and rappelers in fall and winter, Hueco Tanks is never so crowded that visitors can't find a quiet retreat.

For Hueco Tanks take I-10 east to George Dieter (one exit past Lee Trevino Drive), then George Dieter north to Montana Avenue. Drive east on Montana (U.S. 62/180) and watch for the park signs. Go north for 6 miles (10 km) on Rural Route 2775. The drive is about 45 minutes one way. The park opens at 8:00 A.M. and closes at sunset; the office is open daily from 8:00 A.M. to 5:00 P.M. For park and campsite information, Tel: 857-1135.

ON THE MISSION TRAIL

If the Rio Grande had not flooded in 1849, the villages of Ysleta, Socorro, and San Elizario would still be part of Mexico. Now American but by geography only, the once-pastoral and now briskly growing Lower Valley southeast of El Paso maintains its essential Hispanic character. Traditions are firmly tied to a past embodied in three historic sites: the missions for which the three villages were named. Venerated by parishioners and described by

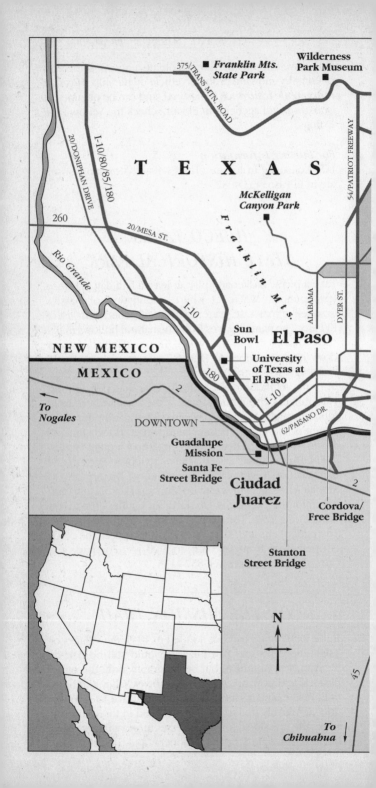

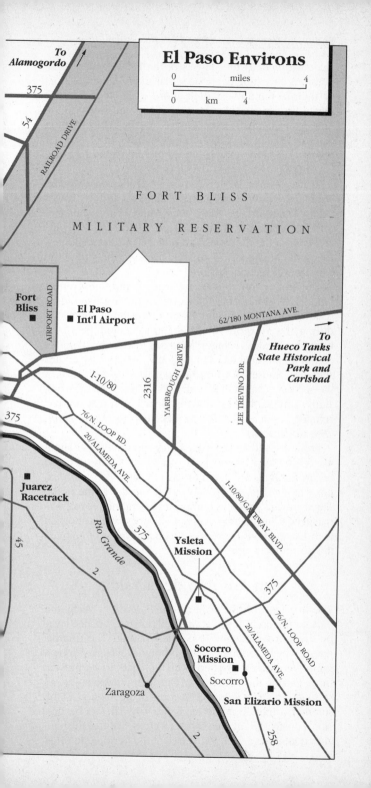

Texas Monthly as the "jewels of the Rio Grande," these missions have long been the social and religious anchors of their communities. Built more than 50 years after Oñate first crossed the Rio Grande, the missions on the American side of the river are predated by Juárez's Misión Nuestra Señora de Guadalupe (Our Lady of Guadalupe Mission), built by Indians under the direction of a Spanish missionary between 1658 and 1659.

El Paso–Juárez Trolley Company's **Trolley on a Mission Tour** is the best way to see the missions and the Lower Valley. The tour takes place every Tuesday and Thursday, April to September, from 10:30 A.M. to 2:30 P.M.; it begins and ends at the El Paso Civic Center. (For information on doing the Mission Trail on your own, see the end of the San Elizario section, below.)

The trolley tour begins by cruising through Chihuahuita (Little Chihuahua), a historic district a few blocks southeast of Civic Center Plaza. Chihuahuita sprang up during the Mexican revolution in 1912 and 1913 as a haven for Mexican refugees who fled from political persecution in Chihuahua. Some of the wealthy expatriates settled in Sunset Heights; the poor took up residence in the section of south El Paso that was considered the worst slum in the country. It was this deprivation that spurred refugee resident Mariana Azuela to write *Los de Abajo* (*The Underdogs*).

From downtown the trolley picks up the Border Highway thought to be the path that Oñate followed as he began the long trek from El Paso to Santa Fe, New Mexico. The road to Pueblo Ysleta del Sur, the home of the Tigua Indians, passes Mount Carmel, an interesting, immaculately maintained cemetery. Every grave is adorned with bouquets of flowers, a surprising burst of color in the desert landscape.

San Antonio de la Ysleta

The first stop on the trolley tour is Mission Ysleta, the oldest mission in Texas. It was built in 1682, washed away by the Rio Grande in 1741, then rebuilt. The original name, which honored Saint Anthony, the Tiguas' patron saint, has been shortened over the years to its present form. During the school year Our Lady of Mount Carmel seventh graders conduct lively tours of the mission; in the summer a trained guide leads the way. The adobe mission, constructed in the shape of a cross, features the high altar common to such structures of the period, the original confessionals (labeled Traditional and Face-to-Face), and a statue of Christ in the Tomb, which is prevalent in contemporary Mexico.

Present-day Tiguas trace their lineage to the Tiwa Indians of Isleta Pueblo in New Mexico. After the Pueblo revolt of 1680 the Tiwas who had been faithful to their Spanish masters fled south from the expected reprisals and founded a new settlement here. Ysleta Pueblo is the only Indian reservation in the country within city limits. A visit to **Pueblo Ysleta del Sur**, a "living pueblo," begins in a courtyard around which shops and galleries are clustered. In the courtyard is a kiva, an Indian ceremonial chamber, and several *hornos* (outdoor ovens made of adobe), used for baking bread. On one side of the kiva is the oldest continuously cultivated plot of ground in the state and a testament to the importance of the region's three traditional staple crops: corn, beans, and squash. Retail operations focus on Tigua arts and crafts, mainly pottery, some small sculptures, wall hangings, and souvenirs. The Ysleta tour ends with lunch, a generous Mexican plate at the **Tigua Restaurant**.

Mission Socorro

Like that of its sister mission in Ysleta, the original name—Our Lady of the Immaculate Conception of the South—has been simplified. Nuestra Señora de la Limpia Concepción de Socorro del Sur (*socorro* means "help" in Spanish) was constructed in 1680 as a temporary shelter; its first permanent structure was built between 1681 and 1691. In 1741 the second building sprang up, but was lost to a flood in 1829. The present mission was constructed in 1840, and around it grew the village of Socorro. The mission features the original cottonwood *vigas* (beams) decorated with Indian painting and hand-carved corbels, while *milagros* (charms) hang in glass cases on either side of a wood altar painted to resemble marble. No longer in use for mass, the mission now hosts weddings and special celebrations.

The use of cement plaster over adobe (a practice that was established in later years) sealed in moisture and initiated the deterioration of the adobe plaster; consequently, both Mission Ysleta and Mission Socorro are under restoration. Adobe bricks are visible where plaster has been stripped away. The tour here includes the highlights of Socorro's galleries and shops: Mexican antiques and Tarahumara pottery. **El Mercadito** (The Little Market), at 10189 Socorro Road, includes six shops that carry handcrafted rustic furniture, Southwestern arts and crafts, leather goods, weaving, jewelry, and gift ideas. **Posada San Miguel** at 10180 Socorro Road (across from El Mercadito) showcases Mexican furniture. Shopping time is limited on the tour; you may have to return on your own.

San Elizario

The last stop is San Elizario, formerly a Spanish presidio. The chapel was built in 1845, burned down in 1935, and was restored between 1940 and 1944. The interior is in superb condition, the exterior under renovation.

In the 1880s the town of San Elizario was the county seat, a bustling community of 1,200 people—three times as large as El Paso at the time. Today, with the resurrection of the Adobe Horseshoe Dinner Theatre and a series of shops owned by Southwestern artisans, sleepy San Elizario is coming back to life.

After a face-lift the old jail house has become a highlight of the tour. Local youngsters enthusiastically reenact a drama in which Billy the Kid breaks into the San Elizario jail to liberate a friend (said to be the only such episode in the Kid's career). The children stage the shootout with greatly exaggerated pratfalls. A visit to the **San Eli gift shop** rounds out the day at San Elizario. San Eli displays Southwestern arts and crafts, but the real treasure is the Christmas shop, filled with traditional Southwestern ornaments.

Independent forays of the Mission Trail are not recommended; a wrong turn can result in your getting lost very easily, for an unplanned trip through the Lower Valley. But if you prefer to do the Mission Trail at your own pace, take I-10 east to Zaragosa Road, nearly 13 miles (21 km) east of downtown. Exit at Zaragosa, go south a little more than 3 miles (5 km) to Alameda Avenue, and turn left (east); after one block turn right onto Old Pueblo Drive. One more block takes you to Mission Ysleta. Continue south on Old Pueblo Drive to Socorro Drive, turn left, and drive 2 miles (3 km) to Mission Socorro. The Chapel of San Elizario is 5½ miles (9 km) south on Socorro Drive.

Complete information, including maps and brochures, is available at the Heritage Tourism office on the east side of the performing-arts hall in the Civic Center. Contact Sheldon Hall; Tel: 534-0630.

GETTING AROUND

The ideal times to visit El Paso are in October and November, or March and April, when daytime temperatures range in the 70s and 80s, humidity is pleasantly low, and evenings are crisp and cool. The mild, short winter begins in mid- to late December and lasts no longer than the first week in March. At night temperatures can drop into the high teens but usually hover around 32°F. Snow falls occasionally and usually melts the following day. El Paso sometimes experiences a winter inversion layer and subsequent heavy smog. Despite its 3,762 foot elevation, the city is located in the Chihuahuan Desert and summers are intensely hot. In June the thermometer consistently climbs above 100°F, the heat offset by dryness. Most of El Paso's nearly eight inches of annual rainfall occurs during the monsoon season in July and August. El Paso's nickname, Sun City, testifies to 340 annual days of sunshine.

El Paso International Airport, the only major air gateway to West Texas and southern New Mexico, is served by the following major airlines: American, America West, British Airways, Continental, Delta, Eastern, Japan Airlines, KLM Royal Dutch Airlines, Northwest, Qantas, Southwest, and United. The airport is 7 miles (11 km) east of downtown, 5 miles (8 km) east of the Cordova Bridge, and 1 mile (1½ km) east of Fort Bliss. From the airport or adjacent car-rental offices and lots, a 2-mile (3-km) drive on Airway Boulevard takes visitors to I-10 and easy access to any part of the city. Most of the major hotel and motel chains provide complimentary shuttle service from the airport; courtesy phones are found on the lower level across from the baggage-claim area.

Taxi service from the airport to downtown El Paso costs about $25. While the mileage charge is consistent at $1.50 per mile, the fee for getting into the cab varies from $1.20 (Texas Cab Company) to $2.70 (Checker Cab Company). Ride sharing is permitted but also varies from company to company. First Class Limousine Service offers 24-hour-a-day chauffeured sedans, limos, and vans from the airport to destinations within a 50-mile radius. Rates range from $35 an hour for a sedan to $50 an hour for a limousine; Tel: 778-2355 in El Paso or (800) 733-0397 outside El Paso. Car-rental companies with desks at the airport include Avis, Budget, and Dollar, all located in the baggage-claim area. Advantage, Alamo, General, Hertz, National, and Thrifty have offices nearby, and provide courtesy pickups from the airport.

At **Union Depot**, a few blocks west of the Civic Center,

Amtrak trains connect El Paso to cities nationwide through Albuquerque and San Antonio. El Paso is served by Greyhound/Trailways Bus System at 111 San Francisco Street; Tel: 544-7200. T. N. M. and O. (Texas, New Mexico, and Oklahoma) Buses, at the same location, connects El Paso to all points north and east; Tel: 532-3404.

El Paso is the only major city in Texas on mountain time, two hours behind eastern standard time and one hour ahead of Pacific standard time. Juárez, located in the central standard zone, is one hour ahead of El Paso from November through March; because the Mexican city does not observe daylight saving, from April through October it is in the same time zone as El Paso.

The city is bisected by two axes: the Patriot Freeway/ U.S. 54 (formerly the North–South Freeway) to Alamogordo, and I-10, from which most of the city's major arteries are accessed, run east to west. Gateway Boulevards East and West (local access roads) run parallel to I-10; Gateway Boulevards North and South run parallel to the Patriot Freeway.

The telephone area code for El Paso is 915.

BIG BEND NATIONAL PARK

Add a fistful of blue sky to a spiny, stone-filled desert, stir in a batch of towering peaks and rugged canyons, then allow the mixture to slow boil in a salubrious climate for a couple of million years. Season to taste with a cornucopia of wild animals, a cool, lovely river, and the most glorious sunsets on earth, and voila: The result is an alluring platter of dramatic natural beauty called Big Bend National Park.

West Texas Indian tribes once claimed that when the Great Spirit created Mother Earth, He dumped all the leftover boulders in what is now Big Bend National Park. Spanish conquistadors knew the region as Tierra Desconocida (Undiscovered Land), and for nearly two centuries it was ignored by explorers and settlers alike. Guarded by slab-sided peaks to the north and by deep, twisting can-

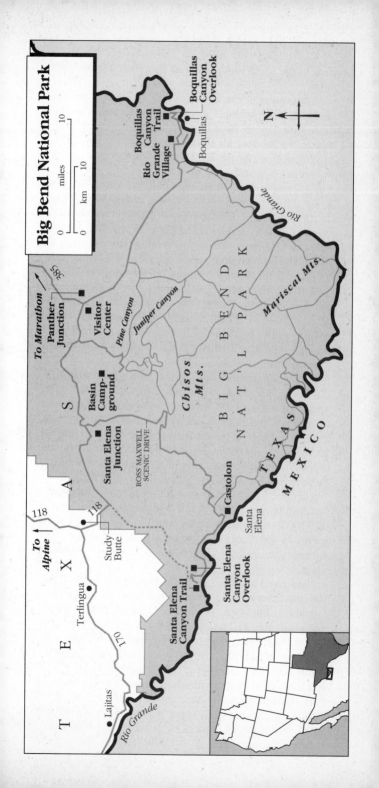

yons to the south, the park is far from being tamed even
today.

Most visitors admit, however, that Big Bend's physical
attributes far outshine its minor inconveniences. For
those who aren't already desert rats—lovers of rattlesnakes, rocks, and all things spiny—a few days spent
exploring this remote West Texas outland will remedy
that situation quickly.

Big Bend is located in the southern "horn" of West
Texas along the inhospitable United States–Mexico border, 300 miles (480 km) southeast of El Paso and about 70
miles (112 km) south of Marathon, Texas. The park is
truly colossal, far too imposing to be measured merely in
acres; land here is computed in square miles—more than
1,100 of them, basted together by the elements into a
haphazard, rock-strewn wilderness. Big Bend's corru-
gated morphology is officially Chihuahuan desert; physio-
graphically, it is a broken landscape of parched earth,
eroded gully, and wind-sculpted rock with mountain
peaks a mile and a half high and canyons more than a
thousand feet deep.

November through April is the most fertile season in
Big Bend. Park wildflowers, especially during March and
April, are at their most glorious, and larger animals tend
to feed and meander in open areas instead of staying in
the shade. Daytime winter temperatures range in the 70s
and 80s, although some January and February days can be
nippy. Snow sometimes falls in the higher peaks during
these two months, but it's uncommon.

Summer in the park is a different story altogether.
Daytime temperatures in July and August almost always
top 100°F, and nights aren't much cooler. Desert flora
seems to wilt under this extreme heat, and seldom will
animals venture from their holes or hideaways except at
night.

Two paved highways enter Big Bend, both south of U.S.
90: one from Alpine, Texas, in the west, the other from
Marathon, due north. From Alpine, travellers can take TX
118 south about 80 miles (128 km) to the desert community of Study Butte, then follow TX 170 east directly to the
park's western boundary. The route from Marathon is on
south U.S. 385, a drive of about 70 miles (112 km). Both
roads meet at **Panther Junction Visitor Center/National
Park Headquarters**, the jumping-off point for most of Big
Bend's sightseeing excursions. Information on road and
weather conditions, park activities, hiking, backpacking,
river rafting, and camping is available here. The visitors'

center also displays a large relief map that clearly details the park's topography and aids in planning an itinerary. Entry into Big Bend is free.

Popular Drives

A 100-mile network of paved roads crisscrosses Big Bend, but most passenger cars can also negotiate the park's far larger assortment of improved dirt and gravel roads. In addition, many primitive roads head into the back-country, suitable for four-wheel-drive vehicles only. The latter are patrolled infrequently, so play it safe and don't try anything you're unsure of. You might also consider buying a copy of *A Road Guide to Backcountry Dirt Roads of Big Bend National Park,* available at the Panther Junction bookstore. The maximum speed in the park, whether driving on dirt or asphalt, is 45 m.p.h.

Persimmon Gap Drive, beginning at the park's north-ern entrance and ending at Panther Junction, requires about one and a half hours (with stops) and is literally a nature trail for motorists. Roadside exhibits examine sci-entific discoveries such as a fossilized Coryphodon (an extinct mammal that lived 50 million years ago), while signs on the side excursion to Dagger Flat identify many of Big Bend's plant species and geological formations.

Another popular trip is **Santa Elena Drive**, which starts at Panther Junction, heads west to Santa Elena Junction, then turns south to the phenomenal Santa Elena Canyon Overlook. Some of the park's most magnificent geologic features can be seen on this day-long sojourn. If you plan to take pictures of Santa Elena Canyon itself, however, go early: Because the chasm is narrow and deep, sun tou-ches its innards for only a few hours each morning.

Basin Drive, a ten-mile stretch of highway from Pan-ther Junction south to the Basin Campground, carries motorists from sparsely wooded lowland desert into the lusher terrain of the spectacular Chisos Mountains. The road is steep in places (watch that your automobile doesn't overheat, a strong possibility if you have the air-conditioning on), but views of Mexico and the surround-ing Chihuahuan Desert from the road's Panther Pass are superb.

Hiking, Backpacking, River Running

Segmented into explorable areas by 800 miles of hiking and river trails, Big Bend offers outdoor-loving visitors a grand opportunity to experience the desert up close. Popular short walks of two miles or less on developed trails include the Window View Trail and Chisos Basin Loop Trail from **Chisos Basin** (10 miles/16 km southwest of Panther Junction); the Rio Grande Village Nature Trail, beginning at **Rio Grande Village** (20 miles/32 km southeast of Panther Junction); the Burro Mesa Pouroff Trail and the Santa Elena Canyon Trail, both beginning near **Castolon** (43 miles/69 km southwest of Panther Junction); and the Boquillas Canyon Trail, starting near the Boquillas Canyon Overlook (25 miles/40 km southeast of Panther Junction). Trailheads for these relatively brief strolls can all be reached by automobile.

For longer, overnight hikes into the park, pick up a copy of the *Hiker's Guide to the Developed Trails and Primitive Routes, Big Bend National Park,* sold at Panther Junction and other park concessions. The guide gives an excellent description of trail and terrain particulars.

Big Bend park rangers recommend that backpackers carry plenty of food and at least one gallon of water per day per person. They also suggest that you wear sturdy hiking boots and carry a well-stocked first-aid kit complete with tweezers for removing cactus thorns. If you want to backcountry camp rather than stay in a campground, you will need a permit, available from any ranger station. Open fires aren't allowed in the park's backcountry, so you'll need a camping stove and fuel. And although reptiles are scarce during the winter, rangers say that in hot months hikers should always be on the lookout for rattlesnakes.

Another popular outdoor attraction in Big Bend is **white water rafting** down the Rio Grande through one of the park's three barely accessible canyons: Santa Elena to the west, Mariscal in the middle, and Boquillas to the east. Deep, narrow, and twisting like sun-crazy snakes along the rugged United States–Mexico border, these awe-inspiring chasms pass through some of the most isolated country in America. Hundreds of species of colorful birds, deer, peccaries, and even mountain lions inhabit the riverbanks and side canyons here, while in the river itself longnose gar and giant catfish weighing up to 50 pounds are common catches.

If you have your own equipment (you can rent rafting paraphernalia in the towns of Study Butte and Lajitas), you'll need to obtain river maps, a free but necessary river-running permit, details on entry/exit points, and information on water conditions and safety procedures at any Big Bend ranger station before starting out. The Rio Grande here is gentle and slow moving for the most part, but there are stretches of rapids—some of them dangerous in high water—in all of the canyons. Consequently, most visitors who want to float the river prefer a guided, organized expedition rather than going it alone. A number of local river-running companies offer river trips through Big Bend ranging in length from one to seven days. Most have offices in the "Western-style" resort town of **Lajitas**, by the Rio Grande 24 miles (38 km) west of the Maverick park entrance on Ranch Road 170, and in the ghost town of **Terlingua**, also on Ranch Road 170 about 12 miles (19 km) west of the Maverick entrance. Most companies furnish transporation to and from the entry/exit points as well as everything you'll need in the way of equipment except personal clothing and cameras.

STAYING IN THE BIG BEND AREA

Overnight lodging is available in motel units and rustic but comfortable cottages at the **Chisos Mountains Lodge**, about 10 miles (16 km) southwest of Panther Junction near the Basin Campground. Reservations are recommended. Contact Basin Station, **Big Bend National Park**, TX 79834; Tel: 477-2291. The *projected* 1993 low-season–high-season rates for a double room, double occupancy are $58 to $70.

Outside the park the nearest accommodations are in **Lajitas**, 24 miles (38 km) west of the Maverick park entrance on Ranch Road 170. There are three motels in town—the **Badlands**, the **Cavalry Post**, and **La Cuesta**—and one hotel, **The Officer Quarters**; all are owned by the same company. For any of these accommodations contact Lajitas on the Rio Grande, Star Route 70, Box 400, **Terlingua**, TX 79852; Tel: 424-3471. $62.

Chisos Basin, Castolon, and Rio Grande Village all have maintained campgrounds where sites are available on a first-come, first-served basis. Drinking water and rest rooms are provided here but the sites are without electricity. Showers and laundry facilities are available at Rio Grande Village.

Additionally, there are scores of primitive campgrounds (no facilities included) located on many of the park's dirt and gravel roads. As only 250,000 people visit Big Bend National Park annually, these off-road campsites are always underused. There's no charge for a primitive campsites, but you will need a free permit, available at any ranger station. For more information on these out-of-the-way sites, simply ask a park ranger.

GUADALUPE MOUNTAINS NATIONAL PARK

The first thing most visitors notice about the landscape of West Texas is how large, empty, and dry this isolated region of America can really be. You can drive for hours here and never pass a car or see another human being. The cloudless sky seems to go on forever, and the horizon looks out of reach. As for moisture, except during a brief, late-summer rainy season, it simply doesn't exist. "Here," wrote Western author-historian George Sessions Perry, "is where Texas travels farthest west and then dies of thirst."

Guadalupe Mountains National Park stands like a deserted island in this dehydrated flatness. Straddling the Texas–New Mexico border a hundred miles northeast of El Paso, this undiscovered gem of a hinterland—encompassing 76,000 acres of mountainous, high-desert terrain—is one of the least utilized wilderness areas in America. Officially established in October 1966, the park is virtually unknown outside the American Southwest. One of the few public reserves in which people are the minority species, it is among the most pristine and least developed of all our national recreation areas. Fewer than 200,000 people visit the park each year, and only 10 percent of those ever leave the main highway or set foot in the dramatic backcountry.

The landscape here is a blend of Alpine peaks, twisting canyons, and prickly-stick desert, all of it basted together by nature into a crazy quilt of haphazard loveliness—but that doesn't begin to convey the true quality of the park's dramatic, complex beauty.

The paramount landmark here is a towering, 2,000-foot-high slab of white limestone guarding the southern-most vistas like a ghostly sentinel: **El Capitan**. Visible more than 50 miles away if you arrive by the park's southern entrance, El Capitan has been a traveller's point of reference for centuries. A bit farther north, and also visible from long distances, is Guadalupe Peak, at 8,679 feet elevation the highest point in Texas. In between, crisscrossing the terrain like a giant, erratic spiderweb, are scores of steep-walled limestone canyons, many of them approaching 1,000 feet in depth. Combine the Colorado Rockies, the Grand Canyon, and the deserts of northern Mexico into a 120-square-mile picture puzzle of tortured earth and jumbled stone and you have some idea of Guadalupe's phenomenal size and scope.

The best time to visit Guadalupe is in the fall (early November, usually), when the river-bottom maple trees in McKittrick Canyon blush red with their annual color change. Panoramic vistas from higher elevations are absolutely breathtaking during this period, and wildlife, particularly the numerous species of colorful desert birds, is fairly easy to spot. The park is also lovely in early spring, when carpets of high-plains wildflowers come into bloom.

You don't have to be a botanist to enjoy the park's wide variety of unusual plants. Lowlands are blanketed with typical desert flora such as cholla, prickly pear, pincushion, and mammillaria cactus; several species of yucca; and scores of different types of wildflowers. Trees, too, are plentiful. Several varieties of maples and other hardwoods flourish in the canyons along the streambeds, while the higher slopes are dominated by ponderosa pine, Texas madrone, Douglas fir, and Chinquapin oak. One of the most interesting plants you'll see here is the agave (a larger specimen is called a century plant), which grows upward in spike form from a nest of needle-sharp, yuccalike leaves. The heart of this plant—also known as mescal—was used for food, liquor, and medicine by the Apaches.

Wild animals are abundant, though often difficult to spot. Nearly 300 species of wildlife are known to inhabit the park, among them Rocky Mountain elk, mule deer, black bears, bald and golden eagles, peccaries, coyotes, and mountain lions. Dozens of species of lizards and snakes also live here, especially in the lower, desert areas. Hikers and backpackers, by the way, are usually warned by Park Service rangers to keep one eye peeled for rattlesnakes while on the trails.

Apache Indians were probably the first to penetrate Guadalupe's rugged terrain, during the 1800s. Historians say that both Geronimo and Victorio, two fierce Apache war chiefs, probably hid among these canyons and peaks while being pursued by the U.S. Army. During the early 20th century several large ranches were established near the base of the mountains, but that land was later purchased by, or given to, the U.S. Park Service for inclusion in the park.

Today the miles of pristine wilderness certainly invite exploration, but Guadalupe is basically a hiker's park; few of its major landmarks can be reached by automobile. Just three roads breach the official boundaries, in fact: U.S. 62/180 from El Paso in the southwest, McKittrick Canyon Road in the northeast, and Dog Canyon Road (NM 137) via NM 408 from Carlsbad, New Mexico, in the north.

Hiking and Backpacking

What Guadalupe lacks in highways it makes up for in hiking, backpacking, and nature-watching opportunities. More than 80 miles of developed trails, ranging from pleasantly level to sweat-popping near-vertical switchbacks, wind through the Guadalupe backcountry. The most popular day hike, especially in the autumn when maple trees are in full color, is through the twisty, vertical-walled **McKittrick Canyon**. The trail, slightly more than nine miles round trip, begins at the **McKittrick Canyon Visitor Center**, 7 miles (11 km) north of the main park visitors' center on U.S. 62/180, then west (left) 4 miles (6½ km); the turnoff is well signposted. The trail meanders west along an icy stream for a few miles, then climbs steeply out of the canyon and into Alpine country.

Two other favorite walks are the trails leading to the base of El Capitan and to the summit of Guadalupe Peak. Both start at **Pine Springs Campground** (a little less than a mile west of the main visitors' center on U.S. 62/180). Each is about ten miles in length, round trip. A shorter but still lovely hike is a two-and-a-half-mile-long loop to Smith and Manzanita springs, beginning at the historic Frijole Ranch (1 mile/1½ km north of the main visitors' center, then west ½ mile/1 km). **Frijole Ranch**, constructed in 1876 and one of the finest examples of early ranch buildings in this part of Texas, houses a wonderful collection of historic photographs and Indian artifacts from the area.

If you're planning to spend a few days in the wilderness, you'll find plenty of primitive backcountry campgrounds scattered along the major park trails. Reservations aren't usually necessary, but you should obtain free backcountry permits and trail maps at the main visitors' center or at the

Dog Canyon Ranger Station before setting out. To reach Dog Canyon drive 50 miles (80 km) north of the main visitors' center on U.S. 62/180, turn west (left) on NM 408 to NM 137, turn left again and follow the signs (about another 60 miles/96 km). Park rangers at both areas will assist you in setting up a hiking itinerary.

Backpacking in the park involves some special preparations. Open fires, for instance, aren't allowed in Guadalupe's fragile backcountry ecosystem, so overnighters must carry a cooking stove. And it's always a good idea to wear or carry clothing suitable for both desert and Alpine weather. Daytime temperatures in the lowlands often reach the upper 90s, while in higher elevations nighttime lows can plummet below freezing. Both day-hikers and backpackers should also carry plenty of water. Streams in the park are few, and rangers recommend carrying at least one gallon of water per day per person.

STAYING IN THE GUADALUPE MOUNTAINS AREA

Tent and RV camping are available at Pine Springs Campground near park headquarters on U.S. 62/180, and at Dog Canyon Campground on the park's northern border. Both areas provide rest rooms and drinking water, tables and grills, but no electric or sewer hookups.

The nearest motel accommodations are about 40 miles (64 km) to the north on U.S. 62/180 at **Best Western Guadalupe Inn**, 17 Carlsbad Caverns Highway, Box 128, White's City, NM 88268; Tel: (800) CAVERNS or (505) 785-2291. The *projected* 1993 rate for a double room, double occupancy is $65. There are also motels in Carlsbad, New Mexico, 60 miles (96 km) north, and of course in El Paso, 100 miles (160 km) southwest.

El Paso accommodations and their contact information are included within the El Paso coverage, above.

SOUTHERN NEW MEXICO

By Lynn Nusom

Lynn Nusom writes a syndicated newspaper column and articles for numerous magazines, including New Mexico magazine. *A resident of Las Cruces in southern New Mexico, he is the author of several books, including* Christmas in New Mexico, The Billy the Kid Cookbook, *and* The New Mexico Cook Book.

From the Texas state line in the south and the east to the Arizona border in the west, the vast landscape of southern New Mexico includes large expanses of bone-dry desert, majestic jagged mountains such as the Floridas (flo-REE-das) and the Organs, and cool pine-clad mountains such as Sierra Blanca. The views along mile after mile of interstate highway are of sand, scrub, an occasional adobe house, or a few head of cattle slowly en route toward a water hole. There are also untold acres of fertile farmland, and vibrant towns and cities with universities, cultural centers, thriving businesses, and plenty of social activities.

For most people, the name "New Mexico" conjures thoughts of Santa Fe, Taos, or Albuquerque. New Mexicans living in the vast geographical area below Albuquerque take this philosophically. Many of us like the fact that the world hasn't found us yet and turned a favorite neighborhood store into a fashionable boutique. However, when visitors do discover this part of New Mexico they find that there are no folks on earth more hospitable or friendly.

Southern New Mexicans are fiercely proud of the uncrowded, wide open spaces here, the many natural wonders, the region's long and often colorful history, and the cultural diversity of their friends and neighbors. The mixture of Spanish, Indian, and Anglo cultures provides visitors with an extremely rewarding travel experience.

Archaeological digs in the Las Cruces area have proven that the Mesilla Valley was inhabited by Pueblo Indians as long ago as 200 B.C. Alvar Nuñez Cabeza de Vaca, after surviving a shipwreck in the Gulf of Mexico and a trek of hundreds of miles in an often barren and hostile environment, found his way into the Mesilla Valley in 1535. In 1598 Don Juan de Oñate marched into New Mexico with a band of conquistadors, livestock, and wagons loaded with families intent on settling the new land. They marched through what is now Las Cruces and Mesilla and then headed north along the Rio Grande, generally bypassing the south in their search for the legendary gold cache of the northern Pueblo tribes.

Large settlements did not arise in this part of the Rio Grande corridor until the middle of the 19th century, when gold and silver were discovered in the area. Mining made boomtowns out of settlements like Silver City. Cattle ranching also flourished here, and the sight of cowboys on the wooden sidewalks became common. The southeastern portion of New Mexico, with its sparse rainfall and endless miles of scrub, provided little incentive to settlers from the East, except for hardy cattlemen and miners, until the discovery of oil and gas created modern boomtowns in the 1980s.

The Indian, Spanish, and Mexican traditions continue to flourish in the lives of the people of southern New Mexico today. For instance, no birthday party for a young boy or girl would be complete without a piñata (originally a clay bowl, but now familiar shapes such as donkeys, sombreros, stars, and even Mickey Mouse made from papier-mâché, covered with brightly colored, shredded tissue paper, and filled with small toys or candy).

Celebrations leading up to the Christmas holidays often combine Indian dances, passed down from generation to generation and originating before Jesus was born, with religious ceremonies introduced into the area by Franciscan friars in the 17th and 18th centuries.

You may run into residents of the area whose families have lived here for generations and who speak only Spanish. Many people with such Anglo-sounding names as Smith and Brown can trace their ancestry directly back to Spain, and families with such Hispanic-sounding names as Garcia may have had a relative who came over on the Mayflower. Such is the mix of cultures in this region.

THE FOOD OF SOUTHERN NEW MEXICO

Another thing that sets this area apart is the food. With its roots in Mexican cooking, mixed with traditional Indian fare, southern New Mexican cooking is not Sonoran, not Tex-Mex, not Northern New Mexican, but a unique cuisine. The food of southern New Mexico has evolved from many influences. The Indians cultivated such crops as corn, squash, peanuts, and beans; their desserts included puddings. Corn was a dietary mainstay, and they were particularly creative in their use of it—in breads or mixed with vegetables such as squash and pinto beans.

Intermarriages between Spaniards, who first opened up New Mexico, and the Indians produced a food tradition that combined pork with red chile peppers, corn, and squash, and laid the foundation for fare served in restaurants and homes throughout southern New Mexico today.

The Rio Grande Valley is the largest chile producer in the United States, with approximately 30,000 acres devoted to growing the state vegetable. (The chile capital is Hatch, on the Rio Grande northwest of Las Cruces.) It is little wonder that chile, in its varying forms, is either the focal point of local recipes or creeps into dishes one would not expect to harbor it in other parts of the country. In addition to tacos, tamales, and enchiladas, chile is coupled with pasta, spinach, and fish. Chile highlights classic French dishes such as quiche here, and even shows up in desserts like apple pie.

The first-time visitor often remarks on the difference in look and taste of dishes served here compared to their same-name counterparts elsewhere in the country. Enchiladas are most often served flat in southern New Mexico, whereas in other areas they are usually rolled. A dish with green chile sauce may be hotter here and, conversely, a dish with red chile might be milder. However, if you are not accustomed to eating chile it pays to ask for the "heat rating" before you sample a particular dish. What you get may be anywhere from mildly spicy to incendiary.

What will strike you most about eating Mexican food in southern New Mexico is the freshness. Because the chile is locally grown the myriad dishes that incorporate it benefit from its fresh, intense flavor.

Some foods may be easier for a new visitor to experiment with than others. *Chile rellenos,* a whole—usually mild—chile stuffed with cheese, dipped in an egg batter, and fried, is delightful served with refried beans, rice, and a salad. *Caldo,* a soup that can be a meal in itself, includes meat and large hunks of vegetables such as potatoes, carrots, and corn on the cob. Do not mistake it, however, for Irish stew. Often flavored with cilantro and red or green chile sauce, it makes a wonderful luncheon dish accompanied by warm flour tortillas.

The more adventuresome might want to try *menudo,* a stew made with tripe and red chile, or *tostadas compuestas,* a corn tortilla deep fried into the shape of a cup and filled with pinto beans and chile con carne (in this part of the country a mixture of red chile sauce and cubed pork), topped off with shredded lettuce, cheese, and chopped fresh tomatoes. Also try *posole,* a stew made with white or yellow hominy, pork, and red or green chile sauce. This dish is a great favorite among all New Mexicans, especially around the holidays.

No trip to this area is complete without sampling some of the wonderful regional dishes; we have included several restaurants where you can enjoy these delights.

TOURING SOUTHERN NEW MEXICO

Southern New Mexico runs to extremes in both terrain and climate. Las Cruces, the second-largest city in New Mexico, lies in the fertile Rio Grande Valley. If you're driving northwest from El Paso on I-10 you'll see urban sprawl at its worst, with homes built in the semi-arid desert or clinging precariously to the sides of mountains. But as you get closer to Las Cruces and neighboring Mesilla you will find high desert with scrub brush and mesquite, and glimpses here and there of yucca plants.

In and around both towns are old mulberry, oak, and pecan trees. Most of the homes have green grassy lawns. The rapidly growing suburbs are like those anywhere except that many a yard offers a view of the Organ Mountains, raw and majestic in summer, swathed in pink and purple at dusk. In the winter the stark gray rock sharply outlines any streaks of snow.

West of Las Cruces, in the direction of Deming and Silver City, you'll traverse miles of boring, flat scrub land, your view broken only by the occasional sighting of cattle, and then the Florida mountains. Deming, like

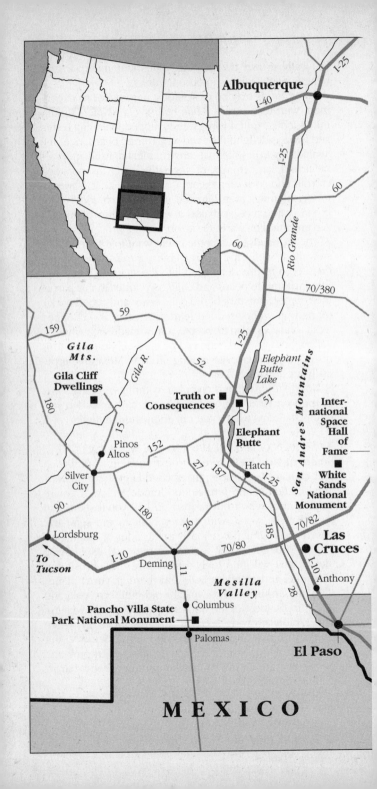

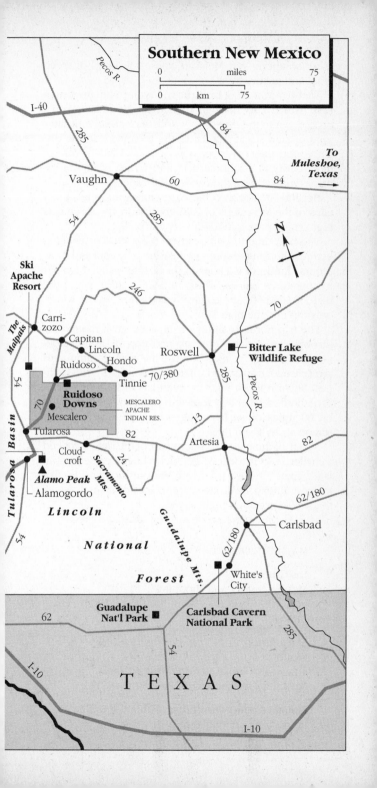

other southern New Mexican cities, is an oasis of green grass and mature trees.

To the northeast of Las Cruces, beyond Saint Augustine Pass, which cuts through the Organ Mountains, you'll drop down to the desert floor and, once again, mile after mile of land stretching flat to the mountains in the distance. You might wonder how Spaniards laden with armor, cowboys on horseback, and pioneers in wagons managed to survive the barren landscape.

Beyond Alamogordo the road climbs into the mountains of the Mescalero Indian Reservation, the scrub gets higher, and pine trees dot the countryside.

The best time to visit southern New Mexico, avoiding extreme heat in the southernmost areas or cold and snow around Ruidoso, is either in the spring or fall. Summer temperatures average in the mid-90s, and in winter the high 50s and 60s; the coldest temperatures in the winter only dip into the high 20s.

The trip north to Albuquerque is by small mountains, through vast stretches of scrub, and atop mesas overlooking pretty, fertile valleys. Because the small communities are spaced far apart and often do not offer tourist facilities, be sure to fill your car with gas in Las Cruces and carry bottled water and something to snack on. You might be 60 miles or so from the nearest restaurant or gas station at any given time.

A tour of the entire southern part of the state is indeed a challenge, because it covers such a huge, sparsely populated area. We have tried to point out those pockets of interest, unexpected oases, and places of natural beauty that will especially delight any visitor.

The telephone area code for New Mexico is 505.

MAJOR INTEREST

Las Cruces
Mesilla: history and shopping

Tularosa Basin (northeast of Las Cruces)
White Sands National Monument
Alamogordo
Cloudcroft
Tularosa's Church of St. Francis de Paula
Mescalero Apache Indian Reservation

Lincoln County (northeast of Tularosa Basin)
Ruidoso mountain resort area

Capitan
The "living museum" of Lincoln

Roswell (east of Lincoln County)
Bitter Lake National Wildlife Refuge

Carlsbad Caverns National Park (east of Las Cruces)

Deming (west of Las Cruces)
Columbus

Silver City (west of Las Cruces)
The old mining town of Pinos Altos
Gila Cliff Dwellings National Monument

Truth or Consequences (north of Las Cruces)
Fort Selden State Monument
Elephant Butte Lake

Southern New Mexico covers a lot of territory, and it is possible to "do" it from many different directions. You can drive in from the west via Arizona on I-10, from the east by way of U.S. 70 through Muleshoe, Texas, from the south through El Paso, Texas (also on I-10), or you can drive in from Albuquerque in the north on I-25.

You can also fly into either El Paso or Albuquerque and rent a car there to tour the area. Las Cruces, Ruidoso, Roswell, and Carlsbad have small regional airports where rental cars are available. But public transportation here is limited, and you will definitely need a car to see all the sights.

One of the best itineraries for touring the region as a whole would be to start with a couple of days in Las Cruces and Mesilla and then make a loop northeast through the towns of the Tularosa Basin (Alamogordo), up to Lincoln County (with a stay in Ruidoso), and then east to Roswell and south to Carlsbad (with an overnight at White's City), before heading back (west) to Las Cruces on U.S. 62/180 past Guadalupe Mountains National Park and through El Paso (see the El Paso chapter for all three). Plan another two days to see the area west of Las Cruces: Deming, Columbus, the Gila Cliff Dwellings, and Pinos Altos (with an overnight stay in Silver City). Finally, Truth or Consequences and Elephant Butte—north of Las Cruces along I-25 on the way to Albuquerque—are an easy day trip from Las Cruces.

LAS CRUCES

You will immediately be struck by the friendly, easygoing mañana attitude of the citizens of Las Cruces, often called the "Crossroads of the Southwest" because of its location at the junction of east–west I-10 (the highway to El Paso to the south and Tucson, Arizona, to the west) and north–south I-25 (which begins its northern trek to Albuquerque, Santa Fe, Denver, and beyond from Las Cruces).

Nestled in the fertile Mesilla Valley east of the banks of the Rio Grande, the site was happened upon in 1598 by a contingent of Spanish conquistadors headed by Don Juan de Oñate.

A forest of crosses here marking the graves of some early-19th-century settlers killed by Apaches, and a row of crosses where another group of hapless travellers met their deaths, represent just two possible reasons why the City of Crosses received its unusual name.

From its incorporation in 1849 Las Cruces remained a sleepy hamlet until political maneuvering brought the Atchison, Topeka & Santa Fe Railway into the heart of town in 1881. The nearby towns, such as Mesilla, that the railroad bypassed fell into economic decline, and Las Cruces became the major city in southern New Mexico. Today it is the second largest in the state, with a population of 62,500.

The city's warm, sunny climate makes it an ideal retirement spot. Its economy is fueled by agriculture; the only nonagricultural industries are the White Sands Missile Range test facility nearby to the northeast and a few small, nonpolluting commercial ventures. Also integral to Las Cruces's economic and cultural life is New Mexico State University, which was founded in the late 1800s as a land-grant school, the New Mexico College of Agriculture and Mechanic Arts. The university is about 3 miles (5 km) southeast of the centrally located Downtown Mall.

Around in Las Cruces

Las Cruces emanates from the **Downtown Mall**, a covered pedestrian promenade seven blocks long that includes a meandering yellow-brick pathway (inevitably referred to as "the yellow brick road"). Main Street, the north–south axis, leads out from the mall, eventually becoming U.S. 70 to the north of town (where it heads northeast to Alamo-gordo, Tularosa Basin, Ruidoso, and Roswell), and U.S.

80/85 to the south, where it eventually intersects with I-10 heading west.

One of the main attractions of Las Cruces is actually its neighbor: the small village of Mesilla, southwest of town via South Main Street and Avenida de Mesilla. There you can walk the same streets that Billy the Kid, Pat Garrett, and Geronimo traversed. Mesilla Plaza has seen a great deal of the history of the Southwest and is lovely for its ambience, historic architecture, spicy food, and shops displaying Indian, Mexican, and Southwestern wares.

A good jumping-off spot to get a feel for Las Cruces's past is the historic **Amador Hotel**, 180 West Amador, a one-way street that runs west at the southern end of the Downtown Mall. Built in 1850 by Don Martin Amador, the hotel has lodged such notorious figures as Billy the Kid, Pat Garrett, and the Mexican revolutionary Benito Juárez. The Doña Ana County Manager's complex is now ensconced here, but you can roam the halls during office hours Monday through Friday to view some of the original art painted directly on the walls, along with framed pictures illuminating the city's past.

Just a few blocks north at 106 West Hadley Avenue (in the 600 block of the Downtown Mall), the **Branigan Cultural Center** showcases a small collection of historic artifacts from the area, including potsherds, military buttons, bottles, and clothing, and hosts changing art exhibits. A gift shop carries items handmade by local artists. Closed Mondays.

On the north end of the mall, at 671 North Main Street, is the **Bicentennial Log Cabin**, circa 1879. Originally located in the Black Mountains northwest of Las Cruces, the cabin was moved here in 1976 for the U.S. bicentennial celebration. Its furnishings and artifacts date from the 1870s through 1900. (It is open mid-June to mid-August, and otherwise by prior arrangement at the Branigan Cultural Center.)

Also on the Downtown Mall, on Wednesday and Saturday mornings local produce growers and craftspeople bring their wares to the **Farmers and Crafts Market**. Especially interesting here are all sorts of items decorated with red and green chiles, stained glass, Indian jewelry, and *santos* (saints) handcrafted from wood.

You can pick up a brochure outlining a self-guided **walking tour** of Las Cruces's two historic districts at the Las Cruces Convention and Visitors Bureau, 311 North Downtown Mall; Tel: 524-8521 or (800) FIESTAS. The first of these tours takes you into the 44-square-block **Mes-**

quite Street Historic District, the oldest neighborhood in
Las Cruces. The site, three blocks east of the Downtown
Mall, was originally surveyed in 1849, and was placed on
the National Register of Historic Places in 1985. Most of
the houses are constructed of adobe and many open
directly onto the sidewalks or the narrow streets. They
are painted in wonderful shades of green, blue, pink, and
terra cotta.

The second tour explores the Alameda Depot Historic
District, an architecturally varied neighborhood two
blocks west of the Downtown Mall that developed after the
arrival of the railroad in the 1880s. The homes are constructed in Mission Revival, Mediterranean Traditional,
French Colonial, Queen Anne, Bungalow, Spanish-Pueblo
Revival, and Italianate styles. The focal point of the Alameda district is the block-square Pioneer Women's Park,
with a gazebo in the center surrounded by large trees.

For golf enthusiasts (great year-round weather makes
Las Cruces a haven) the Las Cruces Country Club has an
18-hole course right in town on North Main Street (U.S.
70). It is open to the public every day except Thanksgiving and Christmas; Tel: 526-9723.

STAYING AND DINING IN LAS CRUCES

There are two excellent dining spots on Las Cruces's restaurant row, El Paseo Road, which begins south of the Downtown Mall and runs from South Main Street to University
Avenue. You don't have to leave your shoes at the door at
Tatsu, which features distinctive Japanese food at number
930; Tel: 526-7144. Aficionados of true Mexican food can
find it in a converted fast-food emporium now called Los
Portales, at number 1609; Tel: 527-1235.

In a large, old house at 523 Idaho Avenue, which
intersects El Paseo Road, Henry J's turns out great hamburgers. The decor is 1940s diner, and although you have
to go to the counter to get your order, it beats the other
burgers in town hands down.

In another old house—this one sprawling and whitewashed at 2605 South Espina Street at the corner of
University Avenue—the Hacienda Restaurant serves the
food of Northern New Mexico. The stars here are blue-
corn tortillas and pork chops *adovada;* Tel: 522-6380.
Another Mexican restaurant, also on South Espina, at
number 363, (at the corner of Amador) is El Sombrero,
known for fast service and hot salsa.

The Santa Fe Restaurant dishes up trendy New Mexican
fare, with the emphasis on the creative use of red and

green chiles. It's worth the trip to 1410 South Solano Drive (corner of Foster Road just south of Idaho Avenue) for the Tabasco onions; Tel: 522-0466.

If you're looking for a casual place where you might run into anybody in town, from the mayor to a local psychic, try the **Pecan Tree Cafe**, at 504 South Solano at the corner of Lohman Avenue. The food here is Americana at its best, with meat loaf and chicken-fried steak heading the list. No rolled or pressed meat at the Pecan Tree; they cook their own turkeys every day for the turkey plates and sandwiches served on homemade bread. Breakfast and lunch only; Tel: 523-9183.

The signature dish at **Guacamoles**, 3995 West Picacho, a short ride west of the Downtown Mall over the Rio Grande and across from the Fairacres Post Office, is a huge burger topped with guacamole. Go in good weather, because all but a handful of seats are outside. Tel: 525-9115.

Halfway between Las Cruces and Mesilla (for which see below) at 1803 Avenida de Mesilla, **Meson de Mesilla** does double duty as a superb bed and breakfast and a full-service restaurant. If you can resist the excellent buffet, order the veal piccata from the menu. This will be your most expensive meal in town, but it's worth it. Reservations are advised; Tel: 525-2380. Meson has rooms and suites, all with private baths. It's best to book well in advance.

Right off I-10 just west of New Mexico State University and east of Mesilla, the **Holiday Inn de Las Cruces**, at the corner of University Avenue and Valley Drive, is not your usual assembly-line model motel. Built around an atrium designed to look like the plaza in a small Mexican town, the hotel displays stagecoaches and 19th-century antiques for good measure. Noted for its relaxing atmosphere, the inn has two restaurants and three bars—two with music. (Rooms facing the inside of the building can be noisy.)

If you want a room with a view of all of Las Cruces, stay at the **Las Cruces Hilton** (ask for a view when making reservations). A high rise decorated with a Southwestern motif, the hotel, just east of I-25 on Telshor Boulevard across from the Mesilla Valley Shopping Mall, has a bar and a coffee shop.

The mall, on the west side of Telshor one block south of Lohman Avenue (not to be confused with the *plaza* in Mesilla or the *Downtown* Mall), is a regional shopping center with several department stores. Quench your thirst while shopping at **O'Ryans Tavern**, a pseudo-Irish pub with fun antique decor and upscale beer on tap.

Craftspeople and artists from all over the Southwest display their wares in early November at the **Renaissance Arts and Crafts Fair** at Young Park (on Walnut Street between Lohman and Idaho avenues). In keeping with the theme, visitors are greeted by laddies and lassies in 15th-century garb.

The crowning glory of **The Whole Enchilada Fiesta** held on the Downtown Mall in early October is the world's largest enchilada. For the two days before this culinary colossus is served, you can sample a host of other foodstuffs, wash them down with beer, and buy souvenirs made by local artisans.

The Indian dances at **Tortugas**, just south of Las Cruces's city limits on South Main (NM 80/85), are not held for tourists. But the Indians don't mind if you're there to watch and the dances, held in conjunction with the **Fiesta of Our Lady of Guadalupe**, which starts on December 10 every year, are great photo opportunities. A meal of local favorites such as *albondigas* (Mexican-style meatballs) and Indian bread is served after the dances, at noon, at the Tortugas Community House, across from the church in the center of town. The dancers eat first; then anyone who comes to the door is served, for free, as long as the food lasts. The volunteers feed more than 1,000 people every year.

Bring stout walking shoes if you wish to accompany those who make the pilgrimage to the top of Tortugas Mountain on the evening of December 11. The faithful carry torches to light the way, and gather wood as they go for a bonfire that will light up the sky at the top.

Mesilla

Mesilla—formerly called La Mesilla and also referred to as Old Mesilla by some residents—is so close to Las Cruces that many find it hard to remember that Mesilla is indeed a separate entity. Going south, turn west (right) off Las Cruces's South Main Street onto Avenida de Mesilla; the street soon becomes two-lane NM 28 and takes you directly into Mesilla (2 miles/3 km). Follow the signs for Historic Plaza; a right turn and two blocks will take you to the central plaza.

Inhabited since the 16th century, Mesilla became a bustling community and a transportation hub about 1850 when the Chihuahua–El Paso del Norte wagon trains and the Butterfield and Wells Fargo stagecoaches stopped here. Saloons and dance halls flourished, merchants prospered, desperadoes such as Billy the Kid made it their stomping grounds, and it was said that Geronimo could be seen wandering the streets.

The Gadsden Purchase was signed in Mesilla Plaza on June 30, 1854. When the Mexican War ended in 1848 and the United States acquired most of what had been Mexican territory north of Sonora and Chihuahua, doubts remained concerning certain areas of the border between the United States and Mexico. To clarify the situation between the two governments and to give the United States a good southern railroad route to the Pacific, James Gadsden, U.S. minister to Mexico, negotiated the sale by Mexico of more than 45,000 square miles of land (in what is now part of Arizona and New Mexico) known as the Gadsden Purchase.

During the Civil War Mesilla was the capital of the Arizona Territory for the Confederacy. In the 1870s it became the county seat of Doña Ana County. On one hot, dusty afternoon during this period, insults were exchanged between Republicans and Democrats, which led to a gunfight that left several people dead on the plaza.

After the Atchison, Topeka & Santa Fe Railway chose to go through Las Cruces in the early 1880s, Mesilla slumbered through the decades until the 1980s, when it was "discovered." It is now a charming tourist attraction.

The century-plus old buildings in the center of town have been lovingly restored, and are now occupied not only by families but also by shops, galleries, restaurants, and bars.

MESILLA PLAZA

A walking tour around Mesilla Plaza begins at San Albino Church, the focal point of the plaza. Built of adobe in 1855, the church was rebuilt in 1906. Services are still given daily in both Spanish and English.

A host of shops surrounds the plaza. On the northwest corner, **Galeria on the Plaza** showcases folk art and Indian rugs, pottery, and jewelry. Handwoven Indian rugs and textiles as well as silver jewelry are the specialties next door at **Del Sol**. **La Zia** features Acoma and Laguna Indian pottery, Navajo rugs, kachinas, and Zuni, Navajo, and Santo Domingo Indian jewelry.

Housed in the building of a former general store, the **Silversmith** has a wonderful array of Indian jewelry, moccasins, and Indian pottery, including the collectible Storyteller (a ceramic depiction of an Indian woman covered with children listening to her spin a yarn).

Specializing in books of the Southwest, the **Mesilla Book Center** is installed in an 1856 mercantile building. Next door, on the southwestern corner, unusual gifts from Mexico and New Mexican souvenirs fill **Thunderbird de Mesilla**, in the oldest documented brick building in New Mexico (built in 1860). Around the corner on Calle de Parian, it's Christmas year-round in Mesilla's Little Christmas Shoppe. San Pasqual Desserts, at the same location, features homemade pastries; their specialty is the *biscocho,* the "New Mexico state cookie."

Walking into **El Patio Bar and Restaurant** on the south side of the plaza is like walking into another era. The locals swear by the food, and there are often several colorful characters at the bar.

Around the corner just behind El Patio, the **Old Fountain Theatre**, built in 1891, serves as both home of the Mesilla Valley Film Society (which shows art films) and as the office and tasting room for Blue Teal Winery, which is open afternoons for the sampling of local wines.

Next door to El Patio, housed in another former general store facing the plaza, is **Nambé** ware, which sells exactly that. The store has a wonderful display of the silver-colored metal plates, platters, and bowls made in the little town of Nambé, just outside of Santa Fe, that attract collectors from all over the world.

On Calle de Parian just steps down from Nambé is the venerable **La Posta Restaurant**, in the old Butterfield Stage building. Parrots in huge cages and piranha in tanks greet guests in the lobby. The same family has been serving Old and New Mexican food here since 1939. The chile they use, in recipes that have been handed down from generation to generation, is on the mild side, and the sopapillas are the best ever; Tel: 524-3524.

Across the street from La Posta, as you head back toward the plaza, is **Casa de Oro**, with one of the largest selections of gold and turquoise jewelry in the state. Next door **La Tienda** offers Zuni, Hopi, and Santo Domingo jewelry and a wide array of other collectibles.

Named after the infamous Billy the Kid, **The William Bonney Gallery** shows one of the finest collections of sculpture, Indian pottery, baskets, and Western art in the region. The **Billy the Kid Gift Shop** is on the southeast corner of the plaza in the courthouse and jail that once housed the gunslinger. Now, instead of justice, the owners dispense a wonderful assortment of Southwestern gifts, including hand-wrought silver jewelry and Southwestern cookbooks. Among the other shops on the east side of the plaza is **J. Eric Chocolatier**. The handmade truffles and other chocolate delights here are not to be missed.

Nouvelle-Southwestern cuisine is the attraction at **Peppers on the Plaza**. Decorated in Santa Fe style, this casual restaurant is known for its oversize margaritas. The same 1850s building also houses the elegant **Double Eagle Restaurant**, furnished with splendid antiques. Dine on steaks and seafood beneath antique crystal chandeliers and a gold-leaf ceiling; Tel: 523-6700.

Around the corner at **Señor Pat's**, at the corner of Calle de Santiago and San Albino, one block east of the plaza, one of Mesilla's most colorful characters hands out samples of his gourmet food items. Señor Pat himself greets and even teases his customers with his jalapeño-stuffed olives. Closed July and August, when Señor Pat holds forth at his shop up in Ruidoso.

East of the church on Calle Santiago, Hopi kachinas, jewelry, and other Indian art are the stars of **Silver Assets**.

To get to the **Gadsden Museum**, a memorial to Colonel Albert Jennings Fountain and five generations of the Fountain family, continue east to NM 28, turn south (right), go to the first intersection and turn left (at Barker Road, also known as Boutz Road). Colonel Fountain, a soldier, Indian fighter, politician, and writer, moved to Mesilla during the Civil War and practiced law here until 1896. He and his eight-year-old son, Henry, mysteriously disappeared while on their way to Las Cruces in a buckboard from Lincoln County, where the colonel had been acting as a special prosecutor. Filled with memorabilia of the life and times of Fountain and of Mesilla, the museum also displays a locally famous painting depicting the signing of the Gadsden Purchase in Mesilla Plaza.

Heading north on NM 28, back toward Las Cruces, you'll find **Mama Marie's Italian Restaurant** in the old converted adobe house at 2190 Avenida de Mesilla. Gourmands drive miles to sample the *caponata* (cold eggplant appetizer) here. Tel: 524-0701.

THE TULAROSA BASIN

Fifty-two miles (83 km) east of Las Cruces on U.S. 70, toward Alamogordo and past the White Sands Missile Range, is the **White Sands National Monument**, at the north end of the Chihuahuan Desert in the heart of the

Tularosa Basin. This 300-square-mile expanse of white gypsum dunes, a beach without an ocean or lake, is one of the world's great natural wonders. The sheer magnitude of the undulating dunes is almost overwhelming.

Turn left off U.S. 70 at the sign for the monument. At the entrance a visitors' center with a gift shop contains a wide array of books on the Southwest. If you wish to tour the dunes, take the drive that circles through the white sands and returns to the visitors' center (the drive takes approximately an hour). Events are scheduled from May 15 to September 7 each year. There's a one-and-a-half-hour nature walk with a ranger who discusses the plants and animals that live in the sand dunes (9:00 A.M. daily from the visitor's center), and a ranger-guided sunset stroll that leaves from the visitors' center an hour and a half before sunset.

ALAMOGORDO

Fifteen miles (24 km) farther up U.S. 70 to the northeast of the national monument turnoff is the city of Alamogordo. Founded in 1898 as a shipping point for lumber, it is now home to Holloman Air Force Base. Alameda Park runs through the center of town for several blocks on the west side of U.S. 70; the park zoo houses a small collection of waterfowl, deer, wolves, monkeys, and lions.

Across from the park at 1480 North White Sands Boulevard is **Si Señor**, a modern restaurant with wonderfully hot and authentic Mexican food. Plan lots of time for Si Señor: A half-hour wait at either lunch or dinner is not unusual; Tel: 437-7899.

Just past the northern boundary of the New Mexico School for the Visually Handicapped—a compound of several large brick buildings on the east side of U.S. 70—you'll come to a stoplight. A right turn off U.S. 70 onto Scenic Drive here will take you to the **International Space Hall of Fame**, which displays satellites, rocket engines, and the Clyde W. Tombaugh Space Theater featuring OMNIMAX and planetarium programs. Tel: 437-2840 or (800) 545-4021. Alamogordo is also home to the Cottonwood Festival, a juried arts-and-crafts show in August.

CLOUDCROFT

Three miles (5 km) north of Alamogordo turn east (right) onto U.S. 82 and drive into the Sacramento Mountains for 16 miles (26 km) to Cloudcroft. This peaceful mountain village was founded in 1889 when surveyors reaching the summit of the Sacramento Mountains caught sight of a single white cloud nestled among the towering pines. They named the spot after the cloud, adding "croft"—an old English word for "meadow." Surrounded by more than a million acres of the Lincoln National Forest, this vacation spot at an elevation of approximately 9,000 feet boasts the southernmost ski area in North America.

After you enter Cloudcroft on U.S. 82, turn south on Wren Place and go six blocks to **The Lodge at Cloudcroft** (it is well signposted). Built by the Southwestern and El Paso Railroad in 1899 as a summer escape for El Paso residents, the lodge burned down a few years later; it was rebuilt and reopened in 1911. This comfortable, cozy resort with its paddle fans, mounted game, and antique fixtures has played host to innumerable celebrities over the years, including Judy Garland and Clark Gable, and propels you into a bygone era. One of its most interesting features is the copper-domed observatory. Located four stories above the hotel and opened by a brass skeleton key, the tower commands a view of 150 miles. All of the 47 rooms here are furnished with antique furniture, and the high beds are covered with down quilts.

The lodge also has one of the highest and most beautiful golf courses in the world, which becomes a challenging terrain for cross-country skiing in winter. Ski equipment and instruction are available at the Ski Chalet in the lodge.

Continental cuisine is the order of the day in the Lodge's **Rebecca's Restaurant**. Breakfast, lunch, and dinner are served in both a fireside room and an airy conservatory named after the resident hotel ghost, said to have been murdered on the property by a jealous lover. A particular treat is dining here at sunset. Reservations are advised; Tel: 842-4216.

Retrace your route to U.S. 82 and head north three blocks; there you will find a skating pond, Zenith Park, the town's tennis courts, and the Chamber of Commerce, where you can obtain information on the festivals held here (see below) and on the area in general (Tel: 682-2733). A little more than 2 miles (3 km) past the Chamber of Commerce building to the east on U.S. 82 is **Ski Cloudcroft**, with 21 different runs and difficulty levels from beginner to expert; Tel: (800) 333-7542.

In addition, Cloudcroft also plays host to quite a few festivals. Near the end of May a juried arts-and-crafts show called **Mayfair** complements a rodeo, chuck wagon dinners, and stage shows. A pie auction, a barbecue, a parade, and a gun-and-knife show highlight the **Western Roundup** in Cloudcroft in mid-June. The **Bluegrass Festival** here, also in late June, is a three-day event that features bluegrass experts from around the country. The rodeo is back in town in late September for a whole weekend; and in October beer and sausage vie for space with more arts and crafts at the **Oktoberfest and Aspencade**.

For the adventuresome interested in (and dedicated to exploring) Territorial architecture, take U.S. 54/70 2 miles (3 km) north of the U.S. 82 Cloudcroft turnoff and head east for **La Luz** (it is marked). Two miles from the highway you will find the oldest still-occupied settlement in the Tularosa Basin. Founded in 1719 when the Franciscans built a chapel here, it is now a tiny, sleepy backwater of tree-lined streets and old adobe buildings. Its residents were said to have given refuge to Billy the Kid.

Thirteen miles (21 km) north of Alamogordo on U.S. 54/70 is another town that was destined to become somnambulant when bypassed by the railroad. Founded in 1863, **Tularosa** has become an oasis of old adobe homes, rosebushes, and gigantic cottonwood trees. The wonderful old Mission architecture of the **Church of St. Francis de Paula** on the main street makes for great photographs. The annual **Rose Festival** in Tularosa in early May includes a parade, arts-and-crafts exhibits, and a salsa contest.

MESCALERO APACHE RESERVATION

On U.S. 70 east from Tularosa toward Ruidoso you drive up into the mountains and enter the 720-square-mile Mescalero Apache Reservation. In the town of Mescalero, the **Old Road Restaurant** serves great New Mexican food. This hard-to-find place is located in a two-story rust-colored adobe a short distance off the highway in the middle of town. There is no sign, so your best bet is to ask any local for directions. *Chile rellenos* and enchiladas head the list of Old Road's great offerings.

Still on the Mescalero reservation, 3½ miles (5½ km) south of Ruidoso, where U.S. 70 changes from a four-lane to a two-lane road, is a sign for the **Inn of the Mountain Gods**. Located on Carrizo Road and run by the Mescalero Indian tribe, this complete resort and convention center features breathtaking mountain views. The main building of the sprawling wood-and-stone complex has a huge lobby with a giant fireplace, and offers a magnificent view of the lake, a piano lounge, a restaurant, a nightclub, and a gift shop. The sleeping rooms are in wings radiating from the lobby.

The inn has its own lake with boating and fishing and an award-winning golf course, and offers trap and skeet shooting, horseback riding, and tennis, bingo, and video-machine gambling. The **Dan Li Ka Dining Room** is an excellent restaurant featuring Continental cuisine and wild game, but it may stretch your budget a bit. Tel: 257-5141, ext. 7555.

LINCOLN COUNTY
Ruidoso

Ruidoso (roo-ee-DOH-soh), just beyond the Apache reservation's northern boundary, has often been called "Texas's playground." Since the early 1900s not only Texans but New Mexicans have sought respite here, at a 7,200-foot elevation, from the sizzling summer temperatures of the Texas and New Mexico flatlands. Today Ruidoso is a sophisticated resort town—but one that tries hard not to look or act like one. One of its great pluses is that, although Ruidoso has amenities similar to those of Taos and Aspen, it doesn't get the horrendous crowds that those towns attract.

Not only can visitors escape the summer heat here (the average July temperature is in the low 70s) and wager at one of the finest horse tracks in the country, but in the winter you can also enjoy some of the best skiing in the Southwest at Ski Apache, which has an average annual snowfall of more than 15 feet (see below).

Be sure to have room reservations on weekends both during the summer and the ski season, as the town and the surrounding area have a limited number of accommodations that fill up quickly.

Ruidoso Downs, on U.S. 70 north of the turnoff west of Ruidoso on NM 48, offers not only some of the best quarter horse racing in the country, but displays great Western art in the **Hubbard Museum** at the track. The museum's collection includes works by such renowned artists as Charles Russell and Frederic Remington. The 30,000-square-foot **Ann Stradling Museum of the Horse**, just east of the grandstand, is packed with more than 10,000 pieces of art relating to horses and their history with people.

The meet at Ruidoso Downs, from mid-May to Labor Day, features some hefty quarter-horse stakes culminating in the richest quarter-horse race in the world: The winner picks up a $1 million purse. The track's grandstand offers varied seating arrangements, some covered, some not. A detailed seating chart with prices for individual seats, tables seating four and six, and grandstand boxes is available at the ticket window. Snack bars in the grandstand serve everything from hot dogs to deli plates and pizza.

The All-American Turf Club and the Jockey Club provide more comfortable seating and full food and beverage service. Runners will even take your bets at your seat so that you don't have to wait in line at the two-dollar window. Turf Club prices are of course higher than those in the grandstand. At the privately owned Jockey Club some seats are available for nonmember purchase for the day by prior arrangement; Tel: 378-4431.

Directly across from the track is a saloon with a huge dance floor. Only country bands perform at **Prime Time**, and the two-step is the "in" dance here. Open evenings only; Tel: 378-4010.

SHOPPING AND DINING IN RUIDOSO

A short distance south of the track, NM 48 runs off U.S. 70 and becomes Sudderth Drive, the main street of Ruidoso, with a host of shops, galleries, and restaurants. (The numbers on Sudderth Drive start at U.S. 70 and get higher as you head west. The **Crazy Cactus** at 410 Sudderth features folk art with a Southwestern flair. At number 524 **Crucis Art Bronze**, a bronze foundry, displays antiques, jewelry, paintings, and sculpture. **Cattle Baron**, 657 Sudderth, a good steak house, albeit with the ubiquitous salad bar as the centerpiece, offers a wide range of beef and seafood choices. (They do not accept reservations.)

The "country bordello" decor of **Ms. Pushy's Romantic Italian Cafe** at number 2103 Sudderth in the Gazebo Shopping Center is an experience. Billed as "Ruidoso's only adult restaurant," the establishment features a romantic "couples only" section and fresh-air dining on the deck, weather permitting. No smoking and no children are allowed. The six-course prix fixe menu is limited and pricey. Reservations only; Tel: 257-5440. Ms. Pushy does not take credit cards.

Wood and leather burnings and pen-and-ink drawings are among the items to be found at **Ernie's Art**, 2442 Sudderth Drive. A touch of the French countryside greets you at **La Lorraine**, at number 2523, a tiny, pricey restaurant run by a husband-and-wife team that serves classic French cuisine. Try the veal and sample their excellent wine cellar. Reservations are necessary; Tel: 257-2954.

Mountain Arts Gallery and Framing at 2530 Sudderth features paintings, prints, pottery, weavings, and Indian artifacts. One of the nation's leading art galleries, **Fentons Art Gallery** at 2629 Sudderth shows off magnificent paintings, bronzes, and outstanding prints by more than 100 of America's leading Southwestern, Indian, and Western artists.

Really good Chinese food is hard to come by in New Mexico, but even people who don't like the cuisines of the Far East are impressed by **The Great Wall of China**. Drive through the intersection of Sudderth and Mechem to 2913 Sudderth. Try anything on the menu with plum sauce. Tel: 257-2522.

The **Blue Goose** is a refreshingly straightforward restaurant that features Old World–style entrées in a converted old home at 2963 Sudderth; Tel: 257-5251.

It has been reported that some visitors to the **Texas Club** at 212 Metz Road (directly behind the Village Lodge on Mechem Drive, see below, 1½miles/2½ km north of the Sudderth–Mechem intersection) enjoy counting the number of luxury automobiles parked outside. True to its name, this relaxed restaurant caters to Texans vacationing in Ruidoso, but the welcome mat is always out for everybody. Tel: 258-3998.

On the right side of Mechem Drive, less than a quarter mile before the ski area is an excellent steak-and-seafood grill, **The Incredible**. Seating is in a greenhouse structure that offers great views by day; at night you can dine under the stars. Reservations are recommended; Tel: 336-4312.

STAYING IN RUIDOSO

A quarter mile (½ km) past the Sudderth–Mechem intersection you'll come to a traffic circle; take the right turn at the arrow to 107 Main Road for **Shadow Mountain Lodge**, charming, relaxed accommodations for couples in a garden setting. All of the 19 units have fieldstone fireplaces, king-size beds, and complimentary coffee, tea, and hot chocolate in the rooms.

A mile and a half (2½ km) from the intersection, at 1000 Mechem Drive, is the **Village Lodge**, an all-suite hotel with 32 units complete with fireplaces and wet bars.

The **Swiss Chalet Hotel** at 1451 Mechem Drive, about 5 miles (8 km) from the Sudderth–Mechem intersection and 1 mile (1½ km) south of the turnoff to the ski area, is built in pseudo–Tudor/Swiss style and commands striking views of the area.

SKI APACHE RESORT

Approximately 6 miles (10 km) north of the Mechem–Sudderth intersection is the well-signposted turnoff for the Ski Apache Resort. You'll enjoy excellent powder skiing here topping off at 11,400 feet above sea level, with 40 trails and runs for all levels of skiers. The long run is approximately 8,000 feet with a vertical drop of 1,800 feet. Lifts include double and triple chairs, a Mighty Mite handle tow, and a four-passenger gondola. Lift tickets are available by writing P.O. Box 220, Ruidoso, NM 88345; Tel: (800) 545-9011. For 24-hour snow-condition reports, Tel: 257-9001.

Ski Apache amenities include snack bars, a bar, a sports shop, a ski-equipment rental shop, and a certified ski school. The road to the ski area is paved and has guard-rails but it's narrow. During the height of the ski season, only traffic heading up to the ski area is permitted in the morning and only traffic coming down in the afternoon.

If you continue on NM 48 approximately 2 miles (3 km) north past the turn to Ski Apache you'll come to a turnoff for two choice places to stay in the Ruidoso area. As you crest the top of the hill a sign indicating the Alto Country Club will be on your right; 100 feet farther you'll see a sign for **Alto Alps Condominium Complex**. Turn left at the minimarket/gas station, go straight past the gate house into the condominium complex, and follow the narrow, paved road until you see the building with the swimming pool and tennis courts (it's the clubhouse and office). One of the very best places to spend some time in the Ruidoso area, this upscale complex nestled in tall pines offers a few one-, two-, and three-bedroom condominiums for rent. All the units have fully equipped kitchens, fireplaces, and large decks, and are elegantly furnished down to the wine glasses. Ask for one of the units that has unsurpassed views of Sierra Blanca.

If you want peace and quiet and a rustic atmosphere that's been cultivated over the past 30 years, take an immediate right (to the north) as soon as you turn at the minimarket, and follow the signs to **La Junta Guest Ranch**, 1 mile (1½ km) from the minimarket. All of the spacious cabins in the seven secluded acres have kitchens and fireplaces and share barbecue pits.

Capitan and Lincoln

About 12 miles (19 km) north of Alto Alps on NM 48 is the town of Capitan, with a claim to fame as the birthplace of the original Smokey the Bear. The famous bear is buried here, in Smokey Bear State Park, which also has a log-structure museum containing memorabilia of Smokey. On July 4 every year the residents of this tiny town host the **Smokey Bear Stampede**, which includes a fun run, a parade, a barbecue, Western dancing, and a rodeo. During the second week of August the Lincoln County Fair is also held here.

Lincoln, 11 miles (18 km) east of Capitan on U.S. 380, became the seat of Lincoln County in 1869, and in the following few years the now-famous rivalry between Englishman rancher and merchant John Tunstall and rancher L. G. Murphy heated to the boiling point. When Tunstall was gunned down, the factions that had supported each man readied themselves for a battle. One of the Tunstall loyalists was Billy the Kid, who had worked for Tunstall as a cowboy and had witnessed the killing of his friend and employer. Billy vowed to avenge his death. The so-called Lincoln County War raged on for a bloody five days, ending with the death on July 19, 1878, of Tunstall's partner and attorney Alexander McSween.

Lew Wallace (the author of *Ben Hur*), then governor of the New Mexico Territory, declared amnesty for everyone involved in the war. Billy is said to have subsequently organized a "gang" that set about terrorizing the countryside and intimidating all the people he thought responsible for Tunstall's death. However, the town of Lincoln itself remained fairly calm during this time, with the help of the Buffalo Soldiers, a black cavalry unit organized during the Civil War. Billy was arrested by Sheriff Pat Garrett, tried in Mesilla, found guilty of murder, and returned to Lincoln, where he was incarcerated. He broke out of jail and after a long siege at Stinking Springs (northeast of Lincoln near Taiban) was shot by Garrett at Old Fort Sumner. The population of Lincoln and of all of New Mexico breathed a collective sigh of relief and went back about its business.

The town of Lincoln is the center of the ten-square-mile **National Historic Lincoln Landmark**. Approximately half of the property in town, including the two-story building from which Billy made his daring escape, is owned by either the Lincoln County Historical Trust or the State of New Mexico. There are no fast-food outlets or kitschy gift shops in Lincoln, and so it is much like what it must have been in the 1880s. The town itself has only one street, approximately four blocks long.

Touring this "living historical museum" makes for a

delightful way to spend an afternoon. Start with a self-guided walking tour of Lincoln at the Historical Center, on the east end of town, after viewing a slide show and an exhibit of tools, weapons, and clothing of the Apache, Spaniards, and Anglos who inhabited the area, as well as uniforms and weapons of the Buffalo Soldiers. Maps indicating the buildings of historical importance in Lincoln are available here, sites such as John Tunstall's store, the courthouse, the home and office of Lincoln County's doctor, and the old Lincoln Hotel—now the Wortley Hotel.

The **Wortley** has a few double rooms. The dining room, filled with country antiques, makes a delightful respite from the outside world. Call ahead to see when and if the Wortley is serving food; Tel: 653-4500. Closed January and February.

The first weekend of August brings Billy the Kid buffs from all over the world to Lincoln for **Old Lincoln Days**, featuring a parade and lectures by experts on the exploits of the Kid.

From Lincoln continue east on U.S. 380 to Hondo and then take U.S. 70/380 a bit farther east to Tinnie, where the main attraction is the **Tinnie Silver Dollar Restaurant**, housed in a magnificent rambling Victorian building with a glass-enclosed ballroom and gazebo. The restaurant, set in the middle of ranching country—where the major sport of the area's residents is polo—serves steak and seafood in a Gay Nineties atmosphere. Dinner is served Wednesday through Sunday and lunch is served weekends only; Tel: 653-4425.

ROSWELL

What is known today as the city of Roswell, 30 miles (48 km) east of Tinnie on U.S. 70/380, is the spot where professional gambler Van C. Smith landed in 1869 after he had picked up stakes in his native Omaha, Nebraska, and headed for the New Mexico Territory. He and his partner, Frank Wilburn, built two adobe buildings to house a post office, general store, and overnight stop and christened their new town Roswell, in honor of Mr. Smith's father.

Now a bustling little city, Roswell is extremely proud of its tree-lined **Downtown Historic District**, with its large stately homes. One of these homes has been turned into the **Chaves County Historical Museum** (at 200 North Lea, right off U.S. 70). Built in 1910 and formerly the palatial home of one of Roswell's early settlers, James Phelps White, it is chock-full of furniture and memorabilia of the era; Tel: 622-8333.

A "must see" in Roswell is the marvelous collection of Indian pottery, Spanish suits of armor, and paintings by such renowned artists as Peter Hurd (who was born in Roswell), Henriette Wyeth, and Georgia O'Keeffe that graces the **Roswell Museum and Art Center** at 100 West 11th Street, just off Main Street; Tel: 624-6744.

Artillery and military artifacts are on view at the **General Douglas L. McBride Museum** (Tel: 622-6250) on the campus of the New Mexico Military Institute on Main Street, between College Boulevard and 19th Street. Situated across from the military institute, the **Roswell Inn**, the city's landmark hotel, has an inviting restaurant, cocktail lounge, and coffee shop.

Anyone who enjoys the atmosphere depicted on television's "Cheers" will like **The Establishment/Mrs. Aris' Restaurant**, 118 East Third Street, near Main. This fun lounge with super drinks and a warm atmosphere serves some of the best Mexican food in town; Tel: 623-5006.

The **Cattle Baron Restaurant** at 12th and Main turns out excellent steak and seafood in relaxing, plant-filled rooms; Tel: 622-2465.

Take U.S. 380 east or U.S. 70 north 13 miles (21 km) from Roswell to the **Bitter Lake National Wildlife Refuge**, a winter haven for migratory waterfowl and cranes, and a draw for photographers and bird-watchers; Tel: 622-6755.

Seventy-six miles (122 km) due south of Roswell on U.S. 285 is the city of Carlsbad, the gateway to the most famous cave in the world: Carlsbad Caverns.

CARLSBAD

In the early 1880s two cowboys looking for stray cattle on a ranch near Eddy (now Carlsbad), New Mexico, saw a large number of bats flying out of a large hole in the ground. Later exploration uncovered one of the greatest caves in the world—today's **Carlsbad Caverns National Park**.

The caverns boast the largest known underground room in America, covering 14 acres and measuring more than 30 stories tall. Two self-guided tours of the cave show off the majestic stalactites and stalagmites and the myriad colors in the rock formations. The three-mile

Blue Tour starts at the main entrance to the cave (20 miles/32 km southwest of Carlsbad on U.S. 62/180, then west on Route 7 at White's City) and wanders through rock chamber after rock chamber, including the Queen's Chamber, the King's Palace, the Whale's Mouth, and the Boneyard.

The Red Tour, which also departs from the main entrance, starts with an elevator ride to the cave's floor, 750 feet below the surface of the earth, and then pursues a predominately flat and circuitous mile-and-a-quarter trail.

Both tours culminate in the big room, which has a cafeteria and a gift shop. The temperature inside the cave is a constant 56°F, so a sweater or light jacket is in order; sturdy walking shoes are a must, especially if you opt for the Blue Tour.

The visitors' center at the entrance to the cave provides both nursery services and air-conditioned kennels for pets. Tel: 785-2107 (24-hour recorded message) or 785-2232.

White's City, a small town at the entrance to Carlsbad Caverns National Park, was founded by a man who was one of the earliest to explore the caverns. The family-owned town has two hotels, the **Best Western Cavern Inn** and the **Guadalupe Inn**. The Cavern Inn contains the **Velvet Garter Restaurant and Saloon**, complete with a painting of a reclining nude over the bar. (White's City is also the nearest town to the Guadalupe Mountains; see the El Paso chapter.)

The city of Carlsbad itself is best known for the nearby caverns. The **Carlsbad Museum and Art Center** at 418 West Fox Street, one block west of Canal Street, displays prehistoric and Indian artifacts in addition to local crafts and paintings; Tel: 887-0276.

Cruises on the Pecos River (which runs through Carlsbad) on the **George Washington Paddlewheel Boat**, built in 1858, are available from Memorial Day to Labor Day; Tel: 887-0512. Carlsbad has two lakes within the city limits: Brantley Lake State Park and Lake Carlsbad, with a 1,000-foot strip of beach.

The **Best Western Motel Stevens**, with a nightclub and a coffee shop, offers genuine Southwestern hospitality at 1829 South Canal Street in Carlsbad.

WEST OF LAS CRUCES
Deming

Sixty miles (96 km) west of Las Cruces on I-10 a billboard announces Deming—the Home of Pure Water and Fast Ducks. This Chamber of Commerce slogan for the small city of Deming, New Mexico, is certainly an attention getter. But what does it mean? The first reference is to the city's water from the underground Mimbres River, which is billed as testing at a higher level of purity even than Ivory Soap, at its famous 99.9 percent pure.

The second half of the claim refers to the fourth weekend of every August, when Deming plays host to the Great American Duck Races, and some 400 ducks race for the gold. There is a full-fledged duckling pageant, with the annual crowning of the Duck Queen, a car show, a rodeo, the Great American Red-&-Green Chile Cookoffs, and an arts-and-crafts fair.

Deming also has the best cultural museum in southern New Mexico: The **Deming Luna Mimbres Museum** at 301 South Silver Avenue has 25,000 square feet of exhibits including fashions from the Gay 90s, a gem and mineral room, early military mementos, a chuck wagon, a quilt room with bedspreads dating to 1847, a large doll collection from around the world, and an extensive array of Mimbres Indian pottery and baskets dating from A.D. 50 to A.D. 1150. A book-and-gift shop is also located within the museum. Tel: 546-2382.

About 35 miles (56 km) south of Deming on NM 11 is **Pancho Villa State Park** at Columbus, New Mexico, at the Mexican border. The visitors' center (in the former customs house, built in 1902) features exhibits of the history of Pancho Villa, his raid on Columbus in 1916, and General Pershing's subsequent punitive expedition; Tel: 531-2711.

The only international port of entry between New Mexico and Mexico is 2 miles (3 km) south of Columbus. **Las Palomas** (The Doves), in Mexico, is an extremely poor border town with dusty unpaved streets, a couple of restaurants, a rather infamous bar, and a pharmacy catering to U.S. citizens. However, visiting Las Palomas is only for the most intrepid traveller.

Silver City

Leave I-10 at Deming, turn northwest on U.S. 180, and head toward the Gila mountains and Silver City.

In 1870 prospectors discovered silver in the hills around this now-gentle, quiet city, and the rush was on. So what better to name the town that developed but Silver City? Unlike many boomtowns that became just a memory when the bust came in the late 1880s, the sturdy brick architecture and the determination of both the Hispanic and Anglo populations here kept Silver City from becoming a ghost town.

To see Silver City start at the six-sided tourist center on NM 90 (1103 North Hudson Street). There are several walking and driving tours from which to choose. An easy town tour begins with the **McComas House** at 500 North Hudson, now the post office. From the turn of the century until the 1960s this was the center of a notorious red-light district. One of the most famous of Silver City's madams, Silver City Millie, has been celebrated in stories and books and has even had hotel rooms named for her.

The former Star Hotel, where, as a child, Billy the Kid waited on tables (he lived with the owners after his mother died), used to stand at the corner of Hudson and Broadway streets.

The spacious **Corner Cafe**, in an old commercial building at Broadway and Bullard streets, serves burgers with sprouts and avocado on homemade buns. You can also buy their homemade bread to take with you.

The Silver City National Bank building at 101 West Broadway was designed in 1923 by the famous architect Henry Trost in the Neoclassical Revival Style. Noteworthy too are the cast-iron details at street level and the pressed metal on the second story of the Italianate building completed by saloon keeper George Bell in 1906, in the 200 block of Broadway.

Anyone interested in late-19th- and early-20th-century architecture will enjoy seeing other examples of the buildings from the city's heyday. Among them is the Martin Maher house at 401 West Market Street. Built in Queen Anne style in 1887, it features a two-story ornamented verandah and is connected by a breezeway to the Stephen Uhi building, built around 1898. The adobe construction of the St. Vincent de Paul Catholic Church at number 412 took place over several years, starting in 1874. The twin towers, the mission-arched façade, and the three round-topped stained glass windows are of particular interest.

The charming, European-style **Palace Hotel** at 106 West Broadway, built in 1882, has recently been restored. Its 22 rooms are furnished with period antiques. A complimentary breakfast is served in the second-floor private garden room among potted palms.

Today the H. B. Ailman House at 312 West Broadway gives shelter to the **Silver City Museum**. Built in Mansard/Italianate style in 1881 from the proceeds of the Naiad Queen silver mine, the building has been used in a multitude of ways over the years, including as a boarding-house. The museum shows off furniture and memorabilia from Silver City's past. A gift shop features poetry and books on New Mexico; Tel: 538-5921.

Pinos Altos

Seven miles (11 km) north of Silver City on NM 15 is the former mining town of Pinos Altos (Tall Pines). Although often relegated to ghost-town status in books and articles, the formerly busy town is still home to any number of folks who live in and around it. After gold was discovered in the area in 1859 Pinos Altos became a boomtown, and the buildings that remain are vestiges of the affluence that the mines brought in.

To reach what is commonly called the "Hearst Church" here, keep to the left when the road divides in town. At the first intersection past the bridge, turn left onto a dirt road, which loops back to the right. There you will find the Gold Avenue Methodist Episcopal Church, or the **Hearst Church**. So labeled in acknowledgment of a large donation from Mrs. Phoebe Hearst (wife of California Senator George Hearst, who owned several lucrative mining interests in the area, and mother of William Randolph, who used that money to build his publishing empire), the adobe structure is now a museum with displays of mining equipment and horse-drawn vehicles, including the funeral hearse of Pat Garrett. Local art exhibits are held in the museum during the summer months.

If you retrace your route to the paved road and turn left, you will find the Rita del Cobre Fort and Trading Post. This three-quarter-scale reproduction of the fort built at the Santa Rita copper mine in 1804 to protect the area from Apache raids was erected in 1980. The Hearst company store was located across the street.

Down the street a few steps on the east side is the **Pinos Altos Opera House**. With their loads of money from the mines, some of Pinos Altos's citizens decided their fellow townsfolk needed culture, and they built an opera house in 1869. Prehistoric Indian artifacts, old mining tools, and household relics from the area as well as photos from the boom times are now on display. Next door visitors can still enjoy a refreshing drink in the Wild West setting at the **Buckhorn Saloon**, where beverages have been flowing since the 1860s.

On the dirt road directly behind the opera house is the cabin of the renowned Indian fighter John McDonald, said to have come to Pinos Altos around 1851.

GILA CLIFF DWELLINGS NATIONAL MONUMENT

The Gila Cliff Dwellings National Monument is 37 miles (59 km) north of Pinos Altos on NM 15, a logging road that has two narrow lanes and many curves, and comes to a dead end at the cliff dwellings; allow at least two hours driving time each way—a long ride but worth it.

The visitors' center's exhibits and pamphlets will prepare you for what you'll see. The mile-long walking trail to the cliff dwellings is fairly steep, and you have to cross a hanging footbridge that spans a small stream. Benches placed strategically along the path provide opportunities for rest.

The earliest people known to inhabit the dwellings were called Mogollon (pronounced "muh-gee-OWN"), and the last were the Anasazi Pueblo Indians. Why they chose this location, one of the least accessible in all of North America, and why they abandoned the site around A.D. 1300 remain mysteries to this day. Call ahead to the visitors' center (Tel: 536-9461), as hours vary with the season and the weather.

NORTH OF LAS CRUCES

The Fort Selden exit 16 miles (26 km) north of Las Cruces on I-25 on the way to Albuquerque takes you directly to **Fort Selden State Monument**. Established in 1865 on the bank of the Rio Grande, this fort was built to guard the villages of Las Cruces and Mesilla and the travellers along the river against Apache raids.

In March 1884 Captain Arthur MacArthur took over command of the fort; for the following two years his son, the future General Douglas MacArthur, lived at Fort Selden with his parents. A visitors' center at the now-ruined fort provides historical facts and information about the fort, which played an important part in southern New Mexico's history.

Truth or Consequences

In the 1950s Truth or Consequences shed its former handle of Mineral Hot Springs in favor of the name of a popular television show. Most New Mexicans refer to the town as "T or C."

T or C is a good one-day trip out of Las Cruces, or a quick stop for gas or a meal off I-25, 70 miles (43 km) from Las Cruces on the way north to Albuquerque and Santa Fe. There are two excellent places to eat on the main street, which runs from one freeway exit up to the next. **La Cocina** serves plate-size sopapillas with their authentic-tasting Mexican food, at 280 Date Street; Tel: 894-6499. The quintessential Western steak house, **Los Arcos Steak and Lobster Restaurant**, at 1400 North Date Street, serves dinner only; Tel: 894-6200.

Elephant Butte Lake, one of the largest lakes in New Mexico, just north of Truth or Consequences, was formed in 1916 by the damming up of the Rio Grande. Facilities here include a marina with boat rentals; you can sail, windsurf, jet ski, water ski, canoe, and swim on the lake— and there's excellent fishing for bass, walleyes, northern pike, blue catfish, and perch. Fishing guides, bait, fishing equipment, and one- or five-day fishing licenses are available. For information call the Elephant Butte Resort Marina, Inc.; Tel: 744-5486.

The **Dam Site**, a bar-restaurant in an old stone building at the marina, provides a welcome refuge from the fun and sun of the lake; Tel: 894-2073.

GETTING AROUND

The most practical and enjoyable way to see southern New Mexico is by car. You can drive into the area on either I-10 (5½ hours from Tucson, Arizona, in the west or 1 hour from El Paso, Texas, to the southeast) or I-25 (4½ hours from Albuquerque to the north).

Aside from a small airport in Las Cruces, the closest entryway to the area for commercial flights is El Paso International Airport, 42 miles (67 km) southeast of Las Cruces. American, Continental, Delta, and Southwest airlines fly into El Paso International. All major car-rental companies have booths in the airport lobby.

Las Cruces Shuttle Service operates nine trips a day to Las Cruces's hotels from the El Paso airport. Reservations are required; Tel: 525-1784 or (800) 288-1784. L & M Limousine offers 24-hour service to Las Cruces from the El Paso airport by advance reservations; Tel: 522-5411. The Yellow Cab & Checker Cab Company also provides 24-hour service from either the El Paso or Las Cruces airports with no reservations necessary; Tel: 524-1711. The company's guided tours of Las Cruces and the surrounding area must be booked in advance; contact Perry.

American, Continental, Delta, Southwest, and United fly into Albuquerque International Airport, 225 miles (360 km) north of Las Cruces. You can connect there with Mesa Airlines flights to Las Cruces, Silver City, or Roswell; Tel: (800) 637-2247. Or you can rent a car from any of the major car-rental companies at the Albuquerque airport and drive south into the area on I-25.

T. N. M. and O. Bus Lines provides service to Las Cruces, Roswell, Ruidoso, and Silver City from El Paso, Albuquerque, and Tucson; Tel: (800) 531-5332.

ACCOMMODATIONS REFERENCE

The rate ranges given here are projections *for 1993. Unless otherwise indicated, rates are for a double room, double occupancy, and do not include meals. Price ranges span the lowest rate in the low season to the highest rate in the high season. As rates are always subject to change, it is wise to double-check before booking.*

The telephone area code for New Mexico is 505.

▶ **Alto Alps Condominium Complex.** P.O. Box 130, **Alto**, NM 88312. Tel: 336-4377 or (800) 962-1420. $90–$140 per day with a two-night minimum (one- to three-bedroom condominiums).

▶ **Best Western Cavern Inn.** 17 Carlsbad Caverns Highway, Box 128, **White's City**, NM 88268. Tel: 785-2291 or (800) CAVERNS; Fax: 785-2283. $60–$75.

▶ **Best Western Motel Stevens.** 1829 South Canal Street, **Carlsbad**, NM 88221. Tel: 887-2851 or (800) 528-1234. $55–$75.

▶ **Guadalupe Inn.** 17 Carlsbad Caverns Highway, Box 128, **White's City**, NM 88268. Tel: 785-2291 or (800) CAVERNS; Fax: 785-2283. $60–$75.

▶ **Holiday Inn de Las Cruces.** 201 East University Avenue, **Las Cruces**, NM 88001. Tel: 526-4411; Fax: 524-0530. $65–$85.

▶ **Inn of the Mountain Gods.** Box 269, **Mescalero**, NM 88340. Tel: 257-5141 or (800) 545-9011. $115–$125.

▶ **La Junta Guest Ranch.** P.O. Box 139, **Alto**, NM 88312. Tel: 336-4361 or (800) 443-8423. $65. Credit cards are not accepted.

▶ **Las Cruces Hilton Hotel.** 705 South Telshor Boulevard, **Las Cruces**, NM 88001. Tel: 522-4300 or (800) 284-0616; Fax: 521-4707. $65–$72.

▶ **The Lodge at Cloudcroft.** 1 Corona Place, Box 497, **Cloudcroft**, NM 88317. Tel: 682-2566 or (800) 395-6343. $70–$100.

▶ **Meson de Mesilla Bed & Breakfast.** 1803 Avenida de Mesilla, Box 1212, **Las Cruces**, NM 88046. Tel: 525-2380. $52–$85.

▶ **Palace Hotel.** 106 West Broadway, **Silver City**, NM 88061. Tel: 388-1811. $30–$50.

▶ **Roswell Inn.** 1815 North Main, P.O. Box 2065, **Roswell**, NM 88202. Tel: 623-4920, (800) 323-0913 (out-of-state), or (800) 426-3052 (in New Mexico). $45–$65.

▶ **Shadow Mountain Lodge.** 107 Main Road, Box 1427, **Ruidoso**, NM 88345. Tel: 257-4886 or (800) 441-4331. $49.50–$77.

▶ **Swiss Chalet Hotel.** 1451 Mechem Drive, Highway 48, **Ruidoso**, NM 88345. Tel: 258-3333 or (800) 47-SWISS. $70–$90.

▶ **Village Lodge.** 1000 Mechem Drive, **Ruidoso**, NM 88345. Tel: 258-5442 or (800) 722-8779; Fax: 258-3041. $49–$89.

▶ **Wortley Hotel.** Highway 380, **Lincoln**, NM 88338. Tel: 653-4500. $53–$58.

TUCSON AND SOUTHERN ARIZONA

By John Stickler

John Stickler, who began his career in communications as a stringer for CBS News in Seoul, Korea, has been a marketing executive at southern Arizona's first destination resort and, for 30 years, a freelance journalist. He is a past president of the Society of Southwestern Authors. Now a fulltime writer, he lives in the desert northwest of Tucson, Arizona.

Travellers searching for the Old West can find it in southern Arizona by applying a little effort and imagination. Traces of the earliest Spanish explorers, the dedicated Jesuit missionaries, the fearful Apache raiders, lawless mining towns, and authentic guest ranches (don't call them dude ranches) are all here—remembered, respected, and ready to be discovered by today's adventurous explorer.

Tucson and its environs offer enough attractions for a week of energetic sightseeing, including a wide variety of dining experiences, magnificent resorts, and a range of performing arts matched only by perhaps a dozen other cities in the country. In Arizona only the Grand Canyon draws more tourists than Tucson's three major attractions: the Arizona–Sonora Desert Museum, Old Tucson Studios, and the controversial new science experiment, Biosphere 2.

Around Tucson, 130 miles to the west there's the former copper-smelting town of Ajo, nearly reduced to a ghost town in 1986 when Phelps Dodge closed the 70-year-old mine there. Between Ajo and the Mexican border lies the largest national monument in the United States, Organ Pipe Cactus National Monument, singular in its vast, desolate beauty. Just south of Tucson, at the eastern edge of the huge Tohono O'odham Indian Reservation (formerly called Papago) stands the "White Dove of the Desert," Mission San Xavier del Bac, the only Spanish colonial church in the United States still serving descendants of its original Indian members.

Farther south, the lush Santa Cruz River Valley leads upstream (south) past the 18th-century missions of Tubac and Tumacacori to the border towns of Nogales, Arizona, and Nogales, Sonora, Mexico. To the southeast of Tucson, Tombstone, "the town too tough to die," still celebrates the famous gunfight at the O.K. Corral. And not far from Tombstone the 19th-century mining town of Bisbee, its huge, gaping Lavender Pit mine closed in 1975, struggles to build a new economy on tourism, history—and a renegade artists' colony.

After discussing Tucson, the main air gateway, we'll continue our coverage at the western end of southern Arizona, in the town of Ajo, and work eastward toward Tucson. We'll cover I-19 south from Tucson to the border at Nogales, and continue east in the border region through Patagonia, Sonoita, Sierra Vista, Bisbee, Tombstone, and Douglas. The final leg moves north on U.S. 666 up to I-10 and west back to Tucson.

The telephone area code for Arizona is 602.

MAJOR INTEREST

Tucson
Downtown Saturday Night/Arts District
University of Arizona
Arizona–Sonora Desert Museum
Old Tucson Studios
Biosphere 2
Sabino Canyon
Pima Air Museum
Mission San Xavier del Bac
The destination resorts
The Mexican food of South Tucson

Southern Arizona
Organ Pipe Cactus National Monument
Kitt Peak observatories
Titan Missile Museum
Historic Tubac and Tumacacori
Nogales: Arizona and Sonora
San Pedro & Southwestern Railway excursion train
Bisbee and the Copper Queen mine tour
Tombstone

Tucson, the major city of southern Arizona, has always been known for its hospitality. The clean, dry air, the constant sunshine (360 days a year), and the desert scenery have long made it a popular place for winter visitors. During the first half of this century there were dozens of guest ranches on the outskirts of town and around southern Arizona. A few remain and still offer a taste of the real West, with horseback riding and cookouts; some even have active cattle ranching that guests are welcome to participate in. The 1980s saw the opening of three major destination resorts that put the Old Pueblo, as Tucson is popularly called, on a different map, the one for national meeting and convention planners.

Spring and fall are ideal times to visit. The weather is warm, the chances of rain (only 11 inches annually) at their lowest. Average high temperatures, December through February are in the mid-60°F (15°C) range, with the average low around 39°F (4°C). March and November both average 72°F (22°C) as a daily high. Summers are hot down here, and seem to be getting hotter. Statistics show, greenhouse effect or not, that eight of southern Arizona's ten hottest years on record occurred in the past decade.

"But it's a *dry* heat." True, 95°F in Tucson with one-digit humidity is much more comfortable than 80 or 85°F in New Orleans or Florida at any time of year. But 105 or 110 degrees even in the shade draws uncomfortable comparisons with the inside of a pizza oven. It used to be that in May, June, or September the temperature rarely broke 100°F. Today it is a common occurrence. And then there are the summer monsoons: July and August downpours that drift up from Mexico, soaking the desert (and everything else) and cooling temperatures as much as 30 degrees. The downpour is heavy, intense, and short-lived leaving arroyos and washes filled with rushing muddy water and the wet desert smelling incomparably fresh.

TUCSON

The city of Tucson was founded on August 20, 1775, when the first Spanish garrison set up a walled fort here, the Tucson Presidio. The name is said to be a Spanish corruption of the Indian word *stjukshon* or *tuqui son,* meaning roughly "spring at the foot of a black mountain"—the perfect description considering its location in a broad valley surrounded by mountain ranges. The closest, immediately to the north, are the Santa Catalinas. The town has lapped up into the foothills, where prestigious home-sites overlook the city from on high. To the east are the Rincons, once miles from town, now forming the eastern edge of the city. Most of the Catalinas and the Rincons are part of the vast Coronado National Forest and are protected from development.

To the west the stately saguaro cactus, part of Saguaro National Monument West, populates the narrow ridge of the Tucson Mountains, and far to the south, on the horizon, is the Santa Rita range. Between the west end of the Catalinas and the north end of the Tucson Mountains, to the northwest, lie the Tortolita Mountains.

Tucson was no more than a remote military outpost serving in the defense against Apache raids, until 1846. That year the United States declared war against Mexico and the Mormon Battalion arrived, took over the garrison, and raised the first American flag over the fort. The walls of the old presidio have long since melted away, but the location is well known and marked by a plaque at the corner of Washington Street and Main Avenue downtown.

The major arteries running east to west are Speedway Boulevard and Broadway. The two streets, which are 1 mile (1½ km) apart, run due east from downtown about 15 miles (24 km) to the base of the Rincon Mountains, with stoplights all the way.

The third major east–west thoroughfare, one mile south of Broadway and parallel, is 22nd Street.

The key north–south streets, starting on the west side, are I-10 (which runs north–south from Tucson to Phoenix, but is signed as east–west because in the big picture it connects El Paso, Texas, with Los Angeles, California); Oracle Road (U.S. 80/89), the route north to Florence; First Avenue; Campbell Avenue; Swan Road; and Craycroft Road. All but I-10 have bridges over the Rillito River, cross River Road, and ascend into the foothills.

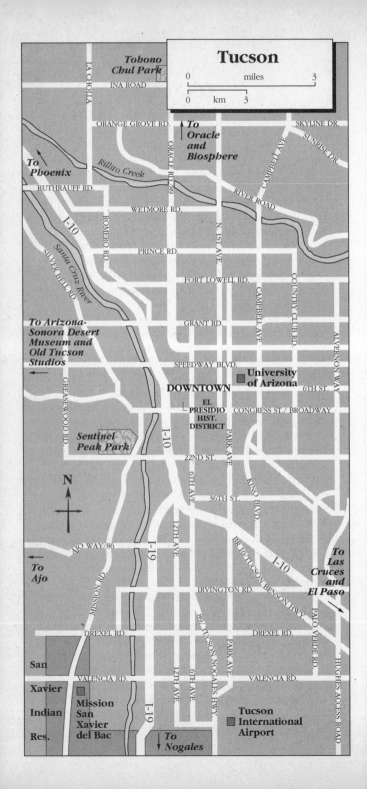

Three distinctive residential neighborhoods will show you how Tucsonans lived before World War II. The Sam Hughes neighborhood, immediately adjacent to the University of Arizona (and a prime location for bed-and-breakfast inns), about 1 mile (1½ km) east of downtown, stretches east along Campbell Avenue between Second and Sixth streets as far as Tucson Boulevard. The older one- and two-story homes here display an eclectic mix of Western styles amid the shade of mature trees and quiet streets with sidewalks. (See below for the university itself.)

The other two neighborhoods are both on Country Club Road, farther east. Colonia Solana, south of Broadway between Country Club and Randolph Park, is a desert setting with homes on large lots shaded by tall palms. The lack of curbs and sidewalks creates a rustic effect. El Encanto also lies east of Country Club, between Broadway and Fifth Street. Here the homes are grander, often with lush lawns and extensive flower beds. Until newer gated communities were built high in the foothills, El Encanto (The Enchanted) was the enclave of choice for Tucson's upper crust.

South Tucson, a one-square-mile mainly Hispanic community, straddles Sixth Avenue south of 22nd Street (see Dining in Tucson, below).

Downtown Tucson

The city's original downtown grew around the Presidio and eventually spread to the east. Downtown today can be defined as the area bounded by the freeway (I-10) on the west, Sixth Street/St. Mary's Road on the north, the Southern Pacific railway tracks on the east, and roughly 16th Street along the southern edge. The grid plan makes it easy to find your way around.

There are three main downtown neighborhoods: the Presidio Historic District (discussed below), and two residential areas (the Barrio Historico, occupying 13 blocks just south of the Tucson Convention Center, and the Armory Park Historic District), which we do discuss.

A fourth area, the recently named Arts District (see below), includes most of commercial downtown and represents an effort by citizens to resurrect the once-decaying city core.

El Presidio Historic District surrounds the site of the original adobe Spanish fort. Listed on the National Register of Historic Places, it is bounded by Church Street on the east, Alameda Street on the south, Grenada Avenue on the

west, and St. Mary's Road on the north. The district is just
north of the city hall and El Presidio Park. The heart of the
district is the walled compound of **Old Town Artisans**,
comprising the block bounded by Court Avenue, Telles
Street, Meyer Avenue, and Washington Street, just northeast of the Tucson Museum of Art. The original building, an
1850s adobe with saguaro-rib ceilings, is now part of a 15-
room complex of art galleries and specialty shops, an ideal
spot to find jewelry, crafts, and paintings by 400 local
artists, at reasonable prices. The complex wraps around a
charming shady garden housing the outdoor dining section of the **Courtyard Cafe**. Two indoor rooms complete
the restaurant, which is open for lunch daily except Sundays and major holidays. As part of Downtown Saturday
Night (see below) Old Town Artisans and the Courtyard
Cafe remain open in the evening the first and third Saturday of each month and provide free open-air concerts. The
restaurant specializes in light meals: homemade soups,
quiches, and sandwiches served in a very informal setting.

The mostly underground **Tucson Museum of Art**, downtown at 140 North Main Avenue, has rotating exhibits of
pre-Columbian art and Spanish Colonial antiques from its
permanent collection, and sponsors travelling shows of
contemporary works; Tel: 624-2333.

For a close-up look at Tucson's early roots, take a
walking tour of El Presidio Historic District. January
through April **Sandpainter Guided Tours** offers a 90-
minute stroll through the 150-year-old neighborhood. A
knowledgeable guide points out the old homes and explains who lived in them and what role they played in the
development of the Old Pueblo. Contact P.O. Box 50501,
Tucson, AZ 85703; Tel: 323-9290.

THE ARTS DISTRICT

Downtown Tucson suffered the fate of many cities when
the traditional department stores departed for the suburbs and the malls: It dried up and died. The city leaders
have worked hard over the past decade to bring it back to
life. New shops, new restaurants, "phantom galleries"
(empty storefronts used temporarily to display local artists' work), the resurrection of old buildings, and even
some new housing has turned the area around and given
it an exciting energy.

This energy is never more apparent than on **Downtown Saturday Night**, the first and third Saturday of each
month, when shops remain open and musicians and

performers entertain on street corners. The *Tucson Citizen* Calendar on Thursday evenings and the *Arizona Daily Star* Starlight section on Friday mornings announce the weekend entertainment. Keep an eye out for performance artist Mat Bevel or the Mat Bevel Company; his one-man-band marching sculpture is indescribable.

The Tucson Convention Center (TCC) is a major entertainment and exhibition complex. The Tucson Symphony Orchestra performs here, as do touring rock musicians, and the complex plays host to sporting events, tractor pulls, and mud-boggers. The TCC fills a four-block area south of Congress Street bounded by Church Avenue and Cushing Street.

Two historic buildings are playing an important role in the downtown comeback. The Carnegie Free Library, built in 1901 with a grant from philanthropist Andrew Carnegie, is one of the finest examples of his library program left in the United States. It stands on its own block, between Sixth and Scott avenues south of 12th Street. For many years known as the Tucson Public Library, it is starting a new career as the **Tucson Children's Museum**; Tel: 884-7511.

Just a block south of the Children's Museum, near the end of Scott Avenue, is the new home of the Arizona Theatre Company. The Spanish-style stuccoed **Temple of Music and Art** is an exact replica of the Pasadena Playhouse, constructed in 1927. (Pasadena patrons of the arts were furious when they learned their architect had sold "their" plans to "hicks" in Arizona.) By the mid-1980s the building had been abandoned and was scheduled for partial demolition. A volunteer group of concerned creatives convinced the city to buy it and restore it as part of Tucson's heritage, both theatrical and architectural. The city did so, completely renovating and modernizing the old facility to create a state-of-the-art, 607-seat performance space. The theater company's season runs from October to May, and the quality of the dramas and musicals usually equals that of Broadway. (One of the 1991–1992 offerings was a world premiere that went on to play in New York.) Tel: 884-8210 (information) or 622-2823 (tickets).

Tucson is rightfully proud of its performing arts. It is one of only 14 cities in the United States with symphony orchestra, ballet, opera, and theater companies. The *Wall Street Journal* has called Tucson a "mini-mecca" for the arts. Information on the performing arts in the city, as

well as movies, art galleries, and more, can be found in
the free tabloid the *Tucson Weekly*. Published every
Wednesday, the paper is available at hundreds of locations around Tucson, including the Visitors' Center, at 130
Scott Avenue.

A sit-down van-bus tour of Tucson usually includes three
downtown historic districts, the University of Arizona, and
a view of the city from atop Sentinel Peak (also called "A"
Mountain), southwest of downtown in Sentinel Peak Park.
Try **Tucson Tour Company**, Tel: 544-2664. The same company offers shuttle service to all major area attractions.

THE UNIVERSITY OF ARIZONA

The educational center of Tucson and southern Arizona,
the University of Arizona was founded in 1888, chartered
in Tucson as a sop for the transfer of the capital to Phoenix. Since then it has grown into a major institution of
higher learning, with over 35,000 students. The campus
lies about one mile northeast of downtown, bordered
roughly by Speedway Boulevard to the north, Campbell
Avenue to the east, Sixth Street on the south, and Park
Avenue on the west, but other university buildings extend
far beyond these boundaries. For information on free
campus tours, Tel: 621-3641.

Photography buffs will enjoy the **John P. Schaefer Center for Creative Photography** on the campus of the University of Arizona. Said to be one of the top three photography
museums in the country, the center offers changing exhibitions of famous photographic works. It also houses an
extensive library and archives of negatives and prints for
scholars doing research in the medium. Parking is free on
weekends, but is limited to pay lots on weekdays. It is best
to call for directions; Tel: 621-7968.

PIMA AIR AND SPACE MUSEUM

The Pima Air and Space Museum attracts aviation buffs
from around the world to its collection of 185 aircraft and
the chance to walk through 80 years of American aviation
history. The nonprofit museum boasts the largest private
collection of planes in the country, kept rust free by the
dry desert air; the latest addition is an SR-71 Blackbird
supersonic spy plane. To get to the museum, which is on
the same road as Tucson International Airport, head
south on I-19 or Kino Boulevard, turn east on Valencia
Road, and continue to number 6000.

Around Downtown Tucson

Tucson, best known for the Arizona–Sonora Desert Museum and Old Tucson Studios, is quickly drawing attention with a new attraction: the new and controversial Biosphere 2.

THE ARIZONA – SONORA DESERT MUSEUM

The Arizona–Sonora Desert Museum is really a misnomer, because almost all of its exhibits are alive. It has been called "one of the top ten zoos in the world," and the *New York Times* has labeled it "the most distinctive zoo in the United States." Because the grounds are extensive and there is so much to see, you should allow two to three hours to take it all in. An indoor section houses all the snakes, scorpions, and gila monsters that first timers to the desert fear; you'll find they are just as frightening as you thought they would be.

The outdoor exhibits carefully re-create natural habitats, as real as modern science can make them. They contain warm-blooded species found (or once found) in the desert that covers Arizona and the northern Mexico state of Sonora. Among the many animals are big-horn sheep, river otters, black bears, mountain lions, coatimundi (related to raccoons), ocelots, javalina (pigs), and prairie dogs. There is an extensive collection of rare Western birds, including owls and hawks, and the newest exhibit, an enclosure filled with various species of hummingbirds.

You haven't really visited Tucson until you've seen this remarkable zoo. It is west of the Tucson Mountains, past Old Tucson Studios. Take Speedway Boulevard west past I-10 through the Saguaro National Monument West (for which see below), over Gates Pass. At Kinney Road turn right. The museum is about a 20-minutes' drive from the freeway, at 2021 North Kinney Road; Tel: 883-2702, Fax: 883-2500.

OLD TUCSON STUDIOS

Old Tucson Studios was built during the 1940s as a movie set to re-create 19th-century Tucson. Many Western films have been shot here over the decades, and today it continues to be an active movie location as well as a Western theme park. (The now-defunct television series "Young Riders" was filmed here for the past few years.) Live shows are performed all day: gunfights, magic acts, and dance-hall routines. There are also rides, games for kids, restaurants, and amusing shops. You can tour the sound-stage if it is not in use.

Old Tucson Studios is also on North Kinney, before the Desert Museum, 15 minutes west of I-10 and down-town, either via Speedway Boulevard or Ajo Way. Just follow the signs. Tel: 883-0100 for filming and special-event information.

BIOSPHERE 2

In September 1991 eight scientists were sealed inside a totally closed environment in the desert for a two-year "mission" to do first-person research on the possibility of human life existing in such an environment. The experiment is known as Biosphere 2 (Biosphere 1 is the world we inhabit). The giant three-acre greenhouse in which the Bionauts are living contains seven "biomes," or habitats: a tropical rain forest, a savannah, a marsh, several types of desert, an intensive agricultural area, and a 25-foot-deep "ocean."

Biosphere 2 is fascinating. Approaching the futuristic glass structure, after touring the nearby experimental rain forest and climate-controlled animal pens that were prototypes, is much like nearing a fictional moon base. The walking tour takes you completely around the lab; lucky guests may glimpse one or more of the four men and four women inside doing their daily chores.

Visitors first watch a video explaining the purposes of the mission, its history, and the scientific rationale behind this massive investment: It is said to have cost over $150 million to build and staff. Most of the financing of the for-profit research has come from Texas multimillionaire Ed Bass. The tour leads to the early Test Module, through the various test greenhouses, and up to the huge glass structure. A new viewing gallery gives an underwater glimpse of the live coral reef in the ocean biome.

Life magazine called it "weird science." The *New York Times* said it is "more akin to Noah's Ark than a laboratory," referring to the 3,800 plant and animal species sealed inside. And some call it a cross between "Star Trek" and Disneyland. Nonetheless, during the first year the scientists inside have contributed to the world's understanding of enclosed, self-sustaining systems. Each of the eight has lost weight on an almost completely vegetarian diet. A great deal of attention has been paid to the buildup of carbon dioxide in Biosphere's atmosphere. In the first eight months oxygen dropped from 20.9 percent to 17 percent; the result is similar to moving up a mountain from sea level to an altitude of 9,000 feet.

Biosphere Cafe here is open for breakfast, lunch, and dinner, indoors or on a patio. The patio offers a panoramic view south over the Canyon Del Oro and the north side of the Catalina mountain range. The **Inn at the Biosphere** makes an overnight stay possible—and at an elevation of 3,900 feet this is not a bad idea for a summer visit. Overnight packages are available, including tours, accommodations, and meals; Tel: 825-6200.

The big event here this year will take place at the conclusion of the Bionauts' two-year period of isolation. The "coming-out party" is set for September 27, and will probably generate as much international media attention as the "closure" did in 1991. There will not be any more two-year missions. Future research teams may be sealed inside for only a year at a time or less.

To get to Biosphere 2 from Tucson, take Oracle Road (U.S. 80/89) north about 25 miles (40 km) to Oracle Junction and AZ 77. Keep to the right on AZ 77 toward Oracle. Five miles (8 km) north of the junction is marker 96; continue ½ mile (1 km) to Biosphere 2 Visitor Center Road, marked by a sign on the right. Turn in here and proceed 2 miles (3 km) along a paved road to the entry gate. It is approximately a 45-minute drive from central Tucson.

SAGUARO NATIONAL MONUMENT

This national monument actually includes two geographically separated sections of land: The larger of the two is at the eastern edge of Tucson in the foothills of the Rincon Mountains, the smaller, tucked into Tucson Mountain Park on the western slopes of the Tucson Mountains, which form the western boundary of the city. Known as Saguaro National Monument East and Saguaro National Monument West, the two sections comprise the best stands of saguaro cactus in the state.

TOHONO CHUL PARK

A gentle, educational introduction to the desert, that's what you'll get at Tohono Chul Park, a nonprofit, 37-acre nature preserve on the northwest side of town. The name means "desert corner" in the Tohono O'odham language. Nature trails here wind through natural desert areas to landscaped gardens, a greenhouse of native plants, and a 50-year-old adobe home converted into a **gallery** for Southwestern artists. Regular lectures and classes continue the park's mission of promoting the conservation and understanding of our desert regions. A new "performance garden" with a view of the Catalina Mountains provides an outdoor space under a canopy of trees for lectures, dramas, storytelling, and miniconcerts. (A donation is requested at the gallery.)

A newer building in the park houses a gift shop, filled with distinctive Southwestern art, jewelry, and wearables, and a cozy restaurant, the **Tohono Chul Tearoom**. Managed by Donna Nordin of Cafe Terra Cotta fame (see Dining in Tucson, below), the tearoom is open daily from 8:00 A.M. to 4:45 P.M., serving breakfast and brunch (all day), lunch, and high tea from 2:30 to 4:30; Tel: 797-1711.

To find Tohono Chul Park, head west from the intersection of Ina and Oracle roads (7 miles/11 km due north of downtown). Turn right at the first light onto Paseo del Norte, and continue past the park's exit to number 7366, the next right turn; it is well marked. Tel: 575-8468.

At the eastern edge of the park is one of Tucson's popular bookstores, the **Haunted Bookshop**, at 7211 North Northern Avenue. During the winter they often have book-signing parties for authors presenting new books. Tony Hillerman, for one, comes here from New Mexico to help launch his novels. Tel: 297-4843.

SABINO CANYON

Another great introduction to the area's wildlife, scenic, tree-lined Sabino Canyon has been preserved in its natural state (except for the nearly four miles of paved road) inside a section of the Coronado National Forest. (Take Speedway Boulevard east to Wilmot Road, turn left and take the right branch—Tanque Verde Road—to Sabino Canyon Road. Turn left and follow the road to the visitors' center.) Sabino Creek runs year-round over water-carved rocks; an open-air shuttle trundles visitors up the canyon and back every day of the year. The narrated tour takes 45 minutes and provides a fascinating look at this rare riparian area. From April through June and September through December, the shuttle goes on moonlight rides on the three nights of the full moon; Tel: 749-2327.

Mission San Xavier del Bac

The first Spanish missionary to visit this area was Jesuit Padre Eusebio Francisco Kino (see also Tubac and Tumacacori, in the Southern Arizona section, below). During the 1680s Kino gradually worked his way up from northern Mexico, bringing Roman Catholicism to the peaceful Indians living in the Santa Cruz River Valley. In 1692, at the invitation of the Pima Indians, the padre travelled down the Santa Cruz River from the settlement at Tumacacori to the Pima Indian village of Bac. With their support and encouragement, the foundation for Mission San Xavier del Bac was laid on April 28, 1700.

Historians disagree on whether the church was built on the site where today's mission stands, or if it was actually a few miles north. In any event, the original building no longer exists; the church we see today was begun by Franciscan missionaries in 1783, and took 14 years to build. (All Jesuits had been expelled from the Spanish empire by King Carlos III in 1767.) For 210 years "the White Dove of the Desert" has been a witness to Arizona history: the Spanish dominion over the native peoples, Mexico's throwing off of Spanish rule, the confiscation of all church property by Mexico in 1829, the war between the United States and Mexico in 1846, and the Gadsden Purchase in 1853, which added this northern slice of Mexico to the United States.

Mission San Xavier's fascinating history is covered thoroughly by Bernice Cosulich in her book *Tucson* (see the Bibliography). The church stands virtually isolated in the northeastern corner of the San Xavier Indian Reservation south of downtown Tucson. It is easy to find; just follow Mission Road south from either Ajo Way or Valencia Road and turn left at the sign. The stark white structure, clearly visible from Mission Road, is especially impressive at sunset. Or take I-10 south to the I-19 turnoff (head south to Nogales), exit at Valencia Road, head west to Mission Road, and turn left.

Thanks to a local fund-raising effort the mission has been undergoing a much-needed renovation. (Because it is still an active church, public funds are not available.) The roof has been recently stabilized, and the ornate interior frescoes cleaned by a team of experts from Italy. A recorded message in English gives the history of the mission for visitors. There is also a new museum, but it is open only on Saturdays and Sundays from 8:00 A.M. to 4:30 P.M.

San Xavier's patron day is December 2, and the annual San Xavier Pageant and Fiesta is held on April 24; ceremonies and pageantry mark both days. In April local Indian tribes re-create the coming of the Spanish missionaries in a silent tableau illuminated by the light of many bonfires; for a fee the public is invited to observe. Catholic mass is held in the church every Sunday and on religious holidays; Tel: 294-2624 for information. Indian jewelry and crafts are available in the little plaza south of the parking lot. On weekends food stalls are set up under mesquite-wood *ramadas,* where vendors sell chili, tacos, and "Papago popovers" (hot Indian fry bread).

Ansel Adams cautioned: "Photographing San Xavier del Bac can start as a half-hour making snapshots and end as a lifetime pursuit; photographers are warned!"

Seasonal Events in Tucson

The Metropolitan Tucson Convention & Visitors Bureau lists more than 117 scheduled annual events in its Official Visitors Guide, not counting the performance schedules of the Arizona Theatre Company (October–May), the Arizona Opera Company (October–March), the Tucson Symphony Orchestra (October–May), the Southern Arizona Light Opera Company (September–May), and Ballet Arizona (October–April).

The one event for which Tucson is most famous is the annual four-day **Fiesta de los Vaqueros**, which always begins on the last Thursday in February. Kicked off Thursday morning by the nation's longest nonmotorized parade, with horses, buggies, stagecoaches, Conestoga wagons, and marchers in Old West costumes, this colorful celebration is a photographer's delight. Afternoons Thursday through Sunday feature the winter's largest outdoor rodeo, held at the Tucson Rodeo Grounds, south of I-10 on Sixth Avenue. Cowboys compete in bareback riding, bull riding, calf roping, and other events. All of Tucson gets into the rodeo spirit during Fiesta. Citizens not wearing cowboy garb may get thrown in the hoosegow and displayed as renegades until they pay a fine or until the vigilantes relent. For a copy of the Fiesta brochure or for ticket information, Tel: 741-2233.

The city's largest event, attracting up to 30,000 people from around the world, is the annual **Gem & Mineral Show**, held sometime around the third week in February. Much of it is exclusively for wholesalers who come to wheel and deal, but the Tucson Convention Center is open to the public with acres of displays and booths providing a fascinating look at the world of rocks, fossils, geodes, crystals, precious stones, and colored gemstones of all sorts; Tel: 791-4266.

The Weiser Lock Copper Bowl football game, broadcast

nationwide, is played the last week of December in the University of Arizona stadium; Tel: 790-5510.

Top names on the PGA pro circuit, around 150 of them, come to Tucson for the annual Northern Telecom Open. The event is usually held at the Tucson National Golf and Conference Resort in January; Tel: 792-4501 or (800) 882-7660.

Year-round, every weekend, you'll find something going on in Tucson or in one of the surrounding towns. Activities slow down a bit during the summer and pick up during the fall and winter.

Staying in Tucson

If you don't count government as an industry, then tourism is Tucson's largest and most important business. About one in five Tucsonans works directly or indirectly in the hospitality field. This means there are myriad choices of places to stay, certainly more per capita than most cities, and for this reason there is something for everyone.

At the top, so far as price is concerned, are three major resorts, followed by two older resorts in the next price range. There are also guest ranches and a health-and-beauty spa on the outskirts of town, two classic hotels in town, and the new phenomenon, at least for Tucson, the bed-and-breakfast inn.

And the next wave in the tourism cycle waits in the wings. The Tucson National Resort and Spa, site of the PGA Tucson Open, has been purchased, saved from bankruptcy, and the new owners are considering the addition of 100 more rooms and new meeting space. Starr Pass golf course also has new owners, who have announced that a guest ranch will open in their Tucson Mountains development some time this year. Hyatt and Stouffers have both made agreements with major Tucson landholders and have new destination resorts on the drawing boards.

The tourist season in Tucson runs from October through May, with the highest rates from January through April. Luckily for the visitor, the hotel business in Tucson is quite competitive, and there are usually accommodations in every price range available year-round.

Because summer is the off-season in Tucson, hotels and resorts offer bargain rates then to generate business. The same room that sells for $200 in the peak season can be had in summer for $75, and often with amenities not even offered in the winter. These add-ons vary each year and at each property, but they may include a complimentary breakfast, a margarita at check in, a free second round of golf (summer golfers tee off early in the morning), or coupon books good for discounts and freebies around the resort. If you're planning an off-season visit call around in advance to determine the best summer deals.

The telephone area code for Tucson and vicinity is 602.

The Resorts

The three big destination resorts are the Loews Ventana Canyon Resort, the Westin La Paloma Resort, and the Sheraton El Conquistador Resort and Country Club. Each has between 400 and 500 rooms, and during the winter season all cater to conventions from back East. (Their dining facilities are discussed below under Dining in Tucson.)

Loews Ventana Canyon Resort opened in 1984 on what was once the Flying V cattle ranch, northeast of downtown. Tucked into the foothills near the east end of the Santa Catalina Mountains, beneath a desert waterfall and overlooking the city of Tucson, Loews wins the critics' award for architecture with its stark, dark, Frank Lloyd Wright look. The golf course, carved from the high, cactus-covered foothills, features demanding carryovers and narrow fairways lined with rocks and stately saguaros.

To get to Loews from downtown, take Speedway Boulevard east to its intersection with Craycroft Road. Turn left and follow Craycroft past its intersection with Sunrise Drive. About 2½ miles (4 km) past Sunrise you'll see a large boulder with Ventana Canyon Resort carved on it. The hotel will be on your left, up Resort Drive (in actuality, their driveway). Valet parking is available at the front entrance, self-parking is on the left as you approach the main building, in front of the ballrooms, or back by the Flying V Nightclub.

7000 North Resort Drive, 85715. Tel: 299-2020 or (800) 234-5117; Fax: 299-6832. $105–$325.

The **Westin La Paloma Resort**, situated about halfway between Campbell Avenue and Swan Road on East Sunrise Drive a few miles west of Loews, was the last of the big three to be built (in 1986). An example of Southwestern Mission Revival architecture, the Westin looks out over Tucson from a spectacular vantage point with views of the city below and the Catalina Mountains to the north. The spacious lobby and public areas feature impressive paintings and sculpture by local artists. Four of the 12 tennis courts are clay. For golfers the Westin is Mecca, thanks to the challenging 27-hole course designed by Jack Nicklaus.

To get to Westin La Paloma, take Speedway Boulevard east to Swan Road. Turn left and head north to Sunrise Drive, and take another left turn (west). Go approximately 2 miles (3 km). At the stoplight (at Via Palomita), a left turn will take you right into the resort.

3800 East Sunrise Drive, 85718. Tel: 742-6000 or (800) 876-3683; Fax: 577-5878. $150–$340.

The architecture of the **Sheraton El Conquistador Resort and Country Club** blends Spanish, Mexican, and Indian influences, and its spacious lobby holds the largest copper mural in the country. The only major resort in Tucson with riding stables on the property, it also has the most extensive golf facilities; with the acquisition of El Conquistador Country Club the Sheraton now offers 45 holes of golf, 31 tennis courts, and two complete fitness centers.

The Sheraton is some 10 miles (16 km) north of Tucson in the town of Oro Valley. Take Oracle Road (U.S. 80/89) north to El Conquistador Way, the first light after Calle Concordia (and three traffic lights after the Ina Road intersection). Take a right turn into the resort's driveway and head toward the towering Pusch Ridge cliffs and the resort.

10000 North Oracle Road, 85737. Tel: 544-5000 or (800) 325-7832; Fax: 544-1224. $80–$180.

Just below these three, in size and price, are two older resorts that are just as comfortable and well run. For the traveller who has visited La Costa Spa north of San Diego, **Tucson National Golf & Conference Resort** may give a sense of déjà vu. The way the clubhouse is situated at the west end of a valley containing a championship golf course is remarkably similar.

For 15 years Tucson National, on the northwest side of town, hosted the PGA Tucson Open every January. The tournament then moved for several years to Randolph Park, the city's downtown golf course. Now it is back at Tucson National.

A major remodeling during the 1980s modernized the 170-room Tucson National, and expanded the spa facilities. Five-day golf schools are held here from October through April, and a number of golf and spa packages are offered year-round. Again, the bargain rates are in the summertime.

Tucson National's dining room, open to the public, offers a comfortable introduction to the resort. To get there, take Oracle Road (U.S. 80/89) north to Ina Road. Turn left and follow Ina to La Cholla Boulevard. Turn right and go past the Foothills Mall to Magee Road, where a left turn will take you to Shannon Road. Turn right on Shannon and ¼ mile (½ km) uphill the first right turn will be into the resort.

2727 West Club Drive, 85741. Tel: 297-2271 or (800) 528-4856; Fax: 297-7544. $85–$205.

The fifth resort does not offer golf, but is known for its tennis facilities and professional instruction. *Tennis* magazine lists it as one of the top 50 tennis resorts in the country. **Westward Look Resort** is situated at the west end of the Catalina foothills overlooking Tucson, west of the Westin La Paloma and a few blocks east of Oracle Road.

The Spanish-style architecture of "the Look," primarily one-story stucco buildings, the lush plantings of palms and bougainvillaea, and the casual atmosphere give visitors the feeling they are guests at a large, comfortable Mexican hacienda. The **Gold Room**, the resort's main dining room, has a reputation for fine Continental food and a great view of the city. Casual dress is acceptable at the Gold Room, but evening reservations are suggested.

245 East Ina Road, 85704. Tel: 297-1151 or (800) 722-2500; Fax: 297-9023. $60–$110.

Hacienda-style Hotels

After Jack Greenway died in Ajo in 1926 (see the Southern Arizona section, below) his young widow, Isabella, came to Tucson, where she set up a rehabilitation clinic for World War I veterans who had suffered lung damage from mustard gas. To keep busy and to earn their keep the men made wooden furniture. Over the years the clinic became **The Arizona Inn**, at 2200 East Elm Street, and many of the 80 rooms are furnished with the tables and chairs hand-crafted by those wounded doughboys.

The Arizona Inn is the only hotel in Tucson on the National Register of Historic Places and the only one with any real feel of history. It covers one square block, a complex of two-story pink stucco buildings enclosing 14 acres of lawns and carefully tended gardens. It boasts one of Tucson's few clay tennis courts and a private (guests only) swimming pool. Located in a quiet residential neighborhood north of Speedway Boulevard and east of Campbell Avenue, just two blocks east of the University Medical Center, the inn can best be described as serene. The subdued dining room is open to the public for three meals a day, and is popular among university professors and Tucson business leaders.

2200 East Elm Street, 85719. Tel: 325-1541 or (800) 933-1093; Fax: 881-5830. $88–$162.

The other choice in Mexican hacienda style is **The Lodge on the Desert**, on North Alvernon Way a few blocks north of Broadway. Before Tucson expanded so much, the 40-room lodge used to be out in the desert east of town, and it still has that casual, guest-ranch feeling. It also has lawns, gardens, and a pool enclosed in a private space. Extended-stay rates are available.

306 North Alvernon Way, 85711. Tel: 325-3366 or (800) 456-5634; Fax: 327-5834. $54–$171.

Guest Ranches

Tucson used to be the hub of dozens of guest ranches, scattered outside the city and throughout southern Arizona. Today only a few are left. The grande dame of the survivors is the **Tanque Verde Guest Ranch**, in the foothills of the Rincon Mountains east of town. Established in 1868 as a working cattle ranch, Tanque Verde claims to have the largest riding stable in Arizona and, with 100 horses, probably does. The ranch offers swimming, tennis, and nature programs (it adjoins the Coronado National Forest), but is best known for its morning breakfast ride. Guests rise early, mount their horses, and ride into the desert to a cookout site where wranglers have prepared a cowboy breakfast over an open campfire.

Not much in Tucson predates 1868, so the sense of history here, preserved in the adobe ranch house and guest *casitas* (little houses), is very apparent. At the same time, owner-manager Bob Cote has modernized the kitchen, dining room, and accommodations to offer the latest in comfort and cleanliness. Even an indoor health spa has been added. Tanque Verde is popular with Europeans, some of whom return year after year for the gourmet dining, the clear desert air, and the opportunity to re-create life in the Old West.

14301 East Speedway Boulevard, 85748. Tel: 296-6275 or (800) 234-3833; Fax: 721-9426. $250–$320, includes meals, horseback riding, and activities.

A bit west of Tanque Verde, closer to the city, **Canyon Ranch Spa** is tucked into the foothills of the Catalina Mountains, south of Sabino Canyon. This luxury health resort, for three consecutive years voted "Best Spa" by the readers of *Condé Nast Traveler* magazine, offers a wide choice of indoor and outdoor fitness activities, relaxing personal services, and innovative stress-reduction programs. Guests at Canyon Ranch can avail themselves of a complete preventive health program administered by a staff of physicians, exercise physiologists, psychologists, and dietitians. The minimum stay is usually one week. The menu in the restaurant does not list prices—those numbers are calories.

8600 East Rockcliff Road, 85715. Tel: 749-9000; Fax: 749-7755. Standard 8-day, 7-night Total Lifestyle Plan: $2,810 (single); $2,290 (double). Rates drop in summer.

The **White Stallion Ranch** is at the opposite end of Tucson, in the far northwest, tucked behind the north end of the Tucson Mountains. This is an active 3,000-acre cattle ranch, with a herd of Texas longhorns, that happens to take in guests. It has 28 rooms—mostly freestanding units—a heated pool, and a former ranch house converted into a dining-and-recreation center. Meals are served family style at long tables, and one night a week the meat is cooked outdoors in an Indian "beehive" oven. Most guests stay for a week or more to enjoy the horseback riding, tennis, volleyball, swimming, rodeos, hayrides, and cookouts here. The ranch adjoins the western section of the Saguaro National Monument, so the mountain and desert views are uninterrupted.

9251 West Twin Peaks Road, 85743. Tel: 297-0252 or (800) 782-5546; Fax: 744-2786. $198–$288, includes meals, horseback riding, and ranch activities. Closed summers.

A guest ranch at Tucson makes a good base of operations if you choose to explore southern Arizona in a series of day trips. For a more complete list of area guest ranches, contact the Metropolitan Tucson Convention & Visitors Bureau; Tel: 624-1817.

Bed-and-Breakfast Inns

Bed-and-breakfast accommodations are a relatively new facet of tourism in southern Arizona. The first one opened in Tucson in 1987, and since then they have been popping up all over town. The best ones offer the comforts of home in a historic setting administered by a dedicated owner-manager. Three of Tucson's centrally located bed and breakfasts are in the university area.

La Posada del Valle (The Inn of the Valley) was the first to open, in 1987, at the corner of Campbell Avenue and

Elm Street, north of the campus and directly across from the University Medical Center. This spacious home was built in 1929 by Josias T. Joesler, who created his own architectural blend of Spanish Colonial and Territorial styles. (It has been copied by Southwestern architects ever since.) Each of the five guest rooms is named after a famous woman of the 1920s—Zelda's room, Isadora's room—and has decor to match. The high-ceilinged living room also acts as a library for guests, and a full breakfast is served in the sunny, north-facing dining room. The flower-filled patio and garden are so picturesque that they are often used for weddings and receptions.

1640 North Campbell Avenue, 85719. Tel: 795-3840. $60–$115.

Less than two blocks from the main gate to the University of Arizona is **Peppertrees Bed & Breakfast Inn**. The proprietor, Marjorie Martin, recently published a cookbook of her own bed-and-breakfast recipes. Guests here may find themselves experimented upon at breakfast as she tests new culinary delights for future editions. The two-story redbrick building was thought to have been built in 1905, but while doing research at the Arizona Historical Society Mrs. Martin found a scratched old photo of the home dated 1902. The main house has two rooms; behind it, past the trickling fountain, are two new two-bedroom apartments.

724 East University Boulevard, 85719. Tel: 622-7167 or (800) 348-5763. $78.

On the east side of the university campus a newly opened bed and breakfast, **The Brimstone Butterfly**, sits on a quiet, tree-shaded street in the Sam Hughes residential neighborhood. The 1930s-era adobe home has been remodeled into a spacious, three-room accommodation with its own private swimming pool. Each room has its own bath. Activities are supervised by one or more cats. A gourmet breakfast is served in the roomy kitchen, under the bougainvillaea out by the pool, or in your room. Owner Maria (pronounced "muh-RYE-uh") Johnstone is also a licensed masseuse; guests may make an appointment for a massage, and also avail themselves of her membership in the Tucson Racquet Club.

940 North Olsen Avenue, 85719. Tel: 322-9157. $59–$95.

A bit of Bavaria has been transported to the west side of town, just to the north of "A" Mountain in Sentinel Peak Park, west of I-10. Gertrude and Hans Herbert Kraus, recent immigrants from Germany, run the **Copper Bell**

Bed & Breakfast, an unusual, lava-rock mansion on Westmoreland Avenue that was just what the couple had been looking for to convert into an inn. Its tall two stories tower over the neighbors' houses in this older, Hispanic neighborhood. Remodel is not the word; resurrect was closer to the job the Krauses faced with this long-abandoned hulk. Now it is a charming five-room accommodation filled with European furnishings and Gertrude's stained glass. Guests may choose their style of breakfast—French, German, or American—and savor the secret-recipe café Vienna served in porcelain cups.

25 North Westmoreland Avenue, 85745. Tel: 629-9229. $65.

Farther west, behind the Tucson Mountains, is the new **Rancho Quieto** (pronounced "kee-EH-toh"). It means "quiet, tranquil, or still," and is a bilingual pun on the owner-innkeeper's name, Corinne Still. The three-unit inn is difficult to describe. It is an outsize, two-story mansion set in the middle of 40 acres of desert, seemingly built to one and a half scale. Huge, rough-hewn beams support the saguaro-rib ceilings, and the exterior is stuccoed like the Taos Pueblo. Three pool areas offer quiet retreats, while balconies and porches provide vistas of the endless desert. An artificial watering hole attracts quail, deer, and javalina at sunset. Each suite includes a private bath, a fireplace, and a patio. Full breakfast is included.

12051 West Fort Lowell Road, 85743. Tel: 883-3300. $95–$125.

Thirty-five miles (56 km) north of Tucson, near the town of Oracle, is the **Triangle L Ranch Bed and Breakfast Retreat**. In the 1880s this was a 2,700-acre cattle ranch homesteaded by William Ladd. During the 1920s it became southern Arizona's first guest ranch, where, it is said, Buffalo Bill Cody was a regular guest. Today it is an 80-acre site blessed with Oracle's largest oak trees. Four of the ranch's many buildings have been restored into complete residences, each with its own view and private setting.

Breakfast is served family style in the huge country kitchen of the original ranch house. In winter the old wood-burning stove heats the room. Antique tins and kitchen utensils, and maybe a cat, sit atop the cupboards beneath the high ceiling. Breakfast may include just-laid eggs from the ranch's hens, waffles, pancakes, homemade breads and pastries, and seasonal fruits and juices. Coffee lovers will enjoy the benefits of the espresso machine; aromatic coffee beans are ground, then combined with live steam and boiling milk to produce espresso, cappuccino, and *latte* by request.

Because the Triangle L is a licensed wildlife rehabilitation center, pets are not allowed. Credit cards are not accepted, but the prices here are competitive with area bed and breakfasts. Smoking is permitted only outdoors.

P.O. Box 900, Oracle, 85623. Tel: 896-2804; Fax: 896-9070. $70–$85.

At an elevation of 4,500 feet, **Oracle** is always cooler than Tucson (at 2,400 feet). Summer visitors should consider an overnight in Oracle, either at the Triangle L or in one of the guest units at Biosphere 2 itself, which is situated in Oracle (see Accommodations Reference, below).

For a list of seven top bed and breakfasts in Tucson, send a stamped, self-addressed envelope to Premiere Bed and Breakfast Inns of Tucson, 3661 North Campbell Avenue, Box 237, Tucson, AZ 85719, Tel: 628-1800.

Dining in Tucson

Like Santa Fe, Tucson is becoming known for the variety of its restaurants and the quality of dining options found here. Former mayor Lew Murphy modestly declared Tucson to be "the Mexican Food Capital of the Universe," claiming the collection of restaurants here to be finer than any in Texas, New Mexico, or California—not to mention Mexico itself. The major resorts offer a choice of posh dining rooms, each competitive at international levels. And Tucson is proud to be home to two restaurants nationally acclaimed as among the birthplaces of nouvelle-Southwestern cuisine.

Add to this a broad mix of authentic Western steak houses, Oriental, Italian, French, and American restaurants and it becomes clear that Tucson can satisfy almost any diner.

The Resorts

It is sometimes said that only a fool picks a hotel dining room over an independent restaurant. In Tucson this saying is simply not true. When the first destination resort, the Sheraton, opened in southern Arizona in December 1982 it faced an immense marketing challenge. Arizona already boasted more first-class resorts than any other state—but not in Tucson. The Sheraton El Conquistador Resort and Country Club was designed to lure major convention business to Tucson. To succeed it had to compete with the established resorts in the Phoenix area and the Valley of the Sun, especially in Scottsdale, 100 miles to the north. Not only did it have to offer accommodations, recreation, and dining comparable to (or better than) those well-known hostelries, but it had to sell Tucson itself, a destination blasé meeting planners had never considered before.

Loews and Westin as well as the Sheraton were up to the challenge. Not only are the facilities they built here among the finest in North America, but all three were eventually named in *Condé Nast Traveler*'s first readers' poll of the top 100 resorts/spas/airlines in the world. Moreover, their dining facilities have received as much corporate attention as the architecture, golf courses, and decor. Sheraton immediately hired the chef from the legendary Arizona Biltmore in Phoenix. Loews and Westin brought in their finest culinary teams. So in the decade from 1982 to 1992, while Tucson achieved international acclaim for its magnificent resorts, its dining facilities developed pari passu. (See the Staying in Tucson section, above, for a description of these resorts and their locations.)

Loews Ventana Canyon Resort is the undisputed leader, among the major resorts, in the culinary department. Its **Ventana Room** boasts an elegant ambience, an outstanding Continental menu, and a romantic nighttime view of Tucson's city lights spread out to the south. The mezzanine-level room features a harpist (in high season), waiters in tuxedos, and gold-plated flatware. The prices match the decor, but for a formal, haute cuisine experience in Tucson the Ventana Room is one of the clear choices. Reservations, jacket, and tie are recommended. Loews also boasts one of the most popular Sunday brunches in town, as voted by the readers of *Tucson Weekly*. The service is impeccable and the buffet bountiful. It's best to call by Saturday for reservations; Tel: 299-2020.

The other big resort overlooking Tucson from a vantage in the foothills is the **Westin La Paloma Resort**, a few miles west of Loews. Three dining choices are offered at La Paloma: **La Villa**, specializing in fresh seafood served in a rather stark room with a view of the city lights (dinner only); the **Desert Garden** in the lobby, with a spectacular view of the Catalina Mountains (Tel: 742-6000 for La Villa and Desert Garden); and the dining room of **La Paloma Country Club**. The country club serves three meals a day (closed Sunday and Monday nights), but is exclusive to guests of the hotel and members of the private club; a jacket is required.

The **Sheraton El Conquistador Resort and Country**

Club is a few miles farther west and north. El Conquistador offers five restaurants under chef Alan Zeman (see the next section), including **Dos Locos Cantina** for Mexican food and entertainment and **The Last Territory Steakhouse. The White Dove**, formerly the gourmet dining room, has recently been repositioned as a grill, offering specialty pizzas. The dining room at El Conquistador Country Club, **La Vista** (recently acquired by the Sheraton), is now the posh facility, and showcases Alan Zeman's innovative touch (see below). La Vista is open to the public and its broad windows expose a sweeping panorama of the city, the golf course, and the Tucson Mountains—where the evening may provide a spectacular sunset. Tel: 544-1980.

Nouvelle-Southwestern Cuisine
In 1987 PBS-TV broadcast a 26-week series of cooking programs entitled "Great Chefs of the West," featuring 60 chefs in 16 cities from Texas to California. The television series and the accompanying book, *Southwest Tastes,* heralded the formal coast-to-coast debut of "contemporary Southwestern cuisine," sometimes called nouvelle-Southwestern cuisine. This new style of cooking represented the regional marriage of Southwestern ingredients and traditional dishes primarily with classic French cooking.

Tucson more than held its own in this pantheon of culinary innovators, with five of the 60 chefs practicing their art here in the Old Pueblo. Two remain. Alan Zeman, first in his class at the Culinary Institute of America, was then at the Tucson Country Club and is now executive chef at the Sheraton El Conquistador. All five of the Sheraton's menus reflect Zeman's extraordinary skills in the kitchen.

The other chef, Donna Nordin, holds court at her unusual restaurant, **Café Terra Cotta**, in St. Philip's Plaza. The plaza is in north-central Tucson, Campbell Avenue at River Road at the foot of the Catalina foothills. Nordin, a graduate of the Cordon Bleu school in France, discovered Tucson in 1983 while travelling around the country giving cooking classes. She fell in love with the desert and opened her café in 1986. It features the only wood-burning pizza oven in Tucson along with an imaginative, eclectic menu. A sample entrée from a recent menu: smoked duck mole tacos with pineapple salsa, black beans, and sour cream. As for pastries . . . well, Donna is famous for concoctions like Devine Madness with espresso ice cream. Tel: 577-8100.

One Tucson chef who should have been included

among the Great Chefs of the West is Janos Wilder. Since 1987 he has surpassed the other two in national recognition, both for his nouvelle-Southwestern cuisine and for his restaurant, located in a National Historic Landmark in El Presidio Historic District. The thick-walled adobe building, on the grounds of the Tucson Museum of Art at 150 North Main Avenue, two blocks northwest of the old County Courthouse, was built between 1859 and 1864 as the home of Hiram Stevens, a pioneer businessman.

Wilder opened his restaurant, called simply **Janos**, in 1983 after receiving classical training in France. His menu, which changes daily, features fresh, locally grown ingredients, French-influenced Southwestern dishes, artistic presentations, and rich, imaginative desserts. The wine cellar holds 2,500 bottles of French and California vintages. Janos is open for dinner Monday through Saturday from mid-November through mid-May, and Tuesday through Saturday mid-May through mid-November. Lunch is served only on Christmas, Valentine's Day, and Secretary's Day. Jackets and reservations are recommended; Tel: 884-9426.

Although he won a gold medal from the American Culinary Federation in 1983, Janos's reputation jumped in 1989 when *Travel Holiday* magazine gave him its Fine Dining Award and *Arizona Trend* magazine gave him its second Golden Spoon Award. Then, in 1990, the James Beard Foundation picked Wilder as a Rising Star of American Cuisine and invited him to prepare a Southwestern dinner for the foundation in New York City. In 1992 the national judges of the Fine Dining Awards, the new "Oscars" of culinary excellence, picked Wilder as one of the top 12 chefs in the United States, and listed Janos as one of the top eight contemporary restaurants in the country.

No list of fine restaurants in Tucson is complete without **The Tack Room**. Originally a home, built in 1938, the property became the Rancho Del Rio resort in 1946; what is now the restaurant was the resort's private dining room. Opened as a separate, fine-dining restaurant in January 1965, the Tack Room sits on a hilltop in a peaceful, 30-acre grove of mesquite trees on the northeastern edge of Tucson at 2800 North Sabino Canyon Road between Tanque Verde Road and the Tanque Verde Wash.

The list of awards, local and national, that the Tack Room has won fills a page and goes back over 16 years. The restaurant is in a class by itself. The wine cellar holds 10,000 bottles, some 40 years old. The à la carte menu is traditional American and Continental, with Southwestern accents. Escargots and Caesar salad lead, for example, into veal Cortez, sautéed au naturel and garnished with bay scallops sautéed in lime and cilantro, all served with asparagus spears and sauce Sonora.

Part of the secret of the Tack Room's classic soups, sauces, and coffee is the water pumped from its own deep wells. Reservations and jackets are recommended (as are deep pockets for paying the bill); Tel: 722-2800.

As this edition went to press, the Distinguished Restaurants of North America announced their awards for 1992–1993. Only five restaurants in Arizona met the strict judging criteria, three in Phoenix and two in Tucson: Janos and the Tack Room.

"The Mexican Food Capital of the Universe"

Tucson devotees of authentic Mexican cooking were aghast when, in 1991, the local press gleefully reported the results of a Mexican-restaurant poll in Phoenix. The Phoenicians had voted a Taco Bell as the best Mexican restaurant in the Valley of the Sun. Cynics announced that people "up there" either had no taste or no good Mexican restaurants.

Tucsonans are justifiably proud of their Mexican cuisine. Former mayor Lew Murphy's declaration that Tucson is the "Mexican Food Capital of the Universe" during a celebratory cooking competition among local restaurants a few years ago led to a contest among Albuquerque, Santa Fe, and other cities irked by the mayor's declaration. But the contest did not go well and will not be reported here. (Who ever heard of escargot tacos, anyway? We are talking authentic.)

The *Tucson Citizen* lists eight Mexican establishments among its editors' choices of the best restaurants in town. The enjoyment of Mexican food is so subjective that this list is as representative as any. Four of the eight are found in the one-square-mile town of **South Tucson**, a separate, mainly Hispanic municipality straddling Sixth Avenue south of 22nd Street. The others are scattered around the city.

Three of the South Tucson four are along Fourth Avenue, south of 22nd Street. First comes **Mi Nidito** (My Little Nest) at 1813 South Fourth Avenue. It is small, usually crowded, short on parking, and authentic in its cuisine. This is the real thing—Sonoran cooking from the northern Mexico state bordering Arizona. Tel: 622-5081. Next, at number 2602, is the **Crossroads**, a South Tucson landmark. Try the shrimp *al mojo de ajo;* Tel: 624-0395.

Farther south, at 2908, is **Micha's**, known for its *chimi-*

changas. (A *burro* is a large, soft flour tortilla wrapped around some kind of filling and served like a package on your plate. If you order it enchilada style it will come with spicy red sauce slathered over it. A burrito is a small *burro*. A *chimichanga* is a *burro* that has been quickly deep fried to give it a crisp crust, and can also be ordered enchilada style.) The content of *burros* and *chimichangas* varies by season and by choice. It may be green chili, red chili, *machaca* (dried, shredded beef), frijoles (refried beans), or various combinations. Micha's "chimis" are so large they can easily serve two people, especially if the meal begins with an appetizer, a large cheese crisp, or a bowl of traditional *menudo* (spicy tripe soup). Mexican restaurants are not known for their salads, except the *topopo* salad, which is like a Mexican chef's salad with chicken or shrimp, tomatoes, avocados, and more. Tel: 623-5307.

The fourth South Tucson choice is on one of the cross streets: **El Torero** (The Bullfighter), at 231 East 26th Street. As you head south on Fourth Avenue, about half a block before 26th Street watch for a sign saying Next Right, El Torero. Turn at the corner and look to the right. Set back off the north side of the street, next to the Stardust Ballroom, is the restaurant, hidden under a giant purple bougainvillaea vine. At El Torero try the summer *topopo* salad, the grilled shrimp taco salad, the shrimp platter Veracruz style, or La Bandera (The Flag), which is three enchiladas (red chili, green chili, and cheese) with refried beans and a flour tortilla; Tel: 622-9534.

The main attraction in South Tucson is the **Tucson Greyhound Park** racetrack, and a Mexican dinner nearby can be a prelude to going to the dogs. Every Wednesday through Sunday lean greyhounds race around the $\frac{5}{16}$-mile track in a little over 30 seconds, chasing a fast-moving "bone." (It used to be an artificial rabbit, but animal-rights activists had it replaced with the phony bone. It is, however, still called Sparky.) Lunch and dinner are served at the park, 2601 South Third Avenue at 36th Street. Upstairs is the glass-enclosed, air-conditioned **Clubhouse**, which holds up to 600 people. The menu features sandwiches, salads, and American and Mexican entrées. Betting is legal and the windows where you place your wagers are right there. The dogs race afternoons and evenings year-round. Tel: 884-7576.

El Charro, at 311 North Court Avenue in El Presidio Historic District, has been a Tucson tradition since 1922.

The home of a French stonemason, Jules Le Flein, in the 1880s, the restaurant was founded by his eldest daughter. It is run today by her grandniece, Carlotta Dunn Flores, and Carlotta's husband, Ray. If you glance up at the entrance you'll see 50 pounds of beef sun-drying in a bird-proof cage on the roof. The beef becomes El Charro's famous *carne seca*. The restaurant serves its own Tucson-style Mexican cuisine and claims to be the originator of the *chimichanga*. Tel: 622-5465.

Of all the Mexican restaurants we suggest, the one with the best combination of atmosphere and food is easily **La Fuente**. Located at 1749 North Oracle Road, a few blocks north of Speedway Boulevard and less than 1 mile (1½ km) east of I-10, La Fuente is the place for people who have time for only one Mexican restaurant during their visit to Tucson. The food is authentic, and every night a mariachi band plays traditional Mexican music. The decor features old photos of Pancho Villa, bullfight posters, and lots of hanging plants. This is one Mexican place that will take reservations—and they are advised; Tel: 623-8659.

The Molina family has run Mexican restaurants in Tucson for years. They are all good. The *Citizen* says the **Molina Midway**, at 1138 North Belvedere Avenue, is the best of the bunch. (Belvedere runs north from Speedway, midway between Columbus Boulevard and Swan Road.) Try the giant cheese crisp before dinner; Tel: 325-9957.

Number eight on our list is different from the others. **La Parrilla Suiza** does not serve Sonoran dishes, but specializes in Mexico City cuisine. It also features a wood-burning grill inside. Located at 5602 East Speedway just east of Craycroft; Tel: 747-4838.

There are any number of additional Mexican restaurants that could be added to this list: The Metropolitan Tucson Convention & Visitors Bureau lists 25 of them among its members, including **El Minuto Cafe**, across the street to the south of the Tucson Convention Center, at 354 South Main (corner of Cushing Street). El Minuto used to be a little family joint serving homemade Sonoran-style food. Then a national magazine quoted Linda Ronstadt as saying it was her favorite place to eat in Tucson, and it had to expand and remodel to handle the increased traffic. The food is still good, but Linda hasn't been spotted there lately. Tel: 882-4145.

One Mexican restaurant is famous not so much for its food but for its music: Back in 1983 Tucson managed to lure the International Mariachi Conference away from San Antonio, Texas—took it and ran with it. Held each year in April, the highly successful conference at that time included musical workshops, a Garibaldi Fiesta, and a competition. Mariachi groups from all over the world came to compete for the title of best band. And each year the same Tucson group, Mariachi America, walked away with the first prize. After several years, when it became clear that no band was ever going to beat them, the annual competition was eliminated and the title retired. Now the annual event features a showcase of mariachi bands instead. (The highlight for the past few years has been the appearance of Linda Ronstadt, the daughter of an old Tucson family, singing "Canciones de Mi Padre" on stage with her father.)

All this by way of introducing **El Mariachi Restaurant**, at 106 West Drachman Street, between Stone Avenue and Oracle Road. At Drachman, the first light north of Speedway and Stone, turn left; the restaurant is on the north side of the street. Mariachi America is alive and well here and plays their "world-acclaimed" music Wednesday through Sunday evenings. Try the tequila shrimp, the green corn tamales, or the mesquite-broiled steaks. Reservations are recommended, especially on weekends; Tel: 791-7793.

Steak Houses

There are at least a dozen good steak houses in Tucson, many which cook their meats over a roaring mesquite-wood fire. The flavor imparted by the mesquite smoke enhances the meats so effectively that Arizona mesquite wood is now shipped all over the country to steak houses striving to be the best. The following three use mesquite fires.

The one with the history is **Li'l Abner's Steak House**, northwest of town at 8500 North Silverbell Road. Take I-10 west (you'll be heading north) to the Ina Road exit. Turn left toward the Tucson Mountains and right at the first stop sign. That's Silverbell. Li'l Abner's claims to be the site of a Butterfield Stagecoach stop back in the 1880s. Dean Armstrong and his country band play outdoors on the patio; Tel: 744-2800.

The one with the best meats is said to be **The Last Territory Steakhouse** on the grounds of the Sheraton El Conquistador Resort. Credit Chef Alan Zeman for selecting only the choicest cuts. Live country music is played here most nights for listening and dancing; Tel: 544-1738.

For the best prices try **Pinnacle Peak**, at 6541 East Tanque Verde Road between Pima and Grant roads. The main attraction of Trail Dust Town, a re-creation of a 19th-century Western street, the busy restaurant is rumored to be owned by a cattle company that brings the fresh steaks and ribs directly from its own ranch. Dinner is served family style at picnic tables, and the huge room is always crowded. Any dude foolish enough to wear a necktie will find it quickly cut off and pinned to the ceiling. Dress is, as you can imagine, casual. Reservations are recommended; Tel: 296-0911.

Other Dining

The Visitors Bureau counts 158 restaurants among its members, and those are the better establishments in town. Serious diners might consider stopping in at the Visitors' Center at 130 South Scott Avenue to pick up a free copy of the Official Visitors Guide, which lists all 158 establishments, with capsule comments and hours. And the monthly *Tucson Lifestyle* magazine always contains an up-to-date restaurant guide.

Vegetarians often have difficulties finding places to eat that meet their needs. Here are two of Tucson's best vegetarian restaurants:

The Good Earth Restaurant & Bakery is in El Mercado at the southeast corner of Wilmot Road and East Broadway, Tucson's eastern center. This popular choice for healthy dining in Tucson is a spinoff, owned and operated by a former executive of the national chain by the same name. Open seven days a week, it serves three meals a day following its own strict rules: no bleached flour, no manufactured chemicals, no refined sugar, no frying, and no pipes or cigars allowed in the smoking section. Breakfast omelets are baked instead of fried, bread is ten-grain or whole grain, and a number of vegetarian dishes are available.

Many entrées are prepared quickly in a wok. The earth burger is a huge, juicy, meatless "hamburger" made of nuts, grains, azuki beans, mushrooms, and exotic spices. The menu features pages of unusual dishes with unusual names, an adventure in culinary reading. Malaysian cashew chicken and various curries lead to more familiar-sounding entrées prepared with a Good Earth twist. Salt-free and wheat-free meals are available on request. Natural fruit shakes, yogurts, and baked-on-site muffins make special desserts. The restaurant does not take reservations for less than eight, and does not accept credit cards. It has a very loyal local clientele and gets crowded at mealtimes; it's best to go early or late to avoid a wait. Tel: 745-6600.

Another, smaller restaurant also offers vegetarian choices among a broader menu. **The Garland Restaurant**, in an old home at 119 East Speedway just east of Stone Avenue and west of the university, is a funky little place reminiscent of Berkeley, California. Garland serves breakfast, lunch, and dinner, with a range of dishes from quiche and brown rice, soups, salads, and sandwiches to crepes, pasta, and Mexican selections. Asterisks dotting the menu indicate which item can be prepared without the use of any animal products. To further reassure vegetarian customers, the menu states that "our meats are separately prepared and stored." Tel: 792-4221.

Nightlife in Tucson

Perhaps because of the high percentage of retirees here, nightlife in Tucson places more emphasis on dining than dancing. Steak houses offer country music; Mexican restaurants have mariachis; sports bars serve continuous televised athletic events with their beer and burgers. But where do the young people go?

Country music is very popular here. The number one local radio station plays only country. The biggest nightclub in town—they say it's the biggest in the Southwest—is the new **Wild Wild West** restaurant and nightclub, less than 1 mile (1½ km) east of I-10 at 4385 West Ina Road. It boasts "an acre of dancin' & romancin.'" With a racetrack dance floor, free buffet meals, games, pool tables, and an old-time photo parlor, it's really a country-and-Western mall. Sometimes WWW books big-name performers and sells tickets. Tel: 744-7744.

Watching couples dance country swing to live music can be almost as much fun as doing it yourself. A popular spot for those who know how is the **Cactus Moon Cafe** at 5470 East Broadway, on the east side of town. They offer dining and dancing with a Southwestern spirit all evening long. Tel: 748-0049.

The top local bands in Tucson perform at the **Club Congress**, at 311 East Congress off the lobby of the Hotel Congress, the heartbeat of the Arts District downtown. There is free parking at the Southern Pacific station across Toole Avenue from the hotel. Naked Prey, One Blood, and others pack the small club and send their rock and reggae beats through the little hotel and out onto the sidewalk. There is a cover charge; Tel: 622-8848.

College students and young professionals frequent **Gentle Ben's Brewing Company**, a restaurant/bar with live music every Friday night near the university campus. An outdoor patio invites leisurely listening while savoring the proprietor's home brews. The music is primarily reggae but varies to include blues, jazz, and soft rock. The beers, brewed on the premises, include Red Cat Amber, Copperhead, and Tucson Blonde. The address is 841 North Tyndall Avenue, near University Boulevard and the west entrance to the campus; Tel: 624-4177.

The oldest bar in the city is said to be **The Shanty**. At the corner of Ninth Street and Fourth Avenue, it qualifies for inclusion in the Tucson Arts District. Tucson's literati hang out here and sample the widest selection of beers in town, domestic and imported.

Entertainment

In addition to the Arizona Theatre Company, mentioned above, there are at least half a dozen other permanent troupes in Tucson, some of which offer performances year-round. The more visible companies are the Borderlands Theatre, the a.k.a. Theatre, Arizona Children's Theatre Company, the Invisible Theatre, and the Dazart Theatre Company. Check the newspaper for current performances.

One acting troupe that operates year-round on its own permanent stage is **The Gaslight Theatre** at 7010 East Broadway, east of Wilmot Road. This is melodrama at its corniest, funny and fun. Each play—they change every few months—is a spoof of one genre or another. It might be a takeoff on Sherlock Holmes, Indiana Jones, Zorro, or rock 'n' roll, and it is always clean humor (appropriate for the whole family). Every night is a sellout, so reservations are a must; Tel: 886-9428. The theatre is dark Mondays and Tuesdays.

Shopping in Tucson

Tucson is not the place to buy designer gowns or trendy Neiman Marcus outfits. (Tucsonans drive up to Scottsdale if they want such stuff.) Perhaps because salaries are low in southern Arizona, shopping tilts toward the bargain end of the price range. Factory outlets are popular.

A number of resale places, many along **North Fourth Avenue**, do quite well selling used clothing, furniture, and toys. Although Fourth Avenue is on the wrong side of the tracks, its merchants insist on being considered part of the Tucson Arts District. The area is west of the university, between the campus and downtown. One of the nicer resale shops, at 531 North Fourth Avenue, **How Sweet It Was** offers clothing, accessories, and textiles from the late 1800s to the 1960s. Goods are not only sold, but bought, too. Tel: 623-9854.

About 60 miles (96 km) north of Tucson in Casa Grande, along the west side of I-10 on the way to Phoenix, is the new strip of **Casa Grande Factory Stores**. Look for exit 194. Thirty-seven brand-name outlets offer 20 to 70 percent off retail prices every day. Nationally known manufacturers of footwear, fashions, leather goods, and gifts sell directly to the consumer here; Tel: 421-0112. Hungry shoppers can refuel at the Yogurt House Eatery. Sixty miles is a long way to go to shop, no matter what the discounts, so a stop here might best be incorporated into a trip to or from Phoenix.

Malls in Tucson are big, in both senses of the word. The **Tucson Mall**, with more than 170 shops and six two-story department stores, is the largest in the state. Sears, Dillard's, Mervyn's, Foley's, JC Penney, and The Broadway anchor the giant complex. Air-conditioned indoor shopping, as here, is always popular in Arizona. Acres of parking surround the mall at 4500 North Oracle Road, alias U.S. 80/89 (the major cross street is Wetmore Road). Tel: 293-7330.

Two miles (3 km) west of Oracle Road via Ina Road, to the north, the **Foothills Mall**, 7401 North La Cholla Boulevard, is anchored by Dillard's and Foley's department stores. **Keaton's Restaurant Grill and Bar** in the mall is known for its fresh seafood. For information on the mall or current museum exhibits, Tel: 742-7191.

If it is difficult to imagine what an abandoned supermarket turned into a bookstore would look like, then a visit to **Bookman's** is an education. Bookman's has two huge outlets in town, both well stocked with used books, paperbacks, magazines, videos, records, and CDs at reasonable prices—great places to find that out-of-print author you've been looking for. The downtown location is at 1930 East Grant Road, near the corner of Campbell Avenue (Tel: 325-5767), and the northwest store is at 3733 West Ina Road, at Thornydale Road (Tel: 579-0303).

For American Western history buffs, one bookstore here ranks as best. Run by a former librarian from the University of Arizona, **Books West Southwest** is one block north of Grant Road, at 2452 North Campbell Avenue, about a mile north of Speedway. Many of the titles in our bibliography may be found here. Tel: 326-3533.

Imports from Mexico

Tucson is a good place to shop for Mexican imports. Some people say that prices here are better than across the border in Nogales. (In Mexico you either haggle or pay more than you should.) **Antigua de Mexico** carries the usual textiles, glassware, and decorative craft items, but also specializes in furniture. The company factory in Nogales produces tables, chairs, and more, both for retail and custom orders. In addition, the store features collectible antiques from all parts of Mexico. The shop in Tucson is at 7037 North Oracle Road, in the Casas Adobes shopping center just south of Ina Road (Tel: 742-7114). There is also a shop in Tubac (see below), on Tubac Road.

Indian Crafts

Indian jewelry—Navajo, Hopi, and Zuni—is probably as popular in Tucson as it is in New Mexico. In fact, most of the jewelry sold in the Southwest comes from Indian craftspeople in New Mexico or on the reservations in northeastern Arizona. Silversmiths from Santa Fe think nothing of driving to Tucson for a weekend fair, or to resupply one of their retail outlets here. Prices vary, so it pays to shop around. At the **San Xavier Mission** it is possible to buy authentic, handcrafted silver directly from the Navajo who made it. Prices may fluctuate by season; they tend to go up in the winter.

Some useful background: "Dead pawn" is jewelry abandoned by the owners in reservation pawn shops, unclaimed after the time limit expires. One warning: Unscrupulous dealers are having Indian designs duplicated in Taiwan for sale to unsuspecting tourists. Try to authenticate any purchase of Indian jewelry.

One respected dealer in Tucson was raised on an Indian reservation in New Mexico and is very knowledgeable and reliable. He has five shops in town, all called **Indian Village**. The oldest one is downtown at 72 East Congress Street; Tel: 623-1162. For the locations of the other four, call the corporate office; Tel: 882-6440.

For an unusual selection of imports from around the world visit **The International Shop of the UN Center** in Decorator Square at the corner of Country Club and Grant roads, northeast of downtown. This shop, run by the United Nations Association of Southern Arizona (proceeds go to educational programs and UNICEF activities), is packed with ethnic clothing, accessories, jewelry, gifts, books, posters, UNICEF cards, and decorative items, all reasonably priced; Tel: 881-7060.

SOUTHERN ARIZONA

Until relatively recently, touring southern Arizona outside Tucson did not offer many attractive options for overnight accommodations. The only hotels of any consequence were the historic Gadsden Hotel in Douglas and the Copper Queen Hotel in Bisbee—and both of those were rather rundown. So visitors were advised to establish Tucson as a base of operations and allocate separate round-trip travel days west to Ajo, south to Nogales, southeast to Sierra Vista and Tombstone, and maybe an overnighter to Bisbee and Douglas farther to the southeast.

Now this picture has changed. In the late 1980s little bed-and-breakfast inns began appearing all across the state. They are still opening up, and offer an attractive alternative to seeing all that southern Arizona has to offer. (Contact Old Pueblo Homestays RSO, A B&B Reservation Service, P.O. Box 13603, Tucson, AZ 85732; Tel and Fax: 790-2399 or 800/333-9776.)

Travellers can put together an east-to-west itinerary, or travel from west to east, threading Ajo, Nogales, Patagonia, Ramsey Canyon, Tombstone, Bisbee, and all the sights along the way into one string (needing at least one overnight) without requiring the luxuries of Tucson. You could save those comforts for later or for a break in your touring itinerary.

Our coverage begins at the western end of southern Arizona in the town of Ajo, moves eastward toward Tucson, and then south via I-19 to the border at Nogales. In the border region we move east through Patagonia, Sonita, Sierra Vista, Bisbee, Tombstone, and Douglas, and then follow U.S. 666 north to I-10 and west back to Tucson.

WEST OF TUCSON
Ajo

The former copper mining town of Ajo (in Spanish "AH-ho") is virtually landlocked. It lies approximately 130

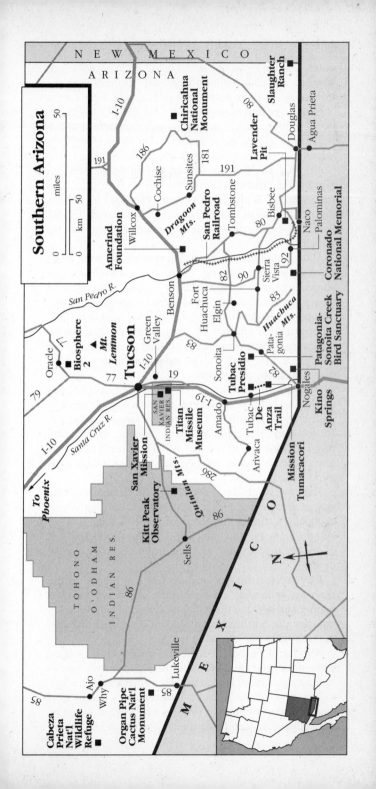

miles (208 km) west of Tucson on AZ 86 in a narrow gap between the giant Tohono O'odham (formerly Papago) Indian Reservation to its east, the Organ Pipe Cactus National Monument to its south, the Cabeza Prieta National Wildlife Refuge to its west, and the Barry M. Goldwater Air Force Range to its north. (Travellers to Ajo from Phoenix drive 120 miles/196 km south on NM 85.)

Ajo lies just 30 miles (48 km) north of the Mexican border (the crossing is at Gringo Pass) and 90 miles (144 km) north of Rocky Point **(Puerto Peñasco)** in Mexico, the northernmost beaches of the Sea of Cortez. (Rocky Point is the "Fort Lauderdale" of Arizona college students on spring break.)

Although *ajo* means "garlic" in Spanish, the town is not named for the seasoning. There are two theories: The name came from a native flower, the Ajo lily, or from a derivation of the Indian word *au'auho,* meaning "paint," because the Tohono O'odham tribe used to collect ornamental pigments from the rocks in this area. Quite possibly the early Spanish residents named the Ajo Mountains after the Indian word, and the indigenous lilies were later named after the mountains.

Copper was discovered here in 1847, the surface ore so rich it could be packed by mules across 90 miles of desert to the Gulf of California, transported by sail around Cape Horn and across the Atlantic, smelted into metal in Swansea, Wales, and still turn a profit. But after one of the ships sank off the coast of South America the mine closed, in 1857.

The town was laid out in 1916 by John Campbell Greenway, general manager of the Calumet and Arizona Mining Company. Calumet merged with Phelps Dodge in 1931 and the mine became the New Cornelia, producing tons of copper ingots until a miners' strike forced its closure in 1985.

Ajo's three main features are less than inspiring: the desolate, mile-wide open-pit mine, the now-smokeless copper smelter, and the white mountain of tailings looming over the northern edge of town, a permanent legacy of the smelter and the pit.

With the closing of the mine, Ajo's population dropped from some 8,000 to 3,000, and the 685 company homes stood empty. Phelps Dodge launched a nationwide marketing effort to sell the houses at bargain prices, and by 1990 had sold most of them to retirees who were attracted by Ajo's climate, among other things. The Chamber of Commerce cleverly claims Ajo is "where the summer spends the winter." (For information on Ajo, contact the Chamber at P.O. Box 507, Ajo, AZ 85321; Tel: 387-7742.)

Aside from the mine pit, the other major attraction here, especially for architecture buffs, is the home of the former general manager, **Greenway Mansion**. It stands on a rocky promontory in splendid isolation, a whitewashed Territorial fortress overlooking the open pit and the stark, stone Greenway Memorial where its erstwhile owner is buried. His young widow, Isabella, built the memorial to honor her husband after he died unexpectedly in 1926. Greenway had been a football hero at Yale, a Rough Rider who fought with Teddy Roosevelt at the battle of San Juan Hill, and the founder of at least five mining towns. He left an indelible imprint on the history of Arizona. After his death Isabella moved to Tucson and later opened the Arizona Inn there (see Staying in Tucson, above).

Although Ajo boasts two motels, and there is talk of reopening the old Cordelia Hotel, the history-seeking traveller will prefer the two bed-and-breakfast inns. The solid, masonry **Mine Manager's House Inn**, built in 1919 for the mine superintendent, sits atop a steep ridge on Greenway Drive overlooking Ajo, an appropriate vantage point for an overseer. The inn has six rooms (only one for smokers), each with private bath, an outdoor hot tub, and a great view of the town. The owners, Micheline and Jean Fournier, serve breakfast on linens and fine china in a sunny, formal dining room.

The 1925 **Guest House Inn Bed and Breakfast**, on Guest House Road, served as the official Phelps Dodge corporate guest house. Owner-managers Norma and Michael Walker oversee the inn's four rooms, each with a Western theme and a private bath. Breakfast is served on the original 20-foot dining room table. No smoking or pets here.

CABEZA PRIETA NATIONAL WILDLIFE REFUGE

Most people visit Ajo not for the now-silent smelter, but only in passing, en route to the Organ Pipe Cactus National Monument or the Cabeza Prieta National Wildlife Refuge. West of Ajo, Cabeza Prieta ("Dark Head," referring to a lava-topped granite peak in the Cabeza Prieta mountain range) is home to desert bighorn sheep and the endangered Sonoran pronghorn antelope. The 860,000-acre refuge is actually the southern portion of the larger

Barry M. Goldwater Air Force Range, and parts of it are still used for gunnery and bombing practice. Therefore, access is strictly prohibited without a refuge-entry permit and a signed military hold-harmless agreement. These may be obtained at the refuge office: 1611 North Second Avenue, Ajo, AZ 85321; Tel: 387-6483, or at the Kofa National Wildlife Refuge, 356 West First Street, P.O. Box 6290, Yuma, AZ 85364; Tel: 783-7861. Entrance to the refuge is 26 miles (42 km) southwest of Ajo on Darby Wells Road.

The refuge is wild and desolate. Bird-watchers have catalogued 197 species of birds here. Of these, 42 are known to nest on this land; the rest are seasonal passersby. Cabeza Prieta has no facilities for gasoline, sanitation, or potable water. Camping is permitted, but hunting is restricted and firearms may be taken in only with special permission, in writing, from the refuge manager. Vehicles with four-wheel drive are recommended; all drivers and vehicles must be licensed.

ORGAN PIPE CACTUS
NATIONAL MONUMENT

The organ-pipe cactus, so named because it looks like organ pipes, resembles a saguaro (sah-WAH-ro) cactus, but is smaller and shorter, with more branches rising from the ground rather than halfway up the trunk. Organ pipes grow 18 to 20 feet tall and have more attractive blooms than their bigger cousins. Nowhere in the world are they found in such profusion as in Organ Pipe Cactus National Monument, the largest national monument in the United States. The headquarters is 35 miles (56 km) south of Ajo on AZ 85, in a 330,000-acre park. Two paved loop roads circle through the monument for sightseeing, and RV spaces are available for 208 vehicles.

The desert here, its black, volcanic hills sprouting with these rare cacti, has been compared to an eerie moonscape or an arid, ancient world. For information contact the Organ Pipe Cactus National Monument, Route 1, Box 100, Ajo, AZ 85321; Tel: 387-6849.

A word of caution: There are service stations in Why, at the junction of AZ 85 and AZ 86 some 10 miles (16 km) southeast of Ajo, and at Lukeville, at the Mexican border crossing 27 miles (43 km) south of Why on AZ 85. Given the choice—and both are a long way from anywhere— you are advised to gas up at Why. Why? Price and service are better.

TOHONO O'ODHAM RESERVATION

Back toward Tucson from Why along AZ 86 it is 121 miles (194 km) to the other, eastern, end of the vast Tohono O'odham Indian Reservation. This is a "green" desert, dotted with scrub brush and prickly pear cactus, and soon becomes monotonous. There are only two points of interest along the way: the Indian town of Sells and Kitt Peak National Observatory.

The Tohono O'odham Indians were traditionally called the Papagos (bean eaters), the name given them by the early Spaniards. In the 1980s the tribe decided it had borne this demeaning title long enough and announced that henceforth they would be called by their own name, Tohono O'odham, or "Desert People." (Each *o* is pronounced separately, and flat as in "odd.")

In **Sells** you will find traditional Tohono O'odham handicrafts, particularly the tightly woven baskets still called papago.

At the eastern edge of the reservation **Kitt Peak National Observatory** looms to the right atop the Quinlan Mountains, at 7,000 feet elevation. Turn south at AZ 386 and follow the paved road about 12 miles (19 km) up to the mountaintop. Kitt Peak was selected as the site of a national observatory because of the clean air in this corner of the country. More telescopes are located here than any other location anywhere: 22, including the largest solar telescope in the world. The observatory is open to the public daily except Mondays; 45-minute lectures are given at 10:30 A.M. and 1:30 P.M. There are guided tours around the peak after the 1:30 lecture on weekdays and after both lectures on weekends. For additional (recorded) information, Tel: 322-3350.

From the intersection of AZ 86 and AZ 386 it is 44 miles (70 km) east to Tucson on AZ 86. The highway becomes Ajo Way along this stretch, and crosses I-19 just south of its merger with I-10.

SOUTH OF TUCSON
Tubac and the Santa Cruz Valley

I-19 spins off from I-10 at the southwest corner of Tucson and follows the Santa Cruz River Valley south 67 miles (107 km) to the Mexican border at Nogales. It is a historic valley, a lush green ribbon of cottonwood trees and tall grasses winding gently through a harsh desert landscape. Jesuit missionary Eusebio Francisco Kino first rode his horse northward along the river in the 1690s, seeking peaceful Indian tribes who would accept his Christian teachings. In October 1775 Juan Bautista de Anza led a major expedition north along the Santa Cruz, escorting Spanish colonists on a grueling trek across the Arizona and California deserts to settle San Francisco and claim it for Spain.

The missions of Tumacacori (see below) and San Xavier (see the Tucson section; the mission is off I-19 just a few miles south of the Ajo Way–I-19 junction), and the remains of the Tubac Presidio (see below), stand today as testaments to the dedication and courage of those early explorers. Fortunately, these churches were solidly built of adobe and have withstood the ravages of time, weather, and Indian attacks.

Just 25 miles (40 km) south of Tucson I-19 passes alongside **Green Valley**, an attractive retirement development of 18,000 people. The golf courses, the climate, and the small-town feeling continue to attract retirees from all over the country. Last year the town was named one of the top 20 retirement communities in the United States by *New Choices* magazine.

Tucked unobtrusively into the northern edge of Green Valley, just half a mile (1 km) west off the interstate at exit 69, is perhaps the county's most unusual attraction—the **Titan Missile Museum**. Opened in May 1986, the museum is an actual U.S. Air Force installation that once held a live nuclear warhead atop a huge Titan missile aimed at a target in the former USSR. (The target has never been revealed.)

Open to the public daily except Mondays and Tuesdays, the installation is a favorite of Cold War buffs. From 1962 to 1984 there were 54 such intercontinental ballistic missile sites around the country, 18 of them in a wide circle around Tucson. This is the only one left, and it has been decommissioned. These sites were manned 24 hours a day by a crew of four from a control center 35 feet below ground. The missile, ten feet in diameter and 105 feet tall, stood nearby in a silo 146 feet deep, ready to fuel and fire upon command from the White House. The nuclear payload packed 214 times the explosive power of the bomb dropped at Hiroshima, more powerful than all the explosives used by both sides in World War II.

The Titan Missile Museum is a branch of the nonprofit Pima Air and Space Museum P.O. Box 160, Green Valley, AZ 85622; Tel: 791-2929. Volunteers lead escorted tours every half hour from 9:00 A.M. to 3:00 P.M.

Just past Arivaca Junction, 34 miles (54 km) south of Tucson on I-19, is the little town of Amado (exit 48). It's not much more than a wide spot in the road, but if you're feeling hungry as you approach consider stopping at Amado's leading restaurant, the **Cow Palace**, at 28802 South Nogales Highway. This landmark has served cowboys and tenderfeet alike since the 1920s, and is renowned for its authentic Western decor and its steaks and burgers.

If lunch can wait another 15 minutes, an alternative is the new **Burro Inn**. Take exit 40 from the interstate, head west, and follow the signs to 70 West El Burro Lane. This former Titan missile site has been developed into an imaginative restaurant and small inn. Before the government could sell the land, demolition teams had to destroy the silo and the command center. The craters were filled with rubble, precluding any use of the Cold War facilities as, say, a Dr. Strangelove wine cellar. The hilltop restaurant's location commands a scenic 360-degree view of the Santa Cruz River Valley. Opened in 1992, Burro Inn features mesquite-broiled steaks, ribs, chicken, and burgers. A live burro, Louie, welcomes customers (in his way) as they pull into the parking area. Tel: 398-2281.

TUBAC

Farther south along I-19, 45 miles (72 km) south of Tucson on the east side of the highway, lies the little village of Tubac. Founded as a garrison in 1752 by early Spanish settlers on the west bank of the Santa Cruz River, Tubac is said to be the oldest European settlement in Arizona. It also claims the first school, the first newspaper, and the first Spanish land grant. Today the **Tubac Presidio State Historic Park and Museum** preserves the history of the site. An underground exhibit reveals artifacts exactly as they were uncovered during archaeological excavation.

A thriving arts-and-crafts center has sprung up between the museum and the highway, with several blocks of attractive galleries, shops, and restaurants. Four places of special interest on Tubac Road (the right fork off the frontage road as you enter Tubac) are **Tortuga Books**, where you can get the *New York Times* and the *Wall Street Journal;* a branch of **Antigua de Mexico** (see Shopping in Tucson, above); the **Artist's Daughter**, a catch-all shop crammed with memorabilia; and the studio of artist Hal Empie, who paints here daily. Both Tubac and Plaza roads lead east to the Presidio and the river. On Plaza Road (the left fork off the frontage road) look for Lee Blackwell's sculpted copper fountains.

Tubac has become the center of activity for the development of a key segment of the **Juan Bautista de Anza National Historic Trail**. On October 23, 1775, de Anza, captain of the Tubac Presidio, led 240 colonists and some 1,000 cattle overland to settle San Francisco, California, before the Russians could establish a colony there and claim it for their czar.

In 1990 the U.S. government passed a law establishing the 1,200-mile-long historic trail, which starts at Nogales and ends in San Francisco. The four-and-a-half-mile segment between Tumacacori Mission to the south and the Tubac Presidio was opened on October 23, 1992. The ten-foot-wide trail accommodates hikers and horseback riders.

For details on this section of the trail, contact the Tubac Presidio State Historic Park, Box 1296, Tubac, AZ 85646; Tel: 398-2252. For information on the entire trail, contact the National Park Service, Division of Planning, Grants, and Environmental Quality, 600 Harrison Street, Suite 600, San Francisco, CA 94107-1372; Tel: (415) 744-3968. Ask for a copy of the newsletter *Noticias de Anza*.

TUMACACORI

Four miles (6½ km) south of Tubac, at exit 29 on I-19, lies the historic **San Jose de Tumacacori Mission**, now a national monument. The site was first used by the Jesuit missionary Father Kino in the 1690s in his attempt to convert the Indians who lived along the river by teaching them agriculture and cattle raising. The ruined church standing here today was actually built around 1800 by Franciscan missionaries. The lovely tree-shaded church compound and its adjoining village was abandoned several times during fierce Indian attacks.

Across the road from the mission the adobe building of the unusual **Santa Cruz Chili & Spice Company and Ranch Museum**, opened in 1943, was once part of a 19th-century land grant, the Baca Float Ranch. The museum displays antiques and memorabilia from the old ranch house. The shelves of the little shop, an adventure in odors, are lined with chile products, natural spices, and gourmet Southwestern foods.

THE TWO NOGALESES

Back on the highway: It is only 20 more miles (32 km) south from Tumacacori to **Nogales**, Arizona, and, just across the border, **Nogales**, Sonora. Both towns are named after the oak trees that used to grow here. At press time the main border crossing was closed to automobile traffic for construction of a new, more efficient gateway. Cars are being routed west along Mariposa Road to the (newer) truck crossing into Mexico until the project is completed. Most visitors prefer to park their cars on the U.S. side and walk across; pedestrians may still use the old checkpoint. On weekends, especially during the winter, parking may be hard to find within two blocks of the border.

For people who have never been to a foreign country, Nogales, Mexico, is worth a trip just to say you've been abroad, though there is not much to see or do, except during the winter when the town's little bullring hosts live bullfights. (For short side trips into Mexico from Nogales, see the chapter following this.)

You can find a few bargains in Mexico. Regular visitors buy the one bottle of liquor they may legally bring back, perhaps some Mexican ground coffee, or certain prescription drugs that are far cheaper than in the United States and available here without prescription. Some tourists are attracted to the brightly colored blankets and piñatas, hammered tin decorations, huge sombreros, clay pots, leather belts, and costume jewelry.

Mexican Nogales's most unusual restaurant, La Caverna, inside a warren of old mine tunnels less than two blocks from the border crossing, burned down about ten years ago and has never been rebuilt. (Every couple of years the Tucson papers announce that it is about to reopen, but it never does.) This leaves the bulk of the tourist business to **La Roca,** a well-run restaurant a few doors south of the ex-Caverna. Upstairs over an antiques shop, La Roca is built into the side of a rock cliff. The architecture is stone and heavy. The restaurant is known for its fresh seafood; no burritos or *chimichangas* here. Do not expect bargain prices either, as this is one of Nogales's finer restaurants.

Probably the main attraction in Nogales, Arizona, is the Primeria Alta Historical Society Museum at 223 Grand Avenue. Housed in what was once the 1914 city hall, it contains photographs and artifacts of the town's history. The U.S. Nogales has been booming lately. Retail space is now said to rent for more than prime Phoenix shops. The reason is the purchasing power of the 200,000 people living on the Sonoran side of the border. Mexican workers come across to spend their hard-earned pesos on the

U.S. side, filling the till of entrepreneurs from Los Angeles who have taken over the retail businesses, importing inexpensive consumer goods from Asia, mostly clothing and household products, and selling them at bargain prices.

Patagonia and Sonoita

From Nogales, AZ 82 heads northeast to Patagonia and Sonoita. This is distinctly un-southern Arizona landscape; the rolling hills are covered with oak trees and cotton-woods, and some stretches are actually green and shady. Just 2 miles (3 km) out of Nogales, on the right, is the winery of **Arizona Vineyards**, run by entrepreneur Tino Ocheltree. The cinderblock building is decorated in bizarre fashion with antiques, concrete gargoyles, and imagination. Step in to sample various vintages or for a tour. Tel: 287-7972.

Just a little farther on, at the bottom of the hill where the road bridges the Santa Cruz River, a turnoff to the right leads to **Kino Springs**, once the 5,000-acre ranch of British movie star Stewart Granger and his movie-star wife, Jean Simmons. They raised registered cattle in this lush grassland. Today it is a golf resort, open to the public, with Granger's spacious ranch house as the clubhouse. You can enjoy lunch or dinner in the very comfortable dining room—the atmosphere is halfway between a posh country club of the 1950s and the set of a Hollywood Western. The bar is decorated with enlarged photos of all the movie stars who used to visit Granger here, escaping for a while the Los Angeles celebrity rat race. John Wayne stayed here so often one of the cabañas is named for him.

PATAGONIA
Patagonia, farther up AZ 82, recently lost its main tourist attraction, the Museum of the Horse, formerly housed near the old railroad station. The trains don't come to Patagonia anymore and the museum reopened in Ruidoso, New Mexico. Only one attraction remains: the Nature Conservancy's **Patagonia–Sonoita Creek Bird Sanctuary**. Tall cottonwoods and mesquite shelter the creek and provide homes to numerous birds, deer, and javalina. Over 300 species of winged creatures have been sighted here, a migratory rest stop on the flyway to Mexico. A new visitors' center and manager's residence are scheduled to open this year. The sanctuary is closed Mondays and Tuesdays.

The first bed and breakfast to open in Patagonia (and in Santa Cruz County, for that matter) was **The Little House**, on Sonoita Avenue. The owner-managers, Don and Doris Wenig, carefully restored an old adobe into two cozy private rooms, each with fireplace, bath, and patio. Tall trees shade the house and the inviting garden. Breakfast, served on the porch of the Wenigs' adjoining adobe home, features homemade breads, freshly ground coffee, and eggs from local hens.

Before leaving the little town, stop in at the Ovens of Patagonia for some fresh-baked bread or pastries.

A choice of four different tours of the area, including wine country, ghost towns, and cattle ranches, is offered by Sonoita operator **Arizona Backroad Tours**; Tel: (800) 967-2227.

SONOITA

Farther northeast on AZ 82 to Sonoita the road emerges into open, gently rolling grasslands. There isn't even a stop sign at the crossroads with AZ 83, but the cluster of commercial buildings makes it clear that this is "downtown" Sonoita. Just to the south of this intersection is the Santa Cruz County Fairgrounds, where many of the activities for this ranching community take place. Quarter horse and thoroughbred races are held the last weekend in April and the first weekend in May, the Sonoita Rodeo takes place each Labor Day weekend, and the Santa Cruz County Fair falls on the third weekend in September. For a schedule of upcoming events contact the Santa Cruz County Fair & Rodeo Association, P.O. Box 382, Sonoita, AZ 85637; Tel: 455-5553.

Just east of the intersection of AZ 82 and AZ 83, in the little row of shops on the north side of the road at number 3084, is an unexpected European pasta restaurant, **Er Pastaro**, run by Giovanni Schifano, formerly with Regine's in New York, and his wife, Karin, a former model. The menu features northern Italian versions of spaghetti, penne, fettuccine, tortellini, and lasagna (most priced under $10). The dish of choice? Spaghetti puttanesca. The wine list features reds and whites imported from Italy. Photos of celebrities cover the walls of the main dining room; most are from Schifano's days in New York, but more and more are of those who have ventured down to this remote part of Arizona for an Italian evening of pasta and wine. Open Wednesday through Sunday, 4:00 to 9:00 P.M. No credit cards; Tel: 455-5821.

Wine Country

South of Sonoita is Arizona's wine country. Thanks to the pioneering work of a University of Arizona soil professor, Gordon Dutt, several small wineries have sprung up in this area. Dr. Dutt, who discovered that the soil and climate conditions here are similar to those in the Burgundy region of France, founded his own winery in 1971, and now offers samples to the public as well as sales. Recognition of Dr. Dutt's efforts took off when Sonoita Vineyards' 1986 Cabernet Sauvignon and 1987 Fumé Blanc were selected to be served at President Bush's 1989 Presidential Inauguration Food and Wine Gala.

To find the winery head south from the Sonoita intersection of AZ 82 and AZ 83, and follow the two-lane road to the Elgin turnoff (at a school), about 4 miles (6½ km) on the left. This is open country; not a tree until Elgin. At Elgin, which is three buildings on the right and one across the creek on the left, the paved road turns left over a little bridge. Instead of crossing it, take the dirt road to the right through a gate with a sign announcing Sonoita Vineyards, 3 Miles. The dirt road leads through rather barren-looking ranchland toward a large metal barn on top of a hill. That is the winery. Open daily 10:00 A.M. to 4:00 P.M.; Tel: 455-5893.

Dr. Dutt's success has led to the opening of two more wineries here. The Santa Cruz Winery Ltd. is Arizona's first kosher grape crusher. The first vintage of the Callaghan Winery, meanwhile, will be available with meals at Karen's café in Elgin (see below).

ELGIN

Karen's Wine Country Café has no actual address, but is the middle building of the three that make up Elgin, Arizona. The café occupies the former Elgin post office, which closed in 1987, and technically *is* Elgin. The building to the south is a small chapel; the building to the north houses a gift shop and the offices of the Santa Cruz Winery.

The café opened in April 1992 and quickly became a popular spot in a county with few places to dine. Karen and Harold Callaghan had a restaurant in Sierra Vista (see below) for several years but claim that this one, far from any urban population, is already more successful. The limited menu features Southwestern sandwiches, imaginative quiches, and a daily special such as smoked-chicken-and-mushroom lasagna with tomato-basil butter.

Besides the home cooking, the other attraction here is the setting. Diners may be served on the front porch, behind an adobe wall. The climate of Elgin, which sits at an elevation of 4,719 feet, is usually pleasant. The view takes in a magnificent stand of tall cottonwood trees shading a lone residence across the road. (The house, once the Elgin railway station, was the location for the classic John Wayne film *Red River*. The train station stood in for the one in Abilene, Kansas.) Beyond the creek and the trees a broad vista of grass-covered ranchland stretches to a ridge of mountains on the eastern horizon. The restaurant is open for lunch on Thursdays and Sundays, lunch and dinner on Fridays and Saturdays. Reservations are recommended for dinner; Tel: 455-5282. No credit cards.

SOUTHEAST OF TUCSON
Sierra Vista and Fort Huachuca

From Elgin cross the bridge over the creek to a two-lane road that heads straight north 5 miles (8 km) to intersect AZ 82. Turn right here and go east for 11 miles (18 km) on AZ 82 to the next intersection, which is with AZ 90. At this point the town of Benson and I-10 are 19 miles (30 km) north, and Sierra Vista and Fort Huachuca are 9 miles (14½ km) south, via AZ 90.

Sierra Vista, formerly sporting the inglorious name Fry, was once primarily a civilian community serving Fort Huachuca (hwa-CHOO-kuh); today the town is developing its own tourism and commercial identity.

Fort Huachuca is the only remaining Arizona frontier outpost still in active use. One of the sergeants from the original Camp Huachuca discovered silver in what later became Bisbee (see below) while tracking escaped Apache Indians in 1877. Huachuca personnel also played a role in the early development of Tombstone. But historically it may be best known as the home of the Buffalo Soldiers, the first all-African–American U.S. Army unit, organized in 1866.

The **Fort Huachuca Museum** documents this era of army history, and is sometimes referred to as the Buffalo Museum. It is located on the army base and is open 9:00 A.M. to 4:00 P.M. weekdays and 1:00 to 4:00 P.M. Saturdays and Sundays. The main gate to the base is easily found just to the right as AZ 90 enters Sierra Vista from the north. To take a vehicle onto the base, the headquarters of the U.S. Army Communications Command, pull into the visitors' area to the right of the gate, where authorities will issue a post pass after confirming your possession of a valid driver's license and vehicle registration.

A few miles south of Sierra Vista on AZ 92, at an elevation of 5,400 feet in the Huachuca Mountains, is the **Ramsey Canyon Preserve**, run by the Nature Conservancy environmental group. Look for the sign on the right and then head up into the mountains on a paved, two-lane road 4 miles (6½ km). A winding stream runs beneath rugged stone cliffs and tall trees, providing a natural habitat to much of Arizona's high-country wildlife. Ramsey Canyon's 280 acres are especially known for their birds, particularly the hummingbirds. During their annual Christmas Count, National Audubon Society birders have logged as many as 100 different species of birds in one day.

The **Ramsey Canyon Inn**, a cozy bed and breakfast next to a trickling stream, adjoins the preserve. Hummingbird feeders hang outside the large dining room window, and guests try to identify the many varieties of iridescent hummers while sipping their morning coffee. Smoking is allowed only on the patio. No children under 13 and no pets are welcome.

Route 92 continues south about 10 miles (16 km) toward the Mexican border and then swings east toward Palominas. Just after the bend, a smaller, two-lane paved road cuts off to the south and then curves west into the Coronado National Forest, heading directly to the **Coronado National Memorial**. This stone monument marks the point where Coronado's expedition entered what is now the United States more than 450 years ago. The view from here encompasses Mexico, the San Pedro Valley to the east, and the San Rafael Valley to the west. There are hiking trails around the memorial. As Stewart L. Udall says in his book *To the Inland Empire*, "In 1540, the Conquistadores entered what's now Arizona near the ranching town of Palominas, southeast of Tucson. The desert days were hot and dry and it is a good bet the horsemen stayed close to the San Pedro River as they headed downstream. This narrow valley is framed by the pine-clad Huachuca Mountains on the west and the low ridges of the Mule Mountains on the east."

Southern Arizona provided the scenic stage for the first act of Spanish conquest of the American West. Francisco Vásquez de Coronado, searching for the legendary Seven Cities of Cíbola as reported by the French missionary Fray

Marcos de Niza, led the longest Spanish expedition of the 16th century. It was essentially a wild-goose chase. With 336 horsemen in gleaming armor and mail, 62 foot soldiers, and 700 "Indian allies," Coronado's trek led from the town of Compostella in northern Mexico up through southeastern Arizona to New Mexico and as far north as Kansas. For four months they forged through wilderness, encountering friendly and unfriendly locals, seeking the Seven Cities, said to be rich Indian pueblos with doors of turquoise and streets of gold.

The golden cities report from Fray Marcos, who may never have even seen New Mexico, let alone any pueblos, proved to be somewhat exaggerated, and Coronado and his men returned empty-handed to their base in colonial Mexico. More than 150 years would pass before Spain developed any interest in this part of the world again.

Today, while driving through Benson and beneath the tall cottonwoods of St. David, it is not difficult to imagine the long column of Spanish conquistadors on horseback, their steel helmets flashing in the spring sunlight, followed by herds of cattle, horses, and sheep tended by the first cowboys—Indians from the tribes of Mexico. The spirit of the Spanish explorers pervades the Southwest, in the language, the place names, and the people who are living evidence of the 400-year domination by Hispanic Mexico.

The San Pedro & Southwestern Railway

Coronado's historic expedition will undoubtedly become more widely known during the next few years, thanks to an exciting new development: an excursion train from **Benson**, north of Sierra Vista on I-10, near the point where it intersects AZ 90 and U.S. 80. Plans are to have a tour-train make a daily 100-mile round trip along the San Pedro River down to the sleepy Mexican border village of **Naco** and back. Possible stops may include points along Coronado's route; the ruins of Santa Cruz de Terrenate, a Spanish presidio abandoned in 1776; an archaeological site where prehistoric men once butchered mammoths; ancient Indian villages; and the abandoned mining town of Charleston.

For details on the excursion train, contact the San Pedro & Southwestern Railway, P.O. Box 1420, Benson, AZ 85602; Tel: 586-2266.

Bisbee

From the Coronado Memorial return to AZ 92 and head east 17 miles (27 km), past Palominas to the mining town of Bisbee on U.S. 80. What land has not been devoured by the open pit mine here over the years remains wedged into two narrow canyons.

Rugged little Bisbee, especially the old downtown, looks much as it did around the turn of the century. The newest structure, which appears obtrusively modern among its stone and brick neighbors, is the 1939 Mercantile Building. The yawning Lavender Pit mine swallowed part of the town over the years, and today the 300-acre hole gapes dead at the sky. The barren, rocky hills looming over the town are riddled with mineshafts.

In May 1877 Army Sergeant Jack Dunn was tracking Apache Indians who had escaped from the San Carlos Reservation. He stopped for water at the spring below Castle Rock and noticed mineral traces indicating silver in Tombstone Canyon (now Bisbee's main street). Later that summer he hired a partner and had him stake claims in the area, and the future of Bisbee was set. Miners poured in to stake their claims, and a settlement sprang up. The town was formalized by the opening of a post office in 1880, and the next year Phelps Dodge Company invested in a copper claim here. The first train chuffed into Bisbee on February 1, 1889. Mining boomed and the population swelled to 20,000.

Bisbee's fortunes ebbed and flowed on the cycle of copper prices. When copper sold high, as during World War I, the town prospered. When the price dropped during the Great Depression, digging stopped and the population fell. In its heyday the town was wild and rowdy. Bars and brothels thrived on the miners' money, and it took some very tough lawmen to maintain order along the infamous Brewery Gulch.

"Texas" John Slaughter was one such man. He earned a national reputation for cleaning up some of the early lawless elements of Bisbee and Tombstone. (See the Douglas and the Chiricahuas section, below, and read *Tombstone,* by Walter Noble Burns, for a detailed account of Slaughter's remarkable career.)

Harry Wheeler, former commander of the Texas Rangers, was another. Sheriff of Cochise County here during a miner's strike in 1917 and only five feet four inches tall, Wheeler was in command in Bisbee on July 12 when the mining companies rounded up 1,200 striking miners and forcibly shipped them into the New Mexico desert in boxcars. It was this infamous, illegal, strike-breaking "deportation" that got the copper mines back into operation during World War I. (*Bisbee '17,* by Robert Houston, gives a fictional yet realistic account.)

Luckily for the town, death came slowly. The Copper Queen mine closed in 1939; the open Lavender Pit was worked until 1974. By June 1975 all mining operations had ceased. Pumps kept water from seeping into the hundreds of miles of underground shafts and tunnels until 1985, when they were finally turned off and the mines allowed to flood.

Artists and hippies discovered Bisbee in the 1960s and 1970s, drawn by low rents, "the best climate in Arizona," and the historic "time trip" atmosphere. The town was incorporated in 1985, and the city fathers have been striving to build a new future on tourism, conventions, and even light industry.

The **Copper Queen mine tour** offers a fascinating trip 75 years into the past, escorted by retired miners. Whatever the outside temperature, the damp tunnels remain at a chill 47°F—a nice respite on a hot summer day. The tour lasts a little longer than an hour, so wear more than a mere tee-shirt. A funny little electric train enters the mountain under an old sign, Copper Queen 1915, and trundles 1,800 feet straight into the darkness. The guide provides a wealth of information on minerals, mining techniques, blind mules, and bobtailed cats. A combined one-hour historic-district bus tour and a Lavender Pit mine tour, as well as a Bisbee walking tour, leave from the same mining shed as the Copper Queen train, on the west side of U.S. 80; Tel: 432-2071.

The **Bisbee Mining and Historical Museum**, at 5 Copper Queen Plaza, is housed in the former Phelps Dodge General Office headquarters, built in 1897 in the center of Old Bisbee. The old mining carts and equipment out front make it easy to find, just below the Copper Queen Hotel. Thanks to a recent grant from the National Endowment for the Arts, the museum has been totally refurbished and gives an excellent presentation of the copper industry and the town's history from 1877 to 1917. The photo archives upstairs contain 12,000 negatives and photographs, often used for historical research.

The old mining town may best be known for its annual bicycle race, **La Vuelta de Bisbee**, sponsored by the U.S.

Cycling Federation and held the last weekend in April. The tough four-day competition climaxes in the Criterium, a race up and down the steep hills of Old Bisbee.

Another effort to attract visitors was launched in July 1992. Modeled after a successful program in Tucson, it is called **Bisbee: Saturday Night Downtown**. All of the galleries and shops downtown remain open the first Saturday of each month. Live music and entertainment are offered on the plaza, creating something like an evening street festival.

As more travellers discover Bisbee's charm, more places to stay spring up and more restaurants and galleries open. Most of them endeavor to fit in with the town's historic atmosphere, making it a fun place to visit. The galleries feature the work of local artists, and numerous antiques shops offer tangible pieces of Old West history. Bisbee author Walter Swan presides over his now-famous One-Book Bookstore.

STAYING IN BISBEE

The traveller who would like to spend the night in Bisbee has numerous options. The grande dame of Bisbee accommodations is the **Copper Queen Hotel**, built by the Copper Queen Mining Company in 1902 and currently being restored, one room at a time, to its original grandeur. (The hotel is such a landmark that the promotional brochure doesn't even give an address.) The 44 rooms here feature high ceilings with circling fans and roomy private baths. Guests have included General "Black Jack" Pershing, young Teddy Roosevelt, and, more recently, Hollywood moviemakers who have discovered Bisbee's particular suitability as a "period" location.

Easily the most unusual accommodation is the **OK Street Jail House Inn**. Bisbee's original, narrow stone jail has been converted into a comfortable "suite," complete with kitchen and Jacuzzi. The two-story jail has a comfortable living room downstairs, in the former drunk tank, and a roomy bedroom with a king-size bed and modern private bath upstairs. The massive barred door swings shut on occupants of the serious offenders' cell who really want to sleep tight. Guests have the entire building at 9 OK Street to themselves.

Bed-and-breakfast inns have proliferated in historic homes and buildings all over Bisbee. For a complete list contact the Greater Bisbee Chamber of Commerce, P.O. Box BA, Bisbee, AZ 85603-0560; Tel: 432-5421. The Chamber lists 11 bed and breakfasts in the area.

Two of the larger establishments are the Oliver House and the Bisbee Inn. The **Oliver House**, at 26 Souls Avenue, is up the hill from the Copper Queen Hotel, reached by crossing a little footbridge. Built in 1909 as the executive hotel and planning center of the Calumet and Arizona Mining Company, the Oliver House has 12 high-ceilinged rooms, wide corridors with wooden floors, and a sunny living room/dining room, where breakfast is served. Clark Gable stayed here once on his way to Tara.

Opened in 1917, the **Bisbee Inn** was originally the LaMore Hotel, and later a miners' boardinghouse. This 18-room, redbrick bed and breakfast was restored by John and Joy Timbers and furnished with period metal bedsteads and tables, chairs, and dressers of oak. Each room has running water, but the toilets and showers are down the hall. The Bisbee Inn is a no-smoking hotel. There are no television sets or telephones in the rooms, much the same state of affairs as when the miners lived here. Breakfast is a major event—not only is it a full breakfast, it is an all-you-can-eat feast. The inn is at 45 OK Street, a few doors uphill from the jail house.

Travellers on a budget may consider the **YWCA**, just up the hill from the Copper Queen Hotel. The Y is in the Grace Dodge Memorial Building, built in 1916, and offers inexpensive rooms and hostel bunks.

South of Bisbee is the "suburb" of **Warren**, where all the mine officials built their mansions, a number of which have been restored as attractive, spacious bed-and-breakfast inns. At 605 Shattuck Street in Warren is the turn-of-the-century **Judge Ross House**, run by Bonnie and Jim Douglass. The two-story, redbrick home has two rooms upstairs, with a shared bath, and a downstairs suite with a bathtub in the middle of the room. The place is furnished with fine art and antiques from the Douglasses' collection. Breakfast is served either in the formal dining room, on the upstairs sun porch, or on the secluded brick patio.

DINING IN BISBEE

Bisbee today offers a wider choice of dining places than in past years. Among the newer restaurants is **Stenzel's**, in what was once a private home, up Tombstone Canyon at number 207. Stenzel's is rather formal and upscale, offering steaks and a generous American menu served on linen tablecloths. The service, the food, and the decor are all first class. Tel: 432-7611.

The reputation of the pasta dishes at the **Wine Gallery Bistro**, 41 Main Street, has spread as far as Tucson. Also served up here are other contemporary Italian, seafood, and vegetarian specials; Tel: 432-3447. Upstairs above the Wine Gallery is **18 Steps**. A casual little place, it is popular for breakfast and lunch. The menu changes daily, but 18 Steps is known for its pastries.

An obvious choice for any meal of the day is the dining room at the **Copper Queen Hotel**, a rather formal room just off the lobby; the window tables offer a nice view of Old Bisbee.

To return to Tucson, about a two-hour, 90-mile (144-km) drive northwest of Bisbee, head north and west on U.S. 80 and I-10, respectively, or drive east to Douglas (see below), north on U.S. 666 via the Sulphur Springs Valley, and west on I-10. If the choice is the former, as in our coverage, on your way to Benson on I-10 you'll pass through the longest tunnel in Arizona, over the Mule Mountains, and, about halfway to Benson, straight to Tombstone.

Tombstone

"Allen Street, with its dilapidated old stores, looks a little forlorn in daylight, despite its asphalt and its automobiles. But when a coyote lifts a weird song in the mesquite and the moon hangs over the Dragoons, it is easy to imagine it the frontier boulevard it used to be. . . . There in the street are the lumber trains coming in from the Chiricahuas. . . . The arcaded sidewalks are crowded. Swing doors of saloons flail back and forth. Laughter of roistering throngs comes from the brightly lighted bars. You hear the click of faro chips, the rattle of roulette wheels. . . . That tall man there with the six-shooters buckled around him is Wyatt Earp. Doc Holliday is lounging in a doorway. Yonder are Virgil and Morgan Earp. Johnny Behan bustles along. And the Clantons and McLowerys and Buckskin Frank and John Ringo in his great buffalo coat, his hands rammed in his pockets on his guns. . . ." That was the Tombstone of Walter Noble Burns (*Tombstone*).

Wyatt Earp, Doc Holliday, and the Clanton gang are forever immortalized in the retelling and reenacting of the infamous shoot-out at the O.K. Corral here. The gunfight really happened, and the corral exists, next to Fly's Photo Parlor. It may be one of the most-analyzed gunfights in American history. Every Sunday the battle is reenacted by professional stuntmen, the bad guys doomed to bite the dust eternally.

Historically, Tombstone is remembered as a wild, lawless mining town of 20,000 people—said to be the largest city between New Orleans and San Francisco during the 1880s. (Denver and Bisbee make the same claim.)

The town got its name when prospector Ed Schieffelin reported he had found signs of silver in the desert. Scout Al Sieber scoffed, "Silver stones? Bah! You'll find nothin' in them hills but yer tombstone." So when Schieffelin struck ore, he called his claim the Tombstone Mine.

What makes Tombstone historically remarkable is that this wild boomtown was so short-lived. Its reputation long outlasted its reality. The boom began in 1877, the population soaring as miners rushed in to stake their silver claims and begin operating their mines. In just a decade a quick one-two punch put the town out of business: By 1888 water had flooded the mines and a disastrous fire had destroyed most of the buildings.

One location actually enables you to step back into the 1880s: The **Bird Cage Theater** was not only the town's favorite watering hole, it also provided a stage for some of the top performers of the age. Opera singers and Broadway beauties like Carlotta Crabtree arrived by stagecoach to entertain the free-spending miners.

When the city burned, the Bird Cage was boarded up. The boards were not removed until the 1930s, revealing an adobe structure that had passed through a 50-year time warp. Luckily, whoever controlled it had no plans for remodeling. It was left virtually untouched for another 60 years, just gathering dust, a repository for 19th-century memorabilia. Today, for a small fee, you can step inside the Bird Cage Theater and, as author Burns suggests, hear the honky-tonk piano, the rowdy miners, the giggles of the "soiled doves" entertaining their guests in the curtained mezzanine boxes, and perhaps a line of can-can dancers up on the creaky stage. Each bullet hole in the walls tells a story.

Allen Street is Tombstone's main drag, where most of the shops are situated and where most of the gunfights take place. A major community project recently removed all of the overhead power and phone lines, burying them underground, to bring the street much closer to its 1880s appearance.

Tombstone is one of the few towns in Arizona where it is *not* legal to wear a gunbelt with a loaded pistol in a holster. This upsets some of the more macho elements in the area, who are attempting to have the law overturned.

Understandably, summer is the off-season in Arizona, and Tombstone does its best to offset the drop in visitors during this period. A series of weekend festivals, all celebrating the Old West, kicks off in early March and continues through the second weekend in November.

Shoot-out reenactments are ongoing events here. On the second and fourth Saturdays of each month the **Tombstone Helldorados** perform at the Helldorados Amphitheater; the first and third Sundays of the month feature the **Wild Bunch** at the O.K. Corral; and the **Vigilantes** give it their best shot on the second, fourth, and fifth Sundays on Allen Street. All performances begin at 2:00 P.M.

Special events begin the first weekend in March with **Territorial Days**, featuring old fire engines, 1880 Championship Fire-Cart Races, and an all-pet parade; Tel: 457-2211 for details. **Wyatt Earp Days** on Memorial Day weekend include gunfights, a chili cook-off, "hangings," fashion shows, a parade, and a dance.

June's **Father's Day Parade** is followed by the annual **Fourth of July** celebration and August's **Vigilante Days**, the second weekend of the month, with mock hangings, cancan girls, a chili cook-off, and a country concert under the stars, among other treats; Tel: 457-3107 for information. The third weekend in August the town honors **Nellie Cashman**, "the Angel of the Camp" who helped many down-on-their-luck folks when Tombstone was a new settlement. Banquets, live entertainment, a ladies' tea, and a Nellie look-alike contest are among the scheduled events; Tel: 457-2212.

The **Rendezvous of Gunfighters**, with competitive shooting and gunfights hosted by the Wild Bunch and Hell's Belles, takes place over the three-day Labor Day Weekend at the O.K. Corral; Tel: 457-3548. From October 15 to 17 **Helldorado Days** offers shoot-outs, street entertainment, a variety show, and a park promenade; Tel: 457-3548.

And the second weekend of November is devoted to celebrating former resident and famous clown Emmett Kelly, Jr., with a clown roundup, a parade, face painting for children, and a children's parade; Tel: 457-3421 for details.

Because of possible scheduling changes, it is wise to call in advance to confirm the above dates. Contact the Tombstone Main Street Program, Tel: 457-3589; or write P.O. Box 266, Tombstone, AZ 85638. Another resource is the Tombstone Tourism Association, P.O. Box 917, Tombstone, AZ 85638; Tel: 457-2211.

TOMBSTONE BED AND BREAKFASTS

Until recently, Tombstone was strictly a day visit sort of place. Tourists would drive in from Tucson or Phoenix or Sierra Vista to watch the gunfights, enjoy Helldorado Days, or any of the town's many scheduled weekend entertainments (see above), and head home before sunset. But this hit-and-run attitude is changing.

Last year two new bed-and-breakfast inns opened up, joining one that debuted two years earlier. Now Tombstone offers historic accommodations that contribute to the town's transformation from an Old West oddity and tourist trap into a more satisfying travel destination. Strolling the quiet streets when the moon is full, or on a quiet morning after a leisurely breakfast, adds a very different dimension to the town.

The first of these establishments to open was the **Tombstone Boarding House**, owned and operated by Shirley and Ted Villarin on North Fourth Street. The pair have laboriously converted two side-by-side 19th-century adobe homes into a spotless bed and breakfast decorated in period style. Ted's remodeling continues, and eventually they will have nine rooms of various sizes. Breakfast is served in their cheerful blue-and-white kitchen.

One short block west, at the corner of Third Street and Safford, stands freshly painted **Priscilla's**, owned and managed by Barbara Arters. This turn-of-the-century, two-story Victorian opened in 1992 with just three rooms, all upstairs and all decorated with lace and Victorian-era furniture.

One more block west, at the corner of Second and Safford, the two-story, 1880 adobe **Buford House** offers five rooms for rent, including the Western Room, the Wicker Room, and the Victorian Room, which has a Jenny Lind bed. The house is crammed with antiques collected by artist-owner Jeanne Hagel, many from Pennsylvania, where she and her husband once ran a bed and breakfast in a 1750 Colonial stone house. A grand piano dominates the living room.

DINING IN TOMBSTONE

Tombstone is a small town and does not offer a wide choice of eating establishments. The oldest restaurant here is the **Nellie Cashman Restaurant and Pie Salon**. Good Samaritan Nellie Cashman (read about her on the back of the menu) purchased the Russ House, at the corner of Fifth and Toughnut streets, on December 19, 1880, and two years later turned it into a hotel and restaurant. Today it is run by Luxembourger Anita Skinner, undoubtedly much as Nellie did. In addition to basic American, Italian, and Mexican fare, the menu features Anita's specialty, homemade fruit pies.

From Tombstone it is 70 miles (112 km) back to Tucson via U.S. 80 North and I-10 West; the highways intersect at Benson. The long way around is southeast to Douglas on U.S. 80 and then north on U.S. 666 to I-10.

Douglas and the Chiricahuas

Douglas, just 23 miles (37 km) southeast of Bisbee on U.S. 80 (all downhill), is another former mining town struggling to recover from the closure of its smelter, in 1987. For most of this century Douglas thrived on the revenues earned from processing copper ore brought by train down from Bisbee and up from the Mexican mines in Nacozari.

The long-abandoned Southern Pacific depot, formerly the El Paso & Southwestern depot, has been turned over by the city to the Douglas police, who are using funds generated by drug-dealer property confiscations to restore the stately building, badly in need of repair. If the planned San Pedro & Southwestern Railway (see above) extends its excursion run past Naco some day, the next stop will be Douglas to the east, and the old terminal may once again become commercially viable.

Douglas has two museums, both open to visitors at no charge. The oldest, featuring Indian and pioneer artifacts, is the **Cochise County Historical and Archaeological Society Museum**, at 1116 G Avenue, Suite 6. For an index of their quarterly magazine, contact them at P.O. Box 818, Douglas, AZ 85608-0818; Tel: 364-5226.

The main exhibit of the second museum, opened in 1991 at 1001 D Avenue, is the 1908 **redwood home** built by Jimmy "Rawhide" Douglas, son of the man for whom the town was named. The home is owned by the Arizona State Historical Society and is open on Tuesdays and Thursdays only from 2:00 to 4:00 P.M.

Douglas's main claim to fame is the **Gadsden Hotel**,

which opened in 1907 and has counted among its guests Eleanor Roosevelt, Alan Ladd, Joseph Cotten, Paul Newman, and every governor of Arizona (except Evan Mecham). Tom Mix is said to have spent his last night here before dying in a highway accident north of Tucson late the following evening.

The imposing lobby boasts a 42-foot Tiffany stained glass mural, four giant rose-colored marble pillars topped with 1,000 ounces of 14-karat gold leaf, and vaulted stained glass skylights. The once-elegant Gadsden has always been the pride of Douglas. Citizens once called it "the last of the grand hotels," the best one ever built between New Orleans and San Francisco. Though it has lost its original glamour, a stay here today offers a glimpse of its once-proud history.

The broad, white marble staircase has a nasty chip in one of the steps, and legend has it that this occurred when Pancho Villa rode his horse into the lobby during his attack on Agua Prieta in 1912. Skeptics point out that the hotel burned down in 1927 and had to be completely rebuilt, precluding any evidence of the bandido's invasion—but then, the staircase couldn't have burned, since it is solid stone.

"Texas" John Slaughter was sheriff of Cochise County from 1886 to 1890, commissioned as a deputy U.S. marshal after he left office, and later elected to the Territorial Legislature in Phoenix. The facts and legends of his picturesque career as a forceful lawman in a virtually lawless era are spellbinding. In 1884 Slaughter purchased a ranch in San Bernardino, 73,240 acres that were originally a land grant awarded to Ignacio Perez by the government of Mexico. The property lay entirely in Mexico before the Gadsden Purchase of 1853 divided it in two. Slaughter retired comfortably to this ranch, overseeing 30,000 cattle under his brand, and died there in 1922.

The **Slaughter Ranch** is open to the public daily from 10:00 A.M. to 3:00 P.M., and visitors can see the adobe ranch house, grainery, wash house, and garage—with Slaughter's Model T still in it. A Disney videotape gives the story of his life and times, and photos and artifacts capture the feel of former days at the ranch. To drive to the property from Douglas, take G Avenue to Tenth Street and head east through town to Airport Road. Turn left on Airport Road to 15th Street and look for the sign saying Geronimo Trail, Slaughter Ranch Road. Turn right there and drive east on the partially paved road for 16 miles (26 km).

Sulphur Springs Valley

U.S. 666 heads north from Douglas through the grassy ranchland of the broad Sulphur Springs Valley. About 37 miles (59 km) north of Douglas, AZ 181 comes in from the east. Follow that road 26 miles (42 km) east to the **Chiricahua National Monument,** a fantasy of rock spires and towers. This is the territory of the infamous Chiricahua Apache Indians, most notably the warriors Geronimo and Cochise. From here they launched attacks against the oncoming pioneers for more than 25 years. The scenic area, part of the much larger Coronado National Forest, was officially declared a national monument in 1924. There is an admission fee to the area, which has a campground, hiking trails, and an eight-mile scenic drive.

Chief Cochise's main hideout was 35 miles west of here, in the **Dragoon Mountains.** To reach it, return to U.S. 666 and go about 10 miles (16 km) north. A dirt road turns off to the west near the little town of Sunsites. (The road is not marked, so it is best to ask directions.) The natural rock fortress is about eight miles up into the mountains. Cochise is said to be buried somewhere in this wilderness, but his grave has never been found.

Also west of Sunsites is one of Arizona's working cattle/guest ranches: **Grapevine Canyon Ranch.** In 1983 Eve and Gerry Searle began taking in guests, and since then have built a Western complex of 11 accommodations. Guests live in comfortable cabins or *casitas* (little houses) among secluded groves of oak and manzanita, eat hearty meals in a ranch-style dining room, ride horseback, and may participate in the working of the cattle ranch. The ranch is at an altitude of 5,000 feet at the foot of the Dragoon Mountains. There is a two-night minimum, and no children under 12 are allowed.

North of Sunsites on AZ 666 the road passes through the little town of Cochise, where the 100-year-old **Cochise Hotel** still takes guests; if you want to dine here you must make reservations; Tel: 384-3156. From here it is only 4 miles (6½ km) north to I-10, at exit 331.

THE AMERIND FOUNDATION

About 6 miles (10 km) north of Sunsites on U.S. 666, before you come to Cochise, Dragoon Road connects from the west. A ride on Dragoon Road will take you past apple, pecan, and pistachio orchards as the road parallels the Southern Pacific Railroad tracks for a distance and then turns north to cross them. Beyond Johnson Road and past the new Dragoon post office, the sign for the Amerind Foundation will appear on the right. The dirt road leads under oak tree branches and between granite boulders before suddenly opening out into a peaceful compound of Spanish-style buildings that resemble a church settlement or a private school with no children. This is the Amerind Foundation. (It can also be reached by taking I-10's exit 318, 16 miles/26 km east of Benson, and heading south on Dragoon Road.)

This nonprofit museum and research center was founded in 1937 by William S. Fulton, who spent his life studying prehistoric and Native American cultures. Displays here chart the beginning of human life in the area and catalogue the vanished tribes of the Hohokam, the Mogollon (muh-gee-OWN), and the so-called Anasazi. Rare artifacts from Fulton's collection of Indian arts and crafts define his life's work. In addition to the articles in the museum, the Amerind Art Galley displays Western art by noted 19th- and 20th-century painters and sculptors. There is an admission fee. The public is invited to bring a lunch and enjoy the scenic picnic grounds on the site. For information contact the Amerind Foundation, P.O. Box 248, Dragoon, AZ 85609; Tel: 586-3666.

Return north or west to I-10 for a straight 64-mile (102-km) run west to Tucson, or an excursion east to Willcox.

Nine miles (14½ km) east of exit 331 on I-10 is the town of **Willcox**, at exit 340. The Willcox area is known for its apples, for the Willcox Cowboy Hall of Fame, and for the **Museum of the Southwest**, which features a cowboy display, Indian artifacts, minerals, and weapons used in the 1880s. The first weekend in October Willcox celebrates its favorite son with Rex Allen Days. For information contact the Willcox Chamber of Commerce & Agriculture, 1500 North Circle 1 Road, Willcox, AZ 85643; Tel: 384-2272.

From Willcox, Tucson is 81 miles (130 km) west on I-10.

GETTING AROUND
Eight airlines serve Tucson through Tucson International Airport south of the city; Tel: 573-8100 for airport information. The carriers that fly into Tucson are AeroMexico, American, America West, Continental, Delta, Northwest, United, and USAir.

Because Tucson is only a spoke of the America West hub in Phoenix, it is usually cheaper to fly in and out of that city and drive to Tucson than it is to fly to Tucson directly. This is especially true for those travelling from California; America West and Southwest airlines are competing for Phoenix–Los Angeles passengers, and the rates of both airlines to and from California are very low. Therefore, when flying to Tucson, it will pay to compare costs of a direct ticket against a fare to Phoenix plus the cost of a rental car down to Tucson.

This imbalance in airfares has produced a new industry: shuttle services between Tucson and the Phoenix Sky Harbor Airport. One such company is the Arizona Shuttle Service, based at the east end of the El Con Mall at 3601 East Broadway. They provide regularly scheduled van service to and from Sky Harbor; Tel: 795-6771 or (800) 888-2749.

Taxis in Tucson tend to be expensive, if only because the city is so spread out. A ride from the airport to one of the destination resorts, for example, runs $25 to $35 because the airport is on the south side of town and the resorts are all on the north side, 30 to 40 minutes away. Airport transfers are provided by the Arizona Stagecoach, which has a desk at the airport, usually at about half the price of taxis; they'll go anywhere in town. Tel: 881-4111.

Thirteen auto-rental companies are registered with the Visitors Bureau. Most will deliver a car to a hotel or a private home on request. You'd best contract for a car before your arrival and arrange for unlimited mileage, especially if you are planning to drive outside of Tucson.

The once-proud Tucson railway station on the eastern edge of downtown, at 400 East Toole Avenue, has fallen into disrepair and is in sad condition. The station does not open every day so you should call for hours; Tel: 623-4442. For Amtrak reservations and information nationwide, Tel: (800) 523-8720.

Greyhound/Trailways Lines has a monopoly on intercity bus service in and out of Tucson. They offer 12 departures per day to Phoenix and 7 per day east to El Paso and beyond. The bus depot is downtown, at the corner of Broadway and Fourth Avenue, a block south of the railway station and the Hotel Congress. For local fare and schedule information, Tel: 792-0972; nationwide, Tel: (800) 531-5332.

Two blocks north of the Temple of Music and Art, at 130 South Scott Avenue, is the two-story Metropolitan Tucson Convention & Visitors Bureau. The glass door on the right is the Visitors' Center, where volunteers provide up-to-date information on every aspect of Tucson and southern Arizona, and have brochures on hundreds of attractions, accommodations, restaurants, tour operators, shops, galleries, and more. The center is open daily except Sundays. Tel: 624-1817 or (800) 638-8350; Fax: 884-7804.

One of the best ways to discover the desert, or the Southwest, is on an escorted tour with an expert guide. Twenty ground excursion operators have registered with the Tucson Visitors Bureau, each offering transportation, knowledgeable guides, and often some specialty. One does camera tours, one takes senior citizens, one serves catered picnics, some are strictly custom tours, most have guides certified by the Southern Arizona Guides Association. It is safe to say that whatever you would like to see in the area, a tour operator will accommodate your party.

Several companies offer jeep rides into the desert, providing an enjoyable introduction to remote sites. **Sunshine Jeep Tours**, Tel: 742-1943, is one of the oldest in Tucson and, they say, the largest in the state. One of their tours takes guests up to the Tortolita Mountains northwest of town, across cactus-covered cattle range, to an archaeological dig and petroglyph sites. The guide gives detailed, educational descriptions of the native flora and fauna, talks about the rocks and the weather, and relates the story of the wild-horse roundup conducted here years ago by the government.

About the July and August monsoons: It is dangerous to drive through dips in Arizona roads during these storms, which often bring a flash-flood alert. Six inches of water can become three feet in seconds. Dangerous washes are usually posted with signs reading Do Not Enter When Flooded. Lightning can be a menace as well. Do not play golf, swim, or row an aluminum boat across a lake when you hear thunder or see lightning, even at a distance.

ACCOMMODATIONS REFERENCE
The rate ranges given here are projections *for 1993. Unless otherwise indicated, rates are for double room, double occupancy. Because the demand for accommodations peaks during the winter, high-season rates occur between January and April. There can be marked differences between winter and summer rates, especially at the larger, convention-oriented resorts. As rates are subject to change, it is wise to double-check before booking.*

Information on the various Tucson accommodations is found in the Staying in Tucson section, following the Tucson narrative.

The telephone area code for Tucson (and all of Arizona) is 602.

► **Bisbee Inn**. 45 OK Street, P.O. Box 1855, **Bisbee**, AZ 85603. Tel: 432-5131. $39.

► **Buford House**. 113 East Safford Street, P.O. Box 38, **Tombstone**, AZ 85638. Tel: 457-3168. $55–$110.

► **Burro Inn**. 70 West El Burro Lane, P.O. Box 4188, **Tubac**, AZ 85646. Tel: 398-09300. $59–$89.

► **Cochise Hotel**. **Cochise**, AZ 85606. Tel: 384-3156. $25.

► **Copper Queen Hotel**. P.O. Drawer CQ, **Bisbee**, AZ 85603. Tel: 432-2216; Fax: 432-4298. $63–$80.

► **Gadsden Hotel**. 1046 G Avenue, **Douglas**, AZ 85607. Tel: 364-4481; Fax: 364-4005. $32–$65.

► **Grapevine Canyon Ranch**. P.O. Box 302, **Pearce**, AZ 85625. Tel: 826-3185 or (800) 245-9202; Fax 826-3636. Peak season, 4-night minimum: $140–$160 per person per night; off-season, 2-night minimum: $120–$140 per person per night. Rates include all meals and horseback riding.

► **Guest House Inn Bed and Breakfast**. 3 Guest House Road, **Ajo**, AZ 85321. Tel: 387-6133. $59.

► **Inn at the Biosphere**. P.O. Box 689, **Oracle**, AZ 85623. Tel: 825-6222. $49–$80; with two meals and tour: $136–$158.

► **Judge Ross House**. 605 Shattuck Street, **Warren**, AZ 85603. Tel: 432-4120 or 432-5597. $60.

► **The Little House**. 341 Sonoita Avenue, P.O. Box 461, **Patagonia**, AZ 85624. Tel: 394-2493. $60.

► **Mine Manager's House Inn**. One Greenway Drive, **Ajo**, AZ 85321. Tel: 387-6505; Fax: 387-6508. $65–$105.

► **OK Street Jail House Inn**. P.O. Box 1152, 9 OK Street, **Bisbee**, AZ 85603. Tel: 432-7435 or (800) 821-0678. One night, $100; two nights, $150; three nights, $200.

► **Oliver House Bed and Breakfast**. 26 Souls Avenue, P.O. Box 1897, **Bisbee**, AZ 85603. Tel: 432-4286; Fax: 432-7877. $45–$75.

► **Priscilla's Bed and Breakfast**. 101 North Third Street, P.O. Box 700, **Tombstone**, AZ 85638. Tel: 457-3844. $55.

► **Ramsey Canyon Inn**. 31 Ramsey Canyon Road, **Hereford**, AZ 85615. Tel: 378-3010. $75–$85.

► **Tombstone Boarding House**. 108 North Fourth Street, P.O. Box 906, **Tombstone**, AZ 85638. Tel: 457-3716; Fax: 457-3038. $55–$65.

► **YWCA**. Grace Dodge Memorial Building, 26 Howell, **Bisbee**, AZ 85603. Tel: 432-3542. $6–$15.

SIDE TRIPS
INTO
MEXICO

By Sam Negri

*Sam Negri, a freelance writer based in Tucson, Arizona,
covered the Southwest and Mexico for more than 20
years as a staff reporter for newspapers in Phoenix and
Tucson. Co-author of* Travel Arizona—The Backroads,
he is a regular contributor to Arizona Highways *magazine and has written articles on the Southwest for numerous publications.*

It was Mexico's president at the turn of the century,
Porfírio Díaz, who lamented that his country was "so
far from God and so near to the United States." Today
his precise meaning may be a matter of conjecture,
but there is no doubt he was at least partially correct.
The evocative countryside of northern Mexico is easily
reached from the United States, and especially from the
Arizona border at Nogales. Within a one- or two-hour
drive south of the border visitors can see the relatively
unchanged terrain that once was the homeland of Opata,
Apache, and Yaqui Indians, as well as the lair of Pancho
Villa. However, if the country was far from God in Díaz's
day, there is every indication, judging from architectural
manifestations and major religious festivals, that that situation has now been remedied.

A visit to some of the rural communities that dot
the landscape of northern Mexico—Magdalena de Kino,
Cucurpe, Cananea, and Arizpe—is not for everyone.

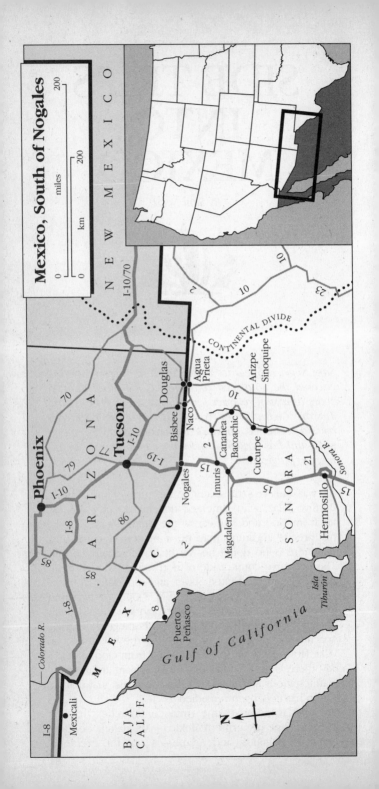

Those seeking luxurious motels and restaurants and crisp efficiency should remain north of the border. The rural ranching and mining towns of Sonora, the Mexican state that borders Arizona, are delightful instead for their architectural simplicity and distinctive ambience, for the omnipresent feel of the past that they evoke, and for the uncompromising faith the people have in age-old myths and legends. It is a place where life moves at the pace of a lethargic burro, especially during the summer months, when afternoon temperatures will often range between 100 and 110°F.

MAJOR INTEREST

Fiesta of St. Francis in Magdalena
Easter pageant in Cucurpe
Cananea jail (museum)
The skeleton in Arizpe's closet

Magdalena

According to local legend, Franciscan friars were passing through Magdalena centuries ago with a statue of Saint Francis loaded on a burro. When the burro got to the middle of town it refused to go on, a situation that convinced the friars that the statue clearly had chosen to remain in Magdalena.

This particular story is told of numerous religious statues in numerous Sonoran towns by people with great conviction. But in Magdalena, partly because of the burros' alleged intransigence and partly because of a pioneering Jesuit priest, the feast day of Saint Francis of Assisi (October 4) is cause for one of the most venerable and frenetic fiestas in Sonora. During the week leading to the saint's day, Magdalena is transformed, as one resident put it, "from a chameleon to an elephant."

The story about the friars and the burro is an entertaining legend, but its tone is consistent with a widely held belief that supernatural events are possible in Magdalena. For several days prior to October 4 all roads into the town are lined with walking pilgrims who attribute magical powers to the statue of Saint Francis that reclines in wooden silence in a chapel of the 160-year-old Church of Santa Maria Magdalena in the town's central plaza.

In 1851 John Russell Bartlett, U.S. boundary commissioner, spent a few days in the town, 56 miles (90 km) south of Nogales on Highway 15, and visited the church.

He happened to arrive on October 4, just as the annual festival was reaching its highest pitch. Bartlett said he saw the faithful approach the statue of Saint Francis and pass ribbons over the various parts of the saint's body in the hope that they would then be able to cure an ailment in their own bodies.

"Some of the worshippers were provided with long pieces of ribbon, which they applied in turn to every part, a knot being tied after each application, making, probably, as one gentleman observed, 'a sort of family medicine chest,'" Bartlett wrote. Today it is just as common to see the faithful approach the statue, place a hand under its head, and attempt to lift it. The general belief is that the statue can tell if a person has been leading a moral life. If you can't lift the statue, they say, there's something wrong with your spiritual purity.

Magic is an integral part of life in Magdalena, and the cult of Saint Francis is its strongest manifestation. During the **Fiesta of St. Francis** booths are set up around the plaza and throughout the narrow streets where curative herbs and magical concoctions are sold to cure everything from gastritis to the evil eye. Carnival rides are set up in and around the plaza, food booths are everywhere, and hawkers sell everything from balloons to "gold" bracelets guaranteed to put the buyers into complete harmony with the cosmos.

About a quarter of the pilgrims are Papago or Yaqui Indians. Yaqui *pascola* dancers (the name given to those who dance at Easter) and deer dancers, wearing headdresses with deer antlers and shell bracelets around their ankles, come to the fiesta with their musicians and, usually to fulfill a vow made when they were ill, dance in front of the church for several days (and then pass the hat).

Otherworldly concerns appear to have played an important part in the town's consciousness, but it was a major historical event that prompted a substantial portion of Magdalena to be rebuilt. On May 21, 1966, archaeologists found the bones of an adventurous Catholic priest, Eusebio Francisco Kino, under the ruins of an old chapel. Kino had spent 24 years, from 1687 to 1711, crisscrossing the desert on foot or horseback, covering the 200 miles between the Rio Magdalena and the Gila River (in present-day Arizona), converting Indians. He left behind a string of some 20 adobe missions—most of which have since disintegrated—as well as the first map of the area (published in 1705) and an extensive memoir. For his physical and intellectual accomplishments, he is often regarded as a local hero.

Historical documents recorded Kino's death in 1711 and identified his burial place under the chapel of San Xavier, which he had just dedicated, but in 1966 no one was certain where that chapel had been located. Everyone knew that the church dominating the central plaza had been built probably 100 years after Kino died and could not be the one where he was buried. In 1966, after comparing information found in historical documents with adobe ruins found in the trenches that had been dug all over the plaza, a team of Mexican and American investigators announced that they had found the ancient chapel and Kino's skeleton about 100 feet north of the present church.

The find led Magdalena to rename itself Magdalena de Kino. It also resulted in the building of an elaborate plaza flanked with Colonial-style arcades and gift shops. And it led to a decision to build a windowed dome over Kino's grave so that visitors could see his skeleton where it was found.

However, it is not Kino but his patron saint, Saint Francis, who motivates the pilgrims. When they get to the side chapel of the church across the plaza from Kino's skeleton, they find the wood-and-plaster statue reclining corpselike on a table. The statue, with a black beard, bare feet, and hands folded on its chest, is draped in the black robes of the Jesuits. In fact, this statue that all of the Indians and cowboys come to venerate on October 4 is not that of Saint Francis of Assisi, but of Jesuit Saint Francis Xavier, whose feast day is not celebrated until December 3. Such details are of no concern to the faithful; one Saint Francis is as good as another, they seem to reason.

STAYING IN MAGDALENA

The quality of accommodations in Magdalena varies considerably. Prices range from U.S. $18 to $44. The Motel Internacional has Jacuzzis in some rooms and is regarded as the most upscale motel in town, though the quality of the rooms is somewhere between a Motel 6 and a Holiday Inn. It is about an eight-block walk from the Internacional to the central plaza. The least expensive hostelry is Motel El Cuervo, a half block from the central plaza, at $19; its rooms are Spartan, though very clean.

Motel Ayabay, Carretera Internacional (a southern extension of Avenida Niños Heroes), offers clean, undistinguished rooms for $24. The independently owned **El Toro Restaurant**, the best in Magdalena, is adjacent to the Ayabay's office; a full meal of beef or shrimp here costs about $10. Tel: (632) 2-0253.

Motel El Cuervo, Avenida 5 de Mayo 316, with clean but small, Spartan rooms, is a half block from the central plaza. Tel: (632) 2-0748. Rooms range from $28 to $38.

Motel Internacional, Avenida Niños Heroes 329 (the main road into town), has 44 rooms built around a court-yard. There is a disco on the first floor, and its sounds echo through the rooms at night. The motel's restaurant is mediocre. Tel: (632) 2-1131. $22 to $38.

Motel Kino, Calle Dr. Ernesto Rivera Magallon, is quiet, plain, and reasonably comfortable, though it is a few blocks' walk to the center of town. Its restaurant is medio-cre. Tel: (632) 2-0998. $22.

Motel Saguaro, Highway 15 south of town, is the new-est motel in the area. Rooms here are comparable to a Motel 6 but lack any Mexican ambience. Rates range from $31.50 for one person to $44 for four. No telephone.

Motel La Suite, Avenida Niños Heroes 310, across the street from the Internacional, offers clean rooms from $31.50 to suites for $36. Tel: (632) 2-0927.

To get to Calle Kino, the road to Cucurpe, from the southern end of Magdalena, take Avenida Niños Heroes back toward Route 15. Calle Kino is a right turn (east) a little more than a quarter mile after the elementary school, which is on the right-hand side of Niños Heroes (there is a whitewashed concrete replica of a mission in front of the school). The road sign is not easily visible, so if you have any trouble ask a local.

Cucurpe

Cucurpe, a small town built on terraces along the side of the Rio San Miguel, 28 miles (45 km) southeast of Magdalena on a narrow paved road off Highway 15, is remarkable for the distance between it and the 20th century.

Approximately 1,000 people live in Cucurpe, and dur-ing Holy Week most of the them are engaged in an Easter pageant. Roman Catholics since the Jesuits established a mission here in 1642, the Cucurpeños usually celebrate Holy Week by carrying statues from the old mission through an abbreviated Way of the Cross. The Jesuit mis-sion was never completed, but the Cucurpeños use it anyway, storing their small hoard of statues and other religious paraphernalia in a room off the sanctuary—the only part of the mission with a roof and a door.

There are a few signs of modern life at Cucurpe, such as pickup trucks, a baseball diamond, and a stone-cutting plant rusting on a hillside above the town, adjacent to the imposing ruins of the mission. Otherwise, it is still 1860 here: men on horseback and fields of ripening winter wheat and barley; a river lined by willows and cottonwoods and hills studded with mesquite and saguaros. There are no motels, restaurants, video stores, or supermarkets.

Cucurpe has grown slightly with the development of a gold mine about ten miles west of town, but by and large it remains a sleepy Western antique that wakes at Easter to demonstrate its faith. The vest-pocket plaza in the center of town is a delightful place to sit at sunset with your favorite beverage. The Cucurpeños are usually intrigued by the arrival of a visitor, and are cheerful conversationalists.

In June of this year the asphalt road that ends at Cucurpe is expected to be extended across the mountains to Sinoquipe (south of Arizpe) and the valley of the Rio Sonora in the east (see below). Until that road is finished, though, you must return to Magdalena for accommodations, or head for any other destinations in Mexico.

The Sonora River Valley

The Bacanuchi and Sonora rivers (the Bacanuchi is a tributary of the Sonora) curve gently through a valley east of the Sonora–Highway 15 corridor where 350 years of conflict and settlement seem like a mural suspended across the landscape. The valley is a relatively untouched history book, where artifacts and architecture link Opata Indian villages, frontier missions, and Mexican communities once dominated by Yaqui and Apache Indians. The widely spaced villages, tucked between sparsely populated rolling hills, resemble woodcuts from the 19th century.

The road through this tranquil countryside begins at Cananea. Drive south on Mexico Highway 15 from Nogales 43 miles (70 km) to the junction of Routes 15 and 2 at Imuris. Turn east there onto Route 2. It is another 51 miles (82 km) to the copper-mining town of Cananea. At the east end of Cananea, Sonora Route 89 leads south through the tiny pueblos of Bacoachi and Chinapa before arriving in historic Arizpe, 55 miles (88 km) south of

Cananea. Gas is available along Sonora Route 89, but no tourist facilities will otherwise be found until you get to Arizpe—and those are minimal.

It is useful to remember that Sonora Route 89 from Cananea to Arizpe, though it is a paved two-lane highway, is a secondary road through cowboy country. That means you may encounter riders on horseback as well as carts being pulled by burros, pedestrians, cows, and tractors. The road is generally in good condition most of the year, but in the period during and just after the summer rains it can be treacherous.

The asphalt on this road is extremely thin, and the combination of heavy rains and the weight of trucks travelling to and from the mines at Cananea and Nacozari de Garcia occasionally turn the road into an obstacle course of fissures, potholes, and small boulders washed off nearby hills.

IMURIS TO CANANEA

Route 2 from Imuris to Cananea traverses a mountainous landscape of high-desert plants, such as saguaro cacti and mesquite and paloverde trees. Approximately 25 miles (40 km) east of Imuris the ruins of **Cocóspera**, a 300-year-old Jesuit mission church that was burned down a few times by Apaches, appears on a hillside to the north. The ruin is a national monument open to visitors, but the narrow dirt road leading up the hill is sometimes badly rutted, and an ordinary passenger car may bottom out.

The 100-year-old copper-mining town of **Cananea** is about 25 miles (40 km) east of Cocóspera. The massive mine itself is visible on the right at the western fringe of the town. Aside from the mine, Cananea's best-known feature is its old **jail**, which is now a museum and national landmark. The jail is widely known in Mexico for two reasons: First, it is the subject of a popular *corrido* (folk ballad), "The Ballad of Cananea." Second, the jail became a symbol of worker repression and resistance during a 1906 strike against the American-controlled mine. The incarceration of more than 2,000 Mexican miners in the Cananea jail is viewed as a regional precursor of the Mexican Revolution of 1910.

The jail is located on Avenida Juárez, on what is known as Cananea's North Mesa. A two-story, redbrick structure, it was built in 1903 and was still in use as a jail in the late 1970s. A few cells, which have been cleaned and filled with murals, historic photos, and antique copper-mining equipment, surround a courtyard. A small gift shop in the lobby sells, among other things, inexpensive collections of minerals found in the Cananea area.

Staying in Cananea

Valle del Cobre Motel, Carretera Cananea Agua Prieta, has 38 excellent rooms, a good restaurant, and a pool, set back off the main highway. (Valle del Cobra means "Copper Valley.") Prices range from U.S. $33 for a double to $57 for a one-bedroom suite with kitchenette. Tel: (633) 2-2888.

Motel El Mesón, across the street from Valle del Cobre, is the newest motel in Cananea. Barrackslike buildings contain 49 comfortable rooms and a decent restaurant. All rooms are $35.

To continue to Arizpe follow Avenida Juárez (an extension of Route 2) east to the junction of Route 89 South. At the Rodeo Café, 55 miles (88 km) south on Route 89, turn left and follow the road to the center of town. Those who prefer not to head south of Cananea to Arizpe can leave Mexico easily without backtracking to Imuris and Nogales. Simply continue east of Cananea 24 miles (39 km) on Route 2 to the cutoff north for Naco. From the cutoff it is about 10 miles (16 km) to the Mexico–Arizona border at Naco, and 6 miles (10 km) north of Naco to Bisbee, Arizona, where all tourist services are available.

ARIZPE

Arizpe is the jewel in the crown of Sonora. With its brightly painted, flat-roofed homes, its 300-year-old Gothic-style church, and a population keenly aware of the town's historic standing, Arizpe projects the ambience of a small town in Spain. A historic landmark, it is a perfectly preserved remnant of Spain's presence in the New World.

On a plateau west of the Río Bacanuchi just north of its junction with the Río Sonora, 55 miles (88 km) south of Cananea, Arizpe was an Opata Indian village when Franciscans from New Mexico province began proselytizing in the area about 1642. A Jesuit began visiting the local residents in 1646, baptismal records were kept as of 1648, the first resident Jesuit missionary arrived in 1650, and the town became capital of New Spain's Frontier Provinces in 1779. At that time it was the most important city between what is now Sonora and San Francisco, California.

As a result, almost anyone who was prominent in the exploration and development of what is now Sonora, New Mexico, Arizona, and California stopped at Arizpe to consult with the General Command. Many of these prominent figures were married in Arizpe's whitewashed church, **La Iglesia de Nuestra Señora de Asunción de Arizpe**, and some were later buried there. Lieutenant Colonel Juan Bautista de Anza, founder of San Francisco, was one of them. Anza died in Arizpe on December 19, 1788, and was buried under the floor of the old church.

In fact, the chief tourist attraction in Arizpe is what is purported to be Anza's skeleton, which lies exposed in a glass-covered, marble sarcophagus in the church floor. In 1962 the City of San Francisco contributed $2,500 toward replacing the floor because it was convinced that what remained of the city's founder would be discovered there. In 1963 a skeleton wearing a lieutenant colonel's uniform was unearthed. Archaeologists from the University of California announced that this was Anza, and the result was a major celebration, with dignitaries from California and Mexico flying between sleepy Arizpe and stylish San Francisco for banquets and interviews.

Nearly 20 years later the Arizpe parish priest who had set this chain of events in motion confessed that he had stolen Anza's death certificate, which clearly identified where the lieutenant was buried in the church, and that he had lived in torment ever since. The priest, now deceased, in effect acknowledged that the skeleton on display is someone else's. That hasn't changed much in Arizpe, however. The plaque at the glass-covered grave still refers to the skeleton as Anza, but a second plaque with Anza's name on it has been installed in a little side chapel, La Capilla de Nuestro Señora de Loreto, on the gospel (or left) side of the church. According to the death certificate, which the priest eventually returned, this is where Anza is really buried.

The church is in the center of Arizpe. Several blocks east of the church, the large, well-kept cemetery is worth seeing for anyone interested in the history of California and what is now the American Southwest, as most of the prominent military and political figures who settled the northern reaches of New Spain's empire 350 years ago are resting here.

Staying in Arizpe

There are two hotels in Arizpe, but both are primitive and would be acceptable only under extreme conditions. Both offer tiny, barely habitable rooms (though at very inexpensive rates). The Hotel Rita (no phone) is in a house on a dirt road just south of the entrance to the town (a sign points the way); the Hotel Anza is in the old colonial plaza directly opposite the church where Anza is buried. There usually is no one at the Anza, and visitors must telephone the owner, who lives down the street, to get service; Tel: 214.

The only restaurant in Arizpe is the **Rodeo Café**, located on the main highway at the entrance to the town. For about U.S. $1.25 you can buy a *machaca* burrito (spicy shredded beef rolled up in a tortilla) and eat it in the ranch-style dining room. In the summertime the only "cooling" in the place comes from a fan that keeps the hot, dry air moving at a more or less constant 95°F.

USEFUL FACTS FOR SONORA, MEXICO

The climate of northern Mexico is governed by rainfall and altitude. Rainfall is scarce, sometimes as little as 11 inches a year. As a result, humidity is almost always very low. In the spring it will often drop to a scant 10 percent, and a day when the temperature is 85°F—a nightmare in a damp climate—can be delightful. Towns in the region vary in altitude from roughly 3,000 to 4,500 feet. In most places springlike weather, with mild days and chilly evenings, are the norm from October to April. June is the hottest month; July and August the wettest.

The best way to see the area is by car. Roads into the region are generally good. Mexico 15, the main highway leading south from Nogales, is a paved route with two lanes in each direction and an abundance of tourist services. Mexico 2, the highway from Imuris (which is on Mexico 15) east to Cananea, is a paved two-lane road that switchbacks over desert mountains before dropping into the Río Sonora Valley. Sonora 89, which begins at Cananea, is a narrow paved road that occasionally crosses through riverbeds as it wends southward through the Rio Sonora Valley to Arizpe.

Cars for use in Mexico can be rented in Tucson, Arizona, 65 miles (104 km) north of the border. In addition to the rental fee, agencies will charge roughly $8 and up per day for Mexican auto insurance. Tourists *must have Mexican auto insurance* as well as a letter from the rental agency authorizing the vehicle's use in Mexico. *Double-check the insurance certificate from the rental agency to be certain that the vehicle identified on the form is the one you are driving*. Mexican authorities have recently started checking such paperwork more closely to prevent stolen vehicles and contraband from entering the country. A permit for the vehicle is obtained at a checkpoint 13 miles (21 km) south of the border. There is a U.S. $10 fee for the permit, which can be paid only with a credit card. Cash is *not* accepted. The permit is good for six months.

Visitors must obtain a Mexican visa at the border in Nogales. A visa will be issued promptly if you present a passport, a birth certificate, or a voter registration card.

Pesos can be purchased at any bank or Casa de Cambio. At the beginning of this year, Mexico adopted new appellations for its currency, dropping three zeros from the amounts. What was previously 60,000 pesos became 60 N, for New Pesos; 4,000 pesos became 4 N.

The international telephone country code for Mexico is 52.

Contact information for the accommodations of the side trips into Mexico is included within the coverage above.

CENTRAL ARIZONA, THE CANYONS REGION, AND LAS VEGAS

PHOENIX

SCOTTSDALE

THE VALLEY OF THE SUN

CENTRAL ARIZONA

GRAND CANYON'S SOUTH RIM

ARIZONA RIVER COUNTRY

SOUTHERN UTAH; CANYONLANDS

GRAND CANYON'S NORTH RIM

LAS VEGAS

PHOENIX AND SCOTTSDALE
THE VALLEY OF THE SUN

By Maggie Wilson

Maggie Wilson, a native of Arizona whose family roots in the state go back to the 1880s, was a columnist and feature writer for the Arizona Republic *for 30 years, and also travel-promotion manager of the Arizona Office of Tourism. A longtime contributor and contributing editor for* Arizona Highways *magazine, she is a widely recognized expert on Indian cultures and crafts, and is a former member of the board of trustees of The Heard—A Museum of Native Cultures and Art in Phoenix, Arizona, where she lives.*

Phoenix was empty, uninhabited land until the first straggling settlers arrived in the late 1860s. Today it is the nation's ninth-largest city—and one of the world's premier desert cities. According to historian John Myers Myers, "No [other] city in the history of the world has moved from scratch to the attainment of such major urban standing within a like period of time."

Most first-time visitors are impressed by three things: The newness of the glass-and-concrete high rises along the Central Avenue and Camelback Road corridors; the park-like, lush green landscaping and fountains of the resort, business, and governmental areas; and the lack of

495

"true" natives. Not native Indians. Just native Arizonans. The great preponderance of residents have come here from "somewhere else."

Phoenix and the 21 cities surrounding it—including Scottsdale, Mesa, and Tempe to the east and Sun City to the northwest—are known collectively as the Valley of the Sun, one of the nation's fastest-growing areas.

The major catalyst for the Valley's growth was air-conditioning, but even with air-conditioned everything—autos, malls, offices, homes—there are two things residents disdain: July and August, when you need oven mitts to open car doors. During those two months daytime temperatures hover around 110°F, with thunderstorms and dramatic lightning displays in the evenings (not to mention accommodations discounted as much as 70 percent).

The trade-off for enduring July and August is shirtsleeve weather in spring and fall, and sunny daytime highs ranging between the 60s and 80s in winter.

The single biggest attraction to vacationing in the desert? Aside from the cultural amenities and art galleries that provide indoor contemplation, it's the sun-drenched, surprisingly green Sonoran Desert itself, and its invitation to outdoor exploration. The desert air (for ten months of the year, anyway) invigorates and tempts even couch potatoes to swim, golf, play tennis, hike, or ride horseback in the mountain preserves surrounding the Valley; take guided jeep tours into the backcountry; raft or water-ski on nearby lakes; venture forth on day trips into Arizona's diverse landscapes and scenery; or simply sit outdoors and soak up sun.

Perhaps a 20th-century genius best captured the desert's mystique and magnetism. "Living in the desert is a spiritual cathartic many people need," said the great architect Frank Lloyd Wright. "I am one of them." And he did live in this desert for half of each year from in the 1920s until his death in 1959.

The telephone area code for Phoenix and the rest of Arizona is 602.

MAJOR INTEREST

Phoenix
Arizona Center: dining, shopping, nightlife
Phoenix Civic Plaza and Symphony Hall

Heritage Square museum and shops, and Rosson House

Museums: The Heard (native cultures) and the Phoenix Art Museum

Pueblo Grande: museum and cultural park (Hohokam ruins)

Papago Park: zoo and botanical gardens

Phoenix South Mountain Park: desert trails

Scottsdale

Old Town

Art galleries and museums

Frank Lloyd Wright's Taliesen West

Paolo Soleri's Cosanti Foundation: the Soleri wind-bells

The resorts

Shopping: Fashion Square, Camelview, The Borgata

Dining

The East Valley

Out of Africa Wildlife Park

Saguaro Lake steamboat cruises

Arizona State University: campus and museums

Old Town Tempe: grazing, browsing, and entertainment

Guadalupe: Yaqui Indian and Hispanic village

Mormon Temple

Mesa Southwest Museum

Champlin Fighter Museum (aircraft)

Historic San Marcos Resort

The West Valley

Metrocenter

Wildlife World Zoo

Sundome Center for the Performing Arts

Day Trips from the Valley

The Apache Trail

Tonto National Monument

Canyon Lake steamboat cruises

Casa Grande Ruins

Wickenburg: frontier-style buildings and guest ranches

PHOENIX

Though Phoenix is a modern metropolitan city, there is nonetheless an interesting bedrock of the old here. Unlike Tucson and southern Arizona, where European contact was established in 1540 (80 years before the Pilgrims landed at Plymouth Rock), Phoenix's first straggle of settlers—Anglos—didn't arrive on the banks of the then-wet Salt River until 1865, practically yesterday.

Even so, it turned out to be the area's second time around as a human habitat. Prehistoric (i.e., pre-Columbian) Hohokam Indians had tamed the Salt River as early as A.D. 300, channeling its waters through intricate networks of canals to fields of beans, corn, squash, and cotton. At their peak, around A.D. 1100, the Hohokam settlements had a population of perhaps 200,000 (compared to the Valley's current 2.2 million), but by 1450 they had mysteriously disappeared or departed. ("Hohokam" is a Pima Indian word meaning "all used up.")

The mission of the first Anglos was to start irrigated hay farms to feed cavalry horses at military posts and dray animals at the far-flung boomtown mines. All they had to do, it turned out, to their delight, was clear the debris from the Hohokam canals and they were in business. Water flow, gradients, holding and diversion canals along the Salt River all functioned. Like the mythical bird for which it was named, Phoenix began to rise from the ashes.

Today the Salt, Gila, Agua Fria, and Verde rivers are dammed upstream to form reclamation lakes, insurance against the inevitable long dry spells. The lakes also serve as recreational places for fishing, water-skiing, boating, tubing, or steamboat dinner cruises on Canyon or Saguaro lakes (see Fountain Hills in the East Valley section and the Apache Trail in the Day Trips from the Valley section, below). The Salt River through Phoenix is a dry riverbed most of the year, but Hohokam canals still transport water to the thirsty city.

The manufacture of electronic components has replaced farming as Phoenix's major industry. Second to manufacturing is tourism, although just three short years ago you could have fired a cannon downtown after office hours and hit nothing more than a palm tree; workers went home to the suburbs and stayed there. No more.

Phoenix is one city where downtown revitalization has worked to produce a vibrant "people" place, thanks mostly to a consortium called Downtown Phoenix Partners—not to mention a $1.1 billion development program that has changed the face of the city's core.

Downtown Phoenix

Flat as a board, downtown Phoenix is a mix of sleek new high rises shouldering enclaves of older, lower buildings. Anything built before 1920 is considered very, very old; families here since the 1920s are rare as hen's teeth, and those predating that period are considered hardy pioneers. This predominance of new people, new things, and new ideas make downtown a spirited place with a lively pace. The fact that Phoenix is the capital of Arizona hasn't hurt, either (most of the state activity is on the west side of downtown).

Central Avenue, stretching 20 miles from huge South Mountain Park to smaller North Mountain Recreation Area, neatly bisects the city. Downtown itself is roughly defined by Washington Street on the south, Seventh Avenue on the west, McDowell Road on the north, and Seventh Street on the east. U.S. 60/AZ 93 and the business loop of I-10 converge within that boundary at Seventh Avenue and Van Buren Street. The State Capitol complex is west of downtown at 17th Avenue and Washington; Sky Harbor International Airport is east of downtown and is bordered by 24th and 44th streets, I-10, and the I-10 business loop.

As you may have deduced about the city's layout: All numbering begins at Central Avenue, a north–south thoroughfare, and Washington Street. Numbered streets west of Central and running parallel to it are avenues; numbered streets east of Central and running parallel to it are streets.

East–west streets also use Central as the dividing line. For example: 1100 West Washington Street is 11 blocks west of Central (and site of the Arizona Office of Tourism), while 1150 East Washington is 11 blocks east of Central (and site of Social Security Administration offices). Van Buren Street is the two-way east–west thoroughfare through downtown. The main uptown east–west street (which to the east leads to Scottsdale) is Camelback Road, about 5 miles (8 km) north of downtown.

Downtown's most heralded attraction, **Arizona Center,**

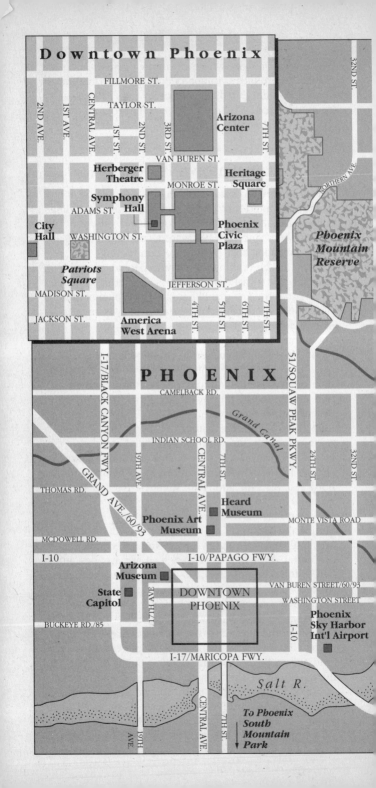

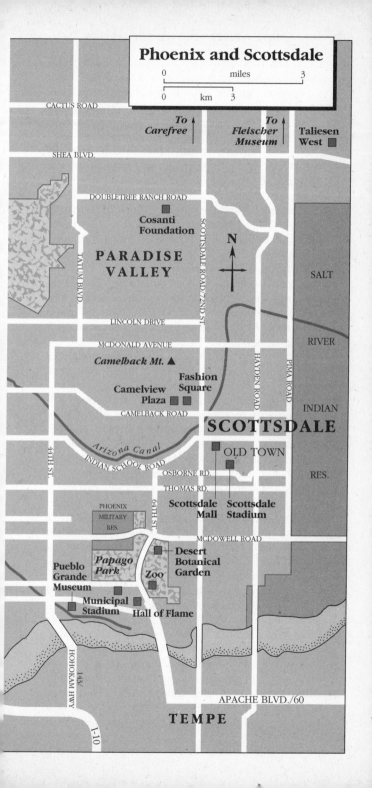

between Third and Sixth streets on East Van Buren, is an eight-block multiphase development of two office towers, specialty shops, vendor carts, and a host of restaurants and night spots including a sports bar, a comedy club, a sing-along bar, a steak house, and a Cajun restaurant. Its spacious grounds are landscaped with lawns, trees, flowers, fountains, walkways, shady nooks, and benches. In spring, fall, and early summer a misting system cools the air as much as 20 degrees, when needed, for outdoor diners.

Outstanding among the specialty shops at the center are **Que Pasa** for Southwestern gifts and folk art, clothing, and home furnishings; **Yippie-Ei-O** for handcrafted gifts, clothes, and accessories, along with some kitschy Western items; and **Catherine's Rare Papers**, for handmade papers, stationery, and gift wrap. **Cheyenne Cattle Company** is the place here for country dancing; **Lombardi's** for upscale Italian food (Tel: 257-8323); and **Sam's Cafe** for lunch featuring a Southwestern grill menu (Tel: 252-3545).

Two blocks south of Arizona Center is the **Herberger Theater Center** at 222 East Monroe, a performing-arts complex that is home to the Arizona Theatre Company, Ballet Arizona, and the Actors Theatre of Phoenix, as well as visiting dance and performance troupes. Across Monroe from the Herberger Theater the 24-acre **Phoenix Civic Plaza** serves as a venue for meetings, conventions, trade shows, and **Symphony Hall**, where the Phoenix Symphony Orchestra and touring groups perform.

Opened last year, **America West Arena**, 201 East Jefferson Street just south of Phoenix Civic Plaza, is a private-public venture between the City of Phoenix and a limited partnership including the NBA Phoenix Suns basketball team. The arena hosts Suns games and other sporting events, pop and rock concerts, circuses, and family shows. In addition to the arena's fast-food court, the popular **The Copper Club** restaurant is open weekdays, but during events is restricted to arena suite holders only. Reservations are recommended; Tel: 379-7777.

Other new additions to downtown include **The Mercado**, across the street from the Civic Plaza (Fifth Street and Monroe), with shops, restaurants, and a Hispanic cultural center in a colorful Mexican market setting, and **Renaissance Square**, two office towers and a landscaped plaza dotted with restaurants and shops two blocks west of Civic Plaza on Central Avenue, between Washington and Adams streets. Facing the side of Civic Plaza at Sixth Street and Monroe is **Heritage Square**, already well known locally for its complex of museums, shops, and restaurants, and for **Rosson House**, a restored 1895 Eastlake-style Victorian edifice on the National Register of Historic Places. Other Heritage Square museums include the Silva House (1900), featuring period furnishings and Salt River Project exhibits; the Burgess Carriage House, an example of Colonial-style architecture similar to that found in Williamsburg, Virginia, and rarely seen this far west; the 1901 Stevens House, which houses the Arizona Doll and Toy Museum; and the 1980 Lath House, built completely of slats typical of early Phoenix architecture (designed for the maximum movement of air).

Patriots Square, at Central Avenue and Washington, is a downtown landmark where brown baggers enjoy entertainment at lunchtime and families congregate in the evenings for the small fry to play with honest-to-gosh laser light for a quarter a turn. The first phase of Margaret Hance Deck Park, about a mile north of Patriots Square on Central Avenue, has been completed, with fountains, an urban plaza, a wooded area, and playground and picnic areas stretching from Third Avenue to Third Street. Both parks are engineering marvels: Patriots Square was built above a 1,500-space underground parking garage; Deck Park, atop the ten-lane I-10 tunnel.

Located on Second Avenue between Washington and Adams streets, two blocks west of Patriots Square, the **New City Hall/Old Orpheum Theater** is expected to open near the end of this year. The new 20-story city hall will connect with the old Orpheum Theater, a historical landmark undergoing renovation. Built in 1929 in Spanish Baroque Revival style and considered the most luxurious playhouse west of the Mississippi River, the theater is to be used for large road shows and musicals.

A 25¢ downtown-area shuttle service, on six purple-and-orange minibuses known as The Dash, runs every five to ten minutes from 6:30 A.M. to 6:00 P.M. weekdays. Stops include the above-mentioned downtown attractions as well as the Hyatt Regency Phoenix hotel and sites in the State Capitol area 17 blocks west along Washington Street (one-way west) and Jefferson Street (one-way east).

Additionally, in season, a dozen "security guides" in purple shirts and khaki pants act as walking information booths, giving out directions, maps, and brochures, and providing information on everything in the city's core, from where to find a hot-fudge sundae to which celebrity is performing where.

Across Second Street from the Civic Plaza, **Hyatt Regency Phoenix** recently overhauled its 711 rooms, renovated its Compass Restaurant (the only revolving rooftop restaurant in Arizona and a fun place for sunset cocktails; Tel: 252-1234), and installed voice-message and modem capabilities in each guest room.

An alternative to downtown hotels, which are devoted essentially to Civic Plaza's meeting and convention delegates, is the old (only 1920s, but these are Phoenix standards), comfy 110-room **San Carlos Hotel**, on North Central Avenue within walking distance of downtown attractions and The Dash. Listed in the National Register of Historic Places, this hotel is adored by nostalgia buffs.

THE DOWNTOWN MUSEUMS

Not far from the city's core is **The Heard—A Museum of Native Cultures and Art,** 22 East Monte Vista Road (three blocks north and one block east of Central Avenue and McDowell Road). The Heard features the best exhibits extant on Southwestern Indian tribes. Start your visit with the beautifully photographed and musically scored audio-visual presentation "Our Voices Our Land," in which Indians of various tribes talk about their lifestyles and cultures. The exhibits interpret the land and people from prehistoric times to the present. Extensive displays show Indian jewelry, most of it created by Navajo, Hopi, and Zuni craftspeople. A collection of Hopi and Zuni carved kachina dolls (icons of tribal deities) fills an entire room. Other collections include pottery, basketry, weavings, paintings, clothing, tools, weapons—even a Navajo abode, called a hogan. Indian dancers, chanters, drummers, and singers provide entertainment most weekends; crafts are demonstrated most days. In the World Cultures Gallery travelling exhibits feature tribal art and artifacts from South America, Africa, Asia, and the Pacific Rim. The **museum gift shop** sells (and certifies as authentic) Indian arts and crafts. Open daily, major holidays excepted.

The **Phoenix Art Museum**, at Central Avenue and McDowell Road, has art collections dating from the Renaissance to contemporary times, with special strengths in its Chinese, Mexican, and contemporary collections and its 18th-century French paintings. A small but select Costume Institute displays 20th-century women's designer clothing, some of them once owned by celebrities and presidents' wives, and a small gift shop features posters and art-oriented collectibles and books. Open daily except Mondays and major holidays.

The museum is notable for its annual show and sale of works by **Cowboy Artists of America**, a group composed of 30 painters and sculptors who have also worked as ranch hands. Like the Taos Ten artists of New Mexico who banded together in the 1930s to enhance awareness and sales of regional works, the CAA was formed in the 1960s for the same purposes. Sales on opening nights of Cowboy Artists shows have never failed to top $1 million, with a portion benefiting the museum.

East of Downtown

Pueblo Grande Museum and Cultural Park, 4619 East Washington Street, is actually a Hohokam ruin occupied from the time of Christ to A.D. 1450. Permanent exhibits feature material excavated from the site and dioramas relating to the building of the ancient Hohokam canal system. Special exhibits highlight other aspects of Indian culture. Open daily.

PAPAGO PARK

Papago Park, tucked into the juncture of Scottsdale and Tempe east of downtown on McDowell Road or U.S. 60, has a public golf course and trails for hiking and rock climbing. It is also the site of several important Phoenix attractions.

The **Phoenix Zoo**, 5810 East Van Buren Street, off Galvin Parkway in the park, is home to 1,300 exotic critters from throughout the world. Most exotic, perhaps, is Ruby the artful elephant, whose abstract paintings and prints are sold to aid the zoo's many conservation projects. (Ruby, who holds brushes in her trunk and selects pigments from a palette, exhibits a remarkable sense of color.) The Safari Train offers an easy way around the extensive grounds.

The **Hall of Flame**, 6101 East Van Buren Street across from the zoo, is the largest museum devoted to fire fighting in the United States. It houses an extensive collection of fire-fighting equipment and memorabilia, some dating back centuries. Daily guided tours; closed Sundays.

Phoenix Municipal Stadium, 5999 East Van Buren, is a lively place during March, when it becomes the spring-training home of baseball's Oakland As. Seven other major-league teams and the As make up the Cactus League, counterpart to Florida's Grapefruit League. Cactus League games are played daily in this and other Valley stadiums during training season.

Also in Papago Park is the **Desert Botanical Gardens**, 1201 North Galvin Parkway, containing arid-land plants from the deserts of the world. A special exhibit shows uses of Sonoran Desert plants as food, shelter, clothing, and medicines by ancient and historic Indian tribes.

South of Downtown

The nation's largest urban park, **Phoenix South Mountain Park**, offers more than 16,000 acres of desert trails for hiking, horseback riding (rentals are available), and picnicking, with sweeping overviews of the Valley. The city lights at night are especially enchanting from here. Entrance to the park is about 5 miles (8 km) south of the city's core via Central Avenue.

Next door to South Mountain Park is **The Pointe Hilton Resort on South Mountain**, ten minutes from the airport and downtown, with easy access to Scottsdale, Tempe, and Interstates 10 and 17. In addition to the dazzling views of the valley, the Pointe offers 700 acres filled with one championship golf course, seven swimming pools, lighted tennis courts, horseback riding and hiking trails, a lavish layout of get-fit equipment in the sports complex, four restaurants, Mediterranean architecture, tiered walkways beside water cascading in hand-carved fountains, and accommodations ranging from poolside to semi-reclusive mountainside suites.

Among the Pointe's restaurants are **Rustler's Rooste**, atop the mountain, offering beef and brew with a view along with country music and two-step dancing; and **Aunt Chilada's**, in an orange grove atop a reflecting pool, serving such authentic northern Mexico standards as tacos, enchiladas, and *chimichangas*—with margaritas, of course. Reservations are advised; Tel: 438-9000.

Like its two sister Pointe resorts in north Phoenix—The Pointe at Squaw Peak, 7677 North 16th Street, and The Pointe at Tapitio Cliffs, 11111 North Seventh Street—this one was built on land thought to be unsuitable for development, but has triumphed in transforming an eyesore into a thriving urban area with enhanced property values. Not to mention adding new chapters to zoning regulations, as well as textbook lessons in harmoniously blending development with natural landforms.

North of Downtown:
The Camelback Corridor

Uptown, along the so-called Camelback Corridor—the royal road east to Scottsdale—the magnet is the area of 24th Street and East Camelback Road. On the northeast corner of the intersection is **Biltmore Fashion Park**, a collection of the city's priciest shops. If you are interested in haute couture you may want to pass up Saks Fifth Avenue, Gucci, Louis, and Ralph for **Femina Boutique**, where finds range from little-known but carefully selected (and less costly) private labels to those of Franco Ferre, Claude Montana, Thierry Mugler, and Bob Mackie. The I. Magnin shop in Biltmore Fashion Park has evolved into a big, glitzy freestanding store with lots of crystal chandeliers and marble accoutrements among its designer boutiques and off-the-rack fashions.

A pleasant break from browsing the 70 shops here is grazing (preferably outdoors in the sunshine) on noshes from **Oscar Taylor's Restaurant, Bakery & Bar**; Tel: 956-5705. More formal is **RoxSand**, a two-story, gallerylike restaurant serving "new American fusion cuisine" (just call it the most imaginative cooking in town); Tel: 381-0444. High tea is served across Camelback Road at **The Ritz-Carlton, Phoenix**, a venue for travelling business executives where tea timers get pomp, circumstance, and white-glove service with the finger sandwiches; Tel: 468-0700.

Specialty shops and moderately priced restaurants may be found across 24th Street from the Ritz-Carlton at **Town and Country Mall** and farther east, at 40th Street and Camelback, at **Camelback Village Center**.

For nouvelle cuisine with a Southwestern flair, the nationally known **Christopher's** and the slightly less expensive **Christopher's Bistro**, side by side across 24th Street from Biltmore Fashion Park, are the city's favorites. Chef Christopher Gross is one of the youngest, most talented culinary artists around, and the young waiters are helpful, handsome, and very Continental. Reservations are advised; Tel: 957-3214.

A half mile (1 km) north of Biltmore Fashion Park on 24th Street at Missouri Avenue is the entrance to the **Arizona Biltmore** hotel and the privately owned mansions of Biltmore Estates. One of the golden oldies among Arizona resorts, this one dates to the days when families with steamer trunks arrived to spend the winter. Staffers kept copious notes about each guest's foibles, favorite furnishings, flowers, drinks, and tee times. Few guests come for the entire season these days, but the traditional grandeur of a grand hotel seems to seep right through the exterior's distinctive three-dimensional block façade designed by Frank Lloyd Wright. In the some-things-never-change category: More than 250,000 flowers are still planted on the grounds each year.

This hotel is an option for the well-to-do who want a resort near town with 36 holes of championship golf, eight lighted tennis courts, a health-and-fitness center, three heated pools, cabañas, a putting green, a croquet court, and lawn chess. There is dining, dancing, and entertainment in the dramatic architectural setting of the **Orangerie**, the award-winning restaurant here. Coat and tie are required from September to May, and reservations are advised; Tel: 955-6600. An alternative is the casual setting and Southwestern fare of **Sonora Restaurant**.

Across 26th Street from Biltmore Fashion Park is **Crown Sterling Suites**, with, well, call it a desert-Deco exterior in buff and brown. The Southwestern contemporary suites here are capacious, the pool is heated, and breakfast and happy-hour cocktails are complimentary.

Some notable restaurants east on Camelback include **Tomaso's**, at number 3225, on the corner of 32nd Street, serving Italian pasta, veal, and seafood dishes (Tel: 956-0836), and **Vincent on Camelback**, number 3930, at 40th Street, an upscale country-French setting with chef Vincent Guerithault's own innovative style of cuisine (Tel: 224-0225). **Garcia's Mexican Restaurants**, home-grown and scattered throughout the Valley, are popular with both residents and visitors, perhaps because the salsa comes in two bowls, hot and mild, and food is served in a Mexican marketplace atmosphere; for the one on Camelback at 44th Street, Tel: 952-8031.

Farther east on Camelback, at 60th Street, is **The Phoenician**, a resort tiered into the flanks of Camelback Mountain, with marble floors and walls, crystal chandeliers, Berber carpets, antiques from Europe, and monumental bronze sculptures by Apache Indian artist Allan Houser. On grounds lined with imported palm trees in acres of manicured lawns there are seven pools (one paved in hand-set mother-of-pearl tiles), ten restaurants, a spa (the Centre for Well-Being), a championship golf course, and the Tennis Garden, with 11 lighted courts.

The Phoenician was built as the proclaimed "crowning accomplishment" of Charles Keating, who has since been jailed for his role in the savings-and-loan scandals. Ostentatious? Yes. Gauche? Not really. In fact, Keating and the Centre for Well-Being aside, you really do get a sense of well-being in the place, even as you drive the mile from entrance gate to lobby past all those palms, lawns, and fountains. Even more so when you dine at **Mary Elaine's**, a gourmet restaurant featuring Mediterranean country cuisine, or the less pricey **Windows on the Green**, with its Southwestern menu and views overlooking the golf course. Reservations are advised for both; Tel: 941-8200.

Camelback Mountain, the rocky pop-up formation in the shape of a kneeling dromedary north of Camelback Road between 44th and 64th streets, is a Valley symbol and landmark that provides a practical, if not cartographic, divider between the contiguous borders of Phoenix, Scottsdale (east), and Paradise Valley (northeast). In the grand Western scheme of things, Camelback is more hill than mountain. Nonetheless, helicopter AirEvac personnel routinely pluck stranded or injured hikers from its stony flanks. A small pinnacle of rock on its west (or head) side has the look and the name of "the praying monk."

SCOTTSDALE

Scottsdale has Palm Springs' resorts, Hilton Head's golf courses, Santa Fe's art galleries, and Rodeo Drive's boutiques—with palm trees, a backdrop of purple mountains majesty, pastel landscapes, and 330 days of sunshine a year. Even so, Scottsdale isn't necessarily Scottsdale. It's as much a state of mind as a municipality. When vacationers say they are going to Scottsdale, many of them really aren't. The Phoenician is in Phoenix, but has a Scottsdale mailing address; Camelback Inn, Mountain Shadows, and La Posada, to name just a few, are in Paradise Valley (basically, north Phoenix), but claim Scottsdale. In the popular view, "Scottsdale" means the good life.

No longer "the West's most Western town," this city has matured since the 1950s when 2,000 people lived in a single square mile; now, 134,000 live in 183 square miles, and the only physical remains of a Western town is Old Town, where some shops are false-front adobes. The

main north–south thoroughfares are Scottsdale Road
(72nd Street) and, to the east, Hayden Road and finally
Pima Road (Scottsdale ends abruptly here). In the downtown area, east–west streets north of Main Street are
numbered avenues; south of Main, numbered streets.
East–west thoroughfares north of Main include Indian
School Road, Camelback Road, Northern Avenue/Shea
Boulevard, and Cactus, Bell, and Pinnacle Peak roads. The
Main Street–Scottsdale Road intersection is a good central location for orientation: This puts you at Gallery Row
and Old Town, and a short stroll from the Scottsdale
Mall—which isn't a suburban-type shopping mall at all,
but rather closer to a New England town green surrounded by shops and commercial property.

Pima Road is the eastern dividing line between Scottsdale and the Pima–Maricopa Salt River Indian Reservation.
The division is dramatic: Indian farmlands and modest
frame houses sprinkled like corn to the chickens on the
road's east side, Scottsdale's compacted commercial and
housing developments on the west side. For insights into
Pima and Maricopa culture visit the reservation's **Hoo-
hoogam Ki Museum**, 10000 East Osborn Road, where
traditional basketry, pottery, historic photos, and artifacts
are displayed.

AROUND IN SCOTTSDALE
Resort Row, where many, but not all, of the resorts are
located, runs north from Camelback Road to Doubletree
Ranch Road. More resorts are west from Scottsdale Road
along Lincoln Drive.

Both resort hopping and gallery hopping (i.e., spending a day or an afternoon going from one to another just
to check them out) are considered prime leisure-time
activities here.

Though there's no such thing as Golf Course Row, golf
courses tend to coincide with Resort Row and the Greenbelt (for which, see below), with additional public and
semiprivate courses scattered throughout the area.

The **Scottsdale Greenbelt**, a flood-control alternative to
a concrete ditch, is a seven-mile-long series of parks,
lakes, golf courses, and jogging trails running roughly
along Hayden Road from 92nd Street and Shea south to
the Tempe city limits.

Scottsdale Mall, between Second Street and Indian
School Road one block east of Scottsdale Road and Old
Town, is downtown's people place, a compact park featur-
ing an outdoor amphitheater, rolling greens, statuary,

fountains, and winding brick walkways overhung with trees. Rimming its open areas are shops, restaurants, bars, galleries, and city offices. The Chamber of Commerce visitor information center is here, and so is the city-funded **Scottsdale Center for the Arts** with its changing visual-arts exhibitions and live performances.

SHOPPING LANDMARKS IN SCOTTSDALE

Shopping (or browsing and grazing, anyway) ranks near the top of Scottsdale activities, leading some comedians to call this city Shopsdale. Twelve malls are part of the scene, not counting the shops of **Old Town,** bounded by Indian School Road, East Main, Brown Avenue, and Scottsdale Road. Wares in Old Town shops include boots, saddles, Indian arts and artifacts, Western wear, and Southwestern home decor. The new **Scottsdale Galleria,** a no-anchor center near Scottsdale and Camelback roads, has 245 specialty shops, restaurants, and an IMAX theater with its super-size wraparound movie screen and live productions in more intimate settings, like the 1960s-style coffeehouses.

Gallery Row, where some of the town's 100 art galleries are concentrated, runs from Scottsdale Road west on Main Street and from Third Avenue north on Marshall Way. Thursday night art walks, a tradition here, are big, ambulatory, arty parties with cheese and wine inside the galleries and entertainment outside on the streets. And they are free, unless you decide to pick up a Warhol print or an original oil by one of the Cowboy Artists of America. Pre–art walk refreshments are served between 5:00 and 7:00 P.M. at the Scottsdale Center for the Arts (see Scottsdale Mall, below).

The best all-around bets for finding anything from collectibles and clothing to toys and tomes are **Camelview Plaza** and **Scottsdale Fashion Square**, side by side on Camelback Road at the northwest corner of Scottsdale Road. **The Borgata,** a walled enclave of strikingly upscale shops and cafés surrounding sunny cobbled courtyards with fountains and shady nooks at 6166 North Scottsdale Road, takes its design and atmosphere from an Italian marketplace.

OUTSIDE CENTRAL SCOTTSDALE

Scottsdale Stadium, 7402 East Osborn Road, is spring-training home of the San Francisco Giants in March and home to the Rattlers football team in summer, as well as venue for various other outdoor sports, concerts, and festival events.

Frank Lloyd Wright's **Taliesin West**, a complex of structures built by the master and his apprentices as his home and studio, still serves as headquarters of the foundation that operates Wright's school of architecture. Built of organic materials, primarily sand and stone collected from the desert floor, Taliesin West is considered an architectural masterpiece. Tours of the buildings and grounds are conducted daily except holidays. Most rewarding of these is the Behind the Scenes tour. For information, Tel: 860-8810; for required tour reservations, Tel: 860-2700. To familiarize visitors with the terrain with which Taliesin West was designed to harmonize, the foundation sometimes offers guided desert hikes of about an hour and a half; call for current information. To reach Taliesin West, go north on Scottsdale or Pima roads to Shea Boulevard, east to Taliesin Way, then north to the complex.

The **Fleischer Museum**, 17207 North Perimeter Drive, houses a privately owned collection dedicated to American Impressionism of the California school. Inspired by European Impressionists, this school flourished in America from the turn of the century until the 1940s. The museum grounds include a sculpture garden; the collection itself boasts paintings by Guy Rose, Franz A. Bischoff, Arthur G. Rider, and William Wendt.

The **Cosanti Foundation**, 6433 East Doubletree Ranch Road (actually in northern Paradise Valley, northwest of Scottsdale), is a unique complex of concrete structures designed and built by the contemporary architect Paolo Soleri. Visitors can tour the studios where the famed ceramic or bronze Soleri wind-bells are made and sold.

Staying in Scottsdale

If you want to stay within walking distance of downtown's attractions, **Scottsdale Marriott Suites**, on Third Avenue, has 250 spacious contemporary-style suites, each with living room, work desk with data port for computer use, king-size bedroom, and private dressing area. The grounds also include a restaurant and a lounge as well as a pool and athletic facilities. **Holiday Inn Scottsdale** on East Indian School Road offers workout attractions including a pool and a tennis court. A restaurant and a lounge complete the facilities. There's a pool at the older **Scottsdale's Fifth Avenue Inn**, and Continental breakfasts here are free.

THE SCOTTSDALE RESORTS

Resorts are a big part of what Scottsdale is all about. Among the nearly three dozen located in the Scottsdale environs, some are large, luxurious, and expensive ($250 and up, per night, in season); most are midrange in size, sumptuousness, and cost (around $175 per night); a few are more like glorified motels, but so are their rates (around $115). Our choices are *highly* selective.

The Big Three

Among the destination resorts, three are exceptional, even by Scottsdale standards. **Marriott's Camelback Inn Resort, Golf Club & Spa**, on East Lincoln Drive, opened in 1936 when its double deluxe room rates were $18, guests could buy margaritas in the Spanish cantina for 30¢, and a children's program called Hopalong College (named after cowboy star Hopalong Cassidy) was an innovation. The inn—not to be confused with Marriott's Mountain Shadows Resort, a bit farther down East Lincoln—was purchased in 1967 by frequent guest J. Willard Marriott, Sr.

The Southwest pueblo architecture is still a trademark, but the inn's original 75 rooms have been upped to 423 guest *casitas* (little houses) including 23 suites and a three-bedroom manor house, all custom furnished in Southwestern decor and with views of Camelback Mountain.

Additionally, the inn now has three pools, four restaurants, 36 holes of USGA championship golf, ten tennis courts, and a 25,000-square-foot European-style health-and-beauty spa in a "hacienda" to service guests, who tend toward the traditional and are often from "old money." Hopalong College continues to keep kids happy—some of them the children of former "college students."

Hyatt Regency Scottsdale at Gainey Ranch, north on Scottsdale Road and east on Doubletree Ranch Road, has the usual spread-out-and-spacious resort stuff: impressively landscaped surrounds of palms, manicured lawns, and flower beds; capacious rooms, suites, and *casitas* in contemporary decor with public rooms to match; a 27-hole championship golf course; eight tennis courts; programs for children and teens; a spa; jogging and biking trails; and four restaurants.

What it has that others do not is a water playground of ten interconnecting pools, a three-story-high water slide, a sand beach, and gondola rides on a lake. This one is the definitive "desert oasis," and is the choice for the well-to-do who have active kids and an active lifestyle.

The 600-room **Scottsdale Princess**, sister of the Acapulco Princess in Mexico and the Southampton Princess in Bermuda, is the Southwest's premier sports resort for those who are into sports big time with big bucks to match. The Princess features two 18-hole Tournament Players Club courses, including the Stadium course where the PGA Phoenix Open is played (yes, the Phoenix Open is in Scottsdale), and nine tennis courts, including the Stadium court, where such players as Ivan Lendl, Jimmy Connors, Andre Agassi, and Michael Chang compete.

Recreational activities at the Princess include indoor-outdoor basketball, sand and water volleyball, croquet, jogging, hiking, biking, fishing, swimming in three pools, and a full-service spa and fitness center. The Princess has four restaurants and *seven* cocktail lounges.

Located on East Princess Drive in north Scottsdale with a backdrop of the McDowell Mountains, the Princess, with its Mexican colonial architecture and antiques, earth-tone colors, arches, fountains, and terra-cotta walkways, especially reflects the Southwestern setting.

The Phoenician would make this the Big Four, but it's technically in Phoenix, west of Scottsdale on Camelback Road (see above). The Arizona Biltmore is also in Phoenix.

Not quite as grand as the previous three resorts but still recommendable are the following:

Stouffers Cottonwoods Resort, next door to The Borgata shopping complex on Scottsdale Road, is a good base if shopping is on your agenda—and even if it is not. The resort grounds, with their shaded walkways and colorful flower gardens, provide a touch of tranquillity. Southwestern in style and decor, the resort offers three heated pools, bicycle and jogging trails, Ping-Pong, water volleyball, tennis, 170 rooms and suites, a lounge, and a restaurant that fits the Stouffer name.

The Registry Resort, 317 units on 76 acres north of Lincoln Drive on Scottsdale Road, is action oriented, with two golf courses, 21 tennis courts, three pools, a health club, four restaurants and lounges, and nightly entertainment.

Days Inn Scottsdale Fashion Square Resort on Scottsdale Road abuts the Fashion Square/Camelview Plaza complex, and has 167 units, a pool, a whirlpool, tennis courts, and a lounge. Pets are allowed.

Dining in Scottsdale

Among upscale restaurants, the **Chaparral Room**, the signature restaurant at Camelback Inn, is the most gracious place for classic Continental cuisine—lobster bisque, steak Diane, and all those dishes you thought were swept away in the nouvelle wave. Reservations are advised; Tel: 948-1700. **Marquesa** at the Scottsdale Princess features the Catalan cuisine of northeastern Spain, meat and fish dishes seasoned with garlic, saffron, chorizo, and other such authentic ingredients. Closed Tuesdays. Reservations advised; Tel: 585-4848.

Café Terra Cotta opened in The Borgata shopping mall (see above) late last year. Based on chef Donna Nordin's way with Southwestern cuisine (and chocolate, chocolate, chocolate) at her Tucson Terra Cotta, this new place should be very "in" by the time you get here. For reservations, Tel: 948-8100.

For a lavish prix fixe Sunday brunch, the **Golden Swan** at Hyatt Regency Scottsdale at Gainey Ranch gets the nod from locals who have tried them all. Be sure to call ahead for reservations; Tel: 991-3388.

Less pricey and less pretentious, but each with their own pluses, are **The Vistas at Oaxaca**, 8711 East Pinnacle Peak Road, where the baby back ribs vie with the spectacular views from the outdoor patio dining room (Tel: 998-2222), and the **Impeccable Pig**, 7042 East Indian School Road, which offers the double whammy of fine dining in an antiques shop (Tel: 941-1141).

Palm Court, 7700 East McCormick Parkway (at Scottsdale Conference Resort), offers a classic upscale menu and much of the fare is prepared tableside. Don't be misled by the "Conference Resort" setting; you won't find rowdy convention-goers in this elegant dining room. Maybe some Fortune 500 executives, though. Tel: 991-3400.

Many travellers come to the Phoenix/Scottsdale resort area hankering for not just an array of "gourmet" rooms that might as well be in Chicago or Atlanta, but for a combination of food, ambience, service, and scenery that fits the Western desert locale. For them—and for knowledgeable Arizonans with maybe at least a whiff of money about them—there is **El Chorro Lodge**, 5550 East Lincoln Drive near Camelback Inn and across the street from the Marriott Mountain Shadows resort. For six decades people have been coming here to the edge of the Paradise Valley desert to enjoy El Chorro's chateaubriand and their sticky buns (despite the name, this is not a Mexican or

"Southwestern" restaurant), especially at one of their outside patio tables. Any wait is a pleasure as you warm yourself against the evening desert chill, drink in hand, in front of the big outdoor fireplace, watching the sun go down over the desert behind the indoor lodge-style dining room. Some people, however, find it hard to tear themselves away from the Western-funky two-room bar—with its own fireplaces—that looks as if it might once have been a stagecoach waystation. There is valet parking, but it's just as easy to park in the desert fringe along the entrance road. Tel: 948-5170.

If you hanker for foreign food, choose from **Jean-Claude's Petit Café**, for French cuisine in a small, intimate downtown restaurant at 7340 East Shoeman Lane (Tel: 947-5288); **Aldo Baldo** in Scottsdale Fashion Square (Tel: 994-0062) for light Italian food with regional accents; the 40-year-old family-owned **Los Olivos**, 7328 Second Street (Tel: 946-2256), for Mexican; and **Daa's Thai Room**, 74th Street and Camelback Road (Tel: 941-9015), for a bit of the Far East.

For Western grub in a rustic setting, with bands for dancing the two-step, try **Pinnacle Peak Patio**, 10426 Jomax Road, a huge place with thousands of necktie ends tacked to the rafters. Your own tie will be unceremoniously whacked off and ceremoniously nailed up if you're foolish enough to wear one. Order a steak well done and you'll get a burned boot on a platter—it's that kind of place (Tel: 585-1599). **Rawhide Steakhouse**, 23023 North Scottsdale Road, is slap dab in the middle of a Western theme attraction, **Rawhide 1800s Western Town**, which is replete with mock shoot-'em-ups, covered wagons, stagecoach rides, false-front shops, board sidewalks, and a museum with Tom Mix's boots, Wyatt Earp's gun, and Geronimo's moccasins. At the steak house they even have fried rattlesnake on the menu (Tel: 563-5600). **Rattler's Steakhouse & Saloon**, 16601 North Pima Road, is in the middle of **WestWorld**, an Old West–type facility for horseback riding, polo, rodeos, concerts, and festivals. Rattler's is another steak, rib, and rattlesnake place with country music for dancing. Or for watching the saloon girls and food servers dance (Tel: 483-8700).

Shopping in Scottsdale

With 12 shopping malls and literally hundreds of specialty shops to choose from, truly dedicated shoppers can have a field day (or week, or month) in Scottsdale. The shops noted here are just some among many—a super-selective list to be used for starters.

The Borgata

In The Borgata, head to **Capriccio** for high-fashion women's clothing in an architectural setting said to be among America's prettiest shopping areas. The large dressing rooms have skylights (the better to view you in natural light, my dear) and easy chairs (with Champagne at the ready) for men who want some say in what the women are selecting. At **Dos Cabezas**, don't make the mistake of thinking the clothing, jewelry, furnishings, and accessories were picked up "as is" in Mexico or Latin America; they came from our neighbors to the south, yes, but designers and craftspeople made them to picky-picky (and wonderful) specifications by the shop owner, Newey DeMille. **Cherubini** here has upscale clothing and gifts for infants to preteens; **Cherubini II** has expensive Victorian-style gifts and antiques. High-fashion men's wear by such designers as Claude Montana, Verri, and Gianni Versace is the draw at **Alta Moda**.

Camelview Plaza/Scottsdale Fashion Square

At Camelview Plaza and the contiguous Scottsdale Fashion Square, Bullock's, Dillards, Robinson's, and Neiman-Marcus department stores are surrounded by scores of specialty shops including **Fogal of Switzerland**, for high-fashion panty hose and legwear in more than 200 styles and 130 colors; the **Museum of Northern Arizona Shop**, a sister of the gift shop at famed Museum of Northern Arizona at Flagstaff, offering high-quality authentic arts and crafts of Southwestern Indian tribes; **Disney Store** and **Warner Bros. Studio Store**, outlets for things such as tee-shirts, toys, collector animation cells, and other products made famous by the mouse and the bunny with the stutter; and **Beauty and the Beast**, with an enormous selection of stuffed animals.

Old Town

If you're in Old Town on East Main, **Old Territorial Shop** is the place to find both antique and contemporary Indian jewelry, rugs, basketry, and pottery. Next door, **Folklorico** offers a mix of Southwestern and Mexican jewelry, folk art, and decorative items; and at the Brown Avenue end of the block, **Shades of the West** is the closest thing Scottsdale has to an Indian trading post, where Navajo silversmiths work while you watch.

Western and Indian Art

As recently as several years ago almost every Scottsdale art gallery had extensive collections of works by regional Indians and Cowboy Artists of America (see The Downtown Museums section, above). Today you have to ferret out their works. For the cowboys there's **Trailside Galleries** in Scottsdale Mall, **Troy's Gallery** at the corner of Scottsdale Road and Main Street, and **The May Gallery** in The Borgata. For contemporary Indian paintings and other arts, try **Lovena Ohls Gallery** at 4251 North Marshall Way, or **O'Brien's Art Emporium** on 7122 Stetson Drive, a block south and west of Camelback and Scottsdale roads, which features creations by regional and nationally prominent contemporary representational artists.

The Desert around Scottsdale

If you come to Arizona to recharge your physical batteries and find some Wild West spirit, there's probably no better way to do it than junketing into the wilderness next door, the Sonoran Desert itself. But with its jumping cactus, creepy crawlers, and dehydrating sunshine it's not a place for the uninitiated to venture alone. (Jumping cactus? It's a variety called cholla, pronounced "CHOY-ah," and its clumps of thorns and tiny stickers seem literally to jump into your skin if you get too close. Removing cholla is a tedious, painful process.)

Guided jeep tours are the answer. The guides have permits to go where ordinary vehicles can't, and they regale you along the way with tales tall but true, romance the living and natural history, and keep you away from those pesky cholla cactus thorns. You might shoot a six-gun, pan for gold, or rope a fence post along the way, maybe even chow down on mesquite-broiled steaks at sundown. Among jeep-tour operators offering full- or half-day trips are **Arizona Bound** (Tel: 994-0580); **Trail Blazer** (Tel: 481-0223); **Wild West** (Tel: 941-8355); and **Arizona Desert Mountain** (Tel: 860-1777).

If price is no object and you want to pack into the Mazatzal Wilderness Area north of the Valley for hunting, fishing, canoeing, or horseback riding for one-day or extended trips (you'll head through untrammeled, roadless landscape beside the wild and scenic Verde River), **Wayward Wind** provides everything but your toothbrush (Tel: 990-0556). **Desert Voyagers Guided Rafting Tours** offers full-day or half-day trips on the Salt River 363 days a year (Tel: 998-RAFT or 800/222-RAFT).

THE VALLEY OF THE SUN

It should be noted that golf courses (125 of them) are never far from anywhere you may be in the Valley. Neither, for that matter, are professional, collegiate, spectator, and participatory sporting events, from rodeos to NASCAR (stock-car racing) and drag-boat races. Art galleries (380 of them) are never very far from where you are, either. Neither are symphony orchestras, ballet, opera, and drama companies, comedy clubs, nightclubs, country-and-western "stomps," or music venues, from those featuring the big-band sound of the 1940s to the world beat of the 1990s. Dinner theaters that serve up whodunits, with a prize to the member of the audience who solves the crime, have proliferated of late.

What follows is a capsule roundup of what's where in the cities surrounding Phoenix/Scottsdale, particularly those in the East Valley. That's where the action is.

THE EAST VALLEY
Carefree

Carefree, north of Phoenix/Scottsdale, probably has more millionaires per capita than any other Arizona community, and this is reflected in street names: Easy Street, Wampum Way, Why Worry Lane. It also is renowned for **The Boulders** resort.

The Boulders consistently gets travellers' nods for best golf, best food, best wines, best hideaway resort, most innovative architecture, most personalized service. In "best" or "most" surveys, Mauna Lani Bay in Hawaii, The Greenbrier in West Virginia, and the Ritz-Carlton Laguna Niguel in California usually rate lower than The Boulders. Designed to blend into the surrounding desert and its massive granite boulders, the resort has 136 adobe-style *casitas,* a main lodge, five restaurants, two pools, six tennis courts, and two 18-hole championship golf courses. Nearby are **El Pedregal Festival Marketplace** and **Spanish Village**, both with specialty shops and cafés in sunny settings with shady nooks.

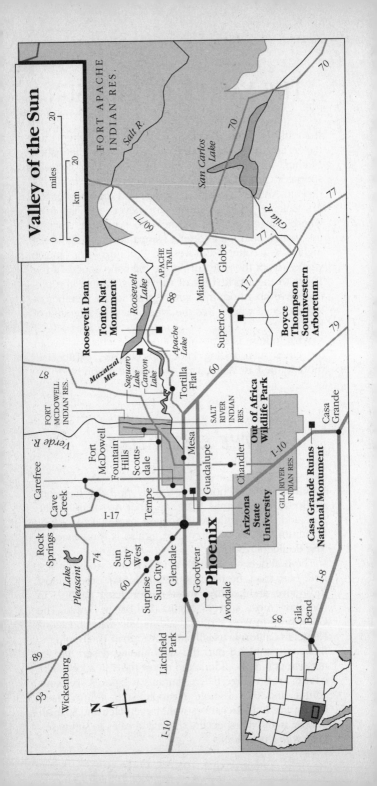

Cave Creek

A study in contrasts to its next-door neighbor, Carefree, which was founded in 1956 as a planned community, Cave Creek is a former stage stop, sheep camp, and gold-mining town that dates back to 1870. Now, as then, it is a town without pretensions. No festival marketplace here; just **Frontier Town** with all-you-can-eat restaurants and fun and funky shops—some given to decorated cow skulls and scorpions-in-plastic bola ties. If it is open (its schedule is unpretentious, too), **Cave Creek Museum** traces the town's history from the Hohokam Indian days.

Fountain Hills

In the far northeast Valley at the junction of Shea Boulevard and AZ 87 is a planned community that makes a splash with its landmark, a fountain that spurts 560 feet in the air from a lagoon in Fountain Park, the town's outdoor community center. The fountain that gives Fountain Hills its name plays for 15 minutes on the hour from 10:00 A.M. to 9:00 P.M. and is illuminated at night.

Other attractions in or near this town of 10,000 include **Out of Africa Wildlife Park** (Beeline Highway/AZ 87), where human beings interact with lions, leopards, tigers, and reptiles in fabulous shows. Visitors get to pet the cubs. Closed Mondays. Just east of Fountain Hills, **Fort McDowell Gaming Center** on the Fort McDowell Indian Reservation where the Yavapai-Apache live is one of several Indian reservations where gambling is permitted, including bingo, keno, and casino games. Open daily.

Saguaro Lake is one of the four man-made water-storage lakes on the Salt River that also is a recreation center for boating, water-skiing, fishing, and picnicking; daytime and dinner cruises along the multicolored cliffs in the **Desert Belle** paddle wheeler are additional highlights here (for reservations, Tel: 827-9144). To reach the lake head south from Beeline Highway/AZ 87 on Saguaro Lake Road to the reservoir.

For an adventurous horseback or jeep ride along the lush Salt or Verde rivers (the excursions venture into the McDowell or Mazatzal wilderness areas on cavalry, outlaw, and Indian trails), or if you just want to dress like a cowboy on Saturday night, contact **Cowboy Adventures** at an honest-to-gosh cowboy ranch far (but not too far; only a half hour) from the madding crowd at Scottsdale. Tel: 873-8585 or 377-8281.

Tempe

Like other Valley cities such as Phoenix, Scottsdale, and Mesa, Tempe, directly south of Scottsdale on U.S. 60, was empty desert in the 1860s. Now it has a population of 145,000 and one of the country's largest schools, **Arizona State University**, with 40,000 students. ASU itself is a barometer of Tempe's evolution. It began in a cow pasture as a four-room brick building called Arizona Normal School; its campus of broad lawns, stately palms, and flowering trees now covers 700 acres.

The ASU campus's **Grady Gammage Auditorium**, designed by Frank Lloyd Wright and heralded by critics as acoustically perfect, is used by symphony orchestras, travelling shows and dance troupes, and celebrity entertainers. The auditorium is the distinctive curved building set into the curve of U.S. 60 (Mill Avenue), which passes through the downtown area. The university's art museum in the new **Nelson Fine Arts Center** houses galleries dedicated to American, contemporary, print, crafts, and changing exhibits, with sculptures displayed on outdoor terraces. Light from the skylights reflects off ten surfaces before illuminating the artwork, protecting the creations from harmful direct sunlight. Nelson Center also includes a playhouse and dance laboratory. In the **Anthropology Museum** the permanent exhibition "La Cuidad: A Hohokam Village" features photographs and artifacts from nearby desert archaeological digs; the **Geology Museum** features a seismograph and displays of gems, minerals, fossils, and shells. (The campus museums are open Monday to Friday.)

Sun Devil Stadium here is home to the ASU Sun Devils, the NFL Phoenix Cardinals, and on New Year's Day, the collegiate Fiesta Bowl. Diablo Stadium, Alameda Drive and 48th Street, is spring-training ground for the California Angels.

Some of the city's oldest buildings are along Mill Avenue between First Street and University Drive. Called **Old Town**, this area has been given an extensive face-lift with shaded sidewalks and archways, gaslights, and attractive landscaping in front of the shops and restaurants in turn-of-the-century buildings. On weekend nights hundreds of people swarm to outdoor rock concerts and street dances. The biggest event of the year is the New Year's Eve Block Party with nonstop entertainment.

Given Old Town's proximity to the ASU campus and the youthful exuberance of the students, there are bound to be some lively, inexpensive clubs and cafés on or near Mill Avenue. **Balboa Cafe**, 404 South Mill, half restaurant, half bar, has lots of brass and glass, good burgers, and live rock groups on weekends; Tel: 966-1300. **Coffee Plantation**, 680 South Mill, offers soups, salads, and sandwiches as well as coffee, espresso, cappuccino, and cheesecake. Live music nights feature mostly jazz; Tel: 829-7878. **Mill Landing**, 398 South Mill, a brick-and-brass place to eat fresh seafood indoors or out, is a tad more expensive than the others; Tel: 966-1700.

Paradise Bar and Grill, 401 South Mill, rates as a long-time favorite watering hole, grazing place, and gathering spot for the college crowd; Tel: 829-0606. **Neon Cowboy**, 1470 East Southern, is a place to kick up your heels to country and Top 40 music and nosh from the free buffet during happy hour; Tel: 752-1700.

Off the path beaten by collegians is a hilltop restaurant affording a panorama of the Valley and serving a regional cuisine that makes for a special event. **Top of the Rock**, located in Westcourt in the Buttes resort, in the notch between two pop-up, rusty-red buttes at 48th Street and Broadway, is circular and dramatically decorated with wood, rock, and live cactus; Tel: 225-9000.

Within walking distance of ASU and Old Town is **Radisson Tempe Mission Palms**, with a restaurant, a lounge, a pool, and tennis courts. Nearby, the moderately priced **Holiday Inn of Tempe/ASU** has a pool, a dining room, a health club, and an attractive sports lounge called **Ducks**, which has great ribs and a super salad bar.

Guadalupe

Just south of Tempe, "minutes away, a world apart," is Guadalupe, where Yaqui Indian and Hispanic cultures meld. **Avenida del Yaqui** here is a street straight out of Mexico with its authentic bakery, fruit stands, and shops selling piñatas, pottery, leather goods, and pickled cactus (properly called *nopalitos,* made from the dethorned and skinned pads of prickly pear cactus, it's a nutritious delicacy in salads). At **El Tianguis**, in a courtyard on the corner of Yaqui and Guadalupe Road, Mexican food is prepared the way it's done in the mother country; live mariachi music accompanies meals on weekends.

The Yaquis, members of a tribe ousted from Mexico, blend their own culture with Catholicism in their 300-year-old tradition of Lenten ceremonies that re-create events leading to the death and resurrection of Jesus, including a battle between good and evil with flowers as weapons for the good guys. The masked dramatizations and dance pageantry take place at Yaqui Temple in the village on weekends during Lent, culminating in the burning of an effigy of Satan. A Guadalupe city ordinance bans reproducing this ceremony in any way. Sketch pads, tape recorders, cameras, and camcorders are forbidden; confiscated, they fuel Satan's funeral pyre.

Next door to Yaqui Temple is the domed and spired Our Lady of Guadalupe Church, built in 1910. It can be visited any day, but is especially beautiful at sunset, when the white building is bathed in a warm glow.

To reach the village go south on I-10 to Baseline Road (exit 155), then head east on Baseline to Avenida del Yaqui; take Yaqui south to the church and temple.

Mesa

Next door to Tempe to the east, and only 15 miles (24 km) east of Phoenix, Mesa was settled in 1877 by 80 Church of Jesus Christ of Latter-Day Saints (Mormon) pioneers and now is Arizona's third-largest city (behind Phoenix and Tucson). Its population of about 220,000 swells in winter when some 50,000 "snowbirds" from cold climates arrive to take up residence in the city's many mobile-home parks, and when the Chicago Cubs' faithful fans arrive in March to watch spring-training games at Hohokam Stadium.

The Mormon influence is still strong and the city's most notable landmark is the church's Arizona Temple, based on classic Greek architecture. The interior is closed to non-Mormons, but visitors are welcome to wander among the exotic plants in the landscaped gardens and to take a free tour of the visitors' center (101 South Lesueur Street). The temple, at 526 East Main, is just east of downtown near the intersection with Mesa Drive.

At **Mesa Southwest Museum**, 53 North MacDonald Street, a re-created cave and village, along with petroglyphs and Salado and Hohokam pottery, show how prehistoric Indians lived. There are also pioneer exhibits, including a stagecoach and an adobe schoolhouse. Kids will enjoy the life-size animated dinosaurs and visits to the authentic old-time jail. A gift shop sells books and souvenirs. Closed Mondays. **Champlin Fighter Museum** at Falcon Field (Mesa Municipal Airport, off McKellips Road), on the northeastern edge of Mesa about 7 miles (11 km) from downtown, has the "hottest" aircraft from World Wars I and II, including the 1911 Rumpler Taube, the world's first combat aircraft from which bombs were thrown by hand; the Fokker Dr-I Triplane, the kind flown by "Red Baron" Manfred von Richthofen; a British Sopwith Camel, which finally downed the Red Baron; and an American P-51 Mustang, said to be the finest fighter plane of World War II. Open daily.

Salt River Recreation, Inc., east of downtown via Main Street to North Bush Highway (at Usery Pass Road), is headquarters for the local pastime of inner tube riding (called tubing by the natives) down the Salt and Verde rivers. Inner tube rentals and shuttle buses from Mesa to the rivers make it easy to enjoy this mid-April to October sport (Tel: 984-3305). Take U.S. 60/89 (Main Street) to **Rockin' R Ranch**, 6136 East Baseline Road, a Wild West town that offers horse-drawn wagon rides, gold panning, a Wild West show, gunfights, entertainment by the Rockin' R Wranglers, and chuck wagon suppers (for reservations, Tel: 832-1539).

Arizona Golf Resort & Conference Center, 7 miles (11 km) east of downtown on Power Road, has kitchenettes, suites, and *casitas*. Their golf course ranks as championship, but if golf is not your sport you can enjoy the pool, their spas, a game of tennis, or bicycling. Food and drinks are served on the outdoor dining patios, in the restaurant, or in the lounge, which features live entertainment. The moderately priced **Rodeway Inn Mesa**, about 8 miles (13 km) east of downtown, has a coffee shop, a restaurant, and a lounge, and for play a pool, tennis, and golf. The budget-priced **Motel 6 Mesa North** is near the Mormon temple.

Bavarian Point, 4815 East Main, has a way with expertly seasoned German dishes that won't weigh you down (Tel: 830-0999). **D's Thai Food**, 2431 East McKellips Road, is a take-out joint dishing up such Thai classics as rice noodles, barbecued chicken with peanut sauce, and ground beef with cabbage leaves. Don't be put off by the gas station it's connected to (Tel: 969-0087). **Armenta's Mexican Food**, 1340 South Country Club, has most of the trappings of small Mexican eateries, including hanging piñatas and a wailing jukebox. But the food is terrific, inexpensive, and runs to the relatively unusual: chicken mole, *nopalitos,* and *chalupas* (Tel: 834-9508).

Chandler

Directly south of Tempe and 25 miles (40 km) southeast of Phoenix, Chandler began as the ranch of Dr. Alexander John Chandler, who arrived in Arizona in 1887. He subdivided his acreage into agricultural plots in 1911 and advertised them for sale. In 1912 the San Marcos Hotel was built here. During the 1920s the San Marcos, the Arizona Biltmore in Phoenix, and The Wigwam in Litchfield Park (see below) evolved into the prototypes of the Valley's luxurious and glamorous golf resorts of today. The Chandler resort was a particular favorite of Hollywood celebrities, including Clark Gable, Errol Flynn, Joan Crawford, Fred Astaire, and Gloria Swanson. Now known as the **Sheraton San Marcos Golf Resort and Conference Center**, the resort is listed on the National Register of Historic Places. Its many renovations have not compromised its Mission Revival architecture. The hotel's cozy wicker-and-chintz fine-dining restaurant, called **1912**, and its high-energy nightclub, **Cibola**, are both open to the public.

Downtown's Chandler Center for the Arts is a venue for both performing and visual arts, and employs a turntable divisible auditorium system allowing three productions to run simultaneously. Compadre Stadium in Chandler is spring-training camp for the Milwaukee Brewers.

THE WEST VALLEY

Metrocenter is b-i-g: five department stores, 37 restaurants, 17 movie theaters, hotels, a miniature golf course, an ice-skating rink, roller coaster, and who knows how many specialty shops—practically a city in itself, though it is actually part of Phoenix. Exit west from I-17 at Dunlap or Peoria avenues.

Crescent Hotel at Koll Center, on Dunlap Avenue, offers easy access to Metrocenter and to I-17. Southwest contemporary is the design here, and the hotel features such sports-minded amenities as a health club, a pool (not necessarily for workouts), and volleyball, tennis, and squash courts. There are also concierge floors. Surrounded by businesses—especially those dealing in computers, microchips, and data processing—and fitted out with an executive business center, the Crescent is popular with business travellers as well as vacationers.

Glendale

Glendale is Arizona's fifth-largest city. A farming community for most of its century-long history, it remains a major shipping point for produce and cotton. On the outskirts of town at 165th and Northern avenues is **Wildlife World Zoo**, which began as a breeding farm for rare and endangered species and just kept growing as the animals and birds multiplied. Among them: exotic birds in a large walk-through aviary; wallabies and kangaroos; such mammals as a white tiger, white rhinos, giraffes, big cats, camels, and zebras; exotic reptiles and monkeys; salt- and freshwater fish, and amphibians. Open daily. Take I-17 north to the Northern Avenue exit and follow Northern west 18 miles (29 km) to 165th Avenue.

Sun City and Sun City West

Begun in 1960, developed by the Del E. Webb company, Sun City is said to be the nation's first "active" adult retirement community. In truth, the first was a more modest enclave down the road a piece at Youngtown. Sun City now has 46,000 residents; the newer Sun City West will have 25,000 residents when all homes are constructed. The active lifestyle here includes classes in jazzercise, golf, arts and crafts, dance, sports, and water ballet, with golf carts for transportation to and from all that activity. **Sundome Center for the Performing Arts** is located in Sun City West; performers are booked based on their appeal to retirement-age patrons.

Surprise

On U.S. 60 northwest of Phoenix, between Sun City and Sun City West, Surprise was founded and named by a 1937 settler, Flora Statler, who said if it became a town it would be a surprise. Two lodgings here are convenient to Glendale and the Sun Cities. **Sun Ridge Communities** has a restaurant, pools, spas, golf, furnished kitchens, and a washer and dryer in each condominium. **Windmill Inn at Sun City West** offers suites with wet bar, refrigerator, and microwave oven; other amenities include a pool, a spa, free bicycle use, free morning coffee, and free muffins and newspapers.

Litchfield Park

Like the West Valley towns of Avondale and Goodyear, Litchfield Park was developed by the Goodyear Tire & Rubber Company as a farming community to produce Egyptian cotton for tire cords. By the late 1920s this town, named for Goodyear's vice president at the time, was growing more than cotton. It was growing greens, as in tees and fairways, around a guest lodge for visiting tire-company honchos. In 1929 the lodge opened to the public as a 13-room resort.

The preeminent Arizona golf resort, **The Wigwam** has evolved into three courses and more than 400 *casitas,* including 20 new tennis *casitas* adjacent to the nine-court racquet club, with stables, trap and skeet shooting, three restaurants, and lounges offering live entertainment. The centerpiece of the 54 holes is the highly acclaimed Gold Course, a 7,074-yard Robert Trent Jones design. A second Jones course and a Red Lawrence 18 round out the field. One of the resort's restaurants, **Arizona Kitchen**, may be the ultimate Arizona restaurant. A mélange of Indian, Mexican, and nouvelle-Southwestern dishes, the menu includes things like pheasant tamales and bittersweet chocolate tacos—all served up in a snazzy Territorial-style setting.

VALLEY-WIDE CELEBRATIONS

January. **Fiesta Bowl Football Classic**, considered among the top five bowl games, matches college football teams New Year's Day at Sun Devil Stadium in Tempe; Tel: 350-0900.

The **Phoenix Open** attracts the finest golfers and 375,000 spectators to this event on the PGA tour, late January at Tournament Players Club of Scottsdale; Tel: 870-0163.

The **Barrett-Jackson Auction** of a $100 million collection of classic, collectible, and celebrity cars takes place in mid-January at Scottsdale's WestWorld; Tel: 273-0791.

February. The **Parada del Sol** rodeo and parade cap weeks of mock gunfights, Western dances, and celebrity country entertainers. The rodeo, in early February, is at Rawhide Arena (in Rawhide 1800s Western Town); the parade (late January) runs through downtown Scottsdale. Tel: 990-3179.

The **Scottsdale Celebration of Fine Arts** is two months'

worth of exhibitions and ongoing demonstrations by 100 regional and national artists. The February–March event takes place under big-top tents, complete with food and entertainment, on the southwest corner of Scottsdale Road and Highland Avenue just north of Scottsdale Fashion Square; Tel: 443-7695.

The **Arizona Renaissance Festival** re-creates a 16th-century Market Faire with hundreds of costumed participants, jousting, games, crafts, food, and music; weekends to mid-March, on the desert east of Apache Junction (for which see Lost Dutchman Days, below). Tel: 463-2700.

The **Great Fair of Fountain Hills** features continuous entertainment, 400 artists and artisans, sky divers, and hot-air balloon rides; late February at Fountain Park. Tel: 837-1654.

Lost Dutchman Days in late February commemorates the legend of the Lost Dutchman Mine, in the nearby Superstition Mountains, and the history of the Apache Junction area with a rodeo, parade, carnival, arts and crafts, and entertainment, east of Phoenix at the intersection of AZ 88 and U.S. 60; Tel: 982-3141.

March. **The Heard Museum Indian Fair and Market** includes a juried show and sale of crafts and fine art by American Indians, along with tribal dances, music, and food, early March; Tel: 252-8840.

The **Chandler Ostrich Festival** commemorates the days (1880s to 1920s) when Valley ostrich farms produced plumage for women's hats and boas; three musical entertainment stages, ostrich races, and the usual food, crafts, and carnival rides in downtown Chandler, mid-March; Tel: 963-4571.

Old Town Tempe Festival, an arts-and-entertainment spring celebration, features 450 nationally and regionally known artists and artisans, traditional and ethnic foods, and continuous entertainment, late March, on Mill Avenue; Tel: 967-4877.

October. **Rodeo Showdown** in early October pits top U.S. cowboys against their Canadian counterparts; a pavilion of retail exhibits includes cowboy clothes, art, gifts, and Western food at Scottsdale's WestWorld; Tel: 946-9711.

November. The **Thunderbird Balloon Classic and Airshow** is one of the Valley's most colorful and photographed events. Along with 200 hot-air balloons rising from Glendale Municipal Airport, there are daily air shows, nightly balloon glows, and street dances, mid-November; Tel: 978-7208.

The **Fine Folk Festival** features 250 artisans, ethnic food booths, name entertainers and local performers, and a Kid's World with pony rides and a petting zoo, Main and MacDonald streets in downtown Mesa, early November; Tel: 890-2613.

The **Checker 500** NASCAR Winston Cup Series showcases premier-level stock-car racing on a one-mile oval that race drivers say is the fastest anywhere, at Phoenix International Raceway in early November; Tel: 252-3833.

December. **Old Town Tempe Fall Festival of the Arts**, rated one of the top 10 festivals by whomever rates such things, has become a kickoff event for Christmas shoppers. Some 500 arts-and-crafts booths, continuous entertainment on four stages, and ethnic and traditional food stalls spread out along Mill Avenue in downtown Tempe in early December; Tel: 967-4877.

Indian Market is show-and-sell time for 700 Indian artisans from 70 tribes; there's also entertainment by tribal singers and dancers and Indian fry bread, tamales, and burritos at Pueblo Grande Museum and Cultural Park east of downtown Phoenix in mid-December; Tel: 495-5645.

The **Fiesta Bowl Parade**, the next-to-last pregame event, brings 300,000 spectators to watch nationally televised marching bands from throughout the nation, equestrian units, and floats; along Central Avenue in Phoenix, Dec. 31; Tel: 350-0900.

The **New Year's Eve Block Party**, the final pregame event, officially welcomes the two Fiesta Bowl teams and fans with 125,000 Valleyites, marching bands, cheer squads, fireworks, food, music, and entertainment. *USA Today* says it's one of the top 10 places in the United States to be on New Year's Eve; Old Town Tempe along Mill Avenue; Tel: 350-8811.

DAY TRIPS FROM THE VALLEY
East of Phoenix

APACHE TRAIL

To make this 160-mile loop trip, begin by taking U.S. 60 east through Superior, head just past Miami, and return via the trail, AZ 88, north and west (counterclockwise) back to U.S. 60 at Apache Junction. This way of doing the route assures wide-angle, downhill views of mountain-to-desert scenery, the string of blue man-made lakes along the Salt River, and the soaring volcanic walls of Fish Creek Canyon.

Though the trail itself is considered one of America's most scenic drives, be aware that some call it the white-knuckle drive because of its twisting hairpin curves and switchbacks.

The **Boyce Thompson Southwestern Arboretum**, on U.S. 60 about 5 miles (8 km) west of Superior, displays desert plants from around the world and has self-guided nature walks. **Tonto National Monument**, on the Apache Trail itself just east of Roosevelt Dam, features cliff dwellings of the 12th-century Salado Indians. There is excellent interpretive material in the visitors' center.

The lakes—Roosevelt, Apache, Canyon, Saguaro—provide year-round water recreation. **Fish Creek Canyon** and **Fish Creek Hill**, about 8 miles (13 km) past the turnoff to Apache Lake Marina, are the trail's most exciting sections—especially for the driver, who must make sharp turns on an up-and-down cliff-face road that rises 1,500 feet in three miles. Atop Fish Creek Hill you'll be rewarded with spectacular views of the canyon below, which is a favorite of hikers. Fish Creek, at the bottom of the hill, usually has a trickle of water but no fish. **Tortilla Flat**, a rustic wayside dining stop on Apache Lake, is known for its killer chili and prickly-pear cactus ice cream you'll find nowhere else. **Dolly's Steamboat** can take you on a leisurely tour of Canyon Lake; board it at the Canyon Lake marina. To pan for gold stop in **Goldfield**, a reconstructed ghost town, after which you'll come back to U.S. 60 at Apache Junction.

South of Phoenix

CASA GRANDE RUINS NATIONAL MONUMENT

The best route to the monument, about 50 miles (80 km) southwest of downtown Phoenix, is via I-10 South, toward Tucson, to Casa Grande (exit 185) and then AZ 387 East. (This also makes a nice little side trip if you're coming up to Phoenix from Tucson.) The well-preserved 600-year-old four-story main Hohokam ruin may have been an observatory, according to rangers leading the frequent guided tours. The visitors' center has exhibits on the Hohokam and a fairly comprehensive bookstore. The shade ramadas near the center are a good spot for a picnic, but you must bring your own food; this site has only a soft-drink machine. Incidentally, if you haven't had your fill of shopping, head south on I-10 to exit 194, where **Casa Grande Factory Stores**, with cut-rate luggage, toys, clothes, china, porcelain, and books, is located right off the exit.

Northwest of Phoenix

WICKENBURG

This picturesque town of guest ranches, golf resorts, and a main drag of frontier-style buildings northwest of Phoenix makes a short, pleasant day trip with some fascinating lore, legend, and sights.

In 1864 Henry Wickenburg, a lone prospector, picked up a rock to throw at a buzzard. The rock happened to be a gold nugget, and a gold rush began. Among the sights at historic **Vulture Mine** and the ghost town of **Vulture City**, recently reopened to visitors, is a hanging tree, ubiquitous in mining camps of the day. Easily $1 million of the mine's first $3.5 million was "high graded" (stolen) by miner-thieves. But high grading stopped when a hanging judge gave "suspended sentences," as he called them, to 20 felonious bad'uns. Eventually more than $20 million in gold was mined at Vulture, but Wickenburg himself died penniless, by his own hand in 1905. To reach the mine and ghost town head west 3 miles (5 km) on Wickenburg Way (U.S. 60), then south 12 miles (19 km) on Vulture Mine Road.

In the town of Wickenburg itself the **Desert Caballeros Western Museum**, 21 North Frontier Street, lavished with love, money, and acquisitions, and supported by volunteer townsfolk and well-to-do winter residents, features outstanding exhibits of Western art, period rooms, a mineral room, an Indian room, and a reconstructed Vulture City street scene. Dioramas commemorate the town's Wild West days.

Boomtowns often grew too fast to build jails; instead, drunks were shackled to so-called jail trees overnight to "sleep it off." Wickenburg's jail tree had its own legend in the person of George ("King of Gunsight") Sayer, said to have been a mountain of a man who bellowed like a range bull. Once, when the tree was filled to capacity, Sayer was chained to a huge log nearby. When he awoke the next morning, he bellowed for a drink but no one obliged, so he picked up the log, marched off to the nearest saloon, and demanded his morning shot of red-eye. He got it, no questions asked. The jail tree, a mesquite, still stands beside the convenience market at the junction of U.S. 93 and U.S. 60.

A visit to Wickenburg might include a meal or an extended stay at the largest and most notable of the local guest ranches, Rancho de los Caballeros, south of U.S. 60 on South Vulture Mine Road. Wickenburg's guest ranches are few now compared to the 1950s, when the town boasted that it was the "Dude Ranch Capital of the World." The remaining ranches are popular with those planning to spend some time in Wickenburg, especially travellers who like desert trail rides and believe that "the backside of a horse is good for the inner man." **Rancho de los Caballeros** offers guest *casitas,* a main lodge, a dining room, a conference center, a pool, and strings of easy-riding horses in the corral. Reservations for dining are required for non-guests; Tel: 684-5484. Closed May to mid-October.

A pleasant route from Phoenix to Wickenburg is north on I-17 to exit 223, west on AZ 74 past Lake Pleasant and forests of young saguaro, and north on U.S. 60 to Wickenburg, about 60 miles (96 km) northwest of Phoenix.

From Wickenburg you can continue northwest on U.S. 93 to the junction with AZ 89 and then northeast on AZ 89 to Prescott (for which see the Central Arizona chapter).

GETTING AROUND
By air. Phoenix Sky Harbor International Airport, immediately southeast of central downtown, is served by Alaska Airlines, American, America West, Continental, Delta, Northwest, Southwest, TWA, United, and USAir.

SuperShuttle provides door-to-door transport from the airport to all Valley locations for $12 and up, depending on the distance. Taxi fare from Sky Harbor to midcity Scottsdale is about $17. Taxi stands are curbside at each of the three terminals. By prior arrangement, some hotels and resorts offer van or limousine airport pickup for their guests.

Aero Services at Scottsdale Airport offers fuel, parking, and maintenance for private aircraft (Tel: 991-0900).

Car rental. Budget Rent-A-Car of Arizona has a desk right at the airport (open 24 hours) and car pickups curbside (Tel: 267-4000 or 800/CARS FOR U). Courtesy vans to nearby rental-car lots are provided by Thrifty Car Rental (Tel: 244-0311); Courtesy Leasing and Rent-A-Car (Tel: 273-7503 or 800/368-5145); and Hertz (Tel: 267-8822 or 800/654-3131).

By foot. Unless you are going to a destination resort from which you do not plan to venture, or unless you are staying in the downtown areas of Phoenix, Scottsdale, Tempe, or Mesa, close to shops, restaurants, and entertainment, you won't do much walking. Valley communities sprawl. They don't lend themselves to walking from one attraction to another.

By public transportation. Phoenix Rapid Transit System runs daily except Sundays to most Valley areas, but not at all Saturdays and Sundays to Tempe and Mesa. Even on weekdays the system has shortcomings. Tel: 235-5000 for schedules and fares.

By car. If you haven't arrived in one, you would be well advised to rent one ASAP. The Phoenix area alone covers 420 square miles. Getting from one point to another with any kind of efficiency makes driving almost mandatory. Even so, "rush hour traffic" here is an oxymoron; there's little "rush" about it.

The fastest way from downtown Phoenix to northeast uptown is via AZ 51—the Squaw Peak Freeway—off I-10 (or pick it up from on-ramps along its route, usually at 18th Street).

Both Seventh Street and Seventh Avenue use the middle turn lanes as traffic lanes during rush hours (southbound, 6:00 to 9:00 A.M.; northbound, 4:00 to 6:00 P.M.). Central Avenue is one-way north through downtown; Third Street is one-way south through downtown.

Tours

Tours in the Air. **Arizona Air** offers "flightseeing" trips combined with ground tours of northern Arizona's Grand Canyon, Sedona, Lake Powell, and Monument Valley (Tel: 991-8252).

Unicorn Balloon Co. offers sunrise and sunset flights daily from November to March (Tel: 991-3666 or 800/468-2478).

Glider flights over the desert are offered by **Turf Soaring School** (Tel: 439-3621) and from **Estrella Sailport** (Tel: 568-2318).

Adventure Sports teaches hang gliding, windsurfing, jet skiing, and canoeing as part of a Rainbow Valley tour (Tel: 788-8959).

Ground Tours. **Vaughn's Southwest Custom Tours** offers Valley cities trips and daily personalized van tours to the Grand Canyon, Sedona, Mexico, Tucson, and the Apache Trail (Tel: 971-1381).

Arizona Travel Experience does daily trips to the

Grand Canyon via Sedona, and tosses in a Continental breakfast and the spectacular film about the Grand Canyon at the IMAX theater there (Tel: 254-9255).

The Trolley Company hops around Tempe during happy hour and does custom tours Valleywide in turn-of-the-century-style trolleylike buses (Tel: 829-1226).

Painted Desert Productions, Inc., offers insider tours of the Arizona art and cultural scene, including artists' studios, galleries, museums, and architectural and archaeological sites, with art experts as guides and Southwest culinary samples included (Tel: 946-8860).

ACCOMMODATIONS REFERENCE

The rates given below are projections *for 1993. Unless otherwise indicated, rates are for a double room, double occupancy, and do not include meals. Price ranges span the lowest rate in the low season (roughly mid-May through December) to the highest rate in the high season (roughly January to mid-May). As rates are always subject to change, it is wise to double-check before booking.*

The telephone area code for Phoenix, Scottsdale, and the Valley of the Sun is 602.

▶ **Arizona Biltmore.** 24th Street and Missouri Avenue, **Phoenix**, AZ 85016. Tel: 955-6600 or (800) 950-0086; Fax: 381-7600. $92–$260; $295–$650 (suites).

▶ **Arizona Golf Resort & Conference Center.** 425 South Power Road, **Mesa**, AZ 85206. Tel: 832-3202 or (800) 528-8282; Fax: 981-0151. $85–$175.

▶ **The Boulders.** P.O. Box 2090, **Carefree**, AZ 85377. Tel: 488-9009 or (800) 553-1717; Fax: 488-4118. $325–$525, M.A.P. (includes breakfast and dinner).

▶ **Crescent Hotel at Koll Center.** 2620 West Dunlap Avenue, **Phoenix**, AZ 85021. Tel: 943-8200 or (800) 423-4126; Fax: 371-2856. $60–$150.

▶ **Crown Sterling Suites.** 2630 East Camelback Road, **Phoenix**, AZ 85016. Tel: 955-3992; Fax: 955-6479. $89–$190.

▶ **Days Inn Scottsdale Fashion Square Resort.** 4710 North Scottsdale Road, **Scottsdale**, AZ 85251. Tel: 947-5411; Fax: 946-1324. $44–$108.

▶ **Holiday Inn of Tempe/ASU.** 915 East Apache Boulevard, **Tempe**, AZ 85281. Tel: 968-3451 or (800) 553-1826; Fax: 968-6262. $59–$87.

▶ **Holiday Inn Scottsdale.** 7353 East Indian School Road, **Scottsdale**, AZ 85251. Tel: 994-9203 or (800) 695-6995; Fax: 941-2567. $49–$140.

▶ **Hyatt Regency Phoenix.** 122 North Second Street, Phoenix, AZ 85004. Tel: 252-1234 or (800) 233-1234. $140–$200.

▶ **Hyatt Regency Scottsdale at Gainey Ranch.** 7500 East Doubletree Ranch Road, Scottsdale, AZ 85258. Tel: 991-3388 or (800) 233-1234; Fax: 483-5550. $115–$295 (contact the resort for suite and *casita* rates).

▶ **Marriott's Camelback Inn Resort, Golf Club & Spa.** 5402 East Lincoln Drive, Scottsdale, AZ 85253. Tel: 948-1700 or (800) 242-2635; Fax: 951-8469. $99–$1,400.

▶ **Motel 6 Mesa North.** 336 West Hampton Avenue, Mesa, AZ 85202. Tel: 844-8899. $38.

▶ **The Phoenician.** 6000 East Camelback Road, Scottsdale, AZ 85251. Tel: 941-8200 or (800) 888-8234; Fax: 947-4311. $150–$425; $430–$1,300 (suites).

▶ **The Pointe Hilton Resort on South Mountain.** 7777 South Pointe Parkway, Phoenix, AZ 85044. Tel: 438-9000 or (800) 528-0428; Fax: 431-6528. $110–$200.

▶ **Radisson Tempe Mission Palms.** 60 East Fifth Street, Tempe, AZ 85281. Tel: 894-1400 or (800) 547-8705; Fax: 968-7677. $58–$135.

▶ **Rancho de los Caballeros.** 1551 South Vulture Mine Road, Wickenburg, AZ 85390. Tel: 684-5484. Open mid-October to May. F.A.P. No credit cards accepted. $192–$324.

▶ **The Registry Resort.** 7171 North Scottsdale Road, Seottsdale, AZ 85253. Tel: 991-3800 or (800) 247-9810; Fax: 948-9843. $205–$220.

▶ **The Ritz-Carlton, Phoenix.** 2401 East Camelback Road, Phoenix, AZ 85016. Tel: 468-0700 or (800) 241-3333; Fax: 468-0793. $155–$250.

▶ **Rodeway Inn Mesa.** 5700 East Main Street, Mesa, AZ 85205. Tel: 985-3600 or (800) 888-3561; Fax: 832-1230. $39–$129.

▶ **San Carlos Hotel.** 202 North Central Avenue, Phoenix, AZ 85004. Tel: 253-4121 or (800) 528-5446. $59–$89.

▶ **Scottsdale Marriott Suites.** 7325 East Third Avenue, Scottsdale, AZ 85251. Tel: 945-1550; Fax: 945-2005. $90–$155.

▶ **Scottsdale Princess Resort.** 7575 East Princess Drive, Scottsdale, AZ 85255. Tel: 585-4848 or (800) 344-4758; Fax: 585-9895. $115–$300 (call for *casita* and suite rates).

▶ **Scottsdale's Fifth Avenue Inn.** 6935 Fifth Avenue, Scottsdale, AZ 85251. Tel: 994-9461 or (800) 528-7396; Fax: 994-0493. $42–$82.

▶ **Sheraton San Marcos Golf Resort and Conference Center.** One San Marcos Place, Chandler, AZ 85224. Tel:

963-6655 or (800) 325-3535; Fax: 899-5441. $90–$190 (includes breakfast and dinner).

▶ **Stouffers Cottonwoods Resort.** 6610 North Scottsdale Road, **Scottsdale**, AZ 85253. Tel: 991-1414. $59–$225.

▶ **Sun Ridge Communities.** 12221 West Bell Road, **Surprise**, AZ 85374. Tel: 583-9800 or (800) 237-9005; Fax: 583-2603. $294–$609 (seven-night minimum).

▶ **The Wigwam Resort.** West Indian School and Litchfield roads, P.O. Box 278, **Litchfield Park**, AZ 85340. Tel: 935-3811 or (800) 327-0396; Fax: 935-3737. $95–$370.

▶ **Windmill Inn at Sun City West.** 12545 West Bell Road, **Surprise**, AZ 85374. Tel: 583-0133 or (800) 547-4747; Fax: 583-8366. $45–$85.

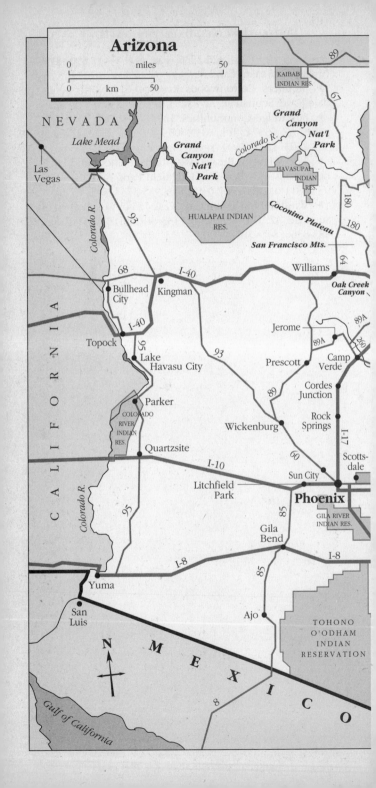

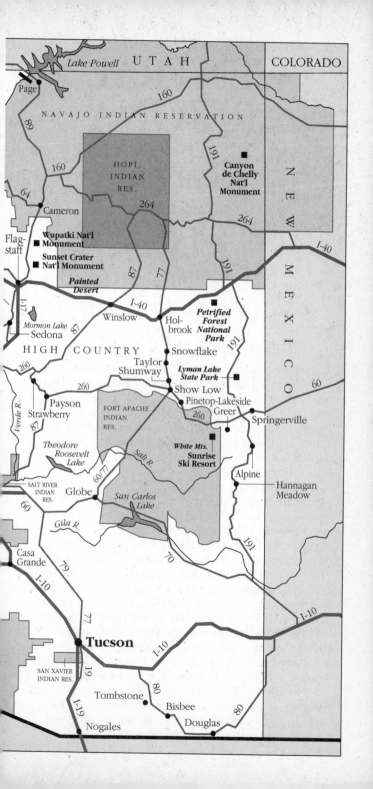

CENTRAL ARIZONA

AND GRAND CANYON'S SOUTH RIM

By Maggie Wilson

First-time visitors to Arizona expect to find nothing but desert and a big scenic gully known as Grand Canyon. But Arizona is not, as one wag put it, "114,000 square miles of kitty litter." True, about one-third of the state is Sonoran Desert, but another third is canyon and mesa country, and a third is forested mountains. For that matter, the Grand Canyon is only one, albeit the best-known, of the state's big scenic gullies.

The state's six life zones range—*very* roughly, south to north—from lower desert to Arctic/Alpine; from tall saguaro cactus "forests" to forests of fir, spruce, and aspen, with the world's largest ponderosa pine forest tucked in along the way. Its highest elevations are above timberline on San Francisco Peaks near Flagstaff, and on Mount Baldy in the White Mountains east of Phoenix near New Mexico. Arizona is home to a rare orchid and to a desert rodent that never needs water. It boasts more boat owners per capita than any other state and is the avowed favorite spot in North America for bird-watchers. It frequently registers both the nation's highest temperature (at Bullhead City on the Lower Colorado River) and the lowest (at Hannagan Meadow in the White Mountains) on the same day.

To its natural scenic wonders, dramatic changes in elevation, and geologic caprices add the scores of man-made lakes throughout the state, including Lake Mead, the nation's largest, in the northwest, and Lake Powell, the second largest, on the north-central border with Utah. Most have been formed by dams on the Colorado, Salt, Verde, Gila, and Agua Fria rivers. Only one tiny lake southeast of Flagstaff is not man-made: Stoneman Lake, formed in the crater of a volcano and fed by snowmelt from the crater's slopes.

Our coverage of Arizona's big middle, along main highways and off-the-beaten-path byways, begins, as most travellers do, by going north from Phoenix on—or branching off from—Interstate 17 up to Flagstaff, the Grand Canyon, or I-40. Along the way we loop through the former territorial capital, Prescott, the mountainside town of Jerome, and the New Age center of Sedona, with its world-famous cliffs, monoliths, and buttes.

Then we cover the I-40 corridor from west to east—taking a side trip west of Flagstaff up to the South Rim of the Grand Canyon—through Flagstaff in the center to the towns that access the High Country in the east. (The North Rim and the so-called Arizona Strip, separated from the rest of Arizona by the Grand Canyon and other canyons, is covered in the Southern Utah chapter.)

After the scenic High Country, with its four seasons, White Mountains, and Fort Apache Indian Reservation, we end with Arizona River Country, at the state's western border with California and Nevada. Water sports and river tours are year-round activities here, but just a few miles away from the life-giving waters you'll find stunning desertscapes.

The telephone area code for Arizona is 602.

MAJOR INTEREST

Along the I-17 Corridor
Arcosanti: prototype city of the future
Montezuma Castle National Monument
Prescott: Whiskey Row and Victorian architecture
Sharlot Hall Museum of Prescott history
Jerome: outdoor architectural museum
Tuzigoot National Monument
New Age energy center of Sedona: famous red-rock monoliths, resorts, specialty shops, and art galleries
Slide Rock State Park
Oak Creek Canyon

The I-40 Corridor and Flagstaff
South Rim Grand Canyon National Park
Flagstaff's Museum of Northern Arizona

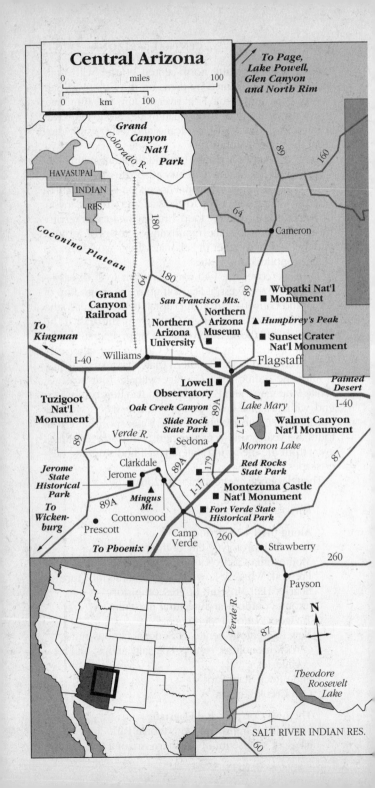

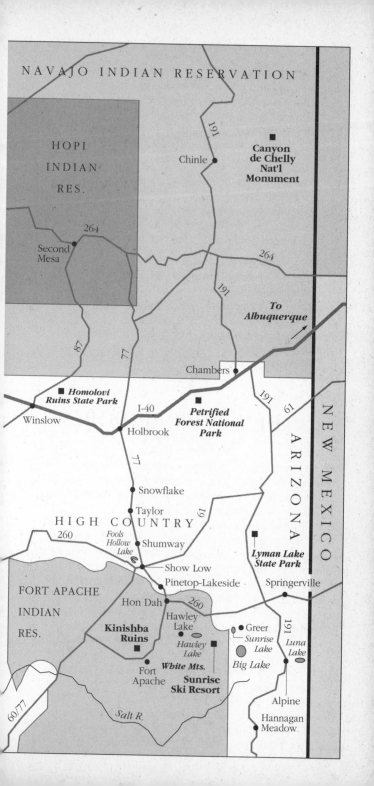

Cameron Trading Post, Navajo Reservation
Wupatki and Sunset Crater national monuments
Lake Powell/Rainbow Bridge
Walnut Canyon National Monument
Petrified Forest National Park in the Painted Desert
Canyon de Chelly National Monument

High Country
Forests, mountains, lakes, streams, trails, and
   scenic drives
Fort Apache Indian Reservation
Casa Malpais archaeological site and museum
Coronado Trail Scenic Highway

River Country
Yuma Territorial Prison State Historic Park
Mexican border town of San Luis
London Bridge and "olde English" villages at Lake
   Havasu City
Gambling (across the river from Bullhead City)

THE I-17 CORRIDOR

Plan to spend three or more days exploring this desert-to-mountain region that exemplifies Arizona's dramatic changes in terrain, vegetation, altitude, and climate—not to mention some indescribable scenery.

As you leave Phoenix heading north on I-17 the road soon begins to climb more and more uphill, until you finally pass the last saguaro cactus and crest the ridge of a plateau covered with a grass not seen just yards to the south. This is Verde Valley and the Sedona area, at the edge of the Colorado Plateau to the north—and where erosion has left the stunning cliffs and buttes that surround Sedona. From there up to Prescott and the Colorado Plateau itself you'll go through another change of terrain, to higher altitudes and cooler climes that produce completely different vegetation: pine and aspen, for example. This all makes for a glorious journey that you will never forget. These are not fussy little microclimates like those of Napa and Sonoma, but full-blown *climates*. For a hundred miles you're in one, then, bang! You're in another. Then, bang! another. Welcome to Arizona.

To the natural scenic majesty of the area add the history of Old Arizona—of Indians, scouts, prospectors, cowboys, cavalrymen, and settlers—and the indoor-outdoor lifestyle of New Arizona: of trail rides, golf carts, backcountry jeep tours, hiking trails, swimming holes, and plain old stump-sitting communion with Mother Nature.

Sedona, in the heart of Red Rock Country, is a one-of-a-kind community where the man-made amenities of resorts, shops, and art galleries are a near match for the natural beauty of the terrain. Prescott, "the Mile-High City," offers passels of territorial history and mountain serenity along with its not-always-serene Whiskey Row.

PHOENIX TO SEDONA

North of Phoenix on I-17 and to the west of the freeway (take exit 242) are the weathered buildings of **Rock Springs**, an old stage stop that now is famed for its smoked meats, its annual output of 20,000 pies (sold whole or by the slice at Penny's Pies), and a delicacy known as mountain oysters. The old hotel here is mostly offices now, but one restored room is said to be the place where Jean Harlow stayed on her way to Prescott to see Tom Mix.

A 1920s copper liquor distiller hangs over the entrance of the **saloon**. Local legend has it that the original owner used it as a business enhancement during Prohibition. Also in the saloon is an ornately carved mahogany Brunswick front and back bar, built in 1856 in Virginia and shipped around the horn of South America to California, then freighted cross-country by 20-mule teams.

Most of the time the town is almost sedate. But on the last Saturday of each month Rock Springs offers 50-cent beer, three country bands, barbecued meats, and mountain oysters. That last, for the uninitiated, is deep-fried animal testicles. Ask the aficionados who arrive on their Harleys or in their Lamborghinis what's so great about mountain oysters and they'll tell you.

At Cordes Junction, exit 262, a frontage road leads about 2 miles (3 km) to **Arcosanti**, an experiment in architecture and ecology called "arcology." The building here, ongoing for the past 23 years, uses alternative methods, including earth-cast forms for concrete construction, designed by architectural innovator Paolo Soleri of Scottsdale.

Arcosanti is being erected by Soleri's apprentices, who believe this experiment to be an urban laboratory for arcological cities of the future. The basic idea: Life, work, and leisure activities are integrated into a community that grows vertically, not horizontally, with solar greenhouses for heating and food production. The city of the future excludes the automobile and the need for it. It is energy efficient because of its compact layout, and encourages interaction with the surrounding natural environment.

A café serves breakfast, lunch, and dinner here. Mockups illustrating Soleri's futuristic philosophy are displayed in a gallery, which also sells the famed bronze or ceramic Soleri wind-bells that are handcrafted here. Tel: 632-7135.

In the town of Camp Verde, 2 miles (3 km) east of the freeway from exit 285, is **Fort Verde State Historic Park,** headquarters of General George Crook during the winter campaign of 1872–1873 that largely ended Indian raids in the region. Like most military posts of the period, Fort Verde wasn't walled, nor did Indians ever attack it. Exhibits in the adobe administration building illustrate the life of the soldiers, their families, Apache Indian army scouts, farmers, and prospectors. Of particular note is a map showing the army's territory-wide communications network of heliographs, a system transmitting the dots and dashes of Morse code by sunshine reflected off mirrors equipped with shutters.

Montezuma Castle National Monument, east of exit 289, is a 12th-century, five-story cliff dwelling erected by a prehistoric Indian tribe anthropologists now call the Sinagua (literally, Spanish for "without water"). The structure was misnamed by early settlers; Montezuma's Aztec realm was far to the south in Mexico.

In New Orleans tour guides tell you that the elegant buildings facing Jackson Square are America's first apartments. Montezuma Castle and many other ruins throughout the Southwest indicate otherwise. Though it would seem demanding enough just to put food in the firepit 800 years ago, the Sinaguas were sophisticated water engineers and artisans as well as builders, as attested by the visitors' center exhibits.

Also near exit 289, at Middle Verde Road, is **Best Western Cliff Castle Lodge.** An alternative to sometimes booked-up accommodations farther north, the lodge offers pleasant Southwestern decor, a pool and Jacuzzi, a lounge, a restaurant, and horseback riding. Some of the staff are Yavapai-Apache Indians, residents of the tiny reservation on which the lodge is situated.

Our coverage returns now to exit 262 at Cordes Junction, which is the exit for AZ 69 running 34 miles (54 km) northwest up to Prescott. From Prescott we'll continue the loop clockwise over Mingus Mountain to Jerome, then to Cottonwood, and into Sedona on AZ 89 Alternate (AZ 89A). If you prefer skipping the Prescott and Jerome loop, or can't spare the extra hours (it would be a misfortune), you can just steam right up I-17 from Phoenix to exit 298 and take AZ 179 to Sedona, a trip of 120 miles (192 km), or a little over two hours. (A direct trip from Phoenix to Flagstaff and the junction of I-17 with I-40 is 164 miles/262 km, or three hours.)

WEST OF I-17

Prescott

The War Between the States had not yet been won when Abraham Lincoln declared Arizona to be a U.S. territory in 1863. The conventional wisdom of the day said that the new territory's capital would be Tucson, then the only settlement of any size. North of the Gila River there were only two non-Indian settlements in the entire territory, Hardyville and Ehrenberg, both steamboat ports on the Lower Colorado River.

But Tucson didn't suit Lincoln. Only the year before, the westernmost battle of the Civil War had been fought at Pichaco Peak just north of that city, and Tucson was known as a hotbed of Secessionists and Confederate sympathizers. Besides, gold was being discovered in the new territory along such little-known rills as Big Bug, Lynx, Granite, and Turkey creeks to the north. And gold was a commodity the Union needed.

Thus, the first capital of the Arizona Territory was a mere spot on a topographical map in a mountain basin near the creeks and beneath a distinctive thumb-shaped butte. Trees and water were plentiful, but it was wilderness—a capital city yet to be built.

Prescott was a planned community from the beginning. Using a prospector's frying pan for a sextant, engineer Robert Groom designed streets around a central plaza. And for that, a riverbed was named Groom Creek to commemorate the city planner.

The territorial legislature had a change of heart in 1867, moving the capital to Tucson until 1877, when it was transferred back to Prescott—before ending up in Phoenix for good in 1889.

Unlike Tucson, which had adobe buildings with a strong Mexican-Spanish flavor, Prescott took its character from settlers who came from New England and the Midwest. Though the Governor's Mansion was of chinked logs, the frame homes that were built later were ornate Victorians, some topped with widow's walks like the homes of Maine whaling skippers. Today Courthouse Plaza, serene tree-shaded streets, and the stately old homes surrounding the downtown district enhance Prescott's claim to be "everybody's hometown."

While this city of 30,000 hosts visitors from around the world, in summer it's a favored cooling-off spot for Arizona's desert-dwelling "flatlanders" (i.e., residents of Phoenix and the Valley of the Sun). Summer camps—of the sports, youth, and church variety—proliferate on the town's outskirts. Many visitors come for special events commemorating area history.

DOWNTOWN PRESCOTT

Courthouse Plaza

Gurley Street is the town's main thoroughfare. Facing it, between Montezuma and Cortez streets, is Courthouse Plaza, surrounded by its own shade trees and benches, and the scene of evening entertainment June through August. A chronology of the city's history—much more interesting than you're probably thinking—is cast in the concrete walkway in front of the monumental bronze statue of "Buckey" O'Neill, a local hero who was variously newspaperman, miner, sheriff, and politician. The nickname Buckey came from "bucking the tiger" (betting against the house) in the gambling game of faro. O'Neill lost his life on the charge up San Juan Hill in Cuba during the Spanish-American War, when he was a member of Theodore Roosevelt's Rough Riders. The statue was created by Solon Borglun, whose brother, Gutzon, carved the presidential faces in Mount Rushmore.

Around Courthouse Plaza

In 1900 Prescott's business district burned to the ground, but even as it did, patrons of the Montezuma Street saloons carried the bars, the gambling tables, and a player piano across the street to the safety of the plaza, where they continued their drinking and gambling. The player piano endlessly ground out—what else?—"There'll Be a Hot Time in the Old Town Tonight," the regimental song of the Rough Riders. The rebuilt business district is what you see today.

Montezuma Street, better known as **Whiskey Row**, was rebuilt with almost as many saloons as it had before the fire, but many of them have now been recycled into shops and restaurants. Three establishments—**Matt's**, **Western**, and **The Palace Bar**—continue to reflect the old-time flavor of ornate back bars and brass foot rails. Nowadays, weekend nights find these joints pulsing to the beat of live (and loud) country music; other nights it's still loud but recorded. Newer, more sedate, and a bit quieter is **County Seat**, also on Whiskey Row.

ELSEWHERE IN PRESCOTT

Two blocks west of Montezuma on Gurley Street is the **Sharlot Hall Museum**, a complex of restored historic buildings and exhibits reflective of the town's still-cherished history of miners, the military, area Indians, ranchers, ramblers, gamblers, gunslingers, and gentlemen. Named for territorial poet-historian Sharlot Hall, the museum comprises buildings ranging from the log Governor's Mansion to the opulent Victorian Bashford House, built in 1877 by a local merchant. Closed Mondays, except holidays.

The well-tended lawns, shade trees, flower beds, gazebo, and benches surrounding the buildings make this block, like Courthouse Plaza, a favored "time out" spot.

The **Phippen Museum of Art**, 4701 Highway 89 North, displays the works of the late George Phippen, a founder of Cowboy Artists of America, and the works of other Southwestern artists.

If Old West history fascinates you—or if you just want a different kind of good time—take the guided walking tour of the original town site (Courthouse Plaza, Whiskey Row, and Victorian structures) offered by Melissa Ruffner's **Prescott Historical Tours**. Members of Ms. Ruffner's family have been Prescott movers, shakers, and raconteurs since 1867 (which is practically the Creation in this part of the Southwest). She conducts her two-hour tours dressed in 1890s attire, and her running commentary is both informative and entertaining. Summer only. Reservations are required; Tel: 445-4567.

Backcountry jeep and horse tours, some with breakfast

and supper cookouts, are offered by **Bradshaw Mountain Backcountry Tours** (Tel: 445-3032).

Among the most popular of the town's busy schedule of annual events are the following: **June** is the month of the Sharlot Hall Folk Art Fair, Territorial Days, Historic Home Tour, and All-Indian Pow-Wow. In **July**, there is Frontier Days Rodeo and Parade (this July 4th event dates back to 1888 and is called the World's Oldest Continuous Rodeo; book lodgings far in advance if you plan to be here over Independence Day). **August** entertainments include the Bluegrass Festival, Mountain Artists' Arts and Crafts Show, and Native American Festival. **September** hosts Faire on the Square and Ranch Tour; **October** is the month of the Governor's Cup Antique Car Rallye from here to the Grand Canyon; and **December** celebrates the Courthouse Plaza Christmas Lighting Ceremony. For details call the Prescott Chamber of Commerce; Tel: 445-2000 or (800) 477-0046.

Five small fishing and boating lakes dot the outskirts of town. One, **Lynx Lake**, rents pedal boats, a favorite of families with children and teenagers. To reach the lake take AZ 69 east 4 miles (6½ km) to Walker Road, turn south (right), and follow the signs to the lake and the rental marina.

Two PGA-sanctioned golf courses around Prescott are open to the public year-round. Thirty-six hole **Antelope Hills Golf Course** is adjacent to the airport on 89 North. (Note: This is not on 89 *Alternate* that branches off from AZ 89 north of town.) Eighteen-hole **Prescott Country Club Golf Course** is 14 miles (22 km) east of town on AZ 69. The horses run on weekends at **Prescott Downs** (take Gurley Street west to Grove Avenue to Miller Valley Road; watch for the entrance sign on the left); the season begins on Memorial Day and ends on Labor Day.

DINING IN PRESCOTT

Murphy's Restaurant, 201 North Cortez, is situated in a downtown mercantile building that escaped the 1900 fire. Though the interior retains its 1890s look, the restaurant has been tastefully redone in shades of gray and burgundy, with etched and beveled glass dividers and brass fixtures. Fresh seafood is flown in daily. Open for lunch and dinner; Tel: 445-4044. The same owners recently opened **Gurley Street Grill**, to similar success. **Penelope Parkenfarker's**, 220 West Goodwin Street, housed downtown in the old Prescott firehouse, has brick walls, high ceilings, lots of glass and greenery, great sandwiches, and a sports bar; Tel: 445-6848.

STAYING IN PRESCOTT

Motels proliferate along the highways leading into town—AZ 69 from the east, AZ 89 from the north and south. The **Sheraton Prescott Resort and Conference Center** is the town's classiest lodging, featuring rooms, suites, and the **Thumb Butte Restaurant** (Tel: 776-1666), decorated in Southwestern pastels and artworks. Townspeople wish the exterior was also pastel, the better to blend into the landscape. As it is, it's a great pile of dark brown rising from a bluff at the intersection of AZ 69 and AZ 89 on the outskirts of town. Because it is on Yavapai Prescott Indian Reservation land, the hotel also has a casino room with slot machines and video poker; machine gambling and bingo are allowed on this and four other reservations around the state.

Among downtown's historic hotels are **Hassayampa Inn** on Gurley Street, a block east of Courthouse Plaza, whose **Peacock Dining Room** (Tel: 778-9434) was recently restored to its 1920s "grand hotel" opulence. Another is **Hotel Vendome**, 230 South Cortez Street, a block and a half south of the plaza; built in 1917 and also attractively restored, it even has its own capricious ghost (replete with melodramatic history). **Hotel St. Michael**, on the corner of Gurley and Montezuma, was built in 1901 following the big fire; it had been abandoned and boarded up until a new owner began renovation in the mid-1980s (some refurbishing is ongoing). The place now fairly exudes Old World charm, with old woods, polished brass, and morning cups of cappuccino in the lobby.

Antiques shops proliferate along Cortez Street; one is a huge consignment complex called **Merchandise Mart Mall**, 205 North Cortez (next door to Murphy's Restaurant), where you'll find everything from sun-purpled glassware and Art Nouveau jewelry to quilts and marble-topped sideboards, with lots of Western kitsch tossed in. If you're looking for Western wear, **The Cattleman's Shop**, across from the plaza on Whiskey Row, is a good choice.

The loop west of I-17 continues from Prescott on AZ 89 at the eastern edge of town. Take AZ 89 north to AZ 89A, which branches to the right a few miles north of town. AZ 89A runs east through Prescott Valley and then up the steep slopes of Mingus Mountain (elevation 7,743 feet). Just on the other side of the crest, perched (just barely) on the seemingly vertical mountainside far above the valley and out toward the Sedona area, is the well-known almost ghost town of Jerome.

Jerome

Plan to spend several hours in Jerome, even if all you do is take in the vistas that go on forever across the Verde Valley to Red Rock Country, rugged Sycamore Canyon, San Francisco Peaks near Flagstaff, and the Mogollon Rim escarpment. (The dwindling western edge of the Mogollon Rim is what you'll pass over on the final leg from Sedona to Flagstaff: the edge of the great Colorado Plateau.)

The shift whistles at this billion-dollar copper camp sounded their last blasts in 1953 when the mines closed. Jerome, clinging precariously to the slopes of Cleopatra Hill, seemed to cling even more precariously to survival. Indeed, its population dwindled from a 1920s peak of 15,000 to a 1950s low of 50, but it never really became a ghost town. Jerome's elevation is about a mile, but the elevation within the town itself varies 1,500 feet from the highest to the lowest points on the hill. Jerome's present population is about 500, mostly artists, artisans, and shopkeepers.

Though townsfolk still boast about the wealth of gold, silver, and copper mined from beneath the town, it is the scenery that keeps Jerome a thriving place, thanks to a steady stream of all-seasons visitors. Old-fashioned buildings, some restored, others abandoned, add to the historic aura of the town. Walking or driving the winding, switchback streets is like wandering an outdoor museum of turn-of-the-century architecture.

From the time the United Verde Copper Company set up shop in 1883, Jerome's fortunes were in boom or bust modes depending upon the price of copper. So many saloons, gambling halls, and brothels lined the street's main drag that a New York newspaper dubbed it "the wickedest town in the West."

During the mine's heyday, underground blasting shook the hillside town so regularly that some buildings fell off their foundations and banks refused to take homes or businesses as collateral. The town's jail slid across a road and down a hillside—where it continues to slide a few inches each year.

Three distinctly different mining museums help visitors get a handle on the town's past and the passé method of underground mining. (Open-pit mining has replaced shaft and tunnel mining.) The most impressive of these is **Jerome State Historic Park**, which includes a museum housed in the former mansion of mining mogul "Rawhide Jimmy" Douglas. To reach the park turn off AZ 89A at milepost 345 at the lower end of Jerome—you can't fully appreciate the import of that "lower" until you get here—and follow the paved road for about 1 mile (1½ km). Ore samples and fascinating old photos are included in displays at **Jerome Historical Society Mine Museum**, at the corner of Main Street (AZ 89A) and Jerome Avenue, in the back of the gift shop. Hoists, pumps, ore cars, and a mineshaft replica are the attraction at **Gold King Mine museum**. Take AZ 89A to the upper switchback in town, turn northwest on Perkinsville Road, and drive for 1 mile (1½ km); you'll pass an open-pit mine on your left.

Outstanding among the many shops in Jerome are Skyfire and Designs on You, both on Main Street, the level below AZ 89A. **Skyfire**, three floors in a replica 1899 building, has pottery, books, handwoven rugs, Southwestern furniture and accessories, and unusual toys. **Designs on You** specializes in fun women's clothing. The store's prints, fabrics, shoes, and hats are from around the world.

Also on Main Street is **Jerome Art Park**, an outdoor gallery showing local artists' works. Exceptional among all the art shops and galleries is **Raku Gallery**, a lulu of a pottery shop in a three-story building on the corner of AZ 89A and Hull Avenue.

Micki's, downstairs in the Historical Society Mine Museum Gift Shop on Main Street, is open for lunch only. (Well, they serve breakfast muffins and scones in the mornings, but no eggs or pancakes.) Specialties include cold zucchini soup, potato tortes, Mexican soufflés, and homemade breads and pastries.

Nancy Russell's Bed & Breakfast on tiny Juarez Street, two levels down from Main, provides spectacular views of Verde Valley from a turn-of-the-century miner's home furnished with antiques of the era. Nancy's breakfasts include homemade breads and fruits from her garden served in cut glass and sterling silver. Accommodations are limited, though, to just two couples per night.

Clarkdale and Cottonwood

After Jerome, AZ 89A winds down the eastern side of Mingus Mountain and into Clarkdale, a town of tree-lined streets and brick homes that is the gateway to the **Tuzigoot National Monument**, a Sinagua Indian village inhabited between A.D. 1125 and 1400. The pueblo-style village (no cliff dwellings) crowns the summit of a ridge that rises 120 feet above the Verde Valley. The original pueblo was two stories high; entry was by way of ladders through openings in the roofs. Displays in the visitors' center provide glimpses of Sinaguan life and suggest a trading network that reached far into Mexico. To reach the ruins take Broadway, which runs between Clarkdale and Cottonwood, then turn east on Tuzigoot Road and continue for a mile (1½ km).

Clarkdale also is the departure and return point for the **Verde River Canyon Excursion Train**, 300 North Broadway. The tracks follow the river up-canyon to Perkinsville, affording views of an otherwise inaccessible portion of Arizona's few remaining pristine riparian habitats. Eagles, Indian ruins, surprisingly lush vegetation along the riverside, and red-walled cliffs are among the sights. A guide narrates various portions of the trip and points out animals of interest on the way up to Perkinsville. Signs in Clarkdale point the way to the depot. The diesel train runs mornings and afternoons year-round, Wednesday through Sunday, and the round trip takes four hours. Moonlight excursions are offered on summer nights of the full moon. Reservations are required; Tel: 639-0010.

The town of **Cottonwood**, a couple of miles past Clarkdale on AZ 89A, was named for a group of trees along the Verde River, which runs through town. Cottonwood was a farm settlement in the late 1870s, and the atmosphere of those earlier days is reflected in **Historic Old Town Cottonwood**, an Old West–style street with high sidewalks and false-fronted buildings.

After Cottonwood AZ 89A continues northeast into Sedona. (Red Rock State Park and Red Rock Crossing/Cathedral Rock, two places of interest off AZ 89A near Sedona on the way from Cottonwood, are covered in the Around Sedona section, below.)

Whether you are coming from Jerome or up AZ 179 from I-17 (the faster way), as you approach Sedona red-rock monoliths begin to appear (in this regard AZ 179 is perhaps a better approach than 89A). All are named. The nearest to the main roads are **Cathedral Rock**, **Bell Rock**, and **Courthouse Butte**.

The stoplight at the intersection of AZ 179 and AZ 89A is known as "the Y" in Sedona. Townspeople give directions to the area's attractions using this junction as the starting point.

SEDONA

Small wonder residents call this "God's country." Small wonder that about four million visitors trek through Sedona annually.

The city (4,400 feet elevation) nestles in a bowl at the bottom of Oak Creek Canyon (for which see Around Sedona, below). The creek itself, meandering through the town, is outlined and canopied by a gallery of old trees. The town is surrounded by red-rock cliffs, buttes, canyons, and monoliths—a statement somewhat comparable to saying Manhattan has office buildings.

Actually, the sandstone formations aren't really red, as in fire engine or apple. Depending upon the time of day and season of the year, they can range from magenta to rosy pink to vermilion. It's the oxidized iron content within the sandstone that causes the coloration; sun and shadow provide the variations. Colorful as the sandstone is, the hues are only skin-deep; underneath, the rock is sand-colored. Oak Creek carved the canyon; the free-standing, pop-up monoliths are like ships adrift from the mooring of the Mogollon Rim.

Supplies for Sedona's handful of residents at the turn of the century came via wagon train from Flagstaff after an arduous six-day journey. Today the 28-mile (45-km) scenic drive on AZ 89A down the switchbacks of Oak Creek Canyon south from Flagstaff to Sedona takes about a half hour. More, of course, for gawkers. From mid-October to mid-November, when the changing leaves provide red, pink, orange, and gold counterpoints to the backdrop of red cliff walls, everybody gawks. (Views are better travelling south from Flagstaff than north from Sedona; see the Around Sedona section, below, for details.)

The author Zane Grey in the 1920s and the artist Max Ernst in the 1950s discovered Sedona for themselves; other writers, photographers, filmmakers, entrepreneurs, retirees, visitors, and artists—especially artists—have been discovering Sedona ever since.

The most recent group to arrive are New Agers, complete with their crystals, pyramids, medicine wheels, and shops relating to such esoterica as past lives, reincarnation, mantras, ESP, and psychic counseling. New Agers say the red rocks abound in energy centers. (To date, so far as is known, no one has managed to measure the alleged vortex energy.)

Sedona's early remoteness and the lack of gold strikes

in the area allowed it to develop without the rough-and-tumble aura of hard-rock miners and brush-busting cowboys. Instead, it evolved as a center of tourism, with full awareness that the remarkable scenery demanded amenities to match. With few exceptions, they do.

Outdoor activities run the full gamut: hiking, golfing, horseback riding, tennis, swimming, fishing, picnicking, and sightseeing. Guided jeep tours are the most popular ways to explore the backcountry; even more spectacular is a hot-air balloon excursion for a bird's-eye view of the red rocks. (See Around Sedona, below.)

With scores of one-of-a-kind shops and boutiques, 40 art galleries, and even a factory outlet center, Sedona is a delight for the shop-till-you-drop crowd. The resorts and restaurant lounges feature a variety of live entertainment including listening or dancing music in the country, jazz, rock, pop, and folk genres, as well as theatrical productions and comedy acts.

SHOPPING IN SEDONA

Don't expect conventional malls or department stores. In Sedona they simply don't exist. Instead, there are specialty shops, boutiques, and galleries, heavy on one-of-a-kind items, in various shopping areas or clusters. Each area has its share of shops devoted to antiques, apparel, art, gifts, decor accessories, furnishings, Indian arts and jewelry, leathers, linens, and pottery.

The most notable of these is **Tlaquepaque Arts and Crafts Village**, fashioned after a walled Mexican market town with brick and stone walkways, old sycamore trees rising from the courtyards, arches, wrought-iron balconies, fountains, flowering bougainvillaea vines climbing the adobe-like walls, and sidewalk cafés and other places to rest in the dappled sunlight—some close enough to hear the plash and gurgle of the creek. In other words, a fun place to go even if shopping isn't on your agenda. One of the many unusual shops here is **Cocopah**, the bead place—with Venetian glass, ethnic, antique, shell, and trade beads, and kits to help you create your own adornments. Outstanding for its Indian jewelry is **Ninibah**. Tlaquepaque is located just south of the Y on AZ 179 at the bridge.

A bit south of Tlaquepaque are other upscale centers: **Hozho**, with architecture resembling pueblo style (inside, **Lanning's** is a major contemporary art gallery); **Artesania Plaza**, a contemporary-style trilevel complex that includes **Kathy Anne's** shop of hand-painted clothes and quilts; and **Hillside**, with its terraced and tiered shops and restaurants, including the **Mineral and Fossil Gallery**, featuring collectibles from nature.

A bit south of Tlaquepaque near the bridge over Oak Creek in a building of its own, **Garland's** houses an outstanding selection of antique and contemporary Navajo rugs, along with collections of Hopi kachina dolls, baskets, and sand paintings. Garland's neighbor is **Touchstone**, "a gallery of wearable art."

The shops of **Uptown Sedona**, another major retail area, along AZ 89A north of the Y, line each side of the street and include **The Worm**, 207 North Highway 89A, a bookstore specializing in Southwestern subjects. At number 320, **Sinagua Plaza** has gift shops and galleries and a restaurant with an "old-time saloon."

Popular among discount shoppers is **Oak Creek Factory Stores**, 6620 Highway 179 in the village of Oak Creek, south of Sedona on AZ 179, offering everything from foundation garments to flatwear—bags, shoes, designer clothing, crystal, china, toys, perfume, and jewelry.

STAYING AND DINING IN SEDONA

As in Phoenix/Scottsdale, "resort hopping" (i.e., staying at one place, taking meals or cocktails at others with different views and vistas) is an acceptable and encouraged practice in Sedona. Be sure to have reservations if you're coming for a weekend or during the peak season (roughly April to November). Prices tend to be on the high side then, but often drop in the winter—the opposite of Phoenix/Scottsdale's seasons. Alternative lodgings may be found at motels in the Cottonwood or Camp Verde areas.

Though almost any lodging you choose will provide views of nature's red-rock spectaculars, an exceptionally desirable setting is **Enchantment Resort** in nearby Boynton Canyon.

Enchantment snuggles into a truly, yes, enchanted red-rock canyon—wide, secluded, and tranquil—worlds away from mundane sights and sounds. The resort comprises the main building with shops, a lounge, a dining room, cocktail terraces, and a spa and fitness center. Surrounding it are six pools, 12 tennis courts, a croquet lawn, a putting green, and adobe-style *casitas* (little houses). While the *casita* arrangement accommodates families or two couples travelling together, singles or couples may opt for a *casita* bedroom only, or a suite with bedroom, living room, and kitchenette.

Enchantment's **Yavapai Room** restaurant offers great

views of Boynton Canyon's red walls along with regional cuisine, including items on the wild side such as rattlesnake chili. There are spectacular Champagne and jazz brunches on Sundays. Reservations are required; Tel: 282-2900.

To reach Enchantment go west from the Y (AZ 89A West) 3 miles (5 km) to Dry Creek Road and turn right. At the T make a left; at the next T turn right to the entrance.

For French elegance in a landscape that has no Gallic counterpart, **L'Auberge de Sedona Resort** is another idyllic hideaway. Romantic luxury cottages or lodge rooms have authentic French country-inn decor with canopied beds, overstuffed love seats, and stone fireplaces. Secluded porches overlook either Oak Creek or flower gardens shaded by cottonwoods and sycamores.

If country-French decor is a bit too froufrou for you, the resort has thoughtfully provided **The Orchards at L'Auberge**, boasting contemporary Southwestern style; the private patios or balconies of these rooms look out on red-rock vistas.

The property's two restaurants reflect the French passion for food. **L'Auberge Restaurant**, beside the creek, serves six-course prix fixe dinners each evening. Reservations are required; Tel: 282-1667. The **Orchards Restaurant**, facing Sedona's main street, offers a more casual setting; Tel: 282-7200.

To reach L'Auberge from the Y, turn right onto AZ 89A North; the entrance is about 200 feet ahead on the right on L'Auberge Lane.

Poco Diablo Resort, the town's first full-service resort, has recently been remodeled in a fresh contemporary style. Its bells and whistles include hot spas, pools, racquetball and tennis courts, and a nine-hole executive golf course meandering among duck ponds and willow trees. Its restaurant, **The Willows at Poco Diablo**, features a view that adds the greens of the golf course to the variegated reds of the rocks. The Southwestern signature dish here: mango chicken. Broiled lamb chops, prepared in a lemon and fresh herb marinade and served with a garlic and basil purée, is another specialty. Reservations are advised; Tel: 282-7333.

From the Y Poco Diablo is south about 2 miles (3 km) on AZ 179.

Los Abrigados is an all-suite resort (living area, bedroom, wet bar, and patio or balcony, some with fireplace and whirlpool) in a setting of Spanish-style plazas and fountains. Winding walkways and bridges connect the

175 suites, restaurant, fitness center, pool, tennis courts, and the neighboring Tlaquepaque Arts and Crafts Village of shops. Nestled beside Oak Creek, the resort property was once a ranch and an early movie location. Sedona's first hotel, a 60-year-old stone building on the property, has been upgraded to a $1,000-per-night two-bedroom "manor."

The resort's restaurant, **Canyon Rose at Los Abrigados**, invites indoor or outdoor dining. (Clay-pot chicken is a favorite here; the place itself is a local favorite for Sunday brunch.) Reservations are advised; Tel: 282-ROSE. **On-the-Rocks Lounge** here is a fun place to watch the sunset while noshing munchies from the appetizer kitchen.

Los Abrigados is on Portal Lane, beside the northern perimeter of Tlaquepaque, just south of the Y on AZ 179.

The rooms at the **Bell Rock Inn**, a pueblo adobe–style lodging, are decorated in soft desert hues. Bell Rock has its own pool, spa, and tennis courts, a restaurant, and a lounge, and offers special packages for golfing at **Sedona Golf Resort** or **Oak Creek Country Club**, both public championship courses located in the nearby village of Oak Creek. The inn is 7 miles (11 km) south of the Y on AZ 179.

The unpretentious **Railroad Inn at Sedona** is an older motel that has recently been refurbished, along with its pool area and its Prickly Pear Depot Restaurant and Cabaret. Of special interest is the Room, Ride, and Meal Deal: a night's lodging, a ride on the Verde Valley Excursion Train, and dinner at the Prickly Pear. The inn is located west of the Y on AZ 89A.

Uptown's **Best Western Arroyo Roble Hotel** on Oak Creek has both hotel rooms and resort "villas." Each villa is a two-bedroom arrangement capable of accommodating six people. The hotel has an indoor-outdoor pool, a spa, an exercise and game room, and handball, racquetball, and tennis courts. It is north of the Y on AZ 89A and within walking distance of shops.

Farther north on 89A, along Oak Creek as it climbs toward Flagstaff, are a number of creekside cottages, cabins, and lodges. Typical among them: **Oak Creek Terrace**, 5 miles (8 km) north, with in-room Jacuzzis, fireplaces, kitchenettes, and television; **Garland's Oak Creek Lodge**, 8 miles (13 km) north, where great food is part of the deal (which is the Modified American Plan); and **Junipine Resort** in the upper canyon, 1 mile (1½ km) north of Slide Rock State Park, with luxury one- and two-bedroom creek houses.

If every resort town has one great restaurant, then

Sedona's is **Rene at Tlaquepaque**, expensive but memorable (Tel: 282-9225). For Mexican food there is **El Rincon**, also in Tlaquepaque Arts and Crafts Village (Tel: 282-4648); for Chinese, try **Mandarin House**, off AZ 179 in Castle Rock Plaza in the village of Oak Creek (Tel: 284-9088); for classic Italian, **Pietro's** on 89A North (Tel: 282-2525); for the Western experience of mesquite-grilled steaks and country music, **Rainbow's End Steak House and Saloon**, 3235 West Highway 89A (Tel: 282-1593).

Around Sedona

Taking a guided jeep tour to the backcountry is almost de rigueur for Sedona visitors, and with good reason. Tour operators have access to parts of Coconino and Prescott national forests that others do not, and the guides are versed in the region's flora, fauna, ecology, geology, and anthropology. Most companies will arrange to pick you up and drop you off at your lodging.

Some guides are comedic enough to do stand-up gigs at the Improv. Two companies with thrill rides and fun guides are **Pink Jeep Tours** (Tel: 282-5000) and **Sedona Red Rock Jeep Tours** (Tel: 282-6826).

Prehistoric Indian ruins riddle the Sedona Verde Valley, and no guides are better at making them meaningful than those of **Time Expeditions** (Tel: 282-2137). "Personal growth" tours to so-called energy vortices are a specialty of **Sedona Adventures** (Tel: 282-3500). **Sue Winters** does photo tours (Tel: 282-4320); **Northern Light Balloon Expeditions** (Tel: 282-2274) gives you a bird's-eye view of Red Rock Country aboard a hot-air balloon; and **Kachina Stables** (Tel: 282-7252) conducts breakfast, lunch, dinner, and full-moon horseback rides on backcountry trails.

Chapel of the Holy Cross, a Catholic church about 3 miles (5 km) south of the Y on AZ 179 and 1 mile (1½ km) east on Chapel Road, was conceived and donated in 1956 by sculptor-painter-heiress Marguerite Brunswig Staude. To her, the world's cathedrals, most of which were of Gothic architecture, signified past glories. Her intent was to create something that would "sing" in bold contemporary language. Originally, Staude's plan was to build a cathedral of the future in Budapest on Mount Ghelert overlooking the Danube, but World War II intervened. This downsized chapel, complemented by the natural beauty of its one-of-a-kind style, has attracted pilgrims from throughout the world.

Red Rock State Park, one of the newest and prettiest of

Arizona's state parks, is located off AZ 89A West on *Lower* Red Rock Loop Road (turn south off the highway). Established as a center for environmental education, the 286-acre park is surrounded by red rocks and has several hiking trails, varying in difficulty from easy to strenuous. Trail maps are available in the visitors' center.

Red Rock Crossing/Cathedral Rock, on *Upper* (as opposed to Lower) Red Rock Loop Road, off AZ 89A West (also a southerly turn), leads to one of the most photographed scenes in the United States. It has been the site of numerous movie locations.

OAK CREEK CANYON

Slide Rock State Park, 8 miles (13 km) north of Sedona in Oak Creek Canyon, provides great views of the red rocks as well as Mother Nature's natural stone water slide in the creek—which makes a big splash with kids. (Be sure they wear jeans or denim shorts over their bathing suits; the slide is rough.) Slide Rock is crowded in summer; ditto in fall when the leaves turn and apples from the park's orchard are sold.

Oak Creek Canyon, said to be one of the most scenic drives in America, offers its best views coming downhill rather than going up. As you descend, the wide vistas open up before you; on the ascent, you sometimes stare only at sky. For that reason this is a popular dry-weather route: Take the turnoff east from AZ 179 a half mile south of the Y at **Schnebley Hill Scenic Drive.** You'll soon leave pavement to wind among red-rock cliffs and overlooks, arriving 12 miles (19 km) later at exit 320 on I-17. Continue north on I-17 to the outskirts of Flagstaff and the junction with AZ 89A. Take 89A south through Oak Creek Canyon's switchbacks and hairpin curves back into Sedona. (If you do decide to drive Oak Creek Canyon from Sedona up to Flagstaff, simply take 89A north at the Y.)

THE I-40 CORRIDOR AND FLAGSTAFF

According to the old Bobby Troup song, folks got their kicks on Route 66. Remember? About St. Looey and how

Oklahoma is mighty pretty, then "Amarillo and Gallup, New Mexico/Flagstaff, Arizona, don't forget Winona, Kingman, Barstow, San Bernardino. . . ."

Route 66, between Chicago and L.A., has been replaced by I-40, but it's still a place to get your kicks. As it passes west to east from California through Flagstaff on to New Mexico, the old "mother road" is the doorway to a mother lode of scenic spectaculars, from the Grand Canyon to the Painted Desert.

We cover the I-40 corridor from west to east, beginning near Las Vegas and Lake Mead, and ending at Canyon de Chelly National Monument near the New Mexico border: first Kingman, 100 miles (160 km) southeast of Las Vegas on U.S. 93 at its intersection with I-40; then Williams, the terminal for the Grand Canyon Railway, and near the I-40 turnoff for AZ 64 toward the Rim (we follow this coverage with a side trip up to the South Rim of the Grand Canyon); Flagstaff, the unofficial capital of Arizona's stretch of old Route 66 is next; then Winslow, Holbrook, and finally Canyon de Chelly. Winslow and Holbrook provide access to Arizona's east-central High Country, which we cover in the section following this one on the I-40 Corridor.

WESTERN CORRIDOR

Kingman

Associations of Route 66 nostalgia buffs exist worldwide. If you're into good old days, stop at the café next to the Route 66 Motel, 2939 East Andy Devine Avenue in Kingman. It's filled to the rafters with stuff to remind you of '59 Cadillacs and glass-topped gas pumps.

Or take the old route 28 miles (45 km) southwest of town (off I-40, exit 44) to the ghost towns of **Goldroad** and **Oatman**. The latter, a former gold-mining town still populated by a few hardy souls, is notable as "the land of the free and home of the bray"—burros roam the streets as freely as the folks do. Oatman gets lively on weekends with mock shoot-'em-ups, live rock and country music blaring from the three saloons, eccentric shopkeepers engrossed in good-natured hucksterism, and visitors riding in on everything from spiffed-up Harleys and ramshackle Chevys to new Porsches. The burros? Turned loose by old-time prospectors, they went forth and multiplied. Gold Camp Days re-creates those thrilling days of

yesteryear with a parade, an international burro-biscuit–
throwing contest, a haystack scramble for kids, and the
like, on Labor Day weekend. Tel: 768-3486 for details.

Williams

At 6,700 feet elevation, here you're in forest country, 120
miles (192 km) east of Kingman and only 30 miles (48
km) west of Flagstaff. Though there is some wintertime
skiing, this town's newest claim to fame is the **Grand
Canyon Railway**. Especially in summer, when Grand Canyon Park Lodges on the South Rim seem to have hung up
a permanent No Vacancy sign, the railway offers an eco-
logically approved alternative for a visit to the canyon and
a night off the premises.

You leave your car at the historic old Williams depot,
climb aboard the Harriman coaches pulled by turn-of-
the-century steam engines, and ride north to the historic
Grand Canyon Village depot right on the canyon's rim.
Up in the morning, back by nightfall. And you'll be
putting one less automobile into that crowded, loved-
nearly-to-death South Rim of the park.

The depot is on Railroad Avenue at the western edge of
town. (Business Route I-40 divides downtown Williams
and becomes Bill Williams Avenue eastbound and Railroad Avenue westbound.) The train ride takes about two
and a half hours one-way. If you have lodgings at the
canyon, you may schedule your return to Williams on the
train according to your own needs; you need not make
the return trip the same day. Grand Canyon Railroad
offers package plans that include train rides, overnight
accommodations, meals, and air or ground tours of the
canyon.

For train schedules and reservations, Tel: (800) 843-
8724. To overnight in Williams try the **Mountain Side Inn**,
within walking distance of the depot. It has a restaurant, a
lounge, a pool and spa, and the hospitality of Bev and Pat
Johnson.

GRAND CANYON'S SOUTH RIM

Many have attempted to describe it, to give voice to the
incredible sights here. It has been said prosaically that the
canyon is a mile deep, up to 18 miles wide, and 280 miles

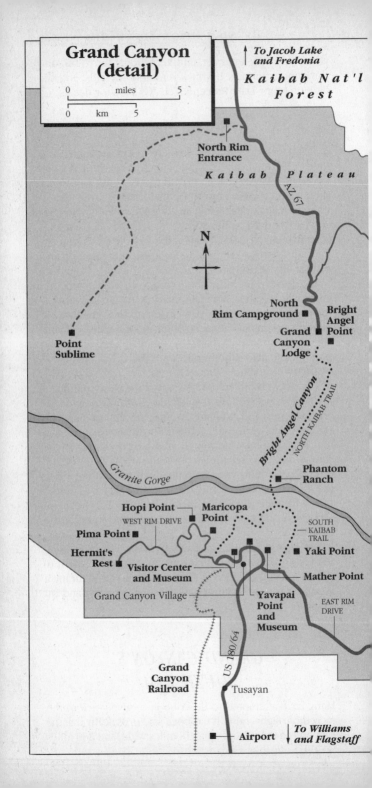

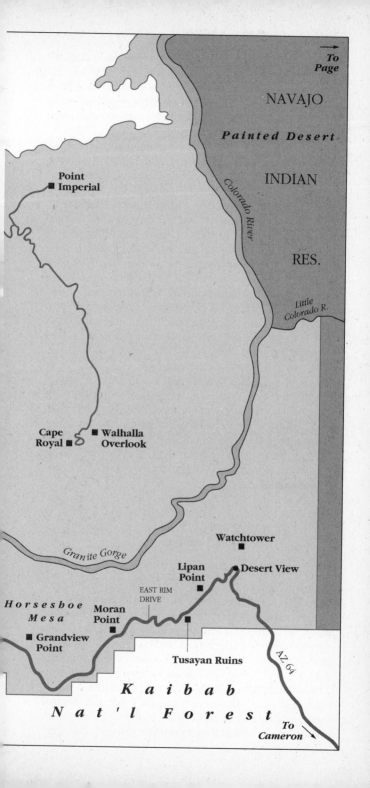

long. It has also been said that the rocks at the bottom are two billion years old and that those at the top are 225 million years old. The colors of the stony strata have been likened to those of gemstones: amethyst, topaz, sapphire, opal, garnet, peridot, and lapis. Here, said one visitor, the eye tap-dances through a dizzying array of rocky terraces, buttes, monoliths, cliffs, and escarpments, and the landscape changes from season to season, minute to minute, in the graceful pas de deux of sunlight and shadow.

But perhaps the poet Carl Sandburg expressed it best. "There," he said, "goes God with an army of banners."

Paintings, photographs, and words (even Sandburg's) pale in comparison to the real thing, the experience of standing on the rim of the immense, colorful, awe-inspiring Grand Canyon. We won't even try. For many visitors it's quite enough to find a viewpoint, sit, and stare at the ever-changing panoramas. For others mule rides, "flightseeing" trips, hikes, National Park Service programs, ruins, smooth-water raft trips, museums, IMAX and "Over the Edge" movies, and shopping are added lures.

To make the most of your time here, stop at the Visitor Center in the park's Grand Canyon Village for a copy of *The Grand Canyon Guide,* published seasonally with information on trails, maps, National Park Service exhibits, activities, and entertaining and informative programs about the geology, anthropology, history, and plants and animals of the area. (We cover the Grand Canyon's North Rim, which is by far less visited than the South Rim, in our Southern Utah chapter.)

Free shuttle service circulates from the lodges (see below) to various points in the village, and also travels the West Rim Drive every 15 minutes in summer when that road is closed to private autos.

RIM VIEWS

West Rim Drive, an 18-mile round trip from the village, includes eight main viewpoints and **Hermit's Rest**, another viewpoint where there is a gift shop, refreshments, and rest rooms. West Rim Drive is closed to autos during the summer months. Shuttles and coach tours are available year-round through the concessionaire. Hikers may get off and on the shuttles at any viewpoint.

South Rim Nature Trail, also served by shuttle, is nearly level and paved between **Maricopa Point** and **Yavapai Point**, making that portion of the trail an easy hike with unparalleled views of the canyon. The rim trail also offers a self-guided nature hike with grand panoramas but without the challenge of canyon descents. This hike is from Hermit's Rest to **Mather Point** in the village. (Get the trail pamphlet in the Visitor Center.)

East Rim Drive, a 46-mile round trip to Desert View from the village, includes such viewpoints as Yavapai and Lipan points and **Moran Point** (the last named for 19th-century landscape painter Thomas Moran, who was inspired by the light, mist, and bright red shale visible from this overlook). At **Desert View** climb the 70-foot **Watchtower** to see spectacular 360-degree views (including the Painted Desert, the Inner Gorge, and the river) from the highest point on this rim.

Desert View Trading Post has refreshments and rest rooms, and sells Indian handicrafts. Desert View Contact Station offers books, maps, and other publications about the canyon.

HIKING

Any trail you take *into* the canyon is rated strenuous to very strenuous. Wear sunshades and sunscreen and carry water and moleskins (for blisters). Remember that every hour you descend requires two hours on the return ascent; consider the canyon an upside-down mountain.

Hard-core hikers try to plan their treks for the spring and autumn months. The reason? The heat. Daytime temperatures at the bottom of the canyon are higher than upon the rim and are the same as those in Phoenix. If it's 110°F (43°C) in Phoenix in July, it's 110° at the bottom of the canyon; 68°F (20°C) in Phoenix in February means 68°F inside the canyon. Winter snows sometimes blanket the uppermost portions of the trails.

For overnights in the canyon's campgrounds, free permits from the Backcountry Reservations Office are required, and must be obtained in person. The office also provides detailed trail information and the necessary reservations for campsites throughout the Inner Gorge. Write Backcountry Office, Box 129, Grand Canyon, Arizona 86023; Tel: 638-7888 for information only—telephone reservations are not accepted.

Bright Angel Trail begins at Bright Angel Lodge in the village and follows switchbacks through the Redwall Formation to Indian Gardens Campground and the Inner Gorge. After Indian Gardens, Bright Angel Trail heads east along the river at the canyon's bottom to the silver suspension bridge leading to Phantom Ranch and Phantom Ranch Campground. Phantom Ranch, where overnighting mule riders stay, offers dormitory beds, cabins, meals, drinks, and snacks, but you must make reservations in advance for meals or accommodations. Bright Angel Trail descends 5,200 feet. One-way distances from the top are 4.6 miles to Indian Gardens (where there is water and a ranger station), 7.8 miles to the Colorado River, and 9.3 miles to Phantom Ranch (which also has water and a ranger station). A very strenuous hike, it requires two days for the round trip.

South Kaibab Trail begins at Yaki Point, 4½ miles (7 km) east of Grand Canyon Village, and drops steeply (5,000 feet in seven miles), following Cedar Ridge toward the river. An emergency telephone is at Tipoff Point, 4.4 miles below the rim, where the trail begins the descent into the Inner Gorge. This hike is rated very strenuous, and is especially grueling in summer because it lacks shade and water. Because of the sweeping views up and down the canyon, many make a day hike from the trailhead only as far as Cedar Ridge, 1.5 miles away, and return. To emphasize: In summer, *nobody* should try to hike the South Kaibab Trail from rim to river and return in a single day.

Grandview Trail begins at Grandview Point on East Rim Drive, 12 miles (19 km) east of the Visitor Center. The highlight of this 3-mile (5-km) trail is its descent onto Horseshoe Mesa, where you'll find various historical mining artifacts (mines proliferated in the canyon before the turn of the century; William Randolph Hearst owned one). You'll also see blue copper ores used by Hopi Indians for paint. Don't be misled by the fact that this is a "mere" 6-mile round trip. The trail is steep, unmaintained, has no water anywhere along the route, and the round trip requires six to eight hours. Very strenuous.

MULE TRIPS

A popular one-day trip, which goes as far as Plateau Point, departs daily from the stone corral at the head of Bright Angel Trail and descends 3,200 feet. From the point you look 1,320 feet down to see the Colorado River. The round trip takes about seven hours.

The two-day trip leaves from the same place, goes to the bottom of the canyon to Phantom Ranch by the river for an overnight stay, and returns the following day. Reservations are recommended for both trips; Tel: 638-7888.

Mules are surprisingly large animals and these well-trained beasts place their feet on the outside edges of the trail. If you fear big animals or heights, you may want to scratch a mule trip.

FLIGHTSEEING TRIPS
Both small planes and helicopters leave from Grand Canyon Airport at **Tusayan,** a small settlement about 5 miles (8 km) south of Grand Canyon Village. Neither kind of aircraft may fly below the rim, but the overviews are terrific. Reservations are recommended; Tel: 638-2631, ext. 6015 for times and fees, or contact the tour desk at any lodge.

OTHER ACTIVITIES
Also in Tusayan is the **IMAX Theatre,** with its 80-foot-high wraparound screen showing a movie about human habitation in the Grand Canyon, both historic and prehistoric. Even people who have just seen the real thing are enthralled by this film.

Yavapai Museum, 1½ miles (2½ km) east of the Visitor Center, offers spectacular panoramic views of the canyon from large observation windows, and has informative exhibits on the park's geological history. Visitors who spend only a few hours in the park say the stop here is well worthwhile.

Photography is obviously quite the thing to do here. The best sunrise photos are taken from Yaki or Yavapai points. Not to be shunned are sunrises at Hopi, Mather, and Lipan points as well. For sunsets, shooting away from the sunset itself is an excellent way to capture the hues of the canyon walls. Hopi, Mohave, Pima, and Lipan points on the West Rim provide good vantage vistas. Midday photography is usually disappointing because the intense sun tends to bleach out the colors unless there is sufficient cloud cover.

For information on **white water rafting** trips down the Colorado River, contact Grand Canyon National Park Service Headquarters (P.O. Box 129, Grand Canyon, Arizona 86023; Tel: 638-7888) for a complete list of the 20 concessionaires. Note: Most trips, which last from three days to three weeks, begin from Lee's Ferry near Page, Arizona (for which locations see the Southern Utah chapter), but a few start at Phantom Ranch.

Harveycar and **Harvey Coach Tours** are available from Grand Canyon Village to the nearby rim drives or as far away as Monument Valley (for which see the Southeastern Utah section of the Four Corners chapter); there's even a 12-hour round-trip package that includes a smooth-water raft trip, a tour of East Rim Drive, and a stop at Cameron Trading Post on the Navajo Reservation (see below). For information, Tel: 638-2401 or 638-2525.

STAYING AND DINING AT THE SOUTH RIM

The first thing to be said about accommodations at the South Rim: Make your reservations well in advance. Take your cue from the fact that lodging reservations are accepted up to 23 months in advance. There are only 900 rooms in Grand Canyon Village to accommodate the canyon's four million annual visitors.

Same-day reservations may be made at the front desk of any lodging facility on a space-available basis, but, particularly in summer, space is seldom available. (Diners may avoid lengthy waits by eating early dinners April through October.)

Grand Canyon South Rim National Park Lodges and their restaurants are operated by a National Park Service concessionaire, Fred Harvey Company.

The priciest accommodations are view suites at El Tovar Hotel on the rim; the most inexpensive are cabins at Maswik Lodge. **Phantom Ranch**, at the bottom of the canyon, has cabins, which are part of the two-day package for mule riders, and dormitories for hikers and backpackers.

El Tovar Hotel, built in 1905 of native stone and Oregon pine in the fashion of European hunting lodges, is called "the architectural crown jewel of the Grand Canyon." Years ago the famous Harvey Girls, outfitted in prim black dresses with white collars and aprons, used to set the standard for genteel hospitality here. Though the hotel is located on the rim, not all rooms and suites afford out-the-window views of the most-photographed sight on earth. **El Tovar Dining Room** offers formal dining and Continental cuisine served by a multilingual staff. Reservations are available only to guests of El Tovar; others wait, sometimes fortified by beverages and piano music in the intimate **El Tovar Lounge**.

El Tovar Hotel and many buildings in the core area of Grand Canyon Village, including the depot, are listed on the National Register of Historic Places. While not "old" in the East Coast scheme of things, they are nonetheless "historic," a fact often overshadowed by the big scenic gully that is their reason for being.

Kachina and **Thunderbird** lodges are identical two-story hostelries just west of El Tovar. No restaurants or lounges.

Bright Angel Lodge, west of Thunderbird and also built of log and native stone but in pioneer style, offers rooms and cabins that nestle on the rim, a restaurant, and a lounge with live entertainment.

Yavapai Lodge, the park's largest facility, is about one-half mile east of the village core, in a pine and juniper forest just east of the Visitor Center, and within a mile walk of the rim. It features cafeteria dining, and music and dancing nightly in the lounge.

Maswik Lodge, at the southwest end of the village, is the newest South Rim facility and offers both rooms and cabins for budget-minded travellers. It has a cafeteria and a sports bar.

Moqui Lodge, 3 miles (5 km) south of Grand Canyon Village, is rustic, offers on-site horseback riding and cook-outs, and has a restaurant and lounge entertainment.

Arizona Steakhouse, just east of Bright Angel Lodge, serves dinners only, in a casual Western setting. Closed January and February. The delicatessen of **Babbitt's General Store**, across from the Visitor Center, offers dine-in or carry-out chicken dinners, sandwiches, and salads. Open daily. **Desert View Trading Post**, 23 miles (37 km) east of the village, has a self-serve cafeteria. Open daily.

SHOPPING AT THE SOUTH RIM

If it's souvenirs, curios, or really good Indian arts and crafts you're after, you'll find them in gift shops at the lodges and at **Verkamp's** and **Hopi House**, just east of El Tovar; **Lookout Studio** (where you'll also find books, fossils, rocks, and photographic prints), west of Bright Angel Lodge; **Hermit's Rest**, 8 miles (13 km) west of Grand Canyon Village at the end of West Rim Drive; and **Babbitt's General Store**, ½ mile (1 km) east of the village core across from the Visitor Center and near Yavapai Lodge. (For descriptions of the jewelry and rugs of Southwestern Indian tribes, see the Shopping In and Around Flagstaff section, below.)

FLAGSTAFF

"Motel City" is a phrase that comes to mind when you first view this hub of Arizona's northland. There's good reason for the lodgings proliferating along the I-40 Business Loop and old Route 66 (Santa Fe Avenue was renamed "66" last year in yet another burst of nostalgia). Travellers use Flagstaff as a base for venturing out on one- or two-day trips to the area's many attractions, including the Grand Canyon. Summer is the high season; winter brings snow sports and ski packages at motels.

Additionally, this 7,000-foot-high city in tall pine country offers in-town attractions ranging from outstanding museums to festivals.

Indians, perhaps the antecedents of today's Hopis, were the Flagstaff area's first settlers, but their villages, represented by ruins at Wupatki and Walnut Canyon national monuments, had long been abandoned when the first mountain men and trappers arrived in the 1820s. With settlement discouraged by hostile bands of Navajos, Apaches, and Paiutes, it wasn't until 1880 that Flagstaff could count a total population of even 67. The following year the place was named Flagstaff after a de-limbed pine tree from which Old Glory flew. (There is ongoing debate among local historians about who flew the flag from a pine tree, where, when—or even if—but the legend persists.)

Today Flagstaff's population is about 46,000. The older, downtown part of the city has many buildings on the National Register of Historic Places, and retains a bit of frontier feeling. A good part of the character and spirit of the city is due to Northern Arizona University, which began as Northern Arizona Normal School in a vacant reform-school building in 1899. The sprawling campus is just south of downtown.

Flagstaff itself is surrounded by Coconino National Forest. North of town the San Francisco Peaks (including Mount Humphreys, at 12,633-feet elevation known as "Arizona's rooftop") are northern Arizona's weather makers, creating air-flow rotations that bring snows in winter and rainstorms in summer.

Santa Fe Avenue (Route 66/I-40 Business Loop) divides the city into north and south; San Francisco Street is the east–west dividing line. The few blocks west of San Francisco are called Santa Fe; four blocks west of San Francisco the road turns south and is known as Route 66. For further orientation of much-used streets: Humphreys is three blocks west of San Francisco; Leroux Street is one block west of San Francisco. Butler Avenue is accessed from exit 198 on I-40. I-17, which enters the city from the south, becomes Milton Road in town. To access the I-40 business route through downtown from the west, take I-40 exit 191; from the east take I-40 exit 201 north to U.S. 89, then turn west. Downtown's specialty shops—selling leather goods, Western wear, Indian crafts, and other regional items—are in a two-block area on North San Francisco Street, beginning at Route 66.

THE MUSEUMS OF FLAGSTAFF

The **Museum of Northern Arizona**, 3 miles (5 km) north of downtown on U.S. 180/Fort Valley Road (take Humphreys Street north from downtown to Fort Valley Road and follow the signs; the museum is right on the road and well marked), combines a research center with exhibit galleries of the archaeology, ethnology, geology, botany, biology, paleontology, and fine arts of the Colorado Plateau. The excellent **museum shop** assures buyers of authentic Indian arts and crafts; the bookshop carries an extensive selection of works on the Southwest. The museum's education department also offers specialized tours throughout plateau country guided by experts, usually from three to five days in length, April to mid-October. The museum is closed Thanksgiving, Christmas, and New Year's Day.

The **Coconino Center for the Arts**, about 1½ miles (2 km) south of the museum on U.S. 180, has revolving art exhibits; dance and drama presentations; and folk, ethnic, classical, and jazz concerts. Its **Gallery Shop** has hand-crafted work ranging from pottery to wearable art. Closed Mondays April through November; Sundays and Mondays November through March; and Thanksgiving, Christmas week, and Easter Sunday.

Lowell Observatory, on Mars Hill overlooking historic downtown at the west end of Santa Fe Avenue, is where Percival Lowell discovered the planet Pluto and helped form the "expanding universe" theory. Tours, lectures, slide shows, and viewing nights are subject to change, so call for current information. For a tape-recorded schedule of events, Tel: 774-2096; for tours and stargazing, Tel: 774-3358.

Northern Arizona University campus, an attraction in itself, makes an inviting summer stroll; in winter its historic district offers a glimpse into the past. On campus, which is just south of downtown, are the Art Museum at Old Main, the NAU Observatory (open for sky viewing most clear Thursday nights), a Natatorium, with an Olympic-size pool open to the public, and the Skydome, a domed stadium covering the football field. NAU's School of Performing Arts offers a year-round schedule of music, drama, and dance; for current presentations Tel: 523-3731. A free shuttle bus loops the campus every 15 minutes weekdays during the main school terms; for scheduled events call the University Union Information Desk (Tel: 523-4636) or the main switchboard (Tel: 523-9011).

STAYING IN FLAGSTAFF

Little America Hotel, on East Butler Avenue off I-40 East at exit 198, has been the mainstay of travellers who want a bit more than a plain vanilla motel room. Its rooms resemble suites in their spaciousness, and the pine-studded grounds include a pool, a two-mile walking or jogging trail, and a large gift shop (open 24 hours).

Old Highway 66's **Best Western Woodlands Plaza Hotel** is an in-town option with Southwestern contemporary decor and a sushi bar among its dining options; amenities include a pool, indoor and outdoor spas, a sauna, and an exercise room. Another Best Western property is **Pony Soldier Motel** on East Route 66, with standard Best Western features.

Also in the "chain" department is **Flagstaff Holiday Inn,** exit 198 off I-40 east to East Lucky Lane, a tad nicer than most properties of this familiar name. Nearby **Rodeway Inn East** has a pool; **Flagstaff Inn,** near Little America, features a pool, coffee shop, sauna, and spa; and near NAU campus, **Flagstaff University/Grand Canyon Travelodge,** on West Highway 66, offers rooms and family suites, hot and cool indoor spas, and a sauna (there are restaurants nearby).

Arizona Mountain Inn, on Lake Mary Road southeast of town, offers cottages and suites in a bed-and-breakfast inn, but a limited number of each. Lake Mary Road is accessed from I-17 about a quarter mile south of the junction with I-40.

DINING AND NIGHTLIFE IN FLAGSTAFF

Nightlife here leans more to cultural than whoop-de-do, but the town is famed far and wide for its **Museum Club,** 3404 East Route 66. Don't let the name fool you. It's a big, old bar and two-step stomping ground with live country music, stuffed animals and animal heads, a stone fireplace, and a dance floor built around the trunks of five trees. Definitely of the whoop-de-do orientation.

Horsemen Lodge Restaurant, 8500 U.S. 89 North, is a rustic steak house decorated with cowboy art. Reservations are advised; Tel: 526-2655. In-town's beef-and-brew place is **Black Bart's Steak House** 2760 East Butler near I-

40 exit 198, where singing waiters stage a musical revue during supper; Tel: 779-3142.

Locals endorse the Sunday brunch at **Little America Hotel**; Tel: 779-2741. The best café with country-French decor is **Chez Marc Bistro**, 503 North Humphreys; Tel: 774-1343. For Continental cuisine in a cute cottage, there is **Cottage Place Restaurant**, 126 West Cottage Avenue. Take San Francisco Street two long blocks south from Route 66 (and south of the railroad tracks) to Cottage Place and turn west. Tel: 774-8431.

For Mexican food try **El Charro Cafe**, 409 South San Francisco, near campus; wandering mariachis wander on Friday and Saturday nights; Tel: 779-0552. The Mexican restaurant **Kachina Downtown**, 552 East Route 66 (Tel: 779-1944), is family-owned and folks in "Flag" like 'em.

Mad Italian, 101 South San Francisco, is a college hangout—make that a loud college hangout—where the pizza is robust; Tel: 779-1820. **Buster's Restaurant and Bar**, 1800 South Milton Road, has a big bar area and seafood and Southwestern cuisine; Tel: 774-5155. **Macy's European Coffee House and Bakery**, 14 South Beaver (two blocks west of San Francisco, two blocks south of Route 66 and the railroad tracks), is a small place favored for breakfasts, with reasonable prices. **Sakura** in the Best Western Woodlands Plaza Hotel (see above) has terrific teriyaki and artistically presented sushi; Tel: 773-8888. Fast-food places abound along South Milton.

SHOPPING IN AND AROUND FLAGSTAFF

A word about traditional Indian jewelry, which you will encounter often during your northern Arizona travels. In general, **Navajo jewelry** features turquoise—in nuggets, slices, cabochons (dome cuts)—and sometimes coral, set in polished silver. Navajo artisans are the silver beads masters, forming a half bead (sometimes stamped with traditional dies) by gently tamping sheet silver into a cup-shaped mold, trimming away the excess silver, and soldering two half pieces together. The expertise of the maker is most easily determined by the smoothness of the "join" between the two halves.

In traditional **Hopi jewelry** stones are used sparingly; silver overlay is the prevalent method. As if in a kind of sandwich, the bottom slice of silver is "buttered" with an oxidizing chemical to turn it black. The top slice has cutout designs of Hopi symbols. When the two pieces are joined the design shows as black against brushed silver.

Zuni jewelry is of three intricate types: The needlepoint or petit point style features many tiny domed pieces of turquoise, each set into its own tiny bezel, and all set into a circular bracelet, brooch, pendant, or ring. Stone-to-stone inlay work uses turquoise, coral, jet, mother-of-pearl, lapis, and other stones to form designs (birds, for instance) within a silver mounting. A variation on stone-to-stone is channel work, which employs thin silver "channels" between the stones. The third Zuni style is carved fetish work, where tiny animal or bird forms are sculpted from various colored stones and strung between tiny "heshe" beads to form necklaces.

Also ubiquitous across Arizona's northland are **Navajo rugs**, which are woven of wool cleaned, carded, and spun by Navajo women, usually from sheep they have herded and shorn. Dyes are of two types: commercial and vegetable. The latter is usually concocted by the weaver from plants and minerals collected on the reservation (though some weavers are now using berries purchased in a supermarket). Judge traditional rugs by the fineness of the weave, symmetry of design, and straightness of sides. Good ones are expensive, but are the product of long, tedious hours.

The best Flagstaff place for those who want authentic Indian crafts and art is at the shop of the Museum of Northern Arizona (see above).

For unusual belts, bags, and artworks from Mexico and Guatemala, Southwest cookbooks, and regional items and books, head for the gift shop at Coconino Center for the Arts (see above).

ANNUAL CELEBRATIONS IN FLAGSTAFF

February. Winter Festival features dogsled races, llama snow games, the Frozen Buns Fun Run, an arts-and-crafts fair, and a stargaze at Lowell Observatory, among other treats, in early February. Tel: 774-9541.

May. Trappings of the American West, a five-week event beginning in mid-May, features exhibits of sculptures, silverwork, metalcraft, paintings, photographs, tooled boots and saddles, and horsehair and rawhide ropes; there are performances by cowboy poets, musicians, and storytellers. Coconino Center for the Arts; Tel: 779-6921.

Zuni Artists Exhibition also includes the sale of pottery, paintings, and sculpture. The show, which highlights Zuni jewelry, also features demonstrations by artists and native dance performances. Museum of Northern Arizona, in late May; Tel: 774-5211.

June. Pine Country Pro Rodeo features 250 professional rodeo cowboys competing for prize money in such events as calf roping, team tying, barrel racing, steer wrangling, and bareback, saddle-bronc, and bull riding. Events during rodeo week include a chili cookoff, a kiddie carnival, and a street dance. Coconino County Fort Puthill Fairgrounds, mid-June; Tel: 774-9541.

The Festival of Native American Arts, a six-week event, highlights contemporary and traditional arts of Indian tribes of the Four Corners region, and includes an outdoor Indian market, song and dance performances, films, and lectures. Coconino Center for the Arts, end of June to the beginning of August (call for daily schedules); Tel: 779-6921.

The 60th Annual Hopi Artist Exhibition (and sale) features kachina dolls, pottery, basketry, jewelry, and paintings. Artists' demonstrations and native dances are also scheduled. Museum of Northern Arizona, late June to early July; Tel: 774-5211.

July. The Festival of the Arts, a five-week event from mid-July to mid-August, includes pop and symphonic concerts, chamber music brunches, theater productions, poetry readings, and art exhibits at various venues; Tel: 774-7750.

August. The Festival in the Pines includes arts-and-crafts booths, food, and continuous entertainment. Coconino County Fort Tuthill Fairgrounds, early August; Tel: 967-4877.

The 44th Annual Navajo Artists Exhibition will show and sell rugs and saddle blankets, pottery, jewelry, fine arts, and a variety of crafts items. Museum of Northern Arizona, beginning of August; Tel: 774-5211.

Around Flagstaff

WUPATKI NATIONAL MONUMENT
A half-day or full-day junket from Flagstaff begins 15 miles (24 km) north of town on U.S. 89 at the turnoff (east) to Wupatki National Monument, the pueblo ruins of a melting pot of prehistoric Southwestern cultures. By continuing south on this 36-mile loop road beyond Wupatki, you'll come down to Sunset Crater National Monument before rejoining U.S. 89 some 10 miles (16 km) north of town.

Wupatki's pueblos sprang up about A.D. 1100 when volcanic ash from an eruption at Sunset Crater made the land arable for Sinagua, Hohokam, and Mogollon Indians from the south, Anasazi from the north, west, and east, and Cohonino from the west. Together, these diverse cultures advanced as never before by sharing construction and farming methods and pottery techniques, and by participating in each other's religious ceremonies and sports competitions.

By 1225 they had all gone away, part of a mass movement evident throughout the Southwest during the 13th century. Though anthropologists theorize, no one yet knows why so many prehistoric tribes were on the move or where they went.

Sunset Crater National Monument

From the main ruins and the Wupatki Visitor Center, continue south on the loop road to Sunset Crater National Monument and the colorful cones and black lava flows of the San Francisco volcanic field. The crater cone itself was formed in 1064 when molten rock sprayed high in the air from a vent in the ground and solidified quickly. Falling to earth as bombs or cinders, the debris formed the 1,000-foot cone.

In its final burst of activity lava containing sulfur and iron shot from the vent. The red and yellow oxidized particles fell onto the cone, and still appear as a permanent "sunset." If you plan to hike the area in summer, wear rugged shoes and a sun hat and carry water. From June through August rangers present nightly campfire programs in the amphitheater near the visitors' center.

TO THE GRAND CANYON

From Flagstaff the most rewarding route to the **Grand Canyon** is north on U.S. 89 past the Wupatki turnoff to Cameron (for which see below), then west on AZ 64. This 100-mile (160-km) route gives you a logical rest stop at an Indian trading post (the real thing) and brings you into the canyon by the most spectacular route—especially if you stop and climb the tower at **Desert View**, just inside the park. It's awe-inspiring. In all directions.

Cameron, on the Navajo Indian Reservation, is a wide spot in the road notable for the 103-year-old **Cameron Trading Post**, where Indian arts and crafts range from mere curios to "good" goods to a detached "collector's hideaway" featuring museum-quality rugs, jewelry, pottery, basketry, and carved kachina dolls. There is a restaurant here, too; try the Navajo tacos for something different.

LAKE POWELL

Another day trip from Flagstaff involves a 260-mile (416-km) round trip, but many travellers consider the driving time inconsequential compared to the experience. Take U.S. 89 north 130 miles (208 km) through Cameron to the town of Page and the water playground of Lake Powell in the **Glen Canyon National Recreation Area**. From Wahweap Lodge on the lake, tour boats leave mornings and afternoons to **Rainbow Bridge National Monument**, 50 miles up the lake. The boat trip is remarkable for its close encounters with sheer red cliff walls rising from the blue waters. Rainbow Bridge is remarkable as another of the area's spectacular geologic caprices. Navajos call it "rainbow turned to stone." Boat-tour reservations are required; Tel: 645-2433 or (800) 528-6154. (For more on the Lake Powell area, see the Southern Utah chapter.)

WALNUT CANYON NATIONAL MONUMENT

Walnut Canyon National Monument is accessed about 7 miles (11 km) east of Flagstaff on I-40. Use exit 204 and drive 3 miles (5 km) south to the visitors' center. Prehistoric Sinagua (Spanish for "without water") Indians arrived about A.D. 1125 and departed by 1250. Unlike the Wupatki pueblos, there are cliff dwellings here built into overhangs on ledges in the canyon walls; the farmlands were on the canyon rims. Evidence shows trading was conducted from as far south as the Gulf of California and the Mexican jungles.

Why did the people leave? Drought? Depleted soil? Warfare with outsiders? Social breakdown from within? Disease? As with all the other departures from established communities during that time, nobody knows.

The ruins may be viewed through binoculars in the visitors' center museum. A three-quarter-mile trail leads to 25 cliff-dwelling rooms, but is not recommended for those with heart conditions or other infirmities.

For day trips south of Flagstaff, see the I-17 corridor section of this chapter above, especially Oak Creek Canyon and Sedona. For professionally guided motor-coach tours, usually including several area attractions in a loop trip, contact **Nava-Hopi Tours**; Tel: 774-5003.

ACTIVITIES IN THE FLAGSTAFF AREA

The San Francisco Peaks

The San Francisco Peaks, north of Flagstaff in Coconino National Forest, are the legendary home of Hopi Indian gods. The Alpine forests here are cool perfection for summer hikes; winters bring downhill or cross-country skiers. Autumns are for enjoying fall foliage, and springs bring the new green of lush grasses to the high meadows.

The **Arizona Snowbowl** on the San Francisco Peaks offers downhill skiing on 32 trails ranging from novice to expert. Some trails exceed two miles. Depending on snowfall, the skiing season is from Thanksgiving to Easter. Though there are no overnight lodgings at Snowbowl, ski schools offer lessons for all levels, equipment rentals, and a pair of day lodges with snacks, beverages, and the welcoming warmth of fireplaces. Because area weather is noted for its unpredictability, call first for snow and road conditions; Tel: 779-4577. For information about instruction, lifts, and rentals, Tel: 779-1951. Summertimes, weekend chair lift rides provide great panoramic views of northern Arizona from the top of the peaks. To reach the Snowbowl from Flagstaff, drive northwest 7 miles (11 km) on U.S. 180 (Fort Valley Road) to the turnoff at Snowbowl Road. In ski season you may take a shuttle bus from the turnoff, or drive the remaining 7 miles.

Flagstaff Nordic Center has groomed trails for cross-country skiing and for all levels of skiers, usually from December to mid-April. The center has ski schools, snacks, rentals, and a busy schedule of winter clinics and races. From May to October the area is a favorite of mountain bikers. Nordic Center is 16 miles (26 km) northwest of Flagstaff on U.S. 180 near milepost 232. For recorded ski conditions, Tel: 774-6216.

Humphreys Trail goes to the top of the highest of the San Francisco Peaks and makes a good day hike in the summer. Though the nine-mile round trip from trailhead to summit and back takes about eight hours, many hikers take shorter walks on this trail through dense forests of spruce, fir, and aspen. The summit itself is above timberline. Deep snows, fierce winds, and subzero cold preclude hiking here most of the year. In summer thunderstorms come without warning, so tuck rain gear into your backpack and carry plenty of water, which is a necessity at these altitudes. At the summit, cloudy days excepted, you'll be able to see most of northern Arizona and some of southern Utah. (It's essentially the same view you get by taking the chair lift to Agassiz Peak, but to outdoor types of the no-pain/no-gain persuasion, it always seems more rewarding as a do-it-yourself project.) Humphreys Trail begins at the Snowbowl, near the Agassiz Peak chair lift, and ascends in a series of challenging switchbacks.

Coconino National Forest includes not only Humphreys Trail but more than 300 miles of other trails for hiking, camping, biking, and horseback riding. For detailed information and trail maps of the area north of Flagstaff, contact the U.S. Forest Service Peaks Ranger District, 5075 North U.S. 89, Flagstaff, AZ 86004; Tel: 526-0866. For the forest and lake areas south of Flagstaff, contact Mormon Lake Ranger District, 4825 South Lake Mary Road, Flagstaff, AZ 86001; Tel: 774-1182.

Lake Mary Road

Lake Mary and Mormon Lake are the two lakes nearest Flagstaff (though there are ten others as well in the forested plateau country southeast of the city). Both are on Lake Mary Road, which runs southeast from I-17 about a quarter mile south of its junction with I-40. **Lake Mary** is really two lakes: Upper and Lower. Upper Lake Mary, beginning 8 miles (13 km) from Flagstaff, is long and deep enough for summertime water-skiing. Boats can be launched from both Upper and Lower Lake Mary, and both have ramadas, grills, and tables for picnicking. Fishing is best on the lower lake. **Mormon Lake**, 25 miles (40 km) southeast from Flagstaff, is both a summertime and wintertime place. Winters are for cross-country skiers and snowmobilers; summers, for hikers, anglers, and horseback riders. Rustic **Mormon Lake Lodge**, at the lake's south end, is famed for beef and beans, live music for two-stepping, accommodations in the lodge or surrounding cabins, and stables offering trail, wagon, and stagecoach rides. Across the road from the lodge the **Mormon Lake Ski Center** offers trails, equipment rentals, and lessons.

Flagstaff's 18-hole public **Elden Hills Golf Course** is east on I-40; take exit 201 south and drive 1½ miles (2½ km). For horseback riding nearby **Don Donnelly Stables** offers year-round rides in the Peaks area; go 3½ miles (5½ km) north on U.S. 89 from I-40 exit 201. **Hitchin' Post Stables** offers trail and hayrides, cowboy breakfasts, and steak-dinner rides; the stables are 4½ miles (7 km) southeast of town on South Lake Mary Road.

EASTERN CORRIDOR

Winslow

This railroad town of the 1880s, 58 miles (93 km) east of Flagstaff on I-40, is a good point of departure for a junket to Second Mesa on the **Hopi Indian Reservation**, 67 miles (107 km) north on AZ 87. The reservation is surrounded by the Navajo Indian Reservation. **Second Mesa**, the middle of three Hopi mesas, each with three villages, provides insights to the Hopi way of life at the museum of the **Hopi Cultural Center**. There is also a motel, a restaurant (Hopi and non-Indian food), and a gift shop at the center. Additionally, some Hopi ceremonials and social dances may be open to the public during the summer months. Call the Office of Public Relations at the tribal headquarters in Kykotsmovi (Tel: 734-2441) or inquire at the motel for current information (Tel: 734-2401). (See the Indian Pueblos and Reservations in New Mexico section of the Northern New Mexico chapter for do's and don'ts at ceremonies. The Hopis are also covered in the Four Corners chapter.)

Homolovi Ruins State Park, just outside Winslow, contains more than 300 archaeological sites—ancestral villages of the Hopis—and many examples of petroglyphs. To visit head east on I-40 to exit 257, then north 1 mile (1½ km) on AZ 87. The park entrance is the first paved road to the left.

If you plan to overnight in Winslow, try the **Best Western Adobe Inn**, which has a restaurant and indoor pool.

Holbrook

The big attraction here, 20 miles (32 km) east of Holbrook on I-40, is **Petrified Forest National Park and Painted Desert**. A wonderland of trees turned to stone, prehistoric Indian sites, and multicolored hills of ever-changing hues, the park is laid out as a 28-mile drive-through arrangement. And that's what most visitors do—drive through, stopping at various overlooks and viewpoints.

Though there are hiking trails in wilderness areas near both the south and north entrances, there is no water in this sere landscape. Park rangers estimate that only one in a thousand visitors strays more than a short distance from their vehicle.

The southern, or "forest" part of the park contains logs from the age of dinosaurs that were washed into a floodplain and covered by mud, silt, and volcanic ash. Gradually, silica-bearing waters seeped into the logs, which crystallized into quartz. Minerals and impurities added bright colors to the petrified wood.

The museum and visitors' center at this end of the park has a replica of the skeleton of a phytosaur, a crocodile-like reptile that lived in the forests and swamps here 225 million years ago; there are also artifacts of prehistoric Indians who made this their home for more than a thousand years, and an exhibit of "bad conscience" wood, stolen and then returned to the park with remorseful letters of apology and recitations of bad luck the miscreants have had since the theft. (Taking *anything* from the park save souvenirs from the gift shops is prohibited.)

The central section of the park contains many Indian ruins and petroglyphs; some of the rock art is now believed to have been used as solar calendars.

The "desert," or northern, part of the park is considered by many to be the most spectacular, "painted" by nature in reds, pinks, mauves, vermilion, even yellow and green—effects of the sun on hills stained by iron, manganese, gypsum, and other minerals.

The visitors' center at the north entrance shows a short movie every half hour on the park's features and the formation of the petrified wood, as well as another display of "conscience wood" and "bad luck" letters.

From Holbrook take U.S. 180 east 20 miles (32 km) to the south entrance, drive through the park, and join I-40 at the north entrance. The best viewing times are sunrise and sunset.

Canyon de Chelly
National Monument

At Chinle, about 120 miles (192 km) north of I-40 on U.S. 191 from Chambers, which itself is 47 miles east of Holbrook on I-40, is Canyon de Chelly, in the heart of the Navajo Nation, a reservation the size of the state of West Virginia with only 600 lodging rooms. Seventy-two of them are on the rim of this monument at **Thunderbird Lodge**, which also offers tours into the canyon with Navajo guides driving safari wagons. (Reservations for lodging and tours are required, preferably well in advance; Tel: 674-5841.) A new full-service resort, **Holiday Inn Canyon de Chelly**, opened this year at Chinle in a restored trading post. Amenities include a dining room, a pool, cable television, and Indian dance and music performances.

At Canyon de Chelly the traveller is presented with a spectacular steep, deep, copper-colored canyon rich in Navajo history; the chance to visit and learn about Navajo culture; a pleasant place to overnight; and maybe the only green lawns in all of slick-rock country—a restful sight after miles of red rocks.

Only one trail leading in may be hiked without a guide. Rim drives, however, provide overlooks of the canyon, its ruins, and legendary Spider Rock, mythical home of Spider Woman, who taught Navajo women to weave.

(As Canyon de Chelly represents a considerable— though unforgettable—departure from the I-40 corridor, our primary coverage of the canyon, in somewhat more detail, is in the Four Corners chapter, its rightful place.)

HIGH COUNTRY

When desert temperatures turn hotter'n a two-dollar pistol, many flatlanders from Phoenix head for High Country to commune with nature and catch the cool.

While it is best known as a summer playground, High Country really is a four-seasons region, complete with spring wildflowers, fall foliage, and winter downhill or cross-country skiing. A traditional getaway for city-soured Arizonans, it is becoming increasingly popular with out-of-state visitors who also respond to the mountain serenity, the outdoor activities—including hiking, biking, fishing, hunting, horseback riding, waterskiing, scenic drives, golfing, skiing, snowmobiling, and ice fishing—but mostly for the nature-at-the-doorstep feel of the place.

High Country is a verdant expanse crammed with mountains, forests, meadows, dozens of lakes, and 800 miles of streams. Its winter snowmelt feeds rivers that eventually empty into Arizona's three largest rivers: the Salt, the Gila, and the Colorado.

Two dramatic topographical features form east-central Arizona's High Country: the Mogollon Rim and the White Mountains. Pronounced "muggy-OWN," the rim is a gigantic escarpment that abruptly separates the lowland deserts to the south from high-country forests to the north. Wrinkling northwest to southeast, this lofty ledge rises to 8,000 feet; the White Mountains atop the rim peak at 11,500 feet.

It was this once-impassable Mogollon Rim that discouraged south-to-north exploration of northeastern Arizona; hence, this area was first explored from east to west, from Santa Fe, New Mexico. Francisco Vásquez de Coronado and his conquistadors, either by accident or design, managed to skirt the rim on their failed search in 1540 for the legendary cities of gold; the real treasure of Coronado's efforts remains today as the scenic Coronado Trail, which we have added in this section as an adjunct to High Country visits.

Just as the San Francisco Peaks are weather makers for the Flagstaff area, the White Mountains do the job for east-central Arizona. In summer, puffy white clouds float above the peaks in morning, bump together, turn leaden, and spit lightning from their rumbling undersides, and in afternoons, the full-blown thunderstorm begins its brief deluge. Then, its efforts spent, it mumbles away to the east, leaving strands of rag-mop clouds and bright sunshine in its wake. Locals call the almost-daily rains gully-washers or toad-chokers. In winter, White Mountain precipitation is snowfall.

Roughly defined by AZ 260 as its east–west axis, High Country stretches through parts of three national forests and a swath of Fort Apache Indian Reservation. While the Mogollon Rim can be said to extend to the Arizona-California-Nevada border, it's not said very often and then only by geologists. Its "classic representation" (i.e., the big, dramatic drop-off) begins at Strawberry on the west and extends to Alpine on the east. The fair-size towns in between are Payson, below the rim, and Show Low, Pinetop-Lakeside, and Springerville, above the rim.

We begin our coverage in the west, at Payson, where AZ 260 starts. Payson is 93 miles (149 km) northeast of Phoenix on AZ 87, and 91 miles (146 km) southwest of Winslow (and I-40), also on AZ 87. Strawberry, on AZ 87 on the way to Payson from Winslow, stands right on the rim.

To the east of Payson, 100 miles (160 km) along AZ 260, is Pinetop-Lakeside, more or less in the middle of High Country, and, nearby, Show Low.

We then discuss the Fort Apache Indian Reservation, south of this stretch of AZ 260, and the scenic area of Greer.

We end near the eastern border of Arizona with New Mexico, at Springerville, Lyman Lake, Alpine, and Hannagan Meadow—that last often the coldest spot in the United States on any given day.

The first order of business in this vast all-of-a-piece area, though, is to choose a base from which to enjoy its scenery and activities.

CHOOSING A BASE IN HIGH COUNTRY

The preferred headquarters for most visitors is the twin-town community of **Pinetop-Lakeside**, because it is mid-point among the sights, and because of its glossy new "condotels" and motels. Every High Country community, however, has its share of cabins, cottages, lodges, and lodgings.

In Pinetop two motels are on Highway 260 (South White Mountain Boulevard) in the middle of town: **Best Western Inn of Pinetop** and **Econolodge of Pinetop**. In Lakeside, **Lake of the Woods** has cabins and a private 12-acre trout lake.

Instead of trying to cover all bases (i.e., "a rustic cabin in the woods by a golf course" or "an upscale motel by a lake close to shopping"), we think it's more helpful, instead, to recommend **White Mountain Tourist Service, Inc.**, which does a superb job of putting you where you want to be. Hiking and biking trail maps, lake locations, and campsite maps are also available through this service. As one staffer says, "Our job is to make your visit easy, pleasant, and as remarkable as our scenery." Tel: 367-4291, or write P.O. Box 128, Pinetop, Arizona 85935.

Or you may choose to stay at the Sunrise Park Resort on the Apache reservation; see below.

Western High Country

Payson is the gateway to High Country from Phoenix (93 miles/149 km northeast of Phoenix on AZ 87); it can also be reached off I-40 from Winslow (91 miles/146 km south of Winslow, also via AZ 87).

Under the rim, Payson had its genesis as an 1870s gold camp that became a major cattle-raising and timbering center. Today its mainstay is tourism, mainly in the summer. Though it is occasionally dusted with snow in winter, it's not a winter-sports mecca as are the Rim and White Mountain towns.

Payson celebrates its past with a country music festival every June; the state championship Chili Cookoff and the state championship Loggers/Sawdust Festival in July; the annual World's Oldest Continuous Rodeo in August; and the state championship Old Time Fiddlers Contest in September. For dates and details, Tel: 474-4515.

Northwest of Payson 17 miles (27 km) on AZ 87 is **Strawberry**, on the Rim. For a taste of the school days of a century ago, visit the one-room schoolhouse that still stands here; when it was built in 1885 it boasted not only store-bought desks, but a clock, a dictionary, and a globe.

Central High Country

Halfway between the twin resort towns of Pinetop-Lakeside, on AZ 260 between mile markers 347 and 348, is the **Mogollon Rim Nature Trail**, a paved, easy walking trail, where markers point out various forest plants and their uses (there's a parking lot at the trailhead). Trail stop number 4 is an eye-binder: a great view from the edge of the Rim, across the jumbled stone and pine canyons of the escarpment to the faraway deserts below.

Pinetop-Lakeside celebrations include **Frontier Days** in late June, with mountain men, gunslingers, chili cookoffs, arts, crafts, food booths, frontier demonstrations, a battle of the bands, and clog dancers; the **White Mountain Native American Art Festival and Indian Market**, with Indian artworks, demonstrations, traditional Indian dancers, musicians, and foods, in July; and the **White Mountain Blue Grass Festival** in August. Get precise dates and details from the Pinetop-Lakeside Chamber of Commerce; Tel: 367-4290.

Show Low, 10 miles (16 km) north of Pinetop-Lakeside on AZ 260, got its name when two owners decided their 100,000-acre ranch wasn't big enough for both of them. Their winner-take-all card game lasted all night. Anxious for a showdown, one said, "Show low and you win." The other drew the unbeatable deuce of clubs and won the ranch. Another result: The town's main drag became known as the Deuce of Clubs. And to this day, when elections here end in ties, a politician must "show low" in a card game to win.

Fools Hollow and Show Low lakes are both stocked with fish and have boat ramps and campgrounds; Show Low Lake also has boat rentals and a store. Fools Hollow Lake is about 4 miles (6½ km) northwest of town off AZ 260; to get to Show Low Lake take AZ 260 south for 4 miles, then head east for about a mile (1½ km) on Show Low Lake Road.

A drive north from Show Low on AZ 77 takes you through farm and dairy country to the small communities of Shumway, Taylor, and Snowflake, where the red-brick buildings of the 1880s are reminiscent of New England. At **Taylor** you may want to take a walk around the quaint town.

Fort Apache Indian Reservation

Sunrise Park Resort, a tribal enterprise on the Apache reservation (take AZ 273 south from AZ 260), is one of the largest ski areas in the Southwest, with 11 chair lifts and 60 trails on three mountains—Sunrise Peak, Apache Peak, and Cyclone Circle. Snow-making machines add to the natural snowpack of the ski runs that wind downhill through pine and aspen forests. Night skiing is a "sometimes" thing on Friday or Saturday nights. Ski rentals, group or private lessons, and child care are available. Snowmobile tours are offered at **Sunrise Sports Center**, a half mile south of the lodge, where cross-country skis are rented in winter and mountain bikes are available in summer.

The resort's lodge, nestled into tall pines beside Sunrise Lake, doubles as a summer retreat for anglers, hikers, mountain bikers, horseback riders, and nature lovers. **Sunrise Marina**, near the lodge, offers boat rentals and fishing supplies. The lodge has a friendly staff, an indoor pool, a restaurant, a lounge with live entertainment in ski season, indoor-outdoor hot tubs, and tennis and volleyball courts. Accommodations go quickly in winter and many skiers stay 15 miles (24 km) east at Greer, 22 miles (35 km) east at Springerville, or 30 miles (48 km) west at Pinetop-Lakeside.

Also on the reservation, at the intersection of AZ 260 and AZ 73, is the travellers' stop **Hon Dah**, Apache for "be my guest." Little more than a wide spot in the junction, Hon Dah, with its restaurant, grocery store, and service station, is a micro commerce center in tall pines for Apaches and visitors.

South 20 miles (32 km) from Hon Dah on AZ 73, the remnants of old **Fort Apache**, from which the U.S. Cavalry and the famed Apache scouts pursued the renegade bands of Geronimo and Natchez, have been turned into a museum of Apache culture and history. Museum director Edgar Perry makes up in tribal wisdom and knowledge for the irreplaceable artifacts that burned in a museum fire. To reach the fort you'll pass **Whiteriver**, the seat of government for the reservation. A giant timber mill on the south edge of town is owned by the tribe. Crack Apache Indian forest fire–fighting teams, known throughout the West, come from this area. Two outstanding Whiteriver events are the July 4 **Mountain Spirit Celebration** and the **Labor Day Rodeo and Tribal Fair**.

Hawley Lake, created strictly for recreation, covers 260 acres of the reservation and is popular for trout fishing in summer, ice fishing in winter. You can get necessary tribal permits right at the lake. Though its elevation is 8,600 feet, the road is kept open year-round. Summertime facilities include a boat dock with rentals and a service station/ grocery store. From Hon Dah, go east 11 miles (18 km) on AZ 260, then turn south 11 miles on AZ 473.

Eastern High Country

Off the reservation, in a pretty valley deep in the woods at 8,500 feet, the hamlet of **Greer**, named for Mormon pioneer Americus Vespucius Greer, comes alive in summers when visitors flock here to enjoy the cool air, forest walks, mountain biking, horseback riding, and fishing in the lakes just north of town or in the Little Colorado River. Winters are busy, too, with cross-country skiers trying the miles of marked trails just outside the village. Though there are rental cabins and lodges here, most are booked from one summer to the next, making them essentially unavailable to first-time visitors.

Greer is 15 miles (24 km) east of Sunrise Lake; from AZ 260 take AZ 373 south for 4 miles (6½ km). **Butler Canyon Trail** is a one-mile self-guided nature walk just north of the village. In the village **Lee Valley Outfitters** offers guided rides (some include cookouts) and mountain-bike rentals. A variety of loop trails for cross-country skiers are in the woods just northwest of Greer. Local businesses, such as **Circle B Market**, rent "skinny skis" for cross-country treks and offer ski-trail maps.

Most non-Indian communities along the rim were settled in the early 1870s by Mormon pioneers sent from Utah by Brigham Young, but at least one, **Springerville**, 40 miles (64 km) east of Pinetop-Lakeside on AZ 260, was settled by outlaws.

The town was named for Harry Springer, who went broke selling feed to cattle rustlers who stole horses in southern Arizona, rebranded them in Round Valley, sold them to northern Arizona ranchers, then reversed the process by rustling in the north and selling in the south.

Springerville today is most noted for **Casa Malpais Pueblo**, an important, recently discovered site of the prehistoric Mogollon people. You may tour the site, even volunteer to do excavation or laboratory work, but the catacombs in the deep underground fissures that were used for ceremonies and burials are off-limits. On the curiosity and excitement scale, American archaeologists equate this find to that of Tutankhamen's tomb.

Excavated artifacts are on display at **Casa Malpais Museum**, 318 East Main Street. The ruins themselves, located just north of town, may be visited *only* on tours sponsored by the city of Springerville. Tours leave from the museum at 9:00 and 11:00 A.M. and at 2:30 P.M., weather permitting. For precise information contact the museum, Tel: 333-5375.

Some 20 miles (32 km) north of Springerville on U.S. 666 is **Lyman Lake State Park**, where buffalo roam near feed racks along the highway and boaters, water skiers, anglers, campers, and picnickers roam around the lake.

If you head 28 miles (45 km) south of Springerville on U.S. 666 you'll come to **Alpine** (population 600), at 8,046-feet elevation. Alpine calls itself "the Alps of Arizona" and boasts that it has no traffic lights on the main drag, but lots of trophy elk, deer, mountain lions, bobcats, javelina, and bears in the backcountry. There are excellent seasonal opportunities for hiking, mountain biking, fishing, hunting, horseback riding, golfing, scenic drives, cross-country, sledding, and snowmobiling in the area. Cross-country ski equipment rentals are available in town at **Alpine Market**, 42651 Highway 180, or the **Tackle Shop**, at the junction of Highways 180 and 191; to rent horses try **Judd's Ranch** (Tel: 339-4326); for golf (including club and cart rentals) there's **Alpine Country Club** (Tel: 339-4944). Nearby **Luna Lake**, east of Alpine off U.S. 180, is a spot for winter ice fishing. Alpine events include Sled Dog Races in January; Logger's Jamboree in July; and Elk Bugling Competition in August. For details contact the Alpine Chamber of Commerce, Tel: 339-4330.

Alpine also is a beginning point of the **Coronado Trail Scenic Highway** (U.S. 191). This route of the conquistadors has breathtaking downhill panoramas: immense forests of evergreen and aspen, sweeps of lush meadows, mountain streams sparkling down the slopes to the desert below. If time doesn't allow the full 100-mile trip (down toward I-10), you won't regret going as far as **Hannagan Meadow**, 23 miles (37 km) south of Alpine. Just as Bullhead City on Arizona's western border is often the hottest spot in the nation, Hannagan Meadow, on this eastern border, sometimes is the nation's coldest.

If you continue on the trail you'll drive straight through the middle of the nation's largest open-pit copper mine at **Morenci**, south of High Country, an amazing place where giant equipment with tires ten feet tall looks like toys in the pit below. The pit itself is as colorful as the Grand Canyon, but because it is man's work, not nature's, many who see it say "the damned thing ought to be covered up." Safford, southwest of Morenci on U.S. 70, with its good selection of motels, is a logical place to overnight.

DINING IN HIGH COUNTRY

Dining well in High Country takes a bit of doing; these suggestions have withstood the taste tests of time: **Bear Pond Inn**, 3 miles (5 km) north of Greer on AZ 373, serves Continental cuisine. Reservations are requested; Tel: 735-7576. **Hannagan Meadow Lodge** on the Coronado Trail (U.S. 191) is a bit out of the way, but a special treat when time is no object; popular for decades for its steaks. Open daily in warm months; Thursday to Sunday in winter. Reservations are advised; Tel: 339-4370. **Casa Territorial**, among the pines in Pinetop just off AZ 260, specializes in New Mexican food, including green chile. A flamenco guitarist plays for dinner patrons during the summer; Tel: 367-3050. **Paint Pony Steakhouse** in the Best Western hotel in Show Low, 581 West Deuce of Clubs, is noted for Western fare of the beef, beans, and brew variety; Tel: 537-5773.

Christmas Tree Restaurant in Lakeside at the corner of Woodland Road and AZ 260 has a year-round display of Christmas tree lights, and is famed for sticky buns fresh from the oven as well as chicken and dumplings; Tel: 367-3107. Rustic **Hilltop House** on AZ 260 in Pinetop is a favored breakfast spot. **Molly Butler Lodge** in Greer has been serving stick-to-your-ribs home cooking since 1910, including prime rib dinners; Tel: 735-7538. **Charlie Clark's**, a steak house on AZ 260 in Pinetop, is a 50-plus-year-old institution—steaks of all kinds; Tel: 367-4900. **Sundowner Restaurant and Saloon** in Alpine on Main Street has steaks, Mexican food, homemade pies, and a Western-art gallery; Tel: 339-4451.

RIVER COUNTRY

The Lower Colorado River forms the Arizona border between California and the southeast tip of Nevada. While there are bigger, wider, more spectacular rivers than the Lower Colorado, few are more used and useful.

A ladder of dams along Arizona's "west coast" has transformed large tracts of Arizona and California desert into rich farmlands and produce fields, and provided tap water for such urban centers as Los Angeles and Phoenix.

Both the lakes and the undammed portions of the river provide blue-water playgrounds for fishing, swimming, boating, and sightseeing—all within the sunny context of the desert that is never far away.

Winter is the busy season in River Country. Thousands of "snowbirds" from cold climes return annually to spend the winter in a plethora of mobile homes and RV parks. Vacationers come for the mix of sunshine and aquatic sports. Collegians transform Lake Havasu City and the Parker Strip into the Dade County of the West during spring breaks. Summer brings new waves of visitors from interior cities of the West who seek the nearest water. The river cities quiet to a mild roar briefly after Labor Day.

From I-8 in the south to I-40 in the north, U.S. 95/AZ 95 is the route of "river rats" and sightseers. Going up the ladder of dams from south to north, the cities and towns along the way include Yuma, Quartzsite, Parker, Lake Havasu City, and Bullhead City. (Above Bullhead City begins the Lake Mead National Recreation Area.) Each spot has its own affable personality; each has its own distinctive twists and shouts.

YUMA

By the time the mighty Colorado gets to Yuma the up-stream dams have reduced it to a placid little stream, though it will be dammed one more time before the remaining waters trickle into the Gulf of California. Because Yuma itself can't been seen from the interstate (I-8), many travellers zip past this city of 60,000.

Time was when Yuma and its ferry across the Colorado were a crossroads of the West. Matériel for military posts was shipped from West Coast ports around Baja California

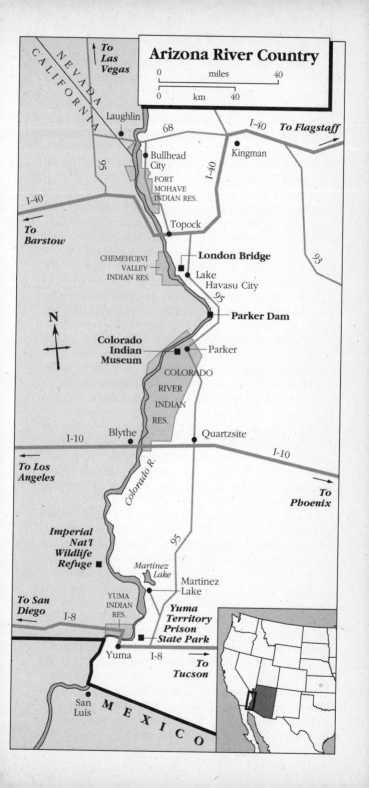

to Yuma to be unloaded and freighted overland—or delivered upstream by steamboats, one of 19th-century Arizona's most innovative enterprises.

To Yuma's military history add a mixture of indigenous Indian tribes, Spanish explorer-priests, Mexican influences, forty-niners, frontiersmen, and farmers. Yumans like to point out that Yuma Crossing was to the Southwest what the Cumberland Gap was to the Midwest and America's westward expansion.

To reach the city from the east on I-8, take the I-8 Business Route at exit 9, which, about 6 miles (10 km) later, turns north on 32nd Street to become Fourth Avenue; or, to quickly get into the downtown area, take the I-8 exit north off Giss Parkway. From the north U.S. 95 becomes 16th Street. Numbered streets run east to west beginning at First Street near the river and extending to 32nd Street. The downtown core, bisected east–west by Giss Parkway and north–south by Main Street, lies between the I-8 Business Route (Fourth Avenue) and I-8.

Downtown's **Main Street Plaza** is the city's people place. Shade trees, brick walkways, and renovated old buildings housing specialty shops and cafés offer a charming blend of the old and new. At **224 Main** you'll find 13 specialty and gift shops whose stock includes collectible dolls and music boxes. In the same area, and next to the Century House (see below), the 250 Madison Avenue Shops include **Stuart and Stuart**, which sells new and estate jewelry and gift items; the **Potting Shed**, with sophisticated women's clothes and accessories; and the **Spice Company**, selling spices as well as gourmet coffee beans and kitchen equipment.

Mexico is 25 miles (40 km)—and a whole other culture—south on U.S. 95 at the border town of **San Luis**, where shopping attracts many visitors. Leather goods are the main products of local artisans here, but shops carry crafts from other regions of Mexico, including pottery, clothing, carved onyx, glassware, and silver jewelry. Most visitors park on the American side and walk across to San Luis, the largest city on the Arizona-Mexico border. (U.S. citizens may shop in San Luis without visas or tourist cards; others should check with U.S. Immigration at the border to be sure of current requirements. Tel: 379-3312.)

Until the proposed Yuma Crossing Park becomes a going concern later this decade, the **Yuma Territorial Prison State Historic Park**, at Giss Parkway and Prison Hill Road, remains the city's best-known historical attraction. A dreadful place on a bluff overlooking the river, the prison tested the theory that one term here would convince the bad guys (and some bad women) to go forth and sin no more. Temperatures in the cells could reach 120° in summer; isolation was an unlit dungeon. Of particular interest today is the collection of inmate art creations that fairly scream of patience and boredom. Open daily.

Century House Museum, 240 South Madison Avenue, a block west of Main Street Plaza in the former home of a Yuma pioneer, is now a museum with Territorial furnishings, photographs, and historical artifacts. Colorful gardens and aviaries with exotic talking birds are maintained here as they were at the turn of the century. Open year-round; closed Sundays, Mondays, and major holidays.

On a hill just across the river in California, the **Quechan Indian Museum** occupies an 1855 building that was once part of Fort Yuma, now known as Fort Yuma Indian Reservation and home to the Quechan tribe. (Follow Fourth Avenue out of Yuma to California to Quechan Boulevard, then follow the signs.) Exhibits illustrate the arrival of the Spanish, the Quechan revolt against Catholic missionaries, and Quechan lifestyles. Artifacts include clay figurines, flutes, gourd rattles, headdresses, and war clubs. Open weekdays.

Also across the river are Sahara-like **sand dunes**, the perfect setting for epic films of the Beau Geste genre and television commercials. (Drive 20 miles/32 km west of Yuma on I-8.) During the 1920s and 1930s a highway made of wooden planks crossed the sands. Occasionally, even now, a section of that board roadway is uncovered by the shifting sands.

Peanut Patch, 4322 East County 13th Street on the outskirts of town, is a peanut farm and store, selling everything peanutty from butter to brittle as well as homemade fudge and other candies. Open October to June. From downtown take Fourth Avenue south to 32nd Street, turn east to Avenue 4E, then south to County 13th Street and follow the signs.

RIVER EXCURSIONS AND SPORTS IN YUMA

The Yuma area's population of 60,000 swells in winter to about 120,000, most of them fleeing the snow; they fill 100 spacious mobile home and RV parks and campgrounds along the river and out on the desert. **Yuma River Tours** offers jet-boat excursions among ruins, petroglyphs, ferry crossings, homesteads, steamboat landings, and mining camps in full, half-day, or sunset dinner cruises. Half-day trips embark from two points on the riverbank at Yuma: just below the Territorial Prison and just below the Quartermaster Depot north of First Street on Second Avenue. The more popular all-day trips embark from Fishers Landing, about 30 miles (48 km) north of town, near Martinez Lake on Martinez Lake Road. Tel: 783-4400 weekdays for reservations.

Yuma Valley Railway provides a ride through time in a 1922 Pullman coach, complete with narrative of the area's lore and legends. The train, powered by a 1941 diesel locomotive, runs November through April; lunch or dinner arrangements may be made. Call for reservations; Tel: 783-3456.

The best—and nearest—lake fishing, bird-watching, canoeing, and water skiing are at **Martinez Lake**, 35 miles (56 km) north of Yuma on U.S. 95, then left on Martinez Lake Road. The lake is part of the Imperial National Wildlife Refuge, a protected area for plants and animals, birds being most prominent. The **Martinez Lake Resort** has a restaurant, motel, marina, and boat rentals.

River fishing is for large-mouth black bass, striped bass, channel catfish, tilapia, bluegill, and crappie. Check fishing regulations with the Arizona Department of Game and Fish; Tel: 344-3436.

Nearby 18-hole **golf courses** are Arroyo Dunes Golf Course, 32nd Street and Avenue A; and Desert Hills Municipal Golf Course, 1245 Desert Hills Drive. For nine-hole par 3 try Ironwood Public Golf Course, 2945 West Eighth Street.

STAYING AND DINING IN YUMA

Short-term visitors have about 2,000 lodging rooms from which to choose, most located along Fourth Avenue. Many, however, are motel properties in the so-so category. The best bets are **Best Western Inn Suites Yuma**, off I-8 north of 16th Street on Castle Dome Avenue, offering complimentary breakfast and happy hour, a lounge, a pool, tennis, an exercise room, and a library; and **Best Western Chilton Inn and Conference Center**, on 32nd Street near Arizona Avenue, with a pool, a restaurant, a lounge, and a fitness center.

Lutes Casino, 221 Main Street (the historic north end of Main Street Plaza) has burgers and brews and lots of tradition. It's the state's oldest pool hall (dominos are also big here). The decor is early eclectic. Or call it interesting junk: A ragged foot seems to be crashing through the ceiling and big posters plastered to the walls feature "The Babe" with his bat, Laurel and Hardy, Bogart, Signal Gas, and Western Union. Also posted: Be Back in a Flash to Snatch Your Cash.

Garden Cafe, beside Century House, serves salads and sandwiches indoors or out. **Mandarin Palace**, 350 East 32nd Street, might be called the town's classiest restaurant, and provides some American dishes for those who want their class without chopsticks; Tel: 344-2805. For Mexican food there is **Chretins**, 485 South 15th Avenue, in an old house, where old-time, down-home food comes from its *cocina*. **Johnny's Other Place**, 432 East 16th Street, with a grill and country music, is the night spot in Yuma.

Quartzsite

This crossroads of AZ 95 and I-10 some 80 miles (128 km) north of Yuma is a little nothing town most of the year. Come winter, though, it becomes an aluminum mélange of mobile homes, trailer homes, and RVs stretched across the desert as far as the eye can see. Call it the world's biggest tailgate party, or maybe the world's biggest swap meet. From January to mid-February it's showtime. Eight major rock and gem shows (with big-name entertainers, helicopter rides, and other diversions) are supplemented with smaller shows set up on any vacant surface available. More than a million people drop in for the goings-on. (Yes, one million—and in a town that numbers 300 in the summer, counting the dogs asleep by the side of the road.) You might want to grab the first parking space you see and walk from there.

West of Quartzsite, across the river on I-10 near Blythe, California, are the **Great Blythe Intaglios**, giant figures engraved in the earth. One human effigy is 170 feet long. Done by prehistoric ancestors of the local Mohave Indian tribe? No one is sure. To find the intaglios, follow U.S. 95 (not AZ 95) 16 miles (26 km) north of Blythe and watch for a stone-and-brass monument on the right side of the road.

Parker

Thirty-five miles (56 km) north of Quartzsite is Parker, gateway to the lakes along the Lower Colorado. En route, you pass through the Colorado Indian Reservation, home to Mohave, Chemehuevi, and relocated Hopi and Navajo

Indians. Two miles (3 km) south of Parker is the Colorado Indian Tribes' **museum**, depicting centuries of Indian life along the river. Open daily, except major holidays.

The Parker Enduro Classic speedboat races draw more than 40,000 spectators to the April event. The **Parker Strip**, between Parker and Parker Dam to the north, is rife with RV parks, marine parks, and campgrounds.

LAKE HAVASU CITY

Barren land until the 1960s and now a city of 35,000, this place is the most popular spot on the Lower Colorado. The transformation began when Robert P. McCulloch, Sr., decided to move his chain-saw plant to healthier surroundings where he could also test boat motors.

When he decided to build a whole town, he formed a partnership with Disney Studios executive C.V. Wood, who became town planner. It was Wood's idea that what the town needed was the **London Bridge**—the one that was falling down, falling down in the childhood song. In truth, it really was falling down into the Thames River of its own weight.

Transplanted block by coded-and-numbered granite block to the Colorado (via the Panama Canal to Long Beach, California, from where it was then shipped by truck), the bridge became the town's showpiece, and an "English village" sprang up around it, Tudor architecture and all. At first the bridge spanned only dry land, so a water channel was cut beneath it that separated what had been known as Pittsburgh Point from the rest of the city, creating an island. The channel is called Bridgewater Channel; the island is still called Pittsburgh Point (by the locals, anyway); the road over the bridge to the island is the town's main thoroughfare, McCulloch Boulevard. In addition to **English Village** at the bridge, **Shambles Village**, a mile northeast, is a re-creation of the medieval Shambles of York.

Water sports—boating, fishing, swimming, parasailing, scuba diving, water skiing, and jet skiing—and houseboating top the what-to-do list in the Lake Havasu City area.

If you haven't brought your own equipment, it can be rented at any number of places. Try **Resort Boat Rentals**, on the water under the London Bridge at English Village for ski, pontoon, deck, fishing, and houseboats; or **Water Sports Centers**, at Nautical Inn, 1000 McCulloch Boulevard, and at Crazy Horse Campground, 1534 Beachcomber Boulevard, for jet skis, scuba gear, and parasail rides.

As for boat tours, the A-1 trip is through the remote, spectacular defile known as **Topock Gorge** (some parts are accessible only by water; there are petroglyphs here, too). Two-hour narrated trips in jet boats, offered by **Bluewater Charters**, leave from London Bridge.

Also available at the bridge are pontoon-boat tours on *Miss Havasupai II* and *Miss Havasupai III,* operated by **Lake Havasu Boat Tours**, and paddle wheel–riverboat tours on *Dixie Belle,* operated by London Bridge Resort (see below).

Golf courses here include two 18-hole courses at London Bridge Golf Club, 2400 Club House Drive; another 18 holes at Nautical Inn Golf Course on the island; and a nine-hole, night-lighted executive course at London Bridge Resort.

Desert walks, bird-watching, and rock hounding are other activities to take advantage of here. Free guided walks are sponsored every other Saturday year-round by the local Lords and Ladies Club (the newspaper and community bulletin boards around town have details). Birds include native, migratory, and water species; rock hunts are for jasper, obsidian, agate, and geodes (obtain guidelines from the local Gem and Mineral Society; Tel: 855-8666, or write P.O. Box 0990, Lake Havasu City, AZ 86405).

Havasu Horse Rentals Inc. guides full- and half-day rides, or provides the horse for a do-it-yourself trip on the trail; Tel: 680-2939.

STAYING, DINING, AND SHOPPING IN LAKE HAVASU CITY

London Bridge Resort, on Queen's Bay Road, closest to the bridge and village, has restaurants, pools, lounges, tennis, an executive golf course, and suites. Its **King's Retreat Restaurant** is noted for prime rib dinners, seafood buffets on Friday nights, and lavish Sunday-morning brunches (Tel: 855-0888 for reservations). Walk or boat in on Bridge-water Channel to **Kokomo's**, the resort's newest libation station, with terraced patios, two bars, tropical drinks, salads and burgers, and a huge outdoor adult pool with water jets and volleyball; deejays spin discs for dancing.

Nautical Inn Resort, on McCulloch Boulevard, grew up with the town and could be called its *other* landmark. All rooms are waterfront; shops, water-sport rentals, and the beach are steps away. Amenities include a pool, a spa, golf, and tennis. **Captain's Table** is the resort's restaurant, featuring lakeside dining on seafood (Tel: 855-2141). **The**

Club Nautical, the resort lounge, offers dancing to top-40 videos and karaoke sing-alongs; adjacent **Tiki Terrace** is a quieter spot overlooking Thompson Bay.

Island Inn Hotel, a new beachfront resort on McCulloch Boulevard on the island, features spacious rooms, panoramic views from its glass elevator, a spa, a heated pool, and golf and tennis. For Continental cuisine try the hotel's **Desert Rose** restaurant; Tel: 680-0606.

The **Lake Havasu Holiday Inn** on London Bridge Road does package deals with London Bridge Golf Course. Its Bridge Room is a popular American-fare restaurant (Tel: 855-4071). The **Reflections Lounge** in the hotel has karaoke sing-alongs and dancing.

Best Western Lake Place Inn on Wings Loop, with a restaurant and a pool, and **Hidden Palms All Suite Inn** on Swanson Avenue, overlooking a central courtyard with pool (and only two minutes away from the lake and bridge), are among the moderately priced lodgings in town.

Get right into the London Bridge mode fast with English-style fish and chips at **Mermaid Inn** under the bridge. At **Hussong's Cantina** in **Casa de Miguel Restaurant**, 1550 South Palo Verde Street (two blocks north of McCulloch Boulevard, off Acoma Boulevard), you get dance music and Mexican fare. A favorite restaurant of the locals is **Krystal's Fine Dining**, 460 El Camino Way (between AZ 95 and London Bridge Road, near South Palo Verde Street), where Maine lobster is a specialty; dinners only. Reservations are advised; Tel: 453-2999.

Three areas qualify as hot spots for specialty shops and eateries: **English Village**, at the bridge; **Island Fashion Mall**, across the bridge on the island; and **Shambles Village**, a mile northeast of the bridge. All have the usual mix of river wear, crazy shirts, wetsuits, and beach accessories. **Thunderbird Indian Trading Post** at Island Fashion Mall is one place to find Indian jewelry, arts and crafts, and designer gifts and prints. **The Golden Unicorn** and **Queen's Pantry** in English Village feature collectibles and gourmet items. **Kites**, in the village, has all kinds and colors of 'em, and is a fun place to browse. For women's river rags, try **River Rags**; for men's, **The Edge**, both in Bashas Shopping Plaza, 1641 McCulloch Boulevard.

Bullhead City

If the name is familiar to you, you've probably heard it on evening newscasts. Often as not, summer and winter,

Bullhead, 65 miles (104 km) north of Lake Havasu City, is the nation's hottest spot. It also happens to be the bedroom community for **Laughlin**, Nevada, across the river. Laughlin's casinos are becoming as splashy as Las Vegas's, and the big-name entertainers here seem to have bigger names each year. The players, though, are apt to be sunburned fishermen taking a break from their boats, or retirees taking a respite from their tour buses.

From Bullhead City you can go east toward the Grand Canyon's South Rim and Flagstaff on I-40, or north to Las Vegas on U.S. 95 across the river, west of Laughlin.

Annual River Country Events

January. The annual Dixieland Jazz Festival at the London Bridge Resort in Lake Havasu City perks up mid-month. For more information, Tel: 855-0888.

Quartzsite gem and mineral shows, where dealers swap and shop, also feature big-name entertainment, camel races, and helicopter rides; one million visitors are drawn to the no-stoplight town from January to mid-February. Call the Chamber of Commerce for details; Tel: 927-5600.

April. Parker Enduro Classic, the granddaddy of powerboat marathons, draws 40,000 to this motorboat race of inboards, outboards, and jet boats; water speeds clock in at 125 m.p.h. Call the Chamber of Commerce for details; Tel: 669-2174.

October. London Bridge Days in Lake Havasu City in early October are ten days of "olde English" festivals, big-name entertainment, water sports, arts and crafts, and folks dressed up in Elizabethan and Victorian costumes. Tel: 855-4115.

November. Lake Havasu Classic Outboard World Championship speedboat races launch from Nautical Inn on Thanksgiving weekend. Tel: 855-2141.

December. During the Christmas Boat Parade of Lights, all kinds of boats light up like—well, Christmas trees. Lights reflect off the water as the boats parade under London Bridge at Lake Havasu City in early December. Tel: 855-1535.

GETTING AROUND

Think of Arizona as a square enclosing a big letter T. The vertical stroke (which is Arizona's portion of I-10 up to Phoenix from Tucson, and I-17 north of Phoenix) starts at Tucson in the south and runs up through Phoenix to

Flagstaff—where it joins the horizontal stroke, which is I-40.

The Colorado River is the left side of the square; Grand Canyon and the Utah Canyonlands are the top. Mexico is the bottom, and New Mexico is the right side.

There is no point in rehashing complicated driving instructions here beyond that basic framework; they are covered in detail in the individual sections above. Phoenix is the main air gateway to Arizona see Getting Around in the Phoenix chapter.

Phoenix–Tucson

By air. Daily departures from Phoenix Sky Harbor International Airport to Tucson International Airport are offered by America West, Delta, Northwest, and USAir. Of these, America West Airlines, headquartered in Phoenix, has the most frequent flights to Tucson.

By ground. Greyhound Bus Lines makes ten trips daily to Tucson; the terminal in Phoenix is at 525 East Washington Street; Tel: 248-4040. Arizona Shuttle Service, Inc. makes 17 round trips daily between the Phoenix and Tucson airports; for information and reservations, Tel: (800) 888-2749. Amtrak trains make three eastbound trips weekly with morning departures for Tucson; the Phoenix depot is at 401 West Harrison and South Fourth Avenue; Tel: (800) 872-7245.

Phoenix–Flagstaff

By air. Flights between Phoenix Sky Harbor International Airport and Pulliam Field in Flagstaff are offered seven times daily by America West, and five times daily by Skywest-The Delta Connection.

By ground. Greyhound Bus Lines has four daily departures to Flagstaff from the terminal at 525 East Washington Street (Tel: 248-4040) in Phoenix; Nava-Hopi Tours makes two trips daily weekdays (three on weekends) between various Valley of the Sun pickup points and Flagstaff (Tel: 800/774-5003). Note: While Nava-Hopi Tours is primarily a northern Arizona sightseeing company, these trips between Phoenix and Flagstaff serve simply as commercial ground transportation.

Grand Canyon's South Rim

There are two entrances to the South Rim: the south entrance on U.S. 180/AZ 64 from Flagstaff or Williams, and the east entrance on AZ 64 from Cameron. The Grand Canyon Railway runs from Williams to Grand Canyon

Village with historic steam engines. Amtrak services Flagstaff, and from there Amtrak's Southwest Chief bus makes morning runs to the canyon, evening returns to Flagstaff (Tel: 800/USA-RAIL). Nava-Hopi Bus Lines offers transport from Flagstaff or Williams (Tel: 774-5003). America West Airlines flies into Grand Canyon Airport at Tusayan, as do "flightseeing" planes (such as Arizona Air) from the Phoenix area. Budget Rent-A-Car is located in the airport (Tel: 638-9360). Hourly shuttles run from Grand Canyon Village to Tusayan and from the village to the airport. Contact the Visitor Center in Grand Canyon Village or the transportation desk at Bright Angel Lodge for rates and schedules.

The High Country

High Country is accessible via AZ 77 south from Holbrook to Show Low; from Phoenix east and north on U.S. 60 to Show Low (the route takes you through deep, colorful Salt River Canyon, so spectacular it is called "the mini Grand"); from Phoenix's East Valley via AZ 87 (the Beeline Highway) north 78 miles (125 km) to Payson, or from I-17 at Camp Verde east on AZ 279, via the General Crook Trail, itself a scenic mountain drive.

Arizona Pacific Airways has weekday flights to and from Show Low Airport and Phoenix Sky Harbor. Weekend flights are Saturday mornings and Sunday evenings only; Tel: 537-7469 or (800) 225-0844. Charlie Clark's Shuttle provides transportation to and from the Show Low airport and anywhere else in the area you might want to go; Tel: 367-4900 or 367-2244. Rental cars from Hatch Motors are available at the airport; Tel: 537-8887. Scenic and photo tours are offered by White Mountain Adventure Tours; Tel: 367-5337.

River Country

Yuma is served by Greyhound Bus Lines with daily trips to Phoenix, Tucson, San Diego, and Los Angeles (Tel: 783-4403). Amtrak trains run three times a week to Phoenix and Los Angeles (Tel: 800/872-7245). From Yuma International Airport, America West makes frequent daily flights to Phoenix and Los Angeles with onward connections (Tel: 800/247-5692). Avis and Hertz have car-rental desks at the airport.

Parker is served by Greyhound Bus to and from Phoenix and Las Vegas daily. For cabs call Parker Taxi (Tel: 669-2811).

Lake Havasu City is served by Mesa Air from Phoenix;

Havasu Airlines flies to Las Vegas and Phoenix. Hertz has rental cars at the airport. Greyhound buses go to Phoenix via Parker and Wickenburg and to Las Vegas.

Note: Some Lake Havasu City hotels offer guests round-trip complimentary river trips to the gambling casinos at Laughlin, Nevada.

ACCOMMODATIONS REFERENCE

The rates given below are projections for 1993. Unless otherwise indicated, rates are for a double room, double occupancy, and do not include meals. Price ranges span the lowest rate in the low season and the highest rate in the high season. Peak season varies in the following properties: Some fall in summer, others in winter. As rates are always subject to change, it is wise to double-check before booking.

The telephone area code for Arizona is 602.

▶ **Los Abrigados.** 160 Portal Lane, **Sedona**, AZ 86336. Tel: 282-1777 or (800) 521-3131; Fax: 282-2614. $195–$350.

▶ **Arizona Mountain Inn.** 685 Lake Mary Road, **Flagstaff**, AZ 86001. Tel: 774-8959. $60–$100.

▶ **L'Auberge de Sedona Resort.** 301 L'Auberge Lane, **Sedona**, AZ 86336. Tel: 282-1661 or (800) 272-6777; Fax: 282-2885. $100–$385. The Orchards at L'Auberge. $120–$165.

▶ **Bear Pond Inn.** P.O. Box 1525, **Eager**, AZ 85925. Tel: 735-7576 (in Phoenix, Tel: 253-2272). Rates do not vary seasonally; lower rates are for weekdays. $41–$55; $70–$100 (cabins).

▶ **Bell Rock Inn.** 6246 Highway 179, **Sedona**, AZ 86336. Tel: 282-4161. $61–$95.

▶ **Best Western Adobe Inn.** 1701 North Park Drive, **Winslow**, AZ 86047. Tel: 289-4638; Fax: 289-5514. $50–$62.

▶ **Best Western Arroyo Roble Hotel.** 400 North Highway 89A, P.O. Box NN, **Sedona**, AZ 86336. Tel: 282-4001. $70–$225.

▶ **Best Western Chilton Inn and Conference Center.** 300 East 32nd Street, **Yuma**, AZ 85364. Tel: 344-1050 or (800) 528-1234; Fax: 344-4877. $65–$79.

▶ **Best Western Cliff Castle Lodge.** P.O. Box 3430/Hwy, I-17 and Middle Verde Road, **Camp Verde**, AZ 86322. Tel: 567-6611 or (800) 622-7853; Fax: 567-9455. $64–$66.

▶ **Best Western Inn of Pinetop.** 404 South White Mountain Boulevard, **Pinetop**, AZ 85935. Tel: 367-6667 or (800) 528-1234; Fax: 367-6672. $59–$70.

▶ **Best Western Inn Suites Yuma.** 1450 Castle Dome Avenue, Yuma, AZ 85364. Tel: 783-8341 or (800) 842-4242; Fax: 783-1349. $59–$135.

▶ **Best Western Lake Place Inn.** 31 Wings Loop, Lake Havasu City, AZ 86403. Tel: 855-2146 or (800) 258-8558; Fax: 855-3148. $55–$64.

▶ **Best Western Pony Soldier Motel.** 3030 East Route 66, Flagstaff, AZ 86004. Tel: 526-2388 or (800) 528-1234; Fax: 527-8329. $42–$72.

▶ **Best Western Woodlands Plaza Hotel.** 1175 West Highway 66, Flagstaff, AZ 86001. Tel: 773-8888 or (800) 528-1234. $59–$109.

▶ **Bright Angel Lodge,** P.O. Box 699, Grand Canyon, AZ 86023. Tel: 638-2401; Fax: 638-9247. Open year-round. $52–$95.

▶ **Econolodge of Pinetop.** 458 South White Mountain Boulevard, Pinetop, AZ 85935. Tel: 367-3636; Fax: 367-1543. $40–$69.

▶ **El Tovar Hotel.** P.O. Box 699, Grand Canyon, AZ 86023. Tel: 638-2401; Fax: 638-9247. $106–$136 (rooms); $174–$250 (suites).

▶ **Enchantment Resort.** 525 Boynton Canyon Road, Sedona, AZ 86336. Tel: 282-2900 or (800) 826-4180; Fax: 282-9249. $145–$460.

▶ **Flagstaff Holiday Inn.** 2320 East Lucky Lane, Flagstaff, AZ 86004. Tel: 526-1150 or (800) 533-2754; Fax: 779-2610. $59–$89.

▶ **Flagstaff Inn.** 2285 East Butler, Flagstaff, AZ 86004. Tel: 774-1821 or (800) 533-8992; Fax: 774-7662. $36–$46.

▶ **Flagstaff University/Grand Canyon Travelodge.** 801 West Highway 66, Flagstaff, AZ 86001. Tel: 774-3381; Fax: 774-1648. $28–$74.

▶ **Garland's Oak Creek Lodge.** Oak Creek Route/P.O. Box 152, Sedona, AZ 86336. Tel: 282-3343. Closed November to April. $134–$154, M.A.P.

▶ **Hassayampa Inn.** 122 East Gurley Street, Prescott, AZ 86301. Tel: 778-9434 or (800) 322-1927. $75 up.

▶ **Hidden Palms All Suite Inn.** 2100 Swanson Avenue, Lake Havasu City, AZ 86403. Tel: 855-7144. $52–$72.

▶ **Holiday Inn Canyon de Chelly.** P.O. Box 1889, Chinle, AZ 86503. Tel: 674-5000; Fax: 674-8264. $59–$99.

▶ **Hotel St. Michael.** 205 West Gurley Street, Prescott, AZ 86301. Tel: 776-1999 or (800) 678-3757; Fax: 776-7318. $33–$72.

▶ **Hotel Vendome.** 230 South Cortez, Prescott, AZ 86303. Tel: 776-0900. $45–$100.

▶ **Island Inn Hotel.** 1300 McCulloch Boulevard, Lake

Havasu City, AZ 86403. Tel: 680-0606 or (800) 243-9955; Fax: 680-4218. $65–$125.

▶ **Junipine Resort.** 8351 North Highway 89A, **Sedona**, AZ 86336. Tel: 282-3375 or (800) 742-PINE; Fax: 282-7402. $160–$236.

▶ **Kachina Lodge.** P.O. Box 699, **Grand Canyon**, AZ 86023. Tel: 638-2401; Fax: 638-9247. $85–$91.

▶ **Lake Havasu Holiday Inn.** 245 London Bridge Road, **Lake Havasu City**, AZ 86403. Tel: 855-4071; Fax: 855-2379. $39–$133.

▶ **Lake of the Woods.** P.O. Box 777, **Pinetop-Lakeside**, AZ 85929. Tel: 368-5353. $40–$87.

▶ **Little America Hotel.** 2515 East Butler, P.O. Box 3900, **Flagstaff**, AZ 86003. Tel: 779-2741 or (800) FLAG-FUN; Fax: 779-7983. $65–$95.

▶ **London Bridge Resort.** 1477 Queen's Bay, **Lake Havasu City**, AZ 86403. Tel: 855-0888 or (800) 624-7939; Fax: 855-2414. $75–$150.

▶ **Martinez Lake Resort.** Route 4, Box 41, **Martinez Lake**, AZ 85365. Tel: 783-9589; Fax: 782-3360. $47.50 (motel); $78.50 (trailers for up to four people); $235 (house, accommodates 12 people).

▶ **Maswik Lodge.** P.O. Box 699, **Grand Canyon**, AZ 86023. Tel: 638-2401; Fax: 638-9247. $46–$89 (cabins closed in winter).

▶ **Molly Butler Lodge.** Box 134, **Greer**, AZ 85927. Tel: 735-7226. $32–$48.

▶ **Moqui Lodge.** P.O. Box 699, **Grand Canyon**, AZ 86023. Tel: 638-2401; Fax: 638-9247. Closed January and February. $63–$73.

▶ **Mormon Lake Lodge.** P.O. Box 12, Mormon Lake, AZ 86038. Tel: 774-0462; Fax: 354-2356. $40–$80.

▶ **Mountain Side Inn.** 642 East Bill Williams Avenue, **Williams**, AZ 86046. Tel: 635-4431 or (800) 462-9381; Fax: 635-2292. $65–$85.

▶ **Nancy Russell's Bed & Breakfast.** 3 Juarez Street, P.O. Box 791, **Jerome**, AZ 86331. Tel: 634-3270. $70.

▶ **Nautical Inn Resort.** 1000 McCulloch Boulevard, **Lake Havasu City**, AZ 86403. Tel: 855-2141 or (800) 892-2141; Fax: 453-5808. $70–$150.

▶ **Oak Creek Terrace Resort.** 4548 North Highway 89A, **Sedona**, AZ 86336. Tel: 282-3562 or (800) 658-5866. $69–$160.

▶ **Poco Diablo Resort.** 1752 South Highway 179, P.O. Box 1709, **Sedona**, AZ 86336. Tel: 282-7333 or (800) 352-5710; Fax: 282-2090. $95–$230.

▶ **Railroad Inn at Sedona.** 2545 West Highway 89A,

Sedona, AZ 86336. Tel: (800) 858-RAIL; Fax: 282-2033. $54 up, not including excursion train fares.

▶ **Rodeway Inn East**. 2350 East Lucky Lane, **Flagstaff**, AZ 86004. Tel: 779-3614 or (800) 228-2000; Fax: 774-5834. $23–$75.

▶ **Sheraton Prescott Resort and Conference Center**. 1500 Highway 69, **Prescott**, AZ 86301. Tel. 776-1666 or (800) 967-4637; Fax: 776-8544. $65–$125.

▶ **Sunrise Park Resort**. P.O. Box 217, **McNary**, AZ 85930. Tel: 735-7676 or (800) 55-HOTEL; Fax: 735-7474. $49–$94.

▶ **Thunderbird Lodge**. Box 548, **Chinle**, AZ 86503. Tel: 674-5841. $79–$84; $140–$152 (suites for up to four people).

▶ **Thunderbird Lodge**. P.O. Box 699, **Grand Canyon**, AZ 86023. Tel: 638-2401; Fax: 638-9247. $85–$91.

▶ **Yavapai Lodge**. P.O. Box 699, **Grand Canyon**, AZ 86023. Tel: 638-2401; Fax: 638-9247. Closed November to February. $68–$78.

SOUTHERN UTAH

CANYONLANDS AND GRAND CANYON'S NORTH RIM

By Richard Menzies

Richard Menzies is a longtime columnist for Utah Holiday *magazine. He lives in Salt Lake City, Utah.*

The venerable Grand Canyon, Zion, and Bryce national parks have long been fixtures on the Southwest tourist trail, but until recently the red-rock badlands of southeastern Utah remained terra incognita. The sole inhabitants were widely dispersed cowboys and Indians, missionaries and visionaries, prospectors, hermits, and outlaws; the average amount of real estate allotted each human occupant was something like ten square miles.

Things began to change with the advent of the atomic age and the big uranium rush of the 1950s. A network of jeep trails spread into erstwhile trackless canyonlands; prospectors and rock hounds started bringing back not just mineral samples but also tales of amazing adventures from "the back of beyond." Many of these jeep trails have since been paved, opening the backcountry to regular motor traffic, which is essentially the only practical way to get around this part of the world unless you plan to spend a great deal of time hiking or on horseback.

Canyonlands, besides being the name of a national park, is also a generic term often applied to the whole quadrant of southeastern Utah bounded on the north by I-70 and stretching south all the way to Monument Valley and the

Arizona border. This generic "canyonlands" includes two national parks, three national monuments, and a number of state parks. It is bracketed by the 12,000-foot La Sal mountain range to the east, and on the west by the forested peaks of the Henry Mountains. In between, the Colorado Plateau is carved and sculpted by the Colorado River, the Green River, which flows into it, and their tributaries. Goose-necks (looping river bends) and plunging gorges, sandstone monoliths and minarets, petrified toadstools, natural arches and bridges, convoluted canyons and slick-rock slopes typify the tortuous topography of the region that is sometimes called Standing-up Country.

Counting the North Rim of Grand Canyon National Park, there are six national parks clustered in the area we will cover, which besides the Canyonlands includes south-western Utah west of the Canyonlands and the corner of Arizona north of the Grand Canyon. The expansive spaces in between national parks contain many state parks, his-torical sites, national monuments, and a wealth of lesser-known scenic attractions—almost too many to name. (Some, no doubt, are still nameless; in 1992, for instance, a vacationing University of Utah professor stumbled upon a natural stone arch in Arches National Park that was uncharted, even though it lay just 200 yards off a major trail.)

Except on the mountaintops, the area is uniformly dry, sparsely vegetated but richly textured with some of the most rugged and unusual topography to be found on earth. Eons of geophysical uplift combined with the ero-sive forces of water, wind, and gravity have sculpted a landscape of towering sandstone cliffs, sheer-walled mesas surrounded by boulder-strewn talus slopes, and deep canyons enclosing shady glades of cottonwood and tamarisk.

Don't be afraid to take the road less travelled here, which in some parts may be the only road available, especially in the southeastern Utah canyonlands. Investi-gate those big blank white spaces on the road map—acreage administered by the United States Bureau of Land Management (BLM). It's all public domain, and chances are you'll find a spot you can have all to yourself.

The main north–south routes through the heart of southeast Utah include UT 95, which trends northwest from Blanding to Hanksville, skirting Canyonlands Na-tional Park and passing Lake Powell at its northernmost tip; and UT 12, which begins at Torrey (just west of Capitol Reef National Park) and ends at U.S. 89 near Bryce

Canyon National Park. UT 24 runs east and west, connecting Torrey and Hanksville, and is the only paved road
crossing Capitol Reef National Park. The significance of
these routes lies in their being all-weather roads crossing
high-desert terrain that epitomizes the Western landscape
of film and folklore.

Southeastern Utah supports a vigorous but relatively
young tourist industry. Not so very long ago the sight of a
stranger in town was cause for commotion in drowsy
villages such as Tropic, Torrey, and Hanksville. Nightlife,
thanks in large part to Utah's Byzantine liquor laws, hovers somewhere between germinal and terminal. Most
liquor stores carry 3.2 beer, which is served in bars and
taverns. Anything stronger, including wine, must be purchased through a state-run liquor store. Some fine restaurants do have wine lists, but are not permitted to show it
unless you first ask to see it. You may carry your own
wine into a restaurant in a brown paper bag provided it is
"cork finished." (If your bottle has a screw-on cap, you'll
have to drink it outside in the parking lot.)

Although innovative changes have lately been made to
accommodate tourists (two-week memberships in private
clubs, the only establishments allowed to serve mixed
drinks, can be bought for $5, for example), Utah remains
for the most part a pretty dry state. Many of her citizens,
non-Mormon in particular, complain loudly about the
situation, but to little avail. Most will agree that whatever
shortcomings Utah may have in the way of creature comforts are more than made up for by a superabundance of
natural beauty.

Virtually all towns and cities in the area were established during the great Mormon colonization movement
of the past century. Each is laid out as a grid of streets
running north and south, east and west, numbered from a
central point in accordance to the pattern established in
Salt Lake City by Brigham Young. Should you get lost,
look for coordinates on the nearest street sign. If you find
yourself standing at the corner of, say, Second (200) West
and Fourth (400) North, it means that you are two blocks
west and four blocks north of the center of town.

Though a model of simplicity, the so-called City of Zion
plan has struck more than one out-of-towner as confus-
ing. "How can it be," they ask, "that Second West Street
runs north and south, and Fourth North runs east and
west?" Like the one about how can I get a drink in this
town, it's a tough question to answer—but one that will

diminish in urgency the longer you stick around and allow the country to weave its mesmerizing spell on you.

MAJOR INTEREST

Scenic drives, especially Routes 95, 24, 12, and 9
Arches National Park
Canyonlands National Park
Grand Gulch Primitive Area
Dark Canyon Wilderness Area
Natural Bridges National Monument
Goblin Valley State Park
Capitol Reef National Park
Bryce Canyon National Park
Cedar Breaks National Monument
Zion National Park
North Rim Grand Canyon National Park
Lake Powell
Rainbow Bridge National Monument

We begin our coverage of Canyonlands country at Arches National Park in the upper Canyonlands, then move in a generally southwesterly direction through Canyonlands National Park and other places around the Colorado River here—an area we call Back of Beyond, which is also accessible from the Four Corners, covered in an earlier chapter of this book. We then take a jog to the northwest to Capitol Reef National Park. From there we go down into south-central and southwestern Utah on U.S. 89, which links Bryce Canyon and Zion national parks, Kanab and (across the border in Arizona) Fredonia, and then goes to the Grand Canyon's North Rim.

We end the chapter at the lower Canyonlands in the area of Lake Powell's Glen Canyon Dam. Because this is an area rich in early Utah history and Mormon culture, we'll make a detour along the way from Zion National Park to the Old World communities of Cedar City and St. George in the southwest corner of Utah (the northern gateway to Las Vegas, Nevada, and the Lake Mead area).

Note: We cover the South Rim and discuss the Grand Canyon itself in our Central Arizona chapter. The Grand Canyon in effect cuts off the North Rim and the so-called Arizona Strip from the rest of Arizona. You can *see* the South Rim clearly from the North, but unless you have a mule's legs you can't get there from here.

A big factor—actually *the* big factor—in travelling

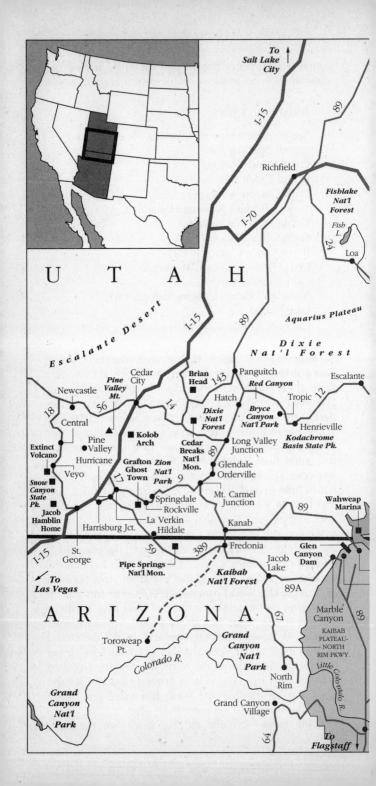

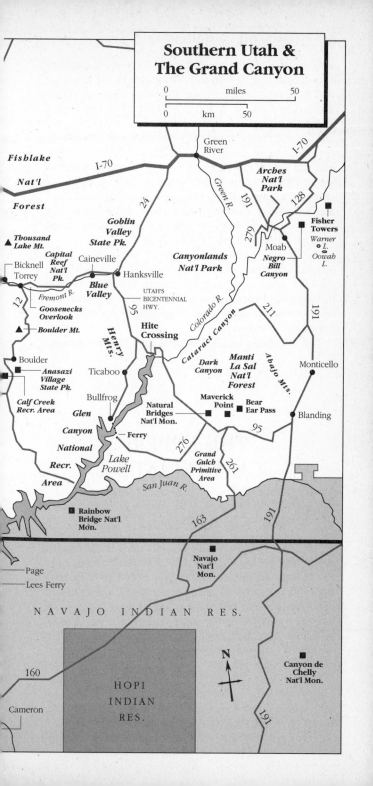

Southern Utah & The Grand Canyon

miles 0 50

km 0 50

Fisblake Nat'l Forest

I-70

Green River

I-70

Arches Nat'l Park

128

Fisher Towers

Thousand Lake Mt.

Goblin Valley State Pk.

24

Green R.

191

279

Warner L. Oowah L.

Capital Reef Nat'l Pk.

Caineville

Moab

Bicknell Torrey

Hanksville

Canyonlands Nat'l Park

Negro Bill Canyon

Fremont R.

Blue Valley

95

UTAH'S BICENTENNIAL HWY.

Colorado R.

211

12

Goosenecks Overlook

Hite Crossing

Cataract Canyon

Manti La Sal Nat'l Forest

191

Boulder Mt.

Henry Mts.

Dark Canyon

Abajo Mts.

Monticello

Boulder

Ticaboo

Maverick Point

Bear Ear Pass

Blanding

Anasazi Village State Pk.

Bullfrog

Natural Bridges Nat'l Mon.

95

Calf Creek Recr. Area

Glen

Ferry

276

Canyon

261

Grand Gulch Primitive Area

National

Lake Powell

Recr.

San Juan R.

Area

Rainbow Bridge Nat'l Mon.

163

191

Page

Lees Ferry

Navajo Nat'l Mon.

NAVAJO INDIAN RES.

N

160

HOPI INDIAN RES.

Canyon de Chelly Nat'l Mon.

Cameron

191

through this area is the Colorado River itself. Between Arches National Park in the northeast and the Las Vegas area hundreds of miles to the southwest, the river can be crossed by car only on UT 95 at Hite and by ferryboat at Hall's Crossing, and at two places near each other just below Lake Powell at the Utah-Arizona border. Moreover, branch canyons created by tributaries of the Colorado, and the topographical realities of the surrounding badlands, mean that in an area roughly the size of Massachusetts, Connecticut, and Rhode Island combined there are few direct routes. Imagine only three roads (not just major roads, but *any* roads) running north–south through all of southern New England.

The result is that our coverage will seem to jump around a bit, and you should be prepared to bring more than the usual amount of skill to charting a trip through this region of the Southwest. But console yourself with the fact that this same difficult topography translates into out-of-this-world scenery.

The telephone area code for Utah is 801, for Arizona 602.

THE UPPER CANYONLANDS

ARCHES NATIONAL PARK

Thirty miles (48 km) south of I-70 and 5 miles (8 km) north of Moab, Utah, off U.S. 191, is Arches National Park, a wonderland of wind- and water-sculpted entrada sandstone. The park boundaries enclose the greatest density of natural stone arches in the world, ranging in size from three-foot windows to the approximately 300-foot span of Landscape Arch. Perhaps the best known is Delicate Arch, the graceful shape of which is featured on Utah's bicentennial auto license plates.

An 18-mile paved road stretches from one end of the park to the other, providing easy access to most of its main attractions, including Double Arch, Balanced Rock, Turret Arch, and Park Avenue—all just a short walk from the pavement. Children will find the scale to their liking, but keep an eye on them; it's amazingly easy to get lost among the many slick-rock fins and folds. Another good reason not to wander off the beaten path is to avoid stepping on a microbiotic crust called cryptogamic soil—literally, living dirt. The stuff is a combination of bacteria, lichen, algae, and fungi, looks something like brown sugar, and serves to retard erosion in the high desert.

An area map locating all roads and foot trails in Arches is issued to everyone who enters the park; thus equipped, you should be able to find your way around, with the exception of the Fiery Furnace section, a maze of convoluted red-rock fins and pinnacles where it's especially easy to get lost or walk right past some of its special attractions, such as Surprise and Twin Arches. The best way to explore Fiery Furnace is to take the ranger-guided tour, for which you must reserve a spot in person at the visitors' center situated at the park entrance off U.S. 191. Overnight camping is available at Devil's Garden on a first-come basis, and sites fill quickly and early in the day. No reservations are taken; Tel: 259-8161.

Indeed, finding a place to stay *anywhere* in the Moab area has been something of a problem lately, thanks to widespread interest sparked by Hollywood films such as *Indiana Jones and the Last Crusade* and *Thelma & Louise,* both of which co-starred the red-rock badlands of Moab and Arches. Makers of off-road sport utility vehicles routinely film their commercials here, and the Philip Morris company relentlessly promotes the area as the epicenter of mythical "Marlboro Country."

Moab

The once-drowsy village of Moab is undergoing a cultural revolution that some of the locals like to disparage as "Aspenization." But to other observers it looks to be more of a shift to outward, rather than upward, mobility. If you want to fit in, the standard-issue outfit here includes a four-wheel-drive vehicle bristling with mountain bikes. Royal Robbins climbing shorts, Birkenstock or Teva sandals, and the obligatory Chums brand sunglasses retainer complete the environmentally correct ensemble.

The current tourist boom is actually Moab's second, the first being the uranium rush of the 1950s, which took off when a down-and-out prospector by the name of Charlie Steen located a radioactive lode he dubbed Mi Vida. Overnight, Steen went from living in a $15-a-month tar-paper shack in Cisco, Utah, to an opulent hilltop mansion overlooking Moab's Spanish Valley. Symbolic of how Moab's economic base has since shifted from mining to tourism, Steen's mansion has become a restaurant, and the so-called Potash Road (UT 279, which parallels the Colorado River south and west of Moab) is now a designated scenic byway. (To give you an idea of what happens to the Colorado River landscape from here south: UT 128 from Moab to Cisco and the short UT 279—both very scenic routes—are the last roads of any size that can run right along the Colorado until you get to the Las Vegas/ Lake Mead area, some 320 *air* miles to the southwest.)

Establishments such as the **Back of Beyond Bookstore** at 83 North Main Street (U.S. 191) stock picture books and literature aimed at refined tastes. Moab is also home to Utah's only commercial winery, **Arches Vineyards**, where visitors are welcome in the tasting room at 2182 South Highway 191. Otherwise, the business district seems to consist entirely of motels and rock shops and two museums, the **Dan O'Laurie Museum** at 118 East Center Street, featuring a small but excellent historical collection detailing geology, ranching, and mining activities in Moab, and the **Hollywood Stuntman's Hall of Fame and Museum** at 100 East 100 North. Housed in an old church building behind a cement walk bearing the boot prints of more than 200 second-unit film performers dating to the silent era and Yakima Canutt, the museum is one of the oddest establishments anywhere. "Look for me falling off the roof!" exclaims exuberant host and veteran stuntman John Hagen, who has doubled in films for Robert Mitchum, among others. A couple of the many unusual exhibits you'll find here are the corset that held up Sally Fields's airborne stunt double in *The Flying Nun* and the dummy heads of Thelma and Louise.

For the most part, however, Moab's main asset is its magnificent setting among the red-rock cliffs of Spanish Valley. Even the municipal landfill southeast of town is lovely; CBS newsman Charles Kuralt once dubbed it "the most scenic garbage dump in the world."

The best place to stay in the Moab area is the **Pack Creek Ranch** on La Sal Mountain Loop Road, 17 miles (27 km) southeast of town. Accommodations are in cozy log cabins, and the Pack Creek Ranch restaurant, offering fine Southwestern fare, is by far the best in the area. The Landmark, Ramada Inn, and Moab Travelodge are safe, comfortable havens in town; the Super 8 on the north end of town has a particularly nice hot tub.

The **Golden Stake Restaurant** at 550 South Main Street

serves a hearty breakfast guaranteed to last you a whole day on the trail. Come suppertime another restaurant, in the **Best Western Greenwell Motel** in the heart of Moab, at 105 South Main, serves enormous, tender porterhouse steaks. The **Main Street Broiler** at 606 South Main is an unpretentious fast-food joint where you can grab an excellent burger and fries any time between dawn and dusk.

Each Easter four-wheel-drive enthusiasts from around the country converge on the region to field test their vehicles on minimal dirt trails with forbidding names like Hell's Revenge. And throughout the spring, summer, and fall, Moab, home of the world-famous Slickrock Trail (see below), is a world-renowned **mountain biking** mecca. Footwear giant Nike even markets a cross-training shoe it dubs the Air Moabb. **Tag-a-Long Tours**, 452 North Main Street, will be happy to take you on a four-wheel-drive tour of the canyonlands area; they also rent flat-water kayaking equipment and will arrange for shuttle service to and from Labyrinth Canyon on the Green River (for which see below). Tel: 259-8946 or (800) 453-3292.

AROUND MOAB

The most popular off-road adventure is mountain biking or hiking the world-famous **Slickrock Trail**, a roller coaster formed of petrified dunes of Navajo sandstone that begins on the outskirts of town not far from the celebrated scenic dump. From Moab, turn east off U.S. 191 onto 300 South, three blocks south of the center of town. Follow this street to its intersection with 400 East and turn right. Two blocks south turn left on Mill Creek Drive, which will soon turn northward and become Sand Flats Road. Follow Sand Flats Road for 2¼ miles (3½ km) until you see the trailhead and parking lot to your left.

The two-mile-long practice loop is a good way to test your wheels if you're new to the sport. The Slickrock Trail itself is a ten-mile round trip that runs north to Icebox Canyon and Updraft Arch, then loops south along Swiss Cheese Ridge before returning to the parking lot. Essentially this is a trail for riders with advanced biking skills; if you're on foot, plan on spending anywhere from two hours to a full day, but stay away on weekends to avoid being trapped in biker gridlock.

For information regarding on- and off-road cycling anywhere in the state, contact Bicycle UT, P.O. Box 738, Park City, Utah 84060. Tel: 649-5806; Fax: 649-8805.

Negro Bill Canyon is an easy four-mile round-trip trek that starts from UT 128 some 3 miles (5 km) upstream from its junction with U.S. 191, and ends at the 250-foot sandstone span of Morning Glory natural bridge.

UT 128 continues on a northeasterly course, running parallel to the Colorado River's south bank to beautiful Castle Valley and Fisher Towers, the tallest of which rises 900 feet above the valley floor. At Castle Valley the **Manti— La Sal Mountain Loop Road** branches off UT 128 at a spot called Richardson. The 61-mile scenic drive will take you high into the forested peaks of the La Sals, past Warner and Oowah lakes, then back down again to join U.S. 191 just south of Moab. The road is mostly paved, reaches altitudes of 8,000 feet and more, and offers a welcome respite from summer heat.

RIVER-RUNNING

Besides being well known for mountain biking, Moab is also a major river-running center. The view from the river here looks very much the same as it did back in 1869, when Major John Wesley Powell and his survey crew passed through in wooden boats on their historic voyage to the Grand Canyon. And no one since has come up with a more agreeable means of transportation.

Float trips on the Colorado River can be taken on everything from jet boats to rubber one-person kayaks, and vary in length from a half day to a week or more. **Cataract Canyon**, downstream in Canyonlands National Park, and **Westwater Canyon**, about 50 miles (80 km) upstream from Moab, are noted for white water. The Green River, south of I-70 from the town of Green River, Utah, flows calmly through **Labyrinth Canyon** and **Stillwater Canyon** into Canyonlands, and the **Colorado River** from Moab south to the confluence with the Green is also without rapids.

One of the more unusual tours is **Canyonlands by Night**, a two-hour evening boat tour down the Colorado from Moab that includes narration, recorded music, and a light show; Tel: 259-5261. An up-and-coming activity is flat-water **canoeing and kayaking** on the relatively un-crowded waters of the Green River through Labyrinth Canyon. Local operators such as Tag-a-Long Tours in Moab rent equipment and offer shuttle service (see above).

A number of other Moab-based outfitters offer a variety of river-running trips, including the **Moab Rafting Company** (Tel: 259-RAFT), **North American River/Canyonlands Tours** (Tel: 259-5865), **Navtec Expeditions** (Tel: 259-7863), and **Adrift Adventures** (Tel: 259-8494). If you'd like to relive Major Powell's adventures on the Colorado without any of the hardships, try **Sheri Griffith Expeditions**; the four-day Expeditions-in-Luxury package includes candlelit dinners with wine and fresh table linens. Tel: 259-2226.

CANYONLANDS NATIONAL PARK

Canyonlands, established as a national park in 1964, is the area around the juncture of the Green and Colorado rivers, south and west of Moab. The park proper is a 338,000-acre preserve surrounding the "Y" formed by the confluence of the two big rivers, which have carved deep canyons that effectively divide the park into three separate sections. The Needles district lies to the east of the Colorado and the Maze district is to the west. (For the Maze district, see the Goblin Valley portion of the Back of Beyond section, below.) The isolated central peninsula at the north end is known as the Island in the Sky. The Needles and Island in the Sky sections now have fully staffed visitors' centers, but don't expect to find much else in the way of creature comforts in the area, or roads that are much more than rudimentary. Canyonlands is the least "civilized" of Utah's national parks, essentially designed for jeeps and backpackers. For information about the park, Tel: 259-7164.

Reach the **Island in the Sky** portion of Canyonlands by taking scenic UT 313, which branches west off U.S. 191 about 13 miles (21 km) north of Moab. The paved road winds southward and eventually forks into two roads, the left one continuing 23 miles (37 km) to Dead Horse Point State Park, the right branch leading to the Island in the Sky. (The visitors' center is about 2 miles/3 km inside the northern park boundary.) **Dead Horse Point** stands 2,000 feet above the Colorado River and commands a spectacular bird's-eye view of the canyonlands region, the Colorado goosenecks, and the La Sal Mountains.

Follow the right fork about 5 miles (8 km) and you arrive at the north end of Canyonlands Park. The road offers sweeping vistas at Grandview Point, White Rim Overlook, Murphy Point, and Green River Overlook. There are a number of easy hiking trails here, including footpaths to Mesa Arch, Aztec Butte, Whale Rock, White Rim, and Grandview overlooks. Of special interest is the mysterious Upheaval Dome, a cavernous depression believed to be either a collapsed subterranean salt dome or the eroded impact crater of an ancient meteorite.

To reach the **Needles** district by automobile from Moab take U.S. 191 south and turn west at the signposted junction of UT 211, some 33 miles (53 km) south of Moab. UT 211 leads first to **Newspaper Rock**, a rock panel bearing inscriptions spanning a thousand years—everything from prehistoric petroglyphs to pioneer graffiti. The road then continues past the Six Shooter Peaks to the Needles Outpost (your last chance to stock up on groceries or take a hot shower) and the visitors' center before dead-ending at **Squaw Flat Campground** (26 primitive sites with water available seasonally; no reservations). Squaw Flat is the trailhead to Big Spring and Squaw Canyon trails, both of which lead to **Chesler Park**, an enchanted area of meadows ringed by walls of standing rocks vaguely reminiscent of Stonehenge. Some other unusual landforms accessible by foot or four-wheel drive from Squaw Flat include Druid Arch and the Devil's Kitchen. All are moderately difficult hikes; be sure to pack water and check in at the ranger station before venturing out.

The trail to the confluence overlook is a bit more strenuous. It begins at Big Spring Overlook, at the end of a road that runs 3½ miles (5½ km) north from Squaw Flat Campground. The round trip is 11 miles; be sure to carry water, food, and an adequate map, which you should pick up at the visitors' center.

You can drive to some good overviews of the Needles district via the canyon-rim drive, which also takes off west from U.S. 191, about 7 miles (11 km) north of the UT 211 junction. The two-lane scenic drive is paved for 22 miles to the spectacular **Needles Overlook**, the closest-to-the-main-road view of Canyonlands. If you're feeling adventurous and don't mind getting dusty, you can turn north at Eight-Mile Rock onto a graded gravel road that leads to Hatch Point and Canyonlands Overlook before dead-ending at **Anticline Overlook**, 1,400 breathtaking feet above the Colorado River.

Monticello

Fifty-three miles (85 km) south of Moab on U.S. 191, nestled against the west flank of the Abajo Mountains, is the small community of Monticello. Monticello is named after Thomas Jefferson's old Virginia home, but in Utah we pronounce it "Mon-ti-SELL-o." It's not as busy as Moab, and not nearly as trendy. Grown men wearing shorts and grandmas wearing hiking boots still turn heads.

Monticello's economy has traditionally been based on

ranching, farming, and mining, but with an unemployment rate that seems fixed at 20 percent the business
community is looking more and more to tourism as a
source of jobs and revenue.

Monticello's motels include the Best Western Wayside,
the Canyonlands Motor Inn, the Days Inn, and the Navajo
Trail National 9 Inn. Bed-and-breakfast inns include the
Grist Mill Inn and the **Home Ranch** (the latter is located
in La Sal, approximately midway between Moab and Monticello on U.S. 191). A working cattle ranch operated by
the descendants of early settlers Charlie and Annaley
Redd, the ranch has played host to everyone from cattle
buyers to British royalty. Sunny Redd's home-baked potatoes and bean salads are widely renowned house specialties, as are Gwen Seely's cole slaw and Annaley Redd's
"Prairie Fire" pinto beans. Like Moab's Pack Creek Ranch,
a similar guest-ranch operation, the Home Ranch is situated in the mountains at an elevation of 7,000 feet, which
makes for pleasant days and cooler nights during the
summer season.

Around Monticello

To find out all the things there are to do in the area, stop
at the Multi-Agency Visitor Center at 117 South Main
Street; Tel: (800) 574-4386. Representatives from San Juan
County, the U.S. Forest Service, the U.S. Department of the
Interior, the BLM, and other agencies provide informa-
tion. Monticello can be either your base for exploring
Canyonlands or your last shot at visitor facilities before
venturing farther into the backcountry.

A pleasant change of scenery during the summer is the
Blue Mountain Loop Road, which heads west from the
center of town into high country, then turns north to join
UT 211 near Newspaper Rock State Park. To the east
stretch cultivated fields as far as the eye can see—almost
as far as Dove Creek, Colorado, self-proclaimed "Pinto
Bean Capital of the World." To the west, the rugged Abajos
drop away into the Dark Canyon Wilderness Area (see
below) and some of the roughest and least-cultivated
country on the continent.

BACK OF BEYOND

Here's where driving through southern Utah starts to get
really interesting—but only if you're willing to make a

few mental adjustments. First, rid yourself of the notion that there just *has* to be a filling station around every bend or a settlement every so many miles. Be prepared to travel *at least* 100 miles between gas pumps, and don't hold out for your favorite brand; take what's available and be grateful for it.

Second, *do* invest in one of those Styrofoam insulated ice chests, if you haven't already. Fill it with ice and soft drinks, or whatever refreshments you prefer. Carry plenty of drinking water and enough groceries to make a picnic lunch or two along the way. And try not to drive at night; there's too much to see, and the only thing you want to miss are the range cows that are perversely fond of grazing the fertile borrow pits and soft shoulders that pass for greenbelts in this part of the country.

South from Monticello follow U.S. 191 through Blanding. (This stretch of highway is also discussed in the Four Corners chapter.) Four miles (6½ km) south of Blanding you'll come to the junction with UT 95, also known as the Trail of the Ancients and Utah's Bicentennial Highway. UT 95 runs west off U.S. 191, skirting the south flank of the Abajos and passing through picturesque high-desert terrain of mesas and buttes for 32 miles (51 km) until it intersects UT 261, which runs south to Mexican Hat.

GRAND GULCH

One of the area's most popular backpacking spots, the Grand Gulch Primitive Area is accessed by a dirt road heading south, about 1 mile (1½ km) west of the junction of Highways 95 and 261, and a mile east of the entrance to Natural Bridges National Monument. Grand Gulch is about 50 miles long from north to south and encloses an abundance of Anasazi ruins, pictographs, and archaeological sites dating to A.D. 1300. Most hikers choose not to trek the whole length of the gulch but rather just a manageable segment, such as the three-day trip from Bullet Canyon to Kane Gulch, or the four-day hike from Collins Spring to Bullet Canyon. Before setting out on any hikes you must register at the Kane Gulch Ranger Station, about 3 miles (4½ km) south of UT 95 on UT 261, where you can also inquire about trail conditions and regulations. Foot traffic through Grand Gulch has increased so much in recent years that the Bureau of Land Management is considering imposing limitations.

DARK CANYON

North of UT 95 and Grand Gulch, the Dark Canyon Wilderness Area encompasses 45,000 acres and a 40-mile-long backpack trail through Woodenshoe, Hammond, Peavine, Dark, and other canyons surrounding Dry Mesa. As with Grand Gulch, an excursion into Dark Canyon calls for adequate preparation and good path-finding skills.

To get to the trailhead turn north off UT 95 at the entrance to Natural Bridges (for which see below; about 2 miles/3 km past the junction with UT 261). Follow the Natural Bridges road for about a mile until you see a graded road branching north (to the right). Follow it to Maverick Point and over Bears Ears Pass. Two miles north of Bears Ears, turn left at the first fork in the road and continue another 4 miles (6½ km) to the trailhead on the east edge of Upper Woodenshoe Canyon.

Natural Bridges National Monument

Natural Bridges National Monument, off UT 95 via UT 275, is home to three of the Southwest's largest natural sandstone bridges, a landform that differs from a natural arch in that it spans a watercourse. The visitors' center and campground at the beginning of the loop road here are situated on a high plateau that takes the shape of a peninsula bounded on the north by White Canyon and on the south by Armstrong Canyon. (The campground's 13 sites are available on a first-come basis.)

Owachomo Bridge is a short hike south from the roadway that runs along the top of the plateau; to have a good look at the other two entails a bit of work. The trail to Sipapu Bridge, which is big enough to span the U.S. Capitol building, is especially steep, descending 500 vertical feet in a half mile via a system of chutes and ladders across cross-bedded sandstone cliffs more than 225 million years old. The second-largest bridge, Kachina, is about three miles southwest of Sipapu and also at the end of a steep foot trail to the bottom of White Canyon. In June 1992 a thousand tons of rock fell from the bridge, making it bigger and "more stable looking," according to park service personnel. Stable looking or not, it's a place you may want to consider not dawdling beneath.

Most visitors end up driving from one trailhead to another, but it's almost as quick to park your car at the Sipapu trailhead and hike the trails that cut across the mesa top through the pygmy forest of piñon and juniper. The best alternative, if you're in no hurry, is to hike the river bottom from one bridge to the next instead of climbing up and down at each one. The round trip is about nine miles, but you can cut it short by exiting at Kachina, the halfway point. Along the way, look for petroglyphs and the **Horsecollar Anasazi ruins**.

Across the Colorado

Refill your canteen at a tap outside the Natural Bridges visitors' center and return the way you came to UT 95, thence right (northwest), resuming your westward course toward the mighty Colorado. In 8 miles (13 km) you'll come to the junction with UT 276, which heads southwest off UT 95 for 42 miles (67 km) to **Hall's Crossing Marina**, where ferry service across Lake Powell to **Bullfrog Marina** is available via Utah's one-ship navy, the *John Atlantic Burr*. The ferry cost is $9 per average-size car. Daytime crossings are scheduled hourly, but in the off-season (October 1 to May 14) be sure you get to Hall's Crossing before 2:00 P.M., your last chance to catch the boat before 8:00 A.M. the next day. If the ferryboat is undergoing repairs, a not infrequent occurrence, the bad news should be posted at the junction of Highways 95 and 276.

Bullfrog has gas, groceries, a restaurant, a yacht club, and the 48-room **Defiance House Lodge**, which has rustic decor with Southwestern accents in gardenside and lakeside accommodations. The near ghost town of Ticaboo, north of Bullfrog on UT 276, has a funny name and what is perhaps the second most scenic trash dump in the world, after Moab's.

From Bullfrog on the west shore of Lake Powell, UT 276 heads along the east flank of the Henry Mountains north 48 miles (77 km) eventually to rejoin UT 95. As an alternate route, if your vehicle has good ground clearance and if you're not timid about dust or solitude, you can take an unpaved road that runs west of the Henrys from Bullfrog 65 miles (104 km) north to Capitol Reef National Park, roughly paralleling a geologic upthrust called the Waterpocket Fold. Besides views of the Fold, the route affords a good look at the isolated Henry Mountains, home of the last free-roaming buffalo herd in the United States. You could call this the "low road" or the back door into Capitol Reef (for which see below).

The "high road" entails staying on UT 95 from Natural Bridges and crossing the Colorado at Hite. The road angles northwest across high plateau country with next to nothing in the way of overnight lodging for 91 miles and only one filling station (at Hite Marina) before you get to Hanksville.

From Natural Bridges, Highway 95 goes north along the top of scenic Mancos Mesa until it drops into the **Glen Canyon National Recreation Area**, skirting the northernmost tip of Lake Powell via three spectacular bridges that span White Canyon, the Colorado River, and the Dirty Devil River. It then wends northward about 50 miles up a rock-walled canyon past Hog Springs, eventually crossing the high, bald expanse of the Burr Desert before it meets up at last with UT 24, also known as Hanksville's main street.

Hanksville

Before it became a refueling stop on the way to Lake Powell, Hanksville wasn't much more than a wide spot along the Outlaw Trail, the route Butch Cassidy and other members of the Wild Bunch Gang used to escape to Robbers Roost, their impregnable desert hideout due east of town near the Dirty Devil River. Besides outlaws, the earliest permanent residents consisted of one or two prospectors and a handful of hardy cattle ranchers, most bearing the surname Ekker.

Turn south of UT 24 in Hanksville at 100 (First) West and follow the road a half mile to the Bureau of Land Management's regional offices. There you can view the historic **Wolverton Mill**, built in the 1920s by a reclusive engineer by the name of Edwin Wolverton. After several years of piloting a steamboat on the Green River around the turn of the century, Wolverton spent the latter part of his life in the Henry Mountains, west of UT 95 below Hanksville, looking for a fabled lost Spanish gold mine. In 1974 the wooden paddle wheel that powered Wolverton's ore-crushing mill was airlifted from Mount Pennell and plopped down in Hanksville, where visitors may examine it today without invoking an old Indian curse said to afflict all those who seek lost gold in the Henrys.

Nailed to a nearby cottonwood tree is a hand-painted sign pointing the way to **Joy's Bed & Breakfast**. Owner Joy Mecham reports business is slow. During the first nine months of operation, in fact, her guest register logged just three names. But she expects business to improve, soon as she can "get me a man to make me a bigger sign."

The rest of Hanksville's minuscule business district is

equally funky; nothing you see conforms to any known pattern or color scheme and nothing is a franchised operation. Hollow Mountain is an underground convenience store blasted into the side of a cliff. **Whispering Sands** is a motel that looks to be a dozen Tuff Sheds yoked together. Inquire about getting a room at Whispering Sands at Stan's Burger Shak next door, where the food counter doubles as the motel desk. The front yard at **Fern's Place** is decorated with everything from sun-bleached animal skulls to "baby rattler" pens—and, yes, even an old kitchen sink.

Strangest of all is **Tropical Jeem's**, a dusty roadside café north of town on UT 24 that upon first glance appears not only closed but abandoned. But—as with most everything else about Hanksville—looks are deceiving. Proprietor Jim Roberts serves up what may be the best New Mexican cuisine this side of New Mexico. His mother and business partner, Evelyn Brown, who holds a master's degree in social work, specializes in traditional American dishes such as peach cobbler and chicken stew with dumplings. Chances are you might be the only customer in the place, but that doesn't mean you'll be able to eat and run. Jim and Evelyn don't like to rush, and they enjoy sitting down and getting acquainted with their clientele. Among his regular customers, Roberts counts actor Howard Hesseman of "WKRP" TV sitcom fame.

Goblin Valley State Park

In the event you have some time left after eating at Tropical Jeem's, consider continuing north on UT 24, at least as far as Goblin Valley State Park. The park is west of the highway at the end of a marked turnoff 22 miles (35 km) north of Hanksville.

Goblin Valley is a storybook land of mushroom- and toadstool-shaped balanced rocks that are just the right size for children. There is virtually no vegetation, but the state of Utah has thoughtfully installed a shaded observation shelter where visitors can find respite from the sun's rays. Other facilities include a 21-unit campground (available on a first-come basis), with modern rest rooms and hot showers. On your way back to the highway, pause to admire Temple Mountain and the spectacular San Rafael Reef, a 50-mile-long tilted sandstone escarpment that resembles the exposed backbone of a stegosaurus. Many believe it will one day be the centerpiece of Utah's sixth national park.

CANYONLANDS NATIONAL PARK'S MAZE DISTRICT

One-quarter mile south of the Goblin Valley turnoff on UT 24, a gravel road heads east 24 miles (38 km) to the west entrance of Canyonlands National Park. This, the Maze district of the park (mentioned above), has been described as "a 30-square-mile puzzle in sandstone." Indian ruins and pictographs, bizarre towers, walls, buttes, and mesas typify the region, which embraces the Flint Trail, Horseshoe Canyon, Ernie's Country, and the Doll House. But the main attraction is probably solitude, the Maze portion of Canyonlands being the least crowded and most rugged national park you'll ever see. Just be sure to carry food and water, and, if it looks like rain, go another day. The claylike dirt that passes for topsoil in this area becomes absolutely treacherous when it gets wet.

West from Hanksville, UT 24 follows the muddy Fremont River through Blue Valley and past the Blue Hills. All of one color, a bluish slate gray, the eroded bentonite landscape here is magnificently desolate. Towering in the distance on the right is Factory Butte, so named because of its resemblance to a smoke-stained industrial plant.

At some point during the 30-mile (48-km) drive from Hanksville to Capitol Reef, you may begin to wonder if you're nearing the end of the earth. If there is such a place, Caineville would certainly be a candidate; it's one of the few places in America without telephone service. In the event you should experience chest pains, run to the farmhouse with the sign out front that reads Public Emergency Radio Available. If the elderly couple who maintain the radio aren't home, don't panic; folks in this part of the country seldom bother to lock their doors. Follow the posted instructions to transmit your SOS, which, if you're lucky, will be intercepted by a shortwave ham stationed at Capitol Reef. The ham will then dial the number of an emergency medical technician in Hanksville, who, if he's in, will pick you up and rush you a hundred miles to the nearest hospital in Richfield. If you're not pronounced dead on arrival, you can later boast to your friends that you survived one of the longest and most scenic ambulance runs anywhere.

CAPITOL REEF NATIONAL PARK

Capitol Reef National Park, about 15 miles (24 km) west of Caineville on UT 24, is so named because of high cliffs that formed a reeflike barrier to early travel. Other settlers thought the domes of Navajo sandstone looked a lot like a man-made landmark in Washington, D.C., hence the name "Capitol."

About 180 million years before the arrival of the first Mormon pioneers the area was a desert of Sahara-like sand dunes that over time were buried and compressed into solid rock. Today those petrified dunes, still bearing the lines etched by ancient winds, have been exposed and, through the process of erosion, are gradually being changed back into sand again. For centuries the Fremont Indians farmed the fertile bottomland between the high cliffs, as did the Mormons, who planted orchards in the place they called Fruita. The orchards are now maintained by the park service, and summer and autumn visitors are welcome to help themselves to a few apples, apricots, cherries, plums, and pears. Please exercise restraint.

Attractions at Capitol Reef include petroglyphs mingled with artifacts left behind by Anglo settlers of the 19th century. Look for Merin Smith's blacksmith shop, the Elijah Behunin cabin, and the little one-room Fruita schoolhouse, idyllically situated amid orchards and soaring sandstone cliffs. Deer are usually browsing among the nearby fruit trees. Geological points of interest in the park include the 133-foot-wide Hickman Natural Bridge, 600-foot-high Chimney Rock, and an 800-foot-deep mini–Grand Canyon, Goose Necks Overlook, carved by the meandering Fremont River.

Near the western entrance, just off UT 24, are park headquarters, which include a visitors' center, a 70-site campground, and a grassy picnic ground shaded by ancient cottonwood trees of immense girth. The entire east–west scenic drive through the park is absolutely delightful, with plenty of roadside pull-offs along the way, including one next to a waterfall. Small crowds and the serene spirit that hovers about the place make Capitol Reef a most relaxing place to spend a day.

Torrey

As at Arches and Canyonlands, if you desire a roof over your head at night that's not made of canvas, you'll have to leave the park boundaries. On a hilltop just west of Capitol Reef stands Al Adamson's Rim Rock Resort Ranch, and just across the road the Best Western Capitol Reef Resort. Or you can continue 11 miles (18 km) west of the park to Torrey and stay either at the Wonderland Inn or the Capitol Reef Inn. The **Wonderland**, at the junction of Highways 24 and 12, is big, new, and one of the few motels in Wayne County with a swimming pool. The **Capitol Reef Inn** on Main Street is a small, older building that's enjoying quite a renaissance under the guidance of its new owner, San Francisco refugee Southey Swede.

For good food, good music, hip company, and interesting reading material, it's hard to beat the **Capitol Reef Cafe**. Stir-fried vegetables, espresso, imported ales, and sensational trout entrées make this unassuming-looking restaurant one of the best eating spots in southern Utah. Europeans love it, as do a growing number of the Teva-sandal set. Across the road from the inn is a reputable restaurant, **La Buena Vida Mexican Cafe**, which is open seasonally, from May until November. Adding to Torrey's cosmopolitan flavor is the Thousand Lakes RV Park at the west end of town, run by former Icelander Vally Reilly. Try Vally's "bag and breakfast" package, which includes a level grassy spot to pitch your tent, and hot coffee and fresh-baked muffins to warm you in the morning.

Bicknell and Loa

Nine miles (14½ km) west of Torrey on UT 24 is Bicknell, named after Thomas Bicknell, an Easterner who offered to donate a library to any town in Utah willing to rename itself in his honor. The library seems to have disappeared, but there *is* a movie house in town that's open on Friday and Saturday nights, and occasional live summer theater is staged in the neighboring hamlet of Teasdale. Next door to Jensen's Grocery is a liquor store, the only one in all of Wayne County. Like all liquor stores in the state, it's run according to guidelines laid down by the Utah State Liquor Commission, an august body made up entirely of teetotalers—some might say prohibitionists. In rural Utah the result is ill-stocked shelves and overpriced inventory where the only decision left to the shopper is whether to buy the red stuff or the white.

Bicknell sits on a high rocky plain between Thousand Lakes Mountain to the northeast and the Aquarius Plateau to the south. The latter, evidently, has nothing to do with the Broadway musical *Hair* or the so-called Age of Aquarius, the mention of which draws only blank stares here. No, the lifestyle in Bicknell is unadulterated country, a fact you'll grasp immediately when you step through the doors of the **Aquarius Cafe** on West Main Street. Decorated from floor to ceiling in a riotous Western Americana motif that includes branding irons, spurs, antlers, skulls, horse collars, barbed wire, beaver traps, "jackalope" postcards, and other cowboy collectibles, the Aquarius is an archetypical Western-style eatery. "Come as a stranger, leave as a friend," is the motto of owner Ted Stallman, who's been known to serenade dinner guests with his harmonica. Another straight-shooting eating establishment here is the **Sunglow Cafe**, on East Main, famous for pecan, pickle, oatmeal, and pinto-bean pies created by pastry chef Cula Ekker. You can buy a slice topped with real whipped cream or order a whole pie to go.

LOA

Bicknell's sister city is Loa, 8 miles (13 km) northwest on UT 24 and district headquarters of the Fishlake National Forest. A mile or two north of Loa is the **Chappell Cheese Company**, where you can buy cheese wholesale (freshly curdled "squeaky" cheddar is a favorite) to go with the pinto-bean pie and Mad Dog Red you picked up earlier in Bicknell.

The big surprise in town is the **Road Creek Inn** at 90 South Main Street. At two stories it's the tallest building in Loa and one of the oldest, dating back to 1912. The inn's 13 rooms and two suites are custom decorated with period furniture and are far and away the most elegant in the area. Tucked away in the basement you'll find a conference room with a big-screen television complete with Dolby sound, as well as an exercise room, a spa, and a billiard with three slate tables. Yes, billiards! The inn's menu is equally impressive, featuring fresh rainbow trout grown at the inn's private ranch. You can order it smoked, charbroiled, sautéed, butterflied, toasted, pâtéed, or on a bun as a trout hoagie. During its first two years of operation the inn changed ownership six times, but current manager Michael Deardon is confident Loa isn't too small to support a luxury hotel. In the works at the nearby Road Creek Ranch are plans for a fly-fishing school and a private upland game-bird hunting preserve.

SOUTHWESTERN UTAH

UTAH ROUTE 12

UT 24 continues west and north from Loa over Fish Lake High Top Plateau for 45 miles (72 km) until it joins U.S. 89/I-70 north of Richfield. But a much better route, especially if you're aiming toward Bryce Canyon and Zion national parks in southwestern Utah, is UT 12 south from Torrey. This all-weather, year-round two-lane road over the east shoulder of Boulder Mountain was only recently paved, and so far it remains a relatively unknown treasure. Three forest campgrounds along the way offer a total of 54 improved sites on a first-come basis: Singletree (18 miles/29 km south of Torrey), Pleasant Creek (8 miles/13 km south of Singletree), and Oak Creek (2 miles/3 km south of Pleasant Creek; not recommended for RVs or camp trailers). Stands of aspens, sprouted from root systems some botanists believe date back 10,000 years, are interspersed with ponderosa forests. Three scenic overlooks command breathtaking views of Capitol Reef, the Waterpocket Fold, the Henry Mountains, the Kaiparowits Plateau, and the Circle Cliffs.

THE BURR TRAIL

Thirty-five miles (56 km) south of Torrey is Boulder, site of one grocery, two gas stations, and the **Anasazi Indian Village State Park**, with excavated foundations, artifact displays, and a model reconstruction of the village. If you turn left at the second gas station, you'll find yourself heading east on a narrow lane known as the Burr Trail, one of the loveliest scenic back roads in Utah, and without a doubt the most controversial. Garfield County commissioners have for years yearned to upgrade and pave this shortcut to Bullfrog and Lake Powell. At the same time, various preservationist groups have worked hard to keep the road unimproved. Court battles and occasional gun battles have resulted, and as of now only the first 20 miles of the trail from Boulder are paved. If you'd like to see what all the shouting (and shooting) is about, it's worth a detour, at least as far as the picnic grounds at Deer Creek. Just be sure to peel that EARTH FIRST! sticker off your bumper before you set out.

ESCALANTE RIVER CANYONS

The 29-mile (46-km) stretch of UT 12 from Boulder south to Escalante abounds with wonders both natural and historic; for instance, you could easily spend your whole vacation just poking around the many narrow canyons of the Escalante River drainage system, which feeds into the Colorado. A petrified forest, cliff dwellings, an extensive wilderness area, two arches, and a natural bridge are just a few of the attractions that could waylay you for days. The most spectacular motoring side trip here is a back road between Boulder and Escalante that follows Hell's Backbone Ridge around the Box-Death Hollow Wilderness Area. The locals say it's passable by regular motorcar; but then, the locals tend to be a fearless bunch. Some backcountry guides who can show you around are **Bob and Sioux Cochran** in Boulder (Tel: 335-7480), **Escalante Canyon Outfitters** (Tel: 335-7311), and **Hondoo Rivers & Trails** in Torrey (Tel: 425-3519).

Calf Creek

If nothing else, you should at least stop at the Calf Creek Recreation Area, just off UT 12, some 9 miles (14½ km) south of Boulder. The signposted exit is at the bottom of a steep twisting downgrade and easy to miss when you're preoccupied with steering and braking. The public campground has an improved rest room with running water and flush toilets, and 12 campsites, which are available on a first-come basis and tend to fill up early in the day.

At the north end of the campground starts the five-mile round-trip trail to **Lower Calf Creek Falls**, a 126-foot-high waterfall and emerald pool at the end of a deep box canyon. Along the way look for brown trout and beaver dams in Calf Creek, eagles, hawks, and the remains of ancient cliff dwellings high on the sandstone walls.

Kodachrome Basin

From Escalante, UT 12 continues southwesterly to the sleepy Mormon village of Henrieville (no relation to Hanksville). Three miles (5 km) west of Henrieville turn south on a paved road to Kodachrome Basin, so named by members of the National Geographic Society, who also christened nearby Grosvenor Arch (after the former editor of *National Geographic* magazine). The basin is distinguished by a number of sandstone arches and something called sand pipes, which are vertical columns of rock extruded upward eons ago by subterranean pressures and then exposed as the surrounding entrada sandstone weathered away. Fresh spring water is available at the improved campground, as are showers and horseback and coach rides. And, of course, Kodak film. Advance reservations for the 26 sites are accepted; Tel: (800) 322-3770.

Tropic

Beyond the Kodachrome Basin turnoff the highway bends northward 5 miles (8 km) to Tropic, which is tropical only in comparison to the higher-elevated Panguitch, another 30 miles (48 km) west. Like Panguitch, Tropic serves as sort of a bedroom community to Bryce Canyon National Park, offering two bed and breakfasts (including **Francisco's**) and the **Bryce Valley Inn**, and, improbably, Argentinean fare at **Doug's Cafe**. The main point of interest in town is the **Bryce Pioneer Village**, which includes a museum and the log cabin of early settler Ebenezer Bryce. Visitors might also want to take a short hike that begins at the bridge on the north end of town and ends at **Mossy Cave**, a natural grotto situated just inside the boundaries of Bryce Canyon National Park.

BRYCE CANYON NATIONAL PARK

The well-marked turnoff to Bryce Canyon, Utah's second-oldest national park, established in 1928, is 9 miles (14½ km) northwest of Tropic, off UT 12. Bryce is not really a canyon, but rather a steep and eroded mountainside that takes its name from Ebenezer Bryce, who allegedly described it as "one helluva place to lose a cow."

Early Paiute Indians saw it differently. One legend says they called the place *Unka timpe-wa-wince-pock-ich,* which roughly translated means "red rocks standing like men in a bowl-shaped canyon." The spectacular maze of anthropomorphic statuary is formed of limestone minerals in a sandstone sediment. It's the minerals—iron and manganese—that give the sediment an estimated 60 varieties of colors ranging from white to vermilion. The park itself takes the shape of an arc that extends north and south along the Paunsaugunt Plateau. The plateau is tilted so that the farther south you go, the higher up you get, all the way from the Upper Sonoran life zone at the Bryce Canyon Lodge, near the north end of the park, to the Canadian life zone at Rainbow and Yovimpa Points, to the extreme south.

Bryce Canyon Trails

Two campgrounds, with a total of 218 units, are available inside the park on a first-come, first-served basis. Back-country camping is prohibited except at designated sites along the Under-the-Rim and Riggs Spring Loop trails. In difficulty these trails range from easy (an along-the-rim trail) to strenuous (any trails that entail going below the rim). The Rim Trail begins at Fairyland Point in the north end of the park and runs south five and a half miles to Bryce Point. This 10-mile round-trip hike takes in the park's three most popular overlooks, Sunrise, Sunset, and Inspiration points, any of which can be the start or finish of your hike. Of the under-the-rim hikes, the easiest is the one-and-a-half-mile Queen's Garden Trail, which begins and ends at Sunrise Point. The Fairyland Loop Trail, the Navajo Loop, and the Peekaboo Loop are all more strenuous; you may find the trip through Queen's Garden a lot more enjoyable from horseback. Contact **Bryce-Zion-Grand Trail Rides** for detailed information; Box 128, Tropic, UT 84776. Tel: 834-5219 in summer; Tel: 679-8665 in off-season.

STAYING AND DINING AT BRYCE CANYON

The 35-mile round-trip Rim Road to Yovimpa Point was completed in 1934, when automobiles weren't very wide. Because of the steep grade and the narrow shoulders, Bryce isn't the greatest place to bicycle. A better idea is to dress up like the Great Gatsby and get decadent at the **Bryce Canyon Lodge**.

The lodge is a prime example of the so-called rustic architectural style originated by Gilbert Stanley Underwood, and the only one of its genre in the area that hasn't burned to the ground at least once. Recently renovated with great attention paid to period authenticity, the lodge sits among ponderosa pines at the north end of the park, within easy walking distance of the Bryce Canyon Amphitheater. Including the Lincoln log–style auxiliary buildings, the lodge offers three deluxe suites, a studio, 70 motel rooms, and 40 cabin units. Dinner in the rustic 1930s-style dining room is by reservation, and if you phone the cashier before 9:00 P.M., the kitchen will prepare a picnic lunch for the morrow's outing.

The lodge opens in mid-April and closes for the winter November 1, and, as with other TWS-operated lodges at Zion and the Grand Canyon (TW Services is the official park concessionaire), is usually booked up months in advance. Of the three lodges, Bryce is the best if what you're looking for is peace and quiet. However, if you've got kids, within about ten minutes they'll be crying, "But what is there to *do* here?"

In that case, go instead to **Best Western Ruby's Inn**, a thriving establishment just beyond the park's north entrance. What began as a forest retreat, built in the early 1930s by Ruben and Minnie Syrett, looks something like Knott's Berry Farm today—or Ma and Pa Kettle gone corporate. The ever-expanding inn now includes a 216-room motel, a steak house, an indoor pool, a trailer park, a convention center, a general store and gas station— even its own film-finishing lab. And unlike the lodge (but like the park), it's open year-round.

Stationed in the lobby you'll find a number of local concessionaires pitching horseback rides, helicopter flights, guided tours, and shuttle services, as well as mountain-bike and car rentals.

Across the road from Ruby's Inn is Old Bryce Town, a recent fabrication of a mythical frontier village that boasts a broad spectrum of Western Americana, including everything from totem poles to cigar-store Indians. You can shop for Native American handicrafts, pose for a sepia-toned portrait of yourself wearing frontier garb, or pan for gold nuggets and sapphires, among other activities. Kids will enjoy visiting the petting zoo and watching Skeeter, the amazing trick pony, and his cowboy-poet partner, Hamilton.

West of Bryce Canyon, UT 12 twists and turns and tunnels its way through beautiful **Red Canyon** before coming to an end 13 miles (21 km) later at the junction with U.S. 89. From here you have a choice of proceeding south on U.S. 89 toward Zion National Park or dallying awhile in the high country of the Markagunt Plateau, west of U.S. 89. Summer and fall are the best times to venture onto the plateau, and often the only times you can count on the roads being clear of snow. First we discuss the plateau— Cedar Breaks and Brian Head—and then we return to U.S. 89 down toward Zion.

CEDAR BREAKS
NATIONAL MONUMENT

Branching west off U.S. 89 some 21 miles (34 km) south of the junction of UT 12 and U.S. 89, **Scenic Byway 14** is gorgeous in late September and early October, when the aspen groves are in their full autumnal splendor. Seven miles (11 km) north of the junction, leading south and west out of the town of Panguitch, **Scenic Byway 143** is equally impressive. Either road will take you to the same place, the top of the Markagunt Plateau and Cedar Breaks National Monument—an eroded amphitheater of castellated limestone outcroppings almost identical to those found at Bryce. The main difference: At 10,000 feet above sea level, Cedar Breaks is higher than Bryce, and there are no foot trails leading to the bottom of the amphitheater, 2,000 feet below the forested rim. There are no rooms or services here either; if you want to stay overnight you'll have to camp out (no reservations taken for the 30-site campground) or drive 8 miles (13 km) north from Cedar Breaks on UT 143 to Brian Head Ski Resort.

Brian Head

Long one of America's best-kept winter recreation secrets, uncrowded Brian Head Ski Resort used to turn into a ghost town each summer after the snow melted. But thanks to aggressive promotion and a full slate of summer and fall activities, the area has lately turned into a bustling year-round resort community and mountain-bike mecca second only to Moab in popularity. The big difference is, at Brian Head you're really biking in the mountains.

There are 13 designated bike trails around 11,307-foot Brian Head Peak, routes that can be taken as a single trip or linked together as a grand tour of the Markagunt Plateau. The trails range from easy to expert, weaving in and out of pine forests, crossing meadows carpeted with wildflowers, and hauling up short of breathtaking redrock drop-offs.

Unlike in other national forests in Utah, rangers of the Dixie National Forest have assisted the fat-tire revolution by grooming bicycle trails and installing dozens of directional signs. For maps, rentals, or information, there are bike shops in town, including **George's Ski Shop**, 612 South Brian Head Boulevard (Tel: 677-2013) and **Mur-**

phy's in the Brian Head Hotel, 223 West Hunter Ridge Drive (Tel: 677-2012).

The resort town itself strives for a laid-back lifestyle that is an improbable hybrid of rock-ribbed Mormon conservatism and southern Californian liberalism. Your chances of finding a room at Brian Head, which boasts a housing base of 3,000 beds, are pretty good. Nicest is the **Brian Head Hotel** with Jacuzzi baths and large, well-appointed rooms. The **Soda Rock Inn** comes in second. Brian Head Hotel's **Summit Dining Room** serves a broad selection of dishes at dinner and has an impressive wine list. If you prefer more moderate altitudes and prices, drive the 12 scenic miles (19 km) down the mountain (north) from Brian Head to Parowan, southern Utah's oldest settlement and a paragon of rustic Mormon charm nestled against the western base of the Markagunt Plateau. The **Best Western Swiss Village Inn and Restaurant** and **Jedediah's Inn & Restaurant** here are both good family-oriented establishments.

BRYCE TO ZION

Bryce Canyon and Zion national parks are commonly thought of as sister destinations, although they are 84 miles (134 km) apart. The usual route to get from one to the other is U.S. 89, which runs along the east side of the Markagunt Plateau through **Long Valley**. It's a delightful drive that winds in and out of sub-Alpine forested hills and alongside irrigated alfalfa fields. In places the eroded red-rock mountainsides look a lot like those at Bryce Canyon and Cedar Breaks. "Must stops" include the well-stocked tourist information booth at the south end of Hatch, a wide spot in the road 8 miles (13 km) south of the junction of UT 12 and U.S. 89.

Overnight accommodations along the way tend to be on the drab side, although if you're camping out the Bryce-Zion KOA campground near Glendale affords one of the best views you'll ever see out your tent flap.

In Glendale, south of Hatch on U.S. 89, Shirley Phelan now operates the historic **Smith Hotel** as a bed-and-breakfast inn, and explains that it was built by an early pioneer who had the same name as Mormon church founder Joseph Smith. The rest of Glendale's meager business district includes an apple-cider outlet and a crafts shop dealing in handmade quilts.

Orderville, 4 miles (6½ km) south of Glendale on U.S.

89, is historically significant as the site of a failed experiment in communism, or what Brigham Young, in 1874, called the United Order. Citizens living under the order were required to work hard and live frugally, turning over all their surplus food and commodities to the bishop's storehouse, from whence it was distributed to other members of the community "according to need." Although the experiment was short-lived, vestiges of the idea can be seen today in the Mormon church's well-organized welfare system.

Today much of downtown Orderville looks as if it could dearly use a handout. Out-of-business storefronts have been turned into warehouses, with eclectic window displays combining old farm implements, dusty saddle tack, mineral samples, plumbing fixtures, and faded religious posters.

At the east end of town, the Daughters of the Utah Pioneers operate a small one-room museum. There are no set business hours, but a sign out front lists two phone numbers you can dial in the event you find the door locked. Call and it will be opened.

SCENIC BYWAY 9

At Mount Carmel Junction, 5 miles (8 km) south of Glendale on U.S. 89, Scenic Byway 9 branches west for 13 miles (21 km), climbing over the Markagunt Plateau before descending into Zion National Park. The central establishment at this unincorporated crossroads is the **Thunderbird Best Western Motel**, a landmark dating to 1931, when Jack and Fern Morrison established a filling station here. Today, besides a gas station, the complex features a 66-room motel, an RV park, a gift shop, a swimming pool, a restaurant, and a golf course.

Scenic Byway 9, also known as the Zion–Mount Carmel Highway, serves as a back door into Zion National Park and is one of the most audacious road-building feats in history, begun in 1927 and completed three years later. From the base of Checkerboard Mesa, the two-lane road descends 3,000 vertical feet, passing through two long tunnels blasted through solid Navajo sandstone before joining UT 9 at the bottom of Zion Canyon.

ZION NATIONAL PARK

Zion National Park is Utah's most popular national park and its oldest, first set aside in 1909 as Mukuntuweap

National Monument. Like Bryce and the North Rim of the Grand Canyon, Zion was heavily promoted as a tourist destination in the early part of the century by the Union Pacific Railroad, and was accorded national park status in 1919. The 147,000-acre reservation ranges in elevation from 3,640 to 8,726 feet, and in several places the gradient is vertical. At the north end of the canyon, for example, the Virgin River runs through a narrow gorge that is 50 feet wide but 2,000 feet deep.

At Bryce you tend to look down at the scenery, but at Zion you'll spend a lot of time craning your neck upward, like a Midwesterner lost in Manhattan. Indeed, towering monoliths such as the Great White Throne resemble nothing so much as nature's own skyscrapers. Here and there the many-hued stone walls recede into alcoves and amphitheaters beneath verdant hanging gardens, from which wispy waterfalls drizzle and drip into shady pools. The first Anglo explorers were moved to name such places Court of the Patriarchs and Angels Landing. It's no wonder; Zion looks a lot like a piece of heaven on earth.

The heart of the park is the deep and narrow Zion Canyon, which trends north to south and is just wide enough to accommodate the Virgin River and a two-lane road. Cottonwoods, maples, and oak trees abound on the canyon floor, while the vegetation on the cliff tops runs to the more desertlike piñons and junipers. At the south end the park headquarters and visitors' center on Route 9 are open year-round with exhibits, book sales, slide programs, and a museum; Tel: 772-3256. Also at the south end are two public campgrounds: **Watchman**, with 229 units, and **South Campground**, with 144 (sites are taken on a first-come basis). Because of the large number of visitors (two million annually), the park service encourages a low-impact approach here to protect the fragile ecosystems. Bicycles are not allowed off the roadways or in the Mount Carmel–Zion tunnels, and due to the heavy auto traffic, bicycling on the roadways can be hazardous.

Just north of the visitors' center, at the far side of a bridge spanning the Virgin River, turn left off UT 9 (the Mount Carmel–Zion Highway) onto the Zion Canyon Scenic Drive that runs north alongside the river to **Zion Lodge**. Built by the Union Pacific Railroad in 1925 and then rebuilt after it burned to the ground in 1960, the lodge is beautifully situated on the canyon floor, encircled by soaring cliffs and pinnacles. Rooms range from motel rooms to Western-style cabins to suites, all managed by TW Services, the official park concessionaire (the same outfit that operates the lodges at Bryce and at the North Rim of the Grand Canyon). Unlike the other two facilities, Zion Lodge is open year-round, and because Zion is such a popular summer-vacation spot, winter may be a good time to book a room.

The lodge includes a gift shop and family restaurant (dinner reservations are necessary, Tel: 772-3213), and serves as the main depot for the open-air shuttle tram, which departs from the parking lot hourly in the summer from 11:00 A.M. to 4:00 P.M. The tram runs north as far as the Temple of Sinawava, passing such sights as the Grotto and the Great White Throne. Another enjoyable mode of transportation initiated by TWS in 1991 is an antique (1936) White touring bus with a rollback canvas top. Inquire at the lodge desk for departure times.

As lovely as Zion is from the road, it's one place you must hike in order fully to appreciate its beauty. The trails range from paved thoroughfares to footpaths into backcountry as rugged and undeveloped as you'll find anywhere. (And don't overlook the **Kolob Canyons**, a separate and relatively uncrowded northern section of the park just east of I-15, about 18 miles/29 km south of Cedar City.)

The half-mile hike from the road to upper and lower **Emerald Pools** is popular but heavily travelled. In order to preserve the area, the park service recently banned swimming in the pools. You may still cool off by wading the ankle-deep waters of the Virgin River into the Narrows—a hike that begins at the north end of the Zion Canyon Scenic Drive and remains the most popular of all Zion trails. Less crowded is the trail to **Angels Landing**, a spectacular overlook 1,500 feet above the canyon floor. A series of 21 switchbacks ("Walters Wiggels") chiseled into solid rock back in 1926, the Angels Landing trail is another of the park's man-made wonders and the pedestrian equivalent of the Mount Carmel–Zion Highway. But it's definitely not recommended for small children or acrophobics.

SPRINGDALE

Hard against the south entrance of Zion park on Scenic Byway 9, the community of Springdale offers a half dozen eateries, a dozen motels, and five bed-and-breakfast inns. Of late the town has attracted a growing population of artists and craftspeople, whose work is displayed alongside rock clocks and lapidary lamps in local gift shops. The towering cliffs that surround Springdale are every bit as spectacular as those inside the park, so if you stay here you won't have to send out for scenery.

The **Under the Eaves Guest House** resembles a cottage transported from merrie olde England; the **Harvest House Bed & Breakfast,** owned and operated by Boston refugees Steven and Barbara Cooper, is especially nice. Barbara's breakfasts, featuring homemade granola and polenta and eggs with tomato sauce, are legendary. Rooms with good views include those at the **Canyon Ranch Motel,** the **Cliffrose Lodge & Gardens,** and the **Best Western Driftwood Lodge.**

The **Bit and Spur Saloon** is an unassuming contender for the title of best Mexican restaurant in Utah; **Flanigan's Inn** and the **Driftwood Restaurant** are good family-dining bets, and the **Bumbleberry Inn** is the *only* place on earth where you can get a slice of the "famous" bumbleberry pie (made with blueberries and whatever other berry is in season).

Springdale is a long, narrow town, and virtually every commercial establishment faces the same street, Zion Park Boulevard (a.k.a. UT 9). Tourism is booming, so plan on making room reservations at least six months in advance.

Grafton

One place that many visitors look for but can't seem to find is the ghost town of Grafton, where scenes from *Butch Cassidy and the Sundance Kid* were filmed. The turnoff isn't marked, but you can get there by turning south off UT 9 in Rockville (4 miles/6½ km south of Springdale) at 200 East, or Bridge Road. Cross the bridge and turn right on Grafton Road. After 4 dusty miles you'll come upon the picturesque adobe schoolhouse where Etta Place, played by Katharine Ross, bided her time while waiting for her lover, Sundance (Robert Redford), and pal Butch (Paul Newman) to show up. Regrettably, the log cabin where Ross and Redford enjoyed their steamy rendezvous burned to the ground in 1988.

On the way back to Rockville pause to reflect on the meaning of life at the pathetic little Grafton graveyard, a windswept and truly bleak testament to the unromantic realities of the real-life frontier. Especially moving is the obelisk marking the final resting place of the Berry family, all "killed by Indians" on April 2, 1866.

UTAH'S DIXIE

All of southwestern Utah's early settlements, with the exception of the rip-roaring mining camp of Silver Reef, were founded in the latter half of the 19th century by Mormon farmers and ranchers. The temperate frost-free winters tempted the colonists to try their hand at growing cotton, silk, sorghum, pecans, pomegranates, and other subtropical crops, hence the common nickname for this region, Utah's Dixie.

ST. GEORGE

St. George, 43 miles (69 km) southwest of Zion park via Scenic Byway 9 and then I-15, is often called "the other Palm Springs," a sunbaked mecca for migratory retirees— snowbirds—who roost here each winter. Come spring-time, thousands of fun-seeking college students on break also descend on the town, which then becomes "the other Fort Lauderdale."

The first and most famous of the snowbirds was Mormon church leader and Utah's first territorial governor, Brigham Young. Young's New England–style winter home here is now preserved as a historical landmark, along with 22 other examples of pioneer architecture included in a nine-block-long **St. George Walking Tour** that begins at the corner of St. George Boulevard and 100 East. Ask for a map and guidebook at the Daughters of the Utah Pioneers Museum (145 North 100 East, Tel: 628-7274) or inquire at the Chamber of Commerce office in the old Washington County Courthouse (97 East St. George Boulevard, Tel: 628-1658).

St. George is a veritable treasure trove of early Mormon buildings, but by far the most impressive is the white alabaster St. George Temple, 300 East and 400 South. Begun in 1871, it was the first Mormon temple built in Utah; the oldest still in use, it stands as a monument to the dedication and ingenuity of its builders. The makeshift pile driver used to firm up the building's foundation, for example, employed a 1,000-pound cast-iron cannon manufactured in France and previously used by Napoleon in his siege of Moscow.

Like all Mormon temples, St. George's is closed to all but church members in good standing. Visitors are welcome to wander about the grounds, however. Guided tours of the Tabernacle (built shortly after the temple), at the corner of Main and Tabernacle streets, are available; Tel: 628-4072.

By way of culture, St. George is home to Dixie College and the **St. George Art Museum**, at 175 East 200 North, which purports to have works on exhibit by such name-brand masters as Van Gogh, Degas, and Rembrandt. You be the judge; Tel: 634-5800. Nightlife consists primarily of teenagers driving up and down St. George Boulevard in search of some Saturday-night action. The oldsters, meanwhile, have already found it in the slot machines and the all-you-can-eat buffets at the **Peppermill Casino**, 26 miles (42 km) south on I-15, just across the border in Mesquite, Nevada.

Otherwise, what folks in St. George do for fun is golf (eight courses) and exercise. St. George hosts the state's biggest marathon and the annual World Senior Games, and is home to one of the nation's ritziest fat farms, the National Institute of Fitness.

Dick's Cafe and Gift Shop at 114 East St. George Boulevard is famous not so much for its American cuisine as for its celebrity clientele. Back in the days when Hollywood Westerns were routinely shot on location in the nearby red-rock foothills, everyone ate at Dick's. St. George also has two sets of golden arches and more fast-food restaurants of all kinds than any other southern Utah city. Many of the sit-down places are the all-you-can-eat-buffet variety, which is such a big draw in Nevada. If your taste buds start to yawn, wake them up at with exquisite Continental cuisine and Italian fare at **McGuire's**, 1235 South Bluff Street. If they're really sleepy, drive 15 minutes north on UT 18 to the one-of-a-kind **Dis I'L Dew Steak House** in Dammeron Valley, where fussy diners are invited to broil their own steaks amid rustic surroundings reminiscent of the Long Branch Saloon. Closed Mondays and Tuesdays, when the cook rides out to wrangle more provisions; Tel: 574-2757.

St. George has an abundance of motels, and your chances of finding a room are good even if you forgot to make reservations, provided it's not spring-break time and no major athletic event is under way. The St. George Holiday Inn Resort Hotel, the Days Inn & Four Seasons Convention Center, the Best Western Coral Hills Motel, the Green Valley Resort, and the Bluffs Motel are all recommendable. An outstanding bed-and-breakfast establishment is the **Greene Gate Village**, a tiny pioneer town surrounded by an elegant courtyard with a swimming pool and garden hot tub. The **Seven Wives Inn** exudes Victorian charm and serves a sumptuous breakfast that'll save you later on lunch.

CEDAR CITY

Cedar City is southwestern Utah's other commercial and cultural hub, situated 50 miles (80 km) northeast of St. George via I-15 (and 18 miles/29 km west of Cedar Breaks via UT 14). Thousands of feet higher in elevation than St. George and with a commensurately cooler climate, Cedar City is where sunbirds from Arizona and Nevada retreat in the summer to get away from the desert heat.

Cedar City was first settled by Mormon pioneers in 1851 as an iron-ore smelting center, but heavy industry has long since yielded to tourism, agriculture, and other nonsmokestack industries. Each June the town hosts a statewide "Olympics" called the Utah Summer Games, and from late June through early September stages the annual **Utah Shakespearean Festival**. What started out years ago as a midsummer night's pipe dream of Southern Utah State University drama teacher Fred Adams has evolved into a major happening that engages nearly every citizen in town and draws acting talent of national stature. For information Tel: 586-7884.

Begin by stopping at the Chamber of Commerce visitors' center at 286 North Main Street (directly east of the Town & Country Inn), where you can restock your glove compartment with free brochures and also pick up a calendar of events; Tel: 586-5124. A free pamphlet outlines a tour of Cedar City's historical sites, but the area isn't as compact—or as interesting—as the one in St. George, since most of the landmarks have been razed and replaced by markers.

History buffs won't be disappointed at the **Iron Mission State Historical Park and Pioneer Museum**, situated about ¾ mile (1 km) north of the Chamber of Commerce at 588 North Main Street (old Highway 91), which houses, among other things, an impressive collection of horse-drawn wagons, buggies, and stagecoaches.

The **Black Swan** at 164 South Main serves "ye olde luncheon fare" in keeping with the Elizabethan summer-theater motif. Seven-course dinners, including lamb, poultry, fish, and pork selections, are available by reservation only; Tel: 586-7873. The **Market Grill** at 2290 West 400 North rustles up steaks and hearty breakfasts at a reasonable price. **Milt's Stage Shop**, a scenic five-mile drive up the canyon (east on UT 14) specializes in steak and seafood dinners. Reservations are recommended; Tel: 586-9344. If you're just looking for a light snack, try the soup, sandwiches, and desserts at **Yogurt Junction**, 911 South Main.

Cedar City is a popular stopover for the interstate motor-home set, which may help to explain the popularity of the **Best Western Town & Country Inn**, a property that sprawls across about ten acres of prime downtown real estate at the junction of UT 56 (200 North) and U.S. 91 (Main Street). If you're looking for a spot to park your big rig within walking distance of everything, this is the place. If your rig is so big you can barely steer it off the freeway, then try the **Cedar City Holiday Inn** at 1575 West 200 North. Another port that will do in a storm is the **Quality Inn** on South Main.

BACK ROADS THROUGH UTAH'S DIXIE

Thanks to Interstates 15 and 70 (dubbed Cocaine Lane by the Utah Highway Patrol in reference to its popularity as a conduit for illegal narcotics), a lot of travellers nowadays just whistle through our Dixie on their way to New York or Los Angeles without bothering to stop for anything unless they're pulled over. That's too bad, because Washington and Iron counties—that is, the St. George/Cedar City region—have some back roads that make excellent scenic detours, especially if you're looking to take a break from the hustle and bustle of the national-parks circuit.

THE CEDAR CITY – ST. GEORGE PINE VALLEY LOOP

Follow UT 56 (200 North Main), which heads due west from Cedar City. In a few miles the suburbs give way to sagebrush and juniper, with not much in the way of fellow travellers except jackrabbits, hawks, and ravens. The highway skirts the south end of the Escalante Desert, part of the all-but-unpopulated portion of Utah known as "the west desert." Savor the solitude, and thrill to the sensation of having the road all to yourself.

About 20 miles (32 km) out you'll come to a marked turnoff to **Old Iron Town**, a ghost town a short distance off the paved road. Iron Town was the site of a pioneer iron-smelting experiment, and several stone foundations and two beehive-shaped smelting ovens survive. This no-fee attraction includes a covered picnic ground; just be careful not to step on any snakes.

Return to the highway and continue west through Newcastle to the junction with UT 18. Turn left and follow the highway, which goes south between alfalfa fields, then gradually ascends Big Mountain and enters the **Dixie National Forest**. At the tiny town of Central, turn left and follow the signs to **Pine Valley**, a sort of landlocked Brigadoon that's 20 miles north of St. George but a world apart climatically. Surrounded by granite peaks and forests of ponderosa pine, it looks more like a lost piece of Northern California's High Sierras than it does the Southwest.

Pine Valley was first settled by Anglos in 1855, after a cowboy by the name of Isaac Riddle stumbled upon the place while looking for a lost cow. The village center-piece is the picturesque white clapboard Pine Valley Chapel, a Mormon meetinghouse built in 1868 and still in use today.

Follow the road that runs east from the chapel into the **Pine Valley Recreation Area**, a lovely forested retreat that consists of four campgrounds, three picnic areas, a babbling brook, and a small reservoir. The only commercial establishment here is the **Pine Valley Lodge**, where you can rent a cabin, ride a horse, or hire a backcountry guide.

Return to Highway 18 the way you came and continue the few miles south to **Veyo**, which, for a tiny town, offers quite a lot to do. There's the Spanish Trail Roller Rink, for instance, and Aunt Effie's Home Cookin', where, according to the sign out front, you can sample the best gravy on earth. Turn left, just past the bridge at the south end of town, onto a narrow lane running east off UT 18, and you'll come to **Veyo Pool Resort**, a swimming hole that looks like something lifted right out of a Larry McMurtry novel.

The resort was founded by homesteader James Cottam in 1927, and has remained in the family ever since. The swimming pool, fed by a 98°F natural hot spring, is the main attraction, but there's also a snack bar, where Melbourne Cottam ("Grampa" to his customers) or his daughter, Joanne Balen, will hand dip you an ice-cream cone or fry up one of their famous pronto pups, more commonly known as hot dogs. Next door is a shady picnic ground tucked away at the bottom of a lava-rock gorge; it's free to the public. Veyo Pool Resort is open 11:00 A.M. to 10:00 P.M., from the last weekend in March until Labor Day.

From Veyo, UT 18 continues south past the cinder cone of an extinct volcano and through the Dammeron Valley to **Snow Canyon State Park**, a near replica of Las Vegas's Red Rock Canyon, but with black-lava rock beds mixed in with the red and mauve crenellated sandstone buttes. Moviegoers may recognize Snow Canyon as the meeting place of Robert Redford and Jane Fonda in *The Electric Horseman*.

A 20-minute hike along a well-marked footpath leads to the Lava Caves, three ancient volcanic tubes that serve as a popular hangout for local spelunkers and bats. At the south end of the park is an improved campground, and just a bit farther south on the right-hand side of the road are riding stables where you can hire a horse by the hour or charter a hayride through the park along a delightful back road that's off limits to motor vehicles.

Five miles (8 km) south of Snow Canyon, UT 18 enters St. George and becomes Bluff Street, from which you can get onto I-15 again at the south end of town.

HURRICANE VALLEY

Another roundabout tour of Utah's Dixie begins 8 miles (13 km) north of St. George. Exit I-15 at Harrisburg Junction and drive east on Scenic Byway 9 for 9 miles (14½ km) to the twin cities of **Hurricane** and—2 miles (3 km) farther north on UT 17—**La Verkin**. The way the locals pronounce the names, the two places rhyme, as in "Hurrikin" and "La Vurrikin."

The two towns are small but bustling. Insect rancher Afton Fawcett of Hurricane, for example, is the biggest exporter of red harvester ants (the kind you find in toy ant farms) in the country. Hurricane is also world headquarters of the Chums corporation, manufacturers of those colorful eyeglass retainers that are de rigueur for fashion-conscious outdoorsmanship.

Get oriented at the **Hurricane Valley Pioneer Heritage Park,** on the corner of Main and State streets in Hurricane, which is run by volunteers of the local Green Thumb Society. Leave your car there and stroll south one block, past the historic Dixie Hotel and Bradshaw Home to the Alamo-esque Chums World Headquarters. Besides eyeglass retainers, you can shop for Hellowear-brand sportswear at the factory outlet, or sample vegetarian cuisine at **Chumley's** restaurant. Admire sleek bodies in clingy Spandex bodysuits peddling past on mountain bikes as you nosh on tofu, sprouts, and whole grains.

Now that good health is on your mind, you might want to check out **Pah Tempe Hot Springs Resort**, situated at the bottom of a gorge off Highway 17 about midway between Hurricane and La Verkin. Just south of the bridge spanning the Virgin River, look for a road called Enchanted Way that leads to the resort. Open daily from 9:00 A.M. until 10:00 P.M., except Tuesdays and Wednesdays, Pah Tempe consists of one swimming pool plus a string of nine natural mineral baths, varying in temperature from 104 to 107°F. Meditation and yoga classes, massage therapy, and vegetarian fare in a tobacco-free environment will soon have you intoning "Ommmm. . . ." If you like you can stay overnight in one of seven motel rooms, or camp out in the resort's **Rain Forest Campground**. (Note: Following a 5.9-magnitude earthquake that jolted southwestern Utah in the fall of 1992, Pah Tempe's hot springs began to run dry. Geologists say the change is the result of a slippage in the Hurricane Fault, but resort owner Ken Anderson alleges human error, and has petitioned the Washington County Water Conservancy District to help turn the water back on. As of press time, no immediate solutions were in sight.)

KANAB

From Hurricane in southwestern Utah it's about 100 miles (160 km) to the North Rim of the Grand Canyon via UT 59, which becomes AZ 389 when it crosses the border (AZ 389 passes through Fredonia, Arizona). Alternately, you can double back through Zion National Park on Scenic Byway 9 to Mount Carmel Junction, and then head south on U.S. 89 to Kanab and on to Fredonia, and, as with the other route, to U.S. 89A. Of the two routes, U.S. 89 through Kanab is infinitely more interesting, passing through the sort of generic Western topography that has served as a backdrop for countless shoot-'em-ups dating back to the time of Zane Grey, who is said to have stayed in Kanab in 1912 while writing *Riders of the Purple Sage*. It's a fair guess that any Hollywood actor who ever sat in a saddle rode into Kanab at one time or another.

Two miles (3 km) north of Kanab in Three Lakes Canyon you'll pass a couple of roadside curiosities worth slowing down for. **Moqui Cave**, with its plaster dinosaur façade suggestive of a set from *Pee Wee's Big Adventure,* bills itself as "the most unique gift shop in Southern Utah." The museum here includes items dating back 140 million years, everything from petrified dinosaur tracks to a black-light mineral display.

A stone's throw north of the cave on the west side of

the road is Montezuma's Campground and RV Park, unremarkable except that it sits beside a pond that is the only known habitat of *Oxyloma haydeni kanabensis*—better known, if at all, as the Kanab ambersnail, an endangered and thus protected species. The snail's natural enemies include largemouth bass and one Brandt Child, the campground's owner. Child is convinced that a fortune in Spanish gold is cached in an underwater cave on his property and he would dearly like to drain the pond to prove his theory. Trouble is, the U.S. Fish & Wildlife Service won't allow it, and the fact that the cave is rumored to be guarded by ghosts doesn't help either. The upshot is that you can camp overnight for six bucks and angle for bass at Three Lakes, but you can't let the water out. And you'd better not mess with the snails or the estimated "2,000 Aztec ghosts on guard duty."

Overnight accommodations in Kanab are like the food, adequate but not destined to be among the highlights of your trip. The **Shilo Inn** is probably the best; the Four Seasons Motor Inn, Quail Park Lodge, and Parry Lodge will do. A better idea is to pass through during daylight hours, spend your time poking around the colorful surrounding countryside, and continue down the road.

A low-budget version of Hollywood's Universal Studio tour can be had at **Lopeman's Frontier Movie Town**, 297 West Center Street. Open from April through October, this make-believe Western town features movie sets, false-front shops, a snack bar, historical exhibits, and occasional gunfights during dinner shows. Because groups are preferred to lone travellers, it's best to call ahead; Tel: 644-5337.

The **Best Friends Animal Sanctuary Thrift Store** at 93 West Center might seem a strange place to go looking for information about many of the historic movie locations and natural wonders in the Kanab area. But it's the best place to find it. Best Friends is a nonprofit outfit dedicated to finding homes for unwanted animals, 1,500 of which are kept at the organization's ranch north of town at a place it calls Angel Canyon. The canyon and ranch are a bit tricky to find, so stop first at the thrift store for a map and inquire about their guided jeep tour, which will take you to old Indian kiva ruins, an underground lake, and other various and sundry "ancient and modern wonders from the dinosaurs to Hollywood."

Among the modern wonders, look for such esoteric attractions as Lone Ranger's Bridge, Mackenna's Trail, and Spiral Rocks, where canine film star Rin Tin Tin stood sentry over the opening credits. Other movies and television series that have been shot in the canyon include *Drums Along the Mohawk, Calamity Jane, Have Gun Will Travel, Gunsmoke, Death Valley Days,* and *The Man Who Loved Cat Dancing.*

NORTHERN ARIZONA

THE FREDONIA AREA

Fredonia, Arizona, 7 miles (11 km) south of Kanab at the junction of AZ 389 and U.S. 89A, is a lonely-looking outpost with an industrial base that includes one petrochemical plant, an idle lumber mill, half a dozen package stores, one steak house, two utilitarian motels, and one bed-and-breakfast inn, the **Jackson House** on North Main Street. Dating to the early 1900s, it was one of the first permanent homes built in Fredonia and served as a center of civic activities, dances, and parties. The inn today is one of the few houses here that does not have wheels, and its main section has been maintained as it was when first built. Because of Arizona's more liberal liquor laws (no need to buy an ersatz private-club membership), Kanabians often drive down to Fredonia to enjoy a cocktail with their dinners.

Like Utah, Arizona keeps mountain standard time, but that can be misleading in the summer because Arizona chooses not to observe daylight saving time. The result is that when you enter Arizona from Utah during daylight saving months you should set your watch back one hour. That is, unless you cross the border at Hildale, 23 miles (37 km) south of Hurricane on UT 59/AZ 389, in which event you should set your clock back a hundred years.

Formerly known as Short Creek, the twin towns of **Hildale**, Utah, and **Colorado City**, Arizona, are home to about 4,000 members of the United Effort Order. An offshoot of the Mormon church, this small sect still practices polygamy in more or less open defiance of the law. The fashion in town is ankle-length gowns and long braided tresses for women, conservative haircuts and traditional Western wear for the menfolk. Like the Amish, adherents of the order are polite but standoffish around strangers, particularly those who ask a lot of nosy questions. So don't inquire as to the number of wives the filling station attendant has, and don't even hazard a guess as to whether there's a wine list at the newly opened family-style **Mark Twain Restaurant**.

Pipe Spring National Monument

Northern Arizona's Highway 389 more or less follows the tracks of the Domínguez-Escalante expedition of 1776, which, having failed to chart an overland route to the Pacific Ocean, retreated to Santa Fe across what is now called the Arizona Strip (the cutoff part of Arizona between the Grand Canyon and the Utah border). From Hildale to Fredonia it's a lot of high, dry, and barren country. You can only imagine what a vision Winsor Castle was to thirst-crazed wayfarers of the past century. Built in the 1870s by Mormon settlers Anson and Emeline Winsor, the castle today is part of Pipe Spring National Monument, 20 miles (32 km) southeast of Hildale and 14 miles (22 km) west of Fredonia. It's a desert oasis where you can fill your canteen from the Winsors' original well, still running all these years at a constant rate of 30 precious gallons a minute. Inside the castle walls during the summer, National Park Service personnel attired in period costumes reenact scenes of daily frontier life. Outside the walls stretches an irrigated oasis of vineyards, orchards, duck ponds, and vegetable gardens.

As in days of yore, the fortress is surrounded by Indians. The headquarters of the Kaibab Paiute tribe is just across the entrance road, and the visitors' center includes a coffee-and-doughnut shop run by Indians. A quarter mile north of the monument is the Paiute-owned Heart Campground and RV Park. Picnicking here is free, although the management requests donations to "pay for the wolf's singing."

GRAND CANYON'S NORTH RIM

TOROWEAP POINT
Six miles (10 km) east of Pipe Spring a dirt road branches south off AZ 389 toward Toroweap Point, 68 miles (109

km) south on the North Rim of the Grand Canyon. This is the most reliable of three access roads leading to Toroweap; the others are a summertime-only trail from St. George south over Mount Trumbull, and a somewhat smoother but slippery-when-wet dirt road south from Colorado City. In good weather all three are deemed passable by the National Park Service, though "only by those adequately prepared to deal with the area and the possible problems associated with desert travel." In addition to that cautionary note, nailed beneath the bullet-riddled mileage sign is another disclaimer: The Kaibab Paiute Tribe Shall Not Be Held Liable For Any Accident, Damages, Injuries, or Loss of Property Incurred On This Road. Is it any wonder Toroweap remains one of the least-visited scenic spots in America?

Those who aren't frightened off and who are able to cope with the many "problems associated with desert travel" will find Toroweap Point to be a most awe-inspiring **overview** of the Grand Canyon. Here, 3,000 feet above Lava Falls, the gorge is at its narrowest, averaging only one mile across. You're so close to the Colorado River you can eavesdrop on the conversations of passing boaters, but chances are that's all you're going to get in the way of human discourse here. There are no houses, no telephones, no nothing at Toroweap except a primitive campground (no water) with a glorious abundance of peace and quiet.

THE KAIBAB PLATEAU

Meanwhile, back on the pavement: U.S. 89A continues on a southeasterly course from Fredonia, gradually ascending to the forested top of the Kaibab Plateau, one of America's premier mule deer habitats, home of the indigenous white-tailed Kaibab squirrel, and a favorite hunting ground of Theodore Roosevelt. The plateau tilts upward, rising to an elevation of 9,000 feet above sea level by the time you get to the North Rim (which is higher than the South Rim). As you drive south, the vegetation changes from pygmy forests of juniper and piñon to groves of aspen, ponderosa, spruce, and fir.

Thirty-two miles (51 km) southeast on U.S. 89A, at the junction with AZ 67, is **Jacob Lake**, site of the rustic **Jacob Lake Lodge**, as well as a restaurant, post office, filling station, and U.S. Forest Service campground—all named after the ambitious Mormon pioneer Jacob Hamblin, whose bigger-than-life portrait hangs over the lodge's fireplace. In the lodge's dining room hearty home-style meals are served, mostly by students recruited from the campuses of Brigham Young University in Provo, Utah, and Ricks College in Rexburg, Idaho.

The forest service's Jacob Lake Campground offers 53 camping spots, each with a cooking grill and water, while Jacob Lake Lodge's RV Campground provides complete hookups. Jacob's "lake" itself is a major disappointment, as it's not much bigger than a bathtub. "It used to be a four-duck pond," laments a resident forest ranger, "but now it's down to two."

After topping off your gas tank, drop in at the new Kaibab Forest Information Center just south of the lodge for news and information and a detailed map of the plateau; Tel: (602) 643-7295. There are several numbered, unpaved forest roads branching off AZ 67 that are passable in good weather; they lead to lesser-known and less-visited **North Rim overlooks** such as **Crazy Jug Point**, **East Rim Viewpoint**, and **Fire Point**, along with historical sites such as the old Jacob Lake Ranger Station and ancient Anasazi ruins and writings. In between these places, the one-and-a-half-million-acre **Kaibab National Forest** affords plenty of primitive camping opportunities for which no fee or permit is required. Just be careful with fire and be sure to pack out what you pack in.

THE KAIBAB PLATEAU – NORTH RIM PARKWAY

AZ 67 south from Jacob Lake to the Grand Canyon is also known as the Kaibab Plateau–North Rim Parkway, Arizona's first designated scenic byway. Characterized by evergreen forests interspersed with lush meadows that are dotted with wildflowers and browsing deer and elk, this scenic drive has been described as "the most pleasant 44 miles in America." The best part, of course, comes at the end, when the land drops abruptly away and you suddenly find yourself standing at the edge of the earth's biggest hole in the ground. It's more than a spectacle; it's a *sensation* of immense spaciousness that can't be equaled anywhere else, even in this land of big spaces. The first thing you'll want to do is just stand there in awe, absorbing the cosmic vibrations of eternity etched in layer upon layer of rock strata dating back millions of years.

Indeed, good vibrations are what the Grand Canyon is all about, and those in the know will tell you the North Rim is the best place to feel them, far from the crowds, traffic, and tourist trappings that clutter the South Rim.

The North Rim gets only about a tenth of the tourists who visit the Grand Canyon each year, in part because the roads are closed in the winter and in part because the North Rim is farther off the beaten track. True, there's not all that much happening at the north end, but that's exactly the point.

For maximum impact, if you've never seen the canyon before, turn left onto the Point Imperial/Cape Royal viewpoints road before you get to the North Rim Lodge. At **Point Imperial** you can drive right up to the canyon's edge, while at **Cape Royal** you park your car and walk a short distance to the **overlook**. Many declare Cape Royal to be the most impressive of all Grand Canyon overlooks— though it's hard, offhand, to name an unimpressive one.

NORTH RIM FACILITIES

To get to the **Grand Canyon Lodge**, stay on AZ 67 until it dead-ends in the parking lot near the lip of Bright Angel Canyon. A faithful reconstruction of the Gilbert Stanley Underwood–designed edifice that burned down only four years after its completion in 1928, the labor-intensive stone fortress evokes the feeling of Roaring Twenties elegance, if not decadence. The tiered lodging accommodations would appeal to Goldilock's Three Bears, beginning at the top end with the Western cabin, which comes with two double beds, a private porch with a great view, a full bathroom, and a telephone. In the midsize range is the frontier cabin, containing a double and a single bed, a shower, and pines all around. Budget class consists of the smaller pioneer cabins and motel rooms.

Unlike the two other TWS-operated lodges at Bryce or Zion parks there are no luxury suites here, but it's still easy to feel like a big shot at the opulent Grand Canyon Lodge—even if you're not a registered guest. Kick back in a genuine leather-cushioned Morris chair in the cavernous sun room and make believe you're relaxing after a hard day of shooting bears and roping mountain lions, Teddy Roosevelt style. The sun room, the enormous dining hall, and various open-air patios all command excellent vistas across the chasm to the South Rim, ten miles distant as the crow flies (though as human beings travel, it's a lot farther: a 215-mile/344-km detour by car via Lee's Ferry and Cameron).

You'll have to reserve a mule or a horse well in advance if you expect to go trail riding, although your chances of finding an empty saddle on the spur of the moment are somewhat better here than at the South Rim. Popular

hiking trails include the half-mile jaunt to Bright Angel Point, the one-and-a-half-mile rim hike along the Transept Trail, and the mile-long round trip to Cliff Springs. For longer hikes try the five-mile Uncle Jim Trail, the ten-mile Widforss Trail, and the ten-mile Ken Patrick Trail, all of which combine forest scenery with breathtaking canyon **overlooks**. The only maintained trail into the Grand Canyon itself on this side is the **North Kaibab Trail**, on which you eventually cross the Colorado River at Phantom Ranch and continue all the way up the other side to the South Rim's Grand Canyon Village, a distance of 22 miles. Very few actually walk the whole distance, however; most hikers on the North Kaibab Trail go as far as Roaring Springs (just over four and a half miles), pause long enough to refill their canteens and drink in the view, and turn back. Allow a full day (six to eight hours) for the round trip. Contact Bryce-Zion-Grand Trail Rides, Box 128, Tropic, UT 84776; Tel: (801) 834-5219 or 679-8665 (off-season).

Information relating to guided tours, children's programs, geology, history, and archaeology lessons, night walks, and night talks is available at the main desk of the Grand Canyon Lodge. If mountain biking is your thing, inquire at rustic, quiet **Kaibab Lodge**, situated at the edge of a meadow just west of AZ 67 and just north of the park entrance. Or contact **North Rim Mountain Bike Tours**, Tel: (602) 638-2389. **Canyoneers Incorporated**, operators of the lodge, rents bikes, runs guided bike tours, and sponsors white-water rafting trips and cross-country ski adventures; Tel: (602) 526-2914. For campsite reservations in the Grand Canyon, Tel: (800) 365-2267.

The North Rim is closed during the winter because of heavy snowfalls. A main number provides information on accommodations (including camping), mule trips, white water rafting, and so on for both the North and South Rims; Tel: (602) 638-7888 for a voice-actuated system (it can take some time to get the information you need).

THE LOWER UTAH
CANYONLANDS AND
THE LAKE POWELL AREA

Backtrack on AZ 67 to the crossroads at Jacob Lake to rejoin U.S. 89A for the last leg of your grand tour. West of

Jacob Lake the road descends off the Kaibab Plateau to lower country, where it runs parallel to the Vermilion Cliffs to your left for 41 miles (66 km) to Marble Canyon. The **Cliff Dwellers Lodge & Trading Co., Inc.** and the **Marble Canyon Lodge** here are your two choices if it's getting dark and you're looking for a roof over your head. If you should see a filling station anywhere along the way, by all means stop and tank up.

This is ruggedly handsome country, somewhat on the desolate side, albeit not nearly as desolate as it used to be before the completion of the 600-foot-long **Marble Canyon Bridge** across the Colorado in 1929. Prior to that, the only way to ford the river was at nearby Lee's Ferry, a proposition that held little allure for the faint of heart. The last three paying customers, in fact, drowned when the ferryboat capsized.

Before the completion of the bridge, Lee's Ferry, about 5 miles (8 km) north of the bridge on the west side of the river, had been in continuous operation for over half a century. It is named after John D. Lee, a fugitive from justice who hid out here for 20 years before being arrested and later executed for his part in the infamous Mountain Meadows Massacre of 1857. Some of Lee's ranch buildings are preserved at **Lonely Dell**, which isn't quite as lonely a spot now that there's a public campground and a boat-launching dock where the ferry used to be.

Since the completion of Glen Canyon Dam, 15 miles (24 km) upriver, the Colorado here runs clear instead of muddy and has become a noted habitat for trophy-size rainbow trout. Call **Arizona Reel Time** in town for tips on the whereabouts of big trout in the Colorado River; Tel: (602) 355-2222. On a hot summer's day the river is also a great place to go wading. Look across the blue-green current and you will see an exposed layer of white limestone angling upward on the opposite bank. This is the same rock layer that forms the uppermost stratum of the Grand Canyon, only 90 miles to the south but 4,000 feet higher.

Lake Powell

Although Lake Powell is only 15 nautical miles up the Colorado River from Marble Canyon, the trip by automobile is a circuitous 37-mile (59-km) drive via U.S. 89A South, and then U.S. 89 north from Bitter Springs to Page, Arizona, and Glen Canyon Dam—which created Lake

Powell in 1963 and changed the face of the lower canyonlands forever. Lake Powell is the second-largest man-
made lake in the nation (Lake Mead downstream is the
largest), and certainly the most unusual. At no point is it
very wide, but it measures 186 miles long as it extends
northeast into Utah—and that's not counting the vast
network of fingerlike coves that back up into 96 major
canyons and countless minor ones. If stretched out, its
convoluted shoreline would extend 1,960 miles, offering
more beachfront than California, Oregon, and Washington combined.

Glen Canyon National Recreation Area surrounds Lake
Powell, which is served by five marinas, all operated by a
federally licensed concessionaire, ARA Leisure Services;
Tel: (800) 528-6154. Boats can be rented or refueled, and
food chests refilled at any of the marinas, all of which,
except Dangling Rope, can also be reached by car.

The main marina is at **Wahweap Bay**, just north of the
dam on the west shore of Lake Powell. Besides the 350
rooms at **Wahweap Lodge and Marina**, facilities include
the adjacent Lake Powell Motel, a 189-unit campground
and RV park, plus ample parking space for mobile homes
and other recreational vehicles. Besides English, travel
brochures at the lodge's front desk are available in Japanese, French, and German, reflecting the international
community of this bustling lake port. Wahweap Lodge's
Rainbow Room offers tables with great views and a broad
range of tasty dishes. Sunset cruises, with or without
dinner, are available aboard the Wahweap-based stern-
wheel paddleboat, *The Canyon King.*

During the summer guided tours depart regularly from
Wahweap and Bullfrog marinas for the 50-mile trip to
Rainbow Bridge, which, before the completion of Glen
Canyon Dam, was perhaps the most remote scenic attraction in the entire Southwest. (For Bullfrog, see also Across
the Colorado in the Back of Beyond section, above.) Although the lake's waters now back up under the bridge,
boaters are required to dock a short distance away and
walk softly the rest of the way in deference to Indian
tradition, which holds the spot sacred. A few hardy souls
still make the arduous two-day overland pilgrimage to the
290-foot-high natural stone bridge, but the religious payoff
is diminished somewhat by the pagan boaters milling
about at the end of the rainbow.

Although the Glen Canyon Recreation Area includes
about 2,000 square miles of dry land, there's virtually no
other way to get to most of it except by boat. The pre-

ferred type of watercraft is the Lake Powell houseboat, which resembles a Winnebago motor home on pontoons. Just as Winnebago owners on vacation often hitch up the family car in the rear, most houseboaters tow along a small skiff for putting ashore. The big 50-footers rent for as much as $2,000 a week during high season, which may not be as outrageous as it sounds provided you've got enough people in your party to share expenses. Factor in what you'll save on lodging and the possibility of catching enough fish to feed the multitude and it may work out to be cheaper than living ashore. All boat rentals at Lake Powell are handled by ARA Leisure Services (see above).

Besides a boat, all you need to enjoy the good life on Lake Powell is an ice chest full of groceries and a two-burner propane stove. If you get weary of "eating out," however, there are a few alternatives. For example, at **Bullfrog Marina**, some 80 miles uplake from the dam, food-and-beverage manager John Kaser, along with chef Steve Price, are available to cater your beach party. The pair offer a selection of beef, seafood, and chicken entrées complemented by soup, salad, side dishes, and ice cream and cheesecake desserts. For the paper-plate and plastic-fork weary, the service, which even includes fresh linens, china, and crystal, will be a highly appreciated respite.

Investigate also ARA's special Explorer Packages, which combine boating with onshore lodging. As with everything else at Lake Powell, prices vary according to the season. The busiest and most popular months are July and August, when you'll almost certainly have to make advance reservations for boats and/or rooms. Other seasons include "budget" (November to March) and "value" (April 1 to 14 and all of October). Those in the know declare Lake Powell is loveliest at "value time," especially October. Not only are boat rentals discounted 20 percent then, but the crowds are gone, the weather's usually superb, and the fishing for striped bass is at its best.

PAGE

Page, Arizona, a community of 6,500 souls at the eastern end of Glen Canyon Dam, came into existence as a power-generation oasis but nowadays depends equally on tourism for subsistence. The main tourist draw is the dam itself, slightly shorter but wider than Hoover Dam. Though blander in character than its Las Vegas counterpart, in many ways it's a more visitor-friendly operation. The guided tour of the dam is free, and if you're squeamish about being packed into a small space with 20 strangers, you can choose to be your own guide and operate the elevator yourself. Picture windows at the Carl Hayden Visitor Center on U.S. 89 at the west end of Glen Canyon Bridge and the pedestrian walk along the bridge afford spectacular overviews of the dam, the lake, and the Colorado River 700 feet below.

The second obligatory tourist stop is the **John Wesley Powell Memorial Museum** on the corner of Lake Powell Boulevard and North Navajo Drive. The museum details the history of Colorado river-running, dating back to Major Powell's historic expedition of 1869. There's also a section on the history of moviemaking in the Page area, where sandstone buttes and pinnacles have co-starred in film productions ranging from *The Greatest Story Ever Told* to a Sears Craftsman lawnmower commercial.

The museum is well stocked with brochures and leaflets describing the many gift shops, trading posts, and hostelries in town. Some good bets for lodging here are the **Inn at Lake Powell**, the **Page/Lake Powell Holiday Inn**, the **Best Western at Lake Powell**, and the **Best Western Weston's Inn**.

A couple of blocks northeast of the museum is the Page Municipal Airport, home base of **Lake Powell Air Services** (901 Sage), which offers a choice of ten scenic flights ranging from a half hour to four hours in length; Tel: (602) 645-2494. Bear in mind that most of the land east of Page belongs to the Navajo Nation, and the winding trails you see leading into the hills aren't scenic byways but probably somebody's driveway. To avoid trespassing, it's better to call **Lake Powell Jeep Tours**, 108 Lake Powell Boulevard; Tel: (602) 645-5501.

Wilderness River Adventures offers half-day float trips down the Colorado River from below the dam, covering the ten miles south to Lee's Ferry through the only part of Glen Canyon that isn't submerged; Tel: (602) 645-3296. They also conduct trips through the Grand Canyon; Tel: (800) 992-8022. If you want to see what you missed because you didn't get here before the dam was built, check out the picture book *The Land Nobody Knew* by photographer Eliot Porter.

From Page to Las Vegas, Nevada, it is 140 miles (224 km) south on U.S. 89 to Flagstaff, Arizona, and the junction with I-40, and then approximately 250 miles (400 km) west on I-40 and (from Kingman, Arizona) U.S. 93.

Otherwise, you have to retrace your route northwest on AZ 89 and UT 9 from Page to St. George, Utah, before heading south on I-15 from St. George to Las Vegas, a trip of about 280 miles (448 km).

GETTING AROUND

Travel in this part of the world requires careful planning. To visit a variety of sites you must drive, and moreover cover a lot of miles. The suggested routes in this chapter are less than direct, but such are the realities of travelling in this area; there are few possible shortcuts because of the vast canyon networks that must be driven around, not through or across. The aim throughout the chapter has been to offer a smorgasbord of possibilities from which you may pick and choose those you find the most appealing. Whatever your choices may be, a certain amount of backtracking is almost certainly inevitable. It is possible to see some of the major attractions such as Arches, Canyonlands, Bryce, and Zion national parks by staying close to I-70 and I-15, but you will miss out on a great deal of incredible scenery if you go that route.

If you start in the Moab area, the closest cities to fly into are Salt Lake City, 250 miles (400 km) to the northwest, or Grand Junction, Colorado, about 100 miles (160 km) to the northeast. Car rentals are available at both locales. From east–west I-70 Moab is 30 miles (48 km) south from Crescent Junction, Utah, or 40 miles (64 km) south from the I-70 exit through Cisco, Utah.

Another possibility is to head for southern Utah from the Four Corners, starting your trip in Blanding, Utah, or Page, Arizona. Yet another option is to start at the South Rim of the Grand Canyon, perhaps forgoing the North Rim leg of this tour. (Because of the 215-mile/344-km road distance between the two, few travellers get to both in the same trip.)

However you decide to approach this vast area, a good road map is essential. Always carry food and water, and top off your gas tank whenever you can; the next gas station may be far away, or closed when you get there. Always inquire locally about road conditions before setting out, particularly in more remote areas.

Summer, which is predictably very warm, with temperatures often topping 100°F, is the primary travel season in this region, but only because it is when most people take their vacations. Reservations will be hardest to come by at that time. Spring is less busy, but late snowstorms and sudden thunderstorms with resulting flash floods make some roads impassable. Those same thunderstorms, combined with spring runoff from the mountains, also make springtime the best for white water rafting, with the highest water levels and the biggest thrills.

In winter, the least-crowded season, many roads are closed by heavy snows, particularly at higher elevations; the list includes AZ 67 from Jacob Lake to the North Rim of the Grand Canyon and scenic loops in the Manti–La Sal and Abajo mountains. As a general rule, all unpaved roads are to be avoided during winter months. Fall is cooler, more comfortable, the least crowded and the most colorful of all the seasons; from mid-September through October aspen leaves are golden and skies are the deepest blue.

For general information about travel in Utah contact the Utah Travel Council, Council Hall, 300 North State Street, Salt Lake City, UT 84114; Tel: (801) 538-1030; Fax: (801) 538-1399. For Utah State Parks information contact Utah Division of Parks and Recreation, 1636 West North Temple, Salt Lake City, UT 84116; Tel: (801) 538-7221; Fax: (801) 538-7315. For a 24-hour road-condition recording, especially useful in the winter, Tel: (800) 492-2400. Arizona travel information is available through the Arizona Office of Tourism, 110 West Washington Street, Phoenix, AZ 85007; Tel: (602) 524-3687.

For information or reservations at Bryce, Zion, and the Grand Canyon Lodge, North Rim, write TW Services, Inc., P.O. Box 400, Cedar City, UT 84721. Tel: (801) 834-5361; Fax: (801) 834-3157.

ACCOMMODATIONS REFERENCE

The rates given below are projections for 1993. Unless otherwise indicated, rates are for a double room, double occupancy, and do not include meals. Price ranges span the lowest rate in the low season and the highest rate in the high season. As rates are always subject to change, it is wise to double-check before booking.

Utah

The telephone area code for Utah is 801.

▶ **Best Western Driftwood Lodge.** 1515 Zion Park Boulevard, **Springdale**, UT 84767. Tel: 772-3262 or (800) 528-1234; Fax: 772-3702. $52–$62.

▶ **Best Western Greenwell Motel.** 105 South Main Street, **Moab**, UT 84532. Tel: 259-6151; Fax: 259-4397. $82.

▶ **Best Western Ruby's Inn.** Utah Highway 63, **Bryce**, UT 84764. Tel: 834-5341 or (800) 528-1234; Fax: 834-5265. $39–$70.

▶ **Best Western Swiss Village Inn and Restaurant.** 580 North Main Street, **Parowan**, UT 84761. Tel: 477-3391 or (800) 528-1234; Fax: 477-8642. $35–$62.

▶ **Best Western Town & Country Inn.** 189 North Main Street, **Cedar City**, UT 84720. Tel: 586-9900; Fax: 586-1664. $53–$69.

▶ **Brian Head Hotel.** 223 Hunter Ridge Road, **Brian Head**, UT 84719. Tel: 677-3000 or (800) 468-4898; Fax: 677-2211. $55.

▶ **Bryce Canyon Lodge. Bryce Canyon National Park**, UT 84717. Tel: 586-7686; Fax: 834-3157. $63–$100.

▶ **Bryce Valley Inn.** 200 North & Main Street, **Tropic**, UT 84776. Tel: 679-8811; Fax: 679-8846. $49–$79.

▶ **Canyon Ranch Motel.** 668 Zion Park Boulevard, **Springdale**, UT 84767. Tel: 772-3357. $40–$60.

▶ **Capitol Reef Inn.** 360 West Main Street, **Torrey**, UT 84775. Tel: 425-3271. $25–$38.

▶ **Cedar City Holiday Inn.** 1575 West 200 North, **Cedar City**, UT 84720. Tel: 586-8888 or (800) 423-8828; Fax: 586-1010. $66–$89.

▶ **Cliffrose Lodge & Gardens.** 281 Zion Park Boulevard, **Springdale**, UT 84767. Tel: 772-3234 or (800) 243-UTAH; Fax: 772-3900. $68–$125.

▶ **Defiance House Lodge.** Bullfrog Marina, **Lake Powell**, UT 84533. Tel: 684-2233 or (800) 528-6154; Fax: 684-2312. $78–$112.

▶ **Fern's Place.** Highway 24, **Hanksville**, UT 84734. Tel: 542-3251. $30–$40.

▶ **Francisco's Bed & Breakfast.** P.O. Box 3, 51 Francisco Lane, **Tropic**, UT 84776. Tel: 679-8721. $60.

▶ **Greene Gate Village Bed and Breakfast.** 76 West Tabernacle Street, **St. George**, UT 87740. Tel: 628-6999 or (800) 350-6999. $40–$95.

▶ **Grist Mill Inn Bed & Breakfast.** 64 South 300 East, P.O. Box 156, **Monticello**, UT 84535. Tel: 587-2597 or (800) 645-3762. $44–$55.

▶ **Harvest House Bed & Breakfast.** 29 Canyon View Drive, **Springdale**, UT 84767. Tel: 772-3880. $60–$75.

▶ **Home Ranch.** P.O. Box 247, Highway 46, **La Sal**, UT 84530. Tel: 686-2223 or (800) 982-1540. $60.

▶ **Jedediah's Inn & Restaurant.** 625 West 200 South, **Parowan**, UT 84761. Tel: 477-3326; Fax: 477-3473. $50–$61.

▶ **Joy's Bed & Breakfast.** 296 South Center Street, **Hanksville**, UT 84734. Tel: 542-3252. $40.

▶ **Pack Creek Ranch.** Off La Sal Mountain Loop, P.O. Box 1270, **Moab**, UT 84532. Tel: 259-5505; Fax: 259-8879. $86–$230 (summer rates include meals).

▶ **Pah Tempe Hot Springs Resort.** 825 North 800 East 35-4, **Hurricane**, UT 84737. Tel: 635-2879 or 635-2353. $48–$75.

▶ **Pine Valley Lodge.** 960 East Main, **Pine Valley**, UT 84722. Tel: 574-2544. $25–$50.

▶ **Quality Inn.** 18 South Main Street, **Cedar City**, UT 84720. Tel: 586-2433 or (800) 221-2222; Fax: 586-7257. $34–$83.

▶ **Road Creek Inn.** 90 South Main Street, **Loa**, UT 84747. Tel: 836-2485 or (800) 388-7688; Fax: 836-2489. $56–$77.

▶ **Seven Wives Inn.** 217 North 100 West, **St. George**, UT 84770. Tel: 628-3737. $45–$100.

▶ **Shilo Inn.** 296 West 100 North, **Kanab**, UT 84741. Tel: 644-2562 or (800) 222-2244; Fax: 644-5333. $40–$66.

▶ **Smith Hotel Bed & Breakfast.** U.S. 89, **Glendale**, UT, 84729. Tel: 648-2156. $40–$50.

▶ **Soda Rock Inn.** 314 Hunter Ridge Drive, **Brian Head**, UT 84719. Tel: 677-2800 or (800) 443-8824; Fax: 677-2504. $60–$70.

▶ **Thunderbird Best Western Motel.** U.S. 89 and UT 9 junction, P.O. Box 36, **Mount Carmel Junction**, UT 84755. Tel: 648-2203 or (800) 528-1234; Fax: 648-2239. $56–$62.

▶ **Under the Eaves Guest House Bed and Breakfast Inn.** 980 Zion Park Boulevard, P.O. Box 29, **Springdale**, UT 84767. Tel: 772-3457. $45–$75.

▶ **Whispering Sands Motel.** Highway 95, **Hanksville**, UT 84734. Tel: 542-3238. $49.

▶ **Wonderland Inn.** Junction of Highways 12 and 24, P.O. Box 67, **Torrey**, UT 84775. Tel: 425-3775; Fax: 425-3212. $38–$78.

▶ **Zion Lodge. Zion National Park**, UT. Tel: 586-7686. $63–$100.

Arizona
The telephone area code for Arizona is 602.

▶ **Best Western at Lake Powell.** 208 North Lake Powell Boulevard, **Page**, AZ 86040. Tel: 645-5988; Fax: 645-2578. $79–$129.

▶ **Best Western Weston's Inn.** 201 North Lake Powell Boulevard, **Page**, AZ 86040. Tel: 645-2451 or (800) 637-9183; Fax: 645-9552. $53–$78.

▶ **Cliff Dwellers Lodge & Trading Co., Inc.** Highway 89A, **Marble Canyon**, AZ 86036. Tel: 355-2228 or (800) 433-2543. $48–$67.

▶ **Grand Canyon Lodge. North Rim Grand Canyon**, AZ 86023. Tel: (801) 586-7686; Fax: (801) 834-3157. $53–$70.

▶ **Inn at Lake Powell.** 716 Rim View Drive, P.O. Box C,

Page, AZ 86040. Tel: 645-2466 or (800) 826-2718. $69–$125.

▶ **Jackson House Bed & Breakfast**. P.O. Box 232, 90 North Main Street, **Fredonia**, AZ 86022. Tel: 643-7702. $40–$45.

▶ **Jacob Lake Lodge**. Jacob Lake, AZ 86022. Tel: 643-7232. $50–$70.

▶ **Kaibab Lodge**. North Rim Grand Canyon, **Jacob Lake**, AZ 86022. Tel: 638-2389 or (800) 525-0924. $45–$87.

▶ **Marble Canyon Lodge**. Box 1, Highway 89A, **Marble Canyon**, AZ 86036. Tel: 355-2225 or (800) 726-1789; Fax: 355-2227. $55–$65.

▶ **Page/Lake Powell Holiday Inn**. 287 North Lake Powell Boulevard, P.O. Box 1867, **Page**, AZ 86040. Tel: 645-8851 or (800) 232-0011; Fax: 645-2523. $75–$110.

▶ **Wahweap Lodge and Marina**. P.O. Box 1597, **Page**, AZ 86040. Tel: 645-2433 or (800) 528-6154; Fax: 645-5175. $54–$120.

Additional Information

Bed and Breakfast Inns of Utah, Inc., P.O. Box 3066, Park City, UT 84060; Tel: (801) 645-8068.

Utah Hotel Association, 9 Exchange Place, Suite 715, Salt Lake City, UT 84111. Tel: (801) 359-0104; Fax: (801) 359-0105.

LAS VEGAS
LAKE MEAD
AND DAY TRIPS

By Lark Ellen Gould

Lark Ellen Gould has worked as a staff reporter and editor for United Press International, the Las Vegas Sun, *and the McClatchy chain of Senior Spectrum newspapers. She lives in Las Vegas, Nevada, where she works as a freelance writer and teaches journalism to college students.*

The action never stops in Las Vegas. Escape begins the moment you enter the glittering, flashing, creeping light show of The Strip, when your mind clicks off and mesmerization sets in. You pan the straightaway view of The Strip, which is guaranteed to make mush of your optic nerves, and then try to single out each attraction one by one.

The attractions here are the hotels. It started with Bugsy Siegel's wild vision to make the Flamingo one of America's premier resort destinations nearly half a century ago. Bugsy died, but the wild vision lives on. The Flamingo still shines on The Strip, with its pink and red neon plumes, but now there's also Caesars Palace with its serenade of fountains, Excalibur with a looming castle and moat, Circus Circus with its veritable big-top effect, the Mirage with volcanic spectacles. The hotels beckon like Greek sirens, each louder than the last.

Las Vegas is a spectacular place. The lights and designer come-ons will shake your senses. Buffets will overwhelm your cravings. Lounge entertainers will woo you and croon into the late-night hours in electrifying performances, all for the cost of a Coke.

665

Las Vegas is technically on Pacific standard time and therefore three hours earlier than New York and Miami. However, time has no meaning here. Try to find a clock in a casino. Try to determine whether it's day or night while you sort out your poker hand. The indoor lighting never flinches; the noise of hyperactive slots never ceases. Food is served around the clock; supermarkets and drugstores stay open 24 hours a day; gas stations pump gas even at 4:00 A.M.; lounge singers cater to insomniacs before they head out into the desert dawn for that long-awaited 49¢ breakfast.

The city is divided into four parts: The Strip, downtown, the east side, and the west side. For visitors, only The Strip and downtown matter; the rest belongs to locals. Las Vegans live from shopping center to mall, embroiling themselves in Strip gridlock only when out-of-town guests insist on seeing the Mirage's volcano. And because the sculptured mountain spits its wrath every 15 minutes from sunset to after midnight, there is a good chance you'll witness the performance while sitting through a series of red lights.

MAJOR INTEREST

Las Vegas
Hotels
Gambling
Big-name entertainment and revues
Museums
Children's entertainment

Day Trips from Las Vegas
Hoover Dam
Lake Mead
Mount Charleston
Red Rock Canyon

Las Vegas derives its name from something it used to have in plenty: water. In fact, the whole state was under water at one time, about 400 million years ago. But the city's name, Spanish for "The Meadows" (not "Lost Wages," as some would tell you), was coined in 1829 by a group of Spanish missionaries en route from Arizona to the coast who happened upon overflowing springs in this otherwise arid region. The springs then became the destination of Anglo explorers and Mormon missionaries bent on tithing the local Paiutes, and eventually became a base for land and gold prospectors who caught the interest of the railroad. Railroad Watering Stop Number 25 was completed here in 1905. A golden spike was driven in Jean, Nevada, about 22 miles west of Las Vegas, to finish the rail route from Salt Lake City to Los Angeles.

Las Vegas was a sleepy, dusty watering hole determined to become an upright town—with the exception of Block 16, a neighborhood of women and whiskey situated where Stewart and Ogden avenues today meet First and Second streets. In 1928 the Boulder Canyon Project Act was created and $168 million in government funding found its way to Las Vegas to build the world's largest dam on the nearby Colorado River, below the Grand Canyon. Three years later the right to gamble in Nevada was signed into law by Governor Fred Balzar, a man who saw liberal gaming as a way to beat the chill of the Great Depression. Games of all fashions were allowed in every area of the state except Boulder City, a town 26 miles southeast of Las Vegas built to house the dam workers. Today Boulder City is still the only town in Nevada where gambling remains off-limits.

The dedication of Hoover Dam in 1936 brought cheap electricity to Las Vegas, and together with the lure of inexpensive land sparked the imaginations of speculators who saw potential for this desert railroad stop to become a destination in its own right. In 1941 Tommy Hull, owner of a chain of motor inns called El Rancho, built a 65-room low rise on the corner of what is now Las Vegas Boulevard and Sahara Avenue. In it he put a steak house, a nightclub, a pool, and palms, and to it came escapees from Southern California and locals looking for relaxation outside the downtown hotel and saloon area. A year later the fancier Last Frontier Hotel was built across the street from El Rancho Las Vegas and prompted a tornado of activity in boom-and-bust speculation, gangster comings and goings, and manager turnarounds, as hotels were built one after another along Highway 91, now The Strip. ("The Strip" was so named, it seems, by a California cop turned Las Vegas casino owner who revered L.A.'s Sunset Strip.) El Rancho doubled in size, then burned to the ground in 1960, but the hotels kept coming. Enter Bugsy Siegel.

Benjamin "Bugsy" Siegel was born about the same time as Railroad Watering Stop Number 25, and started his career in the East with Murder Inc. in the early 1930s. He was sent by mob boss Meyer Lansky to bring the West Coast contingent under control and then to muscle in on the race books in Las Vegas. He soon saw the possibilities for making serious money by putting a lot of glitz "out in the middle of nowhere."

Bankrolled by Lansky and others from New York, Siegel built the Flamingo (on the same site it occupies today) for about $4 million more than budgeted. He gave it the pet name of his mistress and set out to make it a "carpet joint" where only gorgeous people worked and Beautiful People played. His fate was sealed opening night, December 26, 1946. If the Flamingo succeeded, so would he.

It was a rainy, cold night. Jimmy Durante, Xavier Cugat, and Rose Marie entertained, but the evening was not a hit. The Flamingo closed in January. It reopened in March, this time showing a profit, but Siegel met an "untimely" death nevertheless and never lived to see the happy ending of his dream.

In 1948 the Thunderbird opened its doors. In 1950 came the Desert Inn. In 1952 the Sahara and the Sands went up. Within six years, the Riviera, Tropicana, Dunes, Moulin Rouge, Frontier, Hacienda, Mint, and Fremont joined the ranks, each more expensive than the last. The mob moved in for a 15-year reign and put the town on the map for corruption and graft in a high-stakes game; the law enforcers followed. The city's population mushroomed to 65,000.

Right on cue came Howard Hughes, the multimillionaire inheritor of the Hughes Tool Company who had friends in the FBI, IRS, and top university programs. He had just sold Trans World Airlines for $500 million in cash and looked to Vegas to spend his money. He moved into the ninth-floor high-roller suites at the Desert Inn and, when asked to vacate, bought the hotel. He stayed in his room around the clock, protected by an air-purification system and ample supplies of Kleenex (used as buffers between his skin and the things he needed to touch). When he emerged from his room an old man, he had in his possession the Sands, the Castaways, the Frontier, Silver City, the Landmark, North Las Vegas Airport, countless acres of surrounding desert, and a number of other Nevada enterprises. His hotel investments caused a boom of legitimacy and a wave of renewed outside speculation in the Las Vegas resort industry in the 1970s. Soon the Aladdin, Caesars Palace, the Four Queens, Circus Circus, and other major casino hotels were built, shaping the Las Vegas city and skyline of today.

The area code for Las Vegas and all of Nevada is 702.

The Strip

Today the strip of fast speculation runs from the southern-most (farthest from downtown) and newest hotel, Vacation Village, along Las Vegas Boulevard to its northernmost point at Vegas World. After that it's considered the down-town world of "Glitter Gulch," where neon, raunch, and Italian marble offer a blend of old and new Vegas.

In all, over two dozen resort and casino hotels line the three-and-a-half-mile stretch of neon and kitsch called The Strip. A south-to-north walking tour of this route usually begins at the **Tropicana**, at the corner of Tropi-cana Avenue, where enormous replicas of Easter Island godheads—each a 150,000-ton rock carving standing 35 feet tall and 15 feet wide—guard the bamboo-covered entrance to this "island" casino resort. Across The Strip at the **Excalibur** the wonderful world of King Arthur lights up at dusk like the Magic Castle at Disneyland. A walkway from the sidewalk crosses a moat and eventually ends up in a Fantasy Land casino and an honest-to-goodness medi-eval video arcade.

As you head north on the west side of Las Vegas Boule-vard toward the now-defunct Dunes Hotel (the property was recently purchased by hotelier Steve Wynn), don't forget to pay your respects to the life-size Elvis statue, which has been hit pretty hard in recent years by wind and rain, in front of the Boardwalk Hotel and Casino. Across the street, the **Aladdin**'s magic lamp of thousands of minibulbs lights an entrance worthy of celebrities.

At the Dunes you will find yourself in the center of the Vegas spectacle, and you may find yourself stuck, unable to decide whether to cross east to Bally's, northeast to the Flamingo, or to continue due north to Caesars Palace. A simple rule of thumb prevails: Follow the green light. Our tour heads for Caesars. You'll pass 50-foot cypress trees and fountains that spew even higher while reflect-ing the aquamarine lighting of Caesars' grand entrance. There's a lifelike plaster gladiator and slave statues stand-ing under one of the sidewalk rotundas, and a Brahman shrine, strangely out of step with the theme, behind the fountains in the front of the resort hotel. Breathe in the sandalwood incense and bring luck upon yourself by throwing coins at the elephant statues.

Caesars Palace has a second rotunda entrance, which catches the southbound walking traffic. A step onto the moving walkway will lead you into the ancient city of

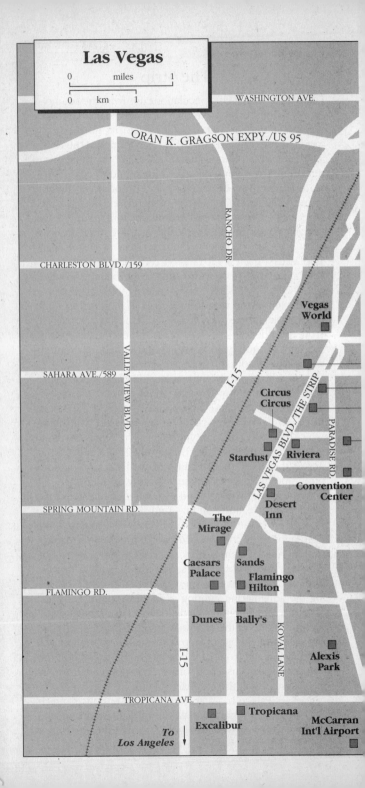

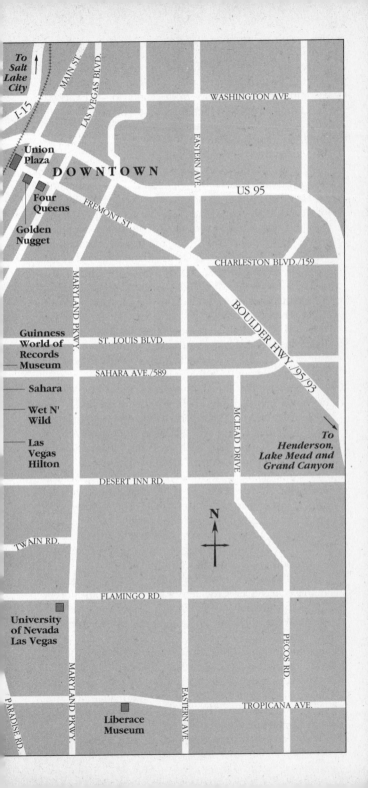

Rome. Special effects using mirrors and holograms suggest the glittering metropolis in magnificent miniatures, accompanied by a message from a Liz Taylor–like Cleopatra. The only problem with this part of the tour is getting stuck on the one-way moving walkway. Unless you're skilled at maneuvering, you'll be on your way into Caesars Palace with no easy way out.

Back out on the sidewalk, you'll see to the north the vintage neon lights of red and pink at Bugsy's dream, now the **Flamingo Hilton**, and a few doors down, **Harrah's** (the former Holiday Inn), shaped like a Mississippi Queen with red and black smokestacks. The theme continues inside, with flocked wallpaper and beaded chandeliers.

But don't cross the street to get to them just yet. A few steps ahead is a megashow in front of the **Mirage**: the volcano. It starts slowly with a few rumbles; a cacophony of nervous chatter escapes from the surrounding rain forest. Then it belches—first fire, then steam. Finally it explodes: Fire spews from the mound, lava bubbles forth, steam hisses, and water cascades, drowning it all in sounds so loud the sidewalk quakes. You can feel the heat. Nightly, every 15 minutes until 1:00 A.M.

Across from the Mirage on the east side of The Strip is the **Sands** marquee and, behind it, a round hotel. The 1952 structure is a throwback to the Rat Pack era that made it famous. The early-1960s movie *Ocean's Eleven,* with Dean Martin, Joey Bishop, Frank Sinatra, Sammy Davis, Jr., and Peter Lawford, was filmed here.

Continue up the west side of the street past the Fashion Show Mall and the **Frontier Hotel and Casino** (the elegant **Desert Inn** is across the street). This is where the funky Vegas begins. Go past the pink-and-blue neon of the **Stardust**, a roomy place to play, and head straight for **Slots A Fun** for your free bag of popcorn, 75¢ Heineken, 99¢ breakfast, hot dogs, and shrimp cocktail.

If you want to gamble but don't want to risk getting emphysema, **Silver City**, across the street from Slots A Fun, is this town's only smokeless casino, a unique venture in Vegas. Butts are left at the door not far from the bike racks.

Circus Circus, at the corner of Sahara Avenue on the west side of The Strip, is easily recognizable by its pink-and-white-striped circus tents (they're the size of the Queen Mary) and a scary-looking clown marquee that looms over Las Vegas Boulevard next to a statue of a topless tightrope walker.

If you cross Sahara and head north half a block you'll

find the not-so-easy-to-spot **Guinness World of Records Museum** (behind Arby's). For $4.95 you'll learn about the world's tallest man and the fattest boy, the average number of calories consumed per capita in Belgium, the world's most tattooed lady, and more, much more. With its lifelike replications and videos, it makes for a pretty amusing hour. The museum's gift shop carries the best postcards in Las Vegas if you're looking for an assortment other than the usual Hoover Dam and Strip offerings. Hours are 9:00 A.M. to 9:00 P.M. daily. Tel: 792-3766.

Now for the trip of The Strip: **Vegas World**. This 1960s space-age setup is worth the walk for the look alone. Entrance into the casino via an abbreviated walkway that looks like an air duct leads into a capsule of light and sound, with space suits and modules hanging from the ceiling, a canopy of twinkling stars in a black sky. Smoked-glass mirrors and plastic illumination rods dangling overhead add to the effect. There's also a display case of a million dollars, stacked in twenties within half-inch Plexiglas. You may get tapped by one of many employees trying to give you coupons for a free this or that. Owner Bob Stupak is a master of self-promotion who knows well how to keep one spouse gambling while the other stands on a long line. Future plans for the hotel are impressive: Stupak intends to build the tallest structure in the world in this fair city, complete with a lion habitat visible from the bar and a sky-high amusement park.

Downtown

The best thing about this section of town, 2 miles (3 km) north of Vegas World, is the lights. You could easily read a dictionary on the street at midnight. Downtown, coined "Glitter Gulch" by the late newspaper publisher Hank Greenspun in the early 1950s, centers on **Fremont Street**. The neon show begins at Fremont and Main streets at the Union Plaza Hotel and ends six blocks to the west at the no-frills El Cortez, a smoke-filled casino hotel built in 1941 (one of its original adobe buildings is still in use as a section of the casino). Fremont Street is the backdrop of hundreds of B-grade movies and television shows, where guns fire and cars skid on empty sidewalks beneath the "Howdy Pardner" wave of Vegas Vic. (The neon sign no longer talks, and the sidewalks are far from empty.) And Glitter Gulch goes on as it always has despite wars, depressions, or feeble attempts to make it a glamour spot. Here is Vegas as it was, the sinful Block 16 when the town was still a railroad watering stop. It is where the cowboys go and the bus tours congregate. It is fun, sassy, and has the best betting odds and minimums of any area in town.

We begin our coverage at the **Union Plaza**, the only hotel in the country with a railroad platform in its lobby. The best views of Fremont Street can be seen here from the **Center Stage** restaurant. Conventional dishes, such as crab legs and New York strip steak, are served beneath a dark-green Plexiglas bubble on the third floor. A great window looks onto the action along Glitter Gulch, and the views are as much fun as the food. Prices here are higher than most midrange restaurants, though.

Your next stop should be **Binion's Horseshoe**, up Fremont on the north side of the street between First Street and Casino Center Boulevard. Ride the glass elevator to the **Sky Room**, where American food and another magnificent view of the downtown wattage are among the offerings. Don't miss having your picture taken at the Million Dollar Horseshoe display on the ground floor near the northeast exit. If the attendant isn't busy, she'll probably take more than one. The free photographs take a few hours to develop, so stick around and pull slots until they're ready, or pick them up later.

Across the street from Binion's is the **Golden Nugget**, sister of the Mirage and the fanciest hotel north of Vegas World. White and gold are its trademark colors, repeated in the brass appointments and marbled floors and pillars. The Nugget's façade imitates a fine European hotel with potted palms and window canopies. Inside, the theme reflects the image of its past, before the current owner took over: turn-of-the-century saloon chic, with a bit of Rodeo Drive thrown in for good measure. You will find here, protected under plate glass, the world's largest golden nugget—a 60-pound chunk found in Australia in 1980, valued at $1 million.

Across Casino Center Boulevard from the Golden Nugget, the **Four Queens** makes its royal presence known with the world's largest slot machine, the Queen's Machine. This mighty contraption, larger than a large U-Haul moving truck, can be played by six people simultaneously for a payoff of $300,000.

The rest of the downtown area is brightly lighted, safe, and fun to walk, especially if you allow time to duck into souvenir shops that suffer no limits when it comes to out-kitsching the inventory of the store next door. Look for the snow shakers with Vegas and desert scenes in glitter water.

Children's Vegas

Yes, there very definitely is such a thing. Las Vegas used to be the place adults went for their first and second honeymoons, leaving children at home or in the casino lobby with a coloring book while the parents gambled. Then Circus Circus entered the game in 1968, and now Las Vegas is touted as a family-vacation destination, where the endless motion of The Strip is as pleasing to children as adults. Most hotels supply a video arcade somewhere around the shopping area and, of course, kids can amuse themselves no end punching buttons for all the floors in the elevator and dropping water balloons out of windows. But a number of more organized entertainment possibilities along The Strip and surrounding Las Vegas make it possible to actually plan excursions for the kids into your vacation schedule.

On The Strip, beginning at the south end at 3765 Las Vegas Boulevard South (in Metz Plaza), **Bethany's Celebrity Doll Museum** is a dream come true for one local little-known entertainer. Bethany Owen Morgan took all the dolls she had been collecting since day one, ordered up another sizable inventory of one-of-a-kind dolls from artists, and opened a museum. She's got excellent miniatures of Marilyn Monroe, Lucille Ball, Desi Arnaz, Katharine Hepburn, Julie Andrews, Judy Garland, Elvis Presley, Debbie Reynolds, Cher, and John Wayne, to name just a few. Copies of most of the dolls are available for purchase at the museum gift shop. The entrance fee is $5.00 for adults and $2.50 for children. Hours are 10:00 A.M. to 5:00 P.M. daily and 1:00 to 5:00 P.M. on Sundays; Tel: 798-3036.

Farther up The Strip the **Tropicana** has a fabulous water park occupying five acres in the center of its complex. The park features three swimming pools, one of them claimed to be the world's largest indoor-outdoor pool. Along the banks are a water slide, five whirlpool spas, a number of waterfalls, lagoons, and, for swim-along parents, Vegas's only swim-up blackjack table complete with bill dryer. Koi fish inhabit the lagoons, and pink flamingos and white and black swans waddle at will around the grounds.

The castle of children's fantasies at **Excalibur**, across The Strip, is a three-tiered design with gaming in the middle tier, dining and shopping on the third level, and an arcade of kiddie delights (The Fantasy Faire) in the basement. Besides the "medieval" shooting galleries and other storybook-themed gaming areas to test your hand-eye coordination, Excalibur sports the city's only Magic Motion Machines. For $2 you can take a three-minute roller coaster ride or bobsled excursion without going anywhere. A bar comes down across your seat and a movie begins. You'll be jerked with every turn or change of direction, making for a thrilling ride if you keep your eyes open and a bumpy bore if you close them. Children may also enjoy King Arthur's Tournament, Excalibur's family-style follies. For $24.95 per person, adult or child, your family can have a cheering, shouting, table-banging workout while rooting for the white or black knight in a football stadium–size arena where Merlin's magic, jousting tournaments, armor-clashing battles, and marriage processions unfold. Merry maids pour endless pitchers of Pepsi while lads distribute the evening's fare: Cornish hen, mashed potatoes, broccoli, and a roll, all served on a pewter tray. It's a hands-on time where you sit on benches and eat on counter tops. No silverware is offered, and extra napkins are hard to get. Two shows "knightly," at 6:00 and 8:30 P.M.; for reservations, Tel: 597-7600.

Caesars Palace, one block north at the corner of Flamingo Road, one-ups the Magic Motion Machines with OMNIMAX, a dome-shaped 57-foot-tall movie screen on the ceiling. The audience, reclining 27 degrees, seems to be right up against a 70-millimeter spectacle. Films such as *Fires of Kuwait* and *The Blue Planet* inundate the senses of sight and sound with engulfing images and informative narration. OMNIMAX presents hourly shows from 2:00 to 10:00 P.M.; $5.00 for adults, $3.00 for children.

A few steps to the north along Las Vegas Boulevard is the **Mirage**. Although the volcano is the hotel's major nighttime attraction, during the day you can visit the dolphin habitat and watch Merlin, Banjo, Duchess, Sigma, and Darla swim around a guarded pool while "dolphinologists" discuss the mammals' thoughts and behavior. An underwater viewing area provides another perspective. There you can watch the wanderings of Squirt, a baby dolphin born in the captive habitat in 1991. Open 11:00 A.M. to 7:00 P.M. during the week and 9:00 A.M. to 7:00 P.M. on weekends and holidays. Also, don't miss the white tigers in a palatial cage near the California Pizza Kitchen restaurant in the Mirage casino (viewing is free).

At **Circus Circus**, at the corner of Sahara Avenue, a second-floor midway complete with clowns, face-painting pits, and shooting galleries keeps children occupied for hours while parents play in a variety of low-minimum gaming areas. The "circus" is not just in name only. High-wire daredevils, trapeze artists, aerialists, cyclists, jugglers, animal trainers, and magicians perform from 11:00 A.M. to midnight throughout the big top.

Across The Strip you'll find an attraction that will make your kids promise to be good for a year: **Wet 'N Wild**. For $16.95 per adult (over ten years old), $13.50 per child (three to nine years old), and half adult price for seniors, you can have a ten-hour day at this water park, which features 12 unlimited-use water rides and plenty of cool activity for the cost of admission. Bring a picnic or buy healthful or fast-food sandwiches here. Plan to slide down the Black Hole—an enclosed blind labyrinth of twisting and dipping water slides—at least five times. Among the other exciting rides are Der Stuka, a steep 100-foot slide that simulates the experience of jumping out of an airplane—as close as you can get without actually doing it. Most of the rides propel you on water through winding tubes at great speeds, ultimately delivering you into well-guarded pools. The park also features a number of shallow-water attractions for small children. Be warned: The sun is strong, shade is limited, and lines are long. Wear a hat plus plenty of sunscreen and consider going between 4:00 and 8:00 P.M., when the rays are weaker and the price of admission drops by $3. Wet 'N Wild is open April to October. Call for hours, which vary; Tel: 734-0088.

Off The Strip, an unusual museum complex may give you something to write home about. To get to the Liberace Foundation return to Tropicana Avenue, turn left, and drive east about 4 miles (6½ km); go past Maryland Parkway four blocks to the light at Spencer Street. Liberace Plaza is on your right.

The **Liberace Foundation** comprises three museums: one for Mr. Showmanship's mirror-tiled Rolls and pianos; one for his rhinestone and mink capes, jewelry, and Baroque-style furniture; and one for his china and crystal. Here is a monument to what becoming insanely rich can lead to. The gift shop is a treat, with gold-wrapped Liberace chocolate coins, rhinestone piano charms, Liberace watches, pens, soaps, calendars, and all the tapes and videos you could possibly want. Hours are 10:00 A.M. to 5:00 P.M. Monday through Saturday and 1:00 to 5:00 P.M. Sundays. Admissions proceeds go to music scholarship funds at 52 colleges and universities in the United States. Tel: 798-5595.

For food-fantasy tours continue along Tropicana Avenue due east about another 3 miles (5 km) to Mountain Vista, and turn right. Follow Mountain Vista about 5 miles

(8 km) to the light at Sunset Way. Turn left into an industrial park and follow the signs to **Ethel M's**. This candy factory, owned by the Mars Corporation, makers of M&Ms and Milky Ways, treats you to a free tour of the production of its famous Ethel M's liqueur-filled candies. This two-minute "tour" is actually a view through a glass wall into two rooms, accompanied by a narrated video. It is rumored that the inheritor to the Mars fortune lives on the top floor of the building. The best part of the tour is the free sample you get at the end (not all contain alcohol) in the gift shop. The grounds are outstanding for their impressive cactus garden, with walkways among prickly things that produce Martian-like blooms in the spring. The gift shop sells chocolates and souvenir cactus in an Ethel M's pot. Hours are 8:30 A.M. to 5:00 P.M. Monday through Friday for the tour; 8:00 A.M. to 7:00 P.M. daily for the cactus garden and gift shop. Tel: 458-8864.

Another candyland tour awaits at the **Kidd Marshmallow Factory**, southeast of the city between Las Vegas and Henderson. Take Sunset Way to Sunset Road, turn left, and follow it 2 miles (3 km) to U.S. 95 South. Follow the freeway until it ends on Lake Mead Boulevard and turn right. On Gibson Road turn right and then right again onto American Pacific Drive, where you'll come to an industrial park and a copper-roofed building housing the factory. See how gelatin is mixed and blown and stretched, dusted, sugared, and chopped to make America's favorite hot-chocolate additive. Free samples are offered at the tour's end in the gift shop. Weekdays from 9:00 A.M. to 4:30 P.M. and weekends from 9:30 A.M. to 4:30 P.M.; Tel: 564-5400.

Far from the madding crowds find **Bonnie Springs**, a family afternoon getaway into the Old West of the surrounding area. From The Strip take I-15 south 3 miles (5 km) to the Blue Diamond exit. Turn right onto NV 160 at the off ramp and head west. Take the right turn for Blue Diamond onto NV 159 and follow it 5 miles (8 km) past Blue Diamond (for which, see West of Las Vegas, below) to Bonnie Springs. There you will find a Vietnamese potbellied pig, a llama, a porcupine, a coyote, and a menagerie of possible petables in a fun mini-zoo. Start with the train ride from the outer parking lot (Saturdays and Sundays only). Disembark and enter Old Nevada, a turn-of-the-century Western façade with a saloon, an opera house, and hourly simulated hangings and shoot-outs. Then sidle through the gateposts to the zoo and onward to the aviary. A restaurant-bar by the duck pond serves decent hamburgers and chili; by decree, ties come off at the door to be hung from the rafters as new property of the management. Bonnie Springs is one of three places near Las Vegas to offer horseback riding by the hour (see Mount Charleston Hotel in the West of Las Vegas section for the others). Be warned, however, that half of that hour may be spent trying to get the horse to move. Tel: 875-4191.

Another route to Bonnie Springs, via the Red Rocks Scenic Route, is to take Las Vegas Boulevard north to its intersection with Charleston Boulevard. Turn left (west) onto Charleston (which becomes NV 159) and drive 23 miles (37 km) to Bonnie Springs, 5 miles (8 km) past the Red Rock Canyon Visitor Center (again, see the West of Las Vegas section, below).

Staying in Las Vegas

Las Vegas is all about hotels: megahotels, resort hotels, resort casino hotels. The largest hotels congregate in two areas: The Strip and downtown. Other fine hotels and non-gaming hotels, such as the Alexis Park Resort, Howard Johnson Plaza Suites, and St. Tropez, make their nests east of The Strip on Harmon Avenue and Paradise Road, across from the Convention Center, a convenient location for the two million or so convention-goers Las Vegas handles each year.

Because the city is such an ideal weekend getaway, its hotel rooms maintain an occupancy rate of 96 percent through most weekends of the year. Therefore, even in a town of 77,000 rooms, finding one can be a tricky business. The best deals are procured through flight/hotel packages found in most Sunday newspaper travel sections or through a travel agent. Gamblers, on the other hand, can get complimentary rooms and food by arranging with the hotel beforehand to play certain games for a predetermined amount of money. Such comps, however, come with a price—of spending much more than intended or being forced to gamble rather than relax by the pool.

Las Vegas is in a state of flux. On the one hand, it lives with constant pressure to build bigger and better hotels in a bizarre battle for such titles as the world's largest and the world's most lavish. Yet several towers on The Strip and downtown are in Chapter 11 bankruptcy proceedings or have recently shut down. The drumbeat pounds on: Preparations are under way to add another 7,000 to

20,000 rooms by next year. A great pyramid named Luxor will take up some of Excalibur's large parking lot with an Egyptian-theme resort, complete with its own Nile and small boats to ferry guests to their rooms. Mirage owner Steve Wynn is well along on his pet project, Treasure Island, which will, of course, have a pirate theme. The granddaddy of worldwide resorts is also slated for a grand opening early next year: the 5,000-room MGM Grand Hotel & Theme Park, under construction across from the Tropicana Hotel. The $1 billion project will contain rides that simulate shooting the rapids of the Grand Canyon, deep-earth exploration, plank walking, and other adventures in an Emerald City motif.

Currently, hotel rooms are still a bargain in Las Vegas, with prices under $30 a night if your timing is right. At the high end you can spend as much as $7,000 a night if you want to take up the top floor of the Las Vegas Hilton or sleep with Elvis's ghost.

We offer a selection of the more prominent hotels with their *projected* 1993 rack rates. They are listed according to location, with The Strip's southernmost hotel choice listed first and with the easternmost downtown selection last. Prices quoted are per-room rates regardless of single or double occupancy. Price ranges span the lowest rate in the low season to the highest rate in the high season. As rates are always subject to change, it is wise to double-check before booking.

The area code for Nevada is 702.

THE STRIP

The Tropicana. This island-theme hotel takes its motif seriously, with an extensive water park, a Kon Tiki marriage hut, and a flock of babbling parrots wandering along hotel walkways. Rooms in the 22-story Island Tower are accessed by glass-enclosed exterior elevators. Some theme suites contain rock waterfalls and Jacuzzis in the living rooms. The casino still wears the Tiffany crown that dates from the gangland era that gave birth to "the Trop."

Dining includes the Island Buffet, which serves authentic Caribbean fare on weekends, and the Tropics restaurant overlooking the water park. The prices at the latter are just above coffee-shop level, but the Polynesian dishes are tasty and ample. For gourmet dining the hotel offers three options: Rhapsody, with Continental entrées; El Gaucho Steak House, for large plates of steak or fish served by candlelight; and Mizunos, which provides a teppanyaki grill table-side knife show.

3801 Las Vegas Boulevard South, 89109. Tel: 739-2222 or (800) 634-4000; Fax: 739-2469. $55–$129.

The Excalibur. It is rumored the executives from Circus Circus checked out 20 castles in Europe to help them create an authentic look here. The 4,032-room hotel is currently pegged as Las Vegas's largest, if not the world's. Most of the accommodations resemble average motel rooms: clean, small, and without bathtubs. However, if you have children along, the hotel makes a convenient and economical choice. Children can entertain themselves by spending their parents' hard-earned winnings at the Fantasy Faire, a basement-level midway, while parents play in the casino. The Excalibur has a small pool area, unimpressive for a hotel its size.

Dining at the Round Table Buffet here is the simplest choice for large families. It serves 1,400 people at a time. For upscale dining **Camelot** is the recommended spot, especially for New York steak. Sir Galahad serves prime rib and Yorkshire pudding in a "ye olde English" setting. Lance-A-Lotta Pasta serves Italian fare. Oktoberfest offers a wiener-and-wurst menu while an oompah-pah band entertains.

3850 Las Vegas Boulevard South, 89109. Tel: 597-7777 or (800) 937-7777; Fax: 597-7040. $20–$150.

Bally's Las Vegas was once the hotel of hotels in Las Vegas—the former MGM Grand—and its history still shows: in the Titian-style nymphs in the carriage fountain, in the famous-name headliners who grace the marquee, in the V.I.P. treatment of guests. The casino is a football field of marble and crystal, rebuilt after a fire swept through the MGM Grand in 1980.

Bally's is always one of the most crowded hotels on The Strip. The casino sets its blackjack minimums at $3 and $5 on weekends and manages to fill all the tables. Possibly this is because of location, possibly because the hotel packs so much entertainment into its quality lounge acts, follies extravaganzas, and celebrity shows. A basement arcade carries some noteworthy concessions, including a Hollywood memorabilia store and a gallery that sells limited-edition Disney cartoon cells.

The **buffet** at Bally's is the city's finest, known for its international variety and Chinese cuisine. Bally's has a half dozen restaurants, and they all serve good food. Its flagship gourmet room is **GiGi**, which offers classic French cuisine in Versailles-style opulence. Grapes describes itself as a California-style wine-and-seafood bar that serves California pizza and wines by the glass. The

Sterling Champagne Brunch is without a doubt the city's best treat on Sundays, served in the ornate setting of Bally's Italian gourmet room, Caruso's.

3645 Las Vegas Boulevard South, 89109. Tel: 739-4111 or (800) 634-3434; Fax: 794-2413. $85–$130.

The Flamingo Hilton. Bugsy's big dream built "out in the middle of nowhere" now sits on the busiest corner in Vegas. The Flamingo's four-floor Oregon Building, where Bugsy Siegel lived, remains intact and continues to welcome guests, though its demise is imminent due to an elaborate remodeling scheme the hotel is about to undertake. The gangster's suite, on the top floor, is occupied by high rollers most nights. The Oregon Building is easily accessible (it's just across the pool from the main high rise) and offers a dramatic sense of what the hotel was like when first built. The decor is a tribute to 1940s Deco, with green-and-gold brocade wallpaper and a massive chandelier that spans two floors. A narrow elevator with black pop-out buttons opens right onto the portico of Bugsy's old suite. Today this building is overshadowed by the Hilton's five 28-story towers decorated in Miami Beach motifs. This hotel caters mostly to the bus and charter-package crowd, and thus maintains a moderate price scale for its rooms and restaurants. Accommodations are modern, clean, and comfortable, but otherwise nondescript, decorated in light charcoals and mauves. The Flamingo's Lindy's Deli serves some of the best lox and bagels in town. The Art Deco Flamingo Room, with pink flamingos and bright pink neon, has wide booths overlooking the pool area.

3555 Las Vegas Boulevard South, 89109. Tel: 733-3111 or (800) 732-2111; Fax: 733-3353. $50–$133.

Caesars Palace, a combination of grace and glitter, is still the hotel of choice for serious gamblers and celebrities. The hotel is big on statues, with marble busts and figures of Roman (and other) personalities in every possible space throughout the hotel property; they've become the trademark of this pagan playhouse. A larger-than-life Joe Louis stands in the Olympic Casino, with an accompanying video of the fighter's better moments in continuous play. In the cocktail lounge you can drink under the serious gazes of Nero and Augustus Caesar. In the Rotunda there's a replica of Michelangelo's David. Gold, too, is worth its weight here, where you will find the world's highest-stakes slots, requiring a minimum $500 gold token for a chance to win a $500,000 jackpot.

What can you say about a hotel that rents Fantasy Suites

(with Roman, Egyptian, or Pompeiian decor) that include a personalized laser show upon entrance and re-create the night sky as it was at the time of Caesar's birth? The more affordable Villa Suites feature private saunas and Jacuzzis and round beds under mirrored ceilings. Each of these 14 suites bears the name of an ancient Roman city rather than a number, and comes with a personal villa captain to take care of every need. Regular rooms are studies in black lacquer with well-appointed Art Deco decor. (Rooms overlooking the lights of Las Vegas may be noisier than those above the pool area.) Statues guard the four corners of the pool, which has a mosaic-tiled bottom. The outdoor Jacuzzi offers contoured seats for comfortable effervescence. The area's "Garden of the Gods" designation somehow seems entirely appropriate at Caesars.

Affordable eating here can be found at La Piazza, a food court where you can get Japanese seafood noodle soup or plunder a salad bar for less than $7. The Forum Shops mall on the casino level (see Shopping, below) includes a few restaurants as well, among them **Spago's** for California-style cuisine, and Boogie's Diner of Aspen for burgers and fries. The Palatium, a Roman-style buffet, carries prawns, all-you-can-eat lox and sturgeon, and a dessert bar of tortes and tarts. Gourmet choices at Caesars can be overwhelming and include the *très* haute Palace Court, the sumptuous Bacchanal Room, the upscale Empress Court for Chinese fare, Primavera for prime Italian cuisine, and Nero's Steak and Seafood.

Dancing has a new twist here. Try **Cleopatra's Barge** for an evening of swaying under blue lights on a rocking boat.

3570 Las Vegas Boulevard South, 89109. Tel: 731-7110 or (800) 634-6001; Fax: 731-7172. $110–$250. Call for suite rates.

At the **Mirage** there's an emphasis on taste in architecture and design—an attempt to change the standard for Strip hotels. The Y-shaped gold and white hotel, with its tiger lair, dolphin habitat, domed rain forest, shark aquarium, and, of course, volcano, has so far outdone most other Vegas hotels inside and out. No neon here, not even a marquee. The volcano replaces all that. Inside, the hotel takes on a Polynesian flair. Comfortable overstuffed rattan chairs make those long rolls on the poker machines easier to manage. Rooms at the Mirage are standard or suite, with tropical decor in the former and a choice of Southwestern or Continental in the latter.

Of the recommended restaurants here, California Pizza

Kitchen is an excellent midprice choice and undoubtedly has something for everyone, including cheeseless pizza with spinach and eggplant, Thai pizza, and pies with gourmet cheeses and tomato sauce.

3400 Las Vegas Boulevard South, 89109. Tel: 791-7111 or (800) 627-6667; Fax: 791-7446. $69–$750.

The Desert Inn, one of The Strip's oldest hotels, may be one of its finest. With "only" 821 rooms it has managed to escape the megaresort frenzy that has overtaken this town in recent years. It caters to an upscale clientele who like to golf as well as gamble (the Desert Inn golf course is considered the best and most beautiful in the city). There are four choices of rooms: deluxe, superior, mini-suite, or one- to four-bedroom suite with whirlpool, bar, and private patio. Garden rooms come with semiprivate patios and outdoor spas. Recommended is the elegant Wimbledon Building, with rooms facing the golf course.

The casino area is small and stately, with brass-ring chandeliers. The lounge usually features recommendable talent. And this hotel comes with the city's best spa facility, which includes salt glow and loofah body scrubs and herbal wraps.

Monte Carlo, with its hand-painted murals, offers pricey French fare in four seatings beginning at 6:00 P.M. The Sunday brunch in the Crystal Room is one of The Strip's most lavish, with omelets and Belgian waffles made to order, fresh strawberries, and lots of lox and bagels.

3145 Las Vegas Boulevard South, 89109. Tel: 733-4444 or (800) 634-6906; Fax: 733-4676. $95–$1,500.

The central location of the **Stardust Hotel**, along with its beacon-bright neon, makes it impossible to miss. Inside the casino, mirrored columns reflect mauve, pink, and saffron-colored lights beneath a starry ceiling. From its 32-story tower, rooms tastefully done in Japanese motifs afford views of The Strip and the mountains. Dining is 1950s style at **Ralph's Diner** in the south end of the resort. Blue-plate specials are served to the tunes of the Van Dells by sock-hopping waitresses.

3000 Las Vegas Boulevard South, 89109. Tel: 732-6111 or (800) 634-6757; Fax: 732-6257. $24–$200.

Elvis is gone, but the **Las Vegas Hilton** lives on—more or less—with Wayne Newton. This hotel has all the tell-tale signs of Vegas: crystal chandeliers imported from Austria, Greco-Roman friezes, an immense gaming area. Rooms are decorated mostly in tropical motifs, some with verandahs that open onto the recreation deck. Plush executive suites are available on every floor. The pool is located on the third-floor rooftop, part of a ten-acre recreation deck that includes tennis courts, an 18-hole putting green, and a comprehensive health club. The Hilton, too, has its share of gourmet restaurants and steak houses. Among them is Le Montrachet, with entrées beginning at $35. At Benihana, with its Japanese garden lounge and animated bird show, dishes are prepared table-side by skilled knife-juggling waiters.

The Hilton also has a Youth Hotel "to provide a complete hotel experience for guests three to 18 years." It offers day services as well; children are attended by trained "play counselors." For Youth Hotel reservations, Tel: 732-5706.

3000 South Paradise Road (east of Las Vegas Boulevard and adjacent to the Las Vegas Convention Center), 89109. Tel: 732-5111 or (800) 732-7117; Fax: 732-5249. $90–$7,000.

Since its recent expansion the **Riviera Hotel** claims title to the world's largest casino, all 125,000 square feet of it. Within this crowded maze of clanking machines and cigarette smoke are four nightclub shows: "Splash," in the Versailles Theatre, is an aquatic revue with beautiful show girls, catchy Broadway tunes, and a few motocross riding stunts (there is no nudity); "Crazy Girls," on the second floor of the Mardi Gras Showroom's three theaters, features nearly nudes with gusto; "An Evening at La Cage" is a comical and riveting show of female impersonations; and "An Evening at the Improv" offers a night of laughs by well-known and not-so-well-known comics.

Dining options here run from Rik Shaw's midprice Chinese cuisine to Kristofer's Mediterranean-style chicken and fish on the rooftop.

2901 Las Vegas Boulevard South, 89109. Tel: 734-5110 or (800) 634-3420; Fax: 794-9230. $59–$440.

Circus Circus is for families. Big families. Lots of them. It's fun, noisy, crowded all the time. It's the place to find nickel slots and poker machines, and $1 and $2 blackjack. The European circus acts performed under the circus tent are entertaining, and the hotel midway on the second floor is full of diversions for children. Some of the rooms are a bit unusual looking, with oddly matched furniture and overly bright colors on the walls and textiles. But the prices and location—at the center of The Strip—make up for all this.

2880 Las Vegas Boulevard South, 89109. Tel: 734-0410 or (800) 634-3450; Fax: 734-5897. $36–$52.

Alexis Park Resort, off The Strip and away from the

action, prides itself on its refined solitude. The tastefully appointed hotel does not have a casino. All rooms are suites, many are as large as a two-bedroom apartment and contain a fireplace, a fully stocked honor bar, and a Jacuzzi. The location is convenient for convention visitors and rock fans, who delight in staying across the street from the Hard Rock Cafe.

375 East Harmon Avenue, 89109. Tel: 796-3300 or (800) 453-8000; Fax: 737-4334. $95–$325.

DOWNTOWN

The Union Plaza presides like a queen over Fremont Street. Its front rooms get a shimmering view of old Las Vegas. The Plaza stands on the site where Las Vegas began in 1905, when William Clark auctioned off the first lots from this very location. The Union Pacific depot is now an Amtrak station built into the hotel where the old platform once stood. Right next to the Greyhound bus station, the Union Plaza has become a favorite with visitors who don't arrive by air or their own wheels. The hotel offers some of the luxuries of Strip hotels, such as a health spa, a swimming pool, tennis courts, a jogging track, and a sports deck. High, dark-green ceilings enhance the spaciousness of the casino, which is done up in saloon-style red with crystal chandeliers.

One Main Street, 89101. Tel: 386-2110, (800) 634-6821 (in California), or (800) 634-6575 (outside California and Nevada); Fax: 382-8281. $30–$130.

The Golden Nugget, quite possibly the most elegant of the downtown hotels, is for people who want Strip service and quality but also want a different taste of Vegas. From the cobblestone entrance to the white marble and gold-leaf details, the hotel (another by Mirage owner Steve Wynn) was done right. All the rooms have been remodeled over the past two years; the decor that used to be turn-of-the-century "neobrothel" is now European contemporary. The Nugget's 27 town suites are split-level accommodations, each with a circular staircase, a sauna and a steam room, and a spa. All other rooms are deluxe, with city or mountain views.

Some things about the casino have not changed from its former days. Nickel slots abound, as do single-deck blackjack and dollar tables. As for dining, the Golden Nugget's gem, **The Buffet**, is considered Las Vegas's best by those who have not yet been to Bally's.

129 East Fremont Street, 89101. Tel: 385-7111 or (800) 634-3403; Fax: 386-8362. $58–$210.

For those who like New Orleans chic **The Four Queens** is heaven. It's even got its own jazz club, **The French Quarter**, where nightly entertainment features singers like the Platters or Della Reese—all for the entrance price of two drinks. Casual listeners are invited to watch from the wings.

The rooms are decorated in New Orleans style. Rooms for the physically impaired and smoke-free accommodations are available on request. **Hugo's**, the Queens' upscale basement restaurant, is a local favorite and one of the best places in town for prime rib. Female dinner guests here receive a rose, which has come to be the restaurant's symbol and the hotel's trademark. Hovering waiters will season your steak for you if you ask. For dessert choose from an incredible selection of fruits dipped in white and dark chocolate with fresh whipped cream.

202 East Fremont Street, 89101. Tel: 385-4011 or (800) 634-6045; Fax: 383-0631. $47–$95.

Dining in Las Vegas

Las Vegas locals love explaining why they don't cook to their out-of-town guests. When you live in a town that practically gives food away to get people to gamble, it doesn't pay to stay home.

Indeed, you will find a great range of dining experiences in Las Vegas, from the 50¢ shrimp cocktail to the $4 buffet chow line (all the shrimp you could ever want) to the $65 seven-course meal—an assortment of dining experiences indeed. However, the food lacks the variety and the finesse you will find in most cities. Las Vegas is not known for Ethiopian restaurants, vegetarian hideaways, or Indian platters. You can count on fillets, prime cuts, and lobster bisques at most gourmet rooms, just as you can count on all-you-can-eat baked ham, roast beef, fried chicken, vegetables, and rolls at most buffets. Las Vegas is American eating, from macaroni and cheese to the catch of the day flown in from New England.

Gone are the years when a Vegas vacation was synonymous with free meals. Gone are the "chuck wagon" days when tuxedoed waiters served complimentary prime rib and rack of lamb from linen-covered pushcarts to hungry gamblers out in the gaming areas. The buffets have taken over, serving guests in high heels, ties, or Bermuda shorts and sneakers without bias.

BEST-FOOD BUFFETS

The best buffets in Vegas are worth the wait. **Bally's Big Kitchen** has yet to be voted the most popular by Vegans, possibly because it is always so crowded most locals have not had the opportunity to eat there. Count on 45 minutes in line and another ten at the register. The best feature is the Chinese kitchen, which cooks up wonderful stir-fry while you wait. There are plenty of pasta salads and there's a fresh-fruit bar of melons and berries. Desserts include a sundae bar with fresh, warm chocolate syrup and a number of minicakes and sweets, among them a delicious pecan pie. All for $10.95. Open 4:30 to 11:00 P.M. Tel: 739-4930.

Bally's Sterling Brunch is the finest buffet dining experience possible without sacrificing a week's salary. The chefs of the major restaurants in the hotel show off their specialties at this brunch, whipping up dishes you've only read about. Try all-you-can-eat truffles, or fresh shrimp, crab, salmon, and octopus sushi by the half dozens. Mussels Provençal for breakfast? Smoked salmon with dill and vodka? Yes, there are the usual waffles with fresh strawberries and whipped cream, and fresh raspberries served with unrefined sugar, but the salmon mousse takes the cake. Cost: $24.95. Sundays 9:00 A.M. to 2:30 P.M. Tel: 739-4111.

The **Golden Nugget** serves all-you-can-eat crab legs and claws by the pound most nights. In a tasteful brass-and-glass dining area, you can eat endless rolls of California sushi (on Wednesdays and Saturdays), smoked salmon, whitefish, and lox (Sundays), and 105 salad items every day. There's always a broiled entrée for cholesterol watchers. The price is $9.50 (children four to ten years old half price). From 4:00 to 10:00 P.M. Tel: 385-7111.

Caesars Palatium Buffet puts you right in the middle of the casino action. Fresh lox, whitefish, and sturgeon as well as shrimp and crab legs with cocktail sauce are served from 4:30 to 10:00 P.M. every day amid the whirling lights and ringing slots. The dessert bar has fresh blueberries and raspberries in season, tarts, pies, and chocolate Italian pastries. All for $11.95. Call for hours; Tel: 731-7110.

Binion's Horseshoe, downtown at 128 Fremont Street, is reputed to have the best seafood buffet in town but actually misses the mark on most dishes when it comes to fresh taste. But it does have a nice *variety* of seafood, including shrimp, crab legs, broiled cod, and other delights, plus an all-you-can-eat pile of raw clams on the half shell—worth the tariff for mollusk lovers (the buffet is the most expensive of the nightly buffets, seafood or otherwise, with the exception of the Sands Garden Terrace Buffet). The charge is $12.95. From 4:00 to 10:30 P.M. Tel: 382-1600.

Fridays-only alternatives for seafood lovers include **Sam Boyd's Fremont Hotel's Friday Seafood Fantasy** for $10.95, which serves crab legs by the bowlful (4:00 to 11:00 P.M.; Tel: 385-3232), or the **Friday Seafood Extravaganza** at the Frontier Hotel for $7.95 (4:00 to 10:00 P.M.; Tel: 794-8200).

BEST-DEAL BUFFETS

If you are feeding a legion of hungry loggers, the following rock-bottom–priced buffets along The Strip may be for you.

Excalibur's **Round Table Buffet** has an active carving station for prime rib, turkey, and ham, and also serves unending portions of pork ribs, all for $4.99, from 4:00 to 10:00 P.M. Tel: 597-7777.

Circus Circus Plate of Plenty dishes out buffet meals to 12,000 people a day for $3.99 per person. Hours are 4:30 to 11:00 P.M. Tel: 734-0410.

Harrah's Galley serves dinners in a Cajun-style setting for $5.49, not including beverage, from 4:00 to 11:00 P.M. (till 10:00 P.M. on Saturdays and Sundays). Tel: 369-5000.

Maxim Hotel, on Flamingo Road behind the Flamingo Hilton, offers an evening buffet from 4:00 to 10:00 P.M. for $4.95, often accompanied by a live piano concert. Tel: 731-4300.

All buffets require some planning in order to avoid a long wait for an empty table. That usually means getting to the register within a half hour of opening, or going late, around 9:30 P.M.

FINE DINING

Chefs from the greatest culinary institutes in the world are attracted to Las Vegas, where so-called gourmet rooms abound in which they can strut their stuff. Diners are usually attracted to gourmet rooms because of the atmosphere, service, and fine dishes, and most come prepared to enjoy the money they are spending or winning. Nearly every hotel maintains a flagship gourmet room, with prices around the city ranging from $12 to $60 per entrée. Here are five special restaurants, some noted for the quality of their preparation, others for their atmosphere. Jackets and ties are usually a must for these dining rooms, and reservations are essential.

Palace Court sits in the crown of Caesars Palace under a domed skylight. A glass-enclosed elevator carries guests to this restaurant, which overlooks the Garden of the Gods pool area, or you can walk up the royal-red carpeted stairs. This is elegance, from the fresh hickory-smoked almonds on the tables in the cocktail room to the individually controlled track lights, adjusted according to your specifications.

The menu, which is classical French cuisine, offers, for example, a quail consommé for starters and a selection of shellfish bisques. All fish is fresh and flown in daily—that goes for the salmon flambé in lemon vodka served in a potato crust. Other specialties are roast duck and herbs, and lamb braised in peppercorns. Entrées average $30 to $35. A wonderful dessert tray and coffee prepared at the table via glass Chemex method top off the dinner. Tel: 731-7547.

Bacchanal, also at Caesars Palace, on the main floor, is an experience that goes beyond food. Inspired by the excesses of Caesars, a meal here begins with dancing women draped in veils who lead guests to their tables, where they are greeted with fruits, nuts, cheeses, and wine (cups are never allowed to empty here). The menu reads like a concert program: seven courses, seven events, with plenty of time in between each. Appetizers are followed by "gifts from the sea," soup, pasta, a Caesar or Cleopatra salad, and then a meat course—a filet mignon, a prime rib, veal or duck prepared with herbs and peppers.

About this time Antony and Cleo make their entrance in full royal Roman regalia just before the unveiling of dessert. It's usually a glass of flaming vanilla ice cream topped with fresh fruits. This dining event, complete with neck massages for the men and hand kissing for the women, costs $65 per person and takes about three hours. Open Tuesday through Saturday, 6:00 to 11:00 P.M. Tel: 731-7731.

Pegasus at the Alexis Park Resort is a quiet affair, with a harpist playing show tunes inside and a rocky waterfall and stream dancing outside. The chef goes all out here, with a medley of rich sauces, and the portions are immense. A recommended meal: the scampi appetizer stuffed with crabmeat in a bisque sauce, lobster bisque laced with Cognac, beef Wellington served with truffles and Madeira sauce, for two (or abalone sautéed in pecan butter for the more adventurous), and ice cream topped with fruit and Grand Marnier. An evening at Pegasus with one bottle of wine can easily cost over $200 per couple before tax and tip. Tel: 796-3353.

Savoia, at 4305 Paradise Road next to the Alexis Park Resort and across from the Hard Rock Cafe, is an affordable delight in California neo-Continental style. The owner, Georges LaForge, has been one of Las Vegas's top maître d's for years, and his menu reflects his love of mixing the whimsical with classics. For starters try the homemade ravioli with either puréed escargots in butter and garlic, or a seafood ravioli in a lobster bisque. The spicy Yucatan duck sausage made with cilantro is an unusual offering. Entrées include pastas, fish and shellfish, corn-fed chicken, and steaks and chops. Recommended is fresh Norwegian salmon broiled in orange honey and mustard seed. For steak lovers the hobo steak cooked in rock salt and fresh herbs is a meal for two (the meats here are unbelievably tender). Salad for the whole table comes in a handsome black oyster shell set upon a plate of condiments. Savoia also provides free limo service to and from the restaurant for the asking. Two people can have an extraordinary culinary experience for under $50, not including wine. Tel: 731-5446.

Pamplemousse, Georges LaForge's other restaurant, is known to most locals simply as the city's best dining establishment. The classical French restaurant sits inconspicuously in a squat white building at 401 East Sahara Avenue, about a mile east of the Sahara Hotel. The dark interior seems to belong in a cottage in the French countryside more than in a restaurant in Las Vegas. Here, after serving an ample basket of crudités, the waiter recites the menu and explains how each dish is prepared. Favorites include fresh salmon with orange and curry, and roast duckling with green peppercorns and Armagnac. Entrées average $30. Tel: 733-2066.

Nightlife in Las Vegas

Las Vegas considers itself the Entertainment Capital of the World, where the names of anyone from Frank Sinatra to Bob Dylan can be found on the marquee. This is the town that once featured Streisand and made gold out of Diana Ross. It's the playground of Shirley MacLaine, Liza Minnelli, and Dean Martin. Liberace settled here, Elvis lived here much of the time, Wayne Newton raises racehorses here, Pia Zadora keeps trying to make it here.

Most of the headliners can be found on The Strip: at Bally's, Caesars, the Desert Inn, and the Riviera. The Hilton gets its share of draws, too, and the Golden Nugget attracts a number of big names. Lounge shows at several hotels feature some names from the past, such as the Platters, the Imperials, Freddy Cannon, Frank Sinatra, Jr., and Roberta Sherwood. (Unless otherwise stated, smoking is not allowed in the headliner theaters.)

At **Bally's** prearranged seating is in place for tickets purchased prior to the show. The theater seats 1,450. Prices range from $39 to $65, not including drinks. Some of the regular performers here are Tom Jones, George Carlin, and Dean Martin. In its Ziegfeld Room you'll find "Jubilee!," a huge stage revue of bare-breasted show girls reenacting such dramas as the sinking of the *Titanic* ($36, not including drinks, 7:30 and 11 P.M. except Wednesdays; Tel: 739-4567). Here, too, is **Catch a Rising Star** comedy club, in the shopping arcade. Shows are at 8:00 and 10:30 P.M., and the price is $12.50 before drinks. Tel: 739-4111.

Caesars Palace brings on blockbusters like Ann-Margret, David Copperfield, Johnny Mathis, and Julio Iglesias in its Roman Circus Maximus nightclub. Prices are $35 to $60, not including bar. Seats can be bought and paid for up to a month before the show, and booths can be reserved for an extra fee. The box office is open from 8:00 A.M. to 10:00 P.M., but phone requests can be made only between 9:00 A.M. and 5:00 P.M. Tel: 731-7333.

The **Desert Inn** has staked its reputation and marketing campaign on its frequent headliners. Regulars include Frank Sinatra, Shirley MacLaine, Liza Minnelli, Debbie Reynolds, Buddy Hackett, and Smokey Robinson. Shows usually start at 8:00 P.M., with tickets ranging from $35 to $75, including drinks. Seats here are assigned by the maître d', so tipping customs demand spending a little more than you bargained for—usually $10 to $20 to guarantee a good comfortable seat ($5 to $10 to the seating assistant will get you to the far left wall behind a pole, and another $5 to $10 will usually secure two chairs closer to, but not facing, the stage).

The **Golden Nugget** has one of the few celebrity rooms that still allows smoking. It brings in such notables as Don Rickles, David Brenner, Yacov Smirnoff, and Mel Tillis. Prices are $27 to $33 and include two drinks. Seating is by the maître d' in this intimate room. Tel: 386-8100.

The room at the **Las Vegas Hilton** is enormous, with seating for 1,650 people—and the shows sell out. Featured performers have included Wayne Newton, Englebert Humperdinck, and Crystal Gayle. Advance purchase is recommended, although locations are only guaranteed for tickets purchased in person. Booths are available without surcharge. The seating price of $34 to $60 includes one drink. Tel: 732-5755.

A number of follies revues, magic shows, stand-up comedy performances, and other live entertainments are standard features of the hotels. The "Folies Bergère" at the **Tropicana** is Las Vegas's longest-running follies and still has a dinner show—something of a dying breed in this town. Tel: 739-2411. "Enter the Night" is the **Stardust's** big show, featuring two hours of laser effects, acrobats, dazzling costumes, and plenty of lilting ladies out of costume. No slow moments in this show; it keeps your ears attuned and your eyes occupied trying to catch it all. A fine, well-executed performance. The $35 price includes taxes and two drinks. Reserved seat locations are purchased prior to the shows, which begin at 8:00 and 11:00 P.M. Tel: 732-6325.

Vegas also offers its share of "Elvis shows" by well-practiced impersonators. The most recommended "Elvis" can be found among the stars in "Legends in Concert" at the **Imperial Palace**, next to the Flamingo Hilton. Performances are at 7:30 and 10:30 P.M. daily except Sundays, and children are welcome. The price of $25 includes two drinks and covers tax and tip. Children 12 and under pay $12. Tel: 794-3261.

For an unusual evening of Texas two-stepping, try the Gold Coast Hotel and Casino and Sam's Town Hotel and Casino. Both hotels are off The Strip, and therefore frequented by locals. You'll spot real and urban cowboys and cowgirls and a lot of muscular construction workers. At the **Gold Coast**, about 1 mile (1½ km) west of Bally's at 4000 West Flamingo Road, there is a spacious dance floor and live music most nights. Call for a schedule; Tel: 367-7111. **Sam's Town** not only features live country music, it also offers free dancing lessons before 9:00 P.M. Sam's Town is about 6 miles (10 km) east of Bally's at the intersection of Flamingo Road, Nellis Boulevard, and Boulder Highway. Drinks are cheap, cover is free, and the action goes on until 3:00 A.M. Tel: 456-7777.

Shopping in Las Vegas

From The Strip, two noteworthy malls are within easy walking distance. The **Forum Shops** at Caesars is something of a Disneyland for upscale shoppers. Seventy restaurants and shops (at last count) with names like Escada, Bernini, Guess, and Gucci make shopping here like spending an afternoon in Milan. But chances are you won't even make it into the shops; what's outside is such appealing entertainment.

Under a massive domed rotunda, every hour on the hour for seven minutes, otherwise stationary statues around a marble fountain come to life in an animated show with lights, music and sounds, and robotics while a laser light show plays on the dome.

At the 90-degree angle of the L-shaped mall is another fountain and piazza, reminiscent of Venice—without the pigeons—where you can people-watch while sipping espresso or Italian mineral water. The painted ceiling of the mall is an extravagant mural of clouds and sky that gradually changes from the tones of sunrise to those of midday, sunset, and then a star-filled night thanks to a coordinated lighting system. Access is by moving sidewalk, which begins at Caesars on the north (Strip) side. However, the only way out is by foot through the casino. The hours of the Forum Shops are 10:00 A.M. to 11:00 P.M. daily.

Farther up The Strip, across from the Mirage, the **Fashion Show Mall** is a good place to pick up bargains at status stores. From Neiman-Marcus and Saks Fifth Avenue to Bullocks and May Co., a number of major stores have found homes here—and run sales more often than not. Clothing carries a 7 percent sales tax in Nevada, which takes something away from the savings, but clothes are still less expensive here than in other major cities, and serious shopping can be accomplished in one stop.

DAY TRIPS FROM LAS VEGAS
The Lake Mead Area

Las Vegas is not only The Strip, the lights, and the entertainment. It is also desert and the quiet mystery that accompanies this ancient and still largely untouched area of earth. The Hoover Dam/Lake Mead area, where Nevada meets Arizona, is an easy half-day trip into the desert. Take Flamingo Road east to the Boulder Highway (which becomes U.S. 93/95), turn right and follow it southeast past Boulder City. (Boulder is the dam's old name.)

Hoover Dam, 30 miles (48 km) east of Las Vegas, straddles the Nevada-Arizona border and two time zones. The ride into the dam area is breathtaking, and the view down the 726-foot concrete wall to the river stirs even the most jaded of travellers. Colossal electrical transformers jut out from the rocks at unsettling angles. For dam buffs the lecture and the ride down into the spillways is an hour well spent. Whether or not Hoover Dam is the eighth wonder of the world, its immensity boggles the mind. Stop at the Alan Bible Visitors' Center 4 miles (6½ km) before the dam on U.S. 93/95, where a continuously playing video gives a historical view of the engineering feat (94 men lost their lives during the construction in the 1930s) and a movie about the desert terrain is available on request. The center also offers nature walks, gives out plenty of free literature about the area, and sells natural-history books. Tel: 293-8907.

A look southward from the dam down the Black Canyon shows a tamed Colorado River. **Black Canyon Inc.'s raft tours** can be booked through Grey Line Tours; Tel: 384-1234. A bus will pick you up at your hotel and take you to Expedition Depot, 1297 Nevada Highway in Boulder City (Tel: 293-3776), near Hoover Dam. From there you will be transported to the embarkation dock and floated from below Hoover Dam down to Willow Beach on a motorized raft while guides regale you with tales of local history. The excursion, which includes lunch, is a relaxing five hours. Tour price: $60 per person; $35 for children 11 and under. This is not a trip for sensitive nonsmokers; many rafting guests prefer to puff away, and seating arrangements are limited.

The **Desert Princess** also cruises the waters, but lakeside. This three-deck steamboat sails from Lake Mead Marina to Hoover Dam and back for a buffet breakfast, scenic midday tour, or sunset dinner dance. The trip takes about two hours, with up to six launchings a day. Smoking is not allowed within the enclosed decks. Prices range from $12 to $32.50 per adult. Tel: 293-6180.

On the north side of Lake Mead, about 60 miles (96 km) from Vegas, you'll find fascinating petroglyphs drawn by the Anasazi Indians between 800 and 4,000 years ago on the exposed sandstone canyons at the **Valley of Fire**. This state park can be reached from I-15 North (exit east on NV 169 and follow the signs) or from the scenic North Shore Road around Lake Mead (NV 167), which is what Lake Mead Boulevard becomes as you follow it northeast out of town. Your best route is to pick up Lake Mead Boulevard East as you drive north on I-15 through town and follow it to the Valley of Fire (about an hour and a half). Your return to Las Vegas can take about an hour if you follow NV 169 out of the park to I-15 South. Stop at

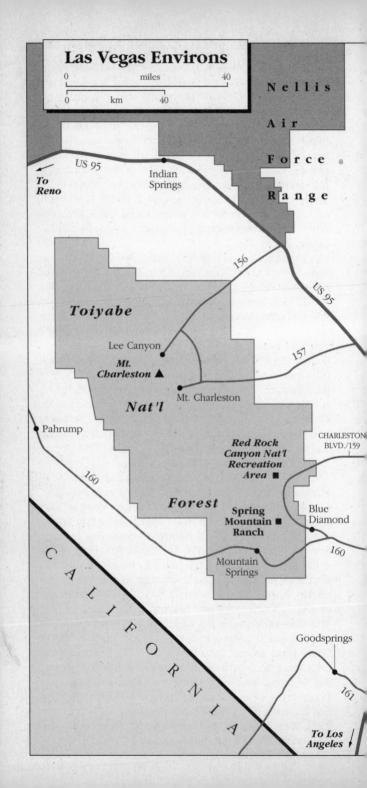

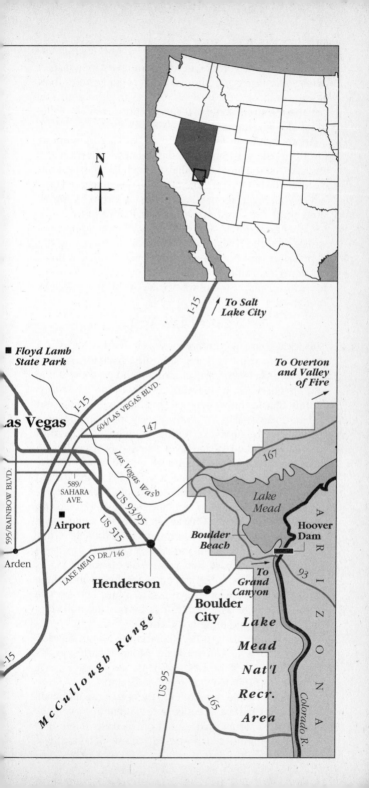

the visitors' center in the middle of the park for a map, a petroglyph dictionary, a flora and fauna guide, and a look at some of those creatures you see only in glass cases. You can also ask about some of the trails and attractions of this moonlike landscape. Tel: 397-2088.

Another draw in the area is the **Lost City Museum** in Overton. Follow I-15 north to the Logandale/Overton exit and take the road into the valley through Logandale to the eastern side of Overton. The museum is well marked up a hill to your right, about 60 miles (96 km) from Las Vegas. Built amid a restored Anasazi village that includes pueblos, the museum is a preserved adobe building constructed by the Civilian Conservation Corps during the depression, and houses not only relics of ancient times but items from Mormon settlements, others of which were lost forever under the flows of Lake Mead. Tel: 367-2193.

West of Las Vegas

The local tourism commission jokes that Las Vegas is a place where you can play golf in the early morning, sail and water-ski in the early afternoon, and go snow skiing and sleigh riding in the early evening. The snow atop **Mount Charleston** sometimes lasts until mid-spring, and the mountain makes for a pleasant escape from the city's heat during the summer. This Alpine mountain slope with its sleepy A-frame villages and marvelous vistas lies an hour northwest of Las Vegas. Pick up I-15 North via any on-ramp from The Strip. Take it to U.S. 95 going toward Reno. Then take the well-marked Mount Charleston turn-off at NV 157. Prepare to stop about 6 miles (10 km) up the road at the **Mount Charleston Hotel** for some coffee and apple pie. The hotel looms large and lodgelike over the side of the mountain and affords a view that pans 50 miles. All rooms have fine views, some have fireplaces and balconies. The lobby's open hearth keeps an inviting fire going in the winter. Live jazz or blues may beckon from the lounge. Two stables nearby provide trail rides on horseback, and these horses move.

For accommodations here contact the Mount Charleston Hotel, 2 Kyle Canyon Road, Mount Charleston, NV 89124. Tel: 872-5500; Fax: 456-3345. Room rates range from $49 to $150 depending on the season.

Continue via the same road to the top of the mountain and **Mount Charleston Lodge**, a restaurant that offers the best views of Mount Charleston from its patio. If the snow is deep, 20-minute sleigh rides give a one-of-a-kind pleasure in southern Nevada. Hiking here is splendid, too. An easy and well-marked trail up Cathedral Rock is the choice of most Sunday amblers. The three-mile uphill trail begins near the ranger station at the very end of NV 157 beyond the turnoff to the lodge. It passes a trickling waterfall and ends up on a ledge that provides the most spectacular view of the mountain you can have without a major workout.

Back at the restaurant join the Dumpkoffs, a German-style sing-along band that also plays at Excalibur's Okto-berfest Restaurant. They play Mount Charleston on Satur-days, Sundays, and holiday afternoons, when the lodge is most crowded. Tel: 386-6899 or (800) 955-1314.

Before returning to Las Vegas take NV 156, by the Mount Charleston Hotel, and mosey over to the **Lee Canyon Ski Area.** A chair lift pulls ski parties up 1,000 feet to the 9,500-foot summit. In non-ski seasons it carries sightseers up the mountain—and takes them back down—for a half hour of relaxed dangling. A snack bar provides hot chocolate and potato chips to hungry skiers; this is not a destination for fine dining. Tel: 872-5462.

From Las Vegas you can also head south and west via I-15 south from The Strip, exiting west onto NV 160. After about 10 miles (16 km) take the branch off to the right onto NV 159 to **Blue Diamond**, a village of 50 or so steadfast families living in two-bedroom bungalows built by the local gypsum mine. The town has a library now, an elementary school, and a prolific clan of wild burros that visit each night. The big tourist attraction of Blue Dia-mond, besides the chance to experience some noncom-mercialized life at a stop on the old Spanish Trail (the historic route that took Spanish missionaries from Mex-ico to California), is **Blue Diamond Bicycles**. Rent trail bikes and helmets, or the whole outfit, for $7 an hour or $25 for the day, and set out for the 13-mile (21-km) scenic loop at Red Rock Canyon, a sandstone wonderland 8 miles (13 km) to the north, discussed below. Blue Dia-mond Bicycles will provide touring directions to Red Rock and elsewhere locally; Tel: 875-4500.

Moments after Bonnie Springs, 5 miles (8 km) past Blue Diamond along NV 159, is **Spring Mountain Ranch**, a 19th-century property that was once owned by Howard Hughes and is now a state park, operated through the kindness of docents. They keep the hearth fires stoked and entertain guests with stories—all true, all for free.

Continue northward along NV 159 as it loops clockwise

back toward Las Vegas and you will come upon **Red Rock Canyon**. Its fire-colored sandstone hills are easy to spot. Begin at the well-marked visitors' center (off Route 159), which houses displays of desert creatures. Then embark on the scenic loop, so marked, just past the visitors' center and enjoy a journey into Red Rock on a well-paved road. All car traffic travels one-way, counterclockwise, and exits about 2 miles (3 km) west of the visitors' center on NV 159. Plenty of well-marked trails make hiking off the loop easy, safe, and well travelled. You'll see magnificent vistas of sandstone abutting limestone in hues of yellow, orange, red, white, pink, and purple, and a rolling outback dotted with Joshua trees leading to the Spring Mountain walls that shadow the canyon to the west. After exiting Red Rock, continue on NV 159 as it veers due east into Las Vegas and becomes Charleston Boulevard. Less than 15 miles (24 km) from the world's largest gambling and indoor-recreation joints, Red Rock Canyon offers a great contrast to Vegas besides being a fine outdoor area in its own right.

If, instead of bearing right onto NV 159 to Blue Diamond you continue on Route 160 west from I-15, you eventually come to the town of Pahrump. There you'll find the **Pahrump Valley Winery and Restaurant**, Nevada's only winery. As owner Jack Sanders puts it, "With a name like Pahrump, we've got to be good."

Pahrump lies about an hour west of Vegas, slightly beyond Mount Potosi. There's not much to this former mining settlement, also remembered as the site of Carole Lombard's plane crash, and most folks miss it completely, but the winery hopes to change all that. Lunch in Pahrump is a relaxing half-day adventure that begins with a tour of the winery and some complimentary tastings of their Symphony vintage before the meal. The owners, refugees from the San Francisco rat race (everything is relative), have put together a menu of croissant sandwiches, healthy home-made soups, and grilled and stir-fried entrées that are served with their award-winning wines. The panoramic views from the plush dining room take in two states and two mountain ranges. The genteel country ambience of the restaurant compensates well for any lack of quality in the menu. Tel: 727-6900 for lunch or dinner reservations.

Among your after-lunch choices are a return to Vegas; a visit to the free hot springs facility at Tecopa (take NV 160 east from Pahrump for about 16 miles/26 km to the Tecopa turnoff on the right; follow that road 34 miles/54 km across the California border to Tecopa); or a trip to check out the Chicken Ranch, less than a mile southeast of Pahrump on NV 160 East and 8 miles (13 km) south down Homestead Road (turn right at Pahrump Valley Winery onto Homestead). Brothels are legal in this part of Nevada, and the Chicken Ranch may be the most notable in the state, or at least in southern Nevada. It opened in 1976, three years after the closing of the Old Chicken Ranch, the 130-year-old Texas brothel that served as the model for the "Best Little Whorehouse in Texas," of literary, theatrical, and cinematic fame. At Chicken Ranch you'll find items from the old ranch plus an entire souvenir line of products such as hats, shirts, beer steins, shot glasses, coffee mugs, and ashtrays, as well as the working ladies. Free round-trip 24-hour limousine service from Las Vegas is available upon request. Tel: 382-7870.

GETTING AROUND

Las Vegas is at least a 5-hour drive from anyplace that smacks of city life. Los Angeles is 295 miles (472 km) southwest on I-15. San Francisco is 600 miles (960 km) to the northwest across Death Valley. Phoenix and Tucson are about 8 hours to the southeast, depending on driving speeds, while Albuquerque is about an 11-hour drive to the southeast. Salt Lake City lies 425 miles (680 km) to the northeast over smooth mountain highways. Amtrak runs through town and even stops at the Union Plaza Hotel. Trains from Salt Lake City, Los Angeles, and San Diego make daily stops in Las Vegas after a full day of travel.

McCarran Airport receives carriers from 17 major airlines, including Air Canada, American, America West, British Airways, Continental, Delta, Hawaiian Air, Northwest, Southwest, TWA, United, and USAir.

The airport sits at the edge of the town, an average seven-minute drive from any hotel on The Strip. It's a promenade of aluminum palm sculptures, moving walkways with recorded warnings delivered by the voices of Don Rickles and Joan Rivers, and video extravaganzas of scenes from Strip shows. The true sounds of Vegas—rows of quarter slots and video poker machines, the likes of which are found in supermarkets, 7-Elevens, and gas stations all over town—clank and ring, accompanying the walking traffic en route to the baggage-claim area.

Be prepared to wait after you've found your luggage. McCarran is one of the few airports in the world that makes a science out of matching luggage tags with tickets. There are only two exits, and the two people charged with this responsibility take their jobs very seriously indeed.

You have two choices for hired transportation into town: taxi and limousine. Las Vegas is not a town that prides itself on convenient and efficient public transportation. Taxis make no bones about the fact that this is where they earn their money—about $9 a trip from airport to hotel, not including tip. Limos, however, will take you to any major hotel for $3 to $5 per person and are available at the curb practically around the clock. Should you choose to travel in style, a stretch and driver can be procured for $24 to $60 an hour, depending on whether your tastes demand high-tech audiovisual entertainment and a well-stocked bar.

Renting a car at the airport is the choice most regulars make, as rates are reasonable and parking is free at most hotels. When renting a car, be aware that some rental contracts require that you limit your driving to Nevada. If you are planning to visit Hoover Dam, which lies squarely on the state border, or if the Grand Canyon is on your itinerary, make sure your rental contract does not restrict this travel. It is best to reserve in advance; most major car-rental companies are located here.

When to Go

Seasons in southern Nevada often dash the hopes of winter sun seekers expecting to escape the cold sting of the East and Midwest with a good book and lounge chair by the pool. Temperatures from November to March dip into the 20s at night before recovering to the high 50s during the day. Las Vegas winters demand a light jacket for most hours of the day and a heavy one at night, although a sweater under day wraps will do. The desert wind can sting as much as the gales off Lake Michigan. However, most days are temperate and cloudless. Las Vegas receives a little over four inches of rain a year. Count on the likelihood of sunshine and a moderate amount of wind, usually enough to cool you off but not enough to cause the cancellation of your golf game.

Tourism has its seasons as well. Las Vegas swells like a hot-air balloon with visitors who come for national holidays and conventions. Las Vegas is nearly always in high season, but the most crowded times of year are New Year's, Fourth of July, Memorial Day, and Labor Day. Also, COMDEX, a major computer exposition, brings in more than 110,000 conventioneers for a week in November, putting hotel accommodations at a premium—assuming a room can be found.

But summer is the main tourist time. This is the season

to revel in the dry heat and strong sun that delivers an almost instant tan. Average midsummer midday temperatures hover at 108°F and drop to a "chilly" 95 at night. Outside Las Vegas on the higher ground of Mount Charleston, an hour north, or in the elevations of southern Utah, two hours north, summer daytime temperatures stay in the 80s and provide a comfortable place for travellers to escape the lower-desert sizzle.

Ask any concierge and you will learn that the best time to visit Vegas is during the holiday gap between Thanksgiving and Christmas. These are the days of short buffet lines, breathable casino air, standing spots at the craps pit, and open seats at the $2 blackjack table. Rooms, too, can be found for a song then, and even bargained into generous upgrades.

Tipping

Las Vegas is a service-industry town. Although the city bills are paid by the megaprofits from hotel casinos, the people working in those casinos pay their bills not so much from salaries earned but from tips. Tips range from the 50¢ gratuity (known in the vernacular as "tokes") for the cocktail waitress delivering your free Scotch and soda while you drop nickels into a slot machine to the $50 bill passed inconspicuously to the maître d' assigning you a center-stage booth for a Frank Sinatra concert. Tipping starts the minute you walk off the plane, whether it's to the limo driver who takes you to your hotel, to the valet who parks your car, or to the bellhop who delivers your luggage. It continues as you gamble, tipping the dealer by placing an extra bet or by pushing $2 chips toward the well when you win. It ends at the airport, where curbside attendants want to see a dollar bill before they will check your luggage. Tipping is considered a necessary good-luck gesture in this town, and in a place where greenbacks feel more like Monopoly paper than bankable receipts, spreading a little luck around can be relatively painless.

Driving in Las Vegas

Those who do not know better use Las Vegas Boulevard to get from one place to another. Wrong. The Strip is gridlocked nearly any time of day, any day. You suffer and sweat behind lost RVs, city buses, and waves of pedestrians. The rule of thumb is to avoid The Strip at all costs, even if that means going eight blocks out of your way.

To accomplish this you need to know that on the east side of The Strip are two or three streets that run parallel to it. First is Koval Lane, which runs from Tropicana Avenue to Twain Avenue. Taking Koval north, followed by a left on Twain (which becomes Spring Mountain Road beyond Las Vegas Boulevard) is an easy way to drive to the Mirage from the Flamingo Hotel, Harrah's, the Sands, and all the places in between (most of these major hotels have back ways that empty onto Koval Lane and other back streets); it's also the easiest way to get to the Fashion Show Mall.

Another street to consider is Paradise Road, a block east of Koval Lane. Paradise Road also runs from Twain Avenue, but it continues on to Sahara Avenue. This is the route to take to get to the Sahara Hotel, to Wet 'N Wild, to the Las Vegas Convention Center (which is on Paradise Road), to the Desert Inn (turn left on Desert Inn Road), and to the Riviera (turn left on Riviera Boulevard). The Paradise Road–Riviera Boulevard route also gives the easiest access to Circus Circus.

To get downtown cross Sahara Avenue on Paradise Road, continuing on Pardise's left fork to St. Louis Boulevard. Take St. Louis Boulevard for a block to a three-way light. You can turn right here (right turn on red is allowed) onto Las Vegas Boulevard and follow it to Fremont Street, or you can wait for the light and take the far right turn on Main Street, which will take you to Union Plaza. (Note: Streets running east and west across The Strip usually lead to their namesake hotel.)

Finally, Maryland Parkway provides a straightaway from Tropicana Avenue to Fremont Street. The street is about 2 miles (3 km) east of The Strip and hits downtown just above all the action.

Las Vegas is the land of free parking. Some hotels, such as the Excalibur and Circus Circus, have such extensive acreage devoted to cars that they offer a tram or a monorail to help people into the casino. Valet parking, by far the easiest way to go, is also one of the best deals in town. You can park your car for four days for a dollar if you want, depending on your generosity toward the valet. Parking at most hotels, otherwise, entails a bit of walking. Parking downtown means either a lot of walking, some travel up and down filthy stairwells, or valet parking. The latter is recommended, not only for safety and convenience, but because street parking is metered and monitored most hours of the day.

The telephone area code for Nevada is 702. Las Vegas accommodations and their contact information are included within the Las Vegas coverage above.

CHRONOLOGY OF THE
HISTORY OF THE
AMERICAN SOUTHWEST

Prehistory

The history of man in the Southwest goes back 10,000 years, a fact discovered in 1926 when a New Mexico cowboy, George McJunkin, found a stone arrowhead made by what is now known as Folsom Man. Apparently two other ancient tribes, so-called Sandia Man and Clovis Man, lived more or less concurrently with Folsom, but links among the three are unclear. The modern Pueblo Indians descend from a group known by the Navajo word for "old ones," Anasazi. The Anasazi created the impressive civilization that has left its ruins in northwest New Mexico, southern Colorado, and eastern Arizona in such places as Mesa Verde, Chaco Canyon, Aztec, New Mexico, Bandelier National Monument, and Canyon de Chelly. These sites were linked by an extensive network of roads and by trade to the Mogollon people in southern New Mexico and to Mexico and California.

What happened to the Anasazi culture is unknown, but it metamorphosed into the Pueblo people, and its cities were abandoned. What is now Santa Fe was inhabited by Pueblo Indians circa A.D. 600 to 1425.

The Navajos and their cousins the Apaches appeared in New Mexico about the same time as the Spaniards. Their ancestors are an Athabaskan people originally from Alaska and northwestern Canada.

The Spanish in the Southwest

New Mexico under Spain was the last outpost of empire. The territory, as vast as it was thinly populated, was kept to protect against the encroachment of the British and the

French into Mexico, to protect the Indians converted to Catholicism, and to advance the faith among the Indians. Although Santa Fe was a capital city, it was neglected and its government never given enough supplies, matériel, or soldiers to safeguard its people. The lives of the Pueblo Indians and the Spaniards were circumscribed by poverty and hardship, as well as unending war against the nomadic Indian tribes.

- **1528–1536**: Alvar Nuñez Cabeza de Vaca and three others, out of an original 400, survive shipwreck on the Texas coast; they eventually work their way back to Mexico. They are the first white men to pass through the Southwest.
- **1539**: Fray Marcos de Niza is the first white man to explore Arizona, during which time his "blackamoor" companion, Estebanico, is killed by Indians. Fray Marcos returns in 1540 with the Coronado Expedition.
- **1540**: Don Francisco Vásquez de Coronado explores New Mexico and parts of present-day Arizona, Texas, Oklahoma, and Kansas in his search for gold. The expedition returns to Mexico two years later empty-handed.
- **1541**: Coronado's expedition discovers the Grand Canyon.
- **1598**: Don Juan de Oñate establishes the first colony in New Mexico, near the pueblo of San Juan; it is abandoned as hopeless in 1604.
- **1610**: Governor Pedro de Peralta founds the second capital of New Spain at Santa Fe.
- **1612–1615**: Fray Isidoro Ordóñez's religious government vies for power with the secular authorities. Fray Ordóñez eventually loses his struggle, but not before setting a tone of conflict for the rest of the century. Government in New Mexico suffers as a result, and the Pueblo Indians bear the brunt of the Spanish government's greed and arrogance.
- **1675**: Forty-seven Pueblo Indians are put to death or whipped for practicing sorcery, i.e., their traditional religion.
- **1680**: Popé, a Pueblo priest who was whipped for his religious practices, organizes a successful revolt that culminates in the retreat of the Spaniards from New Mexico to Juárez.
- **1681–1688**: Spanish soldiers make several unsuc-

cessful attempts to retake the New Mexico province by force.

- **1692–1693**: In two expeditions, the first peaceful, the second forceful, Don Diego de Vargas expels the Pueblo Indians from Santa Fe and reconquers New Mexico. The Spaniards and the Pueblos tentatively agree to live and let live.
- **1692**: Fray Eusebio Kino establishes the first missions in Arizona, at Tumacacori and San Xavier del Bac (outside present-day Tucson).
- **1773**: Spanish explorers open the first overland route from northern Mexico to southern California.
- **1776**: Fray Silvestre Velez de Escalante and Fray Francisco Domínguez explore southern Utah. A *presidio* (fort) is established at Tucson.
- **1779–1786**: Governor Juan Bautista de Anza first defeats the Comanche chief Cuerno Verde, then makes lasting peace with all the Comanche tribes. Outside of this agreement Indians and Spaniards endure constant and unremitting siege by such hostile raiders as the Apaches, the Navajos, and the Utes.
- **1792**: Frenchman Pierre Vial opens the Santa Fe Trail, a trade route from St. Louis, Missouri, to Santa Fe.
- **1806–1807**: Lieutenant Zebulon Pike, in his attempt to explore Spanish territory, discovers Pike's Peak in Colorado, and is arrested by the Spaniards and sent to Mexico. His accounts of the Southwest and its geography are invaluable to American traders later in the century.
- **1810**: Representative government begins in New Mexico when Don Pedro Bautista Pino becomes a delegate to the Spanish *cortes*.

The Mexican Period

The Mexican Republic, like the Spanish government, also ignored New Mexico, for it had troubles of its own. New Mexico was left to eke out a marginal existence under Mexican rule, but was permitted to begin trade relations with the United States, an interaction that relieved some of the material hardship of the people. However, because almost all the Catholic priests had left with the cessation of Spanish rule, the religious needs of the Catholics of this area were not properly served by the Church again until the Territorial period.

- **1821**: Mexico throws off Spanish rule and becomes a republic. New Mexico is given permission to trade with the United States.
- **1822**: The first wagons bring much-needed goods into Santa Fe. Although it is mostly Americans who profit from the Santa Fe Trail, some New Mexicans, especially the great families, also benefit.
- **1824**: Fur trader and mountain man Jim Bridger discovers the Great Salt Lake.
- **1832**: The Bent brothers establish Bent's Fort in Colorado as a post for fur traders and trappers.
- **1836**: Texas wins its independence from Mexico and becomes a republic.
- **1841**: The Republic of Texas tries to enter the Santa Fe Trail trade by force, beginning a long legacy of often justifiable mistrust between New Mexicans and Texans. Texas's armed force becomes humiliatingly lost and then captured by New Mexico Governor Manuel Armijo.

The Territorial Period

The growing influence of the United States brought with it some regularity of governance and law, and connection with the outside world by stage, telegraph, and later by railroad. The U.S. Army eventually provided relief from the depredations of the hostile Indian tribes. However, this period also saw many Spanish-Americans separated from their lands by sharp practices and corruption. Anglo-Americans arrived in greater numbers to mine precious metals and to establish cattle ranches. Few people today realize how recently the Territorial Period ended in the Southwest: in 1912.

- **1845**: Texas becomes the 28th state.
- **1846**: The annexation of Texas precipitates the Mexican War; U.S. General Stephen Watts Kearny invades New Mexico. Governor Armijo disappears into Mexico. American rule begins, as does some real prosperity.
- **1847**: A battalion of Mormon volunteers opens the Gila Trail from New Mexico to California.
- **1848**: The Mexican War ends. By the Treaty of Guadalupe Hidalgo, Mexico cedes to the United States its territory north of the Rio Grande includ-

ing present-day California, Nevada, Utah, and parts of New Mexico, Arizona, Colorado, and Wyoming.

- **1849**: The Mormons, who arrived in 1847 in what is now Salt Lake City, Utah, organize the State of Deseret. Congress ignores this action and instead creates the Utah Territory under the governorship of Brigham Young.

- **1850**: The New Mexico territorial government is established. The alternative of statehood is not considered because of the prejudice of some Americans against "colored" people, Roman Catholics, and Mexicans of "low morals."

- **1851**: Jean Baptiste Lamy, the first Catholic bishop of Santa Fe, arrives in the city and regularizes the practices of Catholics in New Mexico. For the first time since the departure of the Franciscans with Spanish rule, significant numbers of priests are brought in.

- **1852**: The first Spanish-American settlement is established in Colorado, at Conejos in the San Luis Valley.

- **1853**: For $10 million the Gadsden Purchase acquires for the United States portions of New Mexico and Arizona south of the Gila River from Mexico, thereby allowing Americans access to California and its gold fields from the east without having to traverse the mountains.

- **1855**: Brigham Young dispatches 30 Mormons to explore the mountains near present-day Las Vegas. The effort is abandoned when local Indians refuse to convert to Mormonism.

- **1858**: The Butterfield Overland Stage begins twice-weekly service between St. Louis, Missouri, and San Francisco, California, making the Southwest increasingly less isolated. The Colorado Gold Rush brings large numbers of settlers to Colorado for the first time.

- **1861**: The Colorado Territory is formed from northern New Mexico land. Nevada becomes a territory.

- **1862**: The Confederacy launches an attempt to conquer the Western United States, and especially California, by invading New Mexico. Confederate forces are defeated by an army of New Mexicans and Coloradans at the battle of Glorieta near Santa Fe.

- **1863**: President Abraham Lincoln recognizes the

independent governments of the Pueblo Indians by sending them silver-headed canes of authority, similar to those once presented to them by the king of Spain.

- **1863–1886:** The Americans, Kit Carson among them, subdue the Navajos and the Apaches, then move the tribes onto reservations.
- **1863:** Arizona, or Gadsonia as it is temporarily called, becomes a territory separate from New Mexico; its first capital is Fort Whipple.
- **1864:** Nevada becomes the 36th state. Arizonans establish their capital in Prescott. U.S. Army troops force 8,491 Navajo men, women, and children to walk from western New Mexico to the Pecos Valley near Santa Fe, hold them there for four years, then allow them to return home.
- **1866:** Charles Goodnight and Oliver Loving begin a cattle trail that significantly changes the economy of New Mexico. In 1873 John Chisum, the "Cow King of New Mexico," establishes an enormous ranch near Roswell.
- **1867:** By a single vote in the territorial legislature, Tucson becomes the capital of Arizona.
- **1868:** The telegraph reaches Santa Fe.
- **1869:** Major John Wesley Powell explores the Grand Canyon by boat. The Union Pacific and Central Pacific railroads meet at Promontory, Utah, to form the first transcontinental railroad.
- **1870s and 1880s:** Gold fever strikes in New Mexico, but little pans out. Rumors bring development and many Anglo adventurers.
- **1874:** Barbed wire is introduced in the Southwest, marking the end of long cattle drives and open range.
- **1876:** The Centennial State, Colorado, joins the Union as the 38th state.
- **1877:** The Arizona capital is moved from Tucson back to Prescott.
- **1878:** The Lincoln County War begins in southern New Mexico, pitting cattlemen against merchants. Lew Wallace is appointed territorial governor of New Mexico to suppress the violence; he finishes writing *Ben Hur* while living in the Palace of the Governors in Santa Fe. Billy the Kid becomes a hero to many local residents.
- **1879:** Mormon settlers begin colonization of the

San Juan Basin in the present-day Four Corners area.

- **1879–1880**: The railroad reaches Las Vegas, New Mexico, and then Santa Fe; the Santa Fe Trail passes into history.
- **1880**: A Mormon expedition finally reaches the site of present-day Bluff, Utah, where they begin colonization of the southern portion of the territory.
- **1881**: The "Gunfight at the O.K. Corral" takes place in Tombstone, Arizona Territory; three men are killed and three are wounded. Billy the Kid is killed by Pat Garrett in New Mexico.
- **Late 19th century**: Las Gorras Blancas (The White Caps), a clandestine Spanish-American organization, terrorizes the Northern New Mexican countryside with vigilante action aimed at protecting ancient Spanish lands from Anglo encroachment.
- **1886**: Geronimo surrenders in Arizona for the last time. The Apache Indian wars come to an end.
- **1889**: Arizonans again change their seat of government by making Phoenix the new capital.
- **1896**: With the abolition of polygamy, Utah becomes the 45th state.
- **1898**: Artists Ernest Blumenschein and Bert Phillips arrive in Taos by accident when their wagon wheel breaks; they decide to stay and the first seeds of the art colony are planted.

The United States

The 20th century has seen the slow but ineluctable exposure of the Southwest to the outside world. It became a haven for artists and writers, and for those who did not seem to fit in back East. Because of its clean, dry air the Southwest also became a haven for people with tuberculosis.World War II changed the region forever, and the atomic bomb brought it fully into the 20th century. The economy also evolved from its base of farming and ranching and some mining to heavy dependence upon oil, gas, and uranium. The Southwest has become a destination not merely for a few knowledgeable travellers, but for the broad spectrum of Americans and the world.

- **1905**: Las Vegas, Nevada, is founded as a railroad town.

- **1911**: The Roosevelt Dam is constructed on the Salt River in Arizona, becoming the first of many dams in the region that make agricultural irrigation possible. The most famous of these, Hoover Dam, is constructed on the Colorado in 1936.
- **1912**: President William Howard Taft signs statehood bills making New Mexico the 47th state and Arizona the 48th.
- **1916**: Pancho Villa raids Columbus, New Mexico.
- **1922–1924**: Senator Holm Bursum introduces a bill to legalize the holdings of squatters on Pueblo Indian lands. Outraged, the Indians from the All-Pueblo Council protest, and the New Mexican art and literary colonies rally to their defense. The Indian-rights movement attains national stature, as does Eastern social worker and Indian-rights champion John Collier (later Indian Commissioner). The Pueblo Lands Act Bill evicts and compensates the squatters, and confirms the rights of the Indians to their lands.
- **1931**: Las Vegas, Nevada, legalizes gambling and enacts liberal marriage and divorce laws, becoming a haven for those seeking a "quickie" divorce.
- **1941**: El Rancho gambling casino is the first to be built on what is now the famous Las Vegas Strip in Nevada.
- **1941–1945**: New Mexico's isolationist trend ends with involvement in World War II as large numbers of the state's men enter the armed forces. The 200th Coast Artillery, a New Mexican unit, is captured in the Philippines, and hundreds of New Mexicans die on the Bataan Death March in 1942.
- **1943**: The headquarters of the Manhattan Project are established in what had been the Los Alamos Ranch School. Research secrets are later stolen and passed to Soviet agents under a bridge in Santa Fe.
- **1945**: Scientists from the Manhattan Project detonate the first nuclear bomb at Trinity Site, northwest of Alamogordo, New Mexico.
- **1946**: Mobster "Bugsy" Siegel builds the Flamingo (now the Flamingo Hilton) on what is now the Las Vegas Strip.
- **1954**: The Air Force Academy is established in Colorado Springs, Colorado.
- **1970**: President Richard Nixon signs a bill returning the sacred Blue Lake to New Mexico's Taos

Pueblo after decades of lobbying by the Indians and their supporters.

- **1980s:** Santa Fe becomes the "in" vacation destination for the rich and famous. Hollywood also discovers the city, which is soon featured on the covers of *Esquire, National Geographic,* and many other magazines and newspapers. "Santa Fe style" is discovered or, according to some Santa Feans, invented.

—John Pen La Farge

INDEX